Crime, Inequality and the State

Why has crime dropped while imprisonment still grows?

This thoughtful, well-edited volume of ground-breaking articles explores criminal justice policy in light of recent research on changing patterns of crime and criminal careers.

Showing that prison expansion contradicts recent findings of "what works" in reducing crime and reoffending, Mary Vogel situates this development socially and historically to present a very different explanation. She argues that Western societies have shifted in recent years away from chiefly welfarist approaches towards control, surveillance and policing methods. In a context of growing social diversity, this has contributed to a crisis of authority.

Highlighting the role of conservative social and political theory in giving rise to criminal justice policies (from Schmitt and Strauss in the US to Parsons and Levitas in the UK), this innovative book focuses on such policies as "three strikes (two in the UK) and you're out," mandatory sentencing, and widespread incarceration of drug offenders. In addition to comparing this scenario to that in social democratic countries, this volume highlights the costs − in both money and opportunity − of increased prison expansion. Among the factors explored are:

- labour market dynamics;
- the rise of a "prison industry";
- the boost prisons provide to economies of underdeveloped regions;
- the spreading political disenfranchisement of the disadvantaged it has produced.

Throughout, hard facts and figures are accompanied by the faces and voices of the individuals and families whose lives hang in the balance. This volume uses a compelling inter-play of theoretical works and powerful empirical research to present vivid portraits of individual life experiences.

Included are works by: Robert Sampson; Michael Tonry; Eli Anderson; Charles Ogletree; Ben Bowling; Tom Tyler; Jonathan Simon; Tony Jefferson; Lorraine Gelsthorpe; William Julius Wilson; David Farrington; Rosemary Gartner; Jurgen Habermas and Elliott Currie.

Mary E. Vogel is a Reader at King's College London School of Law and Associate Senior Research Fellow at the Institute of Advanced Legal Studies, University of London. Since earning her doctorate at Harvard University, she has taught at several US institutions including the University of Michigan at Ann Arbor and the University of California. She has also been a Visiting Scholar at the American Bar Foundation and the University of Oxford; Bunting Fellow at Harvard University; and John Adams Fellow at the University of London. Vogel is the author of *Coercion to Compromise: Plea Bargaining, the Courts and the Making of Political Authority* as well as numerous articles. Her work won the American Sociological Association Law Section's Article Prize for 2001 and the Law and Society Association's Best Article Prize in 2000.

Crime, Inequality and the State

Edited by

Mary E. Vogel

LONDON AND NEW YORK

First published 2007
by Routledge
2 Park Square, Milton Park, Abingdon, Oxon OX14 4RN

Simultaneously published in the USA and Canada
by Routledge
270 Madison Ave, New York, NY 10016

Routledge is an imprint of the Taylor & Francis Group, an informa business

© 2007 editorial matter and selection, Mary E. Vogel;
the readings, the contributors

Typeset in Perpetua and Bell Gothic by
Newgen Imaging Systems (P) Ltd, Chennai, India
Printed and bound in Great Britain by
TJ International Ltd, Padstow, Cornwall

British Library Cataloguing in Publication Data
A catalogue record for this book is available from the British Library

Library of Congress Cataloging in Publication Data
A catalog record for this book has been requested

ISBN10: 0–415–38269–6 (hbk)
ISBN10: 0–415–38268–8 (pbk)

ISBN13: 978–0–415–38269–4 (hbk)
ISBN13: 978–0–415–38268–7 (pbk)

For

Virginia Vogel McLeod,
my mother,

and for

Tony Long,
orphan at risk who forged adversity into art,

with all my love

Contents

Preface

THIS BOOK BEGAN AS a conversation with Tony Long about how some youth at high risk end up in crime while others do not. Tony had himself lost his father to World War II, grew up in a rough mill town, lived as a small child with his mother and brother in a one-room apartment without hot water, and spent several years in an orphanage. He had lots of rage. Tony became a sculptor. By his 35th birthday he had a solo show of his work at the Centre Georges Pompidou in Paris. Why, we wondered, had his life taken this turn? And had the country, we also asked, changed since the 1980s so that perhaps he would not, despite his gifts, have fared so well today?

The pages that follow present an inquiry and an argument about what accounts for the increasingly punitive turn taken by Anglo-American criminal justice policy in recent decades. This shift, dubbed "the carceral turn," appears to reflect neither rising crime, since crime has dropped, nor recent research about "what works" in rehabilitating and reintegrating offenders. Much excellent work has been done depicting the contours of this "carceral turn" by Feeley and Simon (1992), Garland (2001), Western and Beckett (2001), Bottoms (1987) and Hudson (2002). What this book does is to build on and advance that work by situating this "turn" socio-historically and exploring further the forces that have given rise to it. My argument is presented in the Introduction.

In crafting this book, I have benefited from the contributions and support of many people. My colleague at King's, Ben Bowling, has stimulated my thinking about the links of criminal justice policy to politics through both his own exemplary work and insightful questions. He and my colleague Elaine Player have welcomed me to King's and created the kind of atmosphere where one learns every day. Their commitment to the criminological project is a constant inspiration. Also at King's my colleagues Alan Norrie, Sionaidh Douglas-Scott and Vanessa Munro have extended a warm welcome and challenged me to think more deeply about how social theory can shed light on legal and political events today. I am particularly indebted to Alan Norrie for his lectures on Jacques Derrida and to Sionaidh Douglas-Scott for hers on Carl Schmitt. Their collegiality, intellectual engagement and friendship has in no small part nurtured this book to press.

At Routledge, Gerhard Boomgaarden has from the start been a constant source of enthusiasm, support and encouragement. Someday I may work faster and no doubt be a better person for it. If so, it will be due largely to Gerhard's efforts and patience. Special thanks to him for helping to shape the book and for shepherding it to press. Thanks too to Constance Sutherland, who served as editorial assistant on this project, for her fine work and patience. Her successor, Ann Carter, has big shoes to fill and is certainly doing so. Elisabet Sinkie has been clear and most helpful as production editor on this volume. She herself copyedited the Introduction after Marjorie Leith did a beautiful job of copyediting the text. Last but not least, special thanks to the artists who created, I think, just the right design for the cover.

For my part, the logistics of working transatlantically have created many challenges. That they are overcome is due largely to the intelligence and hard work of freelance associate John Callahan. John tracked down contributors, coordinated the process of gaining permissions to use the articles included in this book, and faxed a continual stream of hard-to-locate articles to me across the Atlantic. For his competence and good humor I am deeply grateful.

This book has had the benefit of comments and consideration from my students, first, at the University of Michigan at Ann Arbor, and then at the University of California at Santa Barbara, the University of Leicester, England, and Kings College London. Their spirited encounter with the ideas I present and, especially, their interest in the rich portraits of lives of offenders in biography, fiction or music has been continually engaging and affirming to me as I wrote. Earlier, I benefitted from Alan Brinkley's inspiring lectures on "America Since 1945" at Harvard, which ignited my interest in this period and, no doubt, contributed to whatever of merit may be found in my approach. Its limitations remain, of course my own.

Most of all, the long process of creating this book benefited from the encouragement of my mother, Virginia Vogel McLeod, who seemed to adopt it as a sort of step-grandchild and take special interest in its development. Tangibly and emotionally, she has helped in ways too numerous to count. Her willingness to laugh, to help out in crucial moments, and to keep faith in hard times means more than words can say. When research speaks of the importance of parenting, it must have in mind such a mother. Equally my sisters, Christine and Virginia, who share that same wonderful capacity to give love and remain steadfast, have been there at each step and encouraging all the way. Last December, we all grieved the loss of Elvira Rigo, a Cuban woman of colour, who, along with our own mother, "mothered" my sisters and I through much of our childhood. Her warmth, humor, love, resilience and sense of abundance amidst scarcity helped inspire this book and will be with me always.

Tony, this book started out as a conversation with you and, like all else, concludes with you. In your capacity to see and make beauty in the most unlikely of ways lies the raison d'etre for this book. Against all odds, you show that courage, authenticity and greatness of heart can sometimes make a difference. This book is for you, Tony, and for those struggling with risk, as have you, to transform their lives. It comes, as always, with deepest love and affection.

Mary Vogel
11 September 2006
Biarritz

Acknowledgements

THE PUBLISHER WOULD LIKE to thank the following for permission to reproduce their works:

NICA and Stephen Donziger for permission to reprint excerpts from S. R. Donziger, 'Crime and policy', in S. R. Donziger (ed.), *The Real War on Crime*, The Report of the National Criminal Justice Commission, pp. 1–44. Copyright © 1996 by NCIA and Stephen Donziger.

Tom R. Tyler for permission to reprint 'Governing amid diversity: the effect of fair decision-making procedures on the legitimacy of government', *Law and Society Review* 28(4) (1994): 809–831.

Reprinted with permission of the Free Press (an imprint of Simon & Schuster Adult Publishing Group) and Robin D. G. Kelley from *Race Rebels: Culture, Politics, and the Black Working Class*, New York: The Free Press, 1994, pp. 183–194. Copyright © 1994 by Robin D. G. Kelley.

Governments and Opposition and Robert D. Putnam for permission to reprint excerpts from R. D. Putnam, 'Civic disengagement in contemporary America', *Governments and Opposition* 36 (2001): 135–156.

Cambridge University Press, Alfred Blumstein and Joel Wallman for permission to reprint excerpts from Alfred Blumstein and Joel Wallman, 'The recent rise and fall of American violence', and Alfred Blumstein, excerpts from 'Disaggregating the violence trends', in Alfred Blumstein and Joel Wallman (eds), *The Crime Drop in America*, 2nd edn, Cambridge: Cambridge University Press, 2006, pp. 13–44. Reprinted with permission of Cambridge University Press.

Oxford University Press for permission to reprint excerpts from Franklin E. Zimring and Gordon Hawkins, *Crime is Not the Problem: Lethal Violence in America*, Oxford: Oxford University Press, 1997, pp. 3–19, 73–83. Copyright © 1997 by Oxford University Press. Reprinted with permission of Oxford University Press.

Northeastern University Press and Scott Christianson for permission to reprint excerpts from Scott Christianson, *With Liberty for Some: 500 Years of Imprisonment in America*, Boston: Northeastern University Press, 1998, pp. 275–305. Copyright © 1998 by Scott Christianson. Reprinted with permission of Northeastern University Press.

Cambridge University Press for permission to reprint excerpts from William Spelman, 'The limited importance of prison expansion', in Alfred Blumstein and Joel Wallman (eds), *The Crime Drop in America*, 2nd edn, Cambridge: Cambridge University Press, 2006, pp. 97–129. Reprinted with permission of Cambridge University Press.

Hart Publishing for permission to reprint excerpts from Katherine Beckett and Bruce Western, 'Crime control, American style', in Penny Green and Andrew Rutherford (eds), *Criminal Policy in Transition*, Oxford and Portland, OR: Hart Publishing, 2000, pp. 15–31.

Malcolm M. Feeley and Jonathan Simon for permission to reprint excerpts from M. M. Feeley and J. Simon, 'The new penology: notes on the emerging strategy of corrections and its implications', *Criminology* 30(4) (1992): 449–474.

American Sociological Review, Christopher Uggen and Jeff Manza for permission to reprint excerpts from Christopher Uggen and Jeff Manza, 'Democratic contraction? The political consequences of Felon disenfranchisement in the United States', *American Sociological Review* 67 (2002): 777–803.

Fox Butterfield for permission to reprint excerpts from Fox Butterfield, *All God's Children: The Bosket Family and the American Tradition of Violence*, New York: Avon Books, 1995, pp. xiv–xv, 135–149, 206–207.

Oxford University Press for permission to reprint excerpts from David P. Farrington, 'Human development and criminal careers', in Mike Maguire, Rod Morgan and Robert Reiner (eds), *Oxford Handbook of Criminology*, 2nd edn, Oxford: Oxford University Press, 1997, pp. 361–408. Reprinted with permission of Oxford University Press.

James Gilligan for permission to reprint James Gilligan, 'Shame: the emotions and morality of violence', in James Gilligan, *Violence: Reflections on a National Epidemic*, New York: Vintage Books, 1997, pp. 103–114. Copyright © 1996 by James Gilligan.

American Society of Criminology, John H. Laub and Robert J. Sampson for permission to reprint excerpts from John H. Laub and Robert J. Sampson, 'Turning points in the life course: why change matters to the study of crime', *Criminology* 31(3) (1993): 301–325.

Random House for permission to reprint Jack Henry Abbott, 'State raised convict', in Jack Henry Abbott, *In the Belly of the Beast*, New York: Random House, 1981, pp. 3–14. Copyright © 1981 by Jack Henry Abbott. Reprinted with permission of Random House, Inc.

Oxford University Press for permission to reprint excerpts from Anthony E. Bottoms and Paul Wiles, 'Environmental criminology', in Mike Maguire, Rod Morgan and

Robert Reiner (eds), *Oxford Handbook of Criminology*, 2nd edn, Oxford: Oxford University Press, 1997, pp. 305–359. Reprinted with permission of Oxford University Press.

American Society of Criminology and Robert Agnew for permission to reprint excerpts from Robert Agnew, 'Foundation for a general strain theory of crime and delinquency', *Criminology* 30(1) (1992): 47–87.

Stanford University Press, Robert J. Sampson and William J. Wilson for permission to reprint excerpts from Robert J. Sampson and William J. Wilson, 'Toward a theory of race, crime, and urban inequality', in John Hagan and Ruth D. Peterson (eds), *Crime and Inequality*, Stanford, CA: Stanford University Press, 1990, pp. 37–54. Copyright © 1990 by the Board of Trustees of the Leland Stanford Junior University. Reprinted with permission of Stanford University Press.

Henry Holt and Company and Elliott Currie for permission to reprint excerpts from Elliott Currie, 'Social action', in Elliott Currie, *Crime and Punishment in America: Why the Solutions to America's Most Stubborn Social Crisis have not Worked – and What Will*, New York: Henry Holt, 1998, pp. 110–148. Copyright © 1998 by Elliott Currie. Reprinted with permission of Henry Holt and Company, LLC.

Cambridge University Press and Scott H. Decker for permission to reprint excerpts from Scott H. Decker and Barrik Van Winkle, *Life in the Gang: Family, Friends, and Violence*, Cambridge: Cambridge University Press, 1996, pp. 1–3, 20–25, 56–83, 144–186. Reprinted with permission of Cambridge University Press.

Oxford University Press for permission to reprint excerpts from Ian Taylor, 'The political economy of crime', in Mike Maguire, Rod Morgan and Robert Reiner (eds), *Oxford Handbook of Criminology*, 2nd edn, Oxford: Oxford University Press, 1997, pp. 265–359. Reprinted with permission of Oxford University Press.

Alfred A. Knopf and Piri Thomas for permission to reprint Piri Thomas, 'How to be a negro without really trying', in Piri Thomas, *Down These Mean Streets*, New York: Vintage Books, 1967, pp. 95–104. Copyright renewed 1995 by Piri Thomas. Reprinted with permission of Alfred A. Knopf, a division of Random House, Inc.

Oxford University Press for permission to reprint excerpts from Coretta Phillips and Ben Bowling, 'Racism, ethnicity, crime, and criminal justice', in Mike Maguire, Rod Morgan and Robert Reiner (eds), *Oxford Handbook of Criminology*, 3rd edn, Oxford: Oxford University Press, 2002, pp. 593–607, 614–619. Reprinted with permission of Oxford University Press.

The Atlantic Monthly and Elijah Anderson for permission to reprint Elijah Anderson, 'The code of the streets', *The Atlantic Monthly* 273(5) (1994): 81–94. Copyright © 1994 by Elijah Anderson. All Rights Reserved.

American Society of Criminology and Dario Melossi for permission to reprint Dario Melossi, 'Overcoming the crisis in critical criminology: toward a grounded labeling theory', *Criminology* 23(2) (1985): 193–208.

Oxford University Press and Loraine Gelsthorpe for permission to reprint, Loraine Gelsthorpe, 'Feminism and criminology', in Mike Maguire, Rod Morgan and Robert Reiner (eds),

Oxford Handbook of Criminology, 3rd edn, Oxford: Oxford University Press, 2002, pp. 112–143. Reprinted with permission of Oxford University Press.

Oxford University Press for permission to reprint, Tony Jefferson, 'Masculinities and crimes', in Mike Maguire, Rod Morgan and Robert Reiner (eds), *Oxford Handbook of Criminology*, 2nd edn, Oxford: Oxford University Press, 1997, pp. 535–552. Reprinted with permission of Oxford University Press.

University of Chicago Press and Michael Tonry for permission to reprint excerpts from Michael Tonry, 'Mandatory penalties', in Michael Tonry (ed.), *Crime and Justice: A Review of Research*, Vol. 16, Chicago: University of Chicago Press, 1992, pp. 243–265.

Yale University Press, Dane Archer and Rosemany Gartner for permission to print excerpts from Dane Archer and Rosemary Gartner, 'Homicide and the death penalty', in Dane Archer and Rosemary Gartner, *Violence and Crime in Cross-national Perspective*, New Haven and London: Yale University Press, 1984, pp. 118–139.

Charles J. Ogletree, Jr. for permission to reprint Charles J. Ogletree, Jr., 'The Rehnquist revolution in criminal procedure', in Herman Schwartz (ed.), *The Rehnquist Court: Judicial Activism on the Right*, New York: Hill and Wang, 2002, pp. 55–69.

Robert J. Sampson and John H. Laub for permission to reprint excerpts from Robert J. Sampson and John H. Laub, 'Structural variations in juvenile court processing', *Law & Society Review* 27(2) (1993): 285–311.

Mary E. Vogel for permission to reprint excerpts from Mary E. Vogel, 'The social origins of plea bargaining: conflict and the law in the process of state formation, 1830–1860', *Law & Society Review* 35(1) (1999): 161–246, and Mary E. Vogel and Elsevier for permission to reprint excerpts from Mary E. Vogel 'Lawyering in an age of popular politics', in Jerry Van Hoy (ed.), *Legal Professions*, London: Elsevier, 2001, pp. 207–252.

Henry Holt and Company and Elliott Currie for permission to reprint excerpts from Elliott Currie, 'Prevention', in Elliott Currie, *Crime and Punishment in America: Why the Solutions to America's Most Stubborn Social Crisis have not Worked – and What Will*, New York: Henry Holt, 1998, pp. 80–107. Copyright © 1998 by Elliott Currie. Reprinted with permission of Henry Holt and Company, LLC.

The Eisenhower Foundation and Lynn A. Curtis for permission to reprint excerpts from Lynn A. Curtis 'What works at the millennium?' in The Eisenhower Foundation, *The Oxbridge Lecture*, Washington, DC: The Eisenhower Foundation.

Transaction Publishers and David F. Greenberg for permission to reprint excerpts from David F. Greenberg, 'Punishment, division of labor, and social solidarity', in William S. Laufer and Freda Adler (eds), *The Criminology of Criminal Law. Advances in Criminological Theory*, New Brunswick, NJ: Transaction Publishers, 1999, pp. 283–359. Copyright © 1999 by Transaction Publishers.

The Institute of Criminology and Anthony Bottoms for permission to reprint Anthony Bottoms (2005), 'Alternatives to prison', *Criminology in Cambridge*, the Newsletter of the Institute of Criminology, University of Cambridge, Issue 6: 3, 14–15.

Westview Press and Jonathan Simon for permission to reprint excerpts from Jonathan Simon, 'Governing through crime', in Lawrence M. Friedman and George Fisher (eds), *The Crime Conundrum: Essays on Criminal Justice*, Boulder, CO: Westview Press, 1997, pp. 171–189. Reprinted with permission of Westview Press, a member of Perseus Books, L.L.C.

Pluto Press for permission to reprint excerpts from Alan Hunt and Gary Wickham, 'Law, government and governmentality', in Alan Hunt and Gary Wickham, *Foucault and Law: Toward a Sociology of Law as Governance*, London and Boulder, CO: Pluto Press, 1994, pp. 52–55.

MIT Press for permission to reprint excerpts from Jurgen Habermas, 'Postscript (1994)', in Jurgen Habermas, *Between Facts and Norms: Contributions to a Discourse Theory of Law and Democracy,* Cambridge, MA: MIT Press, 1996, pp. 447–453. [Originally published by Polity Press, 1991.]

Colin Sumner for permission to reprint excerpts from Colin Sumner, 'Law, legitimation and the advanced capitalist state: the jurisprudence and social theory of Jurgen Habermas', in David Sugarman (ed.), *Legality, Ideology and the State*, London: Academic Press, 1983, pp. 135–140.

Routledge and David Garland for permission to reprint excerpts from David Garland, *The Culture of Control*, London: Routledge, 2001, pp. 75–102.

MIT Press and Jean Cohen for permission to reprint excerpts from Jean L. Cohen and Andrew Arato, *Civil Society and Political Theory*, Cambridge, MA: MIT Press, 1992, pp. 1–3, 15–17.

Introduction

THE IRONY OF IMPRISONMENT
The punitive paradox of the carceral turn and the "micro-death" of the material

■   Mary E. Vogel

CHANGING LANDSCAPES OF CRIME, order and social control are, it is said, inspiring a reimagining of criminology (Loader and Sparks, 2002: 83). Shifts in arrangements of governance, public perceptions of punishment, boundaries between public and private security, orientations to risk, cultural images of crime and disorder, and transnational patterns of offending are all connected with a fundamental rethinking of the nature of social ordering, political institutions and the role of the nation state today (Feeley and Simon, 1992; Beckett and Western, 2001; Garland, 2001; Dryzek, 2002; Hudson, 2002; and Loader and Sparks, 2002). A recurring question among the many raised is in what form, if at all, the nation state will continue to occupy the primary place of sovereignty, security and response to harm and risk in society (Loader and Sparks, 2002: 84). This paper builds on previous research to contribute to the project of situating these transformative changes historically to better understand them – particularly the rich analyses advanced by David Garland (2001) and by Malcolm Feeley and Jonathan Simon (1992), respectively. I suggest some further causal forces at work in criminal justice today en route to shaping what may ultimately be nothing less than a new global order.

In this paper, I focus on the paradox that we see today in criminal justice a growing punitiveness and use of mass imprisonment that has made the United States, since the late 1990s, the country that incarcerates the gretest share of its population of any in the world and Britain among the highest in western Europe (Mauer, 2003). Yet this punitiveness seems to respond neither to trends in crime nor to recent research about what works in reducing offending and reoffending. Recently, such coercive public action has been theorized as reasserting the sovereignty of states that had been weakened in recent years through their inability to assure public and private security. While that makes a compelling claim for the near term, I would like to suggest that something quite different may lie beyond it. My own work explores whether the recent "carceral turn" may, ironically, in the longer term go on to contribute instead to a "hollowing out" or "retreat" of the state – a weakening that breeds *public minimalism* or, perhaps ultimately, the "sunset" of public power – one that could move history beyond the nation state. It may do this by creating a selective and false image of coercive state strength while, in fact, quietly proceeding with the demontage of the institutional infrastructure of liberal democratic goverance in the service of neo-liberalism. I distinguish "public minimalism" from Beveridge's "state minimalism" in that this new form of public power seems to me to entail neither a fixed state role, however limited, nor a necessary stopping point in the shift of power from the public to the private realm.

It is sometimes said that at present there is more law but that public institutions play a lesser role in it (Mulcahy, 2006). Even in criminal justice, where imprisonment is expanding, privatization is widespread. One sees it in private security and policing, privately run prisons, drug treatment centres and non-trial alternatives such as mediation or plea bargaining. One wonders if it is enough to speak of a commingling of public law with private disciplinary practices, as did Michel Foucault, or whether deeper changes are afoot? Besides substitution of private for public regulatory activity, the boundary of privacy that has traditionally limited state power may also be blurring. As rights are called on to protect actions in private, this inherently introduces state power into that realm and risks eroding this boundary. By occupying the boundary between state and non-state and participating in each, are public institutions, either consciously or inadvertently, contributing to a weakening of the public/private boundary or, indeed, its complete eclipse.

Where does such a transformation lead? Is "private prudentialism" emerging in which individuals cluster together to provide security selectively for their families and friends without shouldering the burden of a broader public (O'Malley, 1992)? Are we, instead, heading toward the emergence of parallel systems of largely private governance such as the "lex mercatoria" that shapes international commercial arbitration – all but completely unanchored in the formal institutions of the nation state? Or, where public power continues, are we tolling the end of the nation state – perhaps to see it replaced by formally democratic but, practically speaking, administrative transnational governance (such as the EU, a pan-Arab Union, NAFTA or some version of the UN) while substantively democratic power is devolved to largely symbolic and expressive local governance? Could this unusual punitiveness, then, symptomize far broader changes?

In such times of change, it is always tempting in our anxiety to imagine that we are seeing something completely new. In fact, such times of transformation usually involve elements of both continuity and change. Recently, Rene van Swaaningen and David Downes (2007) have attempted to identify the key factors that explain growing punitiveness. They point to: political will, legislation and policy, the role of penal experts, the media, welfare and political economy, and trust and legitimacy. This is a fine synthesis of the types of causal forces underlying the carceral turn to date. However, the factors themselves do not provide an explanation for the dynamics of this carceral turn. It is such an account that Bottoms (1987 and 1995), Feeley and Simon (1992), Garland (2001) and others are attempting to offer.

In this Introduction, my own work, like that of Garland (2001) and of Beckett and Western (2001), situates the recent rise in punitiveness in a context of global political economy and key strands of American politics since World War II. We should ask, I suggest, "How has democracy been distorted so as to produce such punitiveness?" One must focus on this question, I argue, because this is where the source of the carceral turn lies – in politics. And that, I suggest, is the "irony of imprisonment" today — it is not primarily about punishment. Let us turn now to see what it may involve.

This paper explores how growing punitiveness in criminal justice draws on recognizable strands of post-World War II American politics that are being rewoven in new ways amidst the changes that globalization has wrought. Today, mass imprisonment appears not to be solely, or even primarily, about incapacitating, deterring or rehabilitating offenders. Rather it appears to be driven by broader transformations in power in which criminal justice is being called on to play a key part. The consequence is that a prison expansion so extensive that it has quadrupled the numbers of Americans incarcerated in recent decades and doubled those in Britain may not be caused by a need to reform or punish.

How, one may ask, can a more punitive criminal justice system do anything other than punish? How could this weaken the state? Would it not have exactly the opposite effect of strengthening it? Let us now examine the carceral turn and its causes. In what follows, I begin by considering trends in imprisonment in relation to recent trends in crime and to research findings about what works in reducing crime and reoffending. One finds that, amidst important scholarly work on a risk society, a new penology, penal populism and a structurally conditioned culture of control, policy has varied in ways quite independent of trends in crime and policymakers have tended to bypass research on causes of offending that emphasize the economic and social underpinnings of risk – both in terms of inequality and of poverty. Instead policy decisions have tended to highlight "troublesome" cultural orientations and to point the finger of responsibility at their individual bearers while ignoring the socio-economic forces that shape crime. I then ask why this is so. As we look further, we shall see that what at first seems to be an intellectual gaffe emerges, consciously or not, as part of a political transformation that is occurring as the contours of global power are reworked and the place of the nation state in the twenty-first century is clarified.

In contrast to those policymakers, this volume has three primary purposes. First, it moves to bring the social context of exclusion – most notably inequality, unemployment and poverty – back into the policy discussion about the causes and consequences of crime. Recent research now allows us to see more clearly both direct and indirect effects of economic well-being, both relative and absolute. New research shows how poverty and, especially, the stress it creates works through cultural practices such as parenting, community activity, kinship, subordinated identities, abuse, labelling, schooling, peer group bonding, prenatal care and the diagnosis and treatment of disability, among others things, to create behavioral dispositions that place youths at risk of offending and reoffending. The second primary aim of this work is to suggest that, in talking about crime, offending behavior is only one part of the picture. Laws, policing and the criminal justice process are others which interplay to produce "crime" as a socially constructed phenomenon (Friedman, 1992). In this paper, I explore how a sea change in politics is reshaping Anglo-American criminal justice. In that context, I explore the extent to which punitiveness is reasserting the strength of the state's role or, ultimately, weakening it.

Third, I contemplate an alternative vision of policy, law and politics that is rooted in public power, civic participation, procedural fairness and new welfarist approaches to crime. Parts of this approach have guided the social democratic countries whose crime rates have remained relatively low in recent years while those in more carceral societies have skyrocketed. Implications of this alternate vision are considered both for security and for the democratic exercise of global power. In this book, I suggest that the political reconfiguration taking place, far from being a mere backdrop, is one in which criminal justice policy is playing a major part.

In exploring long term consequences of the recent carceral turn toward a possible minimalism in public governance, I suggest that we may be witnessing in America a process of *autocolonialism* in which the institutions of liberalism are being occupied or "colonized" by the political right to weaken them from within by diluting rights, procedural protections and an agenda of egalitarianism. While much of the growth of imprisonment has been in state institutions so raising questions about the influence of federal strategy, the Republican Party organization has been notably strong and well coordinated at that level. Coerciveness and punitiveness in this scenario mask this evisceration with the appearance of strength. The strength is, however, one of increasingly privatized force rather than the institutional infrastructure that has been the foundation of liberal public governance. Such colonization, where coercive or anti-democratic, may also evoke calls for limitations on state power from liberals themselves. At present, in America, rights, such as that of an accused person to silence, are being distorted and curtailed; the "political" is being reinvented as the "cultural," and "freedom" itself is being reimagined as "lifestyle." In such a setting, the political right quietly devours the procedural substance of the liberal state from within and, through shows of coerciveness, tempts liberals to finish dismantling the empty carapace. In this view, a reassertion of state power may be undertaken not to re-establish the strength of the state but rather to foster a caricature of power that masks on actual weakening and perhaps even to elicit calls for pruning back the apparatus of liberal governance – which the Right may oblige, but in unanticipated ways. If so, the political excesses of recent years assume a new meaning.

Recasting the sublime: deprivation as "unpresentable" dependency

In recent decades, Anglo-American criminal justice policy has undergone what I will call the "micro-death of the material." "Micro-death . . ." was Roland Barthes" acerbic description of his reaction to being photographed for the first time. Barthes bemoaned that photography "froze" wo/man and turned her/him into an object by reducing one to a mere two-dimensional image. He describes passionately "the violent experience of becoming and then being an object ('a micro-experience of death'), of being turned into an Image, nothing but a source for others' use" (Roland Barthes, 1980: 30–31). This was made possible by the fact that photography, like physics, introduced "new natures with a language capable of objectifying many" (Jardine et al., 1988: 125).

Today one sees the power to freeze, reduce and precipitate such a micro-experience of death extending beyond photography to politics and culture. Amidst the landscapes of crime and its control in late modernity, it is now the "frozen" image of appearance that transfixes (Baudrillard, 1995). In this way, we are brought into complicity in the reduction, or "micro-death," of the richness of sociality itself. It is my claim here and throughout this collection that disadvantage has, in recent years, undergone a sort of "micro-death." In it, the realities of life beyond "the face" – for the poor, the unemployed, the homeless – have been lost.

Imparting a negative sense of the "unpresentable"

In a cultural metamorphosis, I suggest that social exclusion has, in Anglo-American criminal justice policy, progressively been detached from its structural moorings in class and ethnicity to be reimagined in terms of "appearance" (Fraser, 1997; West, 1998). Criminality, broken families, problem drug use, lack of work discipline, unemployment, mental disorder and alleged preference for welfare benefits over work now emerge as the ingredients of a cultural pastiche of intergenerational dependency. In the extreme view, this "culture" is seen as breeding characterological flaws (Mead, 1986, 1992 and 1997; Murray, 1994). Like the signs of late-modern middle class affluence typified by gated communities, private (or in Britain, "public") school education and tennis club member-ships, the lifestyle of the poor now supplants the experiences of those struggling with poverty, discrimination and exclusion. "Dependency" with an accompanying image of "moral decay" has become the trope of disadvantage.

By focusing solely on superficial appearances, the image of "dependency" alludes to lives that are, in a deeper sense, unseen. The intimation is one of lives that are "unpresentable" and beyond our gaze. Yet, whereas the "unpresentable" traditionally has signified the sublime (or divine) as a positive ideal to which one aspires, it is now transposed to a sort of negative anti-ideal. It insinuates a shame that polarizes society as it repels the "worthy."

In contrast, this book joins a move to bring exclusion and disadvantage "back in" to prominence in the policy discourse of criminal justice. My quest is not to return to earlier shopworn approaches. Societies clearly now struggle with new challenges of privatization, dispersed power relations and performative conceptions of identity as well as new threats that require rethinking. Instead I explore an improvisation – a re-interpretation of some of the causes and the significance of these carceral policies – akin to that of the jazz musician en route to the new. Let us look now at the extent to which policy corresponds to crime trends or to findings of recent research. What we will see is that this policy shift dubbed by Jonathan Simon the "carceral turn" does not appear to respond strongly to either but, instead, to vary independently or to counter them (Sampson and Laub, 1993; Donziger, 1996; Morgan, 2002; Mauer, 2003).

Looking beyond dependency: three competing arguments

Today we encounter three main competing explanations for the growing punitiveness of Anglo-American criminal justice policy. First, some argue that prison expansion and punitiveness are a product of recent trends and patterns in crime. Though evidence is mixed, a mounting array of findings brings into question the strength or, in some cases, existence of a linkage between recent crime trends and rates of imprisonment (Useem, et al., 1999; Beckett and Western, 2001; Greenberg, 2001). A second argument is that society's increasingly punitive policies might reflect changes in thinking about "what works" in crime prevention, deterrence and offender reintegration. Yet current policy does not appear to relate coherently to recent research findings either (Currie, 1998). With these two explanations challenged, I turn to consider a third set of other explanations for the seemingly paradoxical rise in punitiveness. In recent years, scholars from many disciplines have begun to formulate a series of socio-political accounts that are evoking great interest. I focus, third, on these as it is on this cluster that my own work builds.

The new punitiveness and weak linkage to crime trends

Though it is intuitively appealing to imagine that prison expansion is linked to rising crime, there is growing, though controversial, evidence that such links are weaker than many have previously believed (Donziger, 1996; Beckett and Western, 2001; Greenberg, 2001). Greenberg (2001) urges us to remember, however, that, previously, some authors had found a substantial relationship between prison expansion and crime using rigorous cross-sectional, time-series and panel designs (Michalowski and Pearson, 1987; Jacobs and Helms, 1996; and Greenberg and West, 1998). He notes critically the very high levels of multi-collinearity in Beckett and Western's (2001) study and, because of it, advises that their findings be examined critically. Beckett and Western (2001) do write slightly later than Greenberg and West (1998), however, and might reflect different dynamics of the later "crime drop."

What *was* a problem through the late 1980s and early 1990s in America (and a bit later in England), when imprisonment was rising, was violence. It occurred in cities and its consequences spilled over to the suburbs (Blumstein, 1995). These violent acts were increasingly perpetrated by strangers who were very young – a trait that made them seem frighteningly irrational – and who were armed with guns that made them more lethal (Zimring and Hawkins, 1997; Blumstein and Wallman, 2006). In part, at least, this was associated with gang activity and the drug trade (Blumstein, 1995). It was a time of intense public anxiety about crime. Blumstein suggests that this increased violence by unknown, armed youths may have contributed substantially to the rising fear of crime in America. A similar pattern is now emerging in England with pockets of violence erupting amidst generally falling crime (Hough, 2006).

Perhaps, then, one might ask if the crucial link is that of prison expansion to violence rather than to crime. Again, however, we encounter a problem. Zimring and Hawkins (1997) have shown the difficulty of trying to link rates of imprisonment to rising violence by pointing out that, even under a minimally carceral policy, violent offenders are always likely to be imprisoned. Prison expansion, thus, tends to bring into custody not more violent offenders but other types of less serious offenders. Thus, Zimring and Hawkins suggest that prison expansion seems unlikely to have been caused in any rational sense by violence. Here Greenberg (2001) counters with a methodological reminder that the correlation between violent crime in 1995 and imprisonment in 1996 was strong with a correlation coefficient of 0.7 and had been equally strong a decade earlier. It is worth mentioning, though, that cross-sectional studies of the sort he cites can miss underlying third factors (e.g., severity of law enforcement). Beckett and Western (2001) point to some such factors when they observe that "poor states with high poverty rates and large numbers of minority ethnic groups and that have Republican majorities tend to imprison more people" (2001: 46). Beckett and Western argue that these relationships were stronger in 1995 than in earlier years – leading them to conclude that social and penal policy are closely linked only at certain times "when efforts are made to alter prevailing approaches to social marginality" such as during the Reagan presidency (2001: 46). Yet Greenberg (2001) again responds that the link between imprisonment and violence was equally strong earlier and may, thus, be more fundamental. In England, in contrast, prison growth seems a bit more closely linked to a surge of crime in the late 1980s.

If rising crime does not appear strongly linked to prison expansion, nor did prison expansion abate significantly when crime overall declined. Crime began a fairly sustained drop after 1994 in the United States but prison expansion continued (Donziger, 1996; Mauer, 2003). If mass imprisonment were, instead, a response to violence rather than overall crime, one would expect a softening of policy once violence in America declined in the late 1990s. Yet, while violence dropped after 1998, prison expansion continued (Donziger, 1996; Christianson, 1998; Mauer, 2003). A similar pattern can be seen in England (Maguire, 2002; Morgan, 2002) where prison expansion began during the late 1980s, paused in 1990, and then resumed and continues virtually unabated (after adjusting for changes in recording procedures) to this day. Thus, the extent of any relationship between imprisonment and either crime or violence seems limited at best. Crime worsened in both America and England despite the adoption of tougher policies beginning in the late 1980s and early 1990s and, when crime levels did abate in the mid-1990s, prison expansion continued (Donziger, 1996; Christianson, 1998; Morgan, 2002).

One could argue that prison expansion continues because it has been successful in reducing crime. According to this logic, prison expansion has reduced crime and continuing this punitive policy will cut it even further. Yet, crime rates persisted or rose for years after mass incarceration began though some argue it would have risen more otherwise. Even allowing for a lagged effect, there appears, however, to be evidence of only a limited impact of imprisonment on offending. One reason may be that it is less the severity of penalties and more their swiftness and certainty that deters (Wilson and Herrnstein, 1985). Despite this, some scholars argue that imprisonment inevitably reduces crime somewhat by incapacitating chronic recidivists (Wilson and Boland, 1971). One sophisticated quantitative estimate of the impact of imprisonment on crime rates suggests that approximately 15 to 35 percent of the crime drop throughout the late 1990s may be attributable to mass imprisonment (Spelman, 2000). An improved economy and demographic changes are also pointed to as possible causes. Other very fine work, however, suggests the effect may be much lower or non-existent (Useem, et al., 1999). One obvious problem is that, though each arrest may prevent some number of crimes, the share of crimes that end in arrest and custodial sentence is estimated at well under five percent. Thus, it takes a very great increase in imprisonment to generate a modest reduction in crime. Perhaps the greatest problem of such estimates, however, is that they say little about future recidivism, the children of prisoners, availability of delinquent replacements for those imprisoned or, especially, the persistently high level of violence at the core of the problem in America and, increasingly, England today (Hagan, 1996; Currie, 1998). Nor does it consider whether a crime drop might have been accomplished by more humane means.

When we shift our focus to the impact of prison expansion on violence, Currie (1998) has shown that inequality and the "safety net" a society provides for its most vulnerable members overwhelm imprisonment in their capacity to reduce violence. Countries with wide gaps between rich and poor consistently show higher rates of violent crime (Currie, 1998). Findings are similar for homicide, specifically, with inequality and social security demonstrating the strongest effects in curbing a country's homicide rate (Gartner, 1990). Gartner (1990) found that other factors affecting homicide rates included divorce, ethnic heterogeneity and cultural support for violence.

Similarly, Kenneth Land, Patricia McCall and Lawrence Cohen (1990) found that in America a composite measure of "resource deprivation" that included the proportion of families in poverty, median income, degree of income inequality, percentage of the population that is black, and percentage of children living with a single parent had "by far the strongest and most invariant effect" on homicide rates. Currie (1998) points out that the findings by Kenneth Land and his associates held true across cities, metropolitan areas and states over three decades between 1960 and 1980 (1998: 127). Finally, within deprived groups, it is the most impoverished boys, both in America and in England, who are most prone both to violence and to conviction for it (Farrington, 1989).

Popular punitiveness and recent research on "what works?" in reducing reoffending

One hopes that a regime engaging in mass imprisonment would draw on research about how custody can best prevent delinquency and reduce reoffending. Through most of the twentieth century, rehabilitation was emphasized as a cornerstone of criminal justice in England and America (Walker, 1980). In the mid-1970s, though, Lipton, Martinson and Wilkes (1975) wrote a book with the seemingly innocuous title *The Effectiveness of Correctional Treatment* that sparked vast changes (McGuire, 1999). Their study was widely misinterpreted to say that, when it comes to rehabilitation, "nothing works" (McGuire, 1999). In fact, the authors" conclusion was primarily a methodological one that, if we knew how to rehabilitate offenders, existing methodologies were unable to demonstrate it (Lipton, et al., 1975; Wilson, 1981). Nonetheless, the slogan that "nothing works" took on a life of its own that persisted for decades (Lilly, et al., 1995). Of the evidence that some offenders were being successfully rehabilitated, it was virtually only the efficacy of cognitive behavioral therapy and of practical and emotional skills training that came to light. The striking effectiveness of community-based prevention, such as prenatal care or early childhood education programs like Head Start, were softpedalled by policymakers or, more often, ignored (Currie, 1998).

In retrospect, much of the staying power of the idea that "nothing works" came from its perpetuation by conservative criminologists and policymakers. In the late 1970s, an alternative to rehabilitation as a policy approach emerged (Lilly, et al. 1995). It coincided with the publication by Andrew von Hirsh of his book, *Doing Justice*, and it focused on retribution. A social policy movement, known as the "Neo-Classical Revivial" coalesced around this retributive vision. Neo-Classicists argued against rehabilitation as the prime purpose of punishment – claiming that it violated proportionality and, therefore, justice.

They claimed that rehabilitation espoused a utilitarian sense of the public good that ignored, first, a people's thirst for fairness and, secondarily, the state's need to deter crime. Harking back to Beccaria and the Classical School, Neo-Classicists embraced a retributive approach. They urged that severity of punishment be proportional to the seriousness of a crime. By offsetting perfectly the weight of the crime, punishment could, they claimed, ensure that crime did not pay. This dovetailed with a rational choice theory of crime and, later, a policy of deterrence. Besides adhering to the *lex talionis*, retributivists argued that they communicated a message of fairness because any harm done had been repaid.

As "rational choice theory" developed, biological and psychological traits as well as genetic inheritance were studied for their propensity to produce behavior, such as impulsivity or stimulus-seeking, that might lead youths afoul of the law (Wilson and Herrnstein, 1985). Routine activities theory and situational crime prevention both grew out of this theorizing (Felson, 1994; Clarke and Clarke, 1997; Wilson and Herrnstein, 1985). Each perspective analyzed crime as a choice that some, but not all, youth make – thus highlighting voluntarism. Offenders were depicted as committing crime for some benefit: either "thrills" or another tangible or intangible gain. Crime reduction, according to these views meant ensuring that its costs outweighed any real or perceived benefit. This argument was embraced by a group that went beyond rational choice theory *simpliciter* to designate themselves "conservative criminologists" – most notably James Q. Wilson and Richard Herrnstein in *Crime and Human Nature* (1985).

The Neo-Classical Revival and underlying rational choice theory were used to justify increasingly punitive policies during the late 1980s that marked the start of the "carceral turn." Because de-institutionalization had begun a few years earlier, the prisons began to house both more offenders and, as a last resort, growing numbers of the mentally disordered.

Scope of mass imprisonment and composition of prison populations

Viewing criminal justice policy broadly during this period, one is struck by the extent of the carceral turn. By 1991, the United States had incarcerated more than one million persons at a rate of 426 per 100,000 persons. The country achieved the distinction by the mid-1990s of imprisoning a greater share of its population than any other country in the world – surpassing South Africa at 333 per 100,000 and the former Soviet Union at 268 per 100,000 (Donziger, 1996). By 2001, 1.3 million persons inhabited federal prisons and jails in America – a total that today exceeds 1.5 million (Mauer, 2003). This yielded a U.S. rate of incarceration in 2003 of 702 per 100,000 – still the highest of any nation (Mauer, 2003). The cumulative effect by 2003 was that 5.6 million Americans (or 1 in every 37) were in prison or had served time there (Mauer, 2003).

According to Blumstein and Beck (1999), quantitative analysis suggests that this expansion is primarily due to changes in sentencing policy. Of the expansion, changes in crime explained only 12 percent while new sentencing policies accounted for 88 percent (Blumstein and Beck, 1999). Of that 88 percent, increased rates of imprisonment for a felony contributed 51 percent and longer custodial sentences for felony offenders 37 percent.

Along with more frequent and longer custodial sentences, more than a dozen states in America have longstanding laws that disenfranchise those convicted of a felony. Recently, growing numbers of inmates has meant that those states have been rescinding voting rights at a very sprightly pace (Mauer, 2003; Uggen and Manza, 2006). More than 4 million prisoners or ex-prisoners in America are barred from voting – in twelve states for life (Mauer, 2003). Uggen and Manza (2006) argue that, in some states, the numbers disenfranchised were such that it exceeded the Republican margin of victory in the 2000 Presidential contest. Had those ex-felons voted, the outcome might have been different.

Britain too is now is experiencing a similar rise in punitiveness. England and Wales today incarcerate over 81,000 persons. Two recent reviews of criminal justice in the UK – the Halliday Report and the Auld Report – suggest that the total will climb still higher. Numbers rose modestly in the 1980's, peaked at 50,000 in 1988–89 and then declined to approximately 45,000 from 1990 to 1993. During the mid-1990s, numbers rose dramatically again to 62,000 by 1997, more than 76,000 by 2005 and over 81,000 at present. Between 1980 and 1995, 21 new prisons opened in England to provide more than 10,000 additional places and existing facilities were adapted to produce 7,000 more (Player, 2006). This growth in England and Wales is primarily due to longer sentences being imposed rather than more frequent custodial sentences (Morgan, 2002). Whereas, in the 1940s, only seven percent of prisoners in England and Wales served more than four years, today over half of British prisoners face such sentences.

Minorities have borne the heaviest share of this mass imprisonment in both countries. By the mid-1990s, it was estimated that one in three African-American males was under arrest, imprisoned, on probation or otherwise under the supervision of the criminal justice system (Donziger, 1996). A recent Department of Justice study shows that a black male born recently in America has a 29 percent chance of spending time in prison (Bonczar and Beck, 1997). In deprived areas, the chances are even worse – with estimates that in Washington, D.C. three-fourths of black males will be imprisoned at some point (Braman, 2002). Those imprisoned are consistently drawn from the most disadvantaged social groups. They tend to be extremely poor, unemployed and uneducated. Both in America and in England, they are often homeless, have spent time as a child in state care, and show high rates of physical health problems and mental disorder (Donziger, 1996; Currie, 1998; Wacquant, 2001).

Though women offend at relatively low rates, their rates of imprisonment have begun to increase significantly too (Adler, 1975; Morgan, 2002). One cannot but wonder whether this is a product of more punitive law enforcement. British research suggests that women tend generally to receive more lenient sentences for comparable crimes (Morris, 1987; Hood, 1992). It is worth remembering, though, that these women are far less likely to be violent or to have records of recidivism. British research suggests that in certain kinds of cases, however, women tend to experience a sort of "double jeopardy" that produces longer sentences than men for comparable crimes (Worrall, 1990). According to Worrall (1990) and Carlen (1998), women are given longer sentences mainly in cases where their offending violates male norms of femininity. Thus, they are sometimes effectively punished twice – once for breaking the law and a second time for violating gender norms. Gelsthorpe (2002) terms this "double deviance." The finding of double deviance precedes the recent custodial expansion and so could not have been caused by it. Far newer is an apparent narrowing of the gap in offending between males and females, especially with respect to violence.

Qualitatively, one dramatic change in the prisons has been their privatization and the rise of a "prison industry" (Christie, 1994). In some areas, prisons, whether public or private, are now coveted as generators of employment and economic development (Christianson, 1998). They represent a multi-billion dollar annual industry (Christianson, 1998). Architects, construction crews, surveillance and security specialists, guards, cooks, laundresses, maintenance workers and others build and operate a prison. Hotels, restaurants, transport workers, grocers, clothiers and stationers supply inmates, staff and visitors. It is estimated that in the United States a single maximum security prison cell costs $80,000 to build and more than $30,000 annually to operate (Christianson, 1998). For juvenile facilities, the annual operating costs may double due to the many special services required (Christianson, 1998). If costs in the United States are high, they appear even more so in Britain at £27,566 per year to support each inmate (Morgan, 2002).

The development of "three (two in Britain) strikes" policies has been another major change. These provide for a mandatory life term for a third (or in Britain second) felony conviction. Such policies appear to hold problems for the future. Offenders tend to "age out" of crime with most types of crime peaking during youthful, primarily teen, years (Steffensmeier, 1989). They mostly reduce their criminal activity as they grow older (Steffensmeier, 1989). Though Pampel and Gartner (1995) have questioned whether this pattern extends cross-culturally to societies with "collectivist orientations", it appears quite robust for both the United States and Britain. Thus, as Anglo-Americans implement "tough" mandatory "life" sentences, those imprisoned under it include many who will tend to "age out" of crime soon naturally in any case. Prisons are, thus, likely to find themselves supporting a vast and costly population of inmates – but ones no longer dangerous. Instead, the United States and Britain may soon operate one of the most expensive geriatric systems of social welfare in the history of the western world.

Not only is this mass incarceration enormously expensive and financially debilitating, it imposes enormous collateral costs (Mauer and Chesney-Lind, 2002). It disrupts networks of social relationships that restrain potential offenders from crime and cause active offenders to desist, even in adulthood (Laub and Sampson, 1993). It is now well recognized that not only does prison often fail to reform, but it can cause harm that increases subsequent offending (Abbott, 1981). Imprisonment erodes ties to family and work – prime factors in preventing recidivism (Sampson and Laub, 1993). It may also socialize prisoners into an inmate subculture or prison gang membership that is a "school for crime" (Sykes, 1956; Abott, 1981).

The new penology: from deterrence to incapacitation and beyond

Beginning in America in the late 1980s, public understanding of crime, which by then was grounded in retributivism, once again shifted. Ongoing management of troublesome populations began to be highlighted (Feeley and Simon, 1992). Simultaneously, the social and material circumstances of everyday life were transmuted from a context that might increase a youth's risk of offending to symptoms of lifestyle and (in the extreme version) personal character. It is in these years of the 1990s that the re-imagining of disadvantage as "dependency" appears to have begun to be consolidated.

Criminal offending was recast almost completely in privatized terms of individual responsibility for dependency and crime. Solutions morphed from deterrence and residues of rehabilitation to an increasingly punitive version of incapacitative retributivism. Insulated by long sentences, policymakers sidestepped issues of how unreformed inmates would behave upon release. Instead, populations perceived as constituting an intolerable risk began to be "managed" through lengthy mass incarceration rather than being reformed by any means. In an influential article, Feeley and Simon (1992) dubbed this approach "the new penology." By the late 1990s, the "social landscape" of crime control had changed in England too – in ways that increasingly resembled America (Loader and Sparks 2002). At this point it became meaningful to speak of an "Anglo-American" criminal justice policy. Why these changes occurred is a matter of debate. What is clear is that at the core of this approach was a novel approach to risk. In a telling and well-chosen phrase, Feeley and Simon (1992) describe the new policy approach as providing "actuarial justice." Successful policy implementation became a form of ongoing supervision. It institutionalized those designated as risks and claimed success by re-institutionalizing those who breached parole (or probation) rather than reforming and re-integrating ex-offenders (Feeley and Simon, 1992).

The focus on risk developed at least as rapidly in Britain as in the United States. British risk assessment categorizes those accused on the basis of personal attributes as well as their alleged offences and prior record. These classifications then become a basis for estimating those individuals' probabilities of committing future harm. The probability, rather than deriving from a clinical assessment, is instead based on past behavior by others of similar classification. Early response to an offender is, thus, anchored on the lives of persons unrelated to the accused person and, in fact, unknown to them. In undertaking the risk assessment, individual traits are focused on even though they may be a product of social circumstances beyond the individual's control. For example, violent youths have often been victims of abuse. Such youths are, however, held solely responsible for their behavior and penalized for responding to others as they have been conditioned to.

Alternatives to custody, in particular, place much responsibility for errant behavioral predispositions on the alleged offender. As in Braithwaite and Pettit's (1992) scheme of progressive penalties, an offender who is estimated to present low risk may initially be diverted from custody in favor of community penalties or drug treatment. Yet such programs are individually tailored to require that an extensive menu of conditions be met. Under the new British Drug Treatment and Testing Orders, for example, the accused may be mandated to meet a daunting regime of requirements including frequent testing and counselling. If a condition is breached – for example, an offender fails to take or pass a drug test – the accused is initially warned. Upon subsequent breach, however, he or she would probably be returned to court, labelled a violator and encounter a more punitively inclined judge. There is concern that such offenders might then face a higher tariff than if the Treatment Order were never issued. Thus, the individual is not only classified on the basis of other persons" behaviors but also held to a rehabilitative standard that many non-offenders could not achieve. Behavior does involve choice. Learning and, especially, incentives can, however, also be powerful. Resistance of even the worthy can weaken as many as an otherwise virtuous maid who gave birth en route to the altar can affirm.

This managerialism and also risk assessment largely ignores research recently done that shows how social contexts work not only directly but also indirectly through cultural practices and institutions (Laub and Sampson, 1993; Sampson and Laub, 1993; Farrington, 1995 and 2002; Bottoms and Wiles, 2002). In this way, they shape what appear to be purely "personal" behavior and traits, influence seemingly "individual" choices and, ultimately, heighten or reduce risks of offending (Sampson and Laub, 1993). This research supplements the already powerful work that we examined above on the direct impact of inequality, poverty and a social "safety net" on the propensity for crime and violence. Together these strands of research suggest the importance of weaving disadvantage and social exclusion back into our public policies about crime (Sampson and Laub, 1993; Land, et al., 1996; Currie, 1998; Wikstrom and Loeber, 2000).

All too absent in the policy debate has been a recognition that what gives rise to many destructive human tendencies is conditions in the neighborhood, financial situation, workplace, families, schools or peer groups of delinquents and adult offenders (Sampson and Laub, 1993; Rosenfeld et al., 2001; Sampson et al., 2002; Beyers et al., 2003). Increasingly, research shows, in particular, how a community context of disadvantage works to heighten risks of offending (Andrews and Bonta, 1998; Weatherburn and Lind, 1998; Sampson and Laub, 2003). One major way this occurs is through the creation of stress (Currie, 1998; Rubin, 1976). A second primary way in which community context is formative is in shaping what may, at first glance, appear to be individual characteristics through parenting practices (Sampson and Laub, 1993). A third is the vulnerability to and failure to diagnose and treat physical and psychological disabilities or risk factors (Bartol and Bartol, 1997). Sampson and Laub (2003) has argued that neighborhoods should, for public health purposes, be considered a trait of the individual. Fischer et al.'s (1996) conclusion that neighborhood disadvantage to some extent results from conscious or inadvertent public policy decisions may provide a non-traditional opening for new thinking about responses to crime.

Cool control: risk and a new cultural authoritarianism

Many policymakers interpret this transformation of Anglo-American criminal justice as primarily a cultural phenomenon. Yet, scholarly research has had a strong structural referent. Some researchers, notably Garland (2001) and Bottoms (1995), explicitly see these cultural changes as structurally based while others, such as Feeley and Simon (1992), depict them as a shift in Foucauldian "governmentality," though in a way consistent with structural analysis. What Garland has termed "the penal welfare state," whose institutions and cultural practices were constitutive of crime control throughout the early- to mid-twentieth century, has been re-imagined variously as "risk society" (Beck, 1992), a "new penology" (Feeley and Simon, 1992), a "culture of control" (Garland, 2001), "governing through crime" (Simon, 1997) and "penal populism" (Bottoms, 1995). In each formulation, however, one or more common themes tend to emerge. These include: punitiveness, a plebiscitary role for the public, influence of the media, a changing state stance either through legislation or enforcement, a pre-occupation with risk, and an emphasis on managing what are perceived to constitute prospective threats of harm.

Loader and Sparks (2002) argue that the reasons for this shift in criminal justice are threefold: 1) a sharp rise in recorded crime since World War I such that criminal victimization became "a routine part of modern consciousness"; 2) social and cultural changes in markets and production, the family, media and the social relations of the quotidian coupled with a weakening of the routine acceptance of authority; and 3) New Right governments in the United States and the British Commonwealth that sought to reconfigure the logic and institutions of the state under the mantle of replacing "dependence" with privatization and individual responsibility (Loader and Sparks, 2002: 86). They contend that not only did these developments serve to make public anxiety about crime and fear of disorder defining contours of "late modernity" but they brought the ability of even strong states to provide security for their people dramatically into question (2002: 86). Central to these changes was a focus on risk as a privatizing force, as individuals retained paid security for themselves and associates, and a virulent, but somewhat ineffectual, punitiveness on the part of the state. O'Malley (1993) terms this tendency "private prudentialism."

Imagining ways of predicting and mitigating future harm reoriented criminology's focus and its initiatives as well as its "institutional connections" (Loader and Sparks, 2002: 92). The shift to risk-based prevention has remade the field in ways that, because cultural, are malleable but extremely hard to dispute, stop or even identify (2002: 92). Risk management deploys force in the service of a vision that is inherently speculative. What seems not yet to have occurred to the public imagination is that this has contributed to the opening a new phase (or "face") of Anglo-American politics and of the "culture wars." For Ulrich Beck, who coined the term "risk society," the notion of risk goes beyond the use of practices for estimating future harm to reshape criminal justice for risk management. The key changes, as Beck sees it, are that potential rather than actual harms are designated for attention and that entire groups of persons may be deemed an "intolerable . . . risk" (2002: 95). Beck envisions risk, interestingly, as involving "hazards and insecurities [that may be] induced . . . by modernization itself" and the "globalization of doubt" (Beck, 1992: 21). That is, they are man-made. To some extent uncertainty and anxiety are inherent in the focus on risk since the extent to which *potential* harm will actually be realized cannot be known until it actually happens.

For Beck, as later for Giddens (1994), this vision of impending harm intensifies criminal justice responses for it elicits very intensive action to prevent it. For Beck, one hallmark of "risk society" is "ambivalence" – between belief in "progress" and "reactive traditionalism", reliance on "technical information" and scepticism of "experts", between "authority" and "withdrawal of legitimacy", between "local particularism" and "global utopia", and, finally, between "indifference" and "hysteria" (Loader and Sparks, 2002: 92). Beck warns of the potential for authoritarian tendencies in elites" capacities to deploy expert knowledge for control as well as to mobilize solidarity through cultural tactics of fear mongering and scapegoating (2002: 95). What Beck hints at is a new "cooler," minimal and more elusive form of potentially authoritarian control in the making.

Mary Douglas' "cultural theory of risk" reminds us that "risk" is not an event or "thing" but rather a way of thinking about future potential harm in terms of both its "probability" and the prospective "magnitude," in gain or cost, of its "outcome" (Douglas, 1992: 47). She argues that the nature and sources of threat that a community sees provide insight into its approaches to order and authority (1992: 47). In this book, I build on Douglas' thinking to use an analysis of crime to illuminate changes underway in the contours of Anglo-American criminal justice and governance today.

Building on Beck's argument in *Risk Society*, several authors suggest that anticipation of future harm has combined with rising fear of crime to spur new levels of insecurity and heighten punitiveness. David Garland (2001) has portrayed this as the emergence of a "culture of control." He has attempted to identify the pre-conditions for this shift. Among those he highlights are: "preoccupation with risk; distrust of government and professional elites; neo-liberal political ideology . . . [and] high crime rates becoming accepted as the normal state of affairs" (Garland, 2001; Hudson, 2002: 252). My own work confirms the importance of these factors. What I attempt, though, is to explore further some aspects of the underlying generative process for these dynamics, asking where, when and how the new punitivism arose and examining it for tendencies toward private governance or control and public minimalism.

In his own analysis, Garland links culture with crisis in elaborating an account of the rise of a "culture of control" (Garland, 2001). He argues that change occurs during crisis and that what changes occur ultimately depends on the repertoires of cultural practices available and the way that society is configured at that time (Garland, 2001; Hudson, 2002: 252). Garland (2001) argues that an ongoing state of crisis during the late twentieth century demanded nearly continual innovation. How Garland reconciles this crisis and innovation with a time that gave us the "me generation" and then "generation X," both associated with static self-absorption, is a bit unclear. Among the features that Garland sees reshaping punishment in "late modernity" are: "patterns of . . . [allocating] risk and blame; hyper-individualism and distrust of large and remote power groupings; power of the mass media; the social effects of migration; and the dominance of economic rather than social reasoning" (Garland, 2001; Hudson, 2002: 252).

In contrast with Garland's argument, Bottoms (1987 and 1995) has claimed that "penal populism" is at work in which policies are enacted simply because of their appeal to electoral constituencies. Here Bottoms steers a course close to Cohen's (2003) argument that media-driven public opinion has created a "moral panic" that has demonized offenders. Bottoms suggests that officials respond strongly to such popular sentiments. Offenders have, he argues in a way consonant with Beck, been made scapegoats for politicians" appeals to voters through "get-tough" policies on crime.

Other authors suggest that punitivism may be a response to labor market conditions. In the 1960s, Rusche and Kirchheimer (1939) argued that severity of punishment varies with abundance or scarcity of labor supply. Male punishment, they argued, is less severe when labor demand exceeds supply and a larger free workforce is needed – a claim later taken up by Melossi and Pavarini (1981). While critics warn against oversimplifying the connection, recent studies confirm that rates of imprisonment tend to rise when unemployment is high (Rothman, 1971; Greenberg and West, 1998; Box and Hale, 1982; Melossi, 1985). Western and Beckett's (1999) work also is consistent with this view. They link prison expansion to rates of unemployment – suggesting that rising imprisonment was partly fueled by shunting the unemployed to prisons. They claim that this may explain why inflation remained low despite nearly full employment in the United States during the 1990s – an argument that Greenberg (2001) has challenged on grounds of the form of the models used.

Beckett and Western (2001), working in a similar vein, advance what has come to be known as the "transcarceration" thesis. They observe that societies spending least on social welfare have the highest rates of imprisonment – an argument that is well supported by the literature (Greenberg and West, 2001). Prison and welfare institutions, they argue, have come to comprise a single regime of substitutable treatments for housing and controlling excluded groups. Such persons, Beckett and Western contend, migrate among these "transcarceral" agencies – living out what Hudson (2002: 245) has described as "an institutionally mobile deviant career."

Of special interest has been conceptually related work by Stuart Hall (1980), Phil Scraton (1987) and, most recently, Jonathan Simon (1997) that explores crime control as an emergent form of governance. Writing several decades ago, Hall (1980) and Scraton (1987) seemed to build on Habermas's argument in *Legitimation Crisis* (1973) to observe that the balance between repressive and rehabilitative strategies of punishment shifted fundamentally as a result of an economic recession in the late 1970s in America and the 1980s in Britain. These years, they argued, saw irreversible deindustrialization and flight of jobs overseas. What resulted was a situation in which non-colonial capitalism – no longer offering the tangible rewards of the good life through salaried work – increasingly substituted repressive techniques of surveillance and policing as a means of maintaining conformity and order at home.

To legitimate such action domestically, it was necessary that responsibility for state coercion be seen as lying with "the deviants." Hudson (2002) suggests that a sort of "authoritarian populism" developed according to which those who failed to produce economically by legitimate means or who challenged authority were re-imagined as "enemies within" from whom decent citizens must be protected (Hudson, 2002: 245). Benefit cuts, census undercounts of the unemployed, more repressive (though not necessarily more strictly enforced) rules for immigrants and asylum seekers and prison expansion all contributed to further marginalize disadvantaged and/or excluded groups (2002: 245–6).

With his concept of "governing through crime," Simon (1997 and 2007), brings these issues into the present. Simon draws on Beck (1992) and Foucault (Burchell, et al., 1991) to show that, in this time of intensified insecurity, the state cannot fully assure the security of its people – even in the advanced industrial west. Punitiveness, in this view, results from a state effort to win back and revitalize sovereignty. Public fear of crime calls for mobilization of expanded "power and resources" to combat threat and disorder. This, in turn, bolsters the sovereignty of the nation state (Hudson, 2002: 249). Noting that neo-liberal agendas of the 1990s and early twenty-first century restricted welfarist initiatives just as jobs moved overseas, analysts from this perspective claim that politicians wishing to portray themselves as strong leaders turned to crime fighting – where their mandate was strong and where expensive welfarist programs could be avoided.

Simon's work draws support from Giddens (1994) who shows that dynamics of globalization, which have intensified competitiveness by drawing local producers into world markets, have added to the financial pressures on the welfare state. Many have written about the "fiscal crisis that beset the modern western welfare states during the 1970s and early 1980s (O'Connor, 1973; Offe and Keane, 1984). With the turn to New Right governments committed to neo-liberal principles thereafter, severe retrenchment of welfarism took place. Job flight, de-industrialization and the global "race to the bottom" for lowest-priced labor all increased unemployment in advanced industrial societies. Welfarist states were increasingly unprepared to cope. As globalization created more financial pressure, the cost of local welfare spending came to be seen as requiring a tax burden that would render a society's goods and products non-competitive as that cost was passed on to the consumer. This global competitiveness-driven challenge produced major social welfare cutbacks.

Public minimalism: retreat and the "hollowing out" of the state

We have already examined some competing explanations for the carceral turn. My sense is that prior authors have been right in suggesting that the power and authority of the state had been weakened. I would like to suggest, however, that more remains to be said – especially about recent developments under the influence of the political Right in America. My own claim is that a political "sea change" – it may not be too strong to call it a sort of "revolution" – is underway and that its ultimate port of call is a growth of private self-generating regulatory arrangements – or, in the extreme case, even private governance per se – coupled with public minimalism. It is a transformation in which criminal "justice" is being drawn on to play a key part. This sea change is not a minor one but rather something more fundamental that has quietly begun to recraft the landscape of law and politics in America and, through it, England – though in somewhat different ways. So extensive are the changes that it will take decades to reverse, if reversal is possible. At its core, this transformation began with politics – politics conditioned by unique economic circumstances. It is strongly reminiscent of Richard Nixon's use of politics and involves its use to deliberately polarize voting constituencies along designated social or racial lines. Nixon did this most clearly in the case of affirmative action. He used the policy, which he worked to associate with the Democratic Party, to mobilize opposition among lower-middle and working class whites, who often tend to be Democrats, and to win over their support to the Republicans. The administration of George W. Bush appears to be enacting similarly polarizing policies, notably in criminal justice, and using them in similar ways. Their known consequence, I suggest, is to divide America along racial lines, repress and disenfranchise large segments of the naturally-Democratic black community and marginalize African-American leaders whilst at the same time drawing middle class whites, blacks and Hispanics along with working class and perhaps some poor whites and Hispanics into the Republican Party.

What has prompted this campaign and why is it taking the form that it has? In this paper, I suggest that this is a story about power. Specifically, my claim is that these changes may be about a partial, or perhaps not so parital, transformation of sovereignty. These shifts appear to be beginning to limit the participatory popular sovereignty that has underpinned public power throughout much of the history of the modern West and to supplant it increasingly with self-generating private regulatory arrangements, on the one hand, and minimal public power, on the other. It may be a shift for which the recently observed erosion of the boundary between public and private has helped pave the way.

In part these changes involve a movement towards the transnational as a place of governance. In the public realm, the European Union typifies such movement. Transnational governance has, however, historically been marked by a democratic deficit. It tends inherently towards administrative control. Lacking a *demos*, popular participation has, so far, tended to be weak as the experience of the EU Parliament shows. Global financial groups have also played a part in developing private self-generating regulatory schemes such as the "lex mercatoria" – a voluntary system of binding arbitration to resolve contract disputes in international commercial law (Teubner, 1997; Dezalay and Garth, 1998). Operating largely beyond the reach of the nation state, it provides reasoned decisions by highly knowledgeable experts mutually chosen by the parties to a dispute. Its decisions are enforced, not only by recourse to public bodies, though that is technically possible, but more often, in the manner of a club, through the threat of exclusion from future dealings (Dezalay and Garth, 1998). With arbitrators, who are familiar with the enormous complexity of the enterprise and its procedures, their decision affords a reasonable amount of predictability. One might be tempted at first to argue that private systems, such as the "lex mercatoria," are more responsive to the needs of users than are public arrangements. The drawback is that mechanisms for public accountability are all but absent.

Both nationally and transnationally, the balance of public and private power appears to be shifting in favor of private institutions. Though Foucault long ago showed that we inhabit a world of diffuse and decentralized power relations, we seem to be witnessing something different today. This is that "state authority has [not just dispersed but actually] leaked away, upwards, sideways, and downwards" (Strange, 1996: 7–14) Some suggest this amounts to a "retreat" or "hollowing out" of the state (Strange, 1996; Douglas, 2002). Accelerating technological change "[has] relax[ed] the authority of the state over enterprises [both legal and illegal that are] based . . . [or] directed [both] from inside [and outside] their territorial borders" (Strange, 1996: 7–14). Strange (1996) concludes that "authority over society and economy has become diffused in neo-medieval fashion . . . and [that] some . . . authority once exercised by states is now exercise by no one" or is exercised differently by private parties (1996: 7–14).

Within national borders, we see privatization, to give just a few examples, in the growth of private prisons, the rise of private security guards in gated communities and shopping malls, the rise of private airport and transport police, neighborhood watch networks, volunteer crime prevention patrols, proliferation of private drug treatment facilities, boot camps, CCTV surveillance and even private military contractors. We also see expansion of the private realm in settlements negotiated outside of court, the pervasiveness of plea bargaining and the growth of mediation.

Even as privatization shifts criminal justice activity out of public hands, policy changes are bringing growing numbers of people into this public–private amalgam. Their stays are more extended as a result of longer sentences, mandatory minimums, "truth in sentencing" policies and "three (or two in England) strikes" policies, among others. In England, additional practices are also swelling the ranks of those supervised through apparent net widening and unintended up-tariffing. These other practices include: drug treatment and testing orders, community penalities and the relatively new British antisocial behavior orders (ASBOs). The first two practices appear initially to offer leniency. Yet, attached to each are a menu of conditions whose breach may result in a subsequent custodial sentence. The consequence may be an unintended up-tariffing beyond what would have been imposed at the start. An ASBO, which prohibits behavior that may not itself be criminal, can lead to custody if violated even when the original behavior could not. Because these practices seem to proffer leniency, there may be more willingness than otherwise to bring formal charges. The result may widen the net thrown by the system and draw a greater number of persons into its orb. Thus, criminal justice institutions swell to bursting while its activity gradually shifts into private hands.

Even conceptions of freedom are privatizing. Recent research by Orlando Patterson (2006) has shown that, at least in the United States, freedom is increasingly coming to be understood as a range of personal choice rather than, for example, rights to free expression or political participation. In keeping with the blurring of the boundary between public and private, liberty is thus growing to be understood privately and dissociated from politics. If we distinguish between negative liberty (i.e., the capacity to do as we wish such as speak freely) and positive liberty (i.e., one that we rely on the state to exercise such as welfare rights), this emergent notion shows some affinity with the former. What we see, though, is negative liberty reimagined from autonomy to lifestyle choice.

Are we, then, witnessing a "retreat of the state" in the sense of a permanent decline of public power? Will law and regulation become, like penal institutions, increasingly privatized so that the "lex mercatoria" may preview a new global model of self-generating private governance? Or are we perhaps witnessing a "hollowing out" specifically at the level of the nation state with real power shifting to transnational but still public institutions? What we have seen seems to suggest a strengthening of transnational governance of some sort amidst a neoliberal global market society. It is a picture in which nation states, at least for the time being, continue to play a minimal but vital public role of assuring security and justice. Regulation and control may, according to this scenario, increase even as the role of public institutions at the national level narrows. The limited role that remains focuses the state on social control, surveillance, policing and military intervention (Hall, 1980; Habermas, 1998). Meanwhile, democracy may devolve locally to function expressively. In themselves, these changes to liberal democratic governance are quiet but profound – making these perhaps the most transformative years in most of our lives. Yet, there appears to be more. Though these ideas begin to explain the growing state focus on policing and control, they still do not explain why such punitiveness of approach has developed, why in the particular form it has, particularly for minority communities, and why now. Let us now reconsider the issue of punitiveness and why it has arisen.

Intersubjectivity as a micro-mechanism of change

To say that our sense of self is shaped by our interactions with others has become common wisdom (Mead, 1967; Taylor, 1994). In recent years, scholars of social diversity, in particular, have highlighted the formative power of intersubjectivity. From Hegel's (1807) parable of "lordship and bondage" to Mead's (1967) work on the "generalized other," the message is that our relationships with others and their responses to us shape our selves and behavior (Rosenthal and Jacobson, 1966; Anderson, 1984; Taylor, 1994; Fitzpatrick and Tuitt, 2004). Writings about the experience of colonialism, of war and of occupation demonstrate this with special clarity (Fanon, 1963).

It has been shown that each of these experiences shapes the aggressor as much as it does the victim (Hegel, 1807; Fanon, 1963; Kelley, 2000). For example, Arendt (1973) demonstrated how Western imperialism during the nineteenth century produced changes in Europe that contributed to the rise of totalitarianism during the 1930s. It did this, she claims, by introducing notions of the national particularism of rights and, consequently, of racism. Similarly, in America, the Cold War began amidst a period of intense anxiety following World War II when victory was eclipsed by China's turn to communism, her detonation of an atom bomb and war in Korea. Fear of communism abroad led to the development of a black and white, highly ideological worldview along with a repressive political style at home. Perhaps nothing so represented the quintessence of these years in America as McCarthyism under which dissent was quashed, political non-conformists were blacklisted, privacy was invaded and civil liberties were violated. In the aftermath of the Cold War, Americans saw the world in polarized terms. The language of "friend" and "foe" now fit like an old and comfortable glove. Today, some suggest that another American regime, fresh from war in Iraq in 1991, has embarked on a comparable course of domestic political repression. Others counter, of course, that this style has always slumbered in the current administration. Yet, I suggest that this repression and punitivism has, since 2000, entered a new phase. Possible contributing factors to a climate of punitivism at home include, I suggest, residual traces of a Cold War mentality, the experience of recent wars and military interventions in Iraq, Kuwait and Afghanistan, and the philosophy and ideology that congealed around them.

To explore the sources of these changes more fully, I propose to do three things. First, I will sketch some political background to the policies of the second Bush administration and examine the composition of its inner advisory circle by way of considering the influences shaping its policymaking. Second, given the influences at work, I will probe how one might theoretically understand the recent punitiveness of the Bush and Blair governments – and indeed how the Bush circle itself sees its own political project. Finally, I consider alternative approaches to contemporary criminal justice policy – both in their implication for criminal justice and for our very understanding of democracy.

Roots of political sea change: Nixon, Reagan and the first Bush administration

Let us now revisit the carceral turn in the historical context of post-World War II American politics. In the United States, one can trace the precursors of today's punitiveness through five stages. These are more or less co-terminous with Presidential administrations starting with the second foreshortened term of Richard Nixon that ended in 1973 up to the present one. In Britain, it developed primarily more or less in two stages beginning with the Thatcher and subsequent Major governments a little over half a decade later in the early 1980s and continued with the New Labour government of Tony Blair into the new millennium.

The Nixon government was, by today's standards, seemingly moderate. It highlighted crime control and social order as part of its appeal to middle class voters (whom the President dubbed "the silent majority") who had grown disenchanted with the Democratic Party which presided over race riots, spiralling social welfare spending and the youth culture of the 1960s and early 1970s (Schell, 1976). Nixon promised to refocus social policy back on the interests of the "silent [middle class] majority" – and especially on crime control. Nonetheless, social welfare spending grew during Nixon's years in office. Nixon's apparent moderation was, as we shall see, part of his landmark "Southern Strategy" of fighting each election by highlighting competition for centrist voters and, especially, of attempting to woo moderate Democrats from the southern states and members of the white middle and working classes across the country into the Republican camp. One main tactic of the "Southern Strategy" was a divisive one that involved fostering voting rights for African-Americans and then using black voter registration to depict the Democratic Party as the political home of minority voters in the south – thus prompting white segregationists to switch to the Republican Party. It is at this point that polarization surfaced explicitly as a dominant element in the repertoire of contemporary American politics.

The Carter Presidency, which focused on fiscal responsibility and human rights, appears to have inadvertently strengthened the triggers for division lingering from the Nixon years. By relying on rights litigation rather than welfarism, Jimmy Carter avoided a spurt of social spending. However, the sweeteners to equal opportunity in terms of funding on which Lyndon Johnson had relied were, thus, absent. In that climate, rights litigation such as busing for school desegregation began, as Nixon would have predicted, to produce a vociferous backlash.

Ronald Reagan began his Presidency with an organic conservative vision that directly opposed big government intervention and welfarism. His worldview was of a naturally developed social order in which each person had their place. While very limited on equal opportunity and restrictive on law and order, it was not notably punitive. Everyone did have *a place*. Reagan's vision was symbolically inclusive and paternalistically humane, though far from egalitarian, in gesturing all social groups into an ever more unequal social order. During his term, inequality surged to levels not seen in America since the eve of the Great Depression in 1929 (Galbraith, 1961). As part of Reagan's opposition to social welfare, his budget chief David Stockman (1987) tells us that Reagan planned enormous outlays for defense and crime control that would create deficits which he could use to justify brutal cuts in welfare spending. History shows that those deficits ran out of control leaving a debilitating national debt as a legacy of his administration – one that Bill Clinton wrestled back into balance only to be undone again by George W. Bush who, individually, has created more debt than all American Presidents combined. Under the Reagan administration, the already limited repertoire of American social welfare programs was radically cut back and remains so to this day.

While law and order had been a priority since Nixon, it was under the elder George H. Bush in 1988 that punitiveness was consolidated. I suggest that two factors, in particular, shaped the policies of that administration – first, the mentality of the Cold War in whose later years Bush "pater" had played a leading role at the American Central Intelligence Agency (CIA) and, second, neo-liberal free market ideology. Both unfolded in the late 1980s against a backdrop of rapidly consolidating global financial power. That drama of reconfiguring economic power was one in which, George H. Bush would, with former Secretary of State James Baker, later play a major part through the Carlyle Group.

As a Congressman, ambassador and eventually Director of the CIA, George H. Bush helped implement the post-war American foreign policy known as "containment." This was a strategy crafted by George Kennan after World War II to limit the spread of communism. Initially designed as a political and economic plan to protect American interests in five geographic areas of clear strategic importance, containment was distorted in practice into a doctrine of military intervention that was applied indiscriminately around the globe. The strategy of containment was invoked to support a sustained Allied military presence in Germany and later American military interventions in Laos, Vietnam and Cambodia. Containment was first reinterpreted militarily in the course of American response to what it claimed to be "democratic insurgency" in Greece and Turkey during the 1950s. National Security Council Resolution 68 (NSC-68), which became a cornerstone of the Truman Doctrine, was passed, ostensibly to enable economic and political support for "freedom fighters" resisting "armed subjugation" (Brinkley, 2003). Passage of NSC-68 in 1947 is often used to mark the shift from post-war Détente with the Soviet Union to "containment" and the start of the "Cold War." NSC-68, like containment, was eventually applied militarily as the "domino theory" to limit communist expansion in Southeast Asia. Thus began a series of ill-fated American military interventions around the globe. In the Vietnam years, a tendency of the United States to intervene globally in times of relative peace and to do so militarily was born. It was in this ambience that George H. W. Bush was formed politically and it shaped him, as had been Richard Nixon, as an "internationalist."

Just as these armed interventions of the Cold War had powerful consequences abroad, they also remade life at home. A climate of fear and repression within the United States developed as attention turned to routing out communism within American borders (Rovere, 1996). The approach focused on coercion, rather than persuasion, as exemplified by McCarthyism. Pressure to conform intensified and dissent was attacked (Brinkley, 2003). Thus, the dominant imagery of Presidential power that George H. Bush brought with him to the Oval Office in 1988 was one of militarism and policing, support for free market activity and homogeneity as a measure of patriotism. These were recurrent points of reference in many of his ventures. Internationally, these included: the 1991 Persian Gulf War, rapprochement with China, and encouragement of Russian Glasnost and Perestroika. Domestically, he escalated the issue of crime control through tough law enforcement and harsher sentencing – ultimately declaring a "war on drugs" and recasting policing as a campaign to rout out a new type of domestic threat. Under these policies, police stop and searches increased, racial profiling spread, imprisonment for drug possession surged, arrests among ethnic minorities and the disadvantaged skyrocketed and prison populations soared. Few images so captures the spirit of that administration as the ominous, racialized campaign advertisement featuring Willie Horton, a paroled offender, who murdered after being released. Ultimately, the elder Bush failed to win re-election due to a variety of conditions including a shaky economy, the challenge of Ross Perot and lack of a coherent political "vision." Those lessons would profoundly shape his son's administration as the Cold War had his own. Thus, these years saw the development of a more punitive and, with the onset of the 1991 war in Iraq, also militaristic policy style that highlighted control.

The Clinton administration, in a mirror image of Nixon's "Southern Strategy," moved to the centre to woo moderates back again from the Republicans to the Democratic Party. One crucial element of this approach was an appeal to centrist Republicans through sound management of the economy and a continuation of the commitment of Nixon, Bush and Reagan before him to be "tough on crime." Whereas Nixonian strategy had been to polarize, Clinton sought to include. With the benefit of superb financial guidance, the economy flourished and Americans at all income levels, including the most disadvantaged, gained though inequality was not greatly reduced. Due partly to improved economic conditions, crime dropped beginning in the mid-1990s as did violence by 1998. Yet, Clinton continued the penal policies of the first Bush administration that imposed long sentences and mandatory penalties with the result that prisons continued to grow despite the crime drop.

When George W. Bush acceded to the Presidency in 2000, his advisors were determined not to repeat the mistakes of his father's administration. The old advisory circle, while still prominent at the highest levels, was joined now by a new generation. It was a group notable for the prominence in its ranks of former students from the University of Chicago and, particularly, of Leo Strauss – himself previously a student of the German theorist Carl Schmitt (Norton, 2005). The new generation was closely attuned to the power of divisiveness as a political force and to the potency of culture in bringing change.

The legacy of Carl Schmitt and Leo Strauss: polarization and the culture wars

Political polarization entered the second Bush administration, then, through the influence of Leo Strauss and through lingering memory of Nixonian political strategy. Nixonian memories were undergoing a renaissance in 2000 since the "Monica Lewinsky affair" had been touted as retribution for that President's impeachment decades earlier. In moving to define the Presidency of George W. Bush in 2000, the new advisory circle drew from Ronald Reagan a recognition of the importance of vision, private voluntarism and personal charisma. From Richard Nixon they embraced internationalism, emerging multi-polarity of global leadership, and a sense of the power of political polarization at home. However, these concepts assumed new forms in the hands of the young group of scholars and publicists from Chicago.

In her book *Leo Strauss and the Politics of American Empire*, Anne Norton (2005) brilliantly documents the intellectual pedigree harking back to the University of Chicago of many dozens of Bush advisors and appointees who trace their lineage to Leo Strauss. She demonstrates the growing influence of this circle on the Presidency of George W. Bush. My own interest is in showing how Straussian and Schmittian influences helped to shape the ideological contours of this second Bush Presidency (Douglas-Scott, 2006). Let me begin by sketching a few elements of Schmitt's and Strauss' thought.

Carl Schmitt was a German critic of liberalism who lived in Germany during the 1920s just before the National Socialists came to power. Schmitt provides a critique of liberalism, generally, and, in particular, of the liberal rule of law and of proportional representation (Douglas-Scott, 2006; Schmitt, 2007). Schmitt saw the Weimar government as paralyzed and unable to mobilize citizens. The problem, Schmitt argued, lay in "liberal neutrality" which tended to eviscerate politics. Because liberals tried to incorporate all views, government became bogged down in virtually endless deliberation. Its officials held such diverse ideas that it was very hard to form coalitions. Thus, decision making was impaired. As Schmitt saw it, Germany was mired unnecessarily in stasis.

In response, Schmitt articulated a startlingly new conception of "the political" to provide a basis for strong leadership, an engaged public and decisive political action. Decrying liberal lethargy, Schmitt argued that emergency provisions that enabled a leader to suspend the constitution by declaring a "state of exception" should be used more frequently. "Sovereign is he," stated Schmitt, "who declares the exception" (Schmitt, 2007). In this way, Schmitt depicted the establishment of sovereignty as an act of force. A "state of exception" would, Schmitt believed, open the way for a charismatic figure to bypass enervating neutrality to lead vigorously (Schmitt, 2007). He saw in unfettered executive power a potency not available to deliberative liberalism. Such mobilization, far from undermining democracy, could, he thought, strengthen it. Since democracy centred on the relation of a people to their leaders, Schmitt felt that it could take many forms – even authoritarianism.

According to Schmitt, the essence of "the political" lies in the distinction between "friend" and "foe" (Schmitt, 2007). This distinction can be recognized by a leader. It can arise around any difference that might be intensified to a point that it involved a struggle to the death (Schmitt, 2007). Possibilities vary but the distinction, most often, is one of ethnicity or religion. Once an enemy is designated, a leader can refer to it to engage the imaginations of the people (Schmitt, 2007). While war or death need not follow, politics unfolds in the shadow of that possibility.

As a leader mobilizes a people, he may invoke images from the traditional culture of the "volk" (Schmitt, 2007). Truly engaged politics, according to Schmitt, requires homogeneity (Schmitt, 2007). Heterogeneous elements, which may include religious or ethnic minorities or slaves, for example, should, he suggests, be eliminated (Schmitt, 2007). Whether by indifference, exclusion, banishment or death is debated and unclear. Homogenization will, in Schmitt's view, produce an actively engaged citizenry under strong and decisive leaders. Such leaders, he believed, tend toward expansionism. While Schmitt highlighted executive power, he also debated with Franz Neumann over the role of the judiciary and its place in the rise of Nazism. It is an exchange that has interesting implications today. What Neumann (1957) saw as problematic in the German courts of his day was their inability to regulate concentrated economic power. He also pointed to the hazard of a strong judiciary that was relatively unconstrained procedurally, possessed of broad powers of judicial review and was free to act with discretionary informality. Each of these latter three features, Neumann argued, opened the courts to politicization.

After World War II ended, Leo Strauss built on Schmitt's work to articulate a view of the role of culture in politics (Norton, 2005). A circle of intellectual disciples gathered around him (Norton, 2005). Gradually, their thinking about culture and, especially, about archetypal images in politics formed the groundwork for what has been termed the American "culture wars" (Norton, 2005). Cultural images, Strauss argued, shape cognitive landscapes and spark the imagination (Norton, 2005). Archetypal images, specifically, have the power to inspire fear and can be of great value in mobilizing support for or in undermining a political agenda. Myth rather than truth was recognized as the basis for most action. The Straussian approach affirmed the vast influence of the media and, later, the internet as purveyors of imagery in new more powerful ways (Cohen, 2003). Such media influence is demonstrated by the big part it has played in the recent "moral panic" about crime — one in which public fear has stubbornly persisted despite the fact of falling crime (Cohen, 2003). Straussians have also contributed to reimagining lives of disadvantage as dependency.

As the "culture wars" have unfolded in American electro-politics, Schmitt's reference to "states of exception" has drawn much attention (Agamben, 2005; Douglas-Scott, 2006). Recently, Giorgio Agamben (2005) has argued that the "state of exception," which initially offered a provisional basis for emergency rule, has become permanent and a paradigm for government in the late twentieth century. Agamben argues that constitutional constraints on executive power have been diluted so that leaders" capacities to suspend the law or move outside it by declaring a state of exception is now relatively unchallenged. Thus, since the World Trade Center bombings in 2001, the Bush administration has invoked a state of emergency to detain and interrogate suspected terrorists in ways that skirt both the Geneva Conventions and enacted as well as customary conventions on human rights. The British government, itself a terrorist target, initially attempted similar tactics but encountered more resistance from the courts. The controversial practices include: detention without charge, illegal wiretapping, challenge in America to *habeas corpus*, claims that the Geneva Conventions do not apply to "terrorist suspects" and transfer of prisoners abroad for interrogation where human rights are weak and torture tolerated.

The legacy of "Friend and Foe" in policy: the Bush and Blair governments

Although the Bush and Blair governments cooperate closely on foreign policy, they hold quite different theoretical visions. On the American side, the dominant legacies are those of Carl Schmitt and Leo Strauss. In ways consonant with both these theorists, the Bush administration has an approach to leadership based on a capacity to mobilize people through cultural images and on personal appeal. To distinguish between "friend" and "foe" has been a hallmark of this second Bush administration. This is being done, however, in novel ways as we shall now see. Starting from the President's "with us or against us" language, the administration has since the World Trade Center tragedy cultivated a heightened sense of "the political" in Schmitt's sense. It has appealed too to states of war or emergency to justify its actions. Cultural imagery of the "volk" of the American Bible belt centred on moralism, family values and religious fundamentalism has also been spliced into its rhetoric as a mobilizing force.

In foreign policy, the United States identified Iraq as an enemy, despite its being ostensibly at peace, and allowed the media to fan public fears of hidden means. War was opened in Iraq although no one had definite proof that it possessed means of mass destruction. The United States has also refused support for the International Criminal Court — at least in part to avert efforts to try Americans for military actions against their "foes" as "war crimes." In its "with or against" language to gather support for war, the

Bush government has unabashedly polarized nations and, perhaps inadvertently, religious groups too. This has been done through efforts to marshal support for armed intervention and through the opposition that they have provoked. Interventions in Afghanistan, a second war in Iraq and "war" on terror itself have intensified difference to a point where struggle is clearly to the death through armed aggression and resistance. In international diplomacy, emergency appeals have been used to thrust aside established doctrines of nuclear deterrence and also of "limited [conventional] warfare" that have been the stabilizing framework for the post-World War II nuclear world (Schell, 1976). In their place, we find a newly crafted "Bush Doctrine" of pre-emptive strike wherever threat is believed to exist. In this arena, which is painted in mythic images, even a "one percent chance" that an enemy threat is real is now treated as a "certainty in terms of . . . [American] response" (Suskind, 2007).

Use of strategy and force to divide "friend" from "foe" has also entered domestic politics strongly. Once again, cultural myths and, particularly, archetypal images designed to inspire fear have been used. Nor are these images arcane. Chilling images of rats broadcast subliminally behind the letters "r,a,t" of the word "Democrat" in campaign ads funded by Republican Party supporters are a classic example. Nowhere, however, has this divisiveness and use of frightening archetypal images been clearer than with crime. Here it has been the disadvantaged African-American minority that has borne the brunt of these polarizing tactics. In an updated version of the Southern Strategy, the Bush camp has tried to do with male black offenders what Nixon did with black voters. Every effort has been made to polarize society against them and to associate them with the Democratic Party, thus using them as the basis of an appeal both to middle class voters of all races and, more importantly, to self-described "decent" working class and poor whites and Hispanics.

We have already seen that, under the Bush administration, growing numbers of African-Americans have both been incarcerated and been disenfranchised as ex-felons upon release. One primary means was the enactment in 1986 of a Federal law which made possession of five grams of crack cocaine a felony that carried a mandatory minimum five year sentence. Possession of that same amount of powder cocaine remained a misdemeanor. Since the users of crack were mostly disadvantaged African-Americans while users of powder were middle class whites, it could easily be foreseen that the law would "reshape the racial composition of the prisons" (Donziger, 1996). State laws of long-standing that disenfranchise ex-felons soon began, as a secondary consequence of the new law, to bar large segments of the black community from voting. With welfarist and rehabilitative policies largely truncated, a rational choice approach was increasingly touted to explain patterns of offending. It produced an approach to crime centred on control.

The increasingly Republican-appointed Supreme Court has also created obstacles for mounting a criminal defense by curtailing the rights of those accused and making incursions on privacy. In dozens of small procedural changes – few striking and publicity-worthy in themselves – the Bush administration has quietly dismantled much of the procedural infrastructure of rights, equal opportunity and the "rule of law." This has been done through agency rulemaking, riders to Congressional bills, administrative regulations and court decisions. One recent example is a decision to require that complainants who lose equal opportunity cases pay court costs – a fee which few would risk incurring. Even the record of the new Chief Justice of the U. S. Supreme Court John Roberts is notable mainly for past decisions that support relatively unrestricted use of executive power – a stance unlikely to challenge a Presidential state of exception. Across the board, the camp of George W. Bush has skirted the edges of their own controversial interpretation of the "rule of law" – if not actually violating it outright – to produce two elections so procedurally suspect that it led Fidel Castro to offer his services as an impartial election observer.

Tax cuts for the affluent that, together with the war in Iraq, have created staggering deficits have been the main initiatives of this administration while the middle classes and, especially, the poor struggle to make ends meet. Where Richard Nixon took such steps quietly the Bush government proclaims its actions with mythic claims that lower taxes are good for everyone – gliding by the news that not everyone benefits to the same extent. The standard of what is good for everyone appears, unbeknownst to many, to be what fosters market activity and profit. While much of America has grasped this slowly, "rap music" shows minority communities in the inner cities have understood completely (Kelley, 1996). Nor have they failed to see that federal policies have not only failed to alleviate disadvantage but have sometimes actively fostered "structured inequality" (Fischer et al., 1996).

In contrast to American divisiveness, the Blair government has sought, colonial style, to include and regulate. Its policies have combined modest welfarist measures with efforts to "responsibilize the individual." It too, however, has shifted gradually in the direction of control rather than prevention or reform. Some speak in Britain of the New Labour government having identified an "enemy within" (Hudson, 2002). While citing a "special relationship" with America internationally, Britain also seeks explicitly to learn from her former colony about domestic crime control. Rudolf Giuliani and William Bratton are regularly seen as advisory figures. It seems, however, that the weaknesses of American crime control have come with the good. In England, the limits of liberty are being probed today as extended detention without charge for suspected terrorists is repeatedly debated. Custodial detention has also been proposed, though not yet approved, for mentally disordered dangerous persons who are believed to be highly likely to commit serious future harm – a step not yet formally taken in Washington. This British style has given rise to an inclusive but closely controlled regime.

Consolidating the carceral turn in America: Nixon, the Cold War and the Schmittian Penumbra

If social psychologists and theorists of a politics of recognition are right, then, as we communicate and are responded to, so we tend to become (Rosenthal and Jacobson, 1966; Mead, 1967; Anderson, 1984; Taylor, 1994; Fraser, 1997 and 2003). He who imposes colonialism *becomes* a "colonialist" just as the one whose land is occupied *becomes* the "colonised' (Fanon, 1963; Fitzpatrick and Tuitt, 2004). The adventurer, who brings military occupation, becomes the repressor. The legacy of the Cold War and McCarthyism are, I suggest, reverberating through American militarism and repressive punitivism today.

Since September 11th 2001, the Bush administration has designated terrorists and their supporters "the enemy." Earlier, his father had similarly denounced the then-USSR as an "evil empire." However, more recent rhetoric has intensified and gradually broadened to include much of the Islamic world. Indeed, some suggest that today, despite official denials, the Islamic world in its entirety is under attack. One reason for this broadening may be the lack of a territorial boundary against which to direct anti-terrorist measures. Gradually, a cultural boundary has congealed along largely religious and ethno-cultural lines. Few chances to intensify such distinctions have been missed as the war in Iraq and threatened hostilities toward Iran show. Using the exigencies of "war" as a rationale, George W. Bush has repeatedly cited the "exceptional" events of our day to justify incursions abroad. Such appeals were initially successful in winning the support of Americans. Ultimately, however, George W. Bush's public approval ratings plummeted as low as 29 percent as a result of various policy failures. What was distinctive about the initial mobilization was that it was based on defining and excluding an external enemy.

Domestically, in keeping with a Schmittian emphasis on homogeneity, ethnic minorities have, as we have now seen, been increasingly marginalized. Criminal justice has been a primary arena in which to distinguish "friend" from "foe." This "new penology" has marked off and "warehoused" large swathes of minority communities – achieving a partial purge of the diverse disadvantaged from the visible social world. The homogenizing socio-religious culture of the "volk" of Midwestern and Southern states provides a customary basis of political consolidation. What we see here shaping the carceral turn, thus, appears to be an ideologically grounded political style. If so, the conscious effort to generate fear and crime as problems helps explain why anxiety about crime has long been so at odds with the reality of a crime drop. The "moral panic" that Cohen identified may be a product of conscious political styles and of "culture wars" – "culture wars," as we shall soon see, that have entered a new phase.

At this point, we may be well served to reflect back briefly on Richard Nixon's use of a "politics of positive polarization" in the context of electoral campaigns (Schell, 1976; Skrentny, 1996). This was a strategy, you may recall, that was designed explicitly to divide and mobilize the American electorate in such a way that the lion's share of voters would flock to the Republican cause. Among the primary elements of this approach was Nixon's exploitation not only of black voting rights, as previously shown, but also of policies for affirmative action to remedy employment discrimination. Quite unbeknownst to many, Nixon quietly supported the introduction of affirmative action. Some historians initially pointed to this as a sign of his moderation (Schell, 1976). Yet, Schell (1976) and Skrentny (1996) have subsequently shown how the policy provides crucial insight into Nixon's thinking and his reliance on tactics of division. When he supported affirmative action, Nixon was fully aware of the backlash it would cause among white middle and working class voters (Schell, 1976; Skrentny, 1996). He realized that citizens who normally were sympathetic toward disadvantaged minorities on issues of discrimination and equal opportunity would rebel against a policy that systematically assisted them by disadvantaging the majority. He sought to cultivate that reaction in order to estrange white, Hispanic and middle- and working-class black voters from the Democratic Party – which he painted as the source of affirmative action's strongest support. He planned to use the backlash to help mobilize political support for his campaign for a second term (Schell, 1976; Skrentny, 1996). Nixon referred to this strategy as a "politics of positive polarization" – to polarize the population along a divide as far to the political left as possible, then associate the undesirable policy with the Democratic Party, and mobilize opposition to it so as to carve out the bulk of the electoral centre for his own camp. The strategy worked quite brilliantly and has since become a cornerstone of American politics – replacing efforts to distinguish clearly between leftist and rightist positions. Instead it required that a candidate assume a kind of homogenized and bland centrist position so that nothing would be said to disenchant newly won voters. This is an approach that appears to have been imported by Tony Blair – perhaps through the tutelage of Bill Clinton.

The paradox of the carceral turn seems to be working in a similar way. By promoting racialized images of offenders and by arresting and incarcerating large numbers of African-American males, the Bush administration appears, consciously or not, to be polarizing moderates in opposition to the dependent lifestyle that is the racialized "face" of crime. Middle class blacks along with middle class, working class, and some poor whites and Hispanics tend to reject what appears to be voluntary state-beholden dependency. This opens access for the Republican Party for probably the first time in history to large blocks of disadvantaged whites, Hispanics of all backgrounds and working class African-American voters who have traditionally supported the Democratic Party. These join those of all ethnicities from the middle class who want to dissociate themselves from the dissolution of dependency, crime and moral decay. Association of indolent and racialized disadvantage with crime drives righteous moderates of virtually every class away from the Democratic Party – a Party that is depicted as indulgently tolerating this decadent lifestyle – and toward the Republicans. This is likely to have been part of Bill Clinton's rationale for supporting a "tough on crime" stance. When coupled with the impact of widespread disenfranchisement of ex-felons, the electoral consequence could be massive indeed. This is the "Southern Strategy" carried to an extreme – instead of depicting Democrats as radical as Nixon attempted to do, the effort now is to situate them as defenders of moral depravity, crime, dysfunction and dependency. It draws the line of polarization even farther from the center than did voting rights and its emotional negativity holds comparable power to move voters who are repelled. While the strategy harks back to Nixon, the techniques of its implementation in distinguishing an ethnically defined social "foe" as a means of political mobilization reveals the legacy of Schmitt.

The carceral turn in the UK: declining state support and individualizing choice

In England, the theoretical roots of current policy are quite different. On that side of the Atlantic, it is often said that crime problems appear about half a decade after they surface in America. As a result, our British cousins often borrow heavily to benefit from American experience with crime control. Britain, as we shall soon see, also appears to be situating itself internationally in a global welfarist role that complements but contrasts with an American militarist one. Among the primary theoretical influences on British policy, one finds Talcott Parsons, Amitai Etzioni and Ruth Levitas (McMahon, 2006). Much of the overall policy vision, as Will McMahon (2006) has pointed out, is captured in Ruth Levitas" book *The Inclusive Society* (2005). In it, she distinguishes three different meanings of social inclusion: income, employment and morality. She suggests that earlier welfarist programmes focused too exclusively on redistributing income. The current vision of inclusion is one of paid work and moral self-regulation (Levitas, 2005). From Talcott Parsons, the Blair government borrows an understanding of the historical evolution and growing complexity of societies and, especially, of the role of family as a setting in which an individual develops the capacity for work and self-regulation. Specifically, Parsons points to the family as a primary source of stabilization for the adult personality today. Parsons" focus on family is blended with the writings of Etzioni in the New Labour policy mix. Etzioni contributes a focus on organizations and, especially, a sense of the relation of the individual to the community. He offers a vision of obligations as well as rights in a "responsibilizing communitarianism" that offers an alternative to socialism. These views permeate New Labour's stance on inclusion and, especially, criminal justice. Because citizens have, according to Etzioni, not only rights but also obligations, inclusion means fulfilling those duties. Responsibility for choice and behavioral change is placed with the individual. Penalties of graduated severity meet successive breaches of norms. Most notably, these policies charge the individual with transforming behavior that research shows to be generated largely by the social conditions amidst which one lives. Of course, crime is always *to some degree* a choice. But to what degree?

In Britain, the punitiveness that began in the 1990s has now been coupled with a shift both in youth justice and in parts of adult justice toward an inclusive restorative approach which may or may not be as benign as it first appears. For youth, referral orders have been devised to avert custody for first time offenders who admit their guilt. Contracts are then negotiated, using the language of reciprocity, which specify a host of conditions the offender must meet. These may include community service or other steps to make reparation. The aim of this approach is to repair the damage done and reintegrate the offender (Kemp, 2007). Enormous pressure has also been placed on families as networks of social control to regulate the behavior of their children. One new initiative is a plan to impose penalties on the parents of truants. Yet, this approach seems to miss the power of neighborhood characteristics and socio-economic forces, often working through parenting and socialization by means of dynamics such as stress, to shape youthful behavior and, especially, a propensity for crime.

Despite very different policy stances, the Blair government, like that of George W. Bush, has espoused a relatively unrestricted view of executive power. Within Blairite New Labour, this can be seen in the Prime Minister's initial attempts to use sweeping discretionary executive action to reform of the House of Lords and to abolish the Lord Chancellor's Office. Prime Minister Blair also took Britain into war in Iraq despite sustained vociferous domestic opposition. There was an early effort by David Blunkett too to extend, on a discretionary basis, the time a suspect could be detained without charge though this was modified by Parliament. In each case, the Blair government sought, not necessarily more power, but rather to exercise power in ways that put it outside procedural constraint. This led to a number of resounding collisions with the courts.

American and British foreign policy as a window into domestic politics

American foreign policy today, I suggest, constitutes a crucial context for explaining the paradoxical carceral turn in criminal justice – growing punitiveness in a time of falling crime. Here we find clues as to where more minimal public power may lead. This has grown clearer over the past two years as international criticism over the war in Iraq has mounted and the Bush advisors have revealed more of the philosophy behind their conduct of international affairs (Barnett, 2005). It is here we can find insights into why such a stark polarization with respect to a disadvantaged minority developed.

In its approach to foreign policy as in domestic affairs, I suggest that the Bush administration reflects a Straussian influence in its approach to culture and politics. This has produced a perspective that justifies "foundational violence" as a basis for the occupation of sovereign nations, polarization as a path to global leadership and a clear tendency toward expansionism. At present, the United States and Britain are, for better or worse, playing a prominent and powerful role worldwide. The thinking behind that role, which is dissected by Thomas Barnett in *Blueprint for Action*, provides insight into their actions both at home and abroad. It is a vision in which global financial power, elite leadership and cultural manipulation are remaking the globe as a multipolar playing field for neoliberalism.

Barnett advances a simple vision of political transformation that is anchored in globalization. It draws tacitly on America's experience with "containment" and also on Richard Nixon's foreign policy vision (Schell, 1976). Barnett portrays globalization and the interconnectedness that its eclipse of time and space brings as a positive thing (Giddens, 1994). For his political approach, he seems to owe much to world systems theory and to dependency theorists of economic and political development (Cardoso and Enzo, 1979; Wallerstein, 2004). Barnett seems to reach this positive assessment apparently because globalization promotes the spread of self interest as a motivating force, more stable conditions for market activity, and profit as an ultimate criterion of success. The author argues that globalization already links countries housing two-thirds of the world's population – an area that he optimistically terms the "functioning core" of the globe. One-third of humanity, however, remains, as Barnett puts it, "trapped" outside what he terms "this peaceful sphere" in what he calls the "non-integrating gap." He then advances the highly controversial claim that "since the end of the Cold War, all international war and civil war and genocide has occurred within the gap." Barnett then moves to a bold conclusion. Because all wars and genocide since the early 1990s have occurred within the "gap," he offers a vision for ending war as we know it today, by "shrinking the gap" and making globalization "really global" – thus, "eradicating the disconnectedness that defines danger in the world today." What Barnett is suggesting, he claims, is a strategy for "*helping*" [my emphasis] gap countries join the "existing connectivity" of the globalizing world (Barnett, 2005: xiii). The assumption is that gap states would either want this or could be persuaded to do so. Since integration into the global economy means investment that in turn requires stability which then presumes rules, the effort to bring gap states into global connectivity may, and almost certainly will, require regime change since such rules, now absent, would need to be set in place. Regime change, according to Barnett, may necessitate military intervention.

A "global American century": reimagining the planet — citizens or shareholders?

From this vision of global interconnectivity rises, phoenix-like, a foreign policy strategy for the United States. According to that strategy, the United States equates its national security with "globalization's survival and success." This connects the United States" "national security strategy" with a "global *peace* [my emphasis] strategy." Barnett draws a direct parallel to the Cold War when America's "defense" against the so-called "communist threat" from the Soviet Bloc sought not just American "survival" but "freedom" worldwide. He argues that, once enamored with globalization's march, many countries forgot that the process and the "freedom" it fosters requires protection because some forces in both the gap and even in the core are working against it (Barnett, 2005: xvii). The goals of this global strategy, claims Barnett, are "universal inclusiveness" and "world peace," though on whose terms is not specified (2005: xii).

The origin of this view, Barnett tells us, was the "transforming" experience of the war in Iraq for the American military and, one presumes, the resurrected ghosts of Vietnam too. It has resulted, he suggests, in the development of a new national military strategy [and foreign policy as well] for the United States (2005: 3). This strategy, recently articulated, makes a startling claim. It stipulates that America "will administer the system known as the global economy: policing its bad actors, engaging its failed states, and guiding the rise of its emerging pillars – all the while routing out threats to the [American] homeland at their points of origin" (2005: 3). Note that there is no specification of how this will be done and whether public or private action would be taken. O'Malley's (1993) "private prudentialism" or Strange's (1996) "neo-feudalism" could be presumed as an infrastructure as well as could the nation state.

While the Bush administration entered office in 2001 with a disdain for much of what this new strategy entails, it will, Barnett observes, leave office having adapted the military to its new global environment. The old "core" of North America, Europe, Industrial East Asia and Australia must be defended and must actively engage in that process. Note the reference to regions but not explicitly to nation states here though in what follows the author recognizes the existing prominence of nations. Rising new "core" powers such as India, China, South Korea, Russia, Argentina, Brazil and Chile must be engaged. "Seam" states lying between the "core" and the "gap," including Mexico, Algeria, Turkey and Indonesia must be further integrated. Finally, the "gap," including the Caribbean islands, Andean South America, Africa, the Caucasus, Central Asia, the Middle East and Southeast Asia needs to be "shrunk," as Barnett puts it, "one threat at a time." Barnett does not specify whether "shrinking" ensures continued national integrity. It is a unilateral and interventionist vision that is likely to meet stiff resistance as it is put into action.

The objective is generating a new global security order. In Barnett's words, "it all starts with America and . . . it all starts with security" (Barnett, 2005: 3). Note the customary reference to "America" rather than to the nation that is the United States. While some contend that Bush policies have destabilized the global order, Barnett blithely asserts the opposite. He states: "America stands at the tipping point of possibly the most peaceful period in human history" (2005: 3). "But," he warns, "to achieve these lofty goals . . . we need to . . . shrink the Gap and all its pain and suffering – right out of existence" (2005: 3–4). Is the pain he refers to that of investors facing instability? What role, one wonders, would multi-national corporations play? Is it just a small step further, once all regions are "included," to argue that national boundaries are the prime remaining source of wars and that peace can be had through their erasure – that the nation state is no longer necessary?

What is required for this vision? "We need," argues Barnett, "a military that will wage peace as effectively as it wages war" (2005: 4). He refers here to a military capacity rather than to national armed forces. The aim, Barnett says, is to contextualize our thinking in a process of globalization. Anticipating critics, Barnett notes that many challenge his model as rejecting the post-war "balance of power" and the "realism" or "realpolitik" that it entails. He concedes that they are right to do so for at the center of this new approach lies a new strategic doctrine of "pre-emption." It has replaced nuclear "deterrence" and "massive retaliation" – the post-World War II doctrines that supplanted Dulles" nuclear "brinksmanship" to bring a modicum of stability to the nuclear age (Schell, 1976). "Pre-emption," he argues, "is the big new rule [with which the Bush Administration has] altered global history." Pre-emption can be undertaken publicly or privately. At all costs, a lingering and expensive "standoff" of the sort that marked the Cold War must be averted and pre-emption enables that. To do that, Barnett argues, we need "strong" leaders who will *initiate* [my emphasis] military action against "enemies." Here he strikes almost exactly the tone of Schmitt's (2007) concept of the "political" and echoes Nixon, Reagan and Bush "pater" on the value of initiating military action in times of relative peace.

The end state imagined by Barnett is an emergent multi-lateralism of the United States, European Union, China, Australia and India, among possible others. In the short term, however, the focus is on routing out and destroying terrorists and changing the political environment of the Middle East (Barnett, 2005: 84). Barnett sees terrorism arising as a response to globalization. He reprises Giddens" (1994) argument that it is a product of the confrontation of modern science and reason with pre-modern faith, which resists assimilation. According to Barnett, terrorists seek to disconnect their regions from globalization to foster Islamic empire in their societies (Barnett, 2005: 84–5). Of course, Muslims and many others would question the benign portrait of globalization and would link it with capitalism, regional economic inequality and consumerist values. Iran, with the second largest natural gas reserves in the world, emerges as the biggest unknown for Barnett in this scenario.

Global specialization: welfarist reconstruction and the "peace-waging" role of the UK

What role, you may ask, does Europe play in this vision? In non-military terms, Europe emerges as a standard setter for labor, products and technology that will become global. In military terms, there appears to be a division of labor. At the risk of oversimplifying, the United States will, Barnett contends, specify (and by implication mobilize) what is needed to dismantle rogue states; and Europe will push for definitions of the effort to engage in reconstruction (Barnett, 2005: 228). Barnett sometimes speaks as if all "gap" states are "rogues." If the model sounds a bit black and white, that accurately conveys the tone of the book. Harking back to the model of the Cold War, the scheme is akin to giving Europe responsibility for a Marshall Plan while the United States embarks on military ventures such as were undertaken in Vietnam. Neither approach can, it is now recognized, win separately. What is to be the fate of the "gap" states? Barnett argues that "these states [from the Gap will find they must] trade sovereignty for connectivity, as the influence of foreign powers increases" (2005: 233). Where national self-determination and sovereign integrity stand in this scenario is not clear.

What is particularly interesting is that Barnett emphasizes the tendency, as global connectivity advances, for power to shift from the public to the private realms (2005: 233). Thus, globalization is theorized to naturally abet a "hollowing out of the state" as the power of markets spreads. In its commitment to acting as "protector" of globalization's progress, the United States and, by extension, Britain, thus, appear to be accepting and nurturing a gradual retreat – and conceivably a potential erasure of the public power of the state. If so, this is a significant revelation of the ultimate neoliberal vision.

Hidden meaning: Straussion roots of foreign policy

What these repudiations of "realpolitik" coupled with the drafting of a global master plan seem to me to symptomize is foreign policy clearly rooted in the same Straussian roots as is American domestic policy. Yet it is in the foreign policy vision that the end state becomes most clearly visible. It also illuminates the role of culture. Let us examine Strauss' thinking for a moment in more detail. An iconic figure among neo-conservatives, Strauss built on Schmitt, as we have seen, to explore the role of myth in politics. Strauss argued that myths are needed by all governments to maintain a cohesive society and to give a people meaning and purpose (Strauss, 1978). In *The City and Man* (1978) Strauss outlines his controversial conceptions of "hidden meaning," "noble lies" and a "politics of deception." Favoring a hierarchical view of society, Strauss thought that a natural elite should lead and the masses should follow. This was particularly significant in light of Strauss" approaches to knowledge and truth. Rejecting a fact-value distinction that abstracted reason from "eros," he held that there is neither morality nor absolute truth but only a natural right of the superior to rule the inferior (Drury, 1998). This requires, Strauss argued, "perpetual deception" between the rulers and the ruled (Drury, 1999). It is the challenge of managing this deception that gives rise to the powerful role of myth. Drury (1999) argues that Strauss goes so far, following Machiavelli, as to argue that if no external threat is at hand then one must be created to promote unity. Strauss was unconcerned with the moral character of leaders as long as they could absorb the realization of the absence of absolute truth without descending to nihilism (Drury, 1999).

Though Strauss professed a profound commitment to democracy, he acknowledged that it was not an incontrovertible principle (Drury, 1999). As a result, he is sometimes challenged as an anti-democratic. His elitist conception of democracy also shared more than a little common ground with Carl Schmitt who conceived of democracy flexibly to potentially include authoritarian regimes. Reflecting on his time in the post-World War II years, Strauss viewed human nature as inherently aggressive and believed that such passions were controllable only by a powerful nationalistic state (Drury, 1999). It is on this last point that American conservatives and neo-conservatives today begin to differ.

Religion was of particular interest to Leo Strauss who saw it as a vital means of imposing moral order on masses who elsewise would be ungovernable (Drury, 1998). One interesting implication of this is a possible explanation for why some very secular neo-conservatives emphasize religious commitment and belief so fervently. Straussians, for this reason, contest separation of church and state as weakening order. Where a people are secularized, they argue, it gives rise to individualism and relativism that promote dissent and weaken a society's capacity to respond to external threats (Drury, 1999). Leaders need not be religiously committed, however, since, in Strauss words, it is a "pious fraud." Even under the influence of religion, however, men, due to their nature, can, he argued, ultimately be governed only when they "are united – and they can only be united against other people." Perpetual war, rather than peace, is the Straussian vision (Drury, 1999). Here the legacy of Carl Schmitt's view of the necessity of the "friend"/"foe" distinction and the tendency of the strong charismatic leader to intensify it are evident. In the United States where Strauss' students occupy much of the national security and foreign policy advisory circle, the embrace of belligerent foreign policy to date now appears as no accident though Barnett suggests that is likely to change (Drury, 1999). On the Schmittian vision of "perpetual war," Barnett suggests some conservatives are beginning to differ. Wars no longer have clear ends nor can they be localized. They disrupt enterprise over broader regions and are more costly. National wars also require the expensive maintenance of an "ever-ready" state infrastructure. Given Strauss' impact in America, it is interesting to note that, though he recognized a need for a nation to use military might to realize a glorious destiny, he was chary of ideas of a political world order which he feared would tend inherently to tyranny (Drury, 1999). His thoughts on a neoliberal global order under private governance were not, to my knowledge, made known.

It is perhaps Strauss' concerns about a world order as well as his nationalism that seem in Barnett's book to lead him to give a post-modern turn to Straussian thought as he moves to situate American foreign policy amidst processes of globalization today. What seems to enable this surprising blend is that Strauss and the post-moderns share certain key commitments: rejection of the fact-value distinction and of an absolute conception of truth, recognition of foundational violence as a basis of sovereignty, and embrace of the power of myth.

Reimagining governance and markets: a world without history, social structure or self

Where does Barnett's argument lead, then, and what insight does it provide into the recent paradoxical carceral turn?

First, it gives us a sense of the understanding of sovereignty underlying the Bush administrations' initiatives as one rooted in a foundational act of violence – often bloody, though it may be otherwise. Such a sense of sovereignty stands in contrast with that of popular sovereignty, with roots in the will of a people, of the sort espoused by Rousseau, Habermas and most interpretations of the American Constitution. In Barnett's portrayal of western military intervention, on the one hand, and the coerced surrender of sovereignty by "gap" states, on the other, we find a view of sovereignty as will or "voluntas" rather than one that is popularly based. What Barnett conveys is a conception of sovereignty rooted in power pure and simple. Thus, the US and the UK are pursuing new contours of global power that can be justified by force.

Seyla Benhabib (2002) argues that recent decades have raised three key debates: first, are we witnessing the end of philosophy; second, is this the end of man; and third, have we come to the end of history. She suggests an end to grand, or universal, narrative through which all humans can comprehend and participate in each others' experiences. The alternative is a world of ultimately irreconcilable traditions such that truth is not possible and meanings not mutually comprehensible. It is a world devoid of universal values – a neoliberal world – where the primary justification is profit (i.e., it works) or, sometimes, a capacity to provide security. This has much in common with Strauss' view of the absence of moral absolutes and with the use of cultural myths by the Bush administration for purposes of "noble deception."

To speak of the end of man suggests we are witnessing the problematization of a universal humanity. This yields a new sense of an unstable chameleon-like self that is shaped fluidly in response to its context of dispersed power relations. Here, Barnett highlights the salience of a people's cultural particularity which may stand at odds with ideas of universal human nature, human rights or liberal citizenship. Here we find the intellectual tools for an approach to the evisceration of rights.

Finally the death of history implies an end to Enlightenment ideas of human progress. Barnett seems to hold that such images are an illusion. The opportunity he does see lies in globalization, which, he contends, has liberating tendencies and a power to produce convergence among societies. He sees such changes as likely to occur, however, only if initiated by a people acting unilaterally under a strong leader. If connectivity were fostered by such a leader, however, history would, according to him, be restarted on a new path toward a global order. Lying behind this vision of connectivity is a recurring reference to peace that signals his divergence from Strauss' perpetual war. Barnett sees the world poised on the edge of an historic period of essentially "perpetual peace." What is missing is a consideration of what the contours of the prospective order will be and who, besides investors, will benefit from that peace.

The inhabitants of this globalizing world are portrayed as persons of distinct cultural particularity. Their identity is contingent and contextually shaped. Like cultural meaning, it remains partially hidden. Globalization remakes those formative social contexts. One sees the emergence of disparately contextualized core and gap states that are destined for very different futures. In its emphasis on the cultural, however, the material questions that are consistently softpedalled in this blueprint once again are finessed completely.

The vision Barnett presents operates in binary oppositions, such as core/gap or war/peace. What is interesting is how the boundaries of customary usage for these categories are consistently transgressed and, ultimately, blurred until finally the distinction itself is completely defused. In the end, it appears to be the category itself that is erased. In Barnett's book, the Bush administration seems to have consciously set out to blur the boundaries of war and peace. The language is of "waging peace." By occupying the boundary of war and peace, one participates in both simultaneously so that war and peace are emptied of their traditional meanings. When one cannot tell which is occurring, protest assumes special difficulty. Binaries such as rich/poor, black/white, powerful/oppressed are notable in their absence. What is imagined is a world whose porous, non-oppositional and homogenized categories preclude conflict.

Identity in the re-imagined world whose contours Barnett describes is self-generated in a performative sense from the shreds of one's cultural experience (Butler, 1997; Bhabha, 2004). In embarking on unilateral action to "reinvent" regions, the United States under the Bush administration appears to be performing its own self-proclaimed and particularly imaginative version of advancing "social justice." In it, imperialism is reinvented as "connectivity."

What is offered then is a world whose contours are those of culture in which we, with malleable and somewhat unanchored selves, adapt to a place whose primary dynamic is power (Foucault, 1980). Fluid and unstable selves resist, game or improvise but collective action is likely to be absent as only "imaginaries" could provide an organizing principle. Class and "the material" (i.e., the "economic") are eclipsed. A kaleidoscopic array of identities impedes efforts to work together for change.

So, as the Bush administration embarks on its military ventures abroad, its vision of societies is a malleable cultural one in which "realities" of class, social structure or deprivation are curiously downplayed. Liberty, so frequently touted in presidential speeches, is voided of political participation, dissent and activism in favor of cultural preferences on which one can draw to reinvent oneself. It is a highly subjective view of the world anchored in what may be loosely construed as a performative theory of action. In this way, the global vision of the Bush administration meshes harmoniously with the Straussian thinking that so prominently guides its policies. Religion emerges as both a support for order and as a contour of socio-cultural difference that can be intensified for "political" mobilization as the Bush administration draws on Schmitt and Strauss, the legacy of the Cold War and Nixonian political styles.

It has become a truism in American politics that for a presidency to be seen as successful, it must be strong in the international realm (Neustadt, 1960). This has tended to be especially true, as was the case for Richard Nixon, when a president comes under partisan political attack. For the Bush administration, its priorities, with the exception of taxation, appear to lie far from domestic social policy. Thus, its central preoccupation appears to have been foreign diplomatic and, especially, military and security policy. Given its salience to the Bush White House, the approach taken to international affairs must inevitably color, or at least complement, the administration's policy stance at home. If divisiveness, mythic accounts of truth, elitist political deception and a sort of flamboyant performativity mark its global initiatives, such traits can equally be seen as hallmarks of their approach to social policy within American borders.

Perhaps no question is more vital than that of the form governance might ultimately take as globalization advances. Many elements of Strauss' and Schmitt's views work equally well whether one envisions public governance or self-generating regulatory arrangements of a private sort. An elite can lead, deceive and develop myths to justify their role from within public or private institutions. Never has this been truer than it is now. If arguments regarding the "hollowing out" of the state are correct, then alternate arrangements – perhaps modelled on the "lex mercatoria" – present one model for a new order of the day. This is, of course, partly speculative now. What is distinctive about the current embrace of "public minimalism," however, is that there is no inherent stopping point – no asymptote. It is a point of the utmost importance to consider in that private governance, for its many apparent advantages, affords no public accountability. Other options might include Dryzek's (2002) proposals for multiple, differential jurisdictions for public rule, a bigger role for the social movements of radical democracy, or an extension of the role played by deliberative democracy and non-governmental organizations in human rights to other political domains.

Mythic imagery and the public imagination

One feature of the Bush administration that has been at once fascinating and puzzling is the extent to which major policy initiatives both abroad and at home have been based on constructions of a problem at hand that appear to be factually incorrect. In Iraq this involved claims about weapons of mass destruction despite an inability to find any. Domestically, in criminal justice, the dangers of crime have been much cited while crime itself, including violence, dropped through the late 1990s.

Yet, there is an answer to this dilemma and it lies in the Bush administration's links to Leo Strauss and to Strauss' own student Alan Bloom, whose work *The Closing of the American Mind* inspired the phenomenon of the "culture wars." Drawing on our earlier discussion of Strauss, one can now see in such events what may be more deliberate strategy than might otherwise be so. Committed to elite leadership and to myth as a means of fostering cohesion, it seems likely that the administration would find it prudent to create stories to spark the public imagination. Maintaining a crevasse between fact and public pronouncement could facilitate control of prevailing imagery, often through the use of frightening archetypal figures. It also makes it very hard to challenge them. Such imagery may have taken particularly strong hold since some of it was broadcast subliminally – a practice tested before the U.S. Supreme Court in the course of the 2004 presidential election and allowed as a form of free expression. Here conceptions of freedom and autonomy again are raised since the Court appeared untroubled by any threat such imaging might present to the political autonomy, or freedom of choice, exercised by voters.

In this light, what earlier seemed blunders by the Bush administration may be some-thing else. British "spin" also assumes significance – especially for the fact that those who rapaciously attacked it were the political bedfellows of George Bush. It has sometimes been said that the essence of power is the ability to act arbitrarily. If so, the ever bumbling Bushisms may camouflage something very powerful indeed. With public debate distracted by issues such as weapons of mass destruction that are widely believed to be non-existent, it gives that discourse a sense of unreality that eviscerates political participation and, ultimately, the "public sphere." It also distracts from the real issues of wealth concentra-tion, the effective elimination of an inheritance tax in America, and growing income inequality. In the United States today, those who speak out in dissent against the Bush administration may be attacked with charges ranging from passing "ad hominem" attacks to alleged treasonous failings of patriotism. Gradually an ennui on the part of the populace with myth, and truth alike, has developed.

"Unpresentable" disadvantage: "responsibilizing the individual"

When the Blair government came to power, it vowed to be "tough on crime and tough on the causes of crime." Similarly, the Bush administration has taken a "tough" law and order stance too. Under both regimes, as we have seen, prisons grew exponentially and policy became more punitive. Yet the punitiveness seemed paradoxical in that it emerged largely during years when crime and even violence were stable, or even dropping. In this paper, we have looked at some prior accounts of the causes and consequences of that carceral turn. I have also suggested additional features to consider.

What has been equally striking, along with prison expansion, has been the extent to which both governments have targeted the individual as the focal point for policy. In place of traditional language of disadvantage, we now find one of "individual responsibility." While Feeley and Simon's "new penology" and David Garland's "culture of control" offer excellent accounts of punitivism, they seem to me to leave unexplored some aspects of governments' policies of requiring individual self-transformation from offenders. The "new penology" suggests that the state desists on reform while the "culture of control" anticipates its failure. Each gets at an important part of the picture but more remains, I think, to be said.

In this paper, what I think we have seen is that recent changes in criminal justice are part of a much broader political transformation underway in the United States and, to a lesser extent, Britain. These are changes, however, in which the Bush administration has irrevocably implicated the British. They involve polarizing politics, use of mythic imagery and a conscious strategy of leadership by natural elites. In the course of these shifts, an imagery of dependency and of moral decay has been introduced to supplant with appearances the realities of disadvantaged lives.

This sense of decay is being relied on to justify harsh and non-reintegrative policies and to place responsibility for crime squarely with the individuals who have committed it. In the United States, that onus is rooted in notions of crime as a free choice. In Britain it is one of communitarian obligation on the part of each "responsibilized" member of society. Both accord responsibility for breaches of law primarily to the choices of the individual. Secondarily, they point to "problems" in the family and the home – in the extreme case in character formation. Both ignore important recent research that emphasizes how choices that seem to be vested in the individual are, in fact, not. They ignore evidence suggesting that neighborhood environments as well as qualities of families, schools and workplaces – often working through culture – powerfully shape behavioral dispositions of individuals so as to put them at risk for crime. Thus, individuals, and especially youth, are being "responsibilized" for behavior at least partially beyond their control.

In place of contextually contingent notions of self and offending, we find instead what is actually a sort of "performative" conception of self. According to this view, we can create and then recreate our own unique identity as our own invention out of the varied shreds of our own individual experiences (Messerschmidt, 1997; Bhabha, 2004). Our identities are produced as a sequence of performances over time. Thus, Salmon Rushdie speaks in the *Satanic Verses* of his book as a "lovesong to our mongrel selves" – acknowledging the blended natures of our beings. At the root of the allure of reinvention, is a notion that we, each of us, possess the creative power needed to "reinvent" ourselves. Like Madonna, we can be a "material girl" one day; French courtesan another and religious heretic still another. It gives us a sense of infinite possibility and of freedom. On the down side, what it signals is that those living in "dependency" have voluntarily "invented" those lives. It also implies that the disadvantaged are simply unwilling – perhaps too morally decadent – to trouble to "reinvent" themselves.

Normally such a performative notion of identity does not suggest a self-creation "sui generis" but rather a contextualized creative act. Yet in criminal justice, policymakers seem to have, to some extent, hijacked such images of our capacity for reinvention to suggest complete personal responsibility for the contours of one's life. This goes beyond Foucault's notion of "governmentality" whereby a state diagnoses a social situation, designates a relevant target population and constructs a characterization of its activity as well as a repertoire of potential responses. There Foucault (Burchell, et al., 1991) suggests that our understanding of a group's activity is reimagined. In contrast, I would suggest that today state action goes beyond "governmentality" by imputing to the individual an ostensible capacity for reinvention and responsibility to do so. It implies that those who, unlike Madonna, fail to reimagine their lives are personally reprehensible for choosing crime. Thus, it lays the groundwork for a moral assignment of blame. It also creates a justification for exclusion, according to Ruth Levitas' (2005) scheme, on the basis of failure to morally self-regulate. By building on such a performative conception of self to justify crime as a rational choice, policy today turns a blind eye, at a minimum, to the impact of resource inequalities, social context and human development on human behavior (Jefferson, 1997).

In our western societies, where freedom is increasingly imagined as lifestyle, alternatives to reinvention as a route to change, in fact, look increasingly bleak (Patterson, 2006). A view of liberty as lifestyle means that any prospect of change by means of political mobilization or autonomous political choices through the vote is obstructed. Voting becomes, not a freedom, but an act that may be determined by subliminal advertising or dictated by a party or church mandate as frequently happened in the 2004 American presidential elections. Distracted by efforts to find "true freedom" in choices among leisure activities and a range of flashy consumer goods, citizens allow the "public sphere" to atrophy. This transformation of the American understanding of freedom is one of the most important aspects of the changes now underway.

Another key finding to emerge has been that the factors that explain support for harsh penal policies in the United States are partly racial but, more so, political. While statistical analysis shows that racist beliefs generally have some explanatory effect, the more powerful variables are: Republican Party membership; church-going behavior; and, most powerfully, a belief in individual responsibility (Schaefer and Uggen, 2006). This means that, by depicting African-Americans in the United States and Africans and Afro-Caribbean people in Britain as state-dependent and deficient in responsibility for their own lives, policymakers are conjuring up a moral argument for both the punishment and the exclusion of these minorities. If such groups can be excluded in a way that polarizes the population and thrusts voters into the party of the incumbent, this is from a strategic viewpoint so much the better. Here we begin to grasp the paradox of punitiveness. We come face to face with the irony of imprisonment. This is that it is not about crime.

Democratic crisis and social-democratic crime control

We find ourselves, thus, in late modernity at a particular historical juncture in the West. It has been marked by a move in some western countries away from welfarism and toward heightened control, increased surveillance and harsher policing and sentencing. We have seen that the consequence has been an explosion of the prison population at a time when crime has remained stable or dropped. While globalization, increased competitiveness and fiscal pressures that produced cutbacks in state welfarism have contributed to this shift, not all countries have responded in the same way. Social-democratic and socialist countries, such as the Scandinavian societies, the Netherlands and France, for example, have sustained a preventive welfarist approach with lesser recourse to custodial penalties. To the surprise of some, those societies have, as David Greenberg (1999) and others have ably shown, experienced far lower rates of crime than their more carceral neighbors.

There are various possibilities as to why this is so. One is that work and social provisioning are real alternatives to crime. There is considerable support for this notion from Beckett and Western's work. Another might be that social-democratic societies are more participatory and, so, tend to have stronger communities and institutions that work better – a finding borne out by recent studies of democracy (Putnam, Leonardi and Nanetti, 1994; Cohen and Rogers, 1995; Loader, 2007).

In times of anxiety, one is inclined to imagine that a threat is entirely new but one can find in the current carceral turn elements that hark back to the 1980s and before (O'Connor, 1973; Hall, 1980; Habermas, 1973; Offe and Keane, 1984; Giddens, 1994). Such change, which seems to have begun in the late nineteenth century, has involved a gradual decline in the dialogue essential to democracy and a concomitant rise of a mass culture of consumption. Since bureaucratically administered states tend, as many have shown, toward autonomy and secrecy rather than public consultation and accountability, the weakening of democratic dialogue has been accompanied by a shift toward control, surveillance and policing (Weber, 1978; Habermas, 1984). While critics such as Nancy Fraser have rightly demonstrated that the sphere of public discourse so associated with liberalism has been neither so egalitarian nor so inclusive as Habermas suggests, there remains strong evidence of some degree of change in democratic participation.

During the late nineteenth and the twentieth centuries there had grown up, Habermas claims, a social welfare system that abated the most severe hardships of advanced industrial capitalism. However, during the 1970s, early globalization and increased competitiveness ushered in a fiscal crisis that led to cutbacks in the welfare state. As welfarism has weakened, underlying social conflict and divergence of norms from laws has, as he sees it, grown more apparent. Political participation, particularly in the United States, also seems to have declined (Pateman, 1970; Putnam, 2001). Growing ethnic diversity has also amplified variation in norms – making divergence of customary norms from laws for some social groups inherently more likely. In this way, Habermas (1984) argues, an historically rooted crisis of legitimation emerged. Stuart Hall (1980) has suggested this as a reason for the beginnings of a drift toward a law and order society a quarter of a century ago.

What makes this divergence of laws and norms with its attendant crisis of legitimation especially problematic is the distinctive and somewhat fragile nature of political authority in democracy. Weber (1978) tells us that, whereas power is the ability to impose one's will even over the resistance of another, authority, by contrast, entails a sense of right to command and a duty to obey. This commitment to obey results from subjective acceptance of a command that is recognized as legitimate. This legitimation can take various forms – traditional; charismatic or rational–legal. Whereas the first is based on sacred custom (e.g., tribal elders, mothers) and the second on an heroic strength or special grace of a leader (e.g., Gandhi), the third, rational–legal, roots its claim to obedience in the fact that those uttering commands are lawfully elected or appointed and that the rules of governance are enacted in law (Weber, 1978).

Modern democracies normally rely on the third rational–legal type. This tends to give them a relatively shallow keel since, unlike the powerful pull of traditional response to the claims of royalty or the magnetism of a charismatic personality, rational–legal authority relies on reasoned choice alone to obey a law. Further, if consent is not forthcoming, coercion is not viable. This is because resort to force would undercut the claim of democracy to represent the popular will. Since the root of rational–legal authority in law provides its basis of legitimation, anything that weakens law tends to undercut not only order but political authority itself. Thus, norms that diverge from laws present a uniquely compelling dilemma. While Tyler has proposed that laws, which are seen as made in procedurally fair ways, will tend to be accepted and obeyed even if their content is rejected as unfair, this purely procedural approach still seems partial.

Conclusion

At the paradoxical root of the carceral turn, it seems to me, are an historical conjunction of a long term change in the nature of democratic politics with political strategies consciously oriented to the development of *public minimalism*. It is an eclipse of public power that has no apparent limit. Why, if minimalism is the objective, would punitiveness be used? Partly, the retreat of the state has already occurred through welfare retrenchment, competitive pressures on social spending of global capitalism and the inability of even strong states to assure the security of their people. One sees increasingly a tendency of individuals to provide security for themselves and their families without shouldering the burden of public security for all. Through a pattern, which I call "autocolonialism," neoliberals and other conservatives have, I suggest, occupied the state to advance the work of weakening and dismantling it begun by Ronald Reagan.

Moving in hundreds of small ways, they have accomplished procedural and substantive changes – many of which are discussed by Charles Ogletree – that profoundly affect the way a government does business. While sometimes such actions are taken quietly, the Bush and Blair governments have openly asserted their commitment to change. Acting sometimes under the banner of urgency to claim a state of exception, periods of detention without charge have been extended, the right to silence undermined and incursions on privacy made, among innumerable others. Forward looking risk orientation is fostered that intensifies the public support for strong action. Coerciveness, when evident, may reflect internal weakening due to dismantled procedural constraints. Along with in-house demontage, it may evoke external calls for delimitation of state power that can be met with further dismemberment. The consequence is to eviscerate the public sphere in the name of leadership.

What is occurring is nothing less than a political sea change in which criminal justice is being called on to take a key part. Distinguishing "friend" from "foe," punitive policies have institutionalized the disadvantaged in growing numbers and presented an image of racialized criminality that repels the "worthy." Such disaffiliation serves as a polarizing force that mobilizes centrist voters and woos them to the forces of law and order. Aided by racialized imagery, a mythic public life engages the imagination through Straussian imageries of "noble deception."

It has been paradoxical that mass imprisonment has grown largely during years when crime has dropped. The irony of that vast prison expansion is that it has not been primarily about crime. That this moment occurs as globalization's dynamics are still revealing themselves adds major elements of uncertainty and insecurity to the mix. The timing of these shifts means that they may hold the potential for more extensive and permanent change than might at first seem possible.

It has been notable that American foreign policy has explicitly embraced the advance of globalization and seeks to foster it. Such development appears to be shifting the balance between public and private power in the latter direction. The Bush administration had explicitly claimed it believes that to be globalization's result. Indeed it seems worth reflecting on whether we might witness the end of the nation state or potentially even the end of public institutions of governance altogether. Might we see a return to the privatism of neofeudal arrangements or organized private prudentialism?

On a global scale, we must also ask whether foundational violence is acceptable as a means of transferring sovereignty today. Perhaps more profoundly, could power rather than authority become a basis for governing in the twenty-first century? This is a troubling picture. In contrast to such systematic elitism, Habermas (1998) espouses a sovereignty anchored in popular acceptance and a model of deliberative democracy. Such deliberative democracy, which applies potentially to many different types of public jurisdictions, suggests that freedom is never permanently achieved once and for all. Instead it must be constantly won and rewon – a focus of enduring struggle. It was this realization that inspired the new social movements and radical democratic models of the late 1900s (Cohen and Arato, 1992). Such movements mobilized as self-regulating vehicles through which to pursue civic accountability, democratic dialogue and significant participation. In some cases, such as the Velvet Revolution in the Czech Republic, the leaders of such movements actually took power. What was more common was to provide a means to contest secrecy and coercive policies or procedures as well as to revive democratic deliberation.

The Habermasian model has much in common with the social democratic welfarist approaches of Central and Northern Europe. They have much to teach us about, not only sovereignty but also criminal justice. What we see, at every hand, is considerable evidence of the success of the welfarist and preventive approaches to crime fighting (Currie, 1998). Clearly the social democratic countries have, thus far, fared better with significantly less rising crime, especially violent crime, and far lower rates of imprisonment (Greenberg, 1999). The United States has, however, historically resisted any redistributive policy and embraced only those that benefit all citizens even as they help the most deprived (Weir et al., 1988). Yet, in light of the human costs of the recent carceral turn, the case for rethinking such options is pressing.

Such an approach meshes well with the common law, anchored as it is in mechanisms of discretionary leniency. Common law may have the quality of appearing, perhaps, to work best amidst a people who have both something to hope for and possibly also something tangible to lose. For those with a family, job, home and reputation, criminal conviction represents direct tangible loss. Jobs are terminated, families often break apart, housing cannot be supported, goods are disposed of or destroyed, re-employment is extremely difficult to come by. Though the loss of physical liberty is always a powerful blow, one wonders whether the leniency of the state may be perceived differently on the part of those with little of a tangible sort to lose. Is it possible that, in this circumstance, the tolerance of the courts may be more likely to be perceived simply as weakness and the state regarded with cynicism pure and simple. If so, the more effective criminal justice policy may be, not the more severe effort to assure that crime does not pay, but rather one of investment in people to foster a populace with a greater stake in society than it stands to lose. Wise investment rather than remediation and risk abatement may, at this unique moment, be a most judicious choice.

Bibliography

Abbott, J. (1981) "State-Raised Convict," in *In the Belly of the Beast*. New York: Random House, pp. 3–14.

Adler, F. (1975) *Sisters in Crime*. New York: McGraw-Hill.

Agamben, G. (2005) *States of Exception*. Chicago, IL: University of Chicago Press.

Alexander, G., Balkin, J., Benhabib, S., Bernasconi, R., Brudner, A., Butler, J., Chase, C., Cornell, D., Culler, J., and Dallmayr, F. (1990) "Deconstruction and the Possibility of Justice," 11 *Cardozo Law Review*, Special Issue, nos. 5 and 6.

Anderson, E. (1984) *A Place on the Corner*. Chicago, IL: University of Chicago Press.

Andrews, D. and Bonta, J. (1998) *The Psychology of Criminal Conduct*. Cincinnati, OH: Anderson.

Arendt, H. (1973) *The Origins of Totalitarianism*. New York: Harvest.

Barnett, T. (2005) *Blueprint for Action*. New York: Penguin.

Barthes, R. (1980) *La Chambre Clair*. Paris, pp. 30–31.

Bartol, C. and Bartol, A. (1997) *Delinquency and Justice*. Englewood Cliffs, NJ: Prentice-Hall.

Baudrilliard, Jean and Glaser, S.F. (1995) *Simulacra and Simulation*. Ann Arbor, MI: University of Michigan Press.

Beck, U. (1992) *Risk Society*. London: Sage.

Beckett, K. and Western, B. (2001), "Governing Social Marginality: Welfare Incarceration and the Transformation of State Policy," in D. Garland (ed.), *Mass Imprisonment: Social Causes and Consequences*. London: Sage.

Benhabib, S. (2002) *The Claims of Culture*. Princeton, NJ: Princeton University Press.

Beyers, J.M., Bates, J.E., Pettit, G.S. and Dodge, K.A. (2003) "Neighborhood Structure, Parenting Processes and the Development of Youths' Externalizing Behavior: A Multi-Level Analysis," *American Journal of Community Psychology*, 31: 35–53.

Bhabha, H.K. (2004) *The Location of Culture.* New York: Routledge.

Blumstein, A. (1995) "Youth Violence, Guns and the Illicit Drug Industry," *Journal of Criminal Law and Criminology*, 86(1): 10–36.

Blumstein, A. and Wallman, J. (2006) *The Crime Drop in America.* Cambridge: Cambridge University Press.

Bonczar, T.P. and Beck, A.J. (1997) *Lifetime Likelihood of Going to Federal or State Prison.* Washington, DC: Bureau of Justice Statistics.

Bottoms, A.E (1987) "Reflections on the Criminological Enterprise," *Cambridge Law Journal*, 46/2: 240–63.

—— (1995) "The Philosophy and Politics of Punishment and Sentencing," in C.M.V. Clarkson and Rod Morgan (eds), *The Politics of Sentencing Reform.* Oxford: Clarendon.

Bottoms, A. and Wiles, P. (2002) "Environmental Criminology," in M. Maguire et al. (eds), *The Oxford Handbook of Criminology.* Oxford: Oxford University Press.

Box, S. and Hale, C. (1982) "Economic Crisis and the Rising Prisoner Population in England and Wales," *Crime and Social Justice*, 17: 20–35.

Braithwaite, J. and Pettit, P. (1992) *Not Just Deserts: A Republican Theory of Criminal Justice.* Oxford: Oxford University Press.

Braman, D. (2002) "Families and Incarceration," in M. Mauer and M. Chesney-Lind (eds), *Invisible Punishment: The Collateral Consequences of Mass Imprisonment.* New York: The New Press, pp. 117–135.

Brinkley, A. (2003) *American History: A Survey.* New York: McGraw-Hill.

Burchell, G., Gordon, C. and Miller, P. (1991) *The Foucault Effect: Studies in Governmentality.* Chicago, IL: University of Chicago Press.

Butler, J. (1997) *Excitable Speech: A Politics of the Performative.* London: Routledge.

Butler, R.A. (1974) "The Foundation of the Institute of Criminology at Cambridge," in R. Hood (ed.), *Crime, Criminology and Public Policy.* London: Heinemann.

Cardoso, F.H. and Enzo, F. (1979) *Dependency and Development in Latin America.* Durham, NC: Duke.

Carlen, P. (1998) *Women, Crime and Poverty.* Buckingham: Open University Press.

Christianson, S. (1998) *With Liberty for Some.* Boston, MA: Northeastern University Press.

Christie, N. (1994) *Crime Control as Industry: Towards Gulags, Western Style.* London: Routledge.

Clarke, R.V.G. and Clarke, R.V. (1997) *Situational Crime Prevention.* London: Criminal Justice Press.

Cohen, S. (2003) *Folk Devils and Moral Panics.* London: Routledge.

Cohen, J. and Arato, A. (1992) *Civil Society and Political Theory.* Cambridge, MA: MIT Press.

Cohen, J. and Rogers, J. (1995) *Associations and Democracy.* Cambridge: Verso.

Currie, E. (1998) *Crime and Punishment in America.* New York: Wiley.

deFronzo, J. (1997) "Welfare and Homicide," *Journal of Research on Crime and Delinquency*, 34(3).

Dezalay, Y. and Garth, B. (1998) *Dealing in Virtue: International Commercial Arbitration and the Construction of a Transnational Legal Order.* Chicago, IL: University of Chicago Press.

Donziger, S. (1996) *The Real War on Crime: The Report of the National Criminal Justice Commission.* New York: Harper Perennial.

Douglas, M. (1992) *Risk and Cultural Theory.* London: Routledge.

—— (2002) Purity and Danger. Dallas, TX: Taylor.

Douglas-Scott, S. (2006) Lecture on Carl Schmitt's "The Concept of the Political," King's College School of Law, London, Autumn 2005.

Drury, S. (1998) "Leo Strauss," in *Routledge Encyclopedia of Philosophy*, New York: Routledge.

—— (1999) *Leo Straus and the American Right*. New York: St. Martin's Press.

Dryzek, J. (2002) *Deliberative Democracy and Beyond*. Oxford: Oxford University Press.

Fanon, F. (1963) *The Wretched of the Earth*. New York: Grove.

Farrington, D. (1989) "Early Predictors of Adolescent Aggression and Adult Violence," 4 *Violence and Victims*, 2: 85–86.

—— (1995) "The Development of Offending and Antisocial Behavior from Childhood: Key Findings from the Cambridge Study in Delinquent Development," 360 *Journal of Child Psychology and Psychiatry*, 6: 929–964.

—— (2002) "Developmental Criminology and Risk-Focused Prevention," in M. Maguire et al. (eds), *The Oxford Handbook of Criminology*. Oxford: Oxford University Press.

Feeley, M. and Simon, J. (1992) "The New Penology: Notes on the Emerging Strategy of Corrections and its implications," *Criminology*, 30/4: 449–474.

Felson, M. (1994) *Crime and Everyday Life*. California: Pine Forge.

Fischer, C., Hout, M., Sanchez-Jankowski, J., Lucas, H., Swidler, A., and Voss, K. (1996) *Inequality by Design: Cracking the Bell Curve Myth*. Princeton, NJ: Princeton University Press.

Fitzgerald, F. (1972) *Fire in the Lake*. Boston, MA: Little Brown.

Fitzpatrick, P. and Tuitt, P. (2004) *Critical Beings*. London: Ashgate.

Foucault, M. (1980) *Power/Knowledge*. New York: Pantheon.

—— (1991) "Governmentality," in G. Burchill, C. Gordon and P. Miller (eds), *The Foucault Effect: Studies in Governmentality*. Chicago, IL: University of Chicago Press.

Fraser, N. (1997) *Justice Interruptus*. New York: Routledge.

Fraser, N., Honneth, A., Golb, J. and Ingram, J. (2003) *Redistribution or Recognition: A Political-Philosophical Exchange*. Cambridge: Verso.

Freidel, F. and Brinkley, A. (1982) *America in the Twentieth Century*. New York: Alfred A. Knopf.

Friedman, L.J. (1994) *Crime and Punishment in American History*. New York: Basic Books.

Galbraith, J.K. (1961) *The Great Crash of 1929*. Boston, MA: Houghton Mifflin.

Garland, D. (2001) *The Culture of Control: Crime and Social Order in Contemporary Society*. Oxford: Oxford University Press.

Gartner, R. (1990) "The Victims of Homicide: A Temporal and Cross-National Comparison," 55 *American Sociological Review*: 92–106.

Gelsthorpe, L. (2002) "Feminism and Criminology," in M. Maguire et al. (eds), *The Oxford Handbook of Criminology*. Oxford: Oxford University Press.

Giddens, A. (1994) *Beyond Left and Right*. Stanford, CA: Stanford University Press.

Greenberg, D. (1999) "Punishment, Division of Labor and Social Solidarity," in William S. Laufer and Freda Adler (eds), *The Criminology of Criminal Law*. New Brunswick, NJ: Transaction, pp. 283–359.

—— (2001) "Novus Ordo Saeclorum?: A Commentary on Downes and on Beckett and Western," 3 *Punishment and Society*: 81–93.

Greenberg, D. and West, V. (1998) "Growth in State Prison Populations, 1971–1991" paper presented to the Law and Society Meetings.

—— (2001) "State Prison Population Growth, 1971–1991," *Criminology*, 39(3): 615–654.

Haber, E. and Stephens, J. (2001) *Development and Crisis of the Welfare State.* Chicago, IL: University of Chicago Press.

Habermas, J. (1973) *Legitimation Crisis.* Frankfurt: *Suhrkamp.*

—— (1998) *Between Facts and Norms.* Cambridge, MA: MIT Press.

Hagan, J. (1996) "The Next Generation: Children of Prisoners" in The Vera Institute of Justice, *The Unintended Consequences of Incarceration.* New York: The Vera Institute.

Hall, S. (1980) *The Drift to a Law and Order Society.* London: Cobden Trust.

Hegel, G. (1807) *The Phenomenology of the Spirit.* New York: Oxford University Press. [Reprinted in 1979.]

Hood, R. (1992) *Race and Sentencing.* Oxford: Clarendon Press.

Hough, M. (2006) Seminar presentation, MA Criminology, King's College London, London.

Hudson, B. (2002) "Punishment and Control," in M. Maguire et al. (eds), *The Oxford Handbook of Criminology,* 3rd Edition. Oxford: Oxford University Press.

Jacobs, D. and Helms, R.E. (1996) "Towards a Political Model of Incarceration," *American Journal of Sociology,* 102: 323–357.

Jardine, A., Solomon-Godeau, A., Michard, E. and Sussman, E. (1988) *Utopia Post Utopia: Configurations of Nature and Culture in Recent Sculpture and Photography.* Cambridge, MA: MIT Press.

Jefferson, T. (1997) "Masculinities," in Mike Maguire, et al. (eds), *Oxford Handbook of Criminology.* Oxford: Oxford University Press.

Kelley, R.D.G. (1996) *Race Rebels: Culture, Politics and the Black Working Class.* New York: Free Press.

—— (2000) "A Poetics of Anti-Colonialism," in Aime Cesaire (ed.), *Discourse on Colonialism.* New York: Monthly Review Press.

Kemp, V. (2007) Lecture on Juvenile Justice, Prosecution and Criminal Process Seminar, King's College London, Spring 2007.

Kennan, G. (1967) *Memoirs, 1925–1950.* New York: Pantheon.

Land, Kenneth, McCall, Patricia, and Cohen, Lawrence (1990) "Structural Covariates of Homicide Rates: Are There Any Invariances Across Time and Space?" 95 *American Journal of Sociology*: 922–63.

Laub, J. and Sampson, R. (1993) "Turning Points in the Life Course: Why Change Matters to the Study of Crime," 31 *Criminology*: 301–25.

Levitas, R. (2005) *The Inclusive Society.* London: Macmillan.

Lilly, J. Robert, Cullen, Francis, and Ball, Robert A. (1995) *Criminological Theory.* Thousand Oaks, CA: Sage.

Lipton, D., Martinson, R., and Wilkes, J. (1975) *The Effectiveness of Correctional Treatment.* New York: Praeger.

Loader, I. and Sparks, R. (2002) "Contemporary Landscapes of Crime, Order, and Control: Governance, Risk and Globalization," in M. Maguire et al. (eds), *The Oxford Handbook of Criminology,* 3rd Edition. Oxford: Oxford University Press.

Loader, I. and Walker, N. (2007) *Civilizing Security.* Cambridge: Cambridge University Press.

McGuire, J. (1999) *What Works?: Reducing Reoffending.* London: Wiley.

McMahon, W. (2006) Personal verbal communication at King's College London, Spring 2006.

Maguire, M. (2002) "Crime Statistics: The 'Data Explosion' and Its Implications," in M. Maguire et al. (eds), *The Oxford Handbook of Criminology.* Oxford: Oxford University Press, pp. 322–375.

Mauer, M. (2003) *Comparative International Rates of Incarceration: An Examination of Causes and Trends*. Report of The Sentencing Project presented to the U. S. Commission on Civil Rights, Washington, DC.

Mauer, M. and Chesney-Lind, M. (2002) *Invisible Punishment: The Collateral Consequences of Mass Imprisonment*. New York: The New Press.

Mead, G.H. (1967) *Mind, Self and Society*. Chicago, IL: University of Chicago Press.

Mead, L. (1986) *Beyond Entitlement: The Social Obligations of Citizenship*. New York: The Free Press.

Mead, L. (1992) *The New Politics of Poverty*. New York: Basic Books.

—— (1997) *From Welfare to Work*. London: Institute for Economic Affairs.

Melossi, D. (1985) "Punishment and Social Action: Changing Vocabularies of Motive Within a Political Business Cycle," *Current Perspectives in Social Theory*, 6: 169–197.

Melossi, D. and Pavarini, M. (1981) *The Prison and the Factory: Origins of the Penitentiary System*. Basingstoke: Macmillan.

Messerschmidt, J. (1997) *Crime as Structured Action*. Thousand Oaks, CA: Sage.

Michalowski, R. and Pearson, M. (1987) "Punishment and Social Structure at the State Level: A Cross-Sectional Comparison of 1970 and 1980," 27 *Journal of Research in Crime and Delinquency*: 52–78.

Morgan, R. (2002) 'Imprisonment: A Brief History, the Contemporary Scene and Likely Prospects,' in M. Maguire et al. (eds), *The Oxford Handbook of Criminology*. Oxford: Oxford University Press.

Morris, A. (1987) *Women, Crime and Criminal Justice*. Oxford: Basil Blackwell.

Mulcahy, L. (2006) Comments in response to a lecture given by the author at the WG Hart Conference, Institute of Advanced Legal Studies, University of London, June 2006.

Murray, Charles (1994) *Losing Ground*. New York: Basic Books.

Neumann, F. (1957) *The Democratic and the Authoritarian State*. New York: Free Press.

Neustadt, R. (1960) *Presidential Power*. New York: Wiley.

Norton, Anne (2005) *Leo Strauss and the Politics of American Empire*. New Haven, CT: Yale.

O'Connor, J. (1973) *The Fiscal Crisis of the Welfare State*. New York: St. Martin's Press.

Offe, C. and Keane, J. (1984) *Contradictions of the Welfare State*. Cambridge, MA: MIT Press.

O'Malley, Pat (1992) "Risk, Power and Crime Prevention," *Economy and Society*, 21: 252–275.

—— (1993) "Law-Making in Canada: Capitalism and Legislation in a Democratic State," in R. Hinch (ed.), *Readings in Critical Criminology*. Toronto: Prentice-Hall.

Pampel, F. and Gartner, R. (1995) "Age Structure, Socio-Political Institutions, and National Homicide Rates, " 11 *European Sociological Review*: 243–260.

Pateman, C. (1970) *Participation and Democratic Theory*. London: Cambridge University Press.

Patterson, O. (2006) "Americans' Conception of Freedom," lecture at the London School of Economics, Programme on Cold War Studies.

Player, E. (2006) Seminar presentation on Gender and Criminal Justice, King's College London.

Putnam, R. (2001) *Bowling Alone*. New York: Simon and Schuster.

Putnam, R., Leonardi, R. and Nanetti, R. (1994) *Making Democracy Work*. Princeton, NJ: Princeton University Press.

Rosenfeld, R., Messner, S. and Baumer, E. (2001) "Social Capital and Homicide," *Social Forces*, 80(1): 283–309.

Rosenthal, R. and Jacobson, L. (1966) "Teacher Expectancies: Determinants of Pupils' IQ Gains," 19 *Psychological Reports*: 115–118.

Rothman, D. (1971) *The Discovery of the Asylum*. Boston, MA: Little Brown.

Rovere, R. (1996) *Senator Joe McCarthy*. Berkeley, CA: University of California Press.

Rubin, L. (1976) *Worlds of Pain: Life in the Working Class Family*. New York: Basic Books.

Rusche, G. and Kirchheimer, O. (1939) *Punishment and Social Structure*. New York: Russell and Russell.

Sampson, Robert J. and Laub, John H. (1993) *Crime in the Making*. Chicago, IL: University of Chicago Press.

—— (2003) "Life Course Desisters? Trajectories of Crime Among Delinquent Boys Followed to Age 70," *Criminology*, 41: 555–592.

Sampson, R.J., Morenoff, J.D. and Gannon-Rowley, T. (2002) "Assessing 'Neighborhood Effects': Social Processes and New Directions in Research," *Annual Review of Sociology*, 28: 443–478.

Schaefer, S. and Uggen, C. (2006) "Voting and Civic Re-Integration of Former Prisoners," paper presented at the Annual Meetings of the American Sociological Association, Montreal, Canada.

Schell, J. (1976) *Time of Illusion*. New York: Vintage.

Schmitt, C. (2007) *The Concept of the Political* [Foreward by T. B. Strong; Commentary by L. Strauss; and Translation by G. Schwab]. Chicago, IL: University of Chicago Press.

Scraton, P. (ed.) (1987) *Law, Order and the Authoritarian State: Readings in Critical Criminology*. Milton Keynes: Open University Press.

Skrentny, J. (1996) *The Ironies of Affirmative Action*. Chicago, IL: University of Chicago Press.

Simon, J. (1997) "Governing Through Crime," in Lawrence M. Friedman and George Fisher (eds), *The Crime Conundrum*. Boulder, CO: Westview, pp. 171–189.

—— (2007) *Governing Through Crime*. New York: Oxford University Press.

Spelman, W. (2000) "The Limited Importance of Prison Expansion," in A. Blumstein and J. Wallman (eds), *The Crime Drop in America*. Cambridge: Cambridge University Press. [Reprinted in 2006.]

Steffensmeier, D. (1989) "Age and the Distribution of Crime," 94 *American Journal of Sociology*: 803–31.

Stockman, D. (1987) *The Triumph of Politics: Why the Reagan Revolution Failed*. New York: Avon.

Strange, S. (1996) *The Retreat of the State*. Cambridge: Cambridge University Press.

Strauss, L. (1978) *The City and Man*. Chicago, IL: University of Chicago Press.

Suskind, R. (2007) *The One Percent Doctrine*. New York: Simon and Schuster.

Sykes, G. (1956) *Society of Captives*. Princeton, NJ: Princeton University Press.

Taylor, C. (1994) *Multiculturalism*. Princeton, NJ: Princeton University Press.

Teubner, Gunther (1997) " 'Global Bukowina': Legal Pluralism in the World Society," in *Global Law Without a State*. Aldershot: Dartmouth, pp. 3–28.

Useem, B. and Goldstone, J. (1999) 'Prison Riots as Microrevolutions,' *American Journal of Sociology*, 104(4): 985–1029.

van Swaaningen, R. and Downes, D. (2007) "New Agendas, New Directions," paper presented at the New Directions Conference, Centre for Crime and Justice Studies, King's College London, July 2007.

von Hirsch, A. (1976) "Doing Justice: The Choice of Punishments," *Report of The Committee for the Study of Incarceration*. New York: Hill and Wang.

Wacquant, L. (2001) "Deadly Symbiosis: When Ghetto and Prison Meet and Merge," in D. Garland (ed.), *Mass Imprisonment: Social Causes and Consequences*. London: Sage.

Walker, S. (1980) *Popular Justice*. Oxford: Oxford University Press.

Wallerstein, Immanuel (2004) *World Systems Analysis*. Berkeley, CA: University of California Press.

Weatherburn, D. and Lind, B. (1998) "Poverty, Parenting, Peers and Crime-Prone Neighborhoods," *Trends and Issues in Crime and Criminal Justice*, No. 85. Canberra: Australian Institute of Criminology.

Weber, M. (1978) *Economy and Society*. Berkeley, CA: University of California Press.

Weir, Margaret, Orloff, A.S., and Skocpol, T. (1988) *The Politics of Social Policy in the United States*. Princeton, NJ: Princeton University Press.

West, Cornel (1998) "The New Cultural Politics of Difference," in Charles Lemert (ed.), *Social Theory: The Multicultural and Classic Readings*, second edition. Boulder, CO: Westview Press, pp. 521–531.

Western, B. and Beckett, K. (1999) "How Unregulated is the U.S. Labor Market? The Penal System as a Labor Market Institution," *American Journal of Sociology*, 104: 1030–1160.

Wikstrom, P.-O. and Loeber, R. (2000) "Do Disadvantaged Neighborhoods Cause Well-Adjusted Children to Become Adolescent Delinquents?: A Study of Male Serious Juvenile Offending, Individual Risk and Protective Factors, and Neighborhood Context," 38 *Criminology*: 1109–1142.

Wilson, J.Q. and Boland, B. (1971) in M. Wolfgang and L. Radzinowicz (eds), *Crime and Society*. New York: Basic Books.

Wilson, J.Q. and Herrnstein, R.J. (1985) *Crime and Human Nature*. New York: Simon and Schuster.

Wilson, William J. (1981) *The Declining Significance of Race*. Chicago, IL: University of Chicago Press.

Worrall, A. (1990) *Offending Women*. London: Routledge.

Zimring, F. and Hawkins, G. (1997) *Incapacitation*. Oxford: Oxford University Press.

PART ONE

Bringing inequality back in to crime, law and authority

WHEN THINKING ABOUT CRIME, it is all too easy to forget that it is socially constructed. This means that an act becomes crime because a people have collectively decided that doing it violates the law. In that process of political transformation, however, not all voices are heard equally. Inequality may arise not only from the law as enacted but also its interpretation and implementation. All laws are implemented in settings where scarce resources mean choices are made about what to enforce.

Equally important, law's relation to diverse groups' beliefs and norms of behavior may vary too. An urban inner city youth may find it hard to understand why in some places major financial crimes produce penalties less severe than possession of marijuana for personal use. Conversely, some parents may be mystified as to how hurling rocks through lighted windows can be considered by some youth just a lively night out.

Since it is often the norms of the powerful that are most clearly reflected in law, disadvantaged groups are more likely to view law as out of step with their interests and values. This challenge grows as societies become more ethnically and culturally diverse. Perceptions of such divergence of laws from norms may inspire challenges to the legitimacy of law and, in the extreme case, to political authority itself (Weber, 1978). Robert Putnam shows that a vital part is played by civic engagement and participation in making democracy work.

Because political authority in western democracies is so strongly anchored in law, anything that weakens law has the potential to undercut authority itself. A democratic regime that must have recourse to coercion to uphold order gives the lie to its claim to represent the will of all. Thus, the relation of law on the street to what local communities see as right or wrong is worth thinking about. Diversity makes this an especially difficult task. Interestingly, even where laws do not meet favor substantively, Tyler has shown that laws, which are seen as produced by a process that is procedurally fair, gain more certain acceptance than others.

This research highlights the importance of considering how laws and law enforcement relate to people's norms and beliefs if coercive over-reliance on control, surveillance and policing are to be averted.

Chapter 1

Steven R. Donziger

CRIME AND POLICY

From: Steven R. Donziger (1996), excerpts from 'Crime and Policy', in S. R. Donziger (ed.), *The Real War on Crime*. The Report of the National Criminal Justice Commission, New York: Harper Perennial, pp. 1–44.

AMERICA IS A NATION both afraid of and obsessed with crime. Since the 1960s, hundreds of different crime bills have been passed by Congress and state legislatures. The country has fought a war on drugs. Annual expenditures on police have increased from $5 billion to $27 billion over the past two decades. Prisons have been built to lock up more people than in almost any other country in the world. The United States is the only country in the West to employ capital punishment and to use the death penalty against teenagers. Yet Americans in record numbers still report that they feel unsafe in their streets and in their homes.

We have leveled our supposedly strongest weapons at crime, to the tune of about $100 billion tax dollars per year. . . . Yet still there is the feeling that the criminal justice system is not doing enough. . . . While we continue to take tougher and tougher stances, the underlying problem remains: our criminal justice system is failing to control crime in a way that makes Americans feel safe.

A hoax is afoot. Politicians at every level – federal, state, and local – have measured our obsession, capitalized on our fears, campaigned on "get tough" platforms, and won. . . . Appearances are often deceiving. [. . .]

CRIME RATES: THE NUMBERS DO NOT TELL THE FULL STORY

There is a widespread perception in the United States that crime rates are rising. In most categories, however crime rates over the last two decades have remained remarkably stable. What has changed is the nature of criminal violence. Partly because of the prevalence of firearms, one category of the population—young males in the inner city – is at an extremely high risk of being killed. This danger sometimes spills over to the suburbs and rural areas, creating fear throughout the country. Violence in the inner city is one of the most pressing issues facing the American criminal justice system. [. . .]

Before delving into these issues, we must keep in mind some basic facts. First, crime rates are higher today than they were in the 1950s. This is largely because crime increased significantly in the 1960s. But since the early 1970s, crime rates have remained remarkably stable even though they sometimes go up or down from year to year. . . . Second, the serious violent crime rate for the United States stands 16 percent below its peak level of the mid-1970s. These statistics . . . should not be taken to mean that crime is not a major problem. Crime (particularly homicide) is widespread in this country, and among young people violent crime, after dropping in 1992, 1993 and 1994, increased in the late 1990s.

Two measures of crime

We have found that there is a huge difference between the public *perception* and the *reality* of crime in the United States. . . . Remember that most people perceive crime to have been rising when in reality it has remained remarkably stable for many years.

One major source of confusion about crime rates in the United States is that there are two major methods by which crime is measured, the Uniform Crime Reports (UCR) and the National Crime Victimization Survey (NCVS). It may be startling that these two systems of measurement produce quite different numbers. The UCR is tabulated by the FBI, based on arrest information submitted annually by each of the 17,000 different police departments in the United States. Because it provides a state-by-state break-down of crime rates, the UCR is the measure most cited by the media (who see it as a good local story) and politicians (who talk about it with their constituencies).

However, most criminologists consider UCR figures inaccurate because they tend to exaggerate increases in crime – a fact that is at least partly responsible for the misperception that crime is rising. . . . First, computers have led to marked improvements in police reporting of crime. Thus, "increases" in crime reported by police are often the result of improved recordkeeping rather than criminal activity. [. . .]

The UCR also is flawed because of the way many police departments tabulate their statistics. If two persons are arrested for a single assault, police usually count the two arrests rather than the one assault. Thus, one crime suddenly turns into two. This practice creates the most severe distortions in juvenile crime because juveniles are often arrested in groups.

Moreover, budgetary decisions based on police reports create incentives for police departments to skew their figures upward. The 1994 Federal Crime Control Act, for example, allocates more funds to states with higher levels of crime as recorded by the police. [. . .]

Despite its flaws, the UCR does provide an accurate measure of the homicide rate. This is because murders are rare and serious events that citizens tend to report quickly and accurately to the police, who record them with precision. The UCR indicates that the incidence of murder per capita is lower today than it was in the 1930s, when the rate of incarceration was about one-fifth what it is today. The 1994 homicide rate of 9.3 per 100,000 population is nearly identical to the rate of 9:4 per 100,000 recorded in 1973. . . . Our national murder rate is not increasing nearly as fast as many might claim.

We believe – as do most criminologists' – that the figures produced by the National Crime Victimization Survey are more accurate. To conduct the survey, staff at the Census Bureau telephone a representative sampling of households around the country to determine how many people were victimized by one of seven crimes in the preceding year.

The seven crimes are rape, robbery, assault, personal theft, household theft, burglary, and motor vehicle theft. The NCVS generally is considered more reliable because it uses scientific polling techniques similar to those that determine the Nielson ratings in television. It does not measure murder because the victim cannot be interviewed. The NCVS does not break down crime data by area, thus making it less interesting to members of the news media who want to find a local angle on crime trends.

The threat of violent crime

It is important to distinguish between crime generally and violent crime specifically. Violent crimes are committed against *people* – murders, rapes, robberies, kidnappings, and assaults. Nonviolent crimes are usually committed against *property* – burglaries, auto thefts, embezzlement, check forgery, fraud, and trespassing. [. . .]

Offenses involving the sale or possession of drugs are also nonviolent, but obviously a violent act associated with the sale or possession of drugs (such as a shooting to protect a drug market) would be a violent, crime. Much violence in our society is not a violation of the criminal law. [. . .]

A violent crime is an act of violence that violates a criminal law passed by the Congress or a state legislature.

The vast majority of crime in America is *not* violent. One in ten arrests in the United States is for a violent crime. Only 3 in 100 arrests in the United States are for a violent crime resulting in injury. The distinction between violent and nonviolent crime is critical and helps us understand why the criminal justice system is not more effective at making Americans safe. When people think of locking up criminals, they usually have an image in mind of a violent offender – a murderer or a rapist. But the vast majority of people filling expensive new prisons are nonviolent property and drug offenders.

Violent crime is a major problem in localized areas of the inner city. In those places, firearms violence – especially against young people— has increased dramatically. During the 1980s, teenage boys in all racial and ethnic groups became more likely to die from a bullet than from all natural causes combined. During the time period from 1985 to 1991,

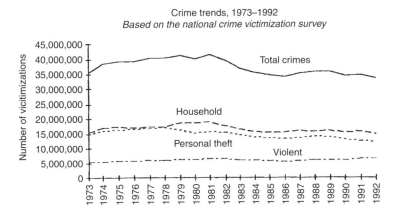

Crime trends, 1973–1992
Based on the national crime victimization survey

Source: U.S. Department of Justice, Bureau of Justice Statistics (July 1994), *Criminal Victimization in the United States: 1973–92 Trends*, p. 9.

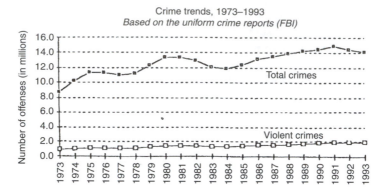

Crime trends, 1973–1993
Based on the uniform crime reports (FBI)

Sources: U.S. Department of Justice, Bureau of Justice Statistics (1994), *Sourcebook of Criminal Justice Statistics – 1993*, p. 352; U.S. Department of Justice, Federal Bureau of Investigation (1994), *Crime in the United States – 1993*, pp. 5, 10.

annual rates of homicide for males aged 15 to 19 years increased 154 percent. For African-American male youths, the homicide rate is eight times that of white male youths. If you live in the inner city and are young – particularly young and African-American – your chance of being the victim of a violent crime is incredibly high. And if you are not living in the inner city, the localized violence of some communities reverberates nationally, making everybody *feel* less safe even though most people are *more* safe than they were in the 1970s.

The media has focused much of its crime reporting on the tragic phenomenon of youth homicide. As a result, a myth has been created and projected that all Americans have a "realistic" chance of being murdered by a stranger. . . . In reality almost all Americans have only a remote chance of being killed or victimized by a stranger. Most violent crime is committed by friends and family. . . . A 1994 government study of 8,000 homicides in urban areas found that eight out of ten murder victims were killed by a family member or someone they knew. [. . .]

Males are more at risk of criminal victimization than females (because males commit much more crime than women, they tend to associate more with criminals and therefore run a higher risk of being victimized by them). Young people – particularly adolescents – are much more at risk than elderly people. [. . .]

U.S. crime rates compared to other countries

Although it is often assumed that the United States has a high rate of incarceration because of a high crime rate, in reality the overall rate of crime in this country is not extraordinary. The one exception is murder. Largely because of the prevalence of firearms, we have about 22,000 homicides per year, about 10 times the per capita murder rate of most European countries. Many comparable countries such as Australia and Canada actually have higher rates of victimization than the United States for some crimes. For the crime of assault with force, 2.2 percent of Americans are victimized each year, compared to 2.3 percent of Canadians and 2.8 percent of Australians. For robbery, 1.7 percent of Americans are victimized annually; in Spain, the number is 2.9 percent.

For car theft, the U.S. rate is 2.3 percent; Australia is at 2.7 percent and England is at 2.8 percent. Thus, it is not our higher violent crime rates that lead to our high incarceration rates – the 22,000 homicides per year cannot account for the 1.5 million people behind bars. Rather, American rates of incarceration are higher because of our exceedingly harsh treatment of people convicted of lesser crimes.

THE KEY TO THE PROBLEM: DISTINGUISHING BETWEEN CRIME AND VIOLENCE

[. . .]

We cannot begin to control violent crime until we recognize that *the primary reason most Americans live in fear is not crime but violence*. The United States does not have more crime than other industrialized countries. Rather, it has a *different character of crime*. Criminologists in the Netherlands and the United Kingdom recently compared crime across industrialized countries. With the exception of homicide, the United States had the highest crime rate in only one of the fourteen offenses measured – attempted burglary. Because of the prevalence of firearms on our streets, however, America leads the world in *the proportion of violent crime resulting in injury*. . . . It is not the amount of *crime* but rather the amount of *violence* that adds to our fear. [. . .]

Crime policy in the United States

[. . .]

Although it is difficult to define the exact parameters of a national crime policy, a national "get tough" trend has been evident over the last fifteen years. Since 1968, six major anti-crime bills have passed Congress and been signed into law by presidents. . . . Many of the bills were used to influence crime policy by withholding money from the states unless they adopted certain "get tough" policies favored by the federal government. For example, under the 1994 federal crime bill, a state can (under "truth in sentencing" provisions) receive part of the $9.7 billion set aside for new prison construction only if it requires inmates to serve at least 85 percent of their sentences before parole (in effect doubling sentences for many classes of offenders). [. . .]

Nonviolent offenders fueled the prison expansion

Since 1980, the United States has undertaken one of the largest and most rapid expansions of a prison population in the history of the Western world. Between 1980 and 1994, the prison population tripled from 500,000 to 1.5 million. The number of people under some form of correctional supervision (in prison or jail, on probation, or on parole) surpassed 5 million people at the end of 1994, or 2.7 percent of the adult population.

Most of the increase in the prison population during this time was *not* accounted for by violent offenders. Fully 84 percent of the increase in state and federal prison admissions since 1980 was accounted for by *nonviolent* offenders. Legislative changes in sentencing laws in the 1980s made it routine to send nonviolent offenders to prison for long terms. A person arrested for a drug offense in 1992 was five times more likely to go to prison than a person arrested in 1980. . . . Even for petty offenses, there has been a tendency to enact criminal rather than civil penalties. A county board in California recently passed legislation imposing thirty days in jail for illegal camping or allowing a dog to run loose. [. . .]

In the federal system, the overwhelming majority of inmates – 89 percent – are convicted of nonviolent offenses. [. . .]

A policy that pretends to fight violence by locking up mostly nonviolent offenders is an inefficient use of taxpayer resources. . . . Criminologists Franklin Zimring and Gordon Hawkins first applied the term "bait and switch" to this aspect of criminal justice policy. Under the bait and switch, people who commit lesser infractions have borne the brunt of the anti-crime fervor by getting sent to prison at much higher rates and serving much longer sentences. [. . .]

"THREE STRIKES AND YOU'RE OUT"

"Three strikes and you're out" is one of the most popular crime control initiatives. Proposals vary state by state, but the general idea behind "three strikes" is to increase the prison sentence for a second offense and require life in custody without parole for a third offense. [. . .]

Michael Garcia shoplifted a package of meat valued at $5.62 from a grocery store in Los Angeles. At the time, Garcia was temporarily out of work and his mother's Social Security check had failed to arrive. . . . For this offense, he faces twenty-five years to life in prison under California's "three strikes" legislation. His other "strikes" also involved small sums of money and no physical injury. [. . .]

We all acknowledge that the crime problem in most cities is severe, and that safety is the primary concern . . . But "three strikes and you're out" threatens to drain billions of tax dollars to incarcerate lesser offenders for long periods of time. . . . A survey by the legislature in California, the state to pass one of the strictest and broadest "three strikes" provisions,

Persons Admitted and in Custody How Many? How violent?

	Population	Violent	Non-violent	Annual admissions	Violent	Non-violent
Jails	490,442	23%	77%	9,796,000	n/a	n/a
State prisons	958,704	47%	53%	431,279	27%	73%
Federal prisons	100,438	11%	89%	38,542	6%	94%
Juvenile	93,851	15%	85%	823,449	n/a	n/a
Total*	1.5 million	35%	65%	11.1 million	n/a	n/a

Notes:
Data are the most recent available. Population figures represent the number of persons under jurisdiction in each category.
* Totals have been adjusted to account for double counting of individuals under more than one Jurisdiction.
n/a not available.
Sources: U.S. Department of Justice, Bureau of Justice Statistics; Federal Bureau of Prisons; Office of Juvenile Justice and Delinquency Prevention.

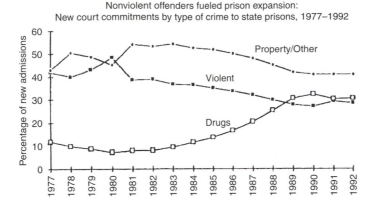

Nonviolent offenders fueled prison expansion:
New court commitments by type of crime to state prisons, 1977–1992

Sources: U.S. Department of Justice, Bureau of Justice Statistics (May 1993), *Prisoners in 1992*, p. 10, Appendix Table 1; Department of Justice, Bureau of Justice Statistics (June 1994), *Prisoners in 1993*, p. 10, Appendix Table 1.

shows that few people sentenced under the new scheme are repeat violent offenders. Fully 70 percent of all second-and third-strike cases filed in California in 1994 were "nonviolent and nonserious offenses." In Los Angeles Country, only 4 percent of second and third felony convictions were cases of murder, rape, kidnapping, or carjacking. [. . .]

The costs run into the billions

The costs of "three strikes" schemes are staggering. Every year an inmate spends in prison — be it under a "three strikes" law or a regular sentence — costs taxpayers an average of $22,000. As the prisoners get older, the cost of maintenance rises, ultimately reaching an average of $69,000 per year per prisoner for those over the age of fifty-five. . . . A study by a Stanford University professor estimated that the cost of a life term for an average. California prisoner is $1.5 million. [. . .]

The Rand Corporation found that the new "three strikes" law will cost between $4.5 and $6.5 billion every year to implement. This is five times more than the state originally estimated. . . . As a result, it is likely that the law will be applied haphazardly across the state. [. . .]

Other unanticipated consequences already are starting to develop. One report concluded that plea bargaining is down because more felony offenders are opting to go to trial rather than risk getting a strike under the new legislation. . . . Moreover, uneven enforcement of the law paves the way for racial and ethnic disparities to develop. Data from the Los Angles Public Defender's office suggests that minorities with roughly the same criminal history as whites are being charged under "three strikes" at seventeen times the rate of whites.

TRUTH IN SENTENCING

Prison populations in many states will increase more rapidly in coming years because of a proliferation of so-called "truth in sentencing" laws. Truth in sentencing requires the prisoner to serve the full sentence without being released early on parole. [. . .]

Under the old "indeterminate" sentencing system, a judge could hand down a sentence within a permissible range. . . . The prospect of early release was designed to induce good behavior so inmates would be easier to manage and more likely to succeed after release. . . . Many politicians now wish to require inmates to serve all or almost all (usually 85 percent) of the full sentence no matter how well they behave in prison. . . . This single change in parole policy would effectively double most prison sentences. . . . Truth in sentencing has become such a powerful slogan that the federal government is trying to impose it on unwilling states. Most of the $10 billion in federal money available to states for prison construction under the 1994 federal crime bill will be contingent on truth in sentencing. [. . .]

MANDATORY MINIMUM SENTENCES

Mandatory minimums were a sentencing reform popular during the late 1980s. The effect of mandatory minimum sentences on the criminal justice system is still being felt by thousands of nonviolent drug offenders, many of whom are spending a decade or more behind bars for relatively modest offenses. The Rockefeller drug laws in New York, passed in the 1970s, have been so harsh on drug offenders that current Republican governor George Pataki has sought to repeal some of their provisions. Mandatory minimums always require offenders to spend time in prison for *at least* a certain number of years. . . . In the federal system, there are currently more than 100 provisions for mandatory minimums. Most states have mandatory minimum sentencing as well. . . . Ninety percent of federal judges and 75 percent of state judges think mandatory minimum sentences are unsound. [. . .]

Mandatory minimums create a number of problems. First, they apply whether or not the punishment fits the crime or the offender. Second, mandatory minimums create what is known as sentencing "cliffs" for drug offenses. For example, possession of five grams of crack is punished with *no more than* one year in prison; possession of 5.01 grams of crack is punished with *no less than* five years in prison. Third, mandatory sentences do not produce an equal sentence for everybody who commits the same offense. If a drug defendant decides to cooperate with the prosecution and turns in other people, the prosecutor will often choose not to charge that person with a crime carrying a mandatory minimum sentence. [. . .]

THE RELATIONSHIP BETWEEN POVERTY, FAMILY BREAKDOWN, AND CRIMINAL JUSTICE

Crime is an act of personal choice and an effective criminal justice system holds individuals accountable for their criminal behavior. Nevertheless, those who wish to prevent crime before it occurs cannot ignore the fact that the majority of the people filling our prisons come from impoverished backgrounds and lack a formal education. Research shows that children from low-income families who are placed in early childhood development programs such as Head Start have lower rates of crime and higher rates of marriage than those who are not in the program. Investing money in early childhood development appears to produce a safer and healthier society over the long run. Unfortunately, the United States is the wealthiest nation on earth but has the highest child poverty rates of any industrialized country. More than fifteen million children live in poverty in the United States, and up to twelve million children are malnourished.

Research consistently demonstrates that a disproportionate amount of violent street' crime occurs in areas that have the lowest incomes and the most desperate living conditions. Furthermore, medical research suggests that children who are malnourished are more apt to engage in high-risk behavior when they get older. Regardless of what one thinks of our high rates of incarceration, it is also clear that they have had a negative impact on family stability. In some cities, more than half of all young men are under criminal justice supervision on any given day. With so many men in prison, the pool of people available for marriage has dwindled. . . . It is two-parent families that are least likely to live in poverty and more likely to cushion young people from the temptation to adopt a criminal lifestyle. Eleven percent of children who live in a two-parent family live in poverty, while 60 percent of children who live with a single parent live in poverty. [. . .]

Poverty is not an excuse for crime, nor is crime the exclusive province of low-income persons. But overall, countries with the highest ratio of poverty have the highest rates of crime. The same correlation holds true for cities. [. . .]

The increase in poverty in the United States during the 1980s was significant. The average rate of poverty in the United States during the decade was 17 percent higher than the average for the 1970s. But this does not begin to capture the overwhelming extent of child poverty, particularly for minorities. The poverty rate for African-American children is an astonishing 44 percent. For Latinos it is 38 percent, and for whites it is 16.2 percent. In Sweden, the poverty rate for children is 2.7 percent; in Canada, it is 13.5 percent; and the overall United States rate is 21.0 percent. . . . The result of our social and criminal justice policies is that today among developed countries, the United States has the highest rates of incarceration, the widest spread of income inequality, and the highest levels of poverty. [. . .]

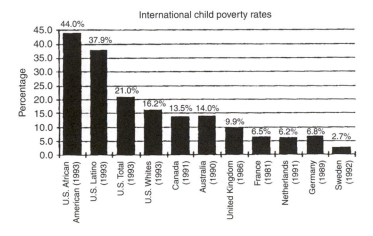

Sources: U.S. Bureau of the Census, Table 21: Poverty Status of Persons, by Age, Race, and Hispanic Origin: 1968–1993; Rainwater, Lee, and Timothy M. Smeeding (August 1995), *Luxembourg Income Study*, Table 3.

YOUTH VIOLENCE AND JUVENILE JUSTICE

[. . .]

Until the 1980s, the biggest threats to young people were car accidents and suicide. In that decade, according to the National Center for Health Statistics, teenage males in all racial and ethnic groups became more likely to die from a bullet than from all natural causes combined. The death rate by homicide in the 1980s of young people aged 15 to 19 increased by 61 percent. Between 1986 and 1992 alone, the number of children in the United States killed by firearms jumped 144 percent, compared to a 30 percent increase for adults.

Although they are shocking at face value, these statistics mask a dramatically higher homicide rate among minorities. For African-American youths, the homicide rate is almost eight times the rate of whites – 34.9 homicides per 100,000 population compared to 4.4 per 100,000 population for 'white male youths'. . . . The increase in juvenile firearms homicide has swept across racial lines: the rate at which white youths are victims of homicide doubled between 1988 and 1992, even though on a per capita basis there are far fewer white homicide victims than African-American homicide victims.

Teenage homicide is the most terrifying element of a much larger geography of juvenile crime. Still, the overwhelming majority of the two million juvenile arrests in the United States each year have nothing to do with violence; only 6 out of 100 juvenile arrests are for violent crimes (for adults, 13 of every 100 arrests are for violent crimes). The most serious crimes of rape and murder account for less than one-half of one percent of juvenile arrests'. Although there has been a dramatic rise in juvenile firearms homicide, we are not in the midst of an *overall* juvenile crime wave. The total rate of arrest for juveniles declined since 1970s.

Nevertheless, because gang killings, drive-by shootings, and high school arms buildups have gained headlines nationwide, we have shaped our policies in response to them. . . . Increasingly, the juvenile justice system has focused on punishing all offenders – violent and nonviolent alike – with harsh sentences while paying lip service to rehabilitation. Our "get tough" policies are perhaps even more severe when we are dealing with children. We try juveniles as adults and allow the death penalty to be imposed against teenagers. But we have failed to solve the problem of juvenile violence. [. . .]

Chronic violent offenders need to be incarcerated for as long as necessary to protect public safety. But that does not change the fact that . . . . the increase in juvenile homicide has given rise to several harsh proposals that . . . will send mostly nonviolent offenders to prison.

The temptation to punish all delinquent youth with harsher penalties because of the violent activities of a few carries real political value. During the debate over the 1994 federal crime bill, one proposal called for spending $500 million to build new juvenile institutions to hold 65,000 delinquent youths. At the time the proposal was made, *all* juvenile facilities in the United States held a total of 63,000 youths, and only about 18 percent of those had been convicted of serious violent crimes. . . . In 1992, over half of the incarcerated children in confinement had committed property or drug crimes and were experiencing their first confinement to a state institution. . . . Most of these would be minorities. [. . .]

Another response to juvenile violence is the call to "waive" minors to adult criminal courts for prosecution. States that allow and encourage such waivers have made a decision that the need to protect the public from juvenile crime outweighs the desire to provide rehabilitation and treatment to youthful offenders (it is virtually impossible for a youth to be sent to a juvenile institution from an adult court). . . . In fact, the greatest increase in juvenile waivers from 1987 to 1991 was for drug cases, which jumped 152 percent. While some repeat drug offenders might be more appropriately handled in adult court, adult waiver is not being used primarily to target violent criminals.

The cost of locking up a young offender in a secure institution can run over $100,000 per child per year. The cost at state-run facilities can range from $35,000 to $70,000 per year. Since youth need more supervision and more educational and treatment services, the cost is usually higher than for adult prisons. [. . .]

Are we missing the problem?

In a survey of inner-city high schools, almost one in four students said that at some point in their lives they had possessed a firearm. So many weapons in the hands of adolescents has had an incendiary effect. . . . An essential element of the problem is that weapons on the streets are more lethal than in the past. In part, this reflects the nature of the drug war. As profits grew, those drug dealers with superior firepower found they could control greater market share and intimidate their competitors. . . . The sophistication of weapons means that the chances of a bullet *killing* rather than *wounding* have grown substantially. [. . .]

Why the increase in youth homicide?

[. . .]

Sociologists and criminologists have tried to explain the impulse to kill with a variety of theories: some cite a chemical imbalance in the brain, others cite an increase in television violence, and others claim it has to do with racism, poverty, and reduced opportunities for upward mobility. In some neighborhoods, carrying a weapon is clearly a way to gain respect and status among peers. This is especially true in communities where traditional opportunities . . . are sorely lacking. "The inclination to violence springs from the circumstances of life among the ghetto poor – the lack of jobs that pay a living wage, the stigma of race, the fallout from rampant drug use and drug trafficking, and the resulting alienation and lack of hope for the future," sociologist Elijah Anderson wrote recently.

Placing juvenile homicide in context

The overwhelming tragedy of youth homicide must not be allowed to overtake our entire approach to juvenile justice. Juvenile courts in 1992 handled more than 1 million criminal cases, but only about 2,500 of them involved a youth accused of homicide. If one subtracts the cases dismissed for lack of evidence, less than 1,000 youths nationwide were convicted of killing somebody in 1992.

There clearly is no reason to build new juvenile institutions just to house youths convicted of murder. . . . How we treat this fraction of youth killers – and how we prevent the many other juvenile offenders from heading in the current direction – is the most important policy issue in juvenile justice today.

DEALING WITH JUVENILE OFFENDERS

The big question is how states can design juvenile justice systems to deal with the violent offender as well as the more numerous lesser offenders. The goal of any juvenile correctional system should be to hold young people accountable for their behavior and to allow them the opportunity to develop the skills and confidence necessary to lead productive lives upon release. Over the past twenty years, a number of states, including Massachusetts, Utah, Missouri, Hawaii, Oregon, Montana, and Arkansas, have tried a more balanced approach with great success. The approach focuses on a combination of smaller facilities for violent youth and community-based programs for lesser offenders. [. . .]

Building smaller facilities for chronic offenders

Utah learned from the failure of its large juvenile training school. Three out of four "graduates" of the state's 166-bed Youth Development Center went on to commit new offenses on the outside. Most of the youths were nonviolent offenders who were being turned into hard-core criminals while incarcerated. [. . .]

In the 1980s, Utah decided to close its juvenile institution. The state built two thirty-bed secure facilities. The smaller facilities were based on the premise that people would respond more positively if their surroundings were more humane. Each youth sent to a locked facility had his or her own bedroom. The common area had soft carpet and living room furniture. Meals were cooked and eaten together in living units of ten. Youths had treatment and educational plans tailored to their particular needs. Group and family counseling were available, as were services for drug treatment and sex offender therapy. The smaller facilities produced impressive results: in one four-year study, recidivism dropped by more than 70 percent. [. . .]

The Massachusetts model

Massachusetts is often cited as a standard-bearer in juvenile corrections. All of its large juvenile institutions were closed in the early 1970s and resources were shifted to privately run community-based programs that focused on rehabilitation. Currently, violent youths who need secure confinement are placed in one of fourteen small facilities around the state. Each of the facilities has between fifteen and thirty beds. Only about 15 percent of juvenile offenders in Massachusetts are placed in these locked facilities. Nonviolent juvenile offenders are placed in group homes and intensive supervision programs that permit staff to individualize treatment services. Regional case managers monitor the youths as they are moved through a spectrum of care and security based on how they respond to treatment at each stage.[. . .]

Researchers have found that both violent and nonviolent youth in Massachusetts were much less likely to commit new crimes upon release than juveniles in other jurisdictions. Even chronic violent offenders showed a significant decline in the incidence and severity of new offenses in the year after release. Although Massachusetts initially spent more money than most jurisdictions in developing its program for violent and serious offenders, the overall system costs are much lower over the long term because expensive secure confinement is used sparingly. It is estimated that Massachusetts saves over $11 million annually.

There are a number of key elements that make the Utah and Massachusetts models effective. The success is due to the continuous case management of each youth, the availability of opportunities to build self-esteem through learning and decisionmaking, clear consequences for misconduct, enriched educational and vocational opportunities, individual and family counseling tailored to the needs of the offender, and an emphasis on making sure the child readjusts to the community *after* his sentence expires. Taken together, they send a strong message to juvenile offenders that society cares about them and wants to bring them into the mainstream.

ADDRESSING THE PROBLEM OF YOUTH VIOLENCE

In 1993, the Office of Juvenile Justice and Delinquency Prevention (OJJDP), a division of the Department of Justice, put forth a document entitled *Comprehensive Strategy for Serious Violent and Chronic Juvenile Offenders*. The prevention approach advocated by the federal government focused on minimizing risk factors (e.g., child abuse) that pushed youth toward delinquency and maximizing protective factors (e.g., family preservation programs) that encouraged youth to lead law-abiding lives. It was based on years of research by juvenile justice experts and represented an emerging consensus in the field. The strategy of the OJJDP proposal was to strengthen those institutions that had the most influence over young people – families, schools, peer groups, and neighborhood and community programs.

RACE AND CRIMINAL JUSTICE

Whites and African-Americans live in different worlds when it comes to the criminal justice system. Three points about race are paramount. First, arrest rates indicate that African-Americans commit more crime than whites relative to the population. Second, there are so many more African-Americans than whites in our prisons that the difference cannot be explained by higher crime among African-Americans – racial discrimination is also at work, and it penalizes African-Americans at almost every juncture in the criminal justice system. Third, whether the cause is higher crime or discrimination or both, this country is on the verge of a social catastrophe because of the sheer number of African-Americans behind bars. [. . .]

While crime rates for African-Americans are somewhat higher than those for whites relative to the population, crime by African-Americans is not getting any worse. Since the mid-1970s, African-Americans have consistently accounted for about 45 percent of those arrested for murder, rape, robbery, and aggravated assault. These numbers tell us that the *proportion* of overall crime committed by African-Americans has not increased for several years. Yet since 1980, the African-American prison population has increased dramatically while the white prison population has increased far less. Something more is at work than changes in crime patterns. [. . .]

THE MAGNITUDE OF MINORITY IMPRISONMENT

[. . .]

The United States imprisons African-American men at a rate six times that of white men. African-Americans are incarcerated at a rate of 1,947 per 100,000 African-American citizens compared to a rate of 306 per 100,000 for white citizens. African-American males make up less than 7 percent of the U.S. population, yet they comprise almost half of the prison and jail population. In 1992, 56 percent of all African-American men aged 18 to 35 in Baltimore were under some form of criminal justice supervision on any given day. In the District of Columbia, the figure was 42 percent. One out of every three African-American men between the ages of 20 and 29 in the entire country – including suburban and rural areas – was under some form of criminal justice supervision in 1994.

The difference between the numbers of minorities and whites in prison has widened as sentences for crimes have gotten longer. In 1930, 75 percent of all prison admissions were white and 22 percent were African-American. That ratio has roughly reversed. In 1992, 29 percent of prison admissions were white, while 51 percent were African-American and 20 percent were Hispanic. Almost three out of four prison admissions today are either African-American or Hispanic. Ninety percent of the prison admissions for drug offenses are African-American or Hispanic. [. . .]

Is there a racial bias?

In 1983, criminologists Alfred Blumstein and Elizabeth Graddy found that 51 percent of nonwhite men in large cities are arrested and charged with a felony in their lifetime. If the study had included the more numerous misdemeanor offenses, the proportion of nonwhite men arrested and charged would have been significantly higher. In the mid-1980s the California Attorney General's office conducted a study that found that two-thirds of non-white California males between the ages of 18 and 30 had been arrested. [. . .]

One way to determine if racial bias has contributed to the minority rate of imprisonment is to look at crime rates of African-Americans. If African-Americans are in prison in higher proportion to their crime rate, it suggests that they may be treated more harshly by the criminal justice system as they are processed through it. We determine crime rates for African-Americans and whites based on their arrest rates. This assessment discounts racial bias that might have occurred *before* arrest . . . but arrest records are the best indication we have of actual crime rates. [. . .]

Relative to population size, about five times as many African-Americans as whites get arrested for the serious index crimes of murder, rape, robbery, and aggravated assault. About three times as many African-Americans as whites get arrested for less serious crimes, which make up the bulk of arrests. [. . .]

If after arrest there were *no* racial bias in the criminal justice system, the racial makeup of the prison population should at least roughly reflect the racial disparity in arrest rates. . . . But the racial difference among African-Americans and whites in prison is overwhelmingly wider than arrest rates suggest it should be absent racial bias. *There are seven African-Americans to each white in prison.*

This evidence strongly suggests that as African-Americans work their way through the system from arrest to punishment, they encounter harsher treatment than whites. This is the *cumulative* effect of racial discrimination on the criminal justice process. For instance, if there is racial discrimination when a person is arrested it can result in a harsher assessment of the offense. This, in turn, can result in a more severe charge and a more severe sentence and thus have an extended impact throughout the process. . . .

This is not to say the criminal justice system is never fair to African-Americans. Some individuals certainly receive fair treatment, but the statistics indicate that African-Americans as a class of offenders receive harsher treatment than whites. . . . This fact has been borne out by studies that show whites are released more often before trial, pay less money to bail themselves out of jail, and receive significantly better deals in plea bargaining. [. . .]

The first place where racial disparities are usually measured is at the point of arrest. . . . A California study found in 1992 that police make *unfounded* (where the suspect was innocent, or there was inadequate evidence, or there was an illegal search or seizure) arrests of African-Americans and Hispanics at sharply higher rates than those of whites. For African-Americans in California, the rate of unfounded arrests was four times greater than that of whites. For Hispanics, the rate was more than double the rate of whites. The disparity was even worse in some urban areas. . . . In Los Angeles, the rate was seven times as great, and in San Diego it was six times the rate of whites. [. . .]

Once they make an arrest, police usually refer the case to a prosecutor, who must decide whether to press charges or dismiss the matter. . . . The majority of available studies conclude that racial discrimination can and often does play a role in the prosecutorial decision. One study of 1,017 homicide defendants in Florida compared the police assessment of the severity of the initial offense with the prosecutorial assessment of the severity. The study found that crimes involving white victims and African-American offenders were much more likely to be upgraded in severity by the prosecutor. [. . .]

Bail also presents problems

A study by the *Hartford Courant* of 150,000 criminal cases in Connecticut found that an African-American or Hispanic man must pay on average *double* the bail of a white man for the same offense. In drug cases, the study found that the average bond for African-Americans and Hispanics in several areas of the state was *four times higher* than the bond for whites. . . . The racial disparities in bail prompted the chief court administrator in Connecticut to charge publicly that judges were using excessive bond to punish minorities who had not been convicted. And as if to compound this problem, a 1989 Connecticut study . . . also found that a failure to obtain release on bond increased both the likelihood of later conviction and the length of sentence.

A similar study in Florida, conducted for the state Department of Corrections, found strong evidence of racial bias in the treatment of African-American defendants before trial. The sample of almost 3,000 adult offenders showed that being African-American significantly increased the likelihood of incarceration before trial. Young unemployed African-American men arrested on "public order" offenses were three times more likely to be kept in jail than unemployed whites arrested on the same charges. They were seven times more likely to be locked up than employed white arrestees.

Plea bargaining and sentencing

More than 90 percent of criminal cases where the defendant faces a prison sentence end in a "deal" in which the defendant pleads guilty to a lesser charge rather than face the risk of trial and a longer sentence. During negotiations between defense attorneys and prosecutors – the plea bargaining process – prosecutors have wide discretion to be tough on some and more generous with others. Evidence suggests that here again it is minorities who get the worst deals.

A comprehensive study of racial bias in plea bargaining was carried out in California by the *San Jose Mercury News* in 1991. A computer analysis of almost 700,000 criminal cases in California from 1981 to 1990 demonstrated that at virtually every stage of pre-trial plea bargaining whites were more successful than minorities . . . at getting charges dropped, getting cases dismissed, avoiding harsher punishment, avoiding extra charges, and having their criminal records wiped clean.

Certainly there are other factors – such as the strength of the evidence – that determine the outcome of the plea bargaining process. But in the criminal justice system, "racially biased decisions add up one by one [to form] an overall dramatic impact," according to Mark Mauer of The Sentencing Project, who analyzed the California data.

The different treatment of minority defendants in the plea bargaining process can stem both from unconscious stereotyping and deliberate discrimination. [. . .]

Although there is no definitive national study, there is evidence that African-Americans and whites are treated differently at sentencing. Florida has a statute that enables prosecu-tors to seek longer sentences for repeat offenders. The state legislature found in 1992 that . . . African-Americans were more than twice as likely to have their sentences lengthened for a nonviolent offense than were whites and for violent offenses, 50 percent more likely. . . . In Florida, African-Americans received longer sentences even though they had engaged in the same criminal conduct and had the same criminal history as whites.

Some of the most blatant racial discrimination in the area of sentencing takes place in the application of the death penalty. The most comprehensive study of the death penalty found in 1983 that *killers of whites were eleven times more likely to be condemned to death than killers of African-Americans*. Since then little has changed. Discrimination in the appli-cation of the death penalty can be seen most vividly by focusing on the race of the *victim*. Prosecutors nationwide – more than nine out of ten of whom are white – tend to seek the death penalty more often if the victim is white. [. . .]

Racial bias through the entire system

The *Harvard Law Review* in 1988 published a comprehensive legal dissection of racial discrimination in the criminal justice system. It is the overall conclusion that is so persuasive: after looking at every component of the criminal justice system, it deter-mined that there is evidence that discrimination exists against African-Americans at almost every stage of the criminal justice process. Other researchers across the political spectrum have reached the same conclusion. A 1994 study of race bias led by researcher Robert Crutchfield concluded that a "growing body of evidence suggests that justice is by no means guaranteed" for minorities in the criminal justice system. Research by criminologists Alfred Blumstein and Jaqueline Cohen compared arrest rates to rates of incarceration and concluded that a significant portion of the racial disparities in prison is accounted for by racial discrimination. According to Norval Morris, there is "measurable racial discrimination in our police practices, in our prosecutorial practices and in our sentencing." Morris concluded that the "whole law and order movement that we have heard so much about is, in operation though not in intent, anti-black and anti-underclass – not in plan, not in desire, not in intent, but in operation."

RACE AND THE WAR ON DRUGS

The "war on drugs" launched in the mid-1980s was a pivotal event in the history of African-American imprisonment in the United States. Amid much media fanfare, President Reagan launched the war on drugs by saying, "The American people want their government to get tough and go on the offensive." . . . What he did not say was that *police enforcement of new drug laws would focus almost exclusively on low-level dealers in minority neighborhoods*. Police found more drugs in minority communities because that is where they looked for them. [. . .]

African-American arrest rates for drugs during the height of the "drug war" in 1989 were five times higher than arrest rates for whites *even though whites and African-Americans were using drugs at the same rate*. African-Americans make up 12 percent of the U.S. population and constitute 13 percent of all monthly drug users, but represent 35 percent of those arrested for drug possession, 55 percent of those convicted of drug possession, and 74 percent of those sentenced to prison for drug possession. [. . .]

The war on drugs did not succeed in its goal of stemming drug use. As the war heated up in the late 1980s, the street price of cocaine should have increased as police interdicted supplies and dealing became riskier. Instead, the street price of cocaine *fell*. . . . But the collateral effects of this "war" on minority communities were devastating. Some of the most striking evidence can be found in Baltimore. Again, remember that African-Americans and whites were using drugs at roughly the same rate all across the country. Of 12,956 arrests in that city for "drug abuse violations" in 1991, 11,107 were of African-Americans. . . . In New York City, 92 percent of drug arrests were of African-Americans or Hispanics. . . . *Today* found that in some cities African-Americans were arrested at as much as 50 times the rate of whites for drug offenses. [. . .]

This pattern helps explain the exploding rate of incarceration among African-Americans. In 1979, only 6 percent of state inmates and 25 percent of federal inmates had been convicted of drug offenses. By 1991, the rate for state inmates had nearly quadrupled to 21 percent, while the proportion of federal inmates so convicted had more than doubled to 58 percent. The overwhelming majority of these new prison admissions for drug offenses were minority men, because that is who the drug war targeted.

Harsher sentences for crack cocaine

One of the most shocking events in the sporting world in 1986 was the cocaine-induced death of University of Maryland basketball star Len Bias. [. . .]

Almost immediately Congress imposed strict mandatory sentences for possessing or selling crack cocaine. . . . Overnight, penalties for the use of "crack" cocaine became up to 100 times harsher than the penalties for powder cocaine. Under federal law, possession of five grams of crack cocaine became a felony that carried a *mandatory minimum* sentence of five years, while possession of the same amount of powder cocaine remained a misdemeanor punishable by a *maximum* of one year. This contrasted with mandatory minimum five year sentences for: 500 grams of powder cocaine, 100 grams of heroin, 10 grams of PCP. Both before and after the law was passed, about 90 percent of "crack" arrests were of African-Americans while 75 percent of arrests for powder cocaine were of whites. [. . .]

Violence and crack cocaine

The different sentences for crack and powder cocaine are hard to justify. Even the U.S. Sentencing Commission has recommended the disparity be eliminated. The media has trumpeted crack cocaine as a highly addictive drug that had the potential to destroy communities and wreak wanton violence, but careful research now tells us that this was largely myth. . . . The violence associated with crack stems more from turf battles between police and crack dealers, and among crack dealers battling to control lucrative markets, than from the narcotic effect of crack itself. [. . .]

PRISONS

Since 1980, the United States has engaged in the largest correctional buildup of any country in the history of the world. During this time the number of Americans imprisoned has tripled to 1.5 million. . . . Hundreds of billions of dollars have poured from taxpayers' checking accounts into penal institutions and the businesses that service them. Several million people have come to depend on the criminal justice system for employment. [. . .]

More than 1.5 million Americans are behind bars

The United States [in 1996] . . . had about 1.5 million people behind bars – one million in state and federal prisons and another [500,000] in local jails. . . . The Rikers Island Correctional Facilities in New York City and the Los Angeles County Jail system are the two largest penal colonies in the world and by themselves have budgets larger than many cities.

In addition to the 1.5 million Americans behind bars, there are also an additional 3.6 million persons on probation or parole. There are thus over 5 million citizens – or almost 3 percent of the U.S. adult population – under the supervision of the criminal justice system. One in thirty-eight adults in the United States and one in twenty-one men, live under the supervision of the criminal justice system. [. . .]

Prison and jail construction in the United States continues at a rapid pace despite evidence that the increase in rates of incarceration failed to reduce crime. More than 600 new prisons have been constructed in the United States since 1980 at a cost of tens of billions of dollars, and this does not include modifications of existing facilities. The 1994 federal crime bill allocated nearly $10 billion for states to build prisons. [. . .]

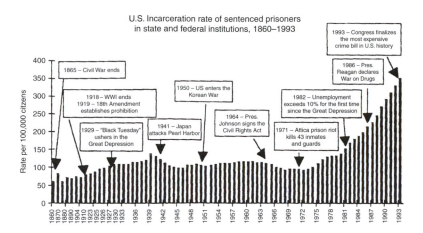

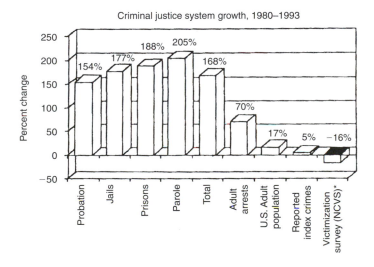

Sources: U.S. Department of Justice, Bureau of Justice Statistics (1994), *Sourcebook of Criminal Justice Statistics—1993*, p. 600; U.S. Department of Justice, Bureau of Justice Statistics (June 1994), *Prisoners in 1993*, p. 2; U.S. Department of Justice, Bureau of Justice Statistics (December 1986), *Historical Corrections Statistics in the United States, 1850–1984*, p. 34.

Sources: U.S. Department of Justice, Bureau of Justice Statistics (1994), *Criminal Victimization in the United States: 1973–1992 Trends*; U.S. Department of Justice, Federal Bureau of Investigation (1994), *Crime in the United States – 1993* and (1981) *Crime in the United States – 1980*; U.S. Department of Justice, Bureau of Justice Statistics Press Release (September 11, 1994), *Parole and Probation Populations Reach New Highs*; U.S. Bureau of the Census (February 1993), *U.S. Population Estimates, By Age, Sex, Race, and Hispanic Origin: 1980 to 1991*; U.S. Bureau of the Census (March 1994), *U.S. Population Estimates, By Age, Sex, Race, and Hispanic Origin: 1990 to 1993*.
Note:
*NCVS percent change is from 1980 to 1992 due to the redesign of the 1993 survey.

Comparing imprisonment across countries

One way to understand the scale of imprisonment in the United States is to compare it to other nations. The US imprisons more people on any given day than any other nation. China, whose population is much larger, has the second biggest prison population of

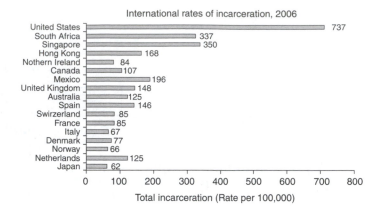

International rates of incarceration, 2006

Sources: Mauer, Marc (September 1994), *Americans Behind Bars: The International Use of Incarceration, 1992–1993* (Washington D.C.: The Sentencing Project): Austin, James (January 1994), *An Overview of Incarceration Trends in the United States and Their Impact on Crime* (San Francisco: The National Council on Crime and Delinquency).

Note: Russia's incarceration rate is estimated to be 558; it has been omitted because of questions of reliability. The incarceration rates include both prison and jail populations.

1,548,498. The United States also leads the world by imprisoning [737] out of every 100,000 of its citizens [in 2006]. The imprisonment rate in the United States is [more than] five times the rate of Canada and Australia and seven times the rate of most European democracies. Yet as we have seen, the overall crime rate in America is no higher than it is in comparable nations. The reason more people are in prison in the United States is because sentences are so much longer for lesser crimes. In most other countries, people who commit nonviolent offenses receive shorter prison terms or noncustodial sanctions such as fines or community service. [. . .]

RATES OF IMPRISONMENT AND CRIME

Academic research has shown little or no correlation between rates of crime and the number of people in prison. States with high rates of imprisonment may or may not have high rates of crime, while states with low rates of crime may or may not have high rates of imprisonment. North Dakota and South Dakota, which are virtually identical in terms of demographics and geography, provide an example. South Dakota imprisons its citizens at three times the rate of North Dakota, but crime between the two states is roughly the same and has been for several decades. This point can also be illustrated by comparing the homicide and incarceration rates in most states. Louisiana, for example, puts more of its citizens in prison per capita than almost any other state – yet it also had the highest homicide rate in 1994. Oklahoma had the third highest incarceration rate but ranked twentieth in its rate of homicide. Nor are dramatic increases in incarceration necessarily followed by declines in crime.

The link between crime and imprisonment creates a great deal of confusion. Because increasing rates of imprisonment will sometimes occur at the same time as declining rates of crime (though sometimes not), those who use the date selectively can make it appear that prisons work to lower crime. In California, the prison population rose in 19 of the past 21 years. In 15 of those 19 years, violent crime rose as well. This would seem to indicate that prisons did not reduce violent crime in California. Yet some elected officials point to the few years that crime fell and claim that additional prison construction is necessary to reduce crime.

This kind of claim is becoming more frequent in the debate over crime policy, particularly since crime rates have declined slightly in each of the last three years. Though one may be gratified crime is dropping, it is impossible to point to an increase in the prison population as the primary reason. In fact nobody can conclusively explain this drop by pointing to one factor. Many experts believe the decline has resulted from a combination of demographic changes (there are fewer criminally active young males) more effective law enforcement, and greater stability in the drug trade (which leads to less violence among drug gangs).

The effects of incarceration

Sending such a high number of Americans through the jailhouse door each year has wide ramifications. . . . Basic survival tactics are necessary to endure even a short stay. Inmates learn to strike first and seek strength in gangs often comprised of dangerous offenders. Sexual assaults are frequent and usually go unpunished. The prison experience is one in which the code is survival of the fittest, in which weakness is a crime, and in which the expression of vulnerable feelings can jeopardize the survival of the prisoner. As ever more young men and women are socialized to the cell blocks and then are returned to the streets, the violent subculture of the correctional facility increasingly acts as a vector for spreading crime in our communities. [. . .]

Some see it as a glamorous rite of passage that earns respect and status. Joanne Page, director of The Fortune Society in New York City, compares the impact of incarceration to post-traumatic stress disorder, which afflicts soldiers returning from war. Many offenders emerge from prison afraid to trust, fearful of the unknown, and with their vision of the world shaped by the meaning that behaviors have in the prison context. For a recently released prisoner, experiences like being jostled on the subway, having someone reach across them in the bathroom to take a paper towel, or staring can be taken as the precursor to a physical attack. Professionals who work with ex-offenders have said it appears prison damages a person's mid-range response to the environment, leaving the choice of gritting one's teeth and enduring, or full-fledged attack to protect oneself from perceived danger. [. . .]

Chapter 2

Tom R. Tyler

GOVERNING AMID DIVERSITY
The effect of fair decision-making procedures on the legitimacy of government

From: Tom R. Tyler (1994) 'Governing amid diversity', *Law and Society Review*, 28(4): 809–831.

The research reported tests the influence of judgments about the fairness of government lawmaking procedures on evaluations of the legitimacy of a national-level governmental authority through studies – two experiments and a survey – examining judgments about Congress. The influence of procedural justice on legitimacy is contrasted with the effects of self-interested judgments indexing agreement with congressional decisions. Although a sizable empirical literature already suggests the importance of procedural justice in shaping reactions to personal experiences with legal, political, and managerial authorities, recent studies have been inconsistent about the degree to which procedural justice findings generalize to national-level institutions. The findings of the studies reported here strongly support the argument that procedural justice judgments influence evaluations of the legitimacy of a national-level political institution. A further exploration seeking to find an influence of ethnicity, gender, education, age, income and/or ideology on the psychology of legitimacy suggests that demographic differences do not influence the criteria respondents use to assess the fairness of decisionmaking procedures. The findings suggest that procedures provide a viable basis for maintaining public support in the face of differences in individuals' policy positions and background characteristics.

IDENTIFYING THE POPULAR BELIEFS that help democratic societies to function effectively is an ongoing goal of legal scholars and social scientists. The key issue is which public beliefs have an important influence on government effectiveness and which do not (Almond & Verba 1963, 1980; Dahl 1971, 1989; Huntington 1984; Inglehart 1990). For example, Dahl (1971) noted five public beliefs that he argued facilitate the development of democracy: (1) belief in the legitimacy of the institutions of government; (2) beliefs about the nature of the authority relationships between governors and governed; (3) confidence in the ability of government to deal with problems effectively; (4) political and interpersonal trust; and (5) belief in the possibility and desirability of political cooperation. The analysis here focuses on the first of these beliefs — judgments about the legitimacy of government authorities. Such beliefs have already been demonstrated to facilitate the effectiveness of government authorities (see Tyler 1990; Tyler & Mitchell 1994). I examine here how public beliefs about legitimacy are affected by those authorities's actions.

Several types of judgments about the actions of authorities potentially underlie public judgments about their legitimacy, including (1) agreement with policies and decisions and (2) judgments about the fairness of decisionmaking procedures. The influence of these beliefs has been examined in a growing empirical literature on national-level legitimacy (Gibson 1989, 1991; Mondak 1993; Tyler & Rasinski 1991). However, studies in that literature disagree about which beliefs are important in producing and maintaining legitimacy, with both models receiving support in some studies.

FAIRNESS AND LEGITIMACY OF GOVERNMENT

I report here . . . [on a study] that explores the relative importance of beliefs about the outcome and procedural justice of lawmaking on the legitimacy of political/legal authorities. . . . The policy issues examined include . . . general evaluations of congressional rules and the congressional rule-making process. . . . The national-level institution is the United States Congress, chosen because it directly confronts conflicts of interest. Prior studies have been conducted using the Supreme Court, which focuses on conflicts over rights, and this report seeks to broaden the scope of the test of procedural justice influence. . . . This research moves beyond prior research by exploring the degree to which there are common criteria for judging the justice of decisionmaking procedures among people who differ in ethnicity, gender, education, age, income, and ideology.

The primary purpose of the research is to test empirically the effectiveness of public beliefs about the justice of government in enhancing the legitimacy of government. The hypothesis tested is that people are influenced by their judgments about the fairness of government decisionmaking procedures. This *procedural justice* argument is developed from the studies of Thibaut and Walker (1975) and has been widely confirmed in studies since 1975 of personal experiences with government and other types of authorities (for reviews, see Lind & Tyler 1988; Tyler & Lind 1992). Research suggests that procedural influences are especially strong on evaluations of third-party authorities and of the institutions they represent (Tyler & Lind 1992). Studies suggest that evaluations of political authorities (Tyler & Caine 1981; Tyler, Rasinski, & McGraw 1985), legal authorities (Tyler 1984, 1990; Tyler, Casper, & Fisher 1989), and managerial authorities (Alexander & Ruderman 1987; Brockner, Tyler, & Cooper-Schneider 1992; Folger & Konovsky 1989) are shaped by judgments about the fairness of their decisionmaking procedures. Further, procedural influences affect the willingness to voluntarily accept third-party decisions (Lind et al. 1993) and voluntarily follow organizational rules (Tyler 1990). [. . .]

The legitimacy of congressional authority

The focus . . . here is the legitimacy of congressional authority. Several aspects of legitimacy are potentially important (Tyler 1990). One aspect of legitimacy is reflected in people's behavioral intentions toward authorities and rules. One element of behavioral intentions is people's willingness to voluntarily accept the decisions made by authorities (Tyler & Lind 1992); another is feelings of obligation to follow the rules and laws enacted by authorities (Tyler 1990). Finally, behavioral intentions are reflected in willingness to act on behalf of authorities, for example, by voting for them (Kelley & Mirer 1974). . . . This study examines feelings of obligation to follow rules.

A second aspect of legitimacy is attitudinal support for authorities, often labeled "trust." Support is assessed through judgments about whether group authorities are viewed as competent and honest (Tyler 1990). A second type of attitudinal support for authorities is the belief that an authority's institutional role is appropriate and should be deferred to (Caldeira & Gibson 1992), or "institutional legitimacy." The study examines supportive attitudes toward congressional authorities. For an examination of the effects of judgments about institutional legitimacy, see Tyler and Mitchell (1994).

The final aspect of legitimacy, not examined here, is actual behavior: whether people pay judgments and obey laws. Previous studies have suggested, however, that both attitudes about legitimacy and behavioral intentions toward law and authorities influence actual behavior (see Tyler 1990).

Bridging differences in ethnicity, gender, income, and ideology

American society is composed of people with diverse values and interests and is rapidly increasing in its multi-ethnic, multicultural composition. Further, both the size of the population and its economic and social polarization are increasing. For these reasons, "[o]ne prediction that can be advanced with sure confidence is that human life on this planet faces a steady increase in the potential for interpersonal and intergroup conflict" (Thibaut & Walker 1975:1). A utilitarian model of governmental legitimacy suggests a discouraging conclusion about the ability of American political and legal authorities to bridge competing values and interests, creating policies that will be viewed as legitimate and be commonly accepted by people and groups differing in their values and self-interests. The procedural justice hypothesis, in contrast, is more optimistic. It suggests that there are ways for authorities to bridge differences by using conflict resolution procedures that all the parties will view as fair.

The success of a procedural justice strategy requires that people who differ in background characteristics such as ethnicity, gender, and income agree on the characteristics of a fair dispute resolution procedure – that there will not be demographic differences in the criteria used to evaluate the justice of procedures. Tyler (1988) examined the influence of demographic differences on the psychology of procedural justice among a sample of citizens, evaluating their personal experiences with police officers and judges. He found no differences due to ethnicity, gender, income, or other personal characteristics. The research reported here extends this analysis to ethnicity, gender, education, income, age, and ideological differences in the evaluation of national-level policy institutions.

DESIGN OF THE RESEARCH

[. . .]

The sample for the study was generated using standard sampling techniques. The first stage of sampling identified a random set of telephone numbers. The goal was to maximize access to all English-speaking adults (age 18 or over) in the San Francisco Bay area. The sample was generated using a stratified, two-phase procedure. The target area was the five-country San Francisco Bay area (all telephone prefixes within the 415 and 510 area codes), plus Santa Clara County (most prefixes in the 408 area code). To generate complete telephone numbers for the sample, four-digit random numbers were appended to each area code and prefix combination corresponding to the target area.

The second stage of the sampling process involved the selection of a respondent from among the residents of households contacted by telephone. One adult was selected at random from each chosen household and designated as the respondent. No substitutions were allowed. Each home was called at least 18 times in an effort to reach that person.

The study . . . screened respondents for ethnicity and only interviewed people who are white or African American and used a statistical procedure that oversampled African Americans by overrepresenting telephone numbers in census tracts known to have greater numbers of African American respondents. The resulting sample is 30% African American. The sample size was 502, with a mean age of 43 (S.D. = 15.60). For other characteristics, see Table 2.1. [. . .]

The study is based on a correlational analysis of the data . . . . Respondents evaluated the general decisionmaking characteristics of Congress: whether it makes decisions which favor them and whether it makes decisions using fair procedures. These judgments are used to predict two aspects of legitimacy: (1) attitudinal support for Congress ("trust") and (2) feelings of obligation to obey federal laws. [. . .]

In this study a broader range of procedural elements was considered, including judgments about the favorability of the outcome; the degree of voice allowed; the neutrality of the decisionmakers and their trustworthiness; and their respect for the public

Table 2.1 Demographic composition of respondents

	Study sample %
Male	47
White	70
High school graduates or less	20
Some college	37
College graduates	22
Some postcollege education	16
Household income	a
$20,000 or less	17
$20,001–$40,000	24
$40,001–$80,000	29
Over $80,000	26

Note:
[a]A few (4%) declined to answer the question about income or did not know their income.

(standing). . . . This study examines the effects of respondent views about five aspects of congressional decisionmaking: the favorability of congressional decisions to the respondent, voice, neutrality, trustworthiness, and standing. . . . The analysis examined the influence of these judgments on procedural justice judgments and on two dependent variables reflecting two aspects of legitimacy: attitudinal support for Congress and feelings of obligation to obey government rules. The underlying issue is whether Congress can gain legitimacy through the use of fair decisionmaking procedures.

The ability of fair procedures to maintain the legitimacy of authorities was examined across six background characteristics: race (African American, white), education, age, income, gender, and ideology (liberal, conservative). This examination explored the role of different aspects of procedures in shaping judgments of procedural fairness. This analysis is important because the ability of procedures to function effectively in a diverse society depends on all groups defining the fairness of procedures in similar ways. [. . .]

Dependent variables

Procedural Justice. Respondents were asked to agree or disagree with: "The way Congress makes decisions is fair" and "The way Congress decides who will benefit from government policies is fair."

Feelings of obligation. Respondents were asked to agree or disagree with four items: "I feel that I should accept the decisions made by government leaders in Washington even when I disagree with them," "People should obey the laws made by Congress even if they go against what they think is right," "There are times when it is all right for people to disobey the government," and "I can think of situations in which I would stop supporting the policies of our government."

Support for Congress. Attitudes about support were assessed via a six-item scale: "Feelings about Congress (cold to warm)," "How much respect do you have for Congress as an institution of government?" "Congress can usually be trusted to do what is right," "Most of the representatives to Congress do a good job," "Many of the people in Congress are basically dishonest," and "The decisions made by Congress are usually fair."

Independent variables

Background

Ideology. Respondents were asked to indicate whether "when it comes to politics" they think of themselves as liberal or conservative. Responses were arranged on a seven-point scale.

Demographics. Respondents' race, gender, age, education, and income were measured by self-report.

Antecedents of procedural justice

Finally, respondents were asked to evaluate the characteristics of congressional decisionmaking. Outcome judgments involve evaluations of the favorability of congressional decisions. Procedural judgments include assessments of voice, neutrality trustworthiness, and standing.

Outcome favorability. Respondents were asked whether the decisions made by Congress "generally favor people like" themselves and whether "Most of the men and women in Congress try to be fair to people in their district – not just to special interest groups."

Voice. Respondents were asked whether there are ways for average citizens to present their views to Congress before policy decisions are made and whether the views of the average citizen influence the decisions made by Congress. (Thibaut & Walker 1975 refer to these elements of control as process control and decision control, respectively.) The responses were combined into a single index in this analysis.

Neutrality. Respondents were asked whether "Congress is generally honest in the way it goes about making decisions," whether "Congress gives equal consideration to the views of all the different groups in America," and whether "Congress gets the kind of information it needs to make informed decisions."

Trustworthiness. Respondents were asked whether "Congress tries to be fair when making its decisions."

Standing. Respondents were asked whether "Congress is concerned about protecting the average citizen's rights."

Results

[. . .]

The concern is with the effects of procedural qualities on procedural justice evaluations and on the legitimacy of the authorities involved. In the analysis two aspects of legitimacy are considered as dependent variables: attitudinal support and feelings of obligation to obey. Procedural qualities are indexed through an assessment of different procedural elements. . . . This analysis considers these two elements and adds the additional elements of trustworthiness and standing, which are drawn from the relational model of authority (Tyler & Lind 1992).

The first question considered is the influence of procedural elements on procedural justice, attitudinal support, and perceived obligation to obey. The analysis is conducted twice, first using only the procedural elements used in studies and then using an expanded set of procedural elements. The results of the analyses, shown in Table 2.2, are the same. Procedural elements influence overall procedural justice judgments, attitudinal support, and perceived obligation to obey. This is true across a variety of procedural elements.

The finding that procedural elements of decisionmaking shaped legitimacy would be of less value if respondents of varying ethnicity, income, gender, or ideology differed in the way that they evaluated the fairness of decisionmaking procedures. In such a situation, respondents would not be able to agree about a common procedure that everyone would regard as just.

To test the degree of common agreement across varying types of respondents, an interaction analysis was performed. That analysis explored the extent to which people with differing demographic characteristics placed a greater or lesser weight on particular issues when defining whether a procedure was fair. For example, women might place greater weight on voice than would men. To test this possibility, an interaction term representing differential influence of voice on procedural justice for men and women was included in a regression equation. A complete test of potential gender influences utilized a regression equation with five main effects for outcome favorability, voice, neutrality, trust, and standing; a main effect to represent the direct influence of gender; and five

Table 2.2 The antecedents of procedural justice and legitimacy

	Procedural justice		Attitudinal support		Obligation	
Outcome favorability	.20***	.10*	.33***	.23***	.08	.04
Voice	.07	.03	.03	−.02	−.07	−.10*
Neutrality	.47***	.31***	.40***	.24***	.33***	.26***
Trust	—	.25***	—	.17***	—	.06
Standing	—	.14**	—	.21***	—	.11*
Age	.00	.01	−.09*	−.08	−.13**	−.13**
Race	−.04	−.06	.06	.05	.12**	.12**
Sex	.05	.05	.01	.01	−.06	−.05
Education	−.05	−.04	−.04	−.03	.08	.09
Income	.04	.03	−.05	−.05	.00	.00
Ideology	.04	.02	.01	.00	−.19***	−.20***
R^2	38%	44%	41%	45%	20%	21%

Notes: Entries are beta weights, which indicate the independent influence of each variable, and adjusted multiple correlation coefficients (R^2), reflecting the percentage of variance explained by all independent variables.
* $p < .05$.
** $p < .01$.
*** $p < .001$.

interaction terms to test the possibility that men and women placed differential weight on each of the five procedural characteristics. A similar regression equation was created for each of the six demographic characteristics: race, gender, education, income, age, and ideology.

Table 2.3 presents the results of the analysis exploring the antecedents of procedural justice judgments among respondents varying in race, gender, education, income, age, and ideology. Consider race. The interaction analysis indicates that procedural justice is influenced by outcome favorability (beta = .15, $p < .05$) but not by voice (beta = .02, n.s.) and standing (beta = .08, n.s.). In addition, there is no direct effect of respondent race, gender, education, income, age, or ideology on procedural justice judgments (beta = −.06, n.s.). Further, these background characteristics do not affect the weight respondents place on outcome favorability (beta = −.07, n.s.), voice (beta = .01, n.s.), neutrality (beta = −.10, n.s.), trustworthiness (beta = .07, n.s.), or standing (beta = .07, n.s.).

The procedural elements studied did not interact significantly with any of the background variables. The results suggest that the same issues are central to procedural justice judgments for all groups: neutrality, trustworthiness, standing, and outcome favorability. Hence, there is general agreement about how fair decisionmaking procedures should be defined. This finding accords with Tyler's (1988) earlier conclusion based on the examination of people's personal experiences with legal authorities.

DISCUSSION

What can hold a society together in the face of conflicts over appropriate social policies? The procedural justice literature suggests that agreements about fair ways of

Table 2.3 Demographic influences on procedural justice

	Race	Gender	Education	Income	Age	Ideology
Outcome favorability	.15*	.16**	.04	.03	.05	.12*
Voice	.02	.00	.06	.09	.00	.08
Neutrality	.39***	.25***	.36***	.38***	.32***	.28***
Trust	.18*	.31***	.19***	.22***	.23**	.38***
Standing	.08	.13*	.18**	.10	.17**	.12
Main effect of interaction term	−.06	−.06	−.04	−.03	−.01	.01
Interaction with outcome favorability	−.07	−.07	.10	.10	.08	−.03
Interaction with voice	.01	.03	−.05	−.07	.05	−.07
Interaction with neutrality	−.10	.06	−.09	−.10	−.03	.03
Interaction with trust	.07	−.10	.09	.02	.01	−.08
Interaction with standing	.07	.03	−.07	.07	−.03	.03
R^2	44%	44%	44%	44%	43%	43%

Notes: Entries are beta weights, which indicate the independent influence of each variable, and adjusted multiple correlation coefficients (R^2), reflecting the percentage of variance explained by all independent variables.
* $p < .05$.
** $p < .01$.
*** $p < .001$.

decision-making can be an effective means for a society to survive differences in values and interests. The studies presented here test this hypothesis using one type of justice judgments – evaluations of the fairness of government decisionmaking procedures. The argument tested is that fair decisionmaking procedures (procedural justice) can legitimize government authorities.

The procedural justice hypothesis builds on a large empirical literature on procedural justice which suggests that fair decision-making procedures can legitimize authorities (Lind & Tyler 1988; Tyler 1990; Tyler & Lind 1992). However, the findings of recent studies of procedural influences on the legitimacy of national authority have been inconsistent, with some studies suggesting minimal influence (Gibson 1989, 1991; Gibson & Caldeira 1993; Mondak 1993) and others suggesting that procedural effects are more substantial (Tyler & Rasinski 1991; Tyler & Mitchell 1994).

The results of the research reported here suggest that the use of fair decisionmaking procedures does enhance the legitimacy of national-level governmental authorities, in this case Congress and its members. To an important extent, it is because Congress makes decisions in fair ways that people regard it as a legitimate political entity. Alternatively, if Congress uses unfair procedures, it will lose its legitimacy. Further, the results of study 3 indicate that these effects occur both with attitudinal support and with feelings of obligation to obey the government. [. . .]

America is, by design, a pluralistic society, which tolerates a diversity of political, social, and religious attitudes. Further, the diversity is increasing as the United States becomes a more multi-ethnic, multicultural society. This diversity of interests and values poses problems for governmental authorities, who must accommodate various interests and create common public policies that will be broadly acceptable to Americans. The findings of these studies suggest an optimistic conclusion about the ability of government to do so. They support the suggestion that government authorities can create common policies across differences in interests if they are viewed as making their decisions in fair ways. [. . .]

References

Alexander, Sheldon, & Andrey Ruderman (1987) "The Role of Procedural and Distributive Justice in Organizational Behavior," 1 *Social Justice Research* 177.

Almond, Gabriel A., & Sidney Verba (1963) *The Civic Culture: Political Attitudes and Democracy in Five Nations*. Princeton, NJ: Princeton Univ. Press.

—— (1980) *The Civic Culture Revisited*. Boston, MA: Little, Brown.

Brockner, Joel, Tom R. Tyler, & Rochelle Cooper-Schneider (1992) "The Influence of Prior Commitment to an Institution on Reactions to Perceived Unfairness: The Higher they are, the Harder they Fall," 37 *Administrative Science Q.* 241.

Caldeira, Gregory A., & James L. Gibson (1992) "The Etiology of Public Support for the Supreme Court," 36 *American J. of Political Science* 635.

Dahl, Robert A. (1971) *Polyarchy*. New Haven, CT: Yale Univ. Press.

—— (1989) *Democracy and Its Critics*. New Haven, CT: Yale Univ. Press.

Folger, Robert, & Mary Konovsky (1989) "Effects of Procedural and Distributive Justice on Reactions to Pay Raise Decisions," 32 *Academy of Management J.* 115.

Gibson, James (1989) "Understandings of Justice: Institutional legitimacy, Procedural Justice, and Political Tolerance," 24 *Law & Society Rev.* 469.

—— (1991) "Institutional Legitimacy, Procedural Justice, and Compliance with Supreme Court Decisions: A Question of Causality," 25 *Law & Society Rev.* 631.

Gibson, James, & Gregory A. Caldeira (1993) "The Legitimacy of Transnational Legal Institutions: Compliance, Support, and the European Court of Justice." Delivered at Law & Society Association annual meeting, Chicago (version 1.2).

Huntington, Samuel P. (1984) "Will More Countries Become Democratic?" 99 *Political Science Q.* 193.

Inglehart, Ronald (1990) *Culture Shifts in Advanced Industrial Societies*. Princeton, NJ: Princeton Univ. Press.

Kelley, Stanley, Jr., & Thad W. Mirer (1974) "The Simple Act of Voting," 68 *American Political Science Rev.* 572.

Lind, E. Allan, & Tom R. Tyler (1988) *The Social Psychology of Procedural Justice*. New York: Plenum.

Lind, E. Allan, Carol A. Kulik, Maureen Ambrose, & Maria V. Park (1993) "Individual and Corporate Dispute Resolution: Using Procedural Fairness as a Decision Heuristic," 38 *Administrative Science Q.* 224.

Mondak, Jeffery J. (1993) "Institutional Legitimacy and Procedural Justice: Reexamining the Question of Causality," 27 *Law & Society Rev.* 599.

Thibaut, John, & Laurens Walker (1975) *Procedural Justice*. Hillsdale, NJ: Erlbaum.

Tyler, Tom R. (1984) "The Role of Perceived Injustice in Defendants' Evaluations of Their Courtroom Experience," 18 *Law & Society Rev.* 51.

Tyler, Tom R. (1988) "What is Procedural Justice? Criteria used by Citizens to Assess the Fairness of Legal Procedures," 22 *Law & Society Rev.* 103.

—— (1990) *Why People Obey the Law*. New Haven, CT: Yale Univ. Press.

Tyler, Tom R., & Andrew Caine (1981) "The Role of Distributional and Procedural Fairness in the Endorsement of Formal Leaders," 41 *J. of Personality & Social Psychology* 642.

Tyler, Tom R., & Gregory Mitchell (1994) "Legitimacy and the Empowerment of Discretionary Legal Authority: The United States Supreme Court and Abortion Rights," 43 *Duke Law J.* 703.

Tyler, Tom R., & Kenneth Rasinski (1991) "Procedural Justice, Institutional Legitimacy, and the Acceptance of Unpopular U.S. Supreme Court Decisions: A Reply to Gibson," 25 *Law & Society Rev.* 621.

Tyler, Tom R., Jonathan D. Casper, & Bonnie Fisher (1989) "Maintaining Allegiance toward Political Authorities," 33 *American J. of Political Science* 629–652.

Tyler, Tom R., & Lind E. (1992) "A Relational Model of Authority in Groups," in M. Zanna, ed., 25 *Advances in Experimental Social Psychology* 115.

Tyler, Tom R., Kenneth Rasinski, & Kathleen McGraw (1985) "The Influence of Perceived Injustice on Support for Political Authorities," 15 *J. of Applied Social Psychology* 700.

Chapter 3

Robin D. G. Kelley

KICKIN' REALITY, KICKIN' BALLISTICS
"Gangsta Rap" and postindustrial Los Angeles

From: Robin D. G. Kelley (1994) excerpt from 'Kickin' Reality, Kickin' Ballistics', in Robin D. G. Kelley, *Race Rebels: Culture, Politics, and the Black Working Class*, New York: The Free Press, pp. 183–194.

In ways that we do not easily or willingly define, the gangster speaks for us, expressing that part of the American psyche which rejects the qualities and the demands of modern life, which rejects "Americanism" itself.

(ROBERT WARSHOW, "The Gangster as a Tragic Hero")

Oppressed peoples cannot avoid admiring their own nihilists, who are the ones dramatically saying "No!" and reminding others that there are worse things than death.

(EUGENE GENOVESE, *Roll, Jordan, Roll*)

FOREWORD: SOUTH CENTRAL LOS ANGELES, APRIL 29, 1992

BELIEVE IT OR NOT, I began working on this chapter well over a year before the Los Angeles Rebellion of 1992, and at least two or three months before Rodney King was turned into a martyr by several police officers and a video camera. Of course, the rebellion both enriched and complicated my efforts to make sense of gangsta rap in late twentieth-century Los Angeles. West Coast gangsta-flavored hip hop – especially in its formative stage – was, in some ways, a foreboding of the insurrection. The previous two years of "research" I spent rocking, bopping, and wincing to gangsta narratives of everyday life were (if I may sample Mike Davis) very much like "excavating the future in Los Angeles." Ice T, truly the "OG" (Original Gangster) of L.A. gangsta rap, summed it up best in a recent Rolling Stone interview:

> When rap came out of L.A., what you heard initially was my voice yelling about South Central. People thought, "That shit's crazy," and ignored it. Then NWA [the rap group Niggas With Attitude] came and yelled, Ice Cube yelled about it.

People said, "Oh, that's just kids making a buck." They didn't realize how many niggas with attitude there are out on the street. Now you see them.

Indeed, though the media believes that the riots began with the shock of the beating of Rodney King, neither the hip hop community nor residents of South Central Los Angeles were really surprised by the videotape. Countless numbers of black Angelenos had experienced or witnessed this sort of terror before. When L.A. rapper Ice Cube was asked about the King incident on MTV, he responded simply, "It's been happening to us for years. It's just we didn't have a camcorder every time it happened." (Subsequently, Cube recorded "Who Got the Camera," a hilarious track in which he asks the police brutalizing him to hit him once more in order to get the event on film.)

Few black Angelenos could forget the 1979 killing of Eula Mae Love, a five-feet four-inch, thirty-nine-year-old widow who was shot a dozen times by two LAPD officers. Police were called after she tried to stop a gas maintenance man from turning off her gas. When they arrived she was armed with a kitchen knife, but the only thing she stabbed was a tree in her yard. Nor could anyone ignore the fifteen deaths caused by LAPD chokeholds in the early eighties, or Chief Darryl Gates's infamous explanation: "We may be finding that in some blacks when [the chokehold] is applied the veins or arteries do not open up as fast as they do on normal people." And then there were the numerous lesser-known incidents for which no officers were punished. Virtually every South Central resident has experienced routine stops, if not outright harassment, and thousands of African American and Latino youth have had their names and addresses logged in the LAPD antigang task force data base – ironically, called a "rap sheet" – whether they were gang members or not.

The L.A. rebellion merely underscores the fact that a good deal of gangsta rap is (aside from often very funky music to drive to) a window into, and critique of, the criminalization of black youth. Of course, this is not unique to gangsta rap; all kinds of "B-boys" and "B-girls" – rappers, graffiti artists, break dancers – have been dealing with and challenging police repression, the media's criminalization of inner-city youths, and the "just-us" system from the get-go. Like the economy and the city itself, the criminal justice system changed just when hip hop was born. Prisons were no longer just places to discipline; they became dumping grounds to corral bodies labeled a menace to society. Policing in the late twentieth century was designed not to stop or reduce crime in inner-city communities but to manage it. Economic restructuring resulting in massive unemployment has created criminals out of black youth, which is what gangsta rappers acknowledge. But rather than apologize or preach, most attempt to rationalize and explain. Virtually all gangsta rappers write lyrics attacking law enforcement agencies, their denial of unfettered access to public space, and the media's complicity in equating black youth with criminals. Yet, the rappers' own stereotypes of the ghetto as "war zone" and the black youth as "criminal," as well as their adolescent expressions of masculinity and sexuality, in turn structure and constrain their efforts to create a counternarrative of life in the inner city.

Indeed, its masculinist emphasis and pimp-inspired vitriol toward women are central to gangsta rap. While its misogynistic narratives are not supposed to be descriptions of everyday reality, they are offensive and chilling nonetheless. Of course, it can be argued that much of this adolescent misogyny is characteristic of most male youth cultures, since male status is defined in part through heterosexual conquest and domination over women.

Part of what distinguishes gangsta rap from "locker room" braggadocio is that it is circulated on compact discs, digital tapes, and radio airwaves. But the story is so much more complicated than this. In order to make sense of the pervasiveness and appeal of the genre's misogyny, I also explore the traditions of sexism in black vernacular culture as well as the specific socioeconomic conditions in which young, urban African American males must negotiate their masculine identities.

Lest we get too sociological here, we must bear in mind that hip hop, irrespective of its particular "flavor," is music. Few doubt it has a message, whether they interpret it as straight-up nihilism or the words of "primitive rebels." Not many pay attention to rap as art – the musical art of, for example, mixing "break beats" (the part of a song where the drums, bass, or guitar are isolated and extended via two turntables or electronic mixers); the verbal art of appropriating old-school "hustler's toasts"; or the art of simply trying to be funny. Although what follows admittedly emphasizes lyrics, it also tries to deal with form, style, and aesthetics. As Tricia Rose puts it, "Without historical contextualization, aesthetics are naturalized, and certain cultural practices are made to appear essential to a given group of people. On the other hand, without aesthetic considerations, Black cultural practices are reduced to extensions of sociohistorical circumstances."

Heeding Rose's call for a more multilayered interpretation of cultural forms that takes account of context *and* aesthetics, politics *and* pleasure, I will explore the politics of gangsta rap – its lyrics, music, styles, roots, contradictions, and consistencies – and the place where it seems to have maintained its deepest roots: Los Angeles and its black environs. To do this right we need a historical perspective. We need to go back . . . way back, to the dayz of the O[riginal] G[angster]s. This, then, is a tale of very recent and slightly less recent urban race rebels, a tale that cannot be totally separated from black workers' sabotage in the Jim Crow South or young black passengers' "acting up" on streetcars in wartime Birmingham. Still, these more recent tales of rebellion, which highlight the problems of gangsta rappers against a background of racial "progress," reveal that the black working class of the late twentieth-century city faces a fundamentally different reality – the postindustrial city.

OGs in postindustrial Los Angeles: evolution of a style

L.A. might be the self-proclaimed home of gangsta rap, but black Angelenos didn't put the gangsta into hip hop. Gangsta lyrics and style were part of the whole hip hop scene from its origins in the South Bronx during the mid-1970s. In Charlie Ahearn's classic 1982 film *Wild Style* about the early hip hop scene in New York, the rap duo Double Trouble stepped on stage decked out in white "pimp-style" suits, matching hats, and guns galore. Others in the film are "strapped" (armed) as well, waving real guns as part of the act. The scene seems so contemporary, and yet it was shot over a decade before the media paid attention to such rap songs as Onyx's "Throw Ya Guns in the Air."

But to find the roots of gangsta rap's violent images, explicit language, and outright irreverence, we need to go back even further. Back before Lightin' Rod (aka Jalal Uridin of the Last Poets) performed toasts (narrative poetry from the black oral tradition) over live music on a popular album called *Hustlers' Convention* in 1973; before Lloyd Price recorded the classic black baaadman narrative, "Stagger Lee," in 1958; even before

Screamin' Jay Hawkins recorded his explicitly sexual comedy "rap" "Alligator Wine." Indeed, in 1938 folklorist Alan Lomax recorded Jelly Roll Morton performing a number of profane and violent songs out of the black vernacular, including "The Murder Ballad" and "Make Me a Pallet on the Floor." Morton's lyrics rival the worst of today's gangsta rappers: "Come here you sweet bitch, give me that pussy, let me get in your drawers/I'm gonna make you think you fuckin' with Santa Claus." In other words, we need to go back to the blues, to the baaadman tales of the late nineteenth century, and to the age-old tradition of "signifying" if we want to discover the roots of the "gangsta" aesthetic in hip hop. Irreverence has been a central component of black expressive vernacular culture, which is why violence and sex have been as important to toasting and signifying as playfulness with language. Many of these narratives are about power. Both the baaadman and the trickster embody a challenge to virtually *all* authority (which makes sense to people for whom justice is a rare thing), creates an imaginary upside-down world where the oppressed are the powerful, and it reveals to listeners the pleasures and price of reckless abandon. And in a world where male public powerlessness is often turned inward on women and children, misogyny and stories of sexual conflict are very old examples of the "price" of being baaad.

Nevertheless, while gangsta rap's roots are very old, it does have an identifiable style of its own, and in some respects it is a particular product of the mid-1980s. The inspiration for the specific style we now call gangsta rap seems to have come from Philadelphia's Schooly D, who made *Smoke Some Kill*, and the Bronx-based rapper KRS 1 and Scott La Rock of Boogie Down Productions, who released *Criminal Minded*. Although both albums appeared in 1987, these rappers had been developing an East Coast gangsta style for some time. Ice T, who started out with the technopop wave associated with Radio and Uncle Jam's Army (recording his first single, "The Coldest Rap," in 1981), moved gangsta rap to the West Coast when he recorded "6 in the Mornin'" in 1986. Less than a year later, he released his debut album, *Rhyme Pays*.

Ice T was not only the first West Coast gangsta-style rapper on wax, but he was himself an experienced OG whose narratives were occasionally semi-autobiographical or drawn from things he had witnessed or heard on the street. A native of New Jersey who moved to Los Angeles as a child, "T" (Tracy Marrow) joined a gang while at Crenshaw High School and began a very short career as a criminal. He eventually graduated from Crenshaw, attended a junior college, and, with practically no job prospects, turned to the armed services. After four years in the service, he pursued his high school dream to become a rapper and starred in a documentary film called "Breaking and Entering," which captured the West Coast break dance scene. When Hollywood made a fictionalized version of the film called "Breakin'," Ice T also made an appearance. Although Ice T's early lyrics ranged from humorous boasts and tales of crime and violence to outright misogyny, they were clearly as much fact as fiction. In "Squeeze the Trigger" he leads off with a brief autobiographical, composite sketch of his gangsta background, insisting all along that he is merely a product of a callous, brutal society.

Even before *Rhyme Pays* hit the record stores (though banned on the radio because of its explicit lyrics), an underground hip hop community was forming in Compton, a predominantly black and Latino city south of Los Angeles, that would play a pivotal role in the early history of gangsta rap. Among the participants was Eric Wright — better known as Eazy E — who subsequently launched an independent label known as Ruthless

Records. He eventually teamed up with Dr. Dre and Yella, both of whom had left the rap group World Class Wreckin Cru, and Ice Cube, who was formerly a member of a group called The CIA. Together they formed Niggas With Attitude and moved gangsta rap to another level. Between 1987 and 1988, Ruthless produced a string of records, beginning with their twelve-inch *NWA and the Posse*, Eazy E's solo album, *Eazy Duz It*, and the album which put NWA on the map, *Straight Outta Compton*. Dr. Dre's brilliance as a producer – his introduction of hard, menacing beats, sparse drum tracks, and heavy bass with slower tempos – and Ice Cube's genius as a lyricist, made NWA one of the most compelling groups on the hip hop scene in years.

A distinctive West Coast style of gangsta rap, known for its rich descriptive story-telling laid over heavy funk samples from the likes of George Clinton and the whole Parliament-Funkadelic family, Sly Stone, Rick James, Ohio Players, Average White Band, Cameo, Zapp and, of course, the Godfather himself – James Brown – evolved and pro-liferated rapidly soon after the appearance of Ice T and NWA. The frequent use of Parliament-Funkadelic samples led one critic to dub the music "G-Funk (gangsta attitude over P-Funk beats)." Within three years, dozens of Los Angeles-based groups came onto the scene, many produced by either Eazy E's Ruthless Records, Ice T and Afrika Islam's Rhyme Syndicate Productions, Ice Cube's post-NWA project, Street Knowledge Productions, or Dr. Dre's Deathrow Records. The list of West Coast gangsta rappers includes Above the Law, Mob Style, Compton's Most Wanted, King Tee, The Rhyme Syndicate, Snoop Doggy Dogg, (Lady of) Rage, Poison Clan, Capital Punishment Organization (CPO), the predominantly Samoan Boo-Yaa Tribe, the DOC, DJ Quick, AMG, Hi-C, Low Profile, Nu Niggaz on the Block, South Central Cartel, Compton Cartel, 2nd II None, W.C. and the MAAD (Minority Alliance of Anti-Discrimination) Circle, Cypress Hill, and Chicano rappers like Kid Frost and Proper Dos.

Although they shared much with the larger hip hop community, gangsta rappers drew both praise and ire from their colleagues. Indeed, gangsta rap has generated more debate both within and without the hip hop world than any other genre. Unfortunately, much of this debate, especially in the media, has only disseminated misinformation. Thus, it is important to clarify what gangsta rap *is not*. First, gangsta rappers have never merely celebrated gang violence, nor have they taken a partisan position in favor of one gang over another. Gang bangin' (gang participation) itself has never even been a central theme in the music. Many of the violent lyrics are not intended to be literal. Rather, they are boasting raps in which the imagery of gang bangin' is used metaphorically to challenge competitors on the microphone – an element common to all hard-core hip hop. The mic becomes a Tech-9 or AK-47, imagined drive-bys occur from the stage, flowing lyrics become hollow-point shells. Classic examples are Ice Cube's "Jackin' for Beats," a humorous song that describes sampling other artists and producers as outright armed robbery, and Ice T's "Pulse of the Rhyme" or "Grand Larceny" (which brags about stealing a show), Capital Punishment Organization's aptly titled warning to other perpetrating rappers, "Homicide," NWA's "Real Niggaz," Dr. Dre's "Lyrical Gangbang," Ice Cube's, "Now I Gotta Wet'cha," Compton's Most Wanted's "Wanted" and "Straight Check N' Em." Sometimes, as in the case of Ice T's "I'm Your Pusher," an antidrug song that boasts of pushing "dope beats and lyrics/no beepers needed," gangsta rap lyrics have been misin-terpreted by journalists and talk show hosts as advocating criminality and violence.

This is not to say that all descriptions of violence are simply metaphors. Exaggerated and invented boasts of criminal acts should sometimes be regarded as part of a larger set of signifying practices. Performances like The Rhyme Syndicate's "My Word Is Bond" or J.D.'s storytelling between songs on Ice Cube's *AmeriKKKa's Most Wanted* are supposed to be humorous and, to a certain extent, unbelievable. Growing out of a much older set of cultural practices, these masculinist narratives are essentially verbal duels over who is the "baddest motherfucker around." They are not meant as literal descriptions of violence and aggression, but connote the playful use of language itself. So when J.D. boasts about how he used to "jack them motherfuckers for them Nissan trucks," the story is less about stealing per se than about the way in which he describes his bodaciousness.

When gangsta rappers do write lyrics intended to convey a sense of social realism, their work loosely resembles a sort of street ethnography of racist institutions and social practices, but told more often than not in the first person. Whether gangsta rappers step into the character of a gang banger, hustler, or ordinary working person – that is, products and residents of the "hood" – the important thing to remember is that they are stepping into character; it is for descriptive purposes rather than advocacy. In some ways, these descriptive narratives, under the guise of objective "street journalism," are no less polemical (hence political) than nineteenth-century slave narratives in defense of abolition. When Ice Cube was still with NWA he explained, "We call ourselves underground street reporters. We just tell it how we see it, nothing more, nothing less."

It would be naive to claim that descriptive lyrics, as an echo of the city, do not, in turn, magnify what they describe – but to say so is a far cry from claiming that the purpose of rap is to advocate violence. And, of course, rappers' reality is hardly "objective" in the sense of being detached; their standpoint is that of the ghetto dweller, the criminal, the victim of police repression, the teenage father, the crack slanger, the gang banger, and the female dominator. Much like the old "baaadman" narratives that have played an important role in black vernacular folklore, the characters they create, at first glance, appear to be apolitical individuals only out for themselves; and like the protagonist in Melvin Van Peebles's cinematic classic, *Sweet Sweetback's Baaadass Song*, they are reluctant to trust anyone. It is hard not to miss the influences of urban toasts and "pimp narratives," which became popular during the late 1960s and early 1970s. In many instances the characters are almost identical, and on occasion rap artists pay tribute to black vernacular oral poetry by lyrically "sampling" these early pimp narratives.

For other consumers of gangsta rap, such as middle-class white males, the genre unintentionally serves the same role as blaxploitation films of the 1970s or, for that matter, gangster films of any generation. It attracts listeners for whom the "ghetto" is a place of adventure, unbridled violence, erotic fantasy, and/or an imaginary alternative to suburban boredom. White music critic John Leland once praised NWA because they "dealt in evil as fantasy: killing cops, smoking hos, filling quiet nights with a flurry of senseless buckshot." This kind of voyeurism partly explains NWA's huge white following and why their album, *Efil4zaggin*, shot to the top of the charts as soon as it was released. As one critic put it, "In reality, NWA have more in common with a Charles Bronson movie than a PBS documentary on the plight of the inner-cities." And why should it be otherwise? After all, NWA members have even admitted that some of their recent songs were not representations of reality "in the hood" but inspired by popular films like *Innocent Man* starring Tom Selleck and *Tango and Cash* starring Sylvester Stallone and Kurt Russell.

While I'm fully aware that some rappers are merely "studio gangstas," and that the *primary* purpose of this music is to produce "funky dope rhymes" for our listening pleasure, we cannot ignore the fact that West Coast gangsta rap originated in, and continues to maintain ties to, the streets of L.A.'s black working-class communities. The generation that came of age in the 1980s was the product of devastating structural changes in the urban economy that date back at least to the late 1960s. While the city as a whole experienced unprecedented growth, the communities of Watts and Compton faced increased economic displacement, factory closures, and an unprecedented deepening of poverty. The uneven development of L.A.'s postindustrial economy meant an expansion of high-tech firms like Aerospace and Lockheed, and the disappearance of rubber and steel manufacturing firms, many of which were located in or near Compton and Watts. Deindustrialization, in other words, led to the establishment of high-tech firms in less populated regions like Silicon Valley and Orange County. Developers and local governments helped the suburbanization process while simultaneously cutting back expenditures for parks, recreation, and affordable housing in inner-city communities. Thus since 1980 economic conditions in Watts deteriorated on a greater scale than in any other L.A. community, and by some estimates Watts is in worse shape now than in 1965. A 1982 report from the California Legislature revealed that South Central neighborhoods experienced a 50 percent rise in unemployment while purchasing power dropped by one-third. The median income for South Central L.A.'s residents was a paltry $5,900–$2,500 below the median income for the black population a few years earlier.

Youth were the hardest hit. For all of Los Angeles County, the unemployment rate of black youth remained at about 45 percent, but in areas with concentrated poverty the rate was even higher. As the composition of L.A.'s urban poor becomes increasingly younger, programs for inner-city youth are being wiped out at an alarming rate. Both the Neighborhood Youth Corps and the Comprehensive Employment and Training Act (CETA) have been dismantled, and the Jobs Corps and Los Angeles Summer Job Program have been cut back substantially.

Thus, on the eve of crack cocaine's arrival on the urban landscape, the decline in employment opportunities and growing immiseration of black youth in L.A. led to a substantial rise in property crimes committed by juveniles and young adults. Even NWA recalls the precrack illicit economy in a song titled "The Dayz of Wayback," in which Dr. Dre and M. C. Ren wax nostalgic about the early to mid-1980s, when criminal activity consisted primarily of small-time muggings and robberies. Because of its unusually high crime rate, L.A. had by that time gained the dubious distinction of having the largest urban prison population in the country. When the crack economy made its presence felt in inner-city black communities, violence intensified as various gangs and groups of peddlers battled for control over markets. In spite of the violence and financial vulnerability that went along with peddling crack, for many black youngsters it was the most viable economic option.

While the rise in crime and the ascendance of the crack economy might have put money into some people's pockets, for the majority it meant greater police repression. Watts, Compton, Northwest Pasadena, Carson, North Long Beach, and several other black working-class communities were turned into war zones during the mid- to late 1980s. Police helicopters, complex electronic surveillance, even small tanks armed with battering rams became part of this increasingly militarized urban landscape. During this same period, housing projects, such as Imperial Courts, were renovated along the lines of minimum security prisons and equipped with fortified fencing and an LAPD substation. Imperial Court residents were now required to carry identity cards and visitors were routinely searched. As popular media coverage of the inner city associated drugs and violence with black youth, young African Americans by virtue of being residents in South Central L.A. and Compton were subject to police harassment and, in some cases, feared by older residents.

All of these problems generated penetrating critiques by gangsta rappers. M. C. Ren, for example, blamed "the people who are holding the dollars in the city" for the expansion of gang violence and crime, arguing that if black youth had decent jobs, they would not need to participate in the illicit economy. "It's their fault simply because they refused to employ black people. How would you feel if you went for job after job and each time, for no good reason, you're turned down?" Ice T blames capitalism entirely, which he defines as much more than alienating wage labor; the marketplace itself as well as a variety of social institutions are intended to exercise social control over African Americans. "Capitalism says you must have an upper class, a middle class, and a lower class. . . . Now the only way to guarantee a lower class, is to keep y'all uneducated and as high as possible." According to Ice T, the ghetto is, at worst, the product of deliberately oppressive policies, at best, the result of racist neglect. Nowhere is this clearer than in his song "Escape from the Killing Fields," which uses the title of a recent film about the conflict in Cambodia as a metaphor for the warlike conditions in today's ghettos.

Gangsta rappers construct a variety of first-person narratives to illustrate how social and economic realities in late capitalist L.A. affect young black men. Although the use of first-person narratives is rooted in a long tradition of black aesthetic practices, the use of "I" to signify both personal and collective experiences also enables gangsta rappers to navigate a complicated course between what social scientists call "structure" and "agency." In gangsta rap there is almost always a relationship between the conditions in which these characters live and the decisions they make. Some gangsta rappers – Ice Cube in particular – are especially brilliant at showing how, if I may paraphrase Marx, young urban black men make their own history but not under circumstances of their own choosing.

"Broke Niggas Make the Best Crooks"

The press is used to make the victim look like the criminal
and make the criminal look like the victim.

(MALCOLM X, "Not Just an American Problem")

In an era when popular media, conservative policy specialists, and some social scientists are claiming that the increase in street crime can be explained by some pathological culture of violence bereft of the moderating influences of a black middle class (who only recently fled to the suburbs), L.A.'s gangsta rappers keep returning to the idea that joblessness and crime are directly related. Consider W.C. and the MAAD Circle's manifesto on the roots of inner-city crime. Its title, "If You Don't Work, U Don't Eat," appropriates Bobby Byrd's late 1960s' hit song of the same title (it, too, is sampled), and replicates a very popular Old Left adage. Describing the song in a recent interview, W.C. explained the context in which it was conceived: "I've got to feed a family. Because I don't have [job] skills I have no alternative but to turn this way. My little girl don't take no for an answer, my little boy don't take no for an answer, my woman's not going to take no for. [. . .]

Chapter 4

Robert D. Putnam

CIVIC DISENGAGEMENT IN CONTEMPORARY AMERICA

From: R. D. Putnam (2001), excerpts from 'Civic disengagement in contemporary America', *Governments and Opposition* 36: 135–156.

OVER THE PAST TWO generations the United States has undergone a series of remarkable transformations. It has helped to defeat global communism, led a revolution in information technology that is fuelling unprecedented prosperity, invented life-saving treatments for diseases from AIDS to cancer, and made great strides in reversing discriminatory practices and promoting equal rights for all citizens. But during these same decades the United States also has undergone a less sanguine transformation: its citizens have become remarkably less civic, less politically engaged, less socially connected, less trusting, and less committed to the common good. At the dawn of the millennium Americans are fast becoming a loose aggregation of disengaged observers, rather than a community of connected participants.

In social science terms, Americans have dramatically less 'social capital' than they had even 30 years ago. Social capital simply refers to the social norms and networks that enhance people's ability to collaborate on common endeavours. These social norms and networks have important consequences, both for the people who share and participate in them and for those who do not. All things being equal, social capital makes individuals – and communities – healthier, wealthier, wiser, happier, more productive and better able to govern themselves peaceably and effectively. [. . .]

What has happened to America's stock of social capital – its civic norms, networks and organizations? My best estimate is that by many different measures the stock has been depleted by roughly one third since the early 1970s. Of course, that broad conclusion masks a lot of variation. Some measures of social capital have declined more; others have declined less. But, broadly speaking, the trends are pronounced and consistent.

Take trust, for example. The degree to which Americans have faith in their government and politics, their social institutions and their fellow citizens has dropped dramatically over the past two generations. In the 1960s, when the American National Election Studies asked Americans whether they trusted the government to do what is right 'just about all' or 'most' of the time, seven out of ten respondents said Yes. In 1999, fewer than two out of ten respondents agreed. That is a 75 per cent drop, reflecting a 30-year erosion of faith in democratic institutions. People have similarly jaded evaluations of the performance of religious institutions and unions and business and universities and so on.

Americans are also far less likely to trust one another – which is logically quite different from trusting public authorities. A variety of different kinds of evidence makes this clear. In round numbers, nearly two-thirds of Americans a generation or two ago said they trusted other people; today, the fraction is closer to one-third. [. . .]

'BOWLING ALONE'

Other indicators of declining connectedness are equally surprising and should be of deep concern to Americans as citizens. Five years ago, in a short article called 'Bowling Alone', I reported familiar trends, such as that Americans are a lot less likely to vote than they were 25 or 30 years ago. There's been about a 25 per cent decline in the fraction of Americans who vote, and that's true at all levels – national, state and local. The article used metaphors like 'bowling' and 'choral societies' to indicate that political participation is embedded in social activity more generally. It is important not to mistake what might be a broad social trend for merely a political trend. And, indeed, the decline in voting is only one of many indicators of civic and social disengagement.

The 'Bowling Alone' article reported, for example, a massive decline in participation in local parent–teacher associations, an especially ominous development given that PTA participation is one of the most common forms of civic engagement in America. The fraction of American parents who belong to a PTA has fallen by roughly half since the 1950s. . . . Simply put, parents have only about half the propensity today that they did in the 1960s.

This is also true for what we might colloquially call the 'animal clubs' – that is, fraternal organizations. In the United States, most men's organizations are named for animals: the Lions, Moose, Elks, Eagles and so on. 'Bowling Alone' showed how all of those organizations have experienced declining membership since the mid-1960s or mid-1970s. Again, these declines reflected a population-adjusted drop in the propensity to join these organizations. The story is the same for women's clubs and also for the group that inspired the article's title, bowling clubs.

Bowling is big in America. The sport consists of throwing a ball down a lane and knocking pins down. The player who knocks the most pins down wins. You can bowl by yourself, as many people do, or you can bowl in teams. Bowling is very popular, the most popular participant sport in America. It is also one of the most egalitarian sports, in the sense that participation is not especially correlated with social class. This is a middle-class and working-class sport. It is a sport that is far more diverse than are many other sports by gender, marital status, race and educational attainment. Because bowling attracts all types, it is an interesting social barometer.

The nature of the game affords important opportunities for face-to-face interaction. Normally, two teams, with five players apiece, square off in a game. But at any given point, there are only two people up at the lane, rolling the ball or getting ready to do so. That leaves eight people who are not doing anything except sitting on a semicircular bench and waiting their turn. Most of the time, they chat about the previous night's game or the latest gossip. But occasionally and inevitably, they will also discuss whether the local bond issue should pass, or whether the trash is picked up promptly, or how the local schools are performing. So, in a profound sense, those eight people sitting in the back are involved in civic deliberation, even if it is not recognized as such at the time. They are having a conversation with other folks that they see regularly, and in a context of mutual understanding.

Bowling is increasingly popular in America. The fraction of people who bowl has risen by roughly ten per cent over the last decade or so. But bowling in leagues, bowling in teams, is down by forty per cent. [. . .]

Here, I update 'Bowling Alone' by presenting new evidence on trends in American civic life. Parenthetically, it would be fascinating to determine whether comparable trends exist in other countries. But for the time being, I address four questions [in my work of which the first three are treated here]:

First, what's been happening to civic life in America?
Second, why?
Third, so what – why should we be concerned?

WHAT HAS HAPPENED TO CIVIC LIFE IN AMERICA?

It turns out that answering this question is more methodologically complicated than it might appear. There are many approaches, but each one has serious drawbacks. For example, examining the membership in fixed-named organizations, such as the Lions or Elks Clubs, provides some sense of the vitality of those particular organizations, and it allows roughly comparable measures of organizational activity over long periods of time. However, that approach does not capture the possible displacement of members from old organizations to new ones. Thus, it is necessary to use myriad approaches to answering the question, on the theory that each approach can make up for the shortcomings in some other approach.

As an initial cut, I have gathered membership data on a large number of voluntary associations over the course of the twentieth century. These were all organizations with local chapters where people met face-to-face, rater than advocacy organizations whose members do not do anything more than send a cheque to national headquarters. [. . .]

Astonishingly, the market share of all of these organizations followed virtually the same trajectory over time. . . . A graph would show a long rise from 1900 to roughly 1960. There is only one notch in that graph, which comes in a dramatic, catastrophic decline in membership in the Depression years, as one might expect. Many organizations lost half of their members in four or five years.

But then, astonishingly, beginning around 1945, America experienced what may well have been the greatest organizational boom in its history. Membership in most groups (as a fraction of the relevant population group) basically doubled between 1945 and 1960. And that is true in virtually all of these organizations after the Second World War. It is perhaps no surprise that there were more members of the American Legion, a veterans' group, right after the Second World War. But it is quite surprising that the Grange, a nineteenth-century organization of farmers, showed a similar boom in membership. The Girl Scouts and Boy Scouts and 4-H, which are all organizations for kids, showed a boom, as did the League of Women Voters, and so on.

Then, in the 1960s, suddenly, surprisingly and mysteriously, all of these groups almost simultaneously began to experience stagnation in their market share. Soon after, their market share began to fall. . . . Of course, what was happening to one organization was happening to all of them, though the declines did not all happen at exactly the same time. [. . .]

Interestingly, these trends also hold for professional organizations, even though it looks on the surface that they could be an exception to the general organizational downturn. . . . But, in terms of the market share – the fraction of professionals who actually belong to their respective professional association – the trend looks exactly like the trend in other voluntary groups. That is, professional associations posted rising membership rates until about 1960 or 1965, and then began a steady decline. [. . .]

But that evidence in itself does not prove anything. Although suggestive, it is not conclusive insofar as membership data from specific organizations do not necessarily reflect an underlying propensity to join groups in general. . . . I had been aware of these problems, but it was not immediately obvious how to get around them. For example, it would be nice to know the number of picnics that people went on every year since 1975, but I knew of no 'national picnic registry'. Likewise, it was not obvious how to find good data on how many club meetings people attended, not just meetings of well-known clubs (where a secretary might be keeping track) but also of new clubs for which no organizational records existed. Astonishingly, just as the methodological situation was looking very dire, two rich new sources of data became available, and between them, they not only confirmed the 'Bowling Alone' story, but also made it much more compelling. [. . .]

The first of these datasets was actually known to exist, but the data were not previously available for analysis. This dataset consists of surveys conducted by a reputable polling firm called the Roper Organization. Roughly every month for 25 years, Roper asked 1,000 Americans – a good nationally representative sample every month – a set of questions that had the following form:

'Now here is a list of things some people do about government or politics. Have you happened to have done any of those things in the past year?'

- 'Attended a public meeting on town or school affairs.' (Note that this asked about any public meeting, and that the meeting could have been about any number of specific issues.)
- 'Served on a committee for some local organization.' Again, note that the question asks about membership in *any* organization, not just in one of a handful of well-established organizations.
- 'Become or served as an officer of some club or organization.'
- 'Written your congressman or senator.'
- 'Held or run for political office.'

[. . .] There are 415,000 people in the Roper dataset. In that large a survey, with that large a sample, you can get statistically reliable estimates of the number of people who run for office, or who have written letters to the editor of the newspaper, or who belong to local good government organizations, or who have signed petitions. In all, the surveys asked about twelve different ways in which one can be politically or civically involved. Unbelievably, according to these surveys, participation in every single one of those activities massively declined over the period. For example, between the early 1970s and the early 1990s, there was a decline of about 40 per cent in the fraction of Americans who served as a club officer, and a decline of 35 per cent in the fraction who attended a public meeting. All told, there was a decline of about 25 per cent in the fraction of Americans who had done any of the twelve activities in the previous year.

The declines were not of equal magnitude across all types of activity. That, in itself, is intriguing, and helps to illuminate how the character of American civil society is changing. The sorts of activities that a citizen can do alone without coordinating with anyone else – activities such as signing a petition or writing a letter to an elected official – are down just 10 to 15 per cent over this period. On the other hand, activities that involve coordinating with somebody else – activities such as public meetings – are down far more sharply, about 40 to 50 per cent. [. . .]

The second newly available dataset is, in many ways, even more useful. Every year since 1975, the market research firm DDB has commissioned a survey that asks 3–4,000 Americans a whole range of 'lifestyle' questions. Most of these questions centre on what brand of car or laundry detergent or some other product they prefer. But 25 years ago, one of the marketers realized that companies could more easily sell products if they knew about the background and tastes of potential customers. Therefore, the surveys contain a lot of questions about people's attitudes toward family, race differences, economic policies, politics and so forth. But the surveys also ask an even more interesting set of questions: how many times, in the course of the last year, did you take part in various specific social activities? . . . Besides inquiring about church attendance, the . . . survey asked:

- How many times last year did you go to a club meeting?
- How many times last year did you have friends over to your house?
- How many times last year did you go to a dinner party?
- How many times last year did you work on a community project?
- How many times last year did you volunteer?
- How many times last year did you play cards?
- And certainly not least, how many times last year did you go on a picnic?

So, it turns out, there is after all a record of picnicking in America. Consistent with other trends, the frequency with which Americans go on picnics has been cut in half over the past quarter-century. Americans went picnicking, on average, four times a year in 1975, but only twice in 1999. [. . .]

Americans are doing other things instead. For example, going to casinos is up. However, casino gambling is anything but a social activity. Casinos consist of hundreds of people in enormous rooms who are sitting and pulling levers by themselves. Some people are choosing to play bridge on the Internet. These are games involving real people, but there is almost never any side-talk. There is no talk about how the players feel about the local schools. [. . .]

Virtually all of the informal social activities – going to club meetings, going to church, having dinner parties, having friends over, going out to bars, going on picnics, etc. – show a substantial decline. The decline is also monotonic, meaning that the prevalence of the activity does not fluctuate from year to year, but rather it just keeps going down in survey after survey. . . . But the most astonishing single finding in this entire dataset concerns how often people have dinner with members of their family. It turns out that the frequency with which people have dinner with their family has declined by nearly one third since the mid-1970s. This is not simply because fewer people are married. This figure refers only to married people, who are increasingly eating alone. [. . .]

WHY IS SOCIAL CAPITAL ERODING?

Looking for social trend hot spots is complicated, however, by the fact that the declines in civic and social activity are remarkably equal across all segments of American society. The trends are down among men and down among women. They are down among the rich, and among the poor and the middle class. They are down among people with graduate education, and they are down among high school drop outs, and among people at all levels in between. The trends are down in central cities, and they are down in suburbs, and they are down in small towns. Even though club meetings and other forms of social capital are more common in small towns than in central cities, the trends are the same in both places. The decline in social capital has also hit all areas of the country: the East Coast the West Coast, the South, and even the comparatively social-capital-rich upper Midwest.

However, there is one bright spot in an otherwise bleak picture. Today's older generation appears to have been somewhat immune from the virus that is depressing social and civic participation. People who are in their 60s and 70s today are nearly as participatory as were people who were in their 60s and 70s several decades ago – and in the case of volunteering in the community, today's seniors are actually much more participatory than were seniors in earlier generations. . . . The generational finding is the only strong clue as to what might have caused the decline in civic participation and social capital over the past 25 or 30 years. But it is a striking clue. [. . .]

In sum, the process of 'generational replacement' is the single most important reason for the erosion of social capital and civic participation. It accounts for about half of the overall decline. [Much of the rest can be explained by TV-watching, urban sprawl and two-career families.] [. . .]

On a positive note, there is some evidence of a slight upturn in civic participation among people now in their twenties. They do not quite match people in their forties and fifties, but the twenty-somethings are more civic than are people in their thirties. So at the very front end of this long-run trend, civic help might be arriving.

SO WHAT?

The erosion of social capital in America matters in many important ways. This is not merely about an ageing generation's nostalgia for the tranquil 1950s. Rather, the stark reality is that, in many measurable ways, the health of our communities and even our own health depends importantly on our stock of social capital.

This investigation of the state of social capital in America is an outgrowth of an earlier study of Italy. That study set out to investigate a rather obscure topic: why some regions of Italy were better governed than other regions were. There were clearly parts of Italy that were poorly governed, and there were other parts of Italy that were well-governed. The research question was, 'What could explain those differences?'

Many hypotheses presented themselves: differences in economic wealth, differences in the education level of the residents, differences in political party systems, and so forth. Some of these factors, such as the level of modernization and economic development, did matter. But it took years of research before it became clear that there was a secret ingredient, a trace element in the soil, that made some regional governments function better than others did. That secret ingredient turned out to be choral societies and football clubs – that is, various forms of community involvement.

Some communities had higher levels of involvement in political life but also in social life. Civic engagement is not purely a matter of politics, which is why 'choral societies' is an effective metaphor and an efficient predictor of good government. Dense networks of civic engagement had given rise to a norm of reciprocity – 'I'll do this for you now, without expecting anything back immediately from you, because down the road, somebody else will do something for me, and anyhow, we'll all see each other on Thursday night at the choral society'. Based on that research, if you tell me how many choral societies there are in a community of Italy, I will be able to tell you, plus or minus three days, how long it will take the average citizen to get his health bills reimbursed. The correlation is strong.

Now communities that have lots of choral societies also turn out to be wealthier, and for some time we thought that this was because wealth produces choral societies. That is, in economically underdeveloped regions, the poor residents do not have the time, energy, or inclination to join choral societies. But, actually, that story is exactly backward. It was not that wealth had produced the choral societies, but rather that the choral societies had produced the wealth. That is, the patterns of connectedness predated the differences in wealth. If a region, for whatever reason, happened to have lots of choral societies, it did not begin wealthier, but it gradually became wealthier. Those more connected regions also had healthier citizens, and happier citizens. [. . .]

It turns out that there is a large body of research on the positive effects of community connectedness. This research shows, among other findings, that educational systems do not perform as well in places where people are not engaged in their communities or schools. And where social capital is weak, people are much more likely to cheat on their taxes.

The crime rate is closely related, too. Suppose a mayor wanted to reduce crime in the city, and she had a choice between two strategies: increase by 10 per cent the number of cops on the beat, or increase by 10 per cent the number of neighbours who know one another's first name. The latter approach – building social capital – is likely to be the more effective crime-fighting strategy. [. . .]

PART TWO

Crime, violence and expanding imprisonment

DURING THE 1990s THE American and British publics widely believed that crime was rapidly rising. In fact, their beliefs were mostly wrong and resiliently so. Media images and "moral panic" to the contrary, show that crime dropped in the United States beginning in 1993 through the late 1990s and into the new millennium. At the time it began dropping, crime overall had been relatively stable in the United States since the 1970s. The American "crime problem" of the late 1980s and early 1990s was, in fact, primarily one of violence in inner cities that was increasingly committed by the very young and visited on strangers.

Nonetheless, policymakers moved to "get tough" through use of mandatory sentences, "truth in sentencing" and "three strikes (in Britain 'two strikes')" laws. This built on a movement in public policy begun in the late 1970s known as the Neo-Classical Revival. Its theoretical base lay in genetic, biological and rational choice theories of crime that, together, have come to be known in the United States as "conservative criminology."

Harking back to the Classical School of Beccaria, the Neo-Classical Revival depicted offenders as reasoning beings who rationally choose crime, sometimes bolstered by biological inheritance. According to this approach, the task of criminal justice is to offset the gains of crime through principled retributiveness and to deter, by means of proportionally severe sentences, those who would choose crime for thrills or because "it pays."

Prison populations expanded as a consequence of these policies. Yet, the extent to which swelling prisons can be said to have reduced crime is questionable. Theoretically, the psychological literature provides no support for the idea that more severe punishment has a greater capacity to deter. Far more important are swiftness and certainty. Empirically, Sampson and Laub (1993) found imprisonment to have little capacity to reduce subsequent adult reoffending. In fact, the collateral destruction of protective social bonds of family and work that often accompanies incarceration raises the question of whether these results might offset any positive effect completely. Scholars such as Spelman, in contrast, find more optimistically that about one-fifth to one-third of the crime drop during the late 1990s may be accounted for by expanded imprisonment. One of the biggest problems in terms of impact on crime of course is that such a relatively small share of crimes, about 2 percent, are ever solved so that an enormous prison expansion would be required to achieve a reduction of even one percent in crime.

Despite doubts about the effect on crime, prisons continued to expand and are still doing so today. By the 1990s the United States had surpassed both South Africa and Russia to achieve the dubious distinction of imprisoning the largest share of its population of any country in the world. England has emerged as among the most carceral of the European nations.

Prison expansion began in the late 1980s in America and the early 1990s in Britain. Paradoxically, it has continued into the new millennium despite a continuing clear drop in crime in both countries. This raises questions about what is causing the expansion.

As a basis for talking about causes of the carceral turn, it is important to paint in broad brush strokes some of the facets of the transformation itself. In the United States, the War on Drugs brought skyrocketing arrests of youth in America's inner cities. The US Supreme Court under Chief Justice Rehnquist moved consistently to expand police powers while limiting the rights of the accused.

Consistent growth of imprisonment despite dropping crime has led scholars to query its causes. Some have pointed to economic dynamics. Scholars, such as Christianson, point to evidence of the growth of a prison industry and to the role of prisons in generating economic development, especially in backwater regions. Western and Beckett explore labor market dynamics, suggesting that imprisonment may explain low unemployment during the 1990s in the United States, and the fact that inflation nonetheless did not rise. They suggest that prison might have been a key factor in strong economic growth.

Among the collateral harms of imprisonment, Uggen and Manza highlight widespread disenfranchisement of felons in many American states. The authors estimate it may have tipped the electoral vote in the American presidential election in 2000.

When looking at both the American and the British prisons, one finds a striking concentration of ethnic minorities, the less educated, the socially excluded and above all, the poor. In America, from city jails to state prisons to federal penitentiaries to death row, inmates reflect disadvantage. British inmates show a comparable social background (Morgan, 2002). Police stop and search, profiling, and deployment to inner city neighborhoods had predictable consequences. At a time when it is increasingly clear that some approaches do "work" in preventing crime and reducing reoffending, Simon and Feeley argue that a "new penology" has given up on rehabilitation to focus on the management of the risk of crime through the "warehousing" of targeted population groups.

Not only does this prison expansion raise questions of lawfulness and fairness, it also entails enormous financial and opportunity cost. Costs for juvenile offenders are more than five times the resources that could fund early childhood education which emerges as a major factor reducing the propensity of youth for crime.

As we contemplate the high concentrations of disadvantaged persons in prison, especially from ethnic minority groups, we need to understand what has produced this further decimation of the life changes of ethnic minorities and the disadvantaged. Why does a democracy embark on racialized incarceration at a rate exceeding that of South Africa under apartheid? And how do policymakers persuade a people that reducing inequality is not an answer – that our challenge is to "responsibilize the individual"?

This research challenges the notion of an escalating crime problem to which anti-social behavior orders, "zero tolerance policing" or "net-widening" can provide answers, and focuses our attention on violence and state response to crime as primary criminological challenges.

Chapter 5

Alfred Blumstein and Joel Wallman

THE RECENT RISE AND FALL OF AMERICAN VIOLENCE

From: Alfred Blumstein and Joel Wallman (2006), excerpts from 'The recent rise and fall of American violence', and Alfred Blumstein, excerpts from 'Disaggregating the violence trends', in Alfred Blumstein and Joel Wallman (eds), *The Crime Drop in America*, 2nd edn, Cambridge: Cambridge University Press, pp. 13–44.

A MERICANS' PRIDE IN THEIR nation's material prosperity, thriving democracy, and often admirable role in world affairs is tempered, for many, by concern and puzzlement over another American distinction – her perennial presence at the top of the list of the most violent industrial nations. Violence has been a major theme in public discussion for decades, and apprehension about it was intensified by the sharp rise in violence in the mid-1980s, a development most pronounced among inner-city minority youth. Despite the remarkable decline in violence that began in the early 1990s, a preoccupation with criminal violence persists among the citizenry as well as among scholars of violence, who are intent on understanding what has happened. [. . .]

DISAGGREGATING THE VIOLENCE TRENDS

The changing rates of violence in the U.S.

The period from 1980 to 1998 has seen some sharp swings in the rate of violence in the United States. The homicide rate in 1980 was at a peak value of 10.2 per 100,000 population, and by 1985 it had fallen to a trough of 7.9. It then climbed a full 24 percent to a peak of 9.8 in 1991, and has been declining markedly since then, reaching a level of 6.3 in 1998, a level that is lower than any annual rate since 1967. The rate of robbery has followed a very similar pattern, oscillating since 1972 between rates of 200 and 250 per 100,000 population, reaching its peaks and troughs within one year of the peaks and troughs of the murder trends. It has also displayed a steady decline since its 1991 peak, and its 1998 rate of 165.2 is lower than any experienced since 1969. These patterns are depicted in Figure 5.1.

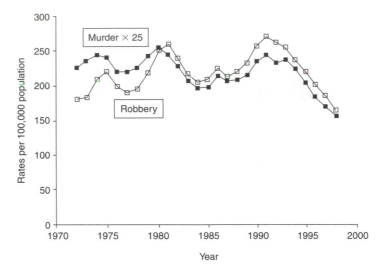

Figure 5.1 UCR murder and robbery rates

This chapter focuses primarily on homicide (the ultimate violent act) and secondarily on robbery (the taking of property by force or threat of force) as the principal indicators of violence. . . . It concentrates primarily on crimes reported to the police . . . and published annually in the FBI's Uniform Crime Reports (UCR). [. . .]

Measuring violence

The mix of violent crime

The rate of violent crime in the United States is typically measured as the sum of the following crimes reported to and recorded by the police: murder and nonnegligent manslaughter, forcible rape, robbery, and aggravated assault. These rates are reported annually by the FBI in the UCR and combined into a *violent-crime index*.

These are very disparate offenses whose rates cover a very broad range. The absolute numbers recorded in a typical year, 1998, display the large disparity across these categories: 16,910 homicides; 93,100 forcible rapes; 446,630 robberies and 974,400 aggravated assaults. The ratio among these is approximately 1, 5, 25, and 50, that is, there are 50 times as many aggravated assaults and 25 times as many robberies as there are homicides. It is evident that even minor fluctuations in the reports of aggravated assault will overwhelm significant changes in the number of murders. For example, even if there is a doubling of the number of homicides, a relatively small 2 percent decrease in aggravated assault will counteract that doubling, and will lead to no change in the reported rate of *violent crime*. [. . .]

Because there tends to be a strong correlation among the various index offenses, these distinctions are often not serious. But there can be occasions when the distinction among them is of serious concern. This is especially true when there are shifts in reporting patterns rather than shifts in the underlying behavior. [. . .]

Forcible rape has been the most difficult of the four violent offenses to measure. Because of stigma associated with rape and because police have often been insensitive to rape victims' emotions, the percentage of rapes reported to the police is about the lowest of the UCR index crimes, and so changes in reporting rates can be an important factor contributing to changes in the UCR rate of rape. Also, the National Crime Victimization Survey (NCVS), which samples over 40,000 households to ask about their victimization experiences, has discovered that typically there are too few cases of rape reported even to the NCVS to provide precise measures of the rate of that offense. Thus, I do not deal further in this chapter with the serious offense of rape.

Aggravated assault

The UCR rate of aggravated assault has displayed a pattern that is quite different from the generally flat trend displayed by homicide and robbery shown in Figure 5.1. The aggravated assault rate, shown in Figure 5.2, grew significantly – by 134 percent – during the twenty-year period from 1972 to 1992 before its more recent decline. But there are reasons to believe that this sharp trend is more artifactual than real. In contrast to murder and robbery, which are relatively well-defined offenses, "aggravated" assault requires discretion on the part of the police taking the report to distinguish it from "simple" assault. . . . And perhaps most important in the current context, there is a good possibility that the nature of this distinction has been changing over time.

Support for this interpretation of the growth in aggravated assault is provided by evidence from the other principal source of crime data in the United States, the NCVS, which asks respondents whether they have been a victim of a crime over the past six months . . . Building on data from a NCVS question that has been largely stable over time. Figure 5.3 shows the responses . . . for the twenty years until 1992. Here, one sees aggravated assault and simple assault with virtually no trend, and even with far less fluctuation than displayed in the police reports. Thus, there is a stark contrast between the rapidly rising trend in aggravated assault based on police reports and the very flat trend based on the victimization survey. The flat trend in the homicide series over this

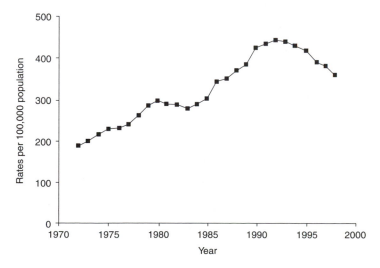

Figure 5.2 UCR aggravated assault rates

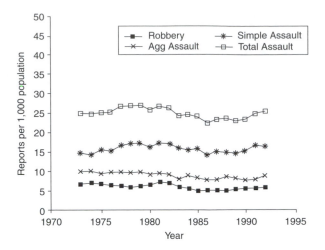

Figure 5.3 Violent victimization rates. Rates per 1,000 population

period is also consistent with the flat trend in the victimization survey. This suggests the reasonable possibility of a fairly stable ratio of aggravated assaults to homicides. [. . .]

The evidence from the victimization survey would appear to be the more compelling, and this calls for some investigation into why the growth in UCR aggravated assaults. It is possible that the chance that an aggravated assault turns into a homicide has been diminished somewhat because of the improved quality of emergency medical services in the United States over the past twenty years, but it would be surprising if that change could account for the doubling of the number of aggravated assaults relative to the number of homicides. Rather, it is much more likely that there has been a steady growth in the reporting of assaults that used to be ignored or dealt with as simple assaults. The principal candidates for this reporting shift are cases of domestic violence. Until relatively recently, police tended to downplay domestic assaults, largely because they were considered more private matters, and the police often chose not to record the crime in order to avoid the frustration of observing the victim recant after the immediate crisis had passed. Recent changes in public attitudes toward domestic assaults, in the attitudes of victims, and in the response by police suggest that these changes are likely to have been major contributors to the growth in the recording of aggravated assaults by the police.

This hypothesis is supported by Figure 5.4, which compares the ratios of the age-specific arrest rates for aggravated assault to those for murder in two years, 1985 and 1994. It is evident that in 1985, that ratio stayed very close to 15 for all ages except ages 15 and 16, where there were many aggravated assaults but relatively few of them resulted in homicides, a manifestation of teenage propensity for fighting, but with relatively low levels of lethality, at least in part because of the relatively low prevalence of firearms then available to teenagers.

The picture changed rather dramatically by 1994. The ratio continued to be close to 15 until age 23, when it began to grow appreciably. It increased to a maximum ratio of 39, and stayed at more than double the previous value of 15 for all the older ages prior to 60. But these are the ages when domestic relationships, and the potential for assault, are more salient in people's lives. It is also the case that the trend to arrest for domestic assault increased appreciably with the shift in policy that grew out of the Minneapolis Spouse Assault experiment conducted in the mid 1980s. This change was reflected in

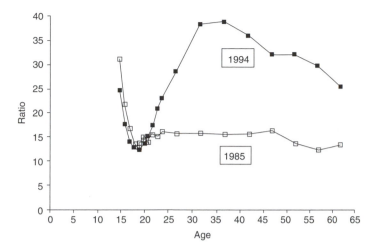

Figure 5.4 Ratio of aggressive assaults to murder rates by age. Arrest rates in 1985 and 1994

many states adopting statues mandating arrest for domestic violence; it also became policy in many police departments, even in the absence of a mandatory statute. Thus, we see this sharp growth in the rate of arrest for aggravated assault at the ages when domestic relationships are most likely. It seems most reasonable, then, to interpret the growth in the UCR rate of aggravated assault in the period between 1985 and 1994 predominantly as a reflection of a growing tendency of police to record incidents of domestic violence as aggravated assaults that would not have been so designated prior to 1985. [. . .]

Homicide and robbery rates

The two crimes that are best measured in the UCR are homicide and robbery, largely because these offenses are reasonably well defined and their definitions have been stable over time. Also, homicide tends to be very well reported to the police, and the rate at which victims have been reporting robberies to the police has been very stable over time.

Although there have been sharp swings up and down, it is striking how trendless these two crimes are. The trend line for homicide is slightly negative, but is not statistically significant. For robbery, the trend line is slightly upward (at an annual trend of 0.87 percent of its mean rate of 223 per 100,000). This stability or relative trendlessness in crime rates is certainly at marked variance with the general view of the American public – and especially the rhetoric of its candidates for political office. [. . .]

This is the case, for example, with age: during the late 1980s, homicides by young people were increasing whereas homicides by older people were decreasing. In other cases, there are important interactions – for example, between race and age. A large increase in homicide with handguns occurred among young African-Americans in the late 1980s, but we observe no such increase for older African-Americans. In such instances, demographic disaggregation is necessary to isolate the effects being examined. A general theme of this chapter is that it is not productive to think of homicide rates as a unitary phenomenon. Rather, recent change in the aggregate homicide rate is the product of several distinct subgroup trends. [. . .]

Many public figures and journalists have offered their own explanations for the recent decline in violence rates. There have been claims, most notably by New York City Mayor Rudolph Giuliani and by William Bratton when he was New York City's police commissioner, that virtually all of the homicide drop in New York resulted from smart and aggressive policing (Butterfield 1995; Kelling and Coles 1997; Krauss 1996; Mitchell 1994). Another view attributes the decline to a change in some of the factors that contributed to the growth, most importantly to a reduction in the high availability of firearms and their use in homicides or robberies by young people. Some of this turnaround may be the result of changes in policing, especially the use of aggressive stop-and-frisk tactics to remove guns from young people, but other factors could well be involved. These could include community efforts to mediate intergang disputes, a greater availability of jobs and income to low-skilled young people in the booming economy, changing drug markets with diminished roles for young people and growing incapacitation effects through increases in the prison population of older offenders. Looking across the nation, one finds that the effects of changes in the large cities have a dominant effect on the aggregate rates.

Differences across age groups

A key factor providing important insight into the changes that have occurred since 1985 is the sharply differing trends in violence associated with different age groups, so this provides the initial departure point for the disaggregation.

Homicide

Elsewhere (Blumstein 1995), I discussed the striking changes between 1985 and 1992 in age-specific arrest rates for homicide. That article explained that, while the rates for persons age 18 and younger more than doubled, the rates for those age 30 and above declined by about 20 to 25 percent. I can now extend that analysis to 1998, and we see some striking changes in the opposite direction for the young people.

Figure 5.5 presents the age-specific arrest rate (known as the age-crime curve) for murder for the years 1985, which was the last year of a fifteen year period of very stable age-specific rates, and 1993, which was the peak year of juvenile age-specific rates. Even though the rates for ages 20 and under had more than doubled over this interval, the rates for those over 30 had indeed declined. Figure 5.6 depicts the same 1993 situation along with the figure for 1998, where we see the rates for all ages decline, with the steepest decline around age 18, where the growth since 1985 had reached the greatest level.

It is instructive to break out these changes in more detail by looking at the time trends for individual ages. Figure 5.7 depicts the trend for the ages traditionally displaying the peak homicide arrest rates – 18 through 24. We see how similar those rates were from 1970 through 1985, and then a divergence beginning in 1986. The rate for the 18 year olds more than doubled by 1991 (for an annual growth rate of 16 percent during this period), dropped in 1992, reached a new peak in 1993, and then continued down for the next five years. The pattern is similar for the other ages depicted in Figure 5.7, although the steepness of the rise in the late 1980s decreases with increasing age, and the decline after 1993 is correspondingly less for the older ages.

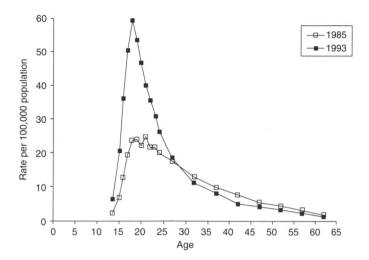

Figure 5.5 Murder arrest rate by age in 1985 and 1993

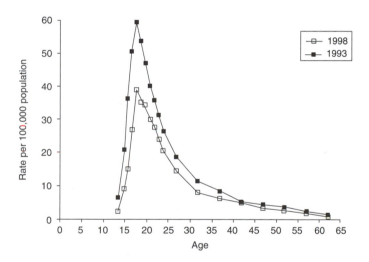

Figure 5.6 Murder arrest rate by age in 1993 and 1998

For youth 18 and under, depicted in Figure 5.8, the pattern is very similar to the pattern at age 18, although the stable base rate in the 1970–85 period was lower. In all these cases of 18 and under, the rate more than doubled by 1993. The pattern for the ages above 24 generally declines after 1975.

These changes for the growth period, 1985 to 1993, and for the decline period, 1993 to 1998, are reflected in Figure 5.9, which depicts for each age the ratio of the age-specific arrest rate for murder to the rates that prevailed in 1985. Points above the heavy line (a ratio of 1.0) represent an increase in the rates, and points below that line represent a decrease. The upper graph portrays the ratio reached in the peak year, 1993, and the lower graph portrays the degree to which the ratio had declined by 1998.

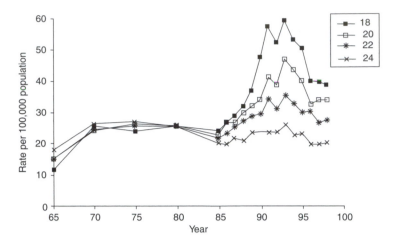

Figure 5.7 Trends in murder arrest rate by age (individual peak ages)

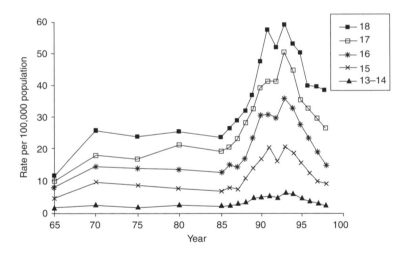

Figure 5.8 Trends in murder arrest rate by age (individual young ages)

The arrest rate for 15-year olds in 1993 was triple the rate that had prevailed in 1985. The growth to 1993 declined with age, but it was more than double the 1985 rate for all ages of 20 and below. In contrast, for the older ages of 30 and above, the 1993 rates were actually about 20 percent lower than the 1985 rates.

The graph of the 1998-to-1985 ratio is clearly below that for 1993, and the greatest decline occurred in the teenage years. But it is clear that the teenage rates in 1998 were still about 40 percent above the 1985 rates that had prevailed since 1970, and so there is still considerable room for improvement. . . .

Also, there was a continuing decline in the homicide rates for the older ages. By 1998, the 25- to 30-year-old group had declined from the 1985 rates by about 20 percent, and the older groups had declined by about 40 percent.

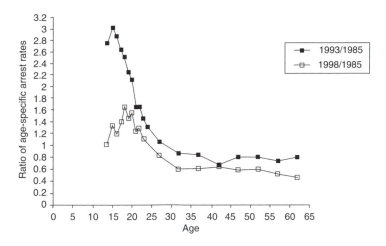

Figure 5.9 Ratios of recent age-specific murder rates (1993 and 1998 murder arrests versus 1985)

These figures underscore the central importance of examining the different roles of the different age groups in explaining the trends in the aggregate homicide rate since 1985. The aggregate rate of Figure 5.1 grew to the 1991 peak solely because the rates of the younger people were increasing faster than the rates for the older people were declining. Between 1991 and 1993, the rates for younger people were generally flat (as reflected in the pattern for the 18 year olds in Figure 5.7), and so the decline by those in the older age groups dominated the aggregate, leading to the downturn that began in 1992. Since the rates of both young and old were decreasing after 1993, the aggregate rate continued to fall.

In sum, all of the increase in the level of homicide in the United States during the growth period of the late 1980s and early 1990s was due to the trends in the younger ages, because homicide rates for those 25 years old and older did not increase. However, the decrease during the decline period since 1993 is due to both the recent sharp drop in offending among young people and to the continuing decline in offending among older people. [. . .]

Robbery

The changes in levels of robbery have many similarities to those associated with homicide, but with some important differences. The time trends in the age-specific arrest rates for robbery based on UCR estimates are depicted in Figures 5.10 (for ages 14 to 18), 5.11 (for ages 18 to 24), and 5.12 (for ages 24 and above).

Over the 1970–85 period, homicide arrest rates were fairly stable and also displayed a flat peak over the 18-to-24 age range as evidenced by the proximity of their trend lines in Figure 5.7. That period saw considerable change in robbery rates, most notably for the youngest age group: a rapid rise through 1975, a relatively flat period from 1975 to 1980, and a strong decline after 1980. In the period before 1985, the rise and the decline were strongest for the youngest group (Figure 5.10), more muted for the middle group (Figure 5.11), and even less pronounced for the oldest group (Figure 5.12), who had much lower rates generally.

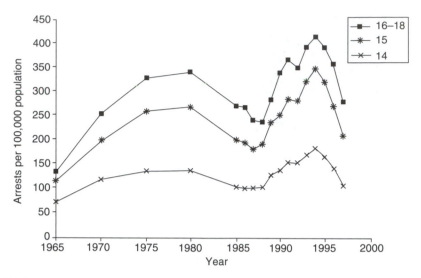

Figure 5.10 Robbery arrest rates ages 14–18

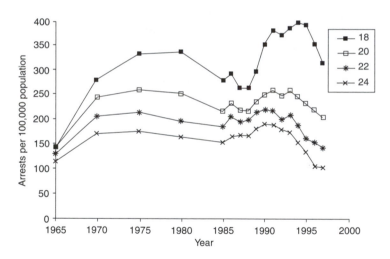

Figure 5.11 Robbery arrest rates ages 18–24

The post-1985 period, which is the dominant period for homicide, also provides some interesting similarities and contrasts with the homicide situation. There was an important post-1985 increase in the robbery arrest rate, especially for the younger age group. For the young people (under age 20), the first noticeable uptick in robbery did not occur until 1989, three years after the increase for homicide (as seen in Figure 5.8). The peak in robbery occurred in 1994, one year after the homicide peak, and the downturn was comparably sharp. For all the ages of 18 and under, the growth in the five years between 1989 and the 1994 peak exceeded 70 percent.

As we examine older people (ages 24 and above in Figure 5.12), we find a rather different pattern: an earlier rise (starting in 1986 rather than 1989) and a much less sharp

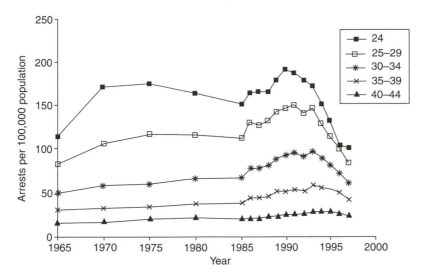

Figure 5.12 Robbery arrest rates age 24 and above

(at most half) rise than that displayed by the young people. But the decline after the peak (between 1990 and 1993) is comparably strong.

Methodological considerations in arrest data

In discussing robbery and homicide trends, arrest data have been used to represent offending patterns by age. . . . In using this approach, it is important to recognize the possibility that arrest rates by age can differ from actual offending rates. That could be a consequence of differential vulnerability to arrest by different demographic groups. For example, it is possible that young offenders are more easily arrested because they are less skillful in avoiding arrest. Or, at least in the case of homicide, they may be less vulnerable to arrest because their victims are more often strangers, and finding the perpetrator in a stranger-homicide is difficult . . . (see Riedel 1993).

As one examines trends in arrests over time within a particular age group, any distortion in the trend pattern because of these differential vulnerabilities must be associated with a *change* in the vulnerability within any age group. Thus, if it were the case that younger people were more vulnerable to arrest than older people, then that difference could contribute to the higher absolute values of the arrest rates associated with the young people. But that difference could not be the cause of the rapid post-1985 rise in the arrest rate of the young people unless there was some reason why there would be a comparable increase in their arrest vulnerability, and there is no indication of any such change.

Another concern about using arrest rates as the proxy for offending rates is the possibility that there might be a greater tendency for multiple arrests in some demographic groups than in others. This might be a consequence of more aggressive police practices in dealing with some groups, leading to multiple arrests for a single homicide. Or it might result because homicide or robbery by some groups, and especially the younger groups, is, in fact, more likely to be committed by multiple offenders than single offenders. Then, a homicide or a robbery committed by a gang, for example, could well result in multiple members of the gang being arrested for the same offense, and that would contribute to a higher arrest rate in the age range typical of gang members. These measurement problems are certainly real, but again, the concern over them is diminished somewhat in examining time trends. [. . .]

Changing demographic composition

Much of the speculation about the recent decline in homicide rates attributes the decline to changing demographics. This may be a holdover from the realization that much of the decline that began in 1980 was attributable to a demographic shift, as the baby-boom generation aged out of the high-crime ages (Blumstein, Cohen, and Miller 1980; Steffensmeier and Harer 1991). But those same demographic effects were not still at work in the early 1990s, since demographic effects do not always have to work in the same direction.

The decline after 1980 was significantly affected by the shrinking size of the cohorts in the high-crime ages, but the United States in the late 1990s was in a period of growing cohort sizes in the late teens and early twenties. . . . It is evident that the smallest age cohort under 40 is about 23, the cohort born in 1976. Each of the younger cohorts is larger than its predecessor until the peak at age six. Thus, if teenage age-specific crime rates were to remain constant, then the aggregate crime rate would increase as a result of the larger cohort sizes. This possibility spurred the warnings of a demographic "crime bomb" set to go off during the 1990s (DiIulio 1996).

Yet, it is important to recognize that these age-composition changes are relatively small, with cohort sizes growing at a rate of about one percent per year. In the face of much larger annual swings in the age-specific crime rates, as much as 10 to 20 percent per year up in the 1980s (16 percent per year for the 18 year olds from 1985 to 1991) as well as down in the 1990s, the one percent change in demographic composition is a minor effect. [. . .]

The role of handguns

There is widespread recognition of the changing role of weaponry in young people's hands. Over the last 15 years, the weapons involved in settling juveniles' disputes have changed dramatically, from fists or knives to handguns – and especially more recently to semiautomatic pistols with their much greater lethality. That growth in lethal weaponry is reflected in the changes in the weapons involved in homicides in different race and age groups (Blumstein and Cork 1996; and Cook 1996, more generally). The FBI's Supplementary Homicide Reports (SHR) provide data to track such changes in homicides. [. . .]

The growth period, 1985–1993

Figures 5.13, 5.14, and 5.15 provide information on the time trends of the weaponry used in homicides by offenders in three age categories: adults, 25 to 45 years old (Figure 5.13); youth, 18 to 24 (Figure 5.14); and juveniles or "kids," 17 and under (Figure 5.15).

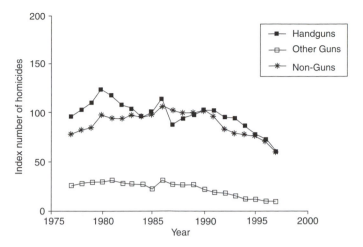

Figure 5.13 Homicide weapons by adults (ages 25–45). 1985 handguns equal 100

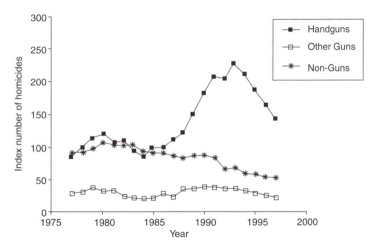

Figure 5.14 Homicide weapons by youth (ages 18–24). 1985 handguns equal 100

The weapons are classified into three groups: handguns, other guns, and nonguns (which includes no weapon). We can see from Figure 5.13 that over the time period shown, 1977–97, there has been a general downward trend in total homicides by adults with all weapons and especially with handguns more recently: overall, however, there has been only little change in the mix of weapons used by adults in homicide.

The situation for youth and juveniles is quite different, however. For both these groups, there was no clear trend until after 1985, and then a significant growth in handgun use began with no comparable growth in the other weapons. With 1985 as the base year, handgun homicide among youth increased by 1993 to an index value of 228 (an increase of 128 percent). The increase in juveniles' use of handguns was dramatically higher, to an index value of 389, almost quadruple the 1985 rate. In these groups, there is a sharp and steady decline following the 1993 peak. This decline is consistent with the

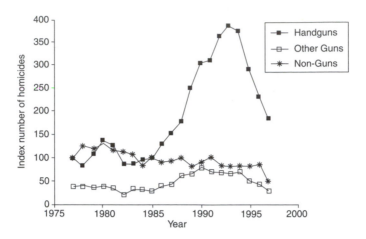

Figure 5.15 Homicide weapons by kids (under 18). 1985 handguns equal 100

decline in homicide arrest rates shown in Figures 5.7 and 5.8. I also note that, despite the sharp declines, the handgun indexes in 1997 were still well above the 1985 level for these groups, 43 percent above for youth and 83 percent for juveniles, an observation also consistent with the young people's arrest rates shown in Figure 5.9.

In all these figures, no appreciable increase has occurred in either the other-gun or the nongun categories. In fact, there has been a steady 40- to 50-percent decline from 1985 to 1997 in the nongun category for all three groups. Thus, there has been some degree of substitution of handguns for other weapons, but the absolute magnitude of non-handgun decline is still small compared to the dramatic growth in the use of handguns by youth and especially by juveniles. Thus, the observation based on Figures 5.5–5.9 that young people under age 25 accounted for all the growth in homicides in the post-1985 period is augmented with the recognition that that growth was accounted for totally by the growth in homicides committed with handguns. Clearly, the sharply increasing presence of handguns in youth and juvenile homicide must be considered of fundamental importance in any explanation of the aggregate homicide increase of the late 1980s and early 1990s. And the counterpart sharp decrease in the handgun homicides by these two groups is an important factor in the decline. But even though their handgun homicide rates are still well above the 1985 level, the continuing decline in homicides by adults, which, by 1997, reached a level almost half that of 1985, contributed to the aggregate decline since 1991.

Some important racial differences in the growth of handgun homicides can also be observed, with the dominant growth being among young African-Americans, as offenders and as victims. Figure 5.16 presents the index number of the weapons involved in homicides committed by black youth, ages 18 to 24. There is an even sharper growth in handgun use than for youth generally (Figure 5.14); the number of handgun homicides more than triples from the low in 1984 to the peak in 1993. There was no comparable growth in the role of the other weapon types.

Although some growth also occurred in handgun homicides by white youth, that growth was far less than among the black youth (see Figure 5.17). . . . There is a strong

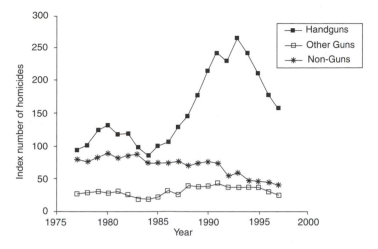

Figure 5.16 Homicide weapons by black youth (ages 18–24). 1985 handguns equal 100

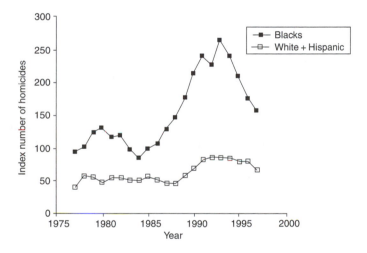

Figure 5.17 Handgun homicides by youth (ages 18–24). 1985 handguns by black youth equal 100

growth in handgun prevalence for black youth, from a low in 1984 to a tripling by 1993. The rise for the white/Hispanic group does not start until 1989, four years after the start of the African-American climb. That growth reaches its peak in 1993, almost a doubling of the rate at the 1988 trough. That growth is attributable predominantly to a growth in handguns in homicides by Hispanics. We also note that the post-1993 decline is much steeper for the black youth than for the white/Hispanic youth.

Firearms have also played an important role in the growth in robberies. There is no incident-based data source for robberies comparable to the SHR for homicide. But there are aggregate statistics for the fraction of robberies that are committed with firearms, and there was indeed a large growth in the fraction committed with firearms during the 1989–91 period. During that time, which was precisely the time of the major increase in the involvement of young people in robbery, there was a 42-percent increase in the total rate of firearm robberies. Over that same period, there was only a 5-percent increase in the rate of nonfirearm robberies. This shift suggests that young people carrying guns found uses for those guns outside the simple role of self-defense. This might help to account for the delay in the rise and the decline in robberies by the younger offenders compared to their older counterparts. For those age 24 and under, the first uptick in robbery did not occur until 1989, whereas for those in their late twenties and thirties, the upturn began three years earlier, in 1986. This may be an indication of the fact that the older people were more likely to include early crack users, and so their rise before the younger robbers may be explained less by their acquisition of guns (which were much less a novelty to them) and more by their use of robbery as means of getting the money to buy drugs. Exploring these issues will require analyses in individual cities, where more detailed information on demographic-specific arrest rates are available.

The decline period, 1993–1996

The steady decline in the handgun homicide rate after 1993 is clearly consistent with the decline in youth homicide rates shown in Figure 5.8, suggesting the importance of the decline in the use of handguns by young people in the decline of the aggregate homicide rate.

The pattern of growth and decline in handgun use is also reflected in Figures 5.18 and 5.19, which depict the time trend in the rate of weapons arrests at the various ages. The pattern here is very similar to the homicide patterns depicted in Figures 5.7 and 5.8, but there is a much more distinct peaking in 1993, with a clear decline subsequently. Changes in the rate of weapons arrests result from a combination of changes in the presence of illegal weapons in the relevant population group and changes in police aggressiveness in pursuing illegal weapons. It is clear from other data that there was considerable growth in weapon prevalence during the late 1980s, and also that police became more concerned about weapons, especially those in the hands of young people. That combination is reflected in the rise in weapons arrests until the peak in 1993. There is no indication that

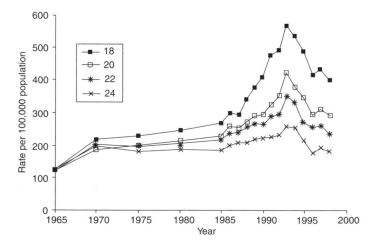

Figure 5.18 Trends: weapons arrest rate by age. Trends for individual ages 18–24

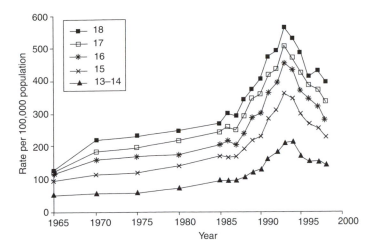

Figure 5.19 Trends: weapons arrest rate by age. Trends for individual young ages

there was any diminution in police aggressiveness in pursuing young people's guns after 1993, and so it seems likely that the decline after 1993 is due much more to a reduction in the carrying of guns than to a slackening of police efforts to capture the guns. [. . .]

The big cities

The largest cities contribute disproportionately to patterns of serious violence for the nation as a whole. The prominent role of the large cities is clearly evident in the trends in homicide. Based on UCR data for 1991, for example, the United States experienced 24,700 homicides. New York City alone provided 2,154 of them, or 9 percent of the total. Since New York City's homicide rate has declined faster than the national rate, its percentage contribution to the total has dropped to a value below 5 percent. Although no other city has as large an effect as New York, the importance of the large cities is reflected in the relative contribution they make to the total homicide picture. . . . In 1991, when New York alone accounted for 9 percent of all U.S. homicides, only seven cities (New York, Los Angeles, Chicago, Detroit, Houston, Dallas, and Washington) were needed to account for a quarter of U.S. homicides.

New York City has been a major contributor to the national decline since the early 1990s. In the national net decline in homicides from 1993 to 1994 (a reduction of 1,200 homicides), New York City's drop of 385 accounted for 32 percent of that change. In the net change from 1994 to 1995 (a national net drop of 1,720 homicides), New York City's drop of 384 accounted for 22 percent of the total decrease. New York City's contribution to the drop since 1995 has been closer to 10 percent, still very large, but smaller than in the earlier years, in part because the smaller cities are beginning to catch up. It is thus clear that what goes on in New York City, or the largest cities more generally, can have a very powerful effect on national statistics.

Examination of the trends over time offers a compelling picture of the saliency of the large cities, both in the rise of homicide in the 1980s and the decline during the 1990s.

Figures 5.20 (for homicides with other than handguns) and 5.21 (for homicides with handguns) use the SHR to estimate the number (not the rate) of homicides in each of four groups of cities (those of one million or more, those in the range of 500,000 to one million, 250,000 to 500,000, and 100,000 to 250,000).[. . .]

Figure 5.20 shows the limited variation associated with the non-handgun homicides. The change was relatively small in the smaller cities, but there was a rather steep and steady decline of almost 50 percent in the large cities from the peak in 1980 to the end of the series in 1997, with the decline accelerating after 1990.

These changes were much smaller than those in the handgun homicides. Figure 5.21 shows that the large cities had a major growth beginning in 1986, increasing 80 percent from 1985 to the flat 1991–93 peak, and then declining over 50 percent to the low in 1997, which was below the 1985 rate.

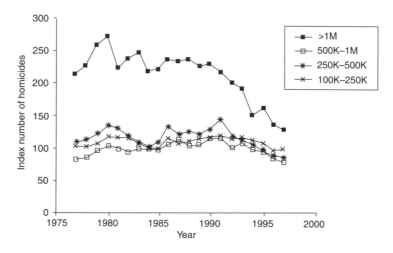

Figure 5.20 Indexed total of nonhandgun homicides by city size. Cities of 500K – 1 million in 1985 equal 100

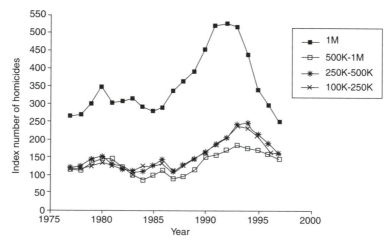

Figure 5.21 Indexed total of handgun homicides by city size. Cities of 500k – 1 million in 1985 equal 100

The smaller cities also had a distinct upturn in the handgun homicides, but that upturn did not begin until 1988, two years later than in the large cities. That upturn was even larger in percentage terms, increasing 110 to 130 percent from the trough in 1987 to the peak in 1993. The more recent downturn began one to two years later than in the large cities, and the drop from the respective peaks was still only about 20 to 30 percent by 1997.

Cork (1999) has shown the connection between the rise in the handgun homicides and the recruitment of juveniles into the crack markets. Using an epidemic model originally used in the marketing literature, he identified in individual cities the time when juvenile arrests for drugs began to accelerate and the corresponding point when juvenile homicides took off. He found most typically a one- to three-year lag between the two, a result consistent with the hypothesis that the rise in juvenile homicides was attributable to the diffusion of guns from the kids recruited into drug markets to their friends and beyond. Cork also showed that crack markets generally emerged first in the largest cities, especially in New York and Los Angeles, and then diffused to the nation's center to smaller cities at a later time, again a result consistent with the lags shown in Figure 5.21. Thus, the observed patterns of handgun homicide are highly consistent with explanations that assign central importance to the rise and decline of crack markets in the United States. [. . .]

The decline in the 1990s is a complicated story, which involves numerous factors. We highlight the necessity to partition the trends by key attributes of the problem. One critical dimension is the age of the offenders. We saw very different patterns across the different age groups, with the crime-rate rise of the late 1980s being composed almost entirely by offenders under age 25, whereas offending rates of older people displayed a steady decline. The sharpest decline in the 1990s has thus occurred among the young offenders. There were also important effects associated with weapons used, largely a growth in the use of handguns, with no comparable growth in other weapon types, and then a rapid decline in handgun use in the 1990s. [. . .]

The role of prisons

One crime-control factor whose effects are especially hard to sort out is incarceration. Following a fifty-year period of impressive stability, incarceration rates in the United States began an enormous increase in the mid-1970s, quadrupling by the end of the century. It would thus be surprising if prisons had not been a factor in the decline in violence. It is clear, however, that so simplistic an analysis as documenting the negative association between incarceration rate and crime rate in the 1990s cannot provide the basis for generating an estimate of its impact. After all, in the 1980s, during the period of the most prodigious growth in imprisonment, violence was increasing most markedly.

William Spelman . . . derives estimates of the elasticity of crime due to incarceration, that is, the percentage change in crime associated with a one-percent change in prison population. . . . Spelman . . . concludes that perhaps 25 percent of the crime drop is attributable to incarceration. [. . .]

The violent crime pattern of adults above age 25 has been quite different from that of those younger. Adult homicide shows a steady decline through the 1980s, when the homicide rate of younger offenders was spiking, and all the way through the 1990s. . . . There are two aspects of the adult homicide decline. One is its generality across both major racial groups, both sexes, and all offender–victim relationships – family member, acquaintance, and stranger. The second is that, for both men and women and blacks and whites the greatest decline is seen in family homicides, a development attributable in part – but only in part – to concurrent declines in marriage rates over the past two decades and to the emergence of a variety of support services intended to reduce domestic violence. [. . .]

Whereas the adult-violence downtrend of the 1990s was a continuation of the previous decade's pattern, a significant fraction of the reduction in youth violence in the 1990s represented an undoing of the growth of youth violence in the late 1980s. Much of that growth resulted from the recruitment of young people into crack markets and the effect of those markets on youth more generally, effects that dominated much of inner-city life in the late 1980s and early 1990s. That the acquisition of firearms spread beyond those directly involved in the crack trade is attested to by youth surveys carried out during this period. These studies documented a rate of gun-carrying far higher than could be explained in terms of participation in drug sales. Geographic diffusion was evident as well – in the upswing in homicide (though of smaller magnitude) seen among white youth some three years after its occurrence in the inner cities, and in the upturn in violence in smaller cities some two years after it occurred in the larger ones. It is no accident that the time difference by city size in the surge in violence maps rather well, with a lag of one to three years, onto the time difference across cities in the beginning of juvenile involvement in crack markets. [. . .]

Johnson, Golub, and Dunlap (2006) credit the antidrug tactics of New York City's police department and its "quality-of-life" campaign with making life more difficult for participants on both sides of the crack market. But the major cause of the decline of crack was an attitude shift among inner-city youth consisting not just of loss of interest in crack but of a positive rejection of the drug and the violence and degenerate lifestyles it engendered. Marijuana, rolled in cigar wrappers as "blunts," has become this generation's illegal substance of preference, which is marketed in ways that seem to avoid the violence of the crack era.

Policing must be a major topic in any consideration of the crime drop, partly because the police are the first line of response to violent activity, but also because the period of the 1990s has been one of substantial innovation in policing. Eck and Maguire (2001) . . . systematically assess evidence for the efficacy of a wide variety of these innovations, including increases in the number of police officers on the street; community, problem-solving, and "zero-tolerance" policing; targeting of drugs and guns; and New York City's Compstat system, which uses geographic displays as a stimulus to interaction between department leadership and precinct commanders in order to hold the latter responsible for the crime in their precincts. Eck and Maguire (2001) looked for differences between jurisdictions that implemented these changes and similar ones that did not. In general, they found that it is difficult to substantiate the often strong and enthusiastic claims made for particular policing strategies, either because the strategy was put in place after crime had already declined or because two or more innovations occurred simultaneously and thus cannot be causally partitioned. They conclude that the best case is to be made for the suite of tactics employed to combat the drug trade, because this campaign at least antedated the drop in crime. [. . .]

Grogger (2001) suggests that individuals weigh the tradeoff between the wages they can earn from crime and the wages they can earn in the legitimate economy and then choose the activity that maximizes their personal utility. This is most readily demonstrable for the case of property crime but can easily be extended to economic crime like drug dealing, and can then be linked to violent crime because of the instrumental role that violence can play in the pursuit of profit. This, he argues, was abundantly evident in the case of crack. For thousands of young men of limited job skills in the inner cities, the steady decline in wages in the legitimate economy in the 1980s, juxtaposed with the easy money possible in the emerging crack trade, forced a clear economic choice.

Forced to operate outside the civil dispute-resolution system, the crack business became a focus of violence. Dealers became a prime target for robbers, and in turn, retaliated whenever they could lest they gain a reputation for vulnerability. Dealers also employed violence to settle bad-debt disputes with customers and business partners, to discipline their employees, and to increase their market share by expanding their territorial dominion. But the violence that initially enhanced the profitability of this pursuit held the seeds of its own decline: the risks from the growing violence raised the cost to both buyers and sellers in the crack market. Grogger believes the increasingly deterrent effect of violence was an important part of the drying-up of the markets and their attendant carnage. That was the push away from illegal wages. The pull toward legitimate employment came with the upturn in the economy in the 1990s, which brought higher wages and more jobs, even for those with low skill levels. [. . .]

Fox (2001) . . . conveys the usefulness of demographic analysis as well as its limitations. The rationale for the demographic approach is that, if all else were equal, crime rates would rise as the fraction of the population in the perennially crime-prone subgroups (young adult males) increased. Thus, Fox was able to predict correctly that violence would peak in 1980 and then decline on the basis of the movement of the baby-boom generation out of the high-crime age range. It is the "all else equal" proviso that limits the predictive value of demography, however. In particular, it is the assumption of stability in crime rates within demographic subgroups that is problematic. We saw this in the late 1980s, when, despite their declining numbers, the young male segment boosted the aggregate rate of violence because of the drastic spike in their per capita rate. This development could not have been – and was not – foreseen by those making predictions based solely on population trends. [. . .]

References

Anderson, David C. 1997. "The Mystery of the Falling Crime Rate." *The American Prospect* (May–June): 49–55.

Blumstein, Alfred. 1995. "Youth Violence, Guns and the Illicit Drug Industry." *Journal of Criminal Law and Criminology* 86(4): 10–36.

Blumstein, Alfred. 1998. "Violence Certainly Is the Problem – and Especially with Hand Guns." *University of Colorado Law Review Symposium Issue* 69(4) (Fall): 945–67.

Blumstein, Alfred and Daniel Cork. 1996. "Linking Gun Availability to Youth Gun Violence." *Law and Contemporary Problems* 59: 5–24.

Blumstein, Alfred, Jacqueline Cohen, and Harold Miller. 1980. "Demographically Disaggregated Projections of Prison Populations." *Journal of Criminal Justice* 8: 1–25.

Butterfield, Fox. 1995. "Many Cities in U.S. Show Sharp Drop in Homicide Rates." *The New York Times*, August 13, p. 1, 10.

Cook, Philip J., ed. 1996. "Kids, Guns, and Public Policy." *Law and Contemporary Problems* 59(1) (Winter).

Cork, Daniel. 1999. "Examining Space-Time Interaction in City-Level Homicide Data: Crack Markets and the Diffusion of Guns Among Youth." *Journal of Quantitative Criminology* 15: 379–406.

DiIulio, John J. 1996. "Why Violent Crime Rates have Dropped." *The Wall Street Journal*, September 6.

Eck, John E. and Edward R. Maguire. 2006. "Have Changes in Policing Reduced Violent Crime: An Assessment of the Evidence." in Alfred Blumstein and Joel Wallman (eds), *The Crime Drop in America*, 2nd edn, Cambridge: Cambridge University Press, pp. 207–65.

Johnson, Bruce D., Andrew Golub, and Eloise Dunlap. 2006. "The Rise and Decline of Hard Drugs, Drug Markets and Violence in Inner-city New York." in Alfred Blumstein and Joel Wallman (eds), *The Crime Drop in America*, 2nd edn, Cambridge: Cambridge University Press, pp. 164–206.

Kelling, George L. and Catherine M. Coles. 1997. *Fixing Broken Windows: Restoring Order and Reducing Crime in Our Communities*. New York: The Free Press.

Krauss, Clifford. 1996. "Crime Rate Drops in New York City." *The New York Times*, December 20, p. A1, B23.

Mitchell, Alison. 1994. "Giuliani Points to Drop in Crime Rate Despite Other Problems." *The New York Times*, September 14, p. A13.

Riedel, Marc. 1993. *Stranger Violence: A Theoretical Inquiry*. New York: Garland.

Sherman, Lawrence W. and Richard A. Berk. 1984. "The Specific Deterrent Effects of Arrest for Domestic Assault." *American Sociological Review* 261:261–72.

Steffensmeier, Darrell and Miles D. Harer. 1991. "Did Crime Rise or Fall During the Reagan Presidency? The Effects of an 'Aging' US Population on the Nation's Crime Rate." *Journal of Research in Crime and Delinquency* 28: 330–59.

U.S. Department of Justice. Federal Bureau of Investigation. 19xx. *Crime in the United States: Uniform Crime Reports, 19xx*. Washington: USCPO. The UCR report for any year is usually published in the fall of the following year.

Chapter 6

Franklin E. Zimring and Gordon Hawkins

CRIME IS NOT THE PROBLEM
Lethal violence in America

From: Franklin E. Zimring and Gordon Hawkins (1997), excerpts from *Crime is Not the Problem: Lethal Violence in America*, Oxford: Oxford University Press, pp. 3–19, 73–83.

WHAT AMERICANS FEAR

B Y LONGSTANDING HABIT, AMERICANS use the terms "crime" and "violence" interchangeably. . . . At the core of this interchangeable usage of crime and violence is the belief that crime and lethal violence are two aspects of the same problem. It is widely believed that there is much more crime of all kinds in the United States than in other developed countries. With so much crime and so many criminals, the high rates of lethal violence in the United States seem all but inevitable to many observers.

The mission of this chapter is to demonstrate that rates of crime are not greatly different in the United States from those in other developed nations and that our extremely high rates of lethal violence are a separate phenomenon, a distinct social problem that is the real source of fear and anger in American life. [. . .]

We identify a process of categorical contagion that leads citizens to fear lethal violence in a broader variety of settings than those that carry any substantial risk to life and limb. To live in an environment where robbery presents a serious hazard to its victims seems to provoke citizens to fear for their lives even from particular forms of crime that do not place their victims at mortal risk. The final section of this chapter shows that general crackdowns on crime are inefficient and potentially self-defeating methods of reducing the risks of lethal violence. [. . .]

New York City and London

New York City is the largest city in the United States with a population at 7 million. London has a city population of 6.6 million. . . . London has more theft than New York City and a rate of burglary 57 percent higher. But the robbery rate in London is less than one-fifth the robbery rate in New York City and the homicide rate in London is less than one-tenth the New York City figure.

The total number of offenses per 100,000 citizens is higher in London than in New York City. If total crime rates were the problem, Londoners should live in fear or New Yorkers in relative complacency. They have the same magnitude of crime. But with death rates eleven times as high as London, the population of New York City is far from comfortable. Lethal violence is New York City's distinctive problem, not crime, and lower rates of general theft are no consolation for huge death toll differences. [. . .]

Twenty countries

We can show clearly that America's special problem is violence and not crime by comparing the results of a twenty-nation survey of citizens about the rate at which they were victims of crime with World Health Organization data on death from assaults for the same nations. Figure 6.1 . . . shows the violent death rates for each group of five nations with the highest crime levels, then the next two highest, and finally the lowest crime categories.

There are several indications that a country's crime rate is substantially independent of its rate of lethal violence. First, the variation in violent death rate is quite large within the separate crime rate categories. Within the group of highest crime nations, the homicide rates vary by a factor of eleven, in the next group by a factor of five, in the third group by a factor of three, and in the lowest crime group by a factor of eight. In contrast, the median homicide rates for the four different crime categories are clustered between 1.3 and 2.2. So knowing which crime rate category a country belongs in does not tell one anything much about what rate of violent death that country suffers.

And knowing a country's violent death rate does not predict much about its crime rate. The lowest death rate country (England) has a crime rate just over average. The next lowest violence nation is Japan, which has the lowest crime rate also. The third lowest death rate country is the Netherlands, in the highest crime rate group. The pattern is just as opaque at the top of the violence distribution. The most violent country, the United States, has a high crime rate as well. The next most violent country, Northern Ireland, is in the lowest crime rate group.

This data set provides a multinational example of the central point that lethal violence is the crucial problem in the United States. It shows the United States clustered with other industrial countries in crime rate, but head and shoulders above the rest in violent death. It also suggests that lethal violence might be the best predictor of citizen fear on a transnational basis. Where would you rather live when examining the map of Figure 6.1? In England with its high crime rate and 0.5 deaths per 100,000 or in Northern Ireland with a much lower crime rate and nine times the death rate? Your money or your life?

Judging from Figure 6.1, the United States has about the same rate of crime and prevalence of criminality as the Netherlands and Australia. But ours is by far the most dangerous country to live in. We currently have a Netherlands-size crime problem and a king-size violence problem that threatens the social organization of our cities. [. . .]

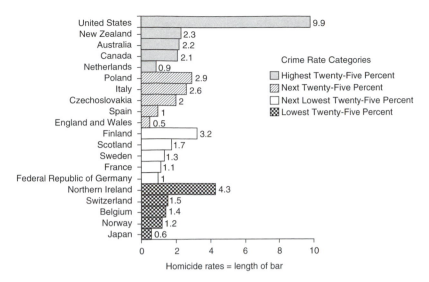

Figure 6.1 Victim survey crime rate categories and homicide rates, twenty countries

Sources: van Dijk and Mayhew 1993 (victim survey crime rates); World Health Organization 1990 (homicide rates).

On the paradoxical impacts of crime wars

The dramatic increase in resources devoted to the punishment of crime in recent years provides a clinical case study of the impact of a general crackdown on crime on policy toward violent crime. The paradox of the crime crackdown is this: When penal resources are scarce, the priority given to more serious offenses means that life-threatening violence will receive a large share of the most serious punishments. No matter how small the prison, we tend to make room for Charles Manson and Willie Horton. But expanding punishment resources will have more effect on cases of marginal seriousness rather than those that provoke the greatest degree of citizen fear. The result is that when fear of lethal violence is translated into a general campaign against crime, the major share of extra resources will be directed at nonviolent behavior.

Serious crime of violence result in prison sentences when offenders are apprehended under most criminal justice policies. Armed robbery, attempted murder, and offenses of equivalent magnitude are seriously punished even before special efforts to increase penal severity are introduced. This pattern of serious punishment means that there is less room left in the system to get tough with this sort of offense.

Instead, crime crackdowns have their most dramatic impact on less serious offenses that are close to the margin between incarceration and more lenient penal sanctions. This pattern of nonviolent offenses absorbing the overwhelming majority of resources in crime crackdowns can be clearly illustrated in the recent history of criminal justice policy in the United States. During the decade 1980–1990, for example, the state of California experienced what might be described as the mother of all crime crackdowns. In ten years, the number of persons imprisoned in California quadrupled, and the population of those incarcerated in the state's prison and jails increased by over 100,000.

As regards the impact of this unparalleled "get tough" policy on the growth in the population confined in the California prison system as a result of conviction for four key offenses, the relative growth in prison population for the two nonviolent offenses is greatly in excess of the growth experienced for robbery and homicide. The relative growth of the number of burglars in prison was over three times that of the number of robbers, and the growth rate of prisoners convicted of theft was six times the rate for robbers.

The relatively modest impact of California's crime crackdown on violent offenders is not a result of lenient attitudes toward robbery and murder in California. Quite the opposite. Since robbery and murder were always seriously punished in California, there was a smaller number of leniently treated robbers and killers who had been spared by the previous regime and were thus available to be swept up by the crackdown.

This tendency for changes in criminal justice policy to have the most profound effect in marginal cases produced a sharp contrast in California's prison system over the decade of its unprecedented expansion. Sixty percent of all California prison inmates in 1980 had been committed for offenses of violence; but only 27 percent of the additional prison space added between 1980 and 1990 was used to increase the number of inmates who had been convicted of violent offenses. If one imagines that the efficiency of an anticrime policy as a way of combating violence can be measured by the proportion of offenders imprisoned for violent offenses, the prison resources available in 1980 could be given a 60 percent efficiency rating, while the additional resources committed to imprisonment during the 1980s were employed with 27 percent efficiency.

The national pattern is less pronounced, but also shows shrinking proportions of violent offenders as prison populations increase. In 1979, 46 percent of the 274,563 persons in state prisons had been convicted of a violent offense. But just under 35 percent of the 429,618 additional prisoners that were present in 1991 had been convicted of crimes of violence. This diminished overlap between imprisonment and violence is in large measure an inevitable consequence of substantial increases in the proportion of felony offenders sentenced to prison. It creates an enormous gap between the motive for crime crackdowns and their effects. [. . .]

Bait and switch

For those who wonder why both violence and the rate of imprisonment increased in the late 1980s, we present the parable of the bait-and-switch advertisement. The practitioner of "bait-and-switch" selling advertises a brand new vacuum cleaner with several attractive features for the unheard of price of $39.95. That advertised product is the "bait" designed to attract customers into the store. When consumers enter the shop, advertisement in hand, they are either told that the advertised special is no longer available or are shown an obviously defective piece of merchandise and actively discouraged from its purchase. The salesperson then attempts to "switch" consumers by interesting them in the $300 vacuum cleaner that the whole scheme was designed to promote.

The "bait-and-switch" character of anticrime crusades occurs in the contrast between the kind of crime that is featured in the appeals to "get tough" and the type of offender who is usually on the receiving end of the more severe sanctions. The "bait" for anticrime crusades is citizen fear of violent crime. Willie Horton is the poster boy in the usual law and order campaign. But the number of convicted violent predators who are not already sent to prison is rather small. In the language of "bait-and-switch" merchandising, the advertised special is unavailable when the customer arrives at the store. The only available targets for escalation in imprisonment policy are the marginal offenders and offense categories. If an increase in severity is to be accomplished, the target of the policy must be "switched." Nonviolent offenders go to prison and citizens wonder why rates of violence continue to increase. [. . .]

NEW PERSPECTIVES ON AFRICAN-AMERICAN VIOLENCE

No aspect of the demography of violence in the United States is more dramatic than the concentration of lethal violence among African-American males. While the statistics on the distribution of violence are clear, however, the significance of those patterns is anything but self-evident.

Every aspect of serious violence in the United States is linked with statistical and policy questions involving race. And very few of the important aspects of race relations are not connected to concerns about violence: its incidence, its consequences, and attitudes toward it. One cannot be concerned about relations between blacks and whites in the United States without also being concerned about African-American violence. One cannot be seriously concerned about violence in the United States without encountering a large number of questions that arise because of the substantial share of American violence that is black violence. [. . .]

Two false inferences

One helpful way to organize a review of the data about violence, race, and crime is to discuss two propositions that are disproved by the existing data about violence among African-Americans:

1 that black violence is just a part of a general tendency for blacks to commit large numbers of criminal offenses, both violent and nonviolent; and
2 that rates of violence in the United States are disproportionately higher than those of other industrial countries only because of the high rates of violence among African-Americans.

Not a crime problem

Just as the high rates of American violence are falsely assumed to be a byproduct of high rates of American crime, there is also a common but false assumption that high rates of African-American violence are simply a byproduct of high crime rates among African-Americans.

Morris and Tonry, for example, write of the "disproportionate black criminality" that is represented by "the black contribution to the totality of crime." And they list the serious crimes in respect of which blacks "are overrepresented" as "rape and robbery, murder and mayhem, burglary and battery" (Morris and Tonry 1984:281–284). Similarly, Wilson and Herrnstein say that "even allowing for the existence of discrimination in the criminal justice system the higher rates of crime among black Americans cannot be denied." In relation to "the higher average crime rates of blacks," they say that "the preponderance of evidence – arrest data, victim surveys, and homicide statistics – confirms the higher rate of most kinds of common crimes among blacks than among whites" (Wilson and Herrnstein 1985:461, 466).

Once black violence is seen as simply a part of "the black contribution to the totality of crime," it is also seen as explicable in the same way as crime in general is explained. Thus, according to Morris and Tonry, the fact that blacks "disproportionately amass serious criminal records" can be accounted for in terms of such things as the "agglomeration of social disadvantages that beset the black areas" and "the long history of cultural adversity and its impact on the black family." In short, "disproportionate black criminality . . . results from the social history of blacks in America" (Morris and Tonry 1984:284).

By contrast, Wilson and Herrnstein list "four major theories of black crime" to explain the "higher black crime rates." They do not endorse any particular theory but say that it is "probably true to say that each theory is partially correct." The four theories are: (1) "there are important constitutional factors at work"; (2) "net economic disadvantage is a cause"; (3) "there is a pattern of cultural pathology rooted in familial experiences"; and (4) "black rage at accumulated injustice is the cause of black crime." There are, they say, "facts and arguments that support each of [these] theories of black crime, but there is not enough systematic evidence to evaluate their claims carefully" (Wilson and Herrnstein 1985:485–486).

What is significant here is not that the explanations suggested by Morris and Tonry and Wilson and Herrnstein are different from each other. It is rather the fact that in both cases those different explanations are advanced as dealing with the same unitary phenomenon. In both cases, they offer what Wilson and Herrnstein call "theories of black crime" (Wilson and Herrnstein 1985:468) to explain "the higher average crime rates of blacks" (Wilson and Herrnstein 1985:461), or "disproportionate black criminality" (Morris and Tonry 1984:281).

John DiIulio of Princeton has produced the most flamboyant compound generalization in this regard – "America does not have a crime problem; inner city America does" – at once defining crime as the problem and the inner city as its sole location (DiIulio 1994:3).

The evidence presented in support of such unitary views of black crime is that the arrest rates of black men for index crimes are higher than the rates of arrest of white men for the same offenses. But a careful examination of the gross aggregate arrest rates that are usually cited suggests that the degree to which black arrest rates exceed those of whites is anything but a unitary phenomenon. Figure 6.2 . . . compares arrest rates for black males with rates for white males for the seven index offenses in the United States in 1992. Since the black–white ratios are the subject of analysis, the black arrest rate is expressed as a whole number that is produced when the white rate of arrest for each offense is restated as 100.

The concentration of arrests among black offenders across the seven index felonies is similar in only one respect: the arrest rates for blacks exceed the arrest rates for whites for all index offenses. But the variation by type of crime in black–white arrest ratios is both substantial and patterned. Arrest rates for burglary and theft are almost three times as high for black men as for white men, while the black arrest rate is more than five times the white rate for rape, more than eight times as large as the white rate for homicide and almost eleven times the white rate for robbery.

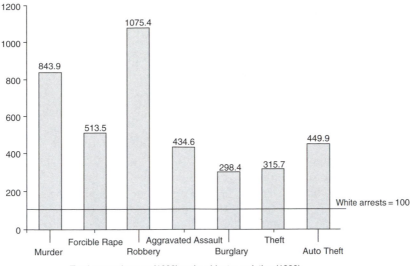

Total arrests by race (1992) and resident population (1990)

Figure 6.2 Comparison of black and white arrest rates

Sources: U.S. Department of Commerce, Bureau of the Census, 1990 (resident population); U.S. Department of Justice, Federal Bureau of Investigation, 1992 (race).

The difference between the concentration ratio for burglary and that for robbery is larger than the difference between the black rates of arrest and white rates of arrest for burglary.

The notable pattern in Figure 6.2 is that the highest ratios of black-to-white arrest are found for violent offenses and not property offenses. Of the four offenses of violence, three of them report a higher concentration among blacks by far than any of the index property offenses. The only overlap between violent and nonviolent offenses occurs because the racial concentration for aggravated assault arrests is slightly lower than the racial concentration for one of the three nonviolent offenses: automobile theft.

Even this is a false impression because the most dangerous forms of assault are more concentrated among black offenders than assaults generally. The ratio of black-to-white arrest rates for the three property offenses is 3.5 to 1, showing that white men are less than one-third as likely to be arrested for property offenses as black men. But the average concentration of violence arrests among black offenders is more than twice as high as the concentration in nonviolent offenses. Blacks are more than seven times as likely as whites to be arrested for offenses of violence.

Yet even this 7-to-1 ratio understates the extent of black offenses of violence. The aggregate national arrest picture tells us that blacks are slightly more than four times as likely as whites to be arrested for serious assault, but more than eight times as likely to be arrested for killing someone. One implication of these contrasting rate's: the extent to which police-reported attacks by blacks have a much higher death rate than assaults, known to the police, by white offenders.

For every fatal attack that results in a black arrest, sixteen nonfatal attacks produce arrests of black suspects. The rate for whites is twice as high, so that there are thirty-one arrests for nonfatal assault for every arrest of a white for criminal homicide. The assaults reported in Figure 6.2 for black offenders are twice as likely to result in a killing as an assault attributed by the police to white offenders. This means that the rate of life-threatening assaults among blacks is probably closer to the 8-to-1 homicide ratio than to the 4-to-1 assault ratio. It also means that for offenses with a high death rate, the concentration among black males for arrest is probably about three times greater than the differential rate of commission of property offenses. The concentration of serious violence among blacks is so much greater than the concentration of other criminal offenses that an observer is on notice that two different patterns are operative.

One more arithmetic exercise can demonstrate how different the distribution of serious violence among blacks is from the pattern of nonviolent criminal offenses. If we assume that white rates of commission of all offenses remain stable at 1992 levels, what would be the impact if black rates of homicide were concentrated at the same level that Figure 6.2 reports for burglary arrests? Under these conditions the black arrest rate for homicide and presumably also the black offense rate would be 2.98 times the white rate rather than 8.44 times the white rate. At 2.98 times the white rate, the homicide rate for blacks in the United States would be 65 percent less than the current homicide rate and the total homicide rate in the United States would be reduced by 35 percent.

A similar numerical thought experiment can be performed by comparing the racial concentration of arrest for robbery and burglary. If rates of white arrests were stable and the concentration of robbery arrests among blacks was 2.98 times the white rate, as was the case in respect of burglary, the total robbery rate among blacks would fall by 72 percent, and the total robbery rate in the United States would fall by 44 percent. So the concentrations of violent offenses among blacks are much larger than the concentration of criminal offenses generally. If robbery and homicide were not more concentrated among black offenders than property offenses, the United States would be a much safer country. [. . .]

Each of the statistical comparisons just mentioned illustrates a significant impediment to looking for a single cause for black crime and violence. The different robbery and burglary arrest patterns found for whites and blacks signal that no unitary theory of crime causation can explain the significant difference in choice between violent and nonviolent means of stealing property. The extraordinary difference in homicide offenses – most of them unrelated to criminal offenses other than assault – are a warning that no plausible explanation of black homicide will be principally concerned with explaining black participation in crime. It is far more likely that the influences that generate grossly disproportionate African-American homicide rates are broadly present in the social structure and behavior of the communities where rates are high. It is the propensity to resolve conflict with maximum personal force rather than any specific commitment to crime that is the precursor to high rates of conflict-motivated homicide.

There are two significant caveats that must be added to our previous remarks when using data on arrests by race to show that violence is not solely a crime problem. First, there is no reason to believe that all the different varieties of violent crime have either the same causes or the same concentrations among blacks. Thus, because it can be demonstrated that all kinds of violent crime have higher concentrations among blacks than among whites, this does not mean that the same factors that produce the difference in one type of violent crime operate with the same intensity and effect for other violent crimes. If lumping together violent and nonviolent offenses to support theories of black crime is a demonstrable aggregation error, that should alert us to the likelihood that lumping together all kinds of violent offenses may also be a fundamental mistake.

To return to the data presented in Figure 6.2, arrests for rape in the Federal Bureau of Investigation statistics are about half as concentrated among black offenders as arrests for robbery. Just because robbery and rape are two subcategories of violent crime, that provides no basis for concluding that rape behavior by African-American offenders should be explained in the same way as robbery behavior by African-American offenders. While rape arrests are more concentrated among blacks than burglary arrests, the concentration noted for rape is closer to that found in burglary than to that found in robbery. So discovering one aggregation error is a poor excuse for spawning a somewhat narrower generalization that might still involve attempting to put very different kinds of eggs into the same basket.

The second caveat that is required for a balanced assessment of racial concentrations in arrest statistics is that race is being used as what scientists call a "marker" for the discussion of differences rather than as an explanation. Substantial differences between races in violence as well as significant differences in pattern by race may tell us a great deal about what sorts of phenomena should be studied. But such differences tell us nothing about what might explain the significant differences in pattern that we observe. We have at best a factor that predicts significant differences in violence but that can explain none of them.

Not a black problem

Whatever the data that we have just reviewed may mean, there is one thing that they do not mean: It is beyond foolishness to regard American violence as solely, or mainly, or even distinctively a black problem. Large segments of the black community in the United States are located in those areas of the social distribution where one would expect a generally higher American propensity to violence to be most concentrated. We will show that the tendencies toward lethal violence documented in the previous section are, in the words of H. Rap Brown's celebrated cliché, "as American as apple pie."

Some observers of crime statistics greet the data showing the extraordinary concentration of violent offenses among African-American males as a definitive exoneration of the general American culture, society, and government from responsibility for the higher overall rates of violent offenses in the United States (see Bonger 1943; Wolfgang and Cohen 1970). What those data are taken to prove is that violence is a black problem. And if violence in the United States can be characterized as a black problem, then perhaps it should not be regarded as a "white" problem. Furthermore, perhaps the general social environment of the country should be regarded as bearing little or even no responsibility for the death rate from violence. Professor DiIulio's refrain bears emphasis in this regard: "America does not have a crime problem; inner city America does." Prior to his 1994 article, these sentiments had never been explicitly stated as a theory in academic criminology or policy analysis. But they constitute a common if not omnipresent subtext in policy discussion and in the opinions held by some governing elites and by segments of the general public.

The only problem with this particular hypothesis is that it is false, contradicted both by the available statistics and by elementary analytic techniques. Statistical analysis should begin with the reported rates of criminal homicide, which can be used both because homicide is the most serious violent crime and because those rates are good indices of the total rate of life-threatening violence. . . . World Health Organization rates of reported homicide in the United States . . . [show] [t]he U.S. homicide rate . . . [to be] 9.4 per 100,000. Fifty-five percent of the 1992 homicide arrests in the United States were of blacks. Assuming that the 55 percent arrest figures means that black offenders were responsible for a similar percentage of homicide would imply a homicide offense rate for non-African-Americans of 4.8 per 100,000. This would be an extremely misleading statistic to use in international comparisons. The national experience of most other countries would benefit greatly if they could exclude their identifiable highest-risk subpopulations from any comparison.

But even with the cosmetic removal of all homicides attributable to black offenders, the U.S. homicide rate would still be a statistical "outlier," far beyond the experience of other industrial democracies [see Figure 6.3]. The "blacks excluded" estimated homicide rate of 4.8 for the United States is well over three times the average homicide rate of the other six [G7 industrial leadership] nations and twice as high as the rate for the second highest nation, Italy.

The concentration of robbery in the United States would be much higher than other Western countries in 1992 if we assumed that black offenders were responsible for the same percentage of robbery offenses as they are of robbery arrests and then erased every robbery in the United States attributable to black offenders. Performing that operation on the data . . ., blacks-excluded robbery in Los Angeles would still be three times the total robbery rates in Sydney, Australia. So the distinctive tendency of Los Angeles

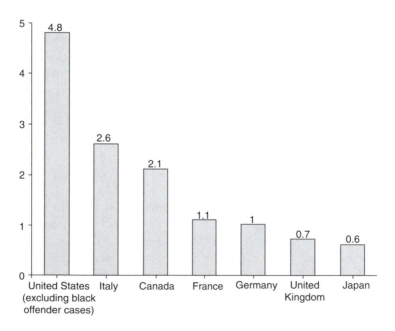

Figure 6.3 Homicide rates (per 100,000) for the United States (excluding black offender cases) and G7 countries, 1990

Source: World Health Organization 1990.

offenders to favor robbery over burglary when compared with offenders in other countries is pronounced for white offenders as well as for blacks.

So, the total exclusion of offenses attributed to blacks would not alter the distinctive position of the United States as an industrial democracy with extraordinarily high rates of high-lethality violence. But it must also be pointed out that "nonblack" rates of homicide and robbery are misleading and nonsensical. The truncation of one group in a national population in an international comparison produces a mythical part-country that cannot meaningfully be compared with real groups and nations. There is no more sense in removing an integrated group from a population in this way than one could amputate a person's leg and then compare that mutilated organism with another whole person.

In this connection, it is important to remember the distinction between factors that predict the distribution of violence in a social unit and the factors that explain levels of violence. . . . [R]ace is like gender and age, a factor that tells us what groups in society will experience higher-than-average rates of violence. That does not imply that increasing the portion of African-Americans in the population would have any impact on rates of violence [see Zimring and Hawkins, *Crime is Not the Problem: Lethal Violence in America*, pp. 217–18]. [. . .]

It will be helpful to contrast two different assumptions that can be made about violent acts committed by blacks in the United States. One assumption is that of social independence, that is, that black violence is an outgrowth of generative processes that have nothing to do with the conditions of American life. This assumption hypothesizes a propensity on the part of blacks for violent attacks, which is both innate and immutable, and for that reason should not be expected to vary much over time or with changing social conditions.

There is no evidence that we know of to support this assumption. Moreover, there is much that contradicts it in the variable nature of both black and white violence in the United States since the midcentury. But this hypothesis of an innate and immutable black propensity for violence is worth mentioning because it describes the only set of circumstances in which a separate "nonblack" rate of American violence would make sense as an analytic tool.

The contrasting and, we believe, correct assumption is that rates of violence among racial and social subpopulations, black and white, are variable over time and with changed circumstances because they grow out of the social experience of American life. In these conditions, the rates of violence experienced by various subpopulations will, in large part, be determined by their location in the American social distribution.

On this assumption, the particular rates of violence of subgroups constitute a dependent variable. And the major social processes they depend on are generated by the social conditions of American urban life. Lethal violence must be regarded as an American problem in this essential respect.

Five-city analysis

Part of the contrast between black and nonblack patterns in the national-level statistics on violence is an artifact of the fact that blacks and whites reside in different types of population areas, and there are substantial variations in standards of reporting and classifying crime in different parts of the country. Black population is concentrated in large urban areas in the

United States. Because the nonblack category is so broad, it represents an aggregation of all community types in the United States. So differences between city populations and populations that reside in suburbs, small towns, and other areas may masquerade as differences between blacks and whites.

To find out how much of the race differences noted in the previous section might stem from different patterns of residence, we examined arrests by race in five U.S. cities: New York City, Los Angeles, Chicago, Houston, and Dallas. . . . When only city populations are analyzed, the contrast between African-American and white arrests changes in two respects.

First, the contrast between assault-to-homicide ratios that existed at the national level all but disappears. The fact that whites have nearly twice as many assault arrests for every homicide arrest as blacks is almost completely the result of policies of police departments outside of cities. In the five-city sample, the eighteen assault arrests per homicide arrest for blacks was 20 percent greater than the 15-to-1 ratio for whites. Eighty percent of the differences between the races in the national statistics disappear when the comparison involves only city populations.

The second substantial finding of the study was that the contrast between black and nonblack violence arrest rates shrinks when the comparison is restricted to city dwellers. While the robbery arrest rate for African-Americans is more than ten times that of whites at the national level, the difference is reduced to 6 to 1 in the five-city comparison. For homicide, the concentration among blacks is cut almost in half, from eight times the non-black rate at the national level to four times the nonblack arrest rate at the city level. So a major element in the explanation of the larger concentration of violence among African-Americans is the fact that they more often reside in cities where violent crime rates are high generally. Here is a concrete demonstration of how the general social structure helps to account for what appears as differences between racial groups. [. . .]

References

Bonger, W. A. 1943. *Race and Crime*. Trans. Margaret M. Hordk, New York: Columbia University Press.

DiIulio, John. 1994. "The Question of Black Crime." *The Public Interest*, Fall, p. 3.

Morris, Norval, and Michael H. Tonry. 1984. "Black Crime, Black Victims." In *The Pursuit of Criminal Justice*, ed. Gordon Hawkins and Franklin E. Zimring. Chicago: University of Chicago Press.

van Dijk, Jan, and Pat Mayhew. 1993. "Criminal Victimization in the Industrialized World: Key Findings of the 1989 and 1992 International Crime Surveys." In *Understanding Crime: Experiences of Crime and Crime Control*, ed. Anna Alvazzi del Frate, Ugljesa Zvekic, and Jan van Dijk. Rome: United Nations Interregional Crime and Justice Research Institute.

Wilson, James Q., and Richard J. Herrnstein. 1985. *Crime and Human Nature*. New York: Simon and Schuster.

Wolfgang, Marvin E., and Bernard Cohen. 1970. *Crime and Race: Conceptions and Misconceptions*. New York: Institute of Human Relations Press, American Jewish Committee.

Chapter 7

Scott Christianson

WITH LIBERTY FOR SOME
500 years of imprisonment in America

From: Scott Christianson (1998), excerpts from *With Liberty for Some: 500 Years of Imprisonment in America*, Boston: Northeastern University Press, pp. 275–305.

PRISON EXPANSION

DESPITE THE RISING CRIME rates and all the tough talk about fighting crime, during the years from 1962 to 1968 the American prison population had actually declined, by 14.3 percent, underscoring a fact generally understood more by criminologists than the general public: that rates of incarceration are not necessarily related to, or a product of, official crime rates. In 1973 or so, changes began to occur. Amidst the abandonment of the Vietnam War, worsening economic conditions, political turmoil, increased federal funding for law enforcement, and a general shift toward harsher criminal justice policies, the numbers of persons in state and federal correctional institutions started climbing sharply.

This rapid swelling occurred despite some contrary developments: the civil rights movements; a continued trend in favor of deinstitutionalization, particularly for mental patients, the developmentally disabled, and juvenile offenders; some major legal victories of the prisoners' rights movement; and decriminalization of or de-emphasis upon some victimless crimes like prostitution, public intoxication, and gambling. It also happened despite the concerted actions of several organizations that had formally begun to seek a halt to expansion of the prison system they said had failed. The National Council on Criminal and Delinquency, a nationwide civic body, and the National Commission on Criminal Justice Standards and Goals, a blue-ribbon presidential panel, argued against the construction of any new correctional facilities until alternatives to incarceration were thoroughly explored. In 1974, with support from the Unitarian Universalist Service Committee, S. Brian Willson, a Vietnam veteran, antiwar activist, and attorney, founded the National Moratorium on Prison Construction, a not-for-profit organization dedicated to stopping prison growth. Grassroots efforts to develop community-based alternatives to incarceration also sprang up around the country, but to little avail. A few reformers had even begun to talk about prison abolition. [. . .]

State and local governments set aside plans to close old and outmoded correctional facilities and rushed instead to build additional prisons and jails. From December 31, 1971, to December 31, 1978, the U.S. prison population increased by 64 percent. From December 31, 1973, to year's end in 1976, it swelled from 204,000 to nearly 281,000. By December 31, 1983, the count of inmates in custody had reached 420,000.

In large measure, the increased number of prisoners was a natural by-product of the war on crime that had been geared up in the 1960s and running ever since. One key part of the national crime control apparatus – the federal Law Enforcement Assistance Administration (LEAA) – pumped hundreds of millions of dollars into domestic crime fighting from the late 1960s until the late 1970s. Its funding of more police, prosecutors, courts, and prisons ensured that there were more, not less, reported crimes and arrests and convictions and prisoners. In October 1970 there were 701,767 criminal justice employees, 146,273 of them in corrections and 507,877 police. By October 1978 there were 1,123,552 employees, 261,385 in corrections and 622,544 police; in October 1983, 1,270,342 employees, 298,722 in corrections and 723,923 police. Criminal justice agencies were also better equipped and trained to go after criminals than ever before.

Even though bolstered by increased assistance to law enforcement, crime fighting was hampered by the insufficient attention paid to the underlying social and economic problems that led to crime and imprisonment in the first place, and overall the problem got worse. Arrests, indictments, and convictions rose to new levels. Prison sentences were made longer. Commitments of persons to prison increased. Support for probation and parole sagged under the weight of rising caseloads. The use of the death penalty was reinstated after a moratorium of several years. Direct corrections expenditures rose from $2.3 billion in 1971 to $5.5 billion in 1978, then to $9.8 billion in 1983, and $16 billion in 1990. But like Vietnam, the war on crime failed to be won. Instead of deterring crime and selectively incapacitating criminals, the nation's greater use of imprisonment and other get-tough responses was accompanied throughout the 1970s and 1980s by even more murders, rapes, robberies, and other serious crimes. This in turn was followed by redoubled calls to "crack down" on criminals.

Through it all, most of the statistics coming out of Washington masked how prison was really being used. Once again, the upsurge was primarily racial. In 1960 about 39 percent of inmates incarcerated in American state prisons were reported as "nonwhite"; by 1974, the percentage had increased to 47 percent "black" and 2 percent "other" nonwhite races. From 1973 to 1979 the incarceration rate for whites in the fifty states and the District of Columbia rose from 46.3 to 65.1 per 100,000. However, the black incarceration rate skyrocketed from 368 to 544 – becoming more than nine times greater than the level for whites. Researchers began to report finding a huge and growing racial gap in the imprisonment rates of every region and state. There was no exception: North, South, East, and West, blacks were many times more likely than whites to be arrested, jailed, convicted, and imprisoned. Some of the jurisdictions with the greatest black incarceration rates tended to be small states with relatively few African Americans in the general population, while those with the highest proportion of black residents tended to have among the lowest rates of African-American imprisonment. Yet, notwithstanding any statistical anomalies, blacks were disproportionately imprisoned in every state, and the disparity was widening fast.

During the span from 1970 to 1990, the overall rate of imprisonment tripled, reaching 455 per 100,000 – the highest level in history to that point. Prison populations continued to grow at record levels, fueled by colossal prison construction that was planned to accommodate the projected waves of blacks and other persons of color who were drowning in a sea of urban cases that were flooding the criminal courts.

By 1990, although blacks comprised only 12 percent of the U.S. population, they accounted for more than 44 percent of those incarcerated in local, state, and federal prisons. Meanwhile, the incarceration rate for black males in the United States grew to 3,370 per 100,000. Among Hispanics, 10.4 percent of the males in the prison-prone age group (20 to 29) were under criminal justice control. On June 30, 1994, according to the United States Department of Justice annual survey, nearly 7 percent of all black men nationwide were in prison or jail, compared to less than 1 percent of white men, marking the first time that the number of black inmates surpassed that of whites.

On a given day that year, nearly one out of every four young African-American men in New York State was under the control of the criminal justice system. That was twice the number of full-time black male college enrollees in the state. Eleven percent of New York's black men between 20 and 29 years of age were in prison or jail. From 1955 to 1992, the white share of the New York State prison population had plummeted from about 50.9 percent to less than 16 percent.

One of the implications of these statistics is that a disproportionately large share of African-American men are disenfranchised as a result of their felony conviction and imprisonment, because the laws in thirteen of the most populous states strip convicted felons of the right to vote, and incarcerated persons are also universally prevented from voting.

Nowhere was the prison system more immense than in California, the former Golden State and one-time land of milk and honey. On December 31, 1977, the prison population there had numbered 19,623, the lowest year-end figure since 1959. But in 1978 the state adopted tough new determinate sentencing laws and the prison admission rate began to increase. By the end of 1979 the number of inmates in custody had risen to 22,500. When graphed on a chart, the next several years looked like a missile launched into outer space. During the 1980s, California carried out what one senator called "the largest prison construction program ever attempted by a government entity," a $6.2 billion expansion. By 1991 it had far and away the most prisoners of any state, with more than 97,000 inmates – 27,000 more than the population of its capital, Sacramento, and more prisoners than in all of western and central Europe. The number of employees of the department of corrections had grown to more than 32,000. Meanwhile, the operational cost of California's prison system, which had been $826 million in fiscal year 1977–78, had ballooned to $2.3 billion.

Nevertheless, in 1991, there was still no end in sight. Even with a massive $3.2 billion capital, construction effort under way, the prison system was packed to 168 percent of its design capacity, and the state was committed to an additional $5.22 billion expansion program just to avoid rising above 130 percent of capacity over the next three years. A blue-ribbon panel projected a population of 136,640 state prisoners in 1994, rising to 173,000 in 1996, as well as 93,003 jail inmates and more than 19,500 inmates in juvenile facilities, for a total of more than 249,000 inmates expected in 1994, when the maintenance cost was expected to reach $4 billion. (As it turned out, the number of prisoners in custody on January 14, 1996, was 135,249.) Yet despite all of the prison expansion, crime in California did not significantly decrease during this period.

The typical California inmate was not a hardened violent predator, but a young, nonviolent, drug-addicted, semi-literate, unemployed minority male. By 1989, one of every three black men between the ages of 20 and 29 in California was either in jail or on probation or parole; the comparable figure for white men that age was one in every nineteen. Five years later, 40 percent of the state's black men in their twenties were under correctional supervision, in contrast to 5 percent of the whites and 11 percent of the Hispanics.

Even as California struggled to stave off fiscal crisis, and some public figures suggested developing cheaper alternatives to incarceration, the ruling powers would not waver from their lock-em-up course. Passage of the "three strikes" law mandated life prison terms for repeat offenders, even the relatively nonviolent. In one notorious case, a twenty-seven-year-old with two prior robbery convictions was sentenced to twenty-five years to life for stealing a slice of pizza. One study of a thousand criminal cases in Los Angeles found that blacks were charged under the new law at seventeen times the rate of whites.

California was not alone in its enormous prison growth. Texas and Florida were not far behind, and several other states expanded their use of imprisonment even more dramatically during the same period. In fact, in 1990 California still ranked only sixteenth among the states in its rate of imprisonment per 100,000 of the population, and twenty-fifth in its proportion of the population under some form of correctional supervision. The number of inmates in the federal prison system grew from 24,000 in 1980 to 95,000 in 1994.

In the 1990s, most American prison inmates were serving time for drug crimes or were known to have histories of serious drug abuse. Bolstered drug sanctions were a major factor responsible for the ongoing record increase of prisoners. In 1985, 38 percent of federal inmates were sentenced for drug offenses. This was up to 58 percent by mid-1991, and reached 62 percent in 1994, according to the Federal Bureau of Prisons. Among state inmates the comparable numbers were 9 percent in 1986 and 21 percent in mid-1991.

In 1994, 58 percent of the federal prisoners were drug offenders, meaning simply that they were serving sentences for drug-related crimes. Forty-two percent of these were serving time for drug trafficking. In state correctional facilities, 21 percent of the inmates were serving time for drug offenses, 13 percent of them for drug trafficking. (Female prisoners were actually more likely to be serving time for drugs: in federal prisons, it was 66 percent of the women, compared to 57 percent of the men; in state facilities, 33 percent of the women and 21 percent of the men were serving time for drug crimes.) According to the 1994 national survey, 42 percent of the federal prisoners and 62 percent of the state prisoners had reported using drugs regularly at some time during their lives. These numbers were generally recognized as being low, and other indications placed the level much higher. Also according to the prisoners' self-reported data, federal inmates were half as likely as state inmates to have been under the influence of drugs or alcohol at the time of their arrest for the crime for which they were incarcerated. For alcohol specifically, 11 percent of the federal inmates and 32 percent of the state prisoners said they had been drinking at the time of their arrest. But many experts believed these numbers too probably under-represented the extent of prior use by prison inmates.

By the late 1980s and the 1990s, many prison inmates were longtime drug addicts and/or alcoholics, some of them having returned to prison after only a brief stint on the streets, followed by a very recent and short span of enforced sobriety (possibly including detoxification) in jail. Under the laws in force in many states, they were often sentenced much more severely as repeat offenders, and in some cases their involvement with illegal drugs even had resulted in life without parole. Drugs kept the revolving door moving briskly, filling the prisons.

By 1991 the United States had more than a million persons behind bars and an incarceration rate of 426 persons per 100,000, the highest rate of imprisonment of any nation in the world. South Africa ranked second with 333, and the Soviet Union was third at 268 per 100,000. The European nations generally ranged from 35 to 120 per 100,000, compared to those of 21 to 140 in Asia. One of the starkest indications of the extent to which imprisonment in the United States had become a racial phenomenon was evident in the fact that its incarceration rate for black males was 3,109 – more than 4.2 times higher than South Africa's before the fall of apartheid. By 1993, after the dissolution of the Soviet Union, Russia reported 558 prisoners per 100,000, and the United States placed second at 519. Canada, meanwhile, had 116; Mexico, 97; England and Wales, 93; Germany, 80; and Japan, 36.

Still, the number of inmates in federal and state correctional facilities continued to grow, reaching a record high of 1.1 million on June 30, 1995, according to the Bureau of Justice Statistics of the U.S. Department of Justice. The census reflected an increase of 89,404, or about 8.8 percent, during the last twelve months, which was the largest one-year growth ever recorded in the United States, and the equivalent of an additional 1,719 new prison beds every week. Females recorded a greater increase (11.4 percent) than did males (8.7 percent). The rate of total growth exceeded ten percent in twenty-three states; it was greatest in Texas (nearly 27 percent), followed by North Carolina (18 percent). The states with the greatest numbers of prison inmates were California (131,342), Texas (127,092), and New York (68,526). The federal prison system held 99,466 inmates on June 30. About 6.3 percent of the nation's total in custody, or 69,028, were women. The one-day count of prisoners in custody at the end of 1994 translated to an incarceration rate of about 403 per 100,000 of the U.S. general population. The highest rates were in the District of Columbia (1,722), Texas (859), and Louisiana (573). The lowest rates were reported in North Dakota (90), Minnesota (103), and Maine (112).

From 1990 to 1995 the nation built 168 state and 45 federal prisons, increasing the number of such institutions to 1,500; the number of prison beds rose by 41 percent to 976,000. During the same period, the prison incarceration rate climbed from 293 to more than 400 per every 100,000 Americans, and by 1996 it was up to 427. Such numbers did not include 3,300 local jails and county or municipal detention centers. By 1991, the jails alone had held 426,479 people, according to the Bureau of Justice Statistics.

Blacks continued to be incarcerated at an increasingly higher rate than whites. In fact, by mid-1995 the incarceration rate for African-American men was almost eight times higher than for white men, and the comparable rate for African-American women was seven times higher. From 1980 through 1994, the total number of persons incarcerated in federal and state prisons and local jails nearly tripled. In other words, four-score and thirty-five years after Lincoln's great Emancipation, and more than two hundred years after the Declaration of Independence, the United States seemed to be heading full circle: it was moving, as a national commission had warned after the Watts riot of 1965, "toward two societies, one black, one white – separate and unequal." This was reflected most graphically in the statistics showing who was in prison and who was not, and who was or was not benefitting from the burgeoning prison system. But that was only part of the alarming picture that was emerging.

THE PRISON BUSINESS

By the mid-1990s, the American penal system consisted of more than five thousand correctional institutions scattered in all the states, including more than thirty-three hundred local jails or holding pens. There was a lockup of some sort in virtually every city, and hundreds more state and federal prisons stood guard far outside the cities in hard-nosed prison towns like Dannemora and Stateville and Chino, dotting the countryside like the new red barns of their time. Prisons seemed to be everywhere, but nobody seemed to notice.

It used to be that localities opposed the siting of a correctional facility within their limits, due to strong protests from homeowners – the NIMBY (or not-in-my-back-yard) phenomenon. But by the late 1980s, in harder economic times, some places, particularly sparsely populated locales, switched to lobbying to get a prospective new prison, thereby converting to a sort of PIMBY (please-in-my-back-yard) movement. "We've been trying to get a prison built here for years," a supervisor of one depressed milltown in upstate New York explained. "It would bring a lot of jobs, and that would be pretty nice for the town."

In Texas, the competition during the early 1990s grew so fierce that some communities offered free country club memberships and other perks to prison officials as an incentive to get them to make the right siting decision. Amused journalists referred to the competitions as "prison derbies." In fact, some Texas towns supported their own, independently financed jail-construction projects in the expectation that any excess space they did not use could be leased out to other jurisdictions at a profit, turning imprisonment into a real moneymaker. . . . For more and more rural communities, prison increasingly had become, by default, both the only show in town and the primary engine of economic development. Prisons were one of the few projects in rural areas that could attract major state investment.

Local representatives of prison towns joined with labor unions and anybody else as staunch opponents of efforts to downsize or close down existing institutions, so much so that it became almost inconceivable for them to think in terms of deinstitutionalization or decarceration. Even the prospect of lowering prison sentences or devising alternative approaches to fighting crime was enough to threaten many prison supporters. On the contrary, they favored getting even "tougher." Instead of gaining expansion of their existing institution, several prison towns in New York State actually lobbied for and obtained additional prisons.

Given their location, prisons often were an area's largest local employer, and consequently the regional economy tended to become inextricably prison based. With little else to turn to, people said they wanted the jobs, the stimulus to the local economy, that prisons offered. Residents were aware that prisons had historically provided jobs of long duration, which seemed to be inflation proof and recession proof, making the institution one of the few enterprises known to humankind that thrived even more in bad times than in good ones. By deciding to build a correctional facility at a particular location, a state committed itself to massive acquisition and initial construction costs, and to very substantial spending over many decades.

In 1994 more than six hundred thousand persons worked for corrections departments alone — a number that did not count many sheriffs' departments and other prison employers — and the total number of others who derived their livelihood from prisons had not been estimated.

Prison employment was the ultimate in job security. There was no danger that the plant would be moved to Mexico, no threat that the industry would become obsolete. Nobody had yet figured out any feasible alternate use or after use for prisons or jails. And there was no incentive to try. In some places, the leading local officials were themselves present or former prison employees or relatives of persons whose livelihood wholly depended on the prison. In such communities, prisoners' families, friends, or supporters were not welcome to linger when they visited or encouraged to take up residence in order to be closer to their loved ones. Programs to help prisoners make the transition from the institution to the community were firmly discouraged. And anything resembling prison reform was considered a dirty word.

Prison expansion has also been aided and abetted by the growth and increasing power of correction officer labor unions. Like their predecessors in criminal justice — the police benevolent associations — these organizations have spearheaded effective campaigns for more jobs and better working conditions, even in the face of budget cuts, layoffs, hiring freezes, and revenue drops in other government programs. Unlike prisoners, whose right to form labor unions has been denied by correction authorities and the Supreme Court, correction officers have generally been allowed to unionize since about the early 1970s. (The first guards' union appears to have been the Correction Officers' Benevolent Association in New York City. In the late 1950s, it became the first correctional employee organization to engage in formal collective bargaining, representing its members in negotiations over a wide range of issues.) [. . .]

Such public employee unions have typically used this power to bolster their employee rosters, substantially raise their members salaries, exercise a strong voice regarding working conditions, and affect efforts to control prison discipline. In some instance, they have gained the right to strike, or, lacking such authorization, they have nevertheless undertaken various actions such as lockdowns and wildcat strikes — sometimes violently. [. . .]

Starting in the 1980s, prison expansion has proved to be a bonanza for architects, builders, hardware companies, electronics firms, and other vendors who, like defense contractors, managed to pull down astronomical profits under the banner of public security. The state, which usually was under intense pressure to create new space to reduce prison overcrowding, sometimes offered construction contractors handsome bonuses for rapid completion, or its officials threw cost containment measures to the wind in order to get the job done in time to accommodate the lines of backlogged prisoners. Cost-plus arrangements were often in effect.

About $80,000 was needed to build a single maximum-security prison cell, more than it took to build a typical middle-class suburban house. An average-sized maximum-security prison generally ran from $30 to $75 million or so, more than what most medium-sized cities spent on education or transportation or recreation, much less the arts.

The financing of this construction was seldom debated or scrutinized. Under many financing arrangements, the costs were usually spread over twenty or thirty years — a whole generation. By the time the bonds were paid off, a single cell could have cost the taxpayers $1 million to create and maintain. Under one increasingly prevalent financing scheme, the state corrections system "leased" a new prison from a state authority (a quasi-private agency that was not as accountable to the public as a regular government agency), which issued bonds through such private underwriters as Merrill Lynch, Goldman Sachs, or Prudential, offering potential investors a much higher rate of return than would be paid by general-obligation bonds. [. . .]

Once a prison was finally built, it constantly required huge amounts of funding to keep running. In fact, operating costs usually exceeded building costs. Keeping a person in prison was more expensive than sending him or her to Harvard or Stanford, but not because the accommodations in a correctional facility were so comfortable or the quality of the services so good. In reality, prison food costs were extraordinarily low – generally less per person per day than the price of one Coke and Big Mac at McDonald's; access to hot water was restricted; expenditures for inmate clothing were minuscule compared even to those on public assistance; and the quality of prison medical care was generally rather low, contributing to interminable health problems, complaints, and litigation. (The director of Hawaii's prison medical services was that state's highest paid public official, but she resigned in protest in 1996 because correction officials persisted in allowing correction officers to override a doctor's prescribed course of medical treatment, because they concluded that security considerations should take precedence over medical ones.)

Nor were expensive rehabilitation programs the reason imprisonment cost so much. Prison education programs, vocational assistance programs, recreational programs, job training programs, drug treatment programs, therapy for sex offenders, and programs to address domestic violence and other problems usually accounted for an infinitesimal share of the corrections budget. Moreover, in many prisons, they hardly existed at all. The lack of adequate drug treatment in prison offered a case in point. After all, most persons were in prison for drug crimes.

By the mid-1990s, the presence of so many drug offenders had begun to pose some sticky political problems, not the least of which was that drug policies appeared to be significantly responsible for the growing racial imbalances within a good number of prison systems. Many critics blamed racial disparities in drug-law enforcement and sentencing. For example, the conviction rate for powdered cocaine was higher for whites and lower for minorities, but minorities were much more likely to be convicted for crack-related offenses, which carried penalties that were one hundred times greater than those involving equivalent amounts of powdered cocaine. In October 1995 convict protests over such policies contributed to disturbances at six federal prisons – at Talladega, Alabama; Memphis, Tennessee; Allenwood, Pennsylvania; El Reno, Oklahoma; Greenville, Illinois; and McKean, Pennsylvania. Some of the inmates involved were serving extraordinarily long prison terms because they had handled crystalline cocaine instead of powder.

According to a national survey, on September 30, 1992, there were an estimated 945,000 clients in specialty substance abuse treatment programs throughout the United States. This translated to about 432 clients per 100,000 of the general population aged twelve years or older. Of those receiving treatment, only 3.2 percent were getting it in correctional facilities. Of the rest, 53.6 percent of the clients were being treated in outpatient facilities, 15.6 percent in community mental health centers, 9.7 percent in general hospitals and veterans' hospitals, 6.8 percent in residential facilities, 2.8 percent in specialized hospitals, 2.4 percent in halfway houses, and 5.8 percent in other settings.

Oddly enough, although drug offenders had became much more prevalent as prison inmates since the late 1980s, in 1980 correctional facilities accounted for a higher share — 4.8 percent — of the drug and alcohol treatment clients, compared to only 3.2 percent twelve years later, meaning that prison-based drug treatment had fallen behind the expansion of other types of treatment. Moreover, according to other data available from federal surveys, on June 29, 1990, state and federal prisons reportedly had drug treatment programs with an estimated capacity of 132,000 persons, of which 100,200 slots were filled. Only 75 percent of the available treatment capacity in state and federal correctional facilities was being used; the rest was "vacant." [. . .]

PRISONS FOR PROFIT

After decades of relative stagnation, the use of prison labor during the 1980s and 1990s began to experience tremendous growth, reviving many age-old issues in prison reform — and prompting new legal concerns about how to safeguard against inevitable abuses. From 1980 to 1984, as the number of prisoners increased by 221 percent, the number of inmates employed in prison industries increased by 358 percent, and sales of prison-made goods grew from $392 million to $1.31 billion. According to the Correctional Industries Association, by the year 2000 fully 30 percent of state and federal inmates would be working, yielding nearly $9 billion in sales.

Such growth of prison industries and privatization appears to have occurred as a result of several factors: a punitive, "get-tougher" mood among many members of the general public; the need to reduce the skyrocketing costs of imprisonment without causing large-scale releases of inmates; the growth of privatization and anti-government and anti-union sentiments; and the appeal of prison as a source of cheap labor and economic development.

By the mid-1990s, prison management was increasingly being turned over to private companies, which operated to make profits and were not subject to the same scrutiny, standards, or controls as government agencies. Privatization, of course, was hardly new in American corrections, and many recent developments appeared to represent a step back into the nineteenth century, to a time before judicial intervention, legal empowerment of inmates, or laws governing the workplace. Convicts can still be, and many are, compelled to work without pay, and very few receive anything close to the minimum wage. Simultaneous with the recent revival of prison privatization, however, there were strong movements to allow prison authorities to govern prison management without interference from the courts or other government agencies. This important deregulation of prison industry, which might permit prison-made goods to be sold at home and abroad on the open market, for example, was occurring with very little public consideration of its implications.

Privatization was one of the stimuli affecting the changes in prison labor. From 1985 to 1995, there was a 500 percent increase in private prisons; 18 companies had rehabilitated 93 private prisons, creating space for some 51,000 prisoners. By 1996 at least 30 states had legalized the contracting out of prison labor to private companies. From 1995 to 2005, the number of prison beds under private management was expected to increase from 60,000 to more than 350,000. Although in its most extreme form privatization may entail having a private company build and operate a prison or jail on behalf of a government entity, other, lesser variants of privatization — although not as easily identified or quantified — commonly involve government contracts with private companies to furnish medical services, food services, bus transportation, program services, and other parts of the corrections operation.

By the mid-1990s, an estimated 10 percent of Arizona's inmates were working for private companies, earning less than the minimum wage, and performing all sorts of tasks, ranging from manual labor and raising hogs to testing human blood. At California's Folsom prison, inmates worked in recycling and made steel tanks for micro-breweries. Hawaiian prisoners packed Spalding golf balls; in Illinois, they sorted inventory for Toys R Us. Nevada convicts converted luxury automobiles into stretch limousines; Oregon's manufactured uniforms for McDonald's. The acting commissioner of New York's Department of Correctional Services announced plans to use inmate labor to help build several new state prisons – a move that until recently would have unleashed an overpowering torrent of opposition from organized labor, but which lately has hardly raised an eyebrow.

Some of the same American politicians who most decry the use of prison labor abroad as a violation of human rights are among the strongest supporters of expanded convict labor and penal servitude at home. Although Americans decried prison labor in China as a major human rights abuse, prison labor at home got less negative publicity, so few consumers were aware they were buying or using prison-made goods. By the mid-1990s, Tennessee inmates were producing $80 custom jeans for the Eddie Bauer company. Women prisoners in Washington State were turning out fashionable clothing under the labels of Eddie Bauer and Union Bay. Oregon, on the other hand, put a different twist on the prison labor scene when it introduced a hip new line of inmate-made casual wear, known as Prison Blues. Sold in five hundred stores nationwide, the line had its own home page on the Internet, where an image of a convict salesman slickly proclaimed, "Prison Blues are as good as you can get in a basic, five-pocket jean." (The program also marketed jackets, bags, and teeshirts.) Oregon Prison Industries, doing business as UniGroup, sold $4.5 million worth of clothes in 1995, thanks to aggressive marketing and a sophisticated appeal to yuppie consumers. The year before, Oregon passed the Inmate Work Act, amending its constitution to provide that if inmates did not "volunteer" to work they could lose good-time credit and other privileges and risk being sent to solitary confinement. Meanwhile, the Beaver State's inmates were paid 28 cents to $8 per hour, but 80 percent of the higher wage was withheld, so that some inmates generated $6,000 a year to defray the cost of their own incarceration. Following Oregon's lead, by 1996 the California corrections system was reportedly considering establishing its own line of casual wear for Japanese markets. It was to be called Gangsta Blues.

Federal Prison Industries, Inc. (UNICOR) produced an assortment of products, ranging from furniture and metal shelving to safety eyewear, which it, too, recently began to sell over its own home page on the Internet. Although UNICOR's primary mission was the productive employment of inmates, it claimed to offer quality products and services at competitive prices, as well as procurement with no bidding necessary.

The Thirteenth Amendment remained the legal cornerstone of prison-labor law, and the provision of the Constitution that set the fundamental parameters for prisoners' rights. For decades following its passage, organized labor gained many important legal restrictions on the use of convict labor, and some states even adopted provisions in their constitutions that limited the ability of prison industry to compete with free labor. The federal Hawes-Cooper Act enabled any state to prohibit within its borders the sale of any goods made in the prisons of another state – a right that most states quickly availed themselves of during the Great Depression. In 1935 the Ashurst-Sumners Act strengthened Hawes-Cooper by prohibiting the transportation of prison products to any state in violation of the laws of that state. Many states adopted laws prohibiting any prison-made goods from being sold on the open market, requiring that they be exclusively sold for state use. Federal law also forbade domestic commerce in prison-made goods unless workers were paid the "prevailing wage." But the law did not apply to exports.

By the early 1990s, however, some of these restrictions were beginning to be changed in ways that favored prison industry. In 1990 California voters approved Proposition 139, allowing the state to use prisoners to make goods that could be sold on the open market. Under the new system, private companies also received various incentives for engaging in prison industry. After 1991, with the state-use system no longer in force, these infant joint ventures with private industry made millions of dollars for private companies and the state's department of corrections.

A San Francisco-based company, DPAS, that opened a data processing operation at San Quentin prison was one such firm that was taking advantage of tax breaks offered under California's Joint Venture Program. Inmates assembled literature for Chevron, Bank of America, and Macy's, for which they received the federal minimum wage of $4.25, minus the 80 percent that was garnished to pay various state deductions. Meanwhile, DPAS received a 10 percent tax credit on the first $2,000 of each inmate's wages. [. . .]

Prison labor continued to be linked to union busting. In Ventura, California, inmates started handling telephone reservations for TWA, as part of the company's response to a strike. Workers at Michigan's Brill Manufacturing Company furniture plant lost their $5.65 per hour jobs to prison inmates who were paid 56¢ to 80¢ per hour without benefits. [. . .]

US VERSUS THEM

Prison benefits one group and one place at the expense of another, somewhat like the convict transportation system in the eighteenth century. Under the present arrangement, urban Democratic politicians generally support tougher sentencing laws to remove more criminals from the cities, while their Republican counterparts co-sponsor legislation to build new prisons in their own rural districts. That way, both interests are served. In one analysis of corrections policy in New York State, the assemblyman who chaired that house's Committee on Corrections found that Republican senate districts with relatively low population densities accounted for 89 percent of the prison employees, housed over 89 percent of the prisoners, and consumed over 89 percent of the state's prison expenditures, while Democratic assembly districts accounted for the overwhelming share of prison inmates. Prison expansion was thus a product of bipartisan collaboration, with the Democrats getting rid of criminals in their districts and Republicans becoming the beneficiaries of prison pork. "It's not only lock them up; it's lock them up in my district," New York assemblyman Daniel L. Feldman explained. One result is a greater number of remote prisons. Whole communities depend for their livelihood upon correctional institutions. Their long-term fate is tied to the prison. [. . .]

During the Reagan-Bush era, prisons were the second fastest-growing item in state budgets, after Medicaid. In fiscal 1991 America spent $20.1 billion on building and operating prisons, and probation and parole costs brought the corrections tab to $26.2 billion.

By comparison, that year the United States spent $22.9 billion on the main welfare program, Aid to Families with Dependent Children. Yet there were 13.5 million women and children who were served by welfare, compared to only 1.1 million persons, mostly men, who were imprisoned. By 1995, state governments' proposed Medicaid costs were projected to grow by 4.9 percent, compared to 8 percent for corrections. In 1996, however, "welfare reform" began a series of massive cuts in welfare spending, while prison costs continued to soar. [. . .]

Another important aspect of the cycle of prison expansion to emerge in the 1990s has been that many state governments suddenly have begun to spend more money on corrections than on higher education. In 1995, as a result of recent sentencing changes and for the first time in history, California voters spent more for prisons than for the two state-supported college systems, the University of California and the California state universities. From 1980 to 1995, the prison share of California's budget increased from 2.0 to 9.9 percent, while the higher education share shrank from 12.6 to 9.5 percent. [. . .]

Rather than provide more and better housing, medical care, education, welfare, and other services to the population most in need of them, the state spends $100,000 or more to build a prison cell and $30,000 to incarcerate one individual in it per year. The billions of dollars thus spent means that these funds are not available to pay for the services to address the problems that contributed to persons being imprisoned in the first place. Lacking those services, more people are pushed toward prison, and the spiral continues. [. . .]

INTERGENERATIONAL IMPACT

Captivity leaves deep, sometimes lifelong, impressions. A leading sociologist identified several major "pains of imprisonment," including material deprivation, denial of heterosexual relationships, loss of autonomy, compromised security and feelings of well-being, and suspended liberty. These of course are among the intended consequences of imprisonment.

Others who have tried to measure some of the unintended long-range consequences of imprisonment have suggested that it may actually strengthen ties to criminals, inculcate a criminal code, promote antisocial behavior, and teach criminal skills. Whether or not by design, imprisonment can injure an inmate's physical health and reduce life expectancy. It can damage psychological well-being and impair an individual's ability to function independently, spawning all kinds of post-traumatic stress disorders. Being imprisoned can attach lasting civil disabilities that will plague a person long after he or she has left through the front gate. And it can shatter personal relationships, dissolve friendships, and disconnect and distress fragile families.

By the time offenders are sent away to prison, stress already has torn some families apart. Often as a consequence of their drug addiction and criminal behavior, some inmates have lost their loved ones and alienated their friends. Although prison rules governing correspondence and visiting have been greatly relaxed since the extreme isolation of the early nineteenth century, such contact remains severely hampered by distance, expense, and intrusive security procedures. Just getting to the prison in time for a visit can entail having to help rent a bus to leave before dawn for a ride that is hundreds of miles each way, which is not an easy proposition for poor people.

Links that were often brittle to begin with sometimes snap as the months and years pass by. Prison visiting can also reopen wounds. According to Gresham Sykes, "This may explain in part the fact that an examination of the visiting records of a random sample of the inmate population, covering approximately a one-year period, indicated that 41 percent of the prisoners in the New Jersey State Prison had received no visits from the outside world." [. . .]

Conservatives and liberals alike agree that the family plays a crucial role in determining whether a person will become delinquent or criminal, regardless of whether the supposed manner is genetic, environmental, moral, or of some other nature. Although it is debatable whether poverty is the cause or the effect of the breakdown of family, it is evident that they go together, and there is general agreement that broken families, poverty, and crime also go together. Yet, there has been little attention given to the extent to which imprisonment may contribute to poverty, delinquency, and criminality on the part of family members in addition to the imprisoned offender. Clearly, the family left behind can become an incubator of social problems.

Chapter 8

William Spelman

THE LIMITED IMPORTANCE OF PRISON EXPANSION

From: William Spelman (2006), excerpts from "The limited importance of prison expansion," in Alfred Blumstein and Joel Wallman (eds), *The Crime Drop in America*, Cambridge: Cambridge University Press, pp. 97–129.

INTRODUCTION

OVER THE PAST TWENTY years, the fifty American states have engaged in one of the great policy experiments of modern times. In an attempt to reduce intolerably high levels of reported crime, the states doubled their prison populations, then doubled them again, increasing their costs by more than $20 billion per year. The states and the Federal government have given up a lot to get to this point: That $20 billion could provide child care for every family that cannot afford it, or a college education to every high school graduate, or a living-wage job to every unemployed youth. But crime levels appear to have (at last) responded, dropping to their lowest level in years. Thus recent history might appear to provide a prima facie case for the effectiveness of prisons.

Not everyone has found this evidence persuasive. Some argue, quite convincingly, that the recent crime reductions had nothing to do with the prison buildup. Crime dropped because the job prospects of poverty-stricken youths have improved, or because police have become more effective at getting weapons off the street, or because neighbors are beginning to watch out for one another again. As usual, correlation does not guarantee causation. If we are to determine the role of the prison buildup in the recent crime reductions, we will need to take a more systematic approach.

There are two ways to measure the effects of prison expansion, corresponding to two, very different approaches to modeling the criminal justice system. *Bottom-up* researchers try to get inside the black box, combining survey information about criminal offenders, published reports on criminal justice system operations, and complex probability models to simulate the detailed workings of the system (Greenwood 1982; Shinnar and Shinnar 1975). Such details are the strength of this approach: Staying close to the facts ensures frequent reality checks. As with any simulation, however, bottom-up prison studies demand an enormous amount of data, some of which is of questionable validity. In addition, these studies only measure the effects of incapacitation, not deterrence and rehabilitation. Thus bottom-up or simulation studies are liable to underestimate the full effects of prison expansion on crime rates.

In contrast, *top-down* researchers work around the black box, using econometric methods and aggregate data on crime rates, prison populations, and other possible causes of crime to link inputs and outputs (Devine, Sheley, and Smith 1988; Ehrlich 1973). Although these methods cannot in general separate the effects of incapacitation from those of deterrence and rehabilitation effects, they are much better suited than the bottom-up methods to capturing the full effect of prisons. And the focus on the behavior of the system, rather than its inner workings, is a strength, in that top-down methods can be used to compare among competing explanations. The fundamental weakness is the flip side of this strength: Because it works around the black box, there are innumerable competing explanations for the system's behavior at any given time. In the absence of a controlled experiment, it is impossible to reject or even account for all these explanations. Thus no matter how persuasive a top-down, econometric study is, it can never be definitive.

In the remainder of this chapter, I describe the principal results of studies using these two approaches and use these results to estimate the extent to which the prison buildup is responsible for the recent crime reductions. I examine the principal threats to validity and limitations on each study's applicability. Although one cannot be certain as to the role of prison expansion, one can use the available information to develop a reasonable estimate.

PREVIOUS FINDINGS AND THE CRIME DROP

The effectiveness of prisons at controlling crime has been an important research issue since at least the late 1960s, when the current prison boom began. Dozens of studies, mostly in the top-down, econometric tradition, were conducted with increasing methodological sophistication (cf. Ehrlich 1973; Gibbs 1968; Logan 1975).

Econometric studies

All econometric studies are based on the statistical method of *multiple regression* – sophisticated curve-fitting. Briefly, prison populations and crime rates for some population are plotted on an *X-Y* chart and the curve that best summarizes the relationship is found. Other variables that may affect crime rates, such as the age distribution of the population or the unemployment rate, can be controlled for statistically according to a formula of the form.

$$C = alpha + beta\ P + gamma\ X \qquad (1)$$

Where C is the crime rate, P is the prison population (somehow defined), and X consists of one or more control variables. [. . .]

For a time, best practice in criminology was defined by Ehrlich's (1973) economic analysis of offender decision making. Ehrlich provided an economic framework for interpreting the results and set a new standard in mathematical sophistication. He also obtained a controversial result: A one-percent increase in prison population would reduce crime rates by anywhere from 0.99 to 1.12 percent. In theory, at least, doubling the prison population would completely eliminate crime.

Ehrlich, of course, made no such claims; no state had ever doubled its prison population in only one year, and diminishing returns would obviously accompany so large a shift. Nevertheless, skeptics took a close look at Ehrlich's data and methods and those of others who obtained similar results. By the late 1970s, some of the cracks in the edifice were showing clearly (Blumstein, Cohen, and Nagin 1978, pp. 22–53).

- For a variety of technical reasons, prison-effectiveness analysts must identify some variables that affect prison populations but *not* crime rates. Ehrlich and others used economic indicators, demographic characteristics, urbanism, region, and similar variables to fill the bill. It is hard to imagine how these variables could *not* be related to crime rates.
- Another to attempt to solve the same problem required the assumption that this year's police expenditures were unrelated to last year's expenditures. More generally, variables that change little from year to year – including crime rates, prison populations, and demographic and social variables – tell us less than they appear to about how one responds to the others.
- Many analysts used so-called ratio variables, such as crimes per population and arrests per crime. Though reasonable in theory, the fact that "crimes" appears in the numerator of one variable and the denominator of the other means that they will appear to be negatively correlated, even if there is no real correlation between them at all.

After reviewing these flaws, the NRC report argued that further studies of the same kind would not help to solve the problem. Instead, analysts should collect better data-sets and use improved statistical methods to identify more robust solutions.

The results of the 1970s were summarized in a report commissioned by the National Research Council (NRC). In several essays (e.g., Cohen 1978; Nagin 1978; Vandaele 1978), researchers reviewed the empirical studies and compared the results. One benefit of the NRC report was to draw researchers' attention to the critical role of the *elasticity* – the percentage change in the crime rate associated with a one-percent change in the prison population. The elasticity was easy to interpret and could be compared among different studies, places, and times. As an added bonus, the elasticity was exceptionally easy to calculate, at least for the econometric studies.

The primary role of the NRC report, however, was to point out the principal objections to the most popular analysis methods, and to show that they provided inaccurate or biased results. This had two effects:

- It raised the bar on econometric studies so high that, for a time, no one tried to jump it. Only in the last ten years have available data and statistical methods improved to the point that these objections can (perhaps) be overcome.
- It shifted attention from the econometric analyses, which had predominated during the 1970s, to bottom-up, simulation studies. The frailties of simulation were less clear at the time.

Simulation studies

All simulation studies are based on a mathematical model developed by Avi-Itzhak and Shinnar (1973) and refined by Shinnar and Shinnar (1975). Briefly, this model combines estimates of the typical offender's

- offense rate per year (sometimes referred to as λ, the Greek letter "lambda"),
- probability of arrest, prosecution, and incarceration per crime committed, and
- average sentence served in jail or prison,

to estimate the likelihood that a typical offender will be incarcerated at any given time. When combined with information about the length of the typical criminal career, it is possible to estimate the proportion of that career that the typical offender spends behind bars. This proportion represents the reduction in the crime rate due to incapacitation. By plugging in different probabilities of arrest, prosecution, or incarceration, or different average sentence lengths, an analyst could estimate the effect of prison expansion, improved police and prosecution, or other criminal justice system improvements.

The NRC report suggested that the simulation model was promising but insufficiently developed to produce accurate estimates (Cohen 1978). For example, the initial model assumed that individual offense rates, arrest and incarceration probabilities, and criminal-career lengths were uncorrelated with one another and did not change over time. No empirical data were available to verify this assumption. Likewise, the model did not distinguish among offenders who committed crimes at different rates, and assumed that incapacitating one member of an offending group would eliminate all offenses committed by members of that group. These assumptions seemed patently untrue. Perhaps more important, data on the operations of the criminal justice system, and particularly on offense rates and career lengths among active offenders, were sorely lacking. In fact, Cohen estimated that the elasticity of crime rates with regard to time spent in prison per crime committed (roughly similar to the elasticity at issue here) could range anywhere from −.05 to −.70, given available data (Cohen 1978, pp. 219–21). That is, for every one-percent increase in the prison population, crime would decline by somewhere between .05 and .70 percent.

The model and the data on which it was based improved in bits and pieces throughout the 1980s. Greenwood (1982) showed how the model could be adapted to include a variety of offense rates. Reiss (1980) provided critical information on the size and behavior of offending groups. Most important, the Rand Corporation conducted a series of studies (Chaiken and Chaiken 1982; Petersilia, Greenwood, and Lavin 1978; Peterson, Braiker, and Polich 1980) that showed that tolerably accurate information on offense rates, arrest and incarceration probabilities, and other critical parameters could be obtained from surveys of incarcerated criminals. These surveys were successfully replicated (DiIulio 1990; Horney and Marshall 1991; Mande and English 1988), providing the knowledge base needed to support policy analysis.

Relying on these and further extensions of the model, DiIulio and Piehl (1991), Spelman (1994), and Piehl and DiIulio (1995) compared the benefits and costs of increased imprisonment. As shown in Table 8.1, these benefits and costs were derived from analysis of a variety of populations, and imply elasticities ranging from −.16 to −.26.

Table 8.1 Summary of recent prison effectiveness analyses

Simulation studies of incapacitation

DiIulio and Piehl (1991)	−.22	Wisconsin, 1989
Spelman (1994)	−.16±.05	Approximates nationwide estimate, 1992
Piehl and DiIulio (1995)	−.26	New Jersey, 1993

Econometric studies of incapacitation and deterrence – national data

Devine, Sheley, and Smith (1988)		
Violent Crimes	−2.84±1.60	
Property Crimes	−1.99±0.88	National time-series, 1948–85
All Index Crimes	−2.20	
Cappell and Sykes (1991)	−.91	National time-series, 1933–85
Marvell and Moody (1997, 1998)		
Violent Crimes	−.79±.29	
Property Crimes	−.95±.20	National time-series, 1958–95
All Index Crimes	−.93	

Econometric studies of incapacitation and deterrence – state data

Marvell and Moody (1994)		
Violent Crimes	−.06±.11	
Property Crimes	−.17±.06	49 states, 1971–89
All Index Crimes	−.16	
Levitt (1996)		
Violent Crimes	−.38±.36	
Property Crimes	−.26±.24	50 states + DC, 1971–93
All Index Crimes	−.31	
Becsi (1999)		
Violent Crimes	−.05±.04	
Property Crimes	−.09±.03	50 states + DC, 1971–93
All Index Crimes	−.09±.03	

Note: Figures shown are elasticities of crimes with respect to increases in prison population. Where available, 95 percent confidence intervals shown after "±".

Given the limited precision of any of these estimates, a more reasonable range might be anywhere between −.10 and −.30.

Recent studies using both approaches have succeeded in overcoming many of the objections to previous efforts. Whether these results are closer to the truth or not, they are certainly more defensible than the estimates of the 1960s and 1970s.

Since the late 1970s, six econometric studies have appeared that respond in part to the NRC challenges. Three of the studies used national crime and prison statistics; because reliable data were not available until the early 1930s, use of national data puts a crimp on the number of cases available for analysis. The other three studies expanded on the national data-set by examining each state separately, in effect multiplying the number of cases by 50 or so. Results are shown in Table 8.1.

Clearly, the studies based on national data obtained results very different from those based on state data. In a separate analysis, Marvell and Moody (1998) found that the national-level elasticities are three times larger than the state-level elasticities. They provide a plausible explanation for some of the difference: Even if one state (say, Missouri) does not increase its prison population at all, increases elsewhere in the country will tend to reduce crime in Missouri because offenders who might have moved there are in prison. Thus Missouri is a "free rider," enjoying a crime reduction it hasn't paid for.

Although this seems reasonable on its face, offenders do not appear to move often enough to account for these results. State arrest records show that the offenders active in the average state commit fully three-fourths of their crimes in that state, even though some of them also commit crimes elsewhere (Orsagh 1992). Thus we should expect that a one-percent increase in the Missouri prison population should reduce crime in Missouri by three times as much as a one-percent increase throughout the rest of the nation, not the other way around. Further, since the 1970s most states have increased their prison populations by about the same rate. Free riders are hard to find.

The most likely explanation for the much higher national-level elasticities is that the national prison population is a proxy for one or more as-yet unmeasured variables. For example, it may track an increase in support for aggressive policing, or the willingness of individuals to prevent crime on their own. More generally, it is dangerous to interpret the clear correlation between the national prison population and state crime rate as causation in the absence of a plausible explanation.

Accordingly, I focus attention on the three state-level studies (with the caveat that they may be underestimating the effect slightly due to a free rider phenomenon). These results cover a relatively narrow range, from $-.05$ to $-.38$. Of the three, the most accurate is probably the largest, produced by Levitt (1996). Levitt's model is the only one to account explicitly for the possibility that, just as prison population influences the crime rate, so can crime rates influence the prison population. For example, politicians may respond to rising crime rates by funding construction of more prison beds; likewise, if crime rates go up, more offenders are liable to be arrested and convicted, increasing the number available to be sentenced to prison. Thus higher crime rates can lead to higher prison populations, a positive relationship. Because more prison presumably leads to less crime (a negative relationship), failing to control for the effect of crime on prison population effectively mixes up two opposing effects, resulting in estimates of the effect of prisons that are systematically biased toward zero. Primarily because it separates these opposing effects, Levitt's model provides estimates of the elasticity that are larger (that is, more negative) than the others. [. . .]

Some have argued that Levitt's estimates are systematically too high (Donohue and Siegelman 1998). Hence a second reason for relying on these results: If estimates based on his elasticities suggest that the prison buildup is still a relatively minor cause of the crime drop, one can be fairly sure that alternative estimates would show the prison buildup to be even less important.

Although all of the studies estimated elasticities separately for violent and for property crimes, none of the differences were statistically significant. In addition, none of the results shown in Table 8.1 are very precise. Thus we should not be very surprised to find that the true elasticity for violent crime was anywhere between $-.10$ and $-.50$. Combined with the results of the simulation studies and the possibility of out-of-state effects, we tentatively conclude that the elasticity is probably in the neighborhood of $-.30$.

Interpreting the elasticities

To help make sense of these elasticities, I put them to use in answering the following question: What would have happened, had the state and Federal governments *not* made an enormous investment in prisons over the last twenty-five years?

Perhaps surprisingly, all that is needed to answer this question are actual changes in prison and crime rates and an estimate of the elasticity. Briefly, one can apply the elasticity estimates to each year's prison expansion and calculate what the crime rate would have been, had that year's expansion not taken place. If one continues these calculations, year after year, one eventually comes up with an estimate of what today's crime rate would have been, had *none* of the previous year's expansions taken place.

An example will show how this works. In 1974, the imprisonment rate (that is, sentenced prisoners per 100,000 population) increased from 97.8 to 103.6 – an increase of 5.9 percent. If the elasticity of violent crime with respect to prison is $-.30$, then the effect of this increase on the crime rate was

$$\Delta VC = -.3 \times 5.9\% = -1.8\% \tag{2}$$

Holding everything else constant, this first step in our twenty-five year prison expansion reduced the violent-crime rate by 1.8 percent. Alternatively, the 1974 violent-crime rate should be 98.2 percent what it was in 1973.

In reality, of course, everything else is never constant. The social, economic, and public policy changes considered elsewhere in this volume act on their own to increase or decrease crime each year. In general, we can separate the effects of prison expansion from the rest of these factors by recognizing that the total percentage change in crime rates will be equal to

$$\Delta VC = \text{prison effect} \times \text{all other effects,} \tag{3}$$

and that the effect of all other factors taken together will be

$$\frac{\Delta VC}{\text{prison effect}} = \text{all other effects.} \tag{4}$$

In 1974, the reported violent crime rate went from 417.4 crimes per 100,000 population to 461.1, an increase of 10.5 percent nationwide. Thus the net effect of all nonprison factors must be

$$\frac{1.105}{0.982} = 1.125, \tag{5}$$

or a net increase in the violent-crime rate of 12.5 percent. Had the 1974 prison expansion never taken place, then, the violent-crime rate would have increased by 12.5 percent – somewhat more than it actually did. If the elasticity was in fact $-.30$, the prison expansion put a damper on what would have been a larger increase in crime rates. If the elasticity were higher or lower, the dampening effect would increase or decrease proportionately.

Similar results are obtained for most years since 1974. Crime rates went up in most of these years, but they would have gone up by more than they did, had prison populations not expanded as they did. Table 8.2 compares the actual change in violent crime to the change due to nonprison factors – roughly, the change in violent-crime rates that *would* have occurred, had prison populations remained constant – for elasticities of −.15, −.30, and −.45.

Now that we have factored out the effects of the prison expansion on an annual basis, it is easy to estimate the cumulative effect. Assuming an elasticity of −.30, Table 8.2 shows that violent-crime rates would have increased by 12.5 percent in 1974, by 8.8 percent in 1975, and so on. In the absence of any prison expansion, the 1975 violent crime rate would have been

$$VC(1975) = 1.125 \times 1.088 = 1.224 \qquad (6)$$

or 22.4 percent higher than it was in 1973; the 1976 violent-crime rate would have been

$$VC(1976) = 1.125 \times 1.088 \times 0.985 = 1.206 \qquad (7)$$

Table 8.2 Estimated changes in violent crime rates in absence of prison expansion[a]

Year	Percent change in rates of		Percent change in violent-crime rates due to nonprison factors at elasticity of		
	Violent crime	Prison	−.15	−.30	−.45
1974	10.5	5.9	11.5	12.5	13.5
1975	5.8	9.1	7.3	8.8	10.3
1976	−4.1	8.8	−2.8	−1.5	−.1
1977	1.7	4.9	2.5	3.2	4.0
1978	4.6	4.7	5.3	6.1	6.8
1979	10.3	.7	10.4	10.5	10.6
1980	8.7	2.2	9.1	9.4	9.8
1981	−.4	10.1	1.1	2.7	4.3
1982	−3.9	11.1	−2.3	−.6	1.2
1983	−5.8	5.3	−5.1	−4.3	−3.6
1984	.3	5.0	1.0	1.8	2.6
1985	3.2	6.4	4.2	5.2	6.3
1986	11.0	8.0	12.3	13.7	15.1
1987	−1.3	5.6	−.5	.4	1.2
1988	4.5	7.0	5.6	6.8	7.9
1989	4.2	11.1	5.9	7.7	9.6
1990	10.3	7.7	11.6	12.9	14.2
1991	3.6	6.2	4.6	5.5	6.5
1992	−.1	6.5	.9	1.9	2.9
1993	−1.4	6.1	−.5	.4	1.4
1994	−4.4	11.1	−2.8	−1.1	.6
1995	−4.1	5.7	−3.2	−2.4	−1.6
1996	−7.0	3.9	−6.5	−5.9	−5.4
1997	−4.0	5.2	−3.3	−2.5	−1.8

Note

a U.S. Department of Justice, Federal Bureau of Investigation (annual); U.S. Department of Justice, Bureau of Justice Statistics (annual); author's calculations.

or 20.6 percent higher than in 1973; and so on. Figure 8.1 shows the actual reported violent-crime rate and three hypothetical violent-crime rates for each year since 1974.

The simplest way to read Figure 8.1 – and the simplest way to interpret the effects of the prison expansion – is to compare the endpoints of the four lines, the actual and predicted values of today's violent-crime rate. In 1997 the violent-crime rate was 610.8 per 100,000 population. If the prison expansion of the last twenty-five years had never taken place, the violent-crime rate would have been somewhere between 775 and 1,260. Thus the prison expansion is responsible for reducing the violent-crime rate by 20 to 50 percent, with a best guess of roughly 35 percent.

Such an effect is more than large enough to account for the recent downturn in violent-crime rates. Can we then claim that the prison buildup is responsible for this downturn? As a careful examination of Figure 8.1 shows, probably not. Consider the experience of the 1990s: Prison populations went up and violent crime went down. So far, so good. But, as shown on the three hypothetical lines on Figure 8.1, violent-crime rates would have gone down in the 1990s even if prison populations had *not* gone up. Further, the hypothetical lines show that the drop would have come at almost exactly the same time, and been almost exactly the same size, as the actual drop. These projections suggest that prison expansion was not responsible for the crime drop.

In fact, violent crime dropped by a little bit more than I have projected that it would have in the absence of a prison buildup – between 4 and 21 percent more. Thus prison expansion during the 1990s increased the size of the crime drop slightly. Nevertheless, the basic result remains: Even had the United States *not* spent $20 billion per year in jails and prisons, violent-crime rates would have gone down, anyway. Between 79 and 96 percent of the violent-crime drop cannot be explained by prison expansion.

In retrospect, this should not be too surprising. The prison boom has been remarkably steady, with the prison population increasing by roughly 6 percent per year, nationwide, for a quarter century. The prison increases of the late 1980s and early 1990s were no larger than they had been at earlier times during the buildup. Unless these prison increases were

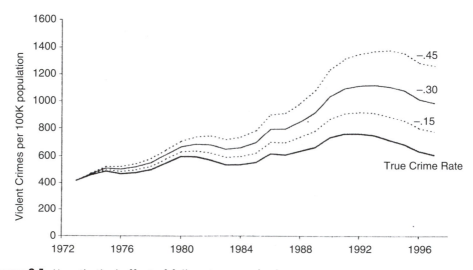

Figure 8.1 Hypothetical effect of failure to expand prisons

somehow more effective than previous increases, one should not have expected to see a downturn in crime rates. Any such downturn must be largely the result of other forces.

Of course, this begs the question of whether prisons are somehow more effective at reducing crime today than they were in the 1970s and 1980s. Has the elasticity increased over time? To find out, I take a closer look at some critical assumptions underlying these conclusions. [. . .]

DID PRISONS BECOME MORE EFFECTIVE?

Increases in the scale of incarceration, in the proportion of crimes committed by adults, and in the selectivity of the criminal justice system [with respect to serious chronic offenders] all suggest that the crime-control effectiveness of prisons, as measured by the elasticity, has increased over the past twenty-five years. As a result, the prison buildup is probably responsible for a larger percentage of the crime drop than estimated earlier. It is difficult to estimate how much larger using bottom-up thought experiments, however. The assumptions required about how offenders commit crimes and are arrested, imprisoned, and ultimately released, and in particular the assumption that prisons only control crime through incapacitation and not through deterrence, are difficult to justify. A more direct means of measuring changes in the elasticity over time would surely be preferable.

The top-down, econometric studies suggest just such a direct measurement. Although previous top-down studies have assumed that the elasticity for a particular crime type is the same for all states and time periods, it is not difficult to relax this assumption. More specifically, one can examine whether the elasticity responds to the shifts over time described previously. If it does, then one must estimate the approximate elasticity at work during each year over the past twenty-five years, apply that time-specific elasticity to our problem, and re-evaluate the effects of the prison buildup on the crime drop.

The best of the top-down studies rely on a panel data-set collected by Marvell and Moody (1994) and improved by Levitt (1996). It covers all fifty U.S. states and the District of Columbia for the period from 1971 to 1997. One important benefit of this data-set is that it contains a wide variety of control variables that can be expected to influence crime rates. By controlling explicitly for the effects of income, unemployment, age structure, and other characteristics, the effect of prisons on crime can be isolated.

At least three sets of results have been obtained from this data-set, corresponding to the specific statistical models used by Becsi (1999), Levitt (1996), and Marvell and Moody (1994). The analysis that follows relies primarily on Levitt's model. As described previously, it is the only model that deals explicitly with the possibility that crime rates affect prison population, and it may provide conservative results by systematically overstating the effect of prisons on crime.

As with most top-down models, the Levitt model controls for a variety of social and economic characteristics. In addition, the model was altered to account for scale, juvenile, and trend effects. Table 8.3 shows the results of four, increasingly complex models.

> Model 1 replicates Levitt's findings, showing the effect of a variety of factors
>   on the violent-crime rate under the assumption that elasticity is a constant;
> Model 2 replaces the constant-elasticity term with one that depends on the
>   scale of imprisonment;

Table 8.3 Estimates of the crime function

	Model 1	Model 2	Model 3	Model 4
Control Variables				
Per Capita Income	*.362*	*.356*	*.352*	*.344*
	(.126)	(.126)	(.126)	(.132)
% Unemployment	.430	.422	.432	.460
	(.298)	(.298)	(.298)	(.304)
% Black	−.028	−.032	−.038	−.046
	(.025)	(.025)	(.026)	(.027)
Police Per Capita	.081	.082	.083	.083
	(.046)	(.046)	(.046)	(.047)
% Urban	.006	.006	.008	.006
	(.012)	(.012)	(.012)	(.012)
% Aged 0–14	−.176	−.170	−.207	−.139
	(.048)	(.047)	(.049)	(.419)
% Aged 15–17	.233	.214	.195	.107
	(.213)	(.214)	(.215)	(.221)
% Aged 18–24	.309	.310	.295	.316
	(.246)	(.245)	(.246)	(.251)
% Aged 25–34	*.724*	*.729*	.706	.596
	(.344)	(.342)	(.343)	(.350)
Prison Elasticity Variables				
Prison Rate (constant)	*−.401*			
	(.150)			
Prison Rate (variable)		*−.082*	*−.089*	−.064
		(.028)	(.029)	(.069)
Prison Rate × Percent Adult Crimes			−.442	−.684
			(.489)	(.543)
Prison Rate Annual Differences			−1.827 to	+1.055
(range of values)			(.866)	(.648)
Summary Statistics				
R^2	.3058	.3069	.3075	.3190
adjusted R^2	.2864	.2875	.2874	.2855
std Error of Estimate	.07204	.07198	.07199	.07208
ΔF			0.818	0.816
$p(\Delta F)$			.366	.638
mean η	−.401	−.428	−.391	−.488
std dev of η	—	.045	.054	.614

Source: Author's calculations, based on data provided by Steven Levitt, University of Chicago, updated to 1997.
Note: In variable sections, first value shown is coefficient; standard error is shown in (parentheses). Statistically significant coefficients ($p < .05$) are shown in italics.

Model 3 also includes a term measuring the proportion of violent crimes
committed by adults;

Model 4 also includes terms measuring other changes in elasticity over time.

Note first that all four models are virtually identical in most respects. The coefficients on
social and economic indicators vary little from one model to the next. In addition, they
all predict the average elasticity to be in the vicinity of $-.40$ – toward the high end of
the expected range, but well within that range. Model 2 is slightly more accurate than
Model 1 (as measured by the standard error of the estimate and the adjusted R^2); the statistical significance of the scale-flexible coefficient in Model 2 is also greater than that of
the constant-elasticity coefficient in Model 1. This alone suggests that the assumption of
constant elasticity is inappropriate. The differences between Model 2 and Model 3 are not
statistically significant, but the adult-proportion coefficient is of the expected sign, and
adding the new term at least does little harm to predictive accuracy. Not so with Model 4:
It is the least accurate predictor, the new terms are not statistically significant, and
perhaps most important, there is no clear pattern in the changes in elasticity over time.
On balance, then, Model 3 (or, perhaps, Model 2) is the most successful of the four.

The elasticity implied by Model 3 differs among states and over time, and can be
expressed as

$$\text{elasticity} = -.089 \log \text{prison rate} - .442 \log p(\text{adult}).$$

As expected, for violent crimes, at least, the elasticity increases (that is, it becomes
more negative) as the scale of imprisonment (here measured by the log of the prison
rate per 100,000 residents) increases. The elasticity also responds to the extent of
juvenile involvement: The elasticity is most negative in the times and places where the
vast majority of crimes were committed by adults. Perhaps most important, elasticity

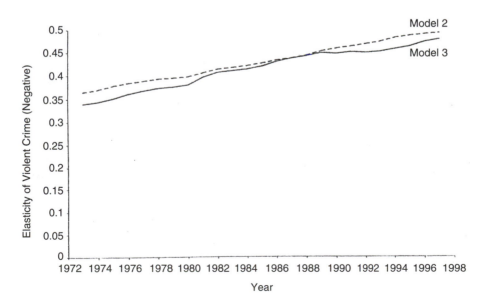

Figure 8.2

does not change significantly or consistently over time, once changes in scale and juvenile involvement have been taken into account. This suggests that any nationwide increases in selectivity are too slight to be identified using these data.

Finally, the equation has no intercept; this is because, at very low values of the prison rate, one can expect that the elasticity is very close to zero.

When this formula is applied to the panel data, the resulting estimates are as shown in Figure 8.2. The elasticity has clearly increased over time, from a low point of $-.34$ in 1973 to a high of $-.48$ in 1997. Even without a specific selectivity effect, it is clear that changes in the scale of imprisonment and the incidence of juvenile violent crime have helped to make prisons more effective (at least on a percentage basis) over time.

CONCLUSION

Armed with direct evidence of increasing elasticity, I return to the original problem. What effect did the prison buildup have on the crime drop? Figure 8.3 shows what happens when the elasticities of Figure 8.2 are applied to the violent-crime and prison data of the last twenty-five years.

The results are very similar to the hypothetical cases of Figure 8.1:

- The violent-crime rate would have dropped, anyway, at almost the same time, but
- The crime drop would have been 27 percent smaller than it actually was, had the prison buildup never taken place.

In short, the prison buildup was responsible for about one-fourth of the crime drop. Other factors are responsible for the vast majority of the drop. [. . .]

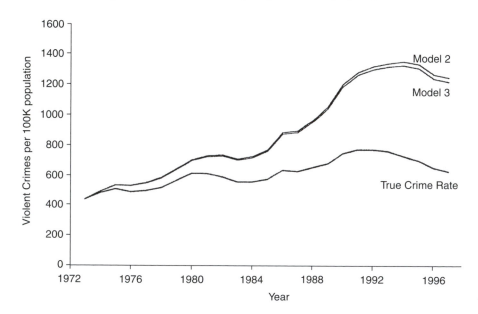

Figure 8.3

Nevertheless, it is hardly the last word on the subject. Over the next few years, researchers should consider making a variety of improvements in this model. Although it allows for random shifts from year to year, the model explicitly considers only scale and juvenile involvement as reasons for changes in elasticity. There may be others, and the methods demonstrated here can be applied to these variables as they are identified. Persistent differences in elasticities among states are beyond the scope of this chapter, but they may be substantial and are of obvious policy relevance. . . . Given the likelihood of changing elasticities over time and the probability of differences among states, the most appropriate policy implications would be very time- and place-specific. [. . .]

One may conclude, . . . that the prison buildup was a contributing factor to the violent-crime drop of the past few years. America would be a much more violent place had billions of dollars not been invested in prison beds over the past two decades; violent crime would not have dropped as far and as fast as it has. Nevertheless, violent crime *would* have dropped a lot, anyway. Most of the responsibility for the crime drop rests with improvements in the economy, changes in the age structure, or other social factors.

References

Becsi, Zsolt. 1999. "Economics and Crime in the United States." *Economic Review of the Federal Reserve Bank of Atlanta* 84 (First quarter):38–56.

Blumstein, Alfred, Jacqueline Cohen, and Daniel Nagin. 1978. *Deterrence and Incapacitation: Estimating the Effects of Criminal Sanctions on Crime Rates*. Report of the Panel on Research on Deterrent and Incapacitative Effects. Washington: National Academy of Sciences.

Chaiken, Jan M., and Marcia R. Chaiken. 1982. *Varieties of Criminal Behavior*. Santa Monica: Rand.

Cohen, Jacqueline. 1978. "The Incapacitative Effect of Imprisonment: A Critical Review of the Literature." In Alfred Blumstein, Jacqueline Cohen, and Daniel Nagin (Eds.), *Deterrence and Incapacitation: Estimating the Effects of Criminal Sanctions on Crime Rates* (pp. 187–243). Washington: National Academy of Sciences.

Devine, Joel A., Joseph F. Sheley, and M. Dwayne Smith. 1988. "Macroeconomic and Social-control Policy Influences on Crime Rate Changes, 1948–1985." *American Sociological Review* 53:407–20.

DiIulio, John J., Jr. 1990. *Crime and Punishment in Wisconsin*. Wisconsin Policy Research Institute Report, Volume 3, No. 7. Milwaukee: Wisconsin Policy Research Institute.

DiIulio, John J., Jr., and Anne Morrison Piehl. 1991. "Does prison pay?" *Brookings Review* (Fall): 28–35.

Donohue John J., III, and Peter Siegelman. 1998. "Allocating Resources among Prisons and Social Programs in the Battle Against Crime." *Journal of Legal Studies* 27:1–43.

Ehrlich, Isaac. 1973. "Participation in Illegitimate Activities: A Theoretical and Empirical Investigation." *Journal Of Political Economy* 81:521–65.

Gibbs, Jack P. 1968. "Crime, Punishment, and Deterrence." *Southwestern Social Science Quarterly* 48:515–30.

Greenwood, Peter W. 1982. *Selective Incapacitation*. Santa Monica: Rand.

Horney, Julie, and Ineke Marshall. 1991. "Measuring Lambda through Self-Reports." *Criminology* 29:401–25.

Levitt, Steven D. 1996. "The Effect of Prison Population Size on Crime Rates: Evidence from Prison Overcrowding Litigation." *Quarterly Journal of Economics* 111:319–51.

Logan, C. H. 1975. "Arrest Rates and Deterrence." *Social Science Quarterly* 56:376–89.

Mande, M. J., and Kim English. 1988. *Individual Crime Rates of Colorado Prisoners: Final Report. 1988*. Denver: Colorado Division of Criminal Justice, Research Unit.

Marvell, Thomas B., and Carlisle E. Moody, Jr. 1994. "Prison Population Growth and Crime Reduction." *Journal of Quantitative Criminology* 10:109–40.

Marvell, Thomas B., and Carlisle E. Moody, Jr. 1997. "The Impact of Prison Growth on Homicide." *Homicide Studies* 1:205–33.

Marvell, Thomas B., and Carlisle E. Moody, Jr. 1998. "The Impact of Out-of-State Prison Population on State Homicide Rates: Displacement and Free-Rider Effects." *Criminology* 36:513–35.

Nagin, Daniel. 1978. "General Deterrence: A Review of the Empirical Evidence." In Alfred Blumstein, Jacqueline Cohen, and Daniel Nagin (Eds.), *Deterrence and Incapacitation: Estimating the Effects of Criminal Sanctions on Crime Rates* (pp. 95–139). Washington: National Academy of Sciences.

Orsagh, Thomas. 1992. *The Multi-State Offender: A Report on State Prisoners Who Were Criminally Active in More Than One State*. Washington: U.S. Bureau of Justice Statistics.

Petersilia, Joan, Peter W. Greenwood, and Marvin Lavin. 1978. *Criminal Careers of Habitual Felons*. Santa Monica: Rand.

Peterson, Mark A., Harriet B. Braiker, and Suzanne M. Polich. 1980. *Doing Crime: A Survey of California Prison Inmates*. Santa Monica: Rand.

Piehl, Anne Morrison, and John J. DiIulio, Jr. 1995. " 'Does Prison Pay?' Revisited: Returning to the Crime Scene." *Brookings Review* (Winter 1995):21–25.

Reiss, Albert J., Jr. 1980. "Understanding Changes in Crime Rates." In Stephen E. Fienberg and Albert J. Reiss, Jr (Eds.), *Indicators of Crime and Criminal Justice: Quantitative Studies* (pp. 11–17). Washington: U.S. Government Printing Office.

Shinnar, Shlomo, and Reuel Shinnar. 1975. "The Effects of the Criminal Justice System on the Control of Crime: A Quantitative Approach." *Law and Society Review* 9:581–611.

Spelman, William. 1994. *Criminal Incapacitation*. New York: Plenum.

U.S. Bureau of Justice Statistics, Annual. *Correctional Populations in the United States*. Washington: U.S. Department of Justice.

Vandaele, Walter. 1978. "Participation in Illegitimate Activities: Ehrlich Revisited." In Alfred Blumstein, Jacqueline Cohen, and Daniel Nagin (Eds.), *Deterrence and Incapacitation: Estimating the Effects of Criminal Sanctions on Crime Rates* (pp. 270–335). Washington: National Academy of Sciences.

Chapter 9

Katherine Beckett and Bruce Western

CRIME CONTROL, AMERICAN STYLE

From social welfare to social control

From: Katherine Beckett and Bruce Western (2000), excerpts from 'Crime control, American style', in Penny Green and Andrew Rutherford (eds), *Criminal Policy in Transition*, Oxford and Portland, OR: Hart Publishing, pp. 15–31.

O VER THE PAST SEVERAL decades, the United States has emerged as the leading example and advocate of the "get-tough" approach to crime. Since 1965, US crime control expenditures have grown from $4.6 billion to over $100 billion and the rate of incarceration in the United States is now one of the highest in the world (Danziger, 1996, 1). Increasingly, politicians agree that policies such as mandatory minimum sentencing laws and capital punishment, as well as aggressive tactics such as "quality-of-life" policing, are the best response to the crime and drug problems. US social policy has also become more punitive in recent years, especially programmes that provided cash and services to the poor. The simultaneity of these developments is not accidental, but reflects the ascendance of the notion that government's primary responsibility is social control rather than social welfare. This shift has, in turn, been facilitated by the construction of the poor as dangerous and undeserving.

Together, the state's expanded penal system and weakened welfare apparatus comprise a novel form of governance, one that has been called a "new government of misery" based on the criminalisation of poverty (Wacquant, 2001). US officials encourage governments around the globe – particularly those undergoing democratisation – to adopt the social and penal policies associated with this new form of governance. In recent years, this approach has been legitimated by apparently low levels of unemployment in the United States which allow the government to argue that the "American model" is far more efficient – and ultimately, more helpful to the poor – than the welfare states of Continental Europe.

This chapter analyses the process by which this mode of governance was adopted in the United States and examines the consequences of its adoption for international policy debates. In Part I, we argue that the ascendance of the "get-tough" approach in the United States is a consequence of the reorientation of government policy around social control rather than social welfare. To support this argument, we show that the discourse of "law and order" has been bound up with the attack on the US welfare state, and that the inscription of this discourse in penal policy and institutions cannot be understood apart from this larger debate over the proper role of government in society.

In Part II, we analyse the impact of growing rates of incarceration in the United States on assessments of the US economy and the welfare states of Western Europe. We argue that the incarceration of large numbers of working-age men in the United States conceals a high level of persistent unemployment, particularly among African-American men. The fact that conventional estimates of unemployment systematically ignore this population – located overwhelmingly at the fringes of the labour market – gives the false impression that the ostensibly unregulated US labour market is more efficient and productive than the welfare states of Continental Europe. This impression has been critical to international debates over social policy and has legitimated US attempts to export the "American model" of governance. We also argue that while, in the short term, the tremendous size of US prisons and jails obscures unemployment, incarceration will increase unemployment in the long run by reducing the job prospects of ex-convicts and disrupting their families and communities. The expansion of the penal apparatus in the United States thus represents a new and unprecedented mode of state intervention in social and economic affairs, one which will have long-lasting adverse consequences.

THE CHANGING FACE OF GOVERNANCE IN THE UNITED STATES

The spread and popularity of "get-tough" policies such as capital punishment and mandatory minimum sentencing statutes is, for many academics and legal professionals, something of a mystery. The most popular explanation of their adoption suggests that such policies reflect the public's preference for "cracking down on criminals." According to this "democracy-at-work" thesis, tough anti-crime measures are politicians' response to widespread popular punitiveness. Although it is certainly the case that segments of the American public have become more punitive, the situation is more complicated than the democracy-at-work thesis implies. In the first place, "Public opinion is not an essentialist thing that exists outside of politics" (Piven, 1998: 459). Attempts to identify the "true nature" of public opinion often reify it, implying that it is based on an experience of the world that is unmediated by culture and politics.

In addition, popular opinion regarding crime, punishment, and social justice remains heterogeneous, fluid and contradictory despite decades of political initiative on these subjects. Enthusiasm for the death penalty, for example, weakens considerably in the presence of alternatives and coexists uneasily with support for rehabilitative ideals (McGarrell and Sandys, 1996; Sandys and McGarrell, 1995). Widespread and growing support for mandatory minimum and three-strikes sentencing laws coexists with ongoing support for policies aimed at crime prevention (Cullen, Clark and Wozniak, 1985; Cullen et al., 1990; Roberts, 1992). In fact, when asked to choose between spending money on punishment or prevention programmes, approximately two-thirds of those polled in the late 1980s chose the latter (Cullen et al., 1990). . . . The fact that much of the public supports prevention and rehabilitation efforts challenges the argument that penal severity is rooted in a new, meaner political culture.

Furthermore, most versions of the "democracy-at-work" thesis cannot explain why public support for punitive anti-crime and drug policies (ambivalent as it is) has become more pronounced in recent years. More simplistic versions of this argument attribute this trend directly to a worsening crime problem, although this argument has become difficult to sustain in the face of consistent and steep declines in rates of crime. Since 1990, for example, the state prison population has grown seven per cent annually, despite significant drops in violent and property crime rates (as reported by both police and victimisation survey data) for seven consecutive years (Butterfield, 1998).

In a more sophisticated version of this argument, Garland (2000b) suggests that relatively high and growing rates of crime in the immediate post-war period mean that more people have directly or indirectly experienced criminal victimisation. Garland also argues that the professional middle classes are now less able to insulate themselves from the threat of crime. When combined with other social developments (including media accounts of crime) that heighten concern about social instability, this popular experience intensified public anxiety and triggered a long-term cultural adaptation to "crime as a normal social fact" that includes heightened efforts to enhance personal security. The punitive policies of the war on crime in the UK and US, Garland argues, are "conditioned by" this cultural context.

Garland's claim that penal policy developments have cultural underpinnings which include the experiences of everyday life is undoubtedly correct, and his emphasis on the culturally mediated nature of this experience enables him to avoid reifying popular "experience" and "public opinion". In addition, the notion that popular measures aimed at enhancing personal security may, in the long run, undermine the sense that the world is a safe and secure place is an interesting one. At a more empirical level, however, Garland's argument exaggerates the fearfulness of the American public, ignores ongoing public support for rehabilitation and prevention efforts, and downplays continued racial, class and geographic differences that shape reactions to crime and punishment (see Beckett and Sasson, 2000). Furthermore, in the absence of any reference to political discourse, Garland's argument does not explain why heightened fear and anxiety (if they in fact exist) would necessarily give rise to greater support for punitive policies (see also Savelsberg, 1999).

Indeed, survey research in the United States suggests that neither concern about crime as a social problem nor fear of personal victimisation necessarily give rise to punitiveness. For example, demographic groups that are relatively unafraid of being victimised typically express the highest levels of support for the "get-tough" approach, while those who are more fearful are often less punitive. Rural white men, for example, feel relatively safe but are quite staunch supporters of law and order policies. By contrast, African-Americans and white women are typically more fearful of being victimised but have historically been less punitive than white men (Stinchcombe et al., 1980). Although recent research suggests that increased risk of victimisation may be the primary cause of growing punitiveness among African-Americans, fear of vicitimisation remains unrelated to punitiveness among whites (Cohn and Halteman, 1991). And although there is evidence that concern about social and familial instability is widespread and related to support for punitive policies (Sasson, 1995; Tyler and Boeckmann, 1997), this connection is not immutable, but rather subject to cultural and political influence (Sasson, 1995).

Another explanation of US punitiveness stresses the fact that the United States is a more crime-ridden and violent place than other industrialised countries. However, according to international crime survey data, the US crime rate in 1995 was average when compared to ten other industrialised nations (Mayhew and van Dijk, 1997). A comprehensive review of both survey and police data concluded that the incidence of non-lethal violence in the United States is similar to that in other English-speaking nations, while US rate of property crime are significantly lower than in comparable countries (Lynch, 1995). Although the rate of lethal assault continues to be exceptionally high in the United States – and it is possible that this contributes to public support for the war on crime (Zimring and Hawkins, 1997) – US punitiveness is not limited to those convicted of violent crimes. In fact, the United States incarcerates a much larger proportion of its property and drug offenders and does so for longer periods of time than other industrialised countries (Lynch, 1995).

To summarise, most accounts of the adoption of punitive anti-crime policies in the United States suggest that such policies are a reflection of popular attitudes, which are based at least to some extent on the experience or incidence of crime. More sophisticated versions of this argument recognise that crime rates do not correspond in any neat way to either cultural practices or policy developments, and that the experience of criminal victimisation is a culturally mediated one (Garland, 2000b). Still, without explicit reference to political struggle and debate, these accounts cannot explain why heightened anxiety about crime and other manifestations of social change and instability – whatever their source – would necessarily lead to punitive penal policies. In what follows, we argue that political discourse on crime and punishment has give expression to these preferences and anxieties in ways that generate support for punitive penal and social policies.

CRIME, PUNISHMENT AND RECONSTRUCTION OF THE STATE

In the late 1950s, Southern governors and law enforcement officials began to use the rhetoric of law and order in an attempt to heighten popular opposition to the civil rights movement. As the debate over civil rights became a national one and welfare rights activists pressured the state to assume greater responsibility for social welfare, the crime issue assumed a central place on the national political agenda. The debates over civil rights and welfare involved the question of whether government is obligated to assume responsibility for creating a more egalitarian society. Without being explicitly identified as such, competing images of the poor as "deserving" or "undeserving" became central components of this debate.

It was in this context that crime-related problems became staples of national political discourse. By drawing attention to the problems of street crime, drug addiction and delinquency, and by depicting these problems as examples of the immorality of the impoverished, conservatives encouraged the public to imagine the poor as dangerous and undeserving. Indeed, over time, race, crime, violence, delinquency and drug addiction became defining features of those now referred to as "the underclass" (Katz, 1993). Of course, the visions of the poor as dangerous and undeserving provides the "vocabulary of punitive motives" (Melossi, 1985) that justifies a more Hobbesian conception of government, according to which the state assumes responsibility for the maintenance of order but not for the reduction of the social inequalities that, ironically, threaten that order.

The politicisation of crime was thus a component of the effort to replace social welfare with social control as the principle of state policy. Toward this end, conservative politicians used discussions of the crime issue to ridicule the notion that criminal (or any other "deviant") behaviour has socio-economic causes, and promoted the alternative view that such behaviour is the consequence of "insufficient curbs on the appetites or impulses that naturally impel individuals towards criminal activities" (Richard Nixon, quoted in Marion, 1994: 70). This neo-classical view that the causes of crime lie in the human "propensity to evil" clearly calls for the expansion of the social control apparatus rather than policies aimed at ameliorating social inequalities.

In the decades that followed, conservatives continued to emphasise "street crime" and to promote individualistic understandings of its causes. President Ronald Reagan's first major address on crime, for example, consisted of a sweeping philosophical attack on "the social thinkers of the fifties and sixties who discussed crime only in the context of disadvantaged childhoods and poverty stricken neighborhoods" (quoted in Gross, 1982: 123). The need to hold individuals – not society – accountable for crime was emphasized again and again in Reagan's speeches on crime:

> Here in the richest nation in the world, where more crime is committed than in any other nation, we are told that the answer to this problem is to reduce our poverty. This isn't the answer . . . Government's function is to protect society from the criminal, not the other way around.
>
> (Reagan, 1984a: 252)

Somewhat contradictorily, conservatives also identified the "culture of welfare" as an important cause of "social pathologies" – especially crime, delinquency and drug addiction. For example, Presidential candidate Barry Goldwater argued in the 1964 election campaign that welfare programmes are an important cause of increased lawlessness and crime (Matusow, 1984: 143). [. . .]

Lest they be perceived as mean-spirited, these critics of the welfare state depicted public assistance programmes as detrimental to the poor themselves and conservatives as the true allies of the impoverished (Reagan, 1985: 1176). [. . .]

Over the years, conservatives continued to argue that welfare programmes such as Aid Families Dependent Children (AFDC) not only reproduce poverty, but accounted, along with lenient crime policies, for the rising crime rate and problems such as drug abuse. Like individualistic interpretations of crime, this argument was used in an effort to legitimate reductions in welfare spending and the adoption of punitive crime and drug policies (Reagan, 1984b: 672). [. . .]

Despite their differences, then, the neo-classical and "culture of welfare" theories of crime initially promoted by conservatives, similarly imply the need to adopt policies that enhance social control and diminish government responsibility for the reduction of social inequality. Initially, the (Democratic) Johnson administration countered the conservative anti-crime campaign by stressing the social causes of crime and by questioning the accuracy of the reported increases in the official crime rate. But by 1965, liberals began to change course, and over time Democratic politicians have become even less likely to challenge the conservative approach to the crime problem. Particularly in response to the Reagan/Bush war on drugs, Democratic Party officials made the conservative rhetoric on crime and drugs their own.

The liberal about-face on crime-related problems reflects, among other things, conservatives' ability to disseminate law-and order rhetoric through the mass media. The presence of the political elites – especially politicians and law enforcement personnel – in news stories that focused on crime and drugs had a significant impact on the way in which the crime and drug problems were framed. [. . .]

While their capacity to shape media representations is not infinite, officials have been quite effective in using the mass media to disseminate images of the crime and drug problems which implied the need for greater punishment and control.

The capacity of elites to mobilise public opinion in favour of "get tough" solutions to the crime problem also reflects the fact that the symbols and rhetoric associated with the discourse of law and order resonate with deep-seated cultural "myths" and help to make sense of lived experience. The neo-classical depiction of crime as a personal and free choice, for example, is consonant with American individualism. Similarly, the argument that welfare programmes encourage family disintegration and crime taps into (and reinforces) widespread concern about social instability and the "breakdown" of the family (see Sasson, 1995). The fact that the discourse of law and order resonates with (and reinforces) these "myths" helps to explain its growing popularity.

The racial sub-text of the decline of "law and order" helps to explain the particular appeal of this rhetoric among those who hold radically and socially conservative views. While many such votes are long-time supporters of the Republican party, others are economic liberals who have historically voted Democrat. In-depth interviews with these "swing" voters reveal that racially charged hostility toward those who "seek something for nothing" – criminals and welfare cheats in particular – is widespread, and that this hostility informs supports for punitive anti-crime and welfare policies (Omi and Winant, 1987; see also Edsall and Edsall, 1991). The strength of these sentiments has had quite significant policy implications, as the Republican and Democratic parties have competed intensely for the loyalty of the these "Reagan Democrats" in recent years.

Finally, while the incidence of violent crime probably did not increase in recent decades, the sense that it was increasingly pervasive and random in nature has generated anxiety and fear among some. When combined with anxiety about social change and instability, calls for "tough" anti-crime policies appear to identify a scapegoat for and resolution of these concerns (Garland, 2000b; Tyler and Boeckmann, 1997).

Although the policies associated with the war on crime are relatively popular, particularly among certain segments of the white population, it is important to recognise that the "success" of the campaign for law and order reflects the resonance of a particular . . . set of images at a specific historic and political juncture. Those who attribute this success instead to a monolithic and immutable "American punitiveness" overlook the political origins of the campaign for law and order, as well as the complexity of popular beliefs about crime and punishment. This complexity is an important resource for progressives who seek to shift the terms of the debates in a more humanitarian and progressive direction. The fact that most members of the public continue to believe that crime has social causes and that rehabilitative programmes are an effective means of responding to crime suggests that the discourses of "root causes" may still be deployed with some success. Similarly, the fact that concern about the "breakdown" of the family (and social fabric more generally) informs assessments of the crime problem (Sasson, 1995) and support for punitive anti-crime policies (Tyler and Boeckmann, 1997) need not work exclusively to the advantage of conservatives; a progressive alternative to the rhetoric of the war on crime might stress the ways in which structural forces such as unemployment, low wages, inadequate medical care and limited access to child care can diminish the capacity of parents to care for their young (Sasson, 1995; see also Currie, 1998).

To sum up, the discourse of law and order has become more entrenched in American political culture and is especially popular among socially and racially conservative voters. Concerns about security, change and stability inform this shift, as do racial tensions and stereotypes. But it is also clear that political elites have played a leading role in calling attention to crime-related problems, in defining these problems as the consequence of insufficient punishment and control, and in channelling popular concerns in ways that generate popular support for punitive anti-crime and welfare policies. This ideological campaign has been a component of a much larger effort to establish social control rather than social welfare as the primary state responsibility.

FROM SOCIAL CONTROL TO SOCIAL WELFARE

The effort to reshape government policy around social control rather than social welfare has had important consequences for US social policy, and in particular, for welfare programmes aimed at the poor. Beginning as a pension programme for widows, Aid Families Dependent Children was gradually transformed into a cash support programme for single mothers after World War II and has remained the main cash assistance programme. In the 1960s, however, policymakers began to challenge means-tested welfare entitlement. In 1967, a Democratic Congress imposed the first work and training requirements on AFDC recipients, and additional work requirements were added in 1971 (Heclo, 1994). The redistributive effect of AFDC was further weakened by its variation across states: poor states offered small benefits with tight eligibility rules, while wealthier states could afford more generous support (Patterson, 1981: 162–3).

The already tenuous position of AFDC in the 1970s foreshadowed the welfare state retrenchment of the 1980s. Two pieces of legislation in the first year of the Reagan administration significantly eroded the redistributive role of American government. The 1981 Economic Recovery Tax Act effected a general 23 per cent cut in marginal tax rates. However, standard deductions and personal exemptions remained unchanged, providing minimal tax relief to low-income families. Because the tax cut was accompanied by a large increase in defence spending, unprecedented budget deficits resulted, placing strong downward pressure on social spending (Danziger and Gottschalk, 1995: 24). The declining economic position of the poor was further undermined by the Omnibus Budget Reconciliation Act (OBRA). Driven by a philosophy of self-reliance and justified by the notion that many welfare recipients were "cheats" or "greedy, not needy", OBRA reduced real spending on employment and training, unemployment compensation, and removed nearly half-a-million working families from AFDC rolls between 1981 and 1983 alone (Danziger and Gottschalk, 1995: 25).

The most recent revisions to the welfare system in the 1996 Personal Responsibility and Work Opportunity Act further tightened work and eligibility requirements. The average benefit payment to families entitled to AFDC has also declined considerably. In response to these cuts in state assistance to the poor, child poverty rates in the 1980s and 1990s have been about one-third higher that in the 1970s (Danziger and Gottschalk, 1995: 67). The severity of poverty has also increased: the average payment required to lift the poor above the poverty line was more than 20 per cent higher in the 1980s and early 1990s than in the 1970s (Danziger and Weinberg, 1994: 33).

The reorientation of government policy has had an equally dramatic effect on penal policy and institutions. Beginning in the mid-1970s, the US incarceration rate began to climb. Between 1980 and 1998, the number of people incarcerated in the United States increased by more than 300 per cent and now totals over 1.8 million (BJS, 1999). Approximately 1.2 million of these inmates are housed in federal and state prisons, up from 266,000 in 1980. The jail population also grew dramatically during this period, from about 183,000 to nearly 600,000 (BJS, 1999). The number of people on probation and parole has grown almost as rapidly as the inmate population, and by 1997 nearly 5.7 million adults (almost three per cent of the population) were under some form of correction supervision (BJS, 1998, Tables 6.1 and 6.2). These developments have had particularly pronounced implications for young, male minorities. By 1995, one out of three (32 per cent) black males aged 20–29 were under some form of state supervision and nearly seven per cent of all black male adults were incarcerated (BJS, 1998).

Keeping these people under governmental supervision is, of course, quite costly. Total criminal justice expenditures increased from approximately $36 billion in 1982 to nearly $94 billion ten years later (BJS, 1995a, Table 1.1). By contrast, only $41 billion was spent on all unemployment benefits and employment-related services in 1992 (Bureau of the Census, 1995, Table 585). While the budgets of all components of the criminal justice system have grown, spending on "correctional" institutions has increased most dramatically. By 1992, the public cost of correctional facilities alone totalled more than $31 billion (BJS, 1995a: 3).

The attack on programmes aimed at the poor has thus occurred alongside an unprecedented expansion of the social control apparatus. The simultaneity of these shifts is not accidental, but reflects a redefinition of the role and responsibilities of the US government that has been legitimated by the image of the poor as dangerous and undeserving. In what follows, we argue that by removing disproportionately working age and minority men from estimates of employment and unemployment levels, the expansion of the penal system has bolstered assessments of US economic performance. These falsely optimistic assessments have, in turn, been a crucial source of legitimation for those promoting the "American model" of governance.

INCARCERATION AND THE DEBATE OVER SOCIAL POLICY

The proper role of the government in social and economic affairs has not just been debated within the United States, but is the subject of intense controversy around the globe. In these debates, the "American model", ostensibly characterised by an unregulated labour market, is contrasted with the co-called "Continental model". Critics of the latter contrast high rates of European unemployment with the apparently strong performance of the US labour market and conclude that the decline of Keynesianism in the United States has produced a more efficient economic system. According to this argument, European welfare states, with their generous unemployment benefits, high levels of unionisation, and strong welfare programmes, are characterised by reduced market flexibility and work incentives and, therefore, high levels of unemployment.

But the estimates of unemployment upon which these arguments rest do not include the prison and jail populations, which in the US are now estimated at nearly 1.8 million. In what follows, we argue that apparently low rates of unemployment in the United States are in part due to the dramatic expansion of its penal system. When the incarcerated population is included in estimates of unemployment, it appears that European economies have had lower levels of male unemployment than has the US for most of the past two decades.

Social policy, penal institutions, and the labour market

It is often observed that the United States lags far behind Western Europe in industrial relations policy and welfare state development (see Table 9.1). The comparative weakness of US industrial relations is illustrated by unionisation and collective bargaining coverage statistics (Columns 1 and 2). Social policy is also less developed in the United States. For example, while approximately one-quarter of the gross domestic product (GDP) is devoted to social welfare in the large European countries, US social spending accounts for only 15 per cent of the GDP (Column 3). Similarly, both coverage of unemployment insurance and spending on employment-related services in the United States are quite low by comparative standards (Columns 4 and 5).

Although welfare and industrial relations statistics do illustrate the weakness of social protection mechanism in the United States, this does not justify the claim that market principles alone drive the superior US employment record. Labour markets are embedded

Table 9.1 Selected industrial relations and social policy characteristics of 12 OECD countries

Countries	Private sectors union density	Collective bargaining coverage	Total social spending	Unemployment benefit coverage	Active labour market spending
Australia	32	80	13	82	0.34
Canada	28	38	19	129	0.68
Denmark	72	—	28	113	1.56
France	8	92	27	98	0.88
Germany	30	90	23	89	1.64
Italy	32	—	25	—	—
Japan	23	23	12	36	0.13
Netherlands	20	71	29	105	1.12
Norway	41	75	29	61	1.14
Sweden	81	83	33	93	3.21
United Kingdom	38	47	24	71	0.59
United States	13	18	15	34	0.25
Average excluding the United States	38	72	24	94	10.3

Source: Western and Beckett, 1999.

Notes: United density and collective bargaining coverage are expressed as a percentage of all employees. Data are for 1988, except for Canada and the Netherlands (measured in 1985) and the United Kingdom (1989). Coverage is expressed as a percentage of all employees. Data are for 1990 except for France (1985), Germany (1992) and Japan (1989). Total social spending is measured as a percentage of GDO. All data are for 1990. Unemployment benefit coverage measures unemployment beneficiaries as a percentage of unemployed recorded in labour force surveys. Data are for 1990–1 except for Denmark (1992) and Sweden (1992). Active labour market spending includes public spending on training, employment services, youth measures and subsidized employment expressed as a percentage of GDP. Data are for 1990–2.

Table 9.2 Numbers of inmates and incarceration rates per 100,000 adult population, selected OECD countries, 1992–1993

Countries	Number of inmates	Incarceration rate
Australia	15,895	91
Canada	30,659	116
Denmark	3,406	66
France	51,457	84
Germany	64,029	80
Italy	46,152	80
Japan	45,183	36
Netherlands	7,935	49
Sweden	5,668	69
United Kingdom	60,676	93
United States	1,339,695	519
US Blacks	626,207	1,947
US Whites	658,233	306
Average excluding the United States	26,988	78

Source: Western and Beckett, 1999.

in and affected by a wide array of social arrangements that extend beyond the regulative mechanisms of the welfare state. As we have seen, market deregulation and welfare state retrenchment have been accompanied by rapid expansion of the criminal justice system in the United States. Public expenditures on the penal system are a significant and costly state intervention comparable in size to the large social programmes of European welfare states. Indeed, due to low levels of unemployment insurance coverage and high rates of incarceration, more American men were incarcerated than received unemployment benefits in 1995.

US incarceration rates are even more striking when compared to those of other industrialised democracies (see Table 9.2). In 1993, the US incarceration rate was five to ten times greater than other OECD countries (Column 1). These high rates correspond to large absolute numbers (Column 2). In the United States, prison and jail inmates are counted in the millions. In European countries, prison populations number in the thousands.

The short-term effect of incarceration on unemployment

By moving more than one million able-bodied men of working age into prisons and jails, US criminal justice policy has had profound effects on estimates of employment trends. Because they are institutionalised, prison inmates are not counted by population surveys as members of the civilian labour force, or even among the jobless – those "not in the labour force". In the short-term, then, incarceration lowers conventional measures of unemployment and joblessness by obscuring significant numbers of working age men from the purview of census takers. These labour market statistics therefore give a falsely optimistic picture of labour utilisation when incarceration rates are high.

To remedy this limitation, we analyse unemployment trends that take account of the size of the incarcerated population. If the number of unemployed is given as U, and the total number of civilian employees E, the usual unemployment rate is calculated by:

$$u = \frac{100U}{(U + E)}$$

To take account of the incarcerated population, P, we also examine the adjusted unemployment rate:

$$u* = \frac{100\,(U + P)}{(U + P + E)}$$

The importance of incarceration as a source of hidden unemployment varies by sex and across counties. More than 90 per cent of prison and jail inmates are male in the United States, so we focus on trends in the labour market conditions of men. From a comparative perspective, the short-term effect of incarceration is tiny in Europe because incarceration rates are so low (see Table 9.3). In most European countries, unemployed males outnumber male prison inmates by between ten and 20 to one. In the United States in 1995 this ratio had fallen to just under 2.2 (Column 3). Differences between the United States and Europe are also reflected in the relative size of the conventional unemployment rate, u, and the adjusted figure that includes the incarcerated, u*. In most European countries, counting prison inmates in estimates of unemployment only changes the unemployment rate by a few tenths of a percentage point. By contrast, prison and jail inmates in the United States added 1.5 points to the usual unemployment rate in 1990 (Column 5) and over two points by 1994.

Table 9.3 Male incarceration and unemployment rates in the Unites States and Western Europe, 1990

	Number unemployed (U)	Number incarcerated (P)	U/P	Unemployment rate (u)	Adjusted unemployed rate (u*)	Difference between conventional and adjusted estimates (in %) u* − u
Austria	63	6.0	10.5	3.0	3.3	0.3
Belgium	143	6.7	21.5	6.1	6.3	0.2
Denmark	121	3.4	35.8	7.8	8.0	0.2
Finland	54	3.4	15.8	4.1	4.3	0.2
France	935	44.7	20.9	7.0	7.3	0.3
Germany	968	49.7	19.5	5.5	5.8	0.3
Italy	1102	11.4	96.7	7.6	7.6	0.1
Netherlands	228	6.2	36.9	5.6	5.7	0.1
Sweden	36	4.8	7.5	1.5	1.7	0.2
UK	1155	51.4	22.5	7.2	7.5	0.3
United States	3799	1087.9	3.5	5.6	7.0	1.5

Source: Western and Beckett, 1999.
Note: Data from all countries are for 1990, except Italy (1986). The unemployed and incarcerated populations are measured in thousand.

Conventional estimates of US and average European unemployment suggest that unemployment in the United States peaked in 1983 at about ten per cent, dropped in the later 1980s, and rose again in the early 1990s – but recovered fairly quickly after each of these recessions. Although European unemployment rates were low compared to the United States until 1984, estimates of unemployment suggest that recovery from the recessions of the mid-1980s and early 1990s in Europe was relatively weak.

But US employment performance looks less impressive once we take the size of the prison and jail population into account. Our adjusted estimate adds inmates to the male unemployment count and shows that male labour market inactivity in the United States never fell below about seven per cent in the 1980s. By 1994, the prison and jail population had become so large that it added about two percentage points to the male unemployment rate. These modified estimates suggest that unemployment in the economically buoyant period of the mid-1990s was about eight per cent – higher than any conventional US unemployment rate since the recession of the early 1980s. When the incarcerated population is included in estimates of unemployment and joblessness, European rates of unemployment are actually lower than those in the United States for 18 of the 20 years between 1975 and 1995.

A more detailed examination of the US data allows us to identify the impact of incarceration on estimates of unemployment and jobless rates among black and white men. Observed unemployment, u, and the adjusted measure, u*, are shown in Table 9.4. In 1983, when the prison population is added to the unemployment count, the resulting unemployment rate for all men is just one percentage point higher. Estimates of unemployment among black men in 1983 increased by four percentage points to 23 per cent. The effect of incarceration on white male unemployment is smaller, raising the unemployment rate by only about half a percentage point. As the prison population grew through the 1980s, however, the labour market effects of incarceration became much larger. For all men, average unemployment in the 1990s was lifted to nearly eight per cent. When the incarcerated population is included in estimates of black unemployment we find that nearly one in five African-American men were without a job throughout the 1990s. Incarceration has a similar effect on estimates of black joblessness, a category that includes those no longer looking for work.

Table 9.4 Conventional and adjusted (incarcerated population included) unemployment and jobless rates for men, 1983–1995

Year	All men		Black men		White men	
	Conventional u	Adjusted u*	Conventional u	Adjusted u*	Conventional u	Adjusted u*
Unemployment Rates:						
1983	9.7	10.6	19.1	23.0	8.6	9.2
1985–9	5.5	6.7	11.6	16.9	4.7	5.5
1990–4	5.9	7.7	11.3	18.8	5.2	6.3
Jobless Rate:						
1983	29.4	29.9	39.5	41.7	28.3	28.6
1985–9	6.2	27.0	34.0	37.0	25.3	25.7
1990–5	27.0	28.1	34.3	38.5	26.2	26.8

Source: Western and Beckett, 1999.

To summarise, the growth of US incarceration through the 1980s and 1990s conceals a high rate of persistent unemployment and joblessness. Adjusted unemployment figures that include the incarcerated population suggest the United States labour market has performed worse than European labour markets for much of the past two decades. Incarceration has particularly strong effects on estimates of black unemployment: when inmates are added to jobless statistics, rates of joblessness among black men have remained around 40 per cent. [. . .]

The long-term effect of incarceration on unemployment

Thus it appears that by removing large numbers of men from the labour force count, incarceration artificially lowers conventional estimates of labour inactivity. However, it is likely that the expansion of prisons and jails will increase unemployment in the long run. Research suggests that the prospects of job applicants with no criminal record are far better than those of demographically similar persons who were convicted and incarcerated. While convicts who acquire educational and vocational skills in prison are able to improve their chances of employment (Irwin and Austin, 1994), resources for education and vocational training in prisons and jails have declined in both absolute and relative terms, and the recent decision to pay inmates Pell grants to pursue higher education suggests that this trend is likely to continue in the future.

Our analysis of data from the National Longitudinal Study of Youth (NLSY) (not presented here) supports the argument that incarceration increases the likelihood of future joblessness. The results of this analysis indicate that youth incarceration reduces annual employment by about five percentage points, or about three weeks per year, controlling for education, work experience and local labour market conditions. The effect is larger for blacks, whose employment is reduced by about eight percentage points (more than four weeks in the year) by juvenile incarceration. In fact, the effects of youth incarceration on adult employment are larger than failure to graduate from high school or living in a high unemployment area. Even after 15 years, respondents who were incarcerated as juveniles worked between five and ten percentage points less than their counterparts who did not experience incarceration. The effects of adult incarceration on employment status are even greater, reducing employment by about one-fifth or about ten weeks per year. A variety of analyses thus strongly supported the conclusion that incarceration has large and extremely long-lasting effects on the job prospects of ex-convicts.

CONCLUSION

Over the past several decades, the crime issue in the United States has played a central role in justifying the reorientation of government policy around social control rather than social welfare. As a result, the already feeble protections offered to the poor have shrunk considerably, while penal institutions have expanded dramatically. In international policy debates, apparently low levels of unemployment in the United States are attributed to this uniquely "American model" of government.

By contrast, our research suggests the US state has made a significant intervention in the labour market by expanding the penal system in the 1980s and 1990s. Consisting mostly of young, unskilled, able-bodied men of working age, large and growing prison and jail populations conceal a high level of joblessness that, if included in labour market statistics, would contribute about two percentage points to the male unemployment rate by the mid-1990s. These effects are especially strong for African-Americans: labour inactivity is understated by about two-thirds, or seven percentage points, by the conventional measure of black male unemployment. Despite claims of "Eurosclerosis" and the successful deregulation of the US labour market, our revised estimates show that unemployment in the United States exceeded average European rates between 1975 and 1993.

While incarceration has the immediate effect of lowering conventional estimates of joblessness and unemployment, it significantly increases the chances of unemployment among ex-convicts. With well over one million men currently in prison or jail, current levels of incarceration annually generate the equivalent of a full year of unemployment for more than 200,000 American men. In the aggregate, then, it appears that the high US incarceration rate will greatly reduce the productivity and employment of the male workforce.

How can these findings be reconciled? If incarceration lowers conventional measures of joblessness in the short-term but increases unemployment in the long-term, why does the US labour market still perform well according to conventional indicators? The steady expansion of the prison and jail population, combined with high rates of recidivism and re-incarceration, helps to explain this paradox. About two-thirds of young state prisoners are re-arrested within three years, removing many of those at risk of unemployment from the labour force. With high rates of recidivism and intensified surveillance of ex-convicts, the short-term negative effect of incarceration on unemployment dominates the long-term positive effect. Under these conditions, the appearance of strong employment performance has been assisted by an ever-increasing correctional population. Thus, far from being unregulated, the distinctively American mode of labour market regulation may be understood as *hyper-regulatory*. By this we mean that a sustained policy effect (low unemployment) depends on a policy intervention of ever-increasing magnitude.

Bibliography

Beckett, Katherine. 1995. "Media Depictions of Drug Abuse: The Impact of Official Sources," *Research in Political Sociology* 7: 161–182.

——. 1997. *Making Crime Pay: Law and Order in Contemporary American Politics*. New York: Oxford University Press.

Beckett, Katherine and Theodore Sasson. 2004. *The Politics of Injustice: Crime and Punishment in America*. (Beverly Hills, CA: Pine Forge Press).

Bureau of the Census. 1995. *Statistical Abstract of the United States, 1992*. Washington, DC: US Government Printing Office.

Bureau of Justice Statistics (BJS). 1995a. *Sourcebook of Criminal Justice Statistics, 1994*. Washington, DC: Bureau of Justice Statistics.

——. 1995b. *Census of Federal and State Correctional Facilities*. Washington, DC: Department of Justice.

——. 1998. *Sourcebook of Criminal Justice Statistics, 1997*. Washington, DC: Bureau of Justice Statistics.

——. 1999. *Prison and Jail Inmates at Midyear, 1998*. Washington, DC: Bureau of Justice Statistics.

Burtless, Gary. 1994. "Public Spending on the Poor: Historical Trends and Economic Limits," in Sheldon H. Danziger, Gary D. Sandefur, and Daniel H. Weinberg (eds) *Confronting Poverty: Prescriptions for Change*. New York: Russell Sage Foundation, pp. 51–84.

Butterfield, Fox. 1998. "Inmates Serving More Time, Justice Department Reports," *New York Times*, January 11, p. A10.

Cohn, Steven Barkan and William Halteman. 1991. "Punitive Attitudes Towards Criminals: Racial Consensus or Racial Conflict?," *Social Problems* 38: 287–296.

Cullen, Francis T., Gregory A. Clark, and John F. Wozniak. 1985. "Explaining the Get-Tough Movement: Can the Public be Blamed?," *Federal Probation* 45(2): 16–24.

Cullen, Francis T., Sandra Evans Skovron, Joseph E. Scott, and Velmer S. Burton, Jr. 1990. "Public Support for Correctional Treatment," *Criminal Justice and Behavior* 17(1): 2–18.

Currie, Elliott. 1998. *Crime and Punishment in America*. New York: Henry Holt and Co., Inc.

Danziger, Sheldon H. and Daniel Weinberg. 1994. "The Historical Record: Trends in Family Income, Inequality, and Poverty," in Sheldon H. Danziger, Gary D. Sandefur, and Daniel H. Weinberg (eds) *Confronting Poverty: Prescriptions for Change*. New York: Russell Sage Foundation, pp. 18–50.

Danziger, Sheldon and Peter Gottschalk. 1995. *America Unequal*. New York: Russell Sage Foundation.

Donziger, Steven R. (ed.). 1996. *The Real War on Crime: The Report of the National Criminal Justice Commission*. New York: HarperPerennial.

Edsall, Thomas B. and Mary Edsall. 1991. *Chain Reaction: The Impact of Rights, Race and Taxes on American Politics*. New York: Norton and Co.

Fox Piven, Francis. 1998. "Politics and Public Opinion," *Contemporary Sociology* 27(5) (September): 457–460.

Garland, David. 2000. "The Culture of High Crime Societies: Some Preconditions of Recent 'Law and Order' Policies," *British Journal of Criminology* 40.

Gross, Bertram. 1982. "Reagan's Criminal Anti-Crime Fix," in Alan Gartner, Colin Greer, and Frank Riessman (eds) *What Reagan is Doing to Us*. New York: Harper and Row.

Heclo, Hugh. 1994. "Poverty Politics," in Sheldon H. Danziger, Gary D. Sandefur, and Daniel H. Weinberg (eds) *Confronting Poverty: Prescriptions for Change*. New York: Russell Sage Foundation, pp. 396–437.

Irwin, John and James Austin. 1994. *It's About Time: America's Imprisonment Binge*. Belmont, CA: Wadsworth.

Katz, Michael B. 1993. "The Urban Underclass as a Metaphor of Social Transformation," in Michael B. Katz (ed.) *The Underclass Debate*. Princeton, NJ: Princeton University Press.

Lynch, James. 1995. "Crime in International Perspective," in James Q. Wilson and Joan Petersilia (eds) *Crime*. San Francisco, CA: Institute for Contemporary Studies, pp. 11–33.

McGarrell, Edmund and Marla Sandys. 1996. "The Misperception of Public Opinion Toward Capital Punishment," *American Behavioral Scientist* 39(4): 500–513.

Marion, Nancy E. 1994. *A History of Federal Crime Control Initiatives, 1960–1993*. Westport, CT: Praeger.

Matusow, Allen J. 1984. *The Unraveling of America: A History of Liberalism in the 1960s*. New York: Harper Torchbooks.

Mauer, Marc. 1994. *Americans Behind Bars: The International Use of Incarceration*. Washington, DC: Sentencing Project.

Mayhew, Pat and Jan van Dijk. 1997. *Criminal Victimization in Eleven Industrialized Countries: key Findings from the 1996 International Crime Victims Survey*. The Hague: Dutch Ministry of Justice.

Omi, Michael and Howard Winant. 1987. *Racial Formation in the United States*. New York: Routledge and Kegan Paul.

Patterson, James T. 1981. *America's Struggle Against Poverty*. Cambridge, MA: Harvard University Press.

Reagan, Ronald. 1984. "Remarks at the Conservative Political Action Conference Dinner," *Public Papers of the Presidents 1983*, Volume I. Washington, DC: US Government Printing Office, pp. 251–254.

———. 1984. "Remarks at a Fundraising Dinner Honoring Former Representative John M. Ashbrook in Ashland, Ohio," *Public Papers of the Presidents 1983*, Volume I. Washington, DC: US Government Printing Office, pp. 670–673.

———. 1985. "Radio Address to the Nation on Proposed Crime Legislation," *Public Papers of the Presidents 1984*, Volume II. Washington, DC: US Government Printing Office, pp. 1175–1177.

Roberts, Julian V. 1992. "Public Opinion, Crime and Criminal Justice," in Michael Tonry (ed.) *Crime and Justice: A Review of Research*, Volume 16. Chicago, IL: University of Chicago Press.

Sandys, Marla and Edmund McGarrell. 1995. "Attitudes Towards Capital Punishment," *Journal of Research in Crime and Delinquency* 32(2): 191–213.

Sasson, Theodore. 1995. *Crime Talk: How Citizen's Construct a Social Problem*. New York: Aldine de Gruyter.

Savelsberg, Joachim. 1999. "Cultures of State Punishment USA–Germany," presented at the meetings of the Law and Society Association, Renaissance Hotel, Chicago, IL, May 27–30.

Stinchcombe, Arthur T., Rebecca Adams, Carol A. Heimer, Kim Lane Scheppele, Tom W. Smith, and D. Garth Taylor. 1980. *Crime and Punishment in America: Changing Attitudes in America*. San Francisco, CA: Jossey-Bass Publishers.

Tonry, Michael. 1995. *Malign Neglect: Race, Crime and Punishment in America*. New York: Oxford University Press.

Tyler, Tom R. and Robert J. Boeckmann. 1997. "Three Strikes and You're Out, but Why? The Psychology of Public Support for Punishing Rule Breakers," *Law and Society Review* 31(2): 237–266.

Van Dijk, Jan J.M., Pat Mayhew, and Martin Killias. 1991. *Experiences of Crime Across the World: Key Findings of the 1989 International Crime Survey*, 2nd edition. Boston, MA: Kluwer.

Wacquant, Loic. 2001. "Blairism: Trojan Horse of Americanism?," in Keijo Rahkonen and Tapani Lausti (eds) *Blairism: A Beacon for Europe?* London: Institute for Public Policy Research.

Western, Bruce and Katherine Beckett. 1999. "How Unregulated is the US Labor Market? The Penal System as Labor Market Institution," *American Journal of Sociology* 104(4) (January): 1030–1060.

Zimring, Franklin and Gordon Hawkins. 1997. *Crime is not the Problem: Lethal Violence in America*. New York: Oxford University Press.

Chapter 10

Malcolm M. Feeley and Jonathan Simon

THE NEW PENOLOGY

Notes on the emerging strategy of corrections and its implications

From: Malcolm M. Feeley and Jonathan Simon (1992), excerpts from 'The New Penology', *Criminology* 30(4): 449–474.

I T IS OFTEN OBSERVED that penal ideology and practice became more conservative during the 1970s and 1980s. This shift is only part of a deeper change in conception – discourse, objectives, and techniques – in the penal process. These shifts have multiple and independent origins and are not reducible to any one reigning idea (e.g., getting tough on criminals). Despite their different origins, the elements of this emerging new conception have coalesced to form a new strategic formation in the penal field, which we call the *new penology*. By *strategy* we do not mean a conscious and coherent agenda employed by a determinate set of penal agents. Rather, the loose set of inter-connected developments that we call the new penology increasingly shapes the way the power to punish is exercised. Foucault's (1978:94) notion that power is both "intentional and nonsubjective" suggests we not deny that people have deliberate strategies but that the overall configuration created by multiple strategies is itself "strategic" without being deliberate (Foucault, 1982:225).

The transformations we call the new penology involve shifts in three distinct areas:

1   The emergence of new discourses: In particular, the language of probability and risk increasingly replaces earlier discourses of clinical diagnosis and retributive judgment. There has been a shift from focusing on the individual, beyond even managing behavior (Cohen, 1985; Wilkins, 1973) to managing segments of the "population."

2   The formation of new objectives for the system are in some sense newly "systemic," such as the efficient control of internal system processes in place of the traditional objectives of rehabilitation and crime control. The sense that any external social referent is intended is becoming attenuated.

3   The deployment of new techniques targeting offenders as an aggregate in place of traditional techniques for individualizing or creating equity.

The new penology has served a significant function in locking together some of the external factors impinging on the criminal justice system and in determining the prevailing responses of the system. Nothing seems as defining as the massive increase in the level of incarceration since the 1970s. Conventional understanding links rise to demographic changes, social changes (like increased drug use), improvement in the efficiency of law enforcement, and increases in the punitiveness of sentencing systems. More can be accomplished with models that allow for the contingent interaction of all these factors (Zimring and Hawkins, 1991:157). A shortfall of this approach, however, is that it holds constant the nature of the penal enterprise while varying external pressures and internal policy shifts. Our analysis of the new penology emphasizes more holistic features of the current penal formation.

The new penology is found among criminal justice practitioners and the research community as a communicative process, a system of discourse having "a life of its own." [. . .]

Unlike the "old" penology which concentrates on individuals as the unit of analysis, the new penology is markedly less concerned with responsibility, fault, moral sensibility, diagnosis, or intervention and treatment of the individual offender. Rather, it is concerned with techniques to identify, classify, and manage groupings sorted by dangerousness. The task is managerial, not transformative (Cohen, 1985; Garland and Young, 1983; Messinger, 1969; Messinger and Berecochea, 1990; Reichman, 1986; Wilkins, 1973). It seeks to *regulate* levels of deviance, not intervene or respond to individual deviants or social malformations.

Although the new penology is much more than "discourse," its language helps reveal this shift most strikingly. It does not speak of impaired individuals in need of treatment or of morally irresponsible persons who need to be held accountable for their actions. Rather, it considers the criminal justice *system*, and it pursues systemic rationality and efficiency. It seeks to sort and classify, to separate the less from the more dangerous, and to deploy control strategies rationally. The tools for this enterprise include "indicators," prediction tables, population projections. Individualized diagnosis and response is displaced by aggregate classification systems for purposes of surveillance, confinement, and control (Gordon, 1991).

DISTINGUISHING FEATURES OF THE NEW PENOLOGY

What we call the new penology is not a theory of crime or criminology but a focus on certain problems and a shared way of framing issues. This strategic formation of knowledge and power offers managers of the system a more or less coherent picture of the challenges they face and the kinds of solutions that are most likely to work. While we cannot reduce it to a set of principles, we can point to some of its most salient features.

The new discourse

A central feature of the new discourse is the replacement of a moral or clinical description of the individual with an actuarial language of probabilistic calculations and statistical distributions applied to populations. Although social utility analysis or actuarial thinking is commonplace enough in modern life – it frames policy considerations of all sorts – in recent years this mode of thinking has gained ascendancy in legal discourse, a system of reasoning that traditionally has employed the language of morality and been focused on individuals (Simon, 1988). For instance, this new mode of reasoning is found increasingly in tort law, where traditional fault and negligence standards – which require a focus on the individual and are based upon notions of individual responsibility – have given way to strict liability and no-fault. These new doctrines rest upon actuarial ways of thinking about how to "manage" accidents and public safety. They employ the language of social utility and management, not individual responsibility (Simon, 1987; Steiner, 1987). [. . .]

There has been a rising trend in the penal system to target categories and subpopulations rather than individuals (Bottoms, 1983; Cohen, 1985; Mathieson, 1983; Reichman, 1986). This partly reflects actuarial forms of representation that promote quantification as a way of visualizing populations. The advance of statistical methods permits the formulation of concepts and strategies that allow direct relations between penal strategy and the population. Earlier generations used statistics to map the responses of normatively defined groups to punishment; today one talks of "high-rate offenders," "career criminals," and other categories defined by the distribution itself. Rather than simply extending the capacity of the system to rehabilitate or control crime, actuarial classification has come increasingly to define the correctional enterprise itself. [. . .]

The new objectives

The new penology is neither about punishing nor about rehabilitating individuals. It is about identifying and managing unruly groups. It is concerned with the rationality not of individual behavior or even community organization, but of managerial processes. Its goal is not to eliminate crime but to make it tolerable through systemic coordination.

One measure of the shift away from trying to normalize offenders and toward trying to manage them is seen in the declining significance of recidivism. Under the old penology, recidivism was a nearly universal criterion for assessing success or failure of penal programs. Under the new penology, the word recidivism seems to be used less often, precisely because it carries a normative connotation that reintegrating offenders into the community is the major objective. High rates of parolees being returned to prison once indicated program failure; now they are offered as evidence of efficiency and effectiveness of parole as a control apparatus. This is especially true for intensive parole and probation supervision programs. [. . .]

It is possible that recidivism is dropping out of the vocabulary as an adjustment to harsh realities and as a way of avoiding charges of institutional failure. However, in shifting to emphasize the virtues of return as an indication of *effective* control, the new penology reshapes one's understanding of the functions of the penal sanction. By emphasizing correctional programs in terms of aggregate control and system management rather than individual success and failure, the new penology lowers one's expectations about the criminal sanction. These redefined objectives are reinforced by the new discourses discussed above, which take deviance as a given, mute aspirations for individual reformation, and seek to classify, sort, and manage dangerous groups efficiently. [. . .]

The importance that recidivism once had in evaluating the performance of corrections is now being taken up by measures of system functioning. Heydebrand and Seron (1990) have noted a tendency in courts and other social agencies toward decoupling performance evaluation from external social objectives. Instead of social norms like the elimination of crime, reintegration into the community, or public safety, institutions begin to measure their own outputs as indicators of performance. Thus, courts may look at docket flow. Similarly, parole agencies may shift evaluations of performance to, say, the time elapsed between arrests and due process hearings (Heydebrand and Seron, 1990: 190–94; Lipsky, 1980:4–53).

Such technocratic rationalization tends to insulate institutions from the messy, hard-to-control demands of the social world. By limiting their exposure to indicators that they can control, managers ensure that their problems will have solutions. No doubt this tendency in the new penology is, in part, a response to the acceleration of demands for rationality and accountability in punishment coming from the courts and legislatures during the 1970s (Jacobs, 1977). It also reflects the lowered expectations for the penal system that result from failures to accomplish more ambitious promises of the past. [. . .]

The new objectives also inevitably permeate through the courts into thinking about rights. The new penology replaces consideration of fault with predictions of dangerous-ness and safety management and, in so doing, modifies traditional individual-oriented doctrines of criminal procedure.

New techniques

These altered, lowered expectations manifest themselves in the development of more cost-effective forms of custody and control and in new technologies to identify and classify risk. Among them are low frills, no-service custodial centers; various forms of electronic monitoring systems that impose a form of custody without walls; and new statistical techniques for assessing risk and predicting dangerousness. These new forms of control are not anchored in aspirations to rehabilitate, reintegrate, retrain, or provide employment, but are justified in more blunt terms: variable detention depending upon risk assessment.

Perhaps the clearest example of the new penology's method is incapacitation, which has become the predominant utilitarian model of punishment (Greenwood, 1982; Moore et al., 1984). Incapacitation promises to reduce the social effects of crime by rearranging the distribution of offenders in society. Incapacitation theory holds that the prison can detain offenders for a time and thus delay their resumption of criminal activity. Moreover, if such delays are sustained for enough time and for enough offenders, significant aggregate effects in crime can take place although individual destinies are only marginally altered.

These aggregate effects can be further intensified, in some accounts, by a strategy of selective incapacitation. This approach proposes a sentencing scheme in which lengths of sentence depend not upon the nature of the criminal offense or upon an assessment of the character of the offender, but upon risk profiles. Its objectives are to identify high-risk offenders and to maintain long-term control over them while investing in shorter terms and less intrusive control over lower-risk offenders.

The new penology in perspective

The correctional practices emerging from the shifts we have identified above present a kind of "custodial continuum." But unlike the "correctional continuum" discussed in the 1960s, this new custodial continuum does not design penal measures for the particular needs of the individual or the community. Rather, it sorts individuals into groups according to the degree of control warranted by their risk profiles. [. . .]

But the same story can be told in a different order. The steady bureaucratization of the correctional apparatus during the 1950s and 1960s shifted the target from individuals, who did not fit easily into centralized administration, to categories or classes, which do. But once the focus is on categories of offenders rather than individuals, methods naturally shift toward mechanisms of appraising and arranging groups rather than intervening in the lives of individuals. In the end the search for causal order is at least premature.

NEW FUNCTIONS AND TRADITIONAL FORMS

It is best to conceive of the new penology as an interpretive net that can help reveal some directions the future may take. Below we re-examine three of the major features of the contemporary penal landscape: (1) the expansion of the penal sanction, (2) the rise of drug testing, and (3) innovation within the criminal process, and relate them to our thesis.

The expansion of penal sanctions

During the past decade the number of people covered by penal sanctions has expanded significantly. Because of its high costs, the growth of prison populations has drawn the greatest attention, but probation and parole have increased at a proportionate or faster rate. The importance of these other sanctions goes beyond their ability to stretch penal resources; they expand and redistribute the use of imprisonment. Probation and parole violations now constitute a major source of prison inmates, and negotiations over probation revocation are replacing plea bargaining as modes of disposition (Greenspan, 1988; Messinger and Berecochea, 1990).

Many probation and parole revocations are triggered by events, like failing a drug test, that are driven by parole procedures themselves (Simon, 1990; Zimring and Hawkins, 1991). The increased flow of probationers and parolees into prisons is expanding the prison population and changing the nature of the prison. Increasingly, prisons are short-term holding pens for violators deemed too dangerous to remain on the streets. To the extent the prison is organized to receive such people, its correctional mission is replaced by a management function, a warehouse for the highest-risk classes of offenders.

From the perspective of the new penology, the growth of community corrections in the shadow of imprisonment is not surprising. The new penology does not regard prison as a special institution capable of making a difference in the lives of individuals who pass through it. Rather, it functions as but one of several custodial options. [. . .]

The new penology's technique of aggregation has been incorporated in a number of sentencing reforms. Minnesota and the U.S. Sentencing Commission have made population an explicit concern. As Alschuler (1991:951) has shown, although these guidelines have been defended as a step toward providing equal justice, in fact they are based upon "rough aggregations and statistical averages," which mask significant differences among offenders and offenses. The guidelines movement marks "a changed attitude toward sentencing – one that looks to collections of cases and to social harm rather than to individual offenders and punishments they deserve . . . [and rather than] the circumstances of their cases."

Drugs and punishment

Drug use and its detection and control have become central concerns of the penal system with increasingly tough laws directed against users and traffickers, well-publicized data that suggest that a majority of arrestees are drug users, and an increasing proportion of drug offenders sent to prison.

The emphasis on drugs marks a continuity with the past thirty years of correctional history. Drug treatment and drug testing were hallmarks of the rehabilitative model in the 1950s and 1960s. The recent upsurge of concern with drugs may be attributed to the hardening of social attitudes toward drug use (especially in marked contrast to the tolerant 1970s), the introduction of virulent new drug products like crack cocaine, and the disintegrating social conditions of the urban poor.

Without dismissing the relevance of these continuities and explanations for change, it is important to note that there are distinctive changes in the role of drugs in the current system that reflect the logic of the new penology. In place of the traditional emphasis on treatment and eradication, today's practices track drug use as a kind of risk indicator. The widespread evidence of drug use in the offending population (Maguire and Flanagan, 1990:459) leads not to new theories of crime causation but to more efficient ways of identifying those at highest risk of offending. From the perspective of the new penology, drug use is not so much a measure of individual acts of deviance as it is a mechanism for classifying the offender within a risk group. [. . .]

Testing also fills the gap left by the decline of traditional intervention strategies. If nothing else, testing provides parole (and probably probation) agents a means to document compliance with their own internal performance requirements. It provides both an occasion for requiring the parolee to show up in the parole office and a purpose for meeting. The results of tests have become a network of fact and explanation for use in a decision-making process that requires accountability but provides little substantive basis for distinguishing among offenders.

Innovation

Our description may seem to imply the onset of a reactive age in which penal managers strive to manage populations of marginal citizens with no concomitant effort toward integration into mainstream society. This may seem hard to square with the myriad new and innovative technologies introduced over the past decade. Indeed the media, which for years have portrayed the correctional system as a failure, have recently enthusiastically reported on these innovations: boot camps, electronic surveillance, high security "campuses" for drug users, house arrest, intensive parole and probation, and drug treatment programs.

Although some of the new proposals are presented in terms of the "old penology" and emphasize individuals, normalization, and rehabilitation, it is difficult to know how these innovations will turn out. Historically, reforms evolve in ways quite different from the aims of their proponents (Foucault, 1977; Rothman, 1971). Thus, we wonder if these most recent innovations won't be recast in the terms we have outlined since many are compatible with the imperatives of the new penology: managing a permanently dangerous population while maintaining the system at a minimum cost. [. . .]

SOCIAL BASES OF THE NEW PENOLOGY

We are not arguing that shifts in the way the penal enterprise is understood and discussed inexorably determine how the system will take shape. What actually emerges in corrections over the near and distant future will depend on how this understanding itself is shaped by the pressures of demographic, economic, and political factors. Still, such factors rarely operate as pure forces. They are filtered through and expressed in terms in which the problems are understood. Thus, the strategic field that we call the new penology itself will help shape the future.

The new discourse of crime

Like the old penology, traditional "sociological" criminology has focused on the relationship between individuals and communities. Its central concerns have been the causes and correlates of delinquent and criminal behavior, and it has sought to develop intervention strategies designed to correct delinquents and decrease the likelihood of deviant behavior. Thus, it has focused on the family and the workplace as important influences of socialization and control.

The new penology has an affinity with a new "actuarial" criminology, which eschews traditional criminological concerns. Instead of training in sociology or social work, increasingly the new criminologists are trained in operations research and systems analysis. This new approach is not a criminology at all, but an applied branch of systems theory. This shift in training and orientation has been accompanied by a shift in interest. A concern with successful intervention strategies, the province of the former, is replaced by models designed to optimize public safety through the management of aggregates, which is the province of the latter.

In one important sense this new criminology is simply a consequence of steady improvements in the quantitative rigor with which crime is studied. The amassing of a statistical picture of crime and the criminal justice system has improved researchers' ability to speak realistically about the distribution of crimes and the fairness of procedures. But, we submit, it has also contributed to a shift, a reconceptualization, in the way crime is understood as a social problem. The new techniques and the new language have facilitated reconceptualization of the way issues are framed and policies pursued. Sociological criminology saw crime as a relationship between the individual and the normative expectations of his or her community (Bennett, 1981). Policies premised on this perspective addressed problems of reintegration, including the mismatch between individual motivation, normative orientation, and social opportunity structures. In contrast, actuarial criminology highlights the interaction of criminal justice institutions and specific segments of the population. Policy discussions framed in its terms emphasize the management of high-risk groups and make less salient the qualities of individual delinquents and their communities.

In actuarial criminology the numbers generate the subject (e.g., the high-rate offender of incapacitation research). Criminals are no longer the organizing referent (or logos) of criminology. Instead, criminology has become a subfield of a generalized public policy analysis discourse. This new criminal knowledge aims at rationalizing the operation of the systems that manage criminals, not dealing with criminality. The same techniques that can be used to improve the circulation of baggage in airports or delivery of food to troops can be used to improve the penal system's efficiency.

The discourse of poverty and the "underclass"

The new penology may also be seen as responsive to the emergence of a new under-standing of poverty in America. Although the term "dangerous classes" was part of early-nineteenth-century penal discourse in England, reflecting a management rather than an individualized approach to crime, the term *underclass* is used today to characterize that segment of society viewed as permanently excluded from social mobility and economic integration. The term is used to refer to a largely black and Hispanic population living in concentrated zones of poverty in central cities, separated physically and institutionally from the suburban locus of mainstream social and economic life in America.

In contrast to groups whose members are deemed employable, even though tem-porarily unemployed, the underclass is understood as a permanently marginal population, without literacy, without skills, and without hope; a self-perpetuating and pathological segment of society that is not integratable into the larger whole, even as a reserve labor pool (Wilson, 1987). So conceived, the underclass is also a dangerous class, not only for what any particular member may or may not do, but more generally for collective potential misbehavior. It is treated as a high-risk group that must be managed to protect society. Indeed, it is this managerial task that provides one of the most powerful sources for the imperative of preventive management in the new penology. [. . .]

The emergence of the new penology in the 1980s reflects the influence of a more despairing view of poverty and the prospects for achieving equality. Rehabilitating offenders, or any kind of reintegration strategy, can only make sense if the larger com-munity from which offenders come is viewed as sharing a common normative universe with the communities of the middle classes – especially those values and expectations derived from the labor market. The concept of an underclass, with its connotation of a permanent marginality for whole portions of the population, has rendered the old penol-ogy incoherent and laid the groundwork for a strategic field that emphasizes low-cost management of a permanent offender population.

The connection between the new penality and the (re)emergent term *underclass* also is illustrated by recent studies of American jails. Irwin (1985) entitled his book, *The Jail: Managing the Underclass in American Society*. His thesis is that "prisoners in jails share two essential characteristics: detachment and disrepute" (1985:2). For Irwin, the function of jail is to manage the underclass, which he reports is also referred to as "rabble," "disorganized," "disorderly," and the "lowest class of people."

The high rates of those released without charges filed, the turnstile-like frequency with which some people reappear, and the pathological characteristics of a high proportion of the inmates, lead many to agree with Irwin that the jail is best understood as a social management instrument rather than an institution for effecting the purported aims of the criminal process. Social management, not individualized justice, is also emphasized in other discussions of the criminal process. Longtime public defender James M. Doyle (1992) offers the metaphors "colonial," "White Man's burden," and "Third World," in an essay drawing parallels between the careers of criminal justice officials and colonial administrators. [. . .]

Whether one prefers Irwin's notion of underclass or Doyle's "colonial" and "third world" metaphors, both resonate with our notion of the new penology. They vividly explain who is being managed and why. But in providing an explanation of these relationships, there is a danger that the terms will reify the problem, that they will suggest the problem is inevitable and permanent. Indeed, it is this belief, we maintain, that has contributed to the lowered expectations of the new penology – away from an aspiration to affect individual lives through rehabilitative and transformative efforts and toward the more "realistic" task of monitoring and managing intractable groups. [. . .]

CONCLUSION

Our discussion has proceeded as if the new penology has contributed to the recent rise in prison populations. Although we believe that it has, we also acknowledge that the new penology is both cause and effect of the increases. We recognize that those conditions we referred to at the outset as "external" have placed pressures on criminal justice institutions that, in turn, have caused them to adapt in a host of ways. Our purpose, however, has been to show just how thorough this adaptation has been. It has led to a significant reconceptualization of penology, a shift that institutionalizes those adaptive behaviors. It embraces the new forms that have arisen as a result of this adaptation. As such, the new language, the new conceptualization, ensures that these new forms will persist independently of the pressures. They appear to be permanent features of the criminal justice system.

Bibliography

Alschuler, Albert. 1991. "The Failure of Sentencing Guidelines: A Plea for Less Aggregation," *University of Chicago Review* 58(3): 901–51.

Bennett, James. 1981. *Oral History and Delinquency: The Rhetoric of Criminology*. Chicago, IL: University of Chicago Press.

Bottoms, Anthony E. 1983. "Neglected Features of Contemporary Penal Systems," in David Garland and Peter Young (eds) *The Power to Punish*. London: Heinemann.

Cohen, Stanley. 1985. *Visions of Social Control: Crime, Punishment and Classification*. Oxford: Polity Press.

Foucault, Michel. 1977. *Discipline and Punish: The Birth of the Prison*. New York: Pantheon.

——. 1978. *The History of Sexuality*, Volume I. New York: Random House.

Foucault, Michel. 1982. "The Subject and Power," in Hubert Dreyfus and Paul Rabinow (eds) *Michel Foucault: Beyond Structuralism and Hermeneutics*. Chicago, IL: University of Chicago Press.

Garland, David and Peter Young (eds). 1983. *The Power to Punish: Contemporary Penalty and Social Analysis*. London: Heinemann.

Gordon, Diana R. 1991. *The Justice Juggernaut: Fighting Crime, Controlling Citizens*. New Brunswick, NJ: Rutgers University Press.

Greenspan, Rosanne. 1988. "The Transformation of Criminal due Process in the Administrative State," paper presented at the annual meeting of the Law and Society Association, Vail, CO.

Greenwood, Peter. 1982. *Selective Incapacitation*. Santa Monica, CA: RAND Corporation.

Heydebrand, Wolf and Carroll Seron. 1990. *Rationalizing Justice: The Political Economy and Federal District Courts*. New York: SUNY Press.

Irwin, John. 1981. *The Jail: Managing the Underclass in American Society*. Berkeley, CA: University of California Press.

Jacobs, James B. 1977. *Stateville: The Penitentiary in Mass Society*. Chicago, IL: University of Chicago Press.

Lipsky, Michael. 1980. *Street Level Bureaucrats*. New York: Russell Sage Foundation.

Maguire, Kathleen and Timothy J. Flanagan. 1990. *Sourcebook of Criminal Justice Statistics, 1989*, US Deaprtment of Justice, Bureau of Justice Statistics. Washington, DC: US Government Printing Office.

Mathieson, Thomas. 1983. "The Future of Control Systems: The Case of Norway," in David Garland and Peter Young (eds) *The Power to Punish*. London: Heinemann.

Messinger, Sheldon. 1969. "Strategies of Control," PhD dissertation, Department of Sociology, University of California at Los Angeles.

Messinger, Sheldon and John Berecochea. 1990. "Don't Stay Too Long, but Do Come Back Soon," proceedings, conference on Growth and its Influence on Correctional Policy, Centre for the Study of Law and Society, University of California at Berkeley.

Moore, M.H., S.R. Estrich, D. McGillis, and W. Spelman. 1984. *Dangerous Offenders: The Elusive Target of Justice*. Cambridge, MA: Harvard University Press.

Reichman, Nancy. 1986. "Managing Crime Risks: Toward an Insurance-Based Model of Social Control," *Research in Law, Deviance and Social Control* 8: 151–72.

Rothman, David. 1971. *Discovery of the Asylum: Social Order and Disorder in the New Republic*. Boston, MA: Little Brown.

Simon, Jonathan. 1987. "The Emergence of a Risk Society: Insurance Law and the State," *Socialist Review* 95: 61–89.

——. 1990. "From Discipline to Management: Strategies of Control Parole Supervision, 1890–1990," PhD dissertation, Jurisprudence and Social Policy Program, University of California at Berkeley.

Steiner, Henry J. 1987. *Moral Vision and Social Vision in the Court: A Study of Tort Accident Law*. Madison, WI: University of Wisconsin Press.

Wilkins, Leslie T. 1993. "Crime and Criminal Justice at the Turn of the Century," *Annals of the American Academy of Political and Social Science* 408: 13–29.

Wilson, William J. 1989. *The Truly Disadvantaged: The Inner City, the Underclass and Public Policy*. Chicago, IL: University of Chicago Press.

Zimring, Franklin and Gordon Hawkins. 1991. *The Scale of Imprisonment*. Chicago, IL: University of Chicago Press.

Chapter 11

Christopher Uggen and Jeff Manza

DEMOCRATIC REVERSAL?

Felon disenfranchisement and American democracy

From: Christopher Uggen and Jeff Manza (2002) excerpts from 'Democratic contraction? The political consequences of felon disenfranchisement in the United States', *American Sociological Review* 67: 777–803.

UNIVERSAL SUFFRAGE IS A hallmark of democratic governance. As levels of criminal punishment have risen in the United States, however, an ever-larger number of citizens have lost the right to vote. We ask whether felon disfranchisement constitutes a meaningful reversal of the extension of voting rights by considering its political impact. We examine data from legal sources, election studies, and inmate surveys to consider . . . whether removing disfranchisement restrictions would have altered the outcomes of U.S. Senate and presidential elections. . . . Because felons are drawn disproportionately from the ranks of racial minorities and the poor, disfranchisement laws tend to take votes from Democratic candidates. We find that felon disfranchisement played a decisive role in U.S. Senate elections, helping to establish the Republican Senate majority of the 1990s. [. . .]

The right to vote is a fundamental element of citizenship in democratic societies, one that "makes all other political rights significant" (Piven and Cloward 2000: 2). Although the sequence of establishing formal voting rights varied from country to country, it was almost always a slow, contested, uneven, and protracted process (e.g. Rokkan 1970: 31–36; Therborn 1977; Bowles and Gintis 1986: 43–44, 56; Rueschemeyer, Stephens, and Stephens 1992; Collier 1999). As Dahl (1998: 89) puts it, "in all democracies and republics throughout twenty-five centuries the rights to engage fully in political life were limited to a minority of adults." Political and economic elites often resisted the extension of voting rights to subordinate groups, including women, youth, the non-propertied, workers, poor people, racial and ethnic groups, and others (Markoff 1996: 45–64; cf. Rogers [1992] and Keyssar [2000] on the U.S. case).

Yet over the course of the nineteenth and twentieth centuries, restrictions on the franchise within countries claiming democratic governance have gradually eroded, and universal suffrage has come to be taken for granted as a key component of democracy in both theory and practice (Dahl 1998: 90). One recent study reports that by 1994, fully

96 percent of nation-states claimed to formally enfranchise adult men and women citizens alike (Ramirez, Soysal, and Shanahan 1997: 735). To proclaim democratic governance today means, at a minimum, universal suffrage for all citizens.

In this paper, we consider a rare and potentially significant counter-example to the universalization of the franchise in democratic societies: restrictions on the voting rights of felons and ex-felons in the United States. Felon disfranchisement may constitute an impediment to American political participation largely because of the extraordinarily rapid rise in criminal punishment since the 1970s. While many other countries – but by no means all – restrict the voting rights of prison inmates, the United States is unique for imprisoning far more of its citizens than all other advanced industrial societies, and for restricting the rights of non-incarcerated felons. The 1995 U.S. incarceration rate was 600 prisoners per 100,000 population, compared to rates of 115 per 100,000 in Canada, 85 per 100,000 in Germany, and 37 per 100,000 in Japan (Mauer 1997a) and many recent analysts have documented this aspect of American penal exceptionalism (e.g. Savelsberg 1994; Lynch 1995; Donziger 1996; Sutton 2000).

Whether felon disfranchisement in the United States constitutes a threat to democracy, however, is not a simple question. Modern democratic governance entails a set of macro-political institutions that register citizens' preferences through (among other things) regular competitive elections (see, e.g. Bollen 1979; Przeworski 1991, chap. 1; Dahl 1998). For democratic governance to be threatened, disfranchisement must reach levels sufficient to change election outcomes. Raw counts of the size of the disfranchised felon population are inconclusive: however much the loss of voting rights matters for affected individuals, there may be no effect on political outcomes and hence, no substantive macro-level impact. Group-level analyses face the same limitations. Some analysts have focused on the disproportionate racial impact of felon disfranchisement (e.g. Shapiro 1993; Harvey 1994), and it has been noted, for example, that approximately one in seven African-American men are currently disfranchised (e.g. Fellner and Mauer 1998). While unquestionably important for many reasons, the disproportionate racial impact of felon disfranchisement cannot by itself address the implications for democracy as a macro-political system. In this paper, we develop an appropriate, macro-level test. We suggest that determining whether felon disfranchisement has had an impact on American democracy requires examining the extent to which it directly alters actual electoral outcomes.

Because felon voting rules are state-specific, the handful of earlier studies of the political consequences of felon disfranchisement estimated the average impact of disfranchisement on turnout rates across the states (Miles 1999; Hirschfield 2001). In the analyses developed in this paper, by contrast, we advance an alternative, counterfactual approach that examines specific elections and tests whether the inclusion of felon voters at predicted rates of turnout and party preference would have been sufficient to change the outcomes. We use data on turnout from the Current Population Survey's Voter Supplement Module, and data on voting intention from the National Election Study, to estimate the likely voting behavior of the disfranchised felon population. We utilize information on felon characteristics from censuses and surveys of prison inmates to estimate the size and social distribution of the felon population. Combining these data sources, we are able to estimate the net votes lost by Democratic candidates in closely contested

U.S. Senate and presidential elections, and to assess the overall impact of felon disfranchisement on the American political landscape. [. . .]

Criminal justice and felon disfranchisement

The possibility that felon disfranchisement is now influencing electoral outcomes is largely tied to changes in the criminal justice regime over the past three decades. For a fifty-year period from the 1920s to the early 1970s, United States incarceration rates fluctuated within a narrow band of approximately 110 prisoners per 100,000 people. The policy consensus accompanying this stability was undergirded by a model of "penological modernism" in which the rehabilitation of offenders was the primary goal of incarceration (e.g. Rothman 1980). Structural elements of the criminal justice system, including probation, parole, and indeterminate sentencing, were designed to reform offenders and reintegrate them into their communities. The model began to break down in the 1960s, as Republican presidential candidates Barry Goldwater (in 1964) and Richard Nixon (in 1968) and other conservative and moderate politicians (such as Nelson Rockefeller in New York) promoted more punitive criminal justice policies (Savelsberg 1994; Jacobs and Helms 1996; Beckett 1997). By the mid-1970s, a rising chorus of conservative scholars, policy analysts, and politicians were advocating punitive strategies of deterrence and incapacitation, dismissing the rehabilitative model as "an anachronism" (Martinson 1974: 50; Wilson 1975). These trends continued in the 1980s and 1990s, with the Reagan, Bush, and Clinton Administrations aggressively focusing the nation's attention on problems associated with drug use and the incarceration of drug offenders (see, e.g. Beckett and Sasson 2000).

The success of the conservative crime policy agenda over the past three decades has had a remarkable impact, producing an enormous increase in felony convictions and incarceration. Since 1970, the number of state and federal prisoners has grown by over 600 percent, from 196,429 to 1,381,892 (USDOJ 1973: 350; 2001a: 1). Other correctional populations have also grown in rate and number, with a four-fold increase in the number of felony probationers (from 455,093 to 1,996,556) and parolees (from 160,900 to 725,527) from 1976 to 2000 (USDOJ 1979; 2001b). When jail inmates are added to state and federal prisoners, approximately 2 million Americans are currently incarcerated, with an additional 4.5 million supervised in the community on probation or parole (USDOJ 2000a), and some 9.5 million ex-offenders in the general population (Uggen and Manza 2006).

Not all of these felons and ex-felons are disfranchised. Ballot restrictions for felons are specific to each state. They were first adopted by some states in the post-Revolutionary era, and by the eve of the Civil War some two dozen states had statutes barring felons from voting or felon disfranchisement provisions in their state constitutions (Keyssar 2000: 62–63). In the post-Reconstruction South, such laws were extended to encompass even minor offenses (Keyssar 2000: 162), as part of a larger strategy to disfranchise African-Americans that also included devices such as literacy tests, poll taxes, and grandfather clauses (e.g. Kousser 1974). In general, some type of restriction on felon voting rights gradually came to be adopted by most states, and at present 48 of the 50 states bar felons – in most cases including those on probation or parole – from voting. At least ten of those states also bar ex-felons from voting, two other states permanently disfranchise recidivists, and one more state requires a post-release waiting period. [. . .]

DATA AND METHODS

Turnout and vote choice

Our analyses of turnout and vote choice utilize standard election data sources. To derive turnout estimates for the disfranchised population, we analyze data from the Voting Supplement of the Current Population Survey (CPS). The CPS is a monthly survey of individuals conducted by the Bureau of the Census. Since 1964, in each November of even-numbered (national election) years, the survey includes questions about political participation. All sampled households are asked, "In any election some people are not able to vote because they are sick or busy or have some other reason, and others do not want to vote. Did [you/another household member] vote in the election on November ___?"

Questions of this type produce slightly inflated estimates of turnout in the CPS series, with the inflation factor ranging from a low of 7.5 percent (1968) to a high of 11.1 percent (1988) in presidential elections between 1964 and 1996 (U.S. Bureau of the Census 1998: 2). Accordingly, after obtaining estimated turnout percentages for the felon population, we reduce them by a CPS inflation factor, multiplying predicted turnout rates by the ratio of actual to reported turnout for each election. Because turnout is most over-reported among better-educated citizens (Silver, Anderson, and Abramson 1986; Bernstein, Chadha, and Montjoy 2001), inflation rates are likely lower among disfranchised felons than among non-felons and this procedure can be expected to produce a conservative estimate.

Our estimates of the expected vote choice of disfranchised felons are developed using National Election Study (NES) data for 1972 to 2000. The NES is the premier source of U.S. voting data, with a rich battery of socio-demographic and attitudinal items and the lengthy time-series needed for this investigation. The biggest drawback of the NES series is that while it asks respondents how they voted in presidential and congressional elections, there are too few respondents (N < 2500) to permit meaningful state-level analyses.

To analyze the expected turnout and vote choice of disfranchised felons, we do not have any survey data that asks disfranchised felons how they would have voted. However, we can "match" the felon population to the rest of the voting age population to derive such an estimate and then test the reasonableness of this approach with a supplementary survey analysis. Our models of political behavior include socio-demographic attributes that have long been shown in voting research to contribute to turnout and vote choice: gender, race, age, income, labor force status, marital status and education (Wolfinger and Rosenstone 1980; Teixeira 1992; Manza and Brooks 1999, chap. 7). We analyze age and education in years as continuous variables. Income is a continuous variable measured in constant dollars. Labor force status, marital status, gender and race are dichotomies (the latter necessitated by the lack of information about Hispanic voters in the NES series prior to the 1980s). We use similar measures for both the turnout analyses (using CPS data) and vote choice analyses (using NES data). Once we have estimated political participation and party preference equations on the general population, we insert the mean characteristics of disfranchised felons into these equations to obtain their predicted rates of turnout and Democratic Party preference. We obtain information on the socio-demographic characteristics of convicted felons from the *Survey of State Prison Inmates* data series (e.g. USDOJ 1993; 2000b).

The dependent variables in both the turnout and voting analyses are dichotomous, so we estimate logistic regressions of the probabilities of participation and Democratic vote choice respectively. In the turnout equations, the outcome is coded "1" for voted, and "0" for not voted. In the voting equations, the outcome is coded "1" for Democratic and "0" for Republican choice. We only consider major party voters, as in Senate elections very few third party or independent candidates have come close to winning office. Results of these regressions are reported in Appendix Table 11.3.

Legal status and correctional populations

In addition to estimating the likelihood of voting and the partisan alignment of felons, we must also determine their absolute numbers in each state. We first examined state statutes and secondary sources documenting the voting rights of offenders to determine which correctional populations to count among the disfranchised population (e.g. Burton, Cullen, and Travis 1986; Olivares, Burton, and Cullen 1996; USDOJ 1996; Mauer 1997b; Fellner and Mauer 1998; Allard and Mauer 1999). To establish the number of disfranchised felons currently under supervision, we sum up the relevant prison, parole, felony-probation, and convicted felony jail populations. The felons under supervision data come from Justice Department publications, such as the *Correctional Populations in the United States* series. We estimate that 3 million current felons were legally disfranchised on December 31, 2000 or slightly less than half of the 6.5 million adults under correctional supervision (USDOJ 2001b). For most states, this is a rather straightforward accounting of the prison, parole and felony probation populations. Convicted felons who serve their sentences in jail represent a smaller but potentially important group not considered in prior estimates (Mauer 1997b). In 1998, for example, 24 percent of felony convictions resulted in a jail sentence (USDOJ 1998). We therefore include a conservative estimate of the number of convicted felons in jail – 10 percent of the total jail population.

These "head counts" are based on excellent data by social scientific standards. Estimating the number of disfranchised *ex*-felons not currently under supervision is a greater challenge, and estimates vary widely with the assumptions made by researchers. Important early work by the Sentencing Project (Mauer 1997b; Fellner and Mauer 1998) based estimates on national felony conviction data and state-level reports of criminal offenses between 1970 and 1995. While valuable, such procedures may make untenable stability and homogeneity assumptions, such as applying national information on racial composition and criminal convictions to individual states. Moreover, they do not account for the mortality of deceased felons or consider those convicted prior to 1970 or after 1995.

We develop alternative estimates based on exits *from* (rather than entry *into*) correctional supervision. We establish the median age of released prisoners using annual data from the National Corrections Reporting Program (e.g. USDOJ 1983–1996). We use recidivism data from national probability samples of prison releasees (USDOJ 1989) and probationers (USDOJ 1992) to establish the number reincarcerated. We then use double-decrement life tables for the period 1948–2000 to obtain the number of released felons lost to recidivism (and therefore already included in our annual head counts) and mortality each year (see, e.g. Bonczar and Beck 1997). Each cohort of disfranchised releasees is thus successively reduced each year and joined by a new cohort of releasees. This allows us to compute the number of ex-felons no longer under correctional supervision for states that disfranchise ex-felons.

THE POLITICAL IMPACT OF FELON DISFRANCHISEMENT

Turnout and party preference

Table 11.1 shows the estimated national participation rates and voting preferences for disfranchised felons by year since 1972. These estimates are based on the voting behavior of those matching felons in terms of gender, race, age, income, labor force status, marital status, and education, reduced for overreporting in the CPS. In short, they provide evidence regarding the likely behavior of hypothetical felon and ex-felon voters. Our estimates of felon turnout range from a low of 20.5 percent (for the 1974 Congressional elections) to a high of 39 percent (for the 1992 presidential election). On average, we predict that about 35 percent of disfranchised felons would have turned out to vote in presidential elections, and that about 24 percent would have participated in Senate elections during non-presidential election years. Although these numbers are well below the corresponding rates among non-felons, they suggest that a non-trivial proportion of disfranchised felons were likely to have voted if permitted to do so.

Table 11.1 Estimated turnout and voting preferences of disfranchised felons

Year	Presidential elections			Senate elections	
	Candidate	Turnout	% Democratic	Turnout	% Democratic
1972	McGovern	38.2%	69.1%	38.2%	68.2
1974				20.5	77.1
1976	Carter	34.3	80.7	34.3	79.6
1978				23.0	80.2
1980	Carter	35.7	66.5	35.7	69.6
1982				26.2	76.8
1984	Mondale	38.2	70.1	38.2	68.9
1986				25.3	73.6
1988	Dukakis	30.0	72.8	30.0	79.4
1990				23.8	80.5
1992	Clinton	39.0	73.6	39.0	74.7
1994				23.1	52.2
1996	Clinton	36.1	85.4	36.1	80.4
1998				23.9	69.7
2000	Gore	29.7	68.9	29.7	76.1

According to our analysis of party choice in Table 11.1, our hypothetical felon voters showed strong Democratic preferences in both presidential and senatorial elections. In recent presidential elections, even comparatively unpopular Democratic candidates such as George McGovern in 1972 would have garnered almost 70 percent of the felon vote. These Democratic preferences are less pronounced and somewhat less stable in senatorial elections. Nevertheless the survey data suggest that Democratic candidates would have received about seven of every ten votes cast by the felons and ex-felons in 14 of the last 15 U.S. Senate election years. By removing those with Democratic preferences from the pool of eligible voters, felon disfranchisement has provided a small but clear advantage to Republican candidates in every presidential and senatorial election from 1972 to 2000.

Impact on individual U.S. Senate elections

We next use these turnout and party preference rates to gauge the impact of felon disfranchisement on U.S. presidential and Senate elections. We obtained information on victory margins and Senate composition from standard election data sources (Congressional Quarterly's *America Votes* bienniel series). Table 11.2 applies the voting behavior estimates from Table 11.1 to these election data, identifying seven elections that may have been overturned if disfranchised felons had been allowed to participate.

To determine the *net* Democratic votes lost to disfranchisement, we first multiply the number of disfranchised felons by their estimated turnout rate (in each state), and the probability of selecting the Democratic candidate. Since some felons would have chosen Republican candidates, we then deduct from this figure the number of Republican votes lost to disfranchisement, which we obtain in a similar manner. For the 1978 Virginia election detailed in the top row of Table 11.2, for example, we estimate that 15,343 of the state's 93,554 disfranchised felons would have voted (16.4 percent). We further estimate that 12,305 of these voters would have selected Andrew Miller, the Democratic candidate (80.2 percent of 15,343), and that the remaining 19.8 percent (or 3,038) would have chosen John Warner, the Republican candidate. This results in a net total of over 9,000 Democratic votes lost to disfranchisement in the 1978 U.S. Senate race in Virginia, almost double the actual Republican victory margin of 4,721 votes.

In recent policy debates over felon disfranchisement, restoring voting rights has been most widely discussed for ex-felons who have completed their sentences (see, e.g. Sengupta 2000; Bush 2001). Yet some analysts have asserted that ex-felon voting restrictions are "electorally insignificant" (*Harvard Law Review* Note 1989: 1303). Is this assumption accurate? The results in Table 11.2 offer a new perspective on this issue. Recall that most states only deprive those currently under some form of correctional supervision of the right to vote, with only 15 states additionally disfranchising some or all ex-felons in 2000 (see Appendix Table 11.1). In only one instance (the late Paul Coverdell's election in Georgia in 1992), however, was a Senate election likely to have been overturned as a result of the disfranchisement of those actively under correctional supervision. Even in this instance, however, the number of current prisoners (25,290) and convicted felony jail inmates (2,163) was too small to affect the election. Rather, it was the large number of felony probationers (80,639, or a full 61 percent of the state's disfranchised population) and parolees (23,819, or 18 percent

Table 11.2 The Impact of felon disfranchisement on U.S. Senate elections 1978–2000

Year	State	Disfranchised population			Estimated voting behavior			Republican victory margin			Senate composition		
		Current felons	Ex-felons	Total	Turnout rate%	Percent dem.%	Net Dem. votes lost	Actual margin	Counter-factual margin	Rep. held seat through	actual[1]	Limited counter-factual	Cumulated counter-factual
1978	Virginia[2]	21,776	71,788	93,564	16.4	80.2	9,268	4,721	−4,547	2002+	58:41-D	60:39-D	60:39-D
1978	Texas[3]	100,707	89,662	190,369	13.4	80.2	15,408	12,227	−3,181	2002+	58:41-D	60:39-D	60:39-D
1980	unchanged										53:46-R	51:48-R	51:48-R
1982	unchanged										54:46-R	52:48-R	52:48-R
1984	Kentucky[4]	20,583	54,481	75,064	38.5	68.9	10,925	5,269	−5,655	2002+	53:47-R	52:48-R	52:48-R
1986	unchanged										55:45-D	52:48-R	50:50 –
1988	Florida[5]	87,264	206,247	293,512	26.5	79.4	45,735	34,518	−11,217	2000	55:45-D	56:44-D	58:42-D
1988	Wyoming[6]	3,013	6,969	9,982	24.5	79.4	1,438	1,322	−116	2006+	55:45-D	58:42-D	60:40-D
1990	unchanged										56:44-D	58:42-D	60:40-D
1992	Georgia[7]	131,911	0	131,911	29.6	74.7	19,289	16,237	−3,052	2000	57:43-D	58:42-D	61:39-D
1994	unchanged										52:48-R	60:40-D	63:37-D
1996	unchanged										55:45-R	51:49-R	54:46-D
1998	Kentucky[8]	31,456	94,584	126,040	25.4	69.7	12,614	6,766	−5,848	2004+	55:45-R	54:46-R	51:49-D
2000	unchanged										50:50 –	51:49-D	55:45-D

Notes:

1 Data on actual senate composition taken from Senate Statistics: *Majority and Minority Parties.*
2 In Virginia, Warner (R) defeated Miller (D) in 1978, Harrison in 1984, Spannaus in 1990, and M. Warner in 1996.
3 In Texas, Tower (R) defeated Krueger (D) in 1978; Gramm (R) defeated Doggett in 1984, Parmer in 1990, and Morales in 1996.
4 In Kentucky, McConnell (R) defeated Huddleston (D) in 1984, Sloane in 1990, and Beshear 1996 (Class 2 election).
5 In Florida, Mack (R) defeated MacKay (D) in 1988, and Rodham in 1994; McCollum (R) defeated Nelson (D) in 2000.
6 In Wyoming, Wallop (R) defeated Vinich (D) in 1988, and Thomas (R) defeated Sullivan in 1994.
7 In Georgia, Coverdell (R) defeated Fowler (D) in 1992, and Coles in 1998. After Coverdell's death in 2000, he was succeeded by Miller (D).
8 In Kentucky, Bunning (R) defeated Baesler (D) in 1998 (Class 3 election).

of disfranchised Georgians) that likely cost the Democrats the election. As this case illustrates, the political impact varies with the particular correctional populations disfranchised. The other reversible cases all include net Democratic vote losses from *ex-felon* voters.

Impact on U.S. Senate composition

Would changes to a handful of elections have had any real impact? Since 1978, there have been over 400 Senate elections, and we find 7 outcomes that would have been reversed. Yet even this small number might have shifted the balance of power in the Senate, which has been fairly evenly divided between the two major parties over this period. To assess this possibility, we recomputed the U.S. Senate composition after each election. Since two Republican seats were overturned in the 1978 elections, the Democratic majority would have increased from 58:41 to 60:39. We followed the beneficiaries of these closely contested elections to see how long their seats remained under Republican control. John Warner of Virginia remains in office today and John Tower's Texas seat also remains in Republican hands (with Phil Gramm currently holding office). Although we cannot know whether the Democratic Party would have held these seats in subsequent elections, this seems likely based on recent voting patterns and the well-known advantages of incumbency. Of the 32 U.S. Senate elections in 1978, the incumbent party retained the seat through at least 1990 in 29 cases (91 percent), through at least 1996 in 27 cases (84 percent) and through at least 2002 in 23 cases (72 percent). Because incumbent parties are unlikely to hold such seats indefinitely, we cumulate the counterfactual using the more reasonable (though untested) assumption that the Democrats would have retained these seats as long as the Republicans who narrowly defeated them. This procedure makes strong *ceteris paribus* assumptions, however, so Table 11.2 also shows "limited counterfactual" results that assume the victor's party would lose the seat immediately after a single six-year term.

After the 1984 elections, the Republicans held a narrow 53:47 Senate majority. Under the cumulated counterfactual scenario in which disfranchised felons had voted, the Democrats may have achieved parity with the Republicans. In the Kentucky election of 1984, the Republican candidate (Mitch McConnell) narrowly defeated the Democratic nominee by 5,269 votes. Since Kentucky disfranchises ex-felons as well as current inmates, parolees, and felony probationers, the total number disfranchised was over 75,000 in 1984. Because 1984 was a presidential election year, turnout was relatively high, and our voting preference model indicates that almost 70 percent of the felon voters would have selected the Democratic candidate. Thus, almost 11,000 Democratic votes were likely lost to disfranchisement in this election, more than twice the 5,269-vote Republican plurality. With the addition of this seat and the Virginia and Texas seats discussed above, the counterfactual Senate composition shows an even 50:50 party distribution.

Pursuing the counterfactual to the present day, we find that Democratic candidates are likely to have prevailed in Florida (1988), Georgia (1992), and in Kentucky's other seat (1998) if felons had been allowed to vote, with a narrower reversal occurring in Wyoming (1988). Our cumulative counterfactual suggests that Democrats may well have controlled the Senate throughout the 1990s (see Table 11.3). Although it is

Table 11.3 Logistic regression predicting 1996 voter turnout and 1996 and 1998 party preference

Voting Predictors	1996 turnout				1996–1998 preference	
	Model 1	Model 2	Model 3	Model 4	Clinton (D)	Ventura (I)
Criminal Sanction						
Any arrest	−.681**	−.264				
	(.217)	(.252)				
Property arrest			−.323	.148	−.242	−.346
			(.326)	(.353)	(.488)	(.597)
Drug/alcohol arrest			−.341	−.171	1.274*	1.599*
			(.342)	(.380)	(.633)	(.789)
Violent arrest			−1.246*	−.851	−.758	.946
			(.501)	(.541)	(.860)	(1.150)
Other arrest			−.065	.145	.582	.198
			(.372)	(.397)	(.589)	(.771)
Voting Predictors						
Nonwhite (vs. white)		−.663**		−.628**	1.216*	−.792
		(.258)		(.261)	(.517)	(.422)
Female		.066		.089	1.231*	−.332
		(.216)		(.215)	(.266)	(.281)
Years education		.415**		.414**	.117	−.536**
		(.063)		(.063)	(.085)	(.102)
Income (in thousands)		.036**		.036**	−.004	.001
		(.012)		(.012)	(.014)	(.016)
Full-time employment		−.257		−.268	−.390	−.592
		(.240)		(.240)	(.313)	(.342)
Married		.088		.018	.130	.076
		(.224)		(.223)	(.293)	(.301)
Constant	.928**	−5.429**	.879**	−5.452**	−1.228	8.778**
	(.107)	(.925)	(.103)	(.923)	(1.281)	(1.554)
Number of Cases	548	548	550	550	354	285
−2 Log Likelihood	673.8**	599.4**	676.1**	603.4**	373.6**	368.7**

Notes: Standard errors in parentheses.
* $p < .05$.
** $p < .01$.

possible that both parties may have shifted course or that other factors would have arisen to neutralize this impact, it seems likely that the Senate deadlock after the 2000 elections would have been broken in favor of the Democrats if the ballot had been returned to disfranchised felons. We discuss the implication of these shifts in the conclusion. [. . .]

DISCUSSION AND IMPLICATIONS FOR AMERICAN DEMOCRACY

In the preceding analysis we estimated the political impact of felon disfranchisement in U.S. Senate and presidential elections. We find that disfranchisement laws, combined with high rates of criminal punishment, may have altered the outcome of seven recent U.S. Senate elections and one presidential election. . . . One startling implication of these findings relates to control over the Senate. Assuming that Democrats who might have been elected in the absence of felon disfranchisement had held their seats as long as the Republicans who narrowly defeated them, the Democratic Party would have gained parity in 1984 and held majority control of the U.S. Senate from 1986 to the present. Changing partisan control of the Senate would have had a number of important policy consequences: in particular, it might have enabled the Clinton Administration to gain approval for a much higher proportion of its federal judicial nominees, and key Senate committees would have shifted from Republican to Democratic control. [. . .]

Although these results are striking, do they signal a true democratic reversal in the United States? Figure 11.1 presents data placing felon disfranchisement in historical context, showing the percentage of states holding felon disfranchisement provisions from the late eighteenth century to present. Most states began to restrict the ballot for felons

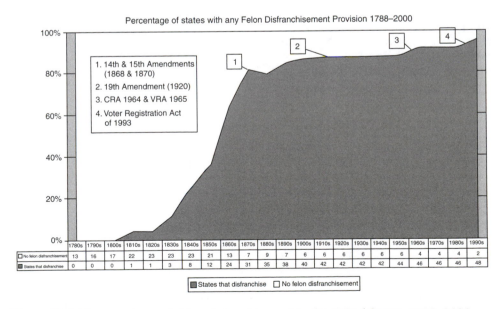

	1780s	1790s	1800s	1810s	1820s	1830s	1840s	1850s	1860s	1870s	1880s	1890s	1900s	1910s	1920s	1930s	1940s	1950s	1960s	1970s	1980s	1990s
No felon disfranchisement	13	16	17	22	23	23	23	21	13	7	9	7	6	6	6	6	6	6	4	4	4	2
States that disfranchise	0	0	0	1	1	3	8	12	24	31	35	38	40	42	42	42	42	44	46	46	46	48

Figure 11.1 The prevalence of felon disfranchisement in the United States, 1788–2000

Appendix Table 11.1 Estimates of disfranchised felons by state 12/31/00

State	Prisoners	Parolees	Felony probation	Jail inmates	Estimated ex felons	Total	Voting Age population	Disf. rate
Alabama	26,225	5,494	30,887	1,214	161,275	225,095	3,333,000	6.75%
Alaska	2,128	507	4,543	212		7,390	430,000	1.72%
Arizona	26,510	3,474	50,897	1,053	65,406	147,340	3,625,000	4.06%
Arkansas	11,915	9,453	29,048			50,416	1,929,000	2.61%
California	163,001	117,647		7,714		288,362	24,873,000	1.16%
Colorado	16,833	5,500		967		23,300	3,067,000	0.76%
Connecticut	13,155	1,868	29,641	520		45,184	2,499,000	1.81%
Delaware	3,937	579	10,808	298	14,384	30,006	582,000	5.16%
Dist. Col	7,456			143		7,599	411,000	1.85%
Florida	71,233	6,046	131,186	5,228	613,514	827,207	11,774,000	7.03%
Georgia	44,232	21,556	217,038	3,451		286,277	5,893,000	4.86%
Hawaii	3,553			150		3,703	909,000	0.41%
Idaho	5,526	1,443	8,774	321		16,064	921,000	1.74%
Illinois	45,281			1,711		46,992	8,983,000	0.52%
Indiana	20,125			1,333		21,458	4,448,000	0.48%
Iowa	7,955	2,763	9,326	330	80,257	100,631	2,165,000	4.65%
Kansas	8,344	3,829		426		12,599	1,983,000	0.64%
Kentucky	14,919	4,909	17,464	1,010	109,132	147,434	2,993,000	4.93%
Louisiana	35,047			2,637		37,684	3,255,000	1.16%
Maine							968,000	0.00%
Maryland	23,538	14,143	22,563	1,115	68,477	129,836	3,925,000	3.31%
Mass.							4,749,000	0.00%
Michigan	47,718			1,600		49,318	7,358,000	0.67%
Minnesota	6,238	3,072	31,644	523		41,477	3,547,000	1.17%
Mississippi	20,241	1,596	15,118	986	82,002	119,943	2,047,000	5.86%
Missouri	27,323	12,357	42,607	725		83,012	4,105,000	2.02%
Montana	3,105			160		3,265	668,000	0.49%
Nebraska	3,895	473	4,828	231	44,001	53,428	1,234,000	4.33%
Nevada	10,012	4,056	8,410	517	43,395	66,390	1,390,000	4.78%
New Hamp.	2,257			159		2,416	911,000	0.27%
New Jersey	29,784	14,899	96,831	1,592		143,106	6,245,000	2.29%
New Mexico	5,342	1,670	7,279	544	63,571	78,406	1,263,000	6.21%
New York	70,198	57,858		3,217		131,273	13,805,000	0.95%
No. Carolina	31,266	3,352	34,701	1,334		70,653	5,797,000	1.22%
North Dakota	1,076			67		1,143	477,000	0.24%
Ohio	45,833			1,628		47,461	8,433,000	0.56%
Oklahoma	23,181	1,825	26,385	698		52,089	2,531,000	2.06%
Oregon	10,630			677		11,307	2,530,000	0.45%
Pennsylvania	36,847					36,847	9,155,000	0.40%
Rhode Island	1,966	353	15,844	132		18,295	753,000	2.43%
So. Carolina	21,778	4,240	25,323	869		52,210	2,977,000	1.75%
South Dakota	2,616			111		2,727	542,000	0.50%
Tennessee	22,166	8,094	30,235	1,934	28,720	91,149	4,221,000	2.16%
Texas	157,997	111,719	250,642	5,609		525,967	14,850,000	3.54%
Utah	5,630	3,266				8,896	1,465,000	0.61%
Vermont							460,000	0.00%
Virginia	30,168	5,148	29,596	1,847	243,902	310,661	5,263,000	5.90%
Washington	14,915	160	109,956	1,078	32,856	158,965	4,368,000	3.64%
West Virginia	3,856	1,112	3,635	272		8,875	1,416,000	0.63%
Wisconsin	20,612	9,430	22,715	1,268		54,025	3,930,000	1.37%
Wyoming	1,680	514	2,760	99	12,797	17,850	358,000	4.99%
Total	1,209,243	444,405	1,320,684	57,708	1,663,689	4,695,729	205,814,000	2.28%

Appendix Table 11.2 Estimates of disfranchised African-American felons by state 12/31/00

State	Black prison	Black parole	Black probation	Black Jail	Est. black ex felons	Total	Voting age population	Disf. rate
Alabama	17,230	2,674	13,248	671	77,932	111,755	800,000	13.97%
Alaska	317	53	585	10		966	17,000	5.68%
Arizona	4,016	543	4,347	143	8,651	17,700	137,000	12.92%
Arkansas	6,595	4,715	10,376			21,686	276,000	7.86%
California	80,490	31,457		2,697		114,644	1,853,000	6.19%
Colorado	4,224	1,639		199		6,063	132,000	4.59%
Connecticut	8,302	1,175	8,689	250		18,417	221,000	8.33%
Delaware	2,524	303	5,069		7,162	15,058	108,000	13.94%
Dist. Col	7,382			131		7,513	230,000	3.27%
Florida	39,427	3,472	43,305	2,774	167,413	256,392	1,600,000	16.02%
Georgia	29,583	14,267	115,711	2,124		161,685	1,577,000	10.25%
Hawaii	201			6		208	27,000	0.77%
Idaho	105	28	141	6		280	7,000	4.00%
Illinois	32,780			1,116		33,895	1,249,000	2.71%
Indiana	8,664			634		9,297	353,000	2.63%
Iowa	2,028	411	1,019	62	7,671	11,192	45,000	24.87%
Kansas	3,218	1,359		117		4,694	112,000	4.19%
Kentucky	5,718	1,377	3,916	312	24,632	35,955	207,000	17.37%
Louisiana	26,820			1,870		28,690	956,000	3.00%
Maine							7,000	0.00%
Maryland	18,228	10,662	13,105	736	42,519	85,251	1,058,000	8.06%
Mass.							270,000	0.00%
Michigan	27,230			572		27,802	977,000	2.85%
Minnesota	2,309	1,841	4,587	128		8,865	106,000	8.36%
Mississippi	15,145	1,130	9,099	698	50,035	76,106	675,000	11.27%
Missouri	12,489	4,964	12,719	300		30,471	425,000	7.17%
Montana	44			4		48	4,000	1.21%
Nebraska	1,155	116	758	47	7,164	9,240	49,000	18.86%
Nevada	3,118	1,331	1,853	154	11,514	17,970	105,000	17.11%
New Hamp.	125			12		138	9,000	1.53%
New Jersey	21,301	8,977	47,666	975		78,920	856,000	9.22%
New Mexico	621	199	515	43	7,750	9,128	37,000	24.67%
New York	38,849	43,638		1,749		84,236	2,309,000	3.65%
No. Carolina	20,480	2,114	17,448	868		40,910	1,173,000	3.49%
North Dakota	27			2		29	4,000	0.72%
Ohio	24,829			720		25,549	895,000	2.85%
Oklahoma	8,336	614	6,108	225		15,283	185,000	8.26%
Oregon	1,506			74		1,580	51,000	3.10%
Pennsylvania	23,104					23,104	820,000	2.82%
Rhode Island	685	100	3,598	35		4,419	36,000	12.27%
So. Carolina	15,262	2,949	13,950	596		32,756	816,000	4.01%
South Dakota	116			3		119	5,000	2.37%
Tennessee	11,277	4,605	12,806	1,125	11,946	41,759	635,000	6.58%
Texas	71,915	44,282	46,546	2,130		164,873	1,800,000	9.16%
Utah	432	244				676	16,000	4.23%
Vermont							4,000	0.00%
Virginia	20,234	3,323	15,085	1,180	121,737	161,559	1,005,000	16.08%
Washington	3,376	23	14,647	205	3,824	22,075	154,000	14.33%
West Virginia	615	218	316	39		1,188	45,000	2.64%
Wisconsin	9,940	4,476	5,920	469		20,805	193,000	10.78%
Wyoming	101	22	85	2	358	567	4,000	14.18%
Total	632,474	199,301	433,216	26,215	550,308	1,841,515	24,635,000	7.48%

Appendix Table 11.3 Logistic regression coefficients for turnout and democratic senate and presidential vote, 1972–2000

Turnout analysis (voted = 1)

	1972	1974	1976	1978	1980	1982	1984	1986	1988	1990	1992	1994	1996	1998	2000
Black	-.061*	-.109***	-.063*	-.033	-.105***	.102***	.161***	.174***	.101***	.058*	-.026	.024	.211***	.263***	.321***
Yrs. of education	.228***	.190***	.245***	.206***	.249***	.211***	.232***	.195***	.283***	.211***	.256***	.238***	.254***	.212***	.277***
Male	-.035*	-.029	-.093***	-.069**	-.126***	-.060***	-.171***	-.073	-.143***	-.089***	-.131***	-.041**	-.153***	-.060***	-.163***
Married	.392***	.517***	.443***	.532***	.528***	.538***	.460***	.541***	.604***	.498***	.418***	.538***	.486***	.535***	.550***
Employed	.291***	.331***	.302***	.266***	.319***	.283***	.261***	.269***	.400***	.260***	.311***	.266***	.229***	.221***	.262***
Age	.031***	.039***	.038***	.041***	.039***	.042***	.034***	.041***	.045***	.039***	.031***	.042***	.036***	.041***	.035***
Constant	-3.753***	-4.653***	-4.384***	-4.763***	-4.464***	-4.754***	-4.149***	-4.4776***	-5.615***	-4.904***	-4.265***	-5.368***	-4.750***	-5.181***	-4.945***

Presidential vote analysis (voted democratic = 1)

	1972	1976	1980	1984	1988	1992	1996	2000
Black	2.553***	2.824***	3.066***	2.375***	2.307***	2.471***	3.241***	2.373***
Yrs. of education	-.006	-.067***	-.064*	-.015	-.004	-.004	-.076**	.033
Male	-.244	-.039	-.358*	-.151	-.162	-.270*	-.439***	-.430**
Married	-.163	.049	-.136	-.070	-.021	-.439***	-.223	-.217
Employed	-.026	.197	.355	-.001	.154	.078	.411*	.137
Age	-.019***	-.010*	.001*	.000	-.003	.007	.004	.000
Income	-.128*	-.276***	-.123	-.303***	-.191*	-.173**	-.160*	-.153*
Constant	.723*	1.817***	.058*	-.716	.916*	.354	1.423**	-.307

Senate vote analysis (voted for democratic candidate = 1)

	1972	1974	1976	1978	1980	1982	1984	1986	1988	1990	1992	1994	1996	1998	2000
Black	1.719***	2.289***	1.852***	1.392***	1.525***	1.729***	1.930***	1.915***	2.049***	2.052***	1.946***	1.029***	2.072***	1.719***	1.906***
Yrs. of education	-.041	-.026	-.027	-.081**	-.027	-.088*	-.041	-.062	-.068*	-.039	-.048	-.023	-.030	-.042	-.021
Male	-.010	-.184	-.151	.706***	.145	-.028	-.076	-.050	-.130	-.156	-.239	-.513**	-.349	-.061	-.237
Married	.017	.393	.117	-.215	-.157	.079	.262	-.163	-.043	-.106	-.339**	-.081	-.569**	.155	-.128
Employed	.218	.516*	-.090	.236	-.116	.179	.076	-.117	.195	.082	-.057	.110	.076	.291	.047
Age	-.015**	-.041*	-.011*	-.007	.005	-.003	-.001	-.003	-.005	-.002	.001	.008	.003	.008	.001
Income	-.260***	-.319**	-.116	-.253*	-.077	-.123*	-.237*	.022	-.195*	-.134	-.035	-.187*	-.230*	-.038	-.115
Constant	1.673***	1.780***	1.589***	1.763***	.482	1.672*	1.092	1.010	1.894***	1.352	1.054*	.409	1.475*	.117	.876

Notes:

* $p < .05$.
** $p < .01$.
*** $p < .001$ (two-tailed tests).

in the mid-nineteenth century, and there is evidence in some states that lawmakers fully appreciated the partisan consequences of their actions (McMillan 1955; Keyssar 2000; Uggen and Manza 2006). Few states rescinded such measures following the enfranchisement of African-American males (with passage of the 14th and 15th amendments to the U.S. Constitution) and women (with passage of the 19th amendment). Nor was felon disfranchisement dismantled during passage of the Civil Rights Act of 1964, Voting Rights Act of 1965, or Voter Registration Act of 1993. Although several states have removed voting restrictions on *ex*-felons since the 1960s (including New Mexico in 2001, Iowa in 2004, Nebraska in 2005, and Maryland and Florida in 2007), most continue to disfranchise prisoners, probationers, and parolees today. In fact, as Figure 11.1 shows, a greater percentage of states disfranchised felons in 2000 than in any prior year.

Although we have specified, political consequences of felon disfranchisement, an argument developed more fully in *ASR*, we have only touched on the origins of these laws and the mass incarceration phenomenon that gives such force to them today (see Manza and Uggen 2006 for more details). These questions are important for situating felon disfranchisement within a broader model of social control of dispossessed groups (see Appendix Table 11.3). Proponents of the "new penology" argue that the focus of criminological interest has recently shifted from the rehabilitation of individual offenders to social control of aggregate groups (Feeley and Simon 1992; Wacquant 2001). The correctional population is subject to a number of exclusions: they are often ineligible for federal grants for education (such as Pell Grants), they have restricted access to social programs, they face sharp disadvantages in the labor market (Western and Beckett 1999), and they must live with the social stigma associated with a felony conviction. Restricted access to the ballot is but a piece of a larger pattern of social exclusion for America's vast correctional population.

References

Allard, Patricia and Mark Mauer. 1999. *Regaining the Vote: An Assessment of Activity Relating to Felon Disenfranchisement Laws*. Washington: Sentencing Project.

Australian Electoral Commission. 2001. *Frequently Asked Questions*. Canberra, ACT: Commonwealth of Australia.

Beckett, Katherine. 1997. *Making Crime Pay: The Politics of Law and Order in the Contemporary United States*. New York: Oxford University Press.

Beckett, Katherine and Theodore Sasson. 2000. *The Politics of Injustice*. Thousand Oaks, CA: Pine Forge Press.

Bernstein, Robert, Anita Chadha, and Robert Montjoy. 2001. "Overreporting Voting: Why It Happens and Why It Matters." *Public Opinion Quarterly* 65:22–44.

Bollen, Kenneth A. 1979. "Political Democracy and the Timing of Development." *American Sociological Review* 44:572–87.

Bonczar, Thomas P. and Allen J. Beck. 1997. *Lifetime Likelihood of Going to State or Federal Prison*. Bureau of Justice Statistics Special Report. Washington: USGPO.

Bowles, Samuel and Herbert Gintis. 1986. *Democracy and Capitalism: Property, Community, and the Contradictions of Modern Social Thought*. New York: Basic.

Burton, Velmer S., Francis T. Cullen, and Lawrence F. Travis III. 1986. "The Collateral Consequences of a Felony Conviction: A National Study of State Statutes." *Federal Probation* 51:52–60.

Bush, Jeb. 2001. "Comment." *Sarasota Herald-Tribune Newscoast*. January 11. Retrieved January 19 (www.newscoast.com/headlinesstory2.cfm?ID=38399).

Collier, Ruth B. 1999. *Paths toward Democracy: The Working Class and Elites in Western Europe and South America*. New York: Cambridge University Press.

Dahl, Robert. 1998. *On Democracy*. New Haven, CT: Yale University Press.

Demleitner, Nora V. 2000. "Continuing Payment on One's Debt to Society: The German Model of Felon Disenfranchisement as an Alternative." *Minnesota Law Review* 84:753–804.

Donziger, Steven R. (ed.). 1996. *The Real War on Crime: The Report of the National Criminal Justice Commission*. New York: Harper Collins.

Ewald, Alec C. 2002. "The Ideological Paradox of Criminal Disenfranchisement Law in the United States." Department of Political Science, University of Massachusetts, Amherst, MA. Unpublished Manuscript.

Feeley, Malcolm M. and Jonathon Simon. 1992. "The New Penology: Notes on the Emerging Strategy of Corrections and its Implications." *Criminology* 30:449–74.

Fellner, Jamie, and Marc Mauer. 1998. *Losing the Vote: The Impact of Felony Disenfranchisement Laws in the United States*. Washington, DC: Human Rights Watch and The Sentencing Project.

Harvard Law Review Note. 1989. "The Disfranchisement of Ex-Felons: Citizenship, Criminality, and 'The Purity of the Ballot Box.' " *Harvard Law Review* 102:1300–17.

Harvey, Alice. 1994. "Ex-felon Disenfranchisement and Its Influence on the Black Vote: The Need for a Second Look." *University of Pennsylvania Law Review* 142:1145–89.

Hirschfield, Paul. 2001. "Losing the Prize: Assessing the Impact of Felon Disfranchisement Laws on Black Male Voting Participation." Paper presented at the 1999 Annual Meetings of the Law and Society Association, Chicago.

Hoffman, Peter B. and Barbara Stone-Meierhoefer. 1980. "Reporting Recidivism Rates: The Criterion and Follow-Up Issues." *Journal of Criminal Justice* 8:53–60.

Honig, Bonnie. 2001. *Democracy and the Foreigner*. Princeton, NJ: Princeton University Press.

Jacobs, David and Ronald E. Helms. 1996. "Toward a Political Model of Incarceration: A Time-Series Examination of Multiple Explanations for Prison Admission Rates." *American Journal of Sociology* 102:323–57.

Keyssar, Alexander. 2000. *The Right to Vote: The Contested History of Democracy in the United States*. New York: Basic Books.

Kousser, J. Morgan. 1974. *The Shaping of Southern Politics: Suffrage Restrictions and the Establishment of the One-Party South*. New Haven: Yale University Press.

Lynch, James. 1995. "Crime in International Perspective." pp. 11–38 in *Crime*, edited by J. Q. Wilson and J. Petersilia. San Francisco: Institute for Contemporary Studies.

Manza, Jeff and Christopher Uggen. 2006. *Locked Out: Felon Disenfranchisement and American Democracy*. New York: Oxford University Press.

Manza, Jeff and Clem Brooks. 1999. *Social Cleavages and Political Change: Voter Alignments and U.S. Party Coalitions, 1950s–1990s*. New York: Oxford Press.

Markoff, John. 1996. *The Abolition of Feudalism: Peasants, Lords, and Legislators in the French Revolution*. University Park, PA: Pennsylvania State University Press.

Martinson, Robert. 1974. "What Works? Questions and Answers About Prison Reform." *The Public Interest* 35:22–54.

Mauer, Marc. 1997a. *Americans Behind Bars: U.S. and International Use of Incarceration, 1995*. Washington, DC: Sentencing Project.

——. 1997b. *Intended and Unintended Consequences: State Racial Disparities in Imprisonment*. Washington, DC: Sentencing Project.

McMillan, Malcolm C. 1955. *Constitutional Development in Alabama, 1798–1901*. Chapel Hill: University of North Carolina Press.

Miles, Thomas J. 1999. "Does the Disfranchisement of Convicted Felons Reduce Electoral Participation?" Department of Economics, University of Chicago, Chicago, IL. Unpublished Manuscript.

Olivares, Kathleen M., Velmer S. Burton, and Francis T. Cullen. 1996. "The Collateral Consequences of a Felony Conviction: A National Study of State Legal Codes 10 Years Later." *Federal Probation* 60: 10–17.

Piven, Frances F. and Richard A. Cloward 2000. *Why Americans Still Don't Vote: And Why Politicians Want it that Way*. Boston: Beacon Press.

Przeworski, Adam. 1991. *Democracy and the Market: Political and Economic Reforms in Eastern Europe and Latin America*. Cambridge: Cambridge University Press.

Ramirez, Franciso O., Yasemin Soysal, and Suzanne Shanahan. 1997. "The Changing Logic of Political Citizenship: Cross-National Acquisition of Women's Suffrage Rights, 1890 to 1990." *American Sociological Review* 62:735–45.

Rogers, Donald W., ed. 1992. *Voting and the Spirit of American Democracy: Essays on the History of Voting and Voting Rights in America*. Urbana, IL: University of Illinois Press.

Rokkan, Stein. 1970. *Citizens, Elections, Parties: Approaches to the Comparative Study of the Processes of Development*. New York: McKay.

Rothman, David J. 1980. *Conscience and Convenience: The Asylum and its Alternatives in Progressive America*. Boston: Little, Brown and Company.

Rueschemeyer, Dietrich, Evelyne Huber Stephens, and John D. Stephens. 1992. *Capitalist Development and Democracy*. Chicago: University of Chicago Press.

Savelsberg, Joachim. 1994. "Knowledge, Domination, and Criminal Punishment." *American Journal of Sociology* 99:911–43.

Sengupta, Somini. 2000. "Felony Costs Voting Rights for a Lifetime in 9 States." *New York Times*, November 3, 2000.

Shapiro, Andrew. 1993. "Challenging Criminal Disenfranchisement Under the Voting Rights Act: A New Strategy." *Yale Law Journal* 103:537–66.

Silver, Brian D., Barbara A. Anderson, and Paul Abramson. 1986. "Who Overreports Voting?" *American Political Science Review* 80:613–24.

Sutton, John R. 2000. "Imprisonment and Social Classification in Five Common-Law Democracies, 1955–1985." *American Journal of Sociology* 106:350–86.

Teixeira, Ruy. 1992. *The Disappearing American Voter*. Washington, DC: Brookings Institute Press.

Therborn, Goran. 1977. "The Rule of Capital and the Rise of Democracy." *New Left Review* 103:3–41.

U.S. Bureau of the Census. 1948–2000. *Statistical Abstract*. Washington: USGPO.

———. 1986–2002. *Voting and Registration in the Election of November 1984* (1992, 1996, 2000). Current Population Reports, ser. P-20, nos. 405, 466, 504, 542. Washington: USGPO.

U.S. Department of Justice. 1973–2001. *Sourcebook of Criminal Justice Statistics*. Washington: USGPO.

———. 1948–1964. "Prisoners in State and Federal Institutions." *National Prisoner Statistics Bulletins*. Washington: USGPO.

———. 1983–1996. *National Corrections Reporting Program*. Washington: USGPO.

———. 1989. *Recidivism of Prisoners Released in 1983*. Washington: USGPO.

———. 1989–1997. *Correctional Populations in the United States*. Washington: USGPO.

———. 1991. *Race of Prisoners Admitted to State and Federal Institutions, 1926–1986*. Washington: USGPO.

———. 1992. *Recidivism of Felons on Probation, 1986–1989*. Washington: USGPO.

U.S. Department of Justice. 1996. Office of the Pardon Attorney. *Civil Disabilities of Convicted Felons: A State-by-State Survey*. Washington: USGPO.

———. 1998. *Felony Sentences in State Courts, 1998*. Washington: USGPO.

———. 2000a *Prison and Jail Inmates at Midyear 1999*. Washington: USGPO.

———. 2000b *Survey of Inmates in State and Federal Correctional Facilities, 1997* [computer file]. Ann Arbor, MI: ICPSR.

———. 2001a. *Prisoners in 2000*. Washington: USGPO.

———. 2001b. *Probation and Parole in the United States, 2000 – Press Release*. Washington: USGPO.

Wacquant, Loic. 2001. "Deadly Symbiosis: When Ghetto and Prison Meet and Mesh." *Punishment and Society* 3:95–133.

Western, Bruce and Katherine Beckett. 1999. "How Unregulated is the U.S. Labor Market? The Penal System as a Labor Market Institution." *American Journal of Sociology* 104:1030–60.

Wilson, James Q. 1975. *Thinking about Crime*. New York: Basic Books.

Wolfinger, Raymond E. and Stephen Rosenstone. 1980. *Who Votes?* New Haven: Yale University Press.

PART THREE

Crime and the life course

THROUGHOUT MUCH OF THE late nineteenth and twentieth centuries, much scholarly research focused on the offender and the causes of delinquent and criminal behavior. Beginning in the 1920s and increasingly from the 1960s on, efforts were made to situate the study of delinquency in the context of the life course of offenders and what were then called their "criminal careers."

Life course research on offending arose initially out of uncertainty about what proportion of all youth engage in criminal offending. When this work began, most previous research had focused exclusively on delinquents and their behavior. This left aside entirely the question of how unique offenders actually were. By looking at youth over time, light was shed on these questions. This longitudinal focus also reflected a growing awareness that a small group of repeat offenders account for quite a large share of crime. More recently, notions of risk and its management have led to the adaptation of "careers" work to anticipate future dangerousness – a move that has generated significant controversy.

Interest in the life course of offenders crystallized in America during the mid-1960s with Marvin Wolfgang's study in Philadelphia of delinquency in a birth cohort. Relying on self-report data, delinquency was found to be far more pervasive than previously thought with approximately one-third of all youth admitting to having offended at least once. Equally important, a high percentage of them desisted naturally after that first offense. Research ongoing in Cambridge, England, in which David Farrington has played a leading role has produced comparable results. These researchers were also able to explore patterns of specialization and chronic reoffending. Both groups of researchers, along with others including Terry Thornberry, went on brilliantly for several decades of follow-up to articulate the risk factors for continued violent and non-violent offending.

In the 1990s, new research by Robert Sampson and John Laub re-analyzed and followed up on data collected decades earlier by Sheldon and Eleanor Glueck in the context of the Cambridge-Somerville Youth Study. Many of their findings proved compatible with those of the British team. On one major point, however, their findings sharply diverged. Whereas Farrington argued that anti-social behavior tended to be established early and to continue into adulthood, Sampson and Laub found evidence of protective factors in adulthood that could exert a powerful influence in reducing recidivism relatively late in life. Two key factors to which they pointed were stable employment and an enduring and engaging domestic partnership. Their work was also striking for its finding that imprisonment tended to exert little significant effect on reducing future reoffending, even as it tended to disrupt the jobs and family in ways that made recidivism more likely.

The findings of these life course studies about causes of delinquency are vividly illustrated as they play out in individual lives in Fox Butterfield's unforgettable portrait of Willie Bosket, "the boy no one could help." Bosket, the most dangerous offender in the history of New York State, was the model for Hannibal Lecter in *The Silence of the Lambs*. Another autobiography, that of Jack Henry Abbott, a writer who was initially taken into custody as a juvenile and eventually lived virtually all his life as a prisoner "in the belly of the beast," suggests reasons embedded in prison subculture why Sampson and Laub found imprisonment to show little capacity to reduce reoffending. Abbott, a remarkable writer, became the subject of a prolonged campaign for his release from prison led by Norman Mailer. Just days after his release, Abbott killed a waiter in an Italian restaurant in Brooklyn who had made a sudden startling move. He raises the question of who is to blame? He had been a prisoner virtually his entire life. Whatever he now was, he argued, was what that institution had made him.

As thinking has developed about the life course of offenders and the limits of what custodial penalties can achieve, some scholars have pointed to shaming and reintegration as a potential remedy. James Gilligan, a clinical psychiatrist, engages the theme of shame and rage among offenders. Contesting the potential of shame for reassimilation, Gilligan argues in his evocative essay, "Dead Souls," that a deep sense of personal shame actually lies at the causal root of much violence.

As attention has focused on risk management, efforts have been made to assess offenders – especially dangerous violent ones – in terms of risk. At the same time, scholars have grown increasingly sensitive to the hazards of thinking predictively about human behavior. The hazard, of course, is an erroneous "false positive" identification. This occurs when probabilistic research findings that describe aggregates are used predictively to designate as "dangerous" individuals who present a high probability of reoffending but, in fact, would actually be one who would not engage in future criminal acts. Such predictions of future dangerousness have recently reached a startling new stage in England, with a proposal in Parliament that government be allowed to detain persons diagnosed with dangerous severe personality disorder who present a significant likelihood of future harm.

The research shows how inequality and disadvantage work through cultural practices to shape the life course of offenders and those who desist.

Chapter 12

Fox Butterfield

ALL GOD'S CHILDREN
The Bosket family and the American tradition of violence

From: Fox Butterfield (1995), excerpts from *All God's Children: The Bosket Family and the American Tradition of Violence*, New York: Avon Books, pp. xiv–xv, 135–149, 206–207.

[. . .]

WILLIE DID NOT LOOK dangerous. He is slight, five feet nine inches tall and at most one hundred fifty pounds, when he is not on a deprivation diet of bread, cabbage, and water. He has cherubic features and a quick, boyish grin accentuated by deep puckish dimples at both corners of his mouth. His large, lively eyes convey an infectious enthusiasm. His voice is strong and deep and persuasive. When he was a boy, some of his teachers thought he could have been president, he had so much charm and intelligence. His IQ breached the genius level.

Unhappily, there was the matter of his criminal record. He had first been sent away to reform school by a judge at age nine. That was after he heaved a typewriter out of a school window at a pregnant teacher.

No reformatory or mental institution could hold him for long. He assaulted his social workers with scissors or metal chairs, set other inmates on fire, or escaped by driving off in state vehicles, his legs seemingly too short to reach the controls and his head not high enough to see over the dashboard. Psychiatrists prescribed antipsychotic drugs; they had no effect.

By the age of fifteen, Willie claimed he had committed two thousand crimes, including two hundred armed robberies and twenty-five stabbings. Even allowing for youthful braggadocio, the figure was impressive.

In the spring of his fifteenth season, Willie shot and killed two men on the subway in Manhattan. The murders should not have happened. Willie was supposed to have been under the supervision of the Division for Youth, New York's juvenile justice agency. Afterward, Willie laughed about the killings. "I shot people, that's all," he said. "I don't feel nothing." He was sentenced to the maximum the law allowed – five years in a state training school.

The murders made Willie a celebrity. Mayor Ed Koch branded him "a mad dog killer." More important, the shootings made Willie a precursor of the terrifying surge of children who kill in the waning hours of the twentieth century. In New York, revulsion over Willie's acts and the brevity of his sentence frightened the legislature into swiftly passing a new law that enabled the state to try juveniles as young as thirteen for murder as if they were adults. It came to be known as the Willie Bosket law; it was the first such statute in the country. Soon, as the epidemic of children with guns spread, other states copied the New York model.

As an adult, Willie continued his campaign of terror even while incarcerated. In 1988, he stabbed a prison guard in the chest with a five-and-a-half-inch shank, a home-made stiletto. Willie picked the visiting room for the assault, in front of more than one hundred people. He had never seen the guard before, nor did he know his victim's name, Earl Porter.

At his trial, Willie cheerfully admitted his guilt. "To this day," he told the jury, "the only regret Bosket has is not having killed Earl Porter and spitting on his corpse." The reason for the stabbing, Willie said, was that he had been incarcerated since he was nine years old and prisons had become his surrogate mother. Consequently, Willie proclaimed, "I am only a monster created by the system." [. . .]

Willie James Bosket Jr. was born on December 9, 1962, shortly after 2 o'clock in the afternoon at Metropolitan Hospital. As a mark of honor, Laura gave him his father's formal name, even though Butch was in jail. It was a full-term pregnancy, no complications with the delivery. Gloria helped bring the baby home in a taxi, holding him in a blue blanket. The very next day, it seemed, Willie began turning over and raising his head. Gloria said to Laura, "You better look out. He's going to grow right up."

Sure enough, Willie began walking at nine months, was potty trained at ten months, and started talking at just over a year, all very early. The family thought he was intelligent, just like his father.

From as far back as anyone could remember, Willie was an active child. He was always running, had trouble sitting still, and was mischievous. At first, his family and the neighbors put his actions down to boyhood pranks, like the times when he walked up behind women on the street and slapped their rear ends, or the occasions when he stole old men's canes. Sometimes he was downright funny, and the neighbors hung out their windows or sat on the stoop to watch him, as if he were the local form of entertainment. Once Willie told Gloria's daughter, Debbie, three years his senior, that he was going to rob an elderly lady. He grabbed the woman's pocketbook, but he had not calculated that she had a chain running from under her sleeve connected to the handbag to foil a robbery. As he struggled to steal her possessions, the woman wrapped the chain around Willie with one arm and hit him repeatedly with her cane with the other arm.

"Oh, Lordy," she shouted over and over, "Jesus is going to get you." Willie came home with no money and covered with little red lumps and splotches.

It was after one such incident that his older sister, Cheryl, gave him the nickname Booby, as in booby trap. It stuck.

Willie was not yet six years old, and he was short and slight for his age, with the face of an angel. He had a beatific smile and big dimples in each cheek. His size and looks only made his behavior more comical in those early years. Debbie, who was his best friend and referred to him as cousin, thought he was trying to be a comedian. Often, she believed, he would do things just to make people laugh, and if you did laugh, he would do it again. Like the time on the subway when he spotted a woman with lots of bright red lipstick and a big pretty wig. As he and Debbie got off the train, he said to her, "Debbie, watch what I do." When the doors closed and the subway began moving. Willie reached through an open window and snatched the wig right off. It turned out the woman was completely bald. She screamed as her hairpiece disappeared, and Willie, Debbie, and the passengers on the train all began laughing. From a young age, Willie had a special thing about the subway.

He also displayed his bravado in their own neighborhood. There was usually a dice game on the corner of 114th Street and Lenox Avenue, where Laura had moved after Willie was born, and he often ran up and grabbed the dice from the players. Or if they saw him coming and protected the dice, he grabbed the money they had put down for bets and ran off with it. It was a risky business. Some of the men were drug pushers, others were pimps, and there were always addicts on the corner, looking to make some money for a score. It was a way for a young boy to show he had nerve, that he understood the code of street life. You earn respect by being the baddest, the toughest person on the block, always ready to use violence to assert your superiority. Early on, Debbie concluded, "Booby had no fear in nothing he did." On the street, that was the highest compliment.

Some of his tricks were endearing. One day, he came by and asked Gloria, whom he called Aunt Mick, "What you cooking today?" Gloria was broke and had no food. So she replied, in her blunt way, "I ain't cooking, Booby." An affable smile softened the expression on her face, which was framed by long, straight, dark hair and a hawk nose that reflected the Cherokee Indian in her ancestry.

"Don't worry, Aunt Mick," Willie reassured her. "My mother is cooking."

Then he went around the corner to a grocery store, loaded up a cart, and went to the checkout counter. When the clerk looked quizzically at him, Willie patted his pocket, as if he were fingering his money. The clerk put the groceries in a bag, and Willie took off without paying. The store owner sent someone to get him, but Willie, who was barely four feet tall and weighed about sixty pounds, said, "You're a lying motherfucker. You ain't seen me. I've been sitting right here on the stoop."

His ability to curse was legendary. The first words he ever learned, said Debbie, were "shit" and "motherfucker." On a street where virtually everyone used this vocabulary, he was king of the cussers. His mother had taught it to him. "If a man threatens you or hits you, this is something you can do to keep your respect," she told him. That was fine until one day when he came into the candy store where Laura worked. For some reason, she was mad at him and told him to stand in the corner. He refused, snapping at her, "Fuck you, you black motherfucker."

Willie did not like to play with the other boys in the neighborhood; he didn't shoot baskets or play baseball in the little concrete park across the street in the Stephen Poster Houses project. He didn't have the patience for teamwork. He was happier being a loner.

From early on, he dreamed about being a policeman. He loved to watch cop shows on television. There were "Adam Twelve," "Mod Squad" and "Hawaii Five O," and later "T. J. Hooker" and "Charlie's Angels." More than most kids, Willie played so hard at his fantasy life that it almost turned into reality. Nearly every day, as Gloria remembered it, Willie asked to use her phone to call the police to report an imaginary robbery in progress, then waited on the stoop to watch the squadrons of police cars arrive with sirens wailing and lights flashing. The local drug pushers got even madder at him than the police, because they were always having to scramble up on the rooftops or down an alley.

One evening, Gloria had an attack of high blood pressure and passed out. Her family called an ambulance, but it never came, a common indignity in their neighborhood. So Willie called the police. "There's some cops got killed in our house," he told them. Several police cars and an ambulance arrived instantly, and policemen poured in through the door with guns drawn.

When they saw what had happened, they chastised Willie. But he was unrepentant: "We told you my aunt was sick and you didn't come, so that was the only way I could get you here. I love my aunt, and I ain't going to let her just stay here and die."

Another time, Willie used the police box on the street to report a robbery under way at a grocery store on the corner of 113th Street and St. Nicholas Avenue. What he didn't know was that there really was a man with a gun in the store. The police arrived just in time to prevent the owner, a man named Raymond, from being shot. Raymond rewarded Willie with a gift of money for saving his life. A year later, Raymond was killed in another robbery.

Willie, Gloria decided, was never predictable. Like the time she took him to the movies, a gangster picture, with her three daughters, Debbie, Joanne, and Eunice, all older than he. Willie was sitting between Debbie and a big, tall, very dark-skinned man, who started laughing at something in the film and knocked the popcorn out of Willie's hand. Willie was only a tiny figure, hardly as tall as the seatback, but the next thing Gloria knew, Willie had jumped up and grabbed the stranger around the neck.

"Aunt Mick, see how I'm going to choke this fucker to death," Willie shouted.

Then he laughed. "I'm only kidding," Willie said, "I just felt like choking somebody."

But that was enough for the man, who got up, shaken, and left the theater. "Bad little Booby," Gloria scolded Willie. "One of these days all this stuff going to come back to haunt you."

In later years, people would try to figure out why such a young boy — he wasn't even in school yet — did these things. Everyone had an explanation, and each theory probably contained some element of the truth.

Laura blamed the neighborhood. She believed she had been a good mother — she worked hard, she saw that her children had a roof over their heads, food to eat, and clothes to wear. But Harlem had deteriorated since she was a girl, she reckoned — lots more drugs and crime and guns.

"There was people out there doing things, and Willie thought he could do the same thing he saw them doing," Laura said.

In truth, it was a tough neighborhood. In the eighteenth and nineteenth centuries, the area had been bucolic farmland, with the Harlem Creek running nearby, but now the local heroin dealer, Miss Emma, lived in the building next door. She often sat with her children on the stoop and talked to Laura and Willie. He grew up knowing the daily details of the drug business the way other American boys knew the box scores in baseball. There was always a congregation of men on the corner, drinking from brown paper bags, or shooting craps, or playing chuck-a-luck, a game with dice and a cardboard box full of handwritten numbers. They hung out at the corner, Willie learned, because that made it easier to spot the police coming down Lenox Avenue, allowing them to disperse up the side streets to escape. "Bulls on the way," the men shouted when they saw a squad car. Sometimes, Willie played chickie for them, serving as their lookout. Broken pieces of green and brown glass from old liquor bottles covered the sidewalk like ersatz grass. Along the curb, people left piles of discarded furniture, parts of wooden chairs or table legs, as if the street were a garbage dump. Sometimes in the morning, when Willie came outside to play, there would be winos asleep on his stoop, or mounds of stinking vomit, or occasionally, the body of a heroin addict who had overdosed, his hands swollen like basketballs.

There was one wino on the block whom the boys liked to tease. They urinated in a wine bottle, then gave it to him to drink when he woke up. In the highly charged atmosphere of the street, Willie always tried to outdo the other boys, who were bigger than he was. It was a matter of preserving his respect. So he took penny nails and stuck them in the man's bare feet.

The first apartment Willie lived in, at 89 Lenox Avenue, by the corner of 114th Street, had only one small bedroom, a radiator that was always exploding in the winter, and holes in the floor where the rats had eaten through. One time the toilet fell through the floor. The Christmas he was five years old, Laura had only enough money for one gift and gave him a toy race car as a present; Willie treasured it. That night, though, a fire struck the building next door. The fire engines arrived too late to put out the flames, but water from their hoses flooded the Boskets' apartment, forcing them out of the building. They moved in with Laura's mother, Nancy, around the corner at 114 West 114th Street. Willie remembered afterward that the race car got lost in the confusion. He could never recall a happy Christmas after that one.

Conditions weren't much better in the new apartment, on the ground floor of a typical turn-of-the-century dumbbell tenement, narrow in width and running back deep through the building. Only a small airshaft separated it from the house next door. Inside, the apartment was perpetually dark. The only windows were in the front room, and the family was too poor to afford more than a couple of bare electric bulbs. Outside, the building was a dingy brown brick. They had no telephone. Most of the time, Willie subsisted on peanut butter and jelly sandwiches. Twice a month, he went with his mother to the welfare center to pick up handouts of United States Department of Agriculture surplus butter and cheese.

Money was always a problem. Once a month, when the white landlord from New Jersey came by to collect the rent, Laura would tell Willie, "Say your mother ain't here." So Willie would go to the door and in his most innocent voice say, "My mother ain't here, mister." Of course, being as smart as he was, he couldn't resist turning around and saying to Laura, "Right, Mommy?" He was playing a joke on both of them. Laura would end up grabbing Willie and slapping him hard.

Some nights, when residents were seated on their stoops talking, they would hear shooting down at the corner, at the Royal Flush bar, and people would come running up the block with others chasing them, firing their guns or throwing bottles. Then the police would arrive and someone would be arrested. Over time, it seemed like sooner or later every boy on that stretch of 114th Street went to reform school and then to jail, or got himself killed. It was a natural fact of life.

Coming up in that neighborhood, Willie had learned the code of the street at a very young age, just as his father had in Augusta – that the secret to survival was a willingness to use violence, to be always ready to fight. But Willie was much smarter than the other kids on his block, and also more driven, more highly motivated. He wanted to be the best. So he took the code of the street to the extreme – he would be the most violent. It would be his ticket; it was the only way Willie knew to get ahead.

Early on, people sensed there was something special at work in Willie, something that came from inside him or his relationship with his family. From his youngest years,

Laura and both his grandmothers, Nancy and Marie, noticed that Willie looked and acted an awful lot like his father. The older he got, the greater the resemblance. Their faces were so similar, they could have been twins, all the women believed. "When you see Willie, you see Butch," they said to one another. And Willie had that same impulsiveness and lack of patience as Butch, when he wanted something, it had to be right away, otherwise he threw a temper tantrum. When that happened, he jumped up and down, cried, cursed, knocked things off the kitchen table, or broke anything he could get his hands on. What was still more remarkable, when Willie got upset or sensed trouble, his eyes bulged out and his jaw began to work, just like his father.

Science has not advanced far enough to say whether Willie inherited any part of his aggressive tendencies from his father. Willie himself often thought so; he believed he could feel something of his father inside him. But you have to be very careful in drawing such conclusions about biology. The poverty and neglect in which Willie grew up, along with the violence on the streets in his neighborhood, were trouble enough to explain what happened. Still, in later years, researchers would find that some traits of temperament, the qualities of personality a person is born with, are often heritable. In particular, studies found that impulsive-aggressive behavior is roughly 25 to 40 percent heritable. If that happened with Willie, it could have given him a predisposition to impulsiveness, to being ready to explode at the slightest provocation. This alone didn't make him violent, but such a predisposition would have magnified in his mind the threatening nature of street life. And it would have made for a powerful combination at work in Willie, the interaction of nature and nurture.

There were also the difficult circumstances of Laura's pregnancy while she was carrying Willie. She had been in Milwaukee when Butch killed the two men, and she had been on the run with him before he got arrested. Years later, scientific studies would find that mothers subjected to high levels of stress during pregnancy, everything from divorce to poverty or violence, ofteh have babies that are hyperactive or unusually irritable. After the fact, there was no way to prove this was the case with Willie. But it, too, could have affected his behavior.

Laura didn't know about these scientific findings, but the more she watched Willie, the more she said to herself, "Yup, that's Butch's son. That's him." This worried her. She began to wonder if Willie was really her child, or was he just Butch's? Laura already had put a brake on her emotions, rationing them out cautiously so she wouldn't get hurt. Now, with Willie turning out like Butch, she withdrew more, putting a distance between herself and her son, a chasm that Willie intuitively felt as a form of rejection.

From the beginning, Laura came right out and told Willie, "You look just like your father." Sometimes, when he acted up, she would also say, "Boy, you bad, just like your father. You sure got the devil in you. You're going to grow up to be no good." It was a heavy load to put on a bright youngster, especially when both his grandmothers constantly repeated the notion.

At first, Willie didn't know exactly what this meant, because Laura didn't tell him the truth about Butch. Instead, when Willie asked where his father was, his mother replied, "He's in the army." She didn't want to tell a little boy that his father was in prison, and she didn't want the other boys in the neighborhood teasing him about an absent father, so she made up a cover story.

This went on for several years, until Willie began to get curious about who his father really was and why he was so bad. Finally, when he was about seven years old and staying at Marie's house one day, he noticed his grandmother holding a black-and-white photograph of a tall man standing beside some weightlifting equipment. The man was dressed in a T-shirt and fatigue pants, revealing a heavily muscled chest and set of arms.

"Who is that man?" Willie asked.

"Your father," Marie replied.

"Where is he?" Willie persisted, his mind racing.

"He's in prison," his grandmother revealed. "He killed some men in a fight. One day, you'll see him, he'll be home."

This was exciting information. In the pecking order of the street, being in prison for murder was first-class, something you could brag about. But his mother's deception also made Willie angry.

In later years, social workers and therapists who worked with Willie would come back to this episode again and again. "When Mrs. Bosket finally admitted to Willie that his father was in prison, he expressed deep anger at her for not telling him the truth before," a psychologist reported when Willie was eleven years old.

"It is further observed that Mrs. Bosket has rejected Willie from birth," the report added. [. . .]

Willie's anger with his mother, and his simultaneous need for her love, were complicated by Laura's relationships with other men. Soon after he was born, she began bringing a series of men to the house, some of whom spent the night, or stayed for a period of weeks. It was as if she were trying to cheer herself out of her depression following the murders by an overdose of romance.

Years later, Willie still remembered some of them, and the giggling in the bedroom at night. His mother never explained anything to Willie, or prepared him beforehand. The first thing he knew, another man was in the house. There was Tommy Robinson, who became the father of his younger sister, Shirley, born three years after him in 1965. Then there was Jose, a tall, very black man, six feet ten inches in height, who lived with Laura for a period. When they got in a fight one day, Jose held her down on the bed, then shoved her against the scalding hot radiator pipe that ran from floor to ceiling. Laura screamed, and when Jose let her down, a patch of her charred skin was stuck to the metal. "Booby saw it and went crazy," Gloria recalled. He picked up an iron pipe and hit Jose, then slashed him with a knife.

Bert was next. He beat Laura up so badly that Nancy had to come and take her to the hospital, where they kept her overnight. She came home with her head bandaged. Willie got so angry he went to Gloria's apartment and told her, "I'm going to burn that motherfucker up." Then he dragged a can of gasoline back to the Boskets' house, pouring it on the living room couch and setting it on fire. Gloria thought to herself, "He sure loves Laura."

He did. But hated his mother, too. It was a complex, tumultuous relationship. Laura had a hard time controlling Willie when he did something bad. Sometimes, she slapped him around with her hand until the veins popped out, or she would give him a whipping with a belt. It wasn't that she hated him; it was just the only form of punishment she knew. But he would shake it right off. Worse, it reinforced Willie's belief that the way to settle things was by getting physical. Watching from across the street, Debbie thought, "There isn't nothing she can do." Laura herself despaired. She was trying hard to be a good mother. But she honestly didn't know what else to do.

One time, after she fought with a boyfriend at home, Willie set fire to his own shirt-sleeve and threatened to stab himself. Another time, when Laura punished him, he shouted, "I hate you. I can't stand you. I wish you wasn't my mother. I'm going to jump in front of the subway and kill myself." She had to run after him and restrain him from going into the subway station.

Sabrina Gaston, the daughter of the local heroin dealer, watched Willie from her window after episodes like this and saw his face dirty with tears. Once, he went outside, picked up a bottle, and smashed a cat in the head and killed it. She thought he was a very sad and angry boy, lost in his own world. [. . .]

The seeds of Willie's problems were planted early. When he was older, he looked back and felt there had always been an anger in him. It started with his childhood hatred of his mother. Then, as the years passed, he identified it as a hatred of the American system. It might all have been the same rage.

After Willie turned six, Laura enrolled him in first grade at P.S. 207, a few blocks from their house. School was a nightmare from the start. It wasn't that Willie lacked intelligence; in fact, the teachers all agreed he was unusually bright. He just couldn't sit still in class, or follow the teachers' instructions, which made it hard to learn. He was always throwing temper tantrums, and when the teachers tried to discipline him, Willie hit them. He also fought with the other students, ran out of the classroom into the hallway, pulled the fire alarms, and stole supplies like crayons and construction paper. The principal quickly put Willie in a special class for destructive children – that worked for a while. His teacher now was Mrs. House, a soft-spoken, gentle black woman who wasn't afraid of him. She controlled him with a mix of firmness and affection. If he acted up, she hit him and said, "Come here, give me an Eskimo kiss." Willie adored her as the mother he had always wanted.

But he soon had another teacher, and his behavior deteriorated again. Willie began playing hooky, just as his father had. Laura would walk him to school in the morning, and as soon as she dropped him at the front door, he would run out the back door. That was especially embarrassing to Laura, because she had begun to work at the school as a teacher's side. One day, as he was escaping, he spotted several of his mother's fellow workers walking toward him, so he dashed out into the street to avoid them and was hit in the head by a car. The impact knocked him out and threw him to the far side of the street. He woke up in Lenox Hill Hospital, where he complained of headaches for several days, but X-rays showed no damage. In the future, some psychiatrists wondered if the accident contributed to his behavior; a number of extremely violent criminals have suffered damage to their brains when young.

After the accident, the school recommended that Laura take Willie to a psychiatrist. She did, once, but saw no improvement and thought it was a waste of time. "The stupid public school thinks he's crazy, but he's not," she told Gloria.

By now, Willie was eight years old and in second grade, technically, at least. It got so the teachers often told him he was crazy right to his face, which made Willie laugh. On the street, being called a "crazy nigger" was high praise. A "crazy nigger" was someone who developed a reputation for being unpredictably violent and aggressive. You had to show deference to a person like that. Willie discovered that if he acted crazy, people were afraid of him and he could get what he wanted, like being sent home for bad behavior. Willie was a human nuclear chain reaction – the worse he acted, the more people said bad things about him, and then the more impossible he behaved. One time a teacher Willie called Mr. Sauerkraut, because of his German-sounding name, took him aside and told him he was no good and was going to grow up to be no good. Afterward, Willie and another boy broke into a storeroom on the school's third floor, which was normally kept locked. In the forbidden area, they found stacks of textbooks that were fun to throw around, a mimeograph machine that was asking to be smashed, and a nice big typewriter sitting on a desk. Willie picked it up, carried it to a window, and hurled it out. The type-writer just missed hitting a pregnant teacher who was walking below.

That was the final straw for the school. Willie was expelled, and the city school board ordered Laura to take him for psychiatric observation to Bellevue Hospital, where both his father and his grandfather had been sent, though no one was aware of the fact.

Laura brought Willie to Bellevue on March 8, 1971, a bad day for her. The same morning, the police took her older daughter, Cheryl, now thirteen, to Zarega, one of four juvenile detention centers in New York where children were sent while awaiting the outcome of their cases in Family Court. At Laura's reluctant insistence, Cheryl had been charged with running away from home and consorting with older boys. She was wild in school, sitting in class throwing pumpkin seeds and cursing her teachers. Now she was also playing hooky and disappearing from home for long stretches of time. Her neigh-bor and schoolmate, Sharon Parker, thought Cheryl was full of anger at her mother for the way she was raised and was trying to get back at Laura. Whatever the reason, many nights Laura and Gloria set out frantically to search for Cheryl, so Laura had finally been persuaded by the Bureau of Child Welfare that the best course was to bring her before the Family Court. To Gloria, Laura seemed like a tiny raft on the ocean being tossed about by huge waves; she was at the mercy of larger forces. Butch had married her, then set off on a spree that ended in murder and her abandonment while pregnant. Just getting through each day was a trial, like being flooded out of her apartment on Christmas Day. Now nothing she did with Willie or Cheryl worked. She sensed she had lost control of her children.

Laura and Willie took the bus to get from Harlem down to Bellevue, at First Avenue and Thirtieth Street. It was an old green bus, with hard seats, and they sat diag-onally across from the driver. The bus ride seemed to take hours for Willie, and he had a premonition that his life was changing forever. His mother had told him the doctors in Bellevue wanted to keep him for thirty days. He hated being controlled, and he didn't understand how he could be separated from his mother and deprived of his freedom. Only grown men got locked up, in jail, he believed. It would be his first taste of a lifetime of institutionalization. [. . .]

The psychiatrist who saw Willie was Dr. Mahin Hassibi, the doctor in charge of the children's unit. Slight and short, with narrow eyes, straight dark hair, and a gentle, self-composed manner, she looked like a figure in a miniature Persian painting from her native Iran. She thought Willie was very handsome but the saddest little boy she had ever seen. It wasn't something she had to interpret. He looked sad and frightened all the time. He talked to no one, and when he walked into the room to meet her, he just straight out said he didn't want to be alive. In fact, Willie told her he was going to jump in front of a subway train and kill himself. He was quite capable of doing it, she thought. Usually, in Dr. Hassibi's experience, kids would be sad when they were admitted to Bellevue, but the sadness would lift after a few days. Willie remained depressed the whole time he was in the hospital.

Willie also told the psychiatrist about his father. "He's in prison for killing two men," Willie said accurately, now that he knew the story. Dr. Hassibi mentally calculated the effect that must have had on him. She believed Willie was an abused child, which was why he was so depressed and suicidal. "Not physically abused necessarily, but an abused, neglected child," she told her colleagues. Dr. Hassibi met Laura, too, and got the impression his mother "did not really care for him. Not only did she not care for him, she had identified him with his father and she was quite sure that he was not going to end up anyplace else. She foresaw only a bad future for her son."

After seeing Laura, Dr. Hassibi was even more upset. She tried to explain her findings, that Willie was very sad and might try to hurt himself.

"I'll beat the craziness out of him," Laura responded.

After consulting with other doctors on the staff, Dr. Hassibi wrote out her conclusion: "Diagnosis – Hyperkinetic reaction of childhood with depressive features."

The first part of the diagnosis was common enough. In current psychiatric terms, it meant Willie was suffering from attention deficit disorder, that he was hyperactive. But the reference to "depressive features" was unusual. At the time, psychiatry did not yet recognize depression in children. The assumption was that a period of depression in a child was an isolated event that the child would soon outgrow, with no lasting effect. But Dr. Hassibi had seen something so deep in Willie that she wanted to call attention to it. In hundreds and thousands of charts of children she saw over the years at Bellevue, he was the only one with that diagnosis.

Despite everything, however, Dr. Hassibi believed there was a softness in Willie, an openness, that a good therapist could work on. He was still only eight. It was important to act quickly, because she had seen children much like Willie, sad and frightened youngsters, who turned into violent, aggressive kids to deal with their fear. Their anxiety was so great that if you touched them, they thought you were going to kill them, and they reacted violently, in self-defense. They had to be defused. So Dr. Hassibi recommended that Willie be kept for further observation after the initial thirty-day commitment and then be sent to a residential facility where he could receive intensive treatment.

But Willie was working on his mother. He cried and screamed when she came to visit and told her a male nurse had attacked him. He accused her of betraying him by leaving him there, playing on her guilt. Finally, his entreaties were too much, and she told the hospital that she was signing him out, against the hospital's advice. Dr. Hassibi was concerned. She notified the Bureau of Child Welfare that Laura's action constituted neglect. The bureau opened a file on Willie, but it was swamped with far more serious cases, so there was no follow-up. Willie, though, had learned another lesson about the power of manipulation – he could get what he wanted by staging a fit.

After he was released from Bellevue, things went downhill abruptly, Willie's school refused to take him back, and he figured out ways to play hooky from the new special school he was supposed to be enrolled in. He began spending a lot of time in a neighbor's apartment across the street, with three girls who were twelve, thirteen, and fourteen years old, and also playing hooky. The girls were experimenting with sex, and Willie was the happy guinea pig. They each had a room, and they would take turns with him, calling him in, then showing him how to do it, where to put his penis. It took several tries, but they finally got it right. Some days, Willie got tired and said, "It's the next one's turn." But one of the girls would shout, "I ain't done yet. Just a little bit more." And Willie would plead, "No, no more I'm getting sore." They called it "doing it." Willie was just shooting dog water, of course. He was only nine years old.

About the same time, his grandfather, James Bosket, who was now fifty years old, began taking Willie for weekends to the apartment he rented in Queens. Willie didn't much like going with James. It was a long, tedious ride on the subway, and then the bus, and it was ten blocks from James's house to the nearest candy store where he could steal things. James drank a lot, and Willie was always afraid he would suffer one of his epileptic fits and fall on the floor. That embarrassed Willie. James had recently been released from the city prison on Rikers Island, where he had served a year for kidnapping and sodomizing a young boy, though no one had told Willie about that. In the evenings, on those weekends at James's apartment, they watched television, and then James had Willie sleep in the bed with him.

"I'm going to teach you about sex," James told his grandson. "Your father loved having sex, and the ladies loved him. He was a regular Casanova."

Then James lay on the bed and told Willie to penetrate him with his penis. He used Vaseline as a lubricant. "This is how you do it with girls," James told him. "It will be our little secret."

The fourth time this happened, James also beat Willie, so he ran out of the house, to the nearest store he knew about, and the store manager called the police. Willie never told any of the psychiatrists who saw him about his adventures with the three girls, or about his experience with his grandfather. But a therapist would have concluded that all this sexual stimulation at the young age of nine was a lot for a young boy to handle. It was another form of abuse, and it might have added to the rage and agitation already burning inside him.

Willie's file with the Bureau of Child Welfare was rapidly growing longer in 1971 and early 1972 when he was eight and nine. The police reported that he snatched a woman's pocketbook, stole a car, set several fires, pointed a knife at a girl one day when he did attend school, and was truant most of the time. But many of the things he did were never reported. Like the hot summer evening he and Debbie and Debbie's boyfriend, Arthur Habersham, and a few other friends were in Central Park. The sun was just going down in a big red ball and they were getting ready to go home when they spotted a black man lying on a bench asleep. Willie gathered up some newspapers and wadded them under the bench, where the man's shirtsleeve was hanging down. Then he set the papers on fire. Pretty soon, the man felt his arm burning, jumped up, and ran straight for a little lake. As he ran, the flames billowed out all over him. He screamed and jumped in the lake. Willie was standing there laughing, a deep laugh for a small boy.

Laura was trying to get her life in order. She was now working as a security guard for a private agency at City College, only a few blocks from the family's apartment on 145th Street. When Willie had . . . come home from the halfway house, she figured the Division for Youth had let him go. No one contacted her to tell her differently.

Laura had a new boyfriend, "Charles," a tall, thickset, very dark-skinned man who at forty-eight was eleven years older than Laura. He acted as the superintendent of their building and ran the pool hall on the first floor, Al Clark's Billiards. Charles also watched over the building next door, a front for drug pushers. Given his line of work, Charles always carried a gun, and he wasn't shy about using it. One night soon after Willie came home, Laura, Shirley, and Willie were looking out the window of their second-floor apartment when they saw a man named Gangster running out of the pool hall. He was trash-talking about how he wasn't going to pay for the games he played, and what he was going to do to Charles, Charles pulled out his pistol and shot Gangster in the kneecap.

Willie was awed by Charles. To Willie, he was the baddest dude on the street and the first man he met who might have been as tough as his father. By this time, Charles had moved in with Laura, bringing his collection of guns – fifty or sixty revolvers, automatics, and shotguns: a regular arsenal. The local drug dealers gave them to Charles to hold for safekeeping, and he stored them in the bedroom closet.

Willie was having trouble with two boys – Leroy, an older boy who lived in the neighborhood (Willie was fifteen), and Ricky, a drug dealer and trained boxer. Leroy and Ricky enjoyed taunting Willie, calling him a punk and challenging him to fight.

"Yo, my man, don't disrespect me," Willie told them. "Do I disrespect you?" When the two older boys persisted, Charles offered Willie a gun to even the odds.

"The next time you see them," Charles counseled Willie, "you show them this gun and you let them know what's going to happen if they start picking on you. They won't disrespect you."

It was the code of the streets again, the code that descended from the old Southern notion of honor. A man had to be ready to fight to prove himself in the eyes of others. Southern whites had called it honor; Willie's great-grandfather Pud had talked about reputation; and his father, Butch, had spoken of respect. Now on the streets of Harlem, the term was undergoing another metamorphosis – it was being referred to as disrespect. Whatever word was used, it was still a lethal credo, especially for poor African-American boys like Willie with scant chance for a good education or a decent job and little to look forward to but a life in prison. And Willie, so bright and driven, had carried the code of violence to the extreme. For him, violence was like a sport, a competition, and victory went to the most violent. So what Charles said struck a powerful chord in Willie, an echo of the voices of his ancestors.

On February 1, 1978, Willie was hanging out at Intermediate School Number 10, a large, yellow-brick building that had been constructed on top of the subway yards at 148th Street and Lenox Avenue, not far from his house. While Willie was trying to talk with a pretty brown-skinned girl who messed around with Leroy, she insulted Willie, disrespecting him. He slapped her in the face.

That was a serious challenge to Leroy. He gave Willie an ultimatum that evening: "You can fight it out alone with Ricky, or we will both kill you." Leroy led him up to the roof of their five-story tenement, where Ricky was waiting. Willie knew he was overmatched.

When Ricky started throwing punches, there was no time to think. The language of the street was action, and Willie pulled out the gun Charles had given him. Ricky jumped backward in fear, toward the edge of the roof. Willie gave him a kick, knocking him down the narrow air shaft between the building they were on and its neighbor. Leroy turned and ran.

The next morning, Charles found Ricky's body lying in the bottom of the air shaft and told Willie he had to get rid of it. People often dumped their garbage out there, and someone might find the corpse and call the police. Willie said he would get some gas and burn it. [. . .]

Chapter 13

David P. Farrington

HUMAN DEVELOPMENT AND CRIMINAL CAREERS

From: David P. Farrington (1997), excerpts from 'Human development and criminal careers', in Mike Maguire, Rod Morgan and Robert Reiner (eds), *Oxford Handbook of Criminology*, 2nd edn, Oxford: Oxford University Press, pp. 361–408.

THE AIM OF THIS chapter is to review what is known about human development and criminal careers. A 'criminal career' is defined as the longitudinal sequence of offences committed by an individual offender. 'Offences' in this chapter are defined as the most common types of crimes that predominate in the official *Criminal Statistics*, including theft, burglary, robbery, violence, vandalism, and drug use. 'White collar' crime is not included here, because there has been little attempt as yet to study it from the perspective of human development and criminal careers. [. . .]

The criminal career approach is essentially concerned with human development over time. However, criminal behaviour does not generally appear without warning; it is commonly preceded by childhood antisocial behaviour (such as bullying, lying, truanting, and cruelty to animals) and followed by adult anti-social behaviour (such as spouse assault, child abuse and neglect, excessive drinking, and sexual promiscuity). [. . .]

In studying development, it is important to investigate developmental sequences over time, for example where one behaviour facilitates or acts as a kind of stepping stone to another. It is desirable to identify non-criminal behaviours that lead to criminal behaviours, and long-term developmental sequences including types of offending. For example, hyperactivity at age 2 may lead to cruelty to animals at 6, shoplifting at 10, burglary at 15, robbery at 20, and eventually spouse assault, child abuse and neglect, alcohol abuse, and employment and accommodation problems later on in life. Typically, a career of childhood anti-social behaviour leads to a criminal career, which often coincides with a career of teenage anti-social behaviour and leads to a career of adult anti-social behaviour. . . . A deeper understanding of the development of the criminal career requires a deeper understanding of the wider anti-social career. [. . .]

CONCEPTUAL AND METHODOLOGICAL ISSUES

The antisocial syndrome

[. . .]

The results obtained in criminal career research depend on the methods of defining and measuring crime that are adopted. Most criminal career researchers focus on official records of arrests or convictions for relatively serious offences rather than on self-reports of relatively trivial infractions.

DEVELOPMENT OF OFFENDING

Prevalence at different ages

One of the distinctive contributions of criminal career research has been to demonstrate the high cumulative prevalence of arrests and convictions of males (for a review, see Visher and Roth, 1986). In the Cambridge Study, 40 per cent of London males were convicted for criminal offences up to age 40, when these were restricted to offences normally recorded in the Criminal Record Office (Farrington, 1995). In Newcastle-upon-Tyne, 31 per cent of males and 6 per cent of females were convicted of non-traffic offences up to age 32 (Kolvin *et al.*, 1988). Similarly, a longitudinal follow-up of a 1953 English birth cohort in official records (Home Office Statistical Bulletin, 1995) found that 34 per cent of males and 9 per cent of females were convicted of non-traffic offences up to age 39.

Similar results have been obtained in other countries. In the Philadelphia cohort study, Wolfgang *et al.* (1987) showed that 47 per cent of males were arrested for non-traffic offences up to age 30, including 38 per cent of Caucasians and 69 per cent of African Americans. In Sweden, Stattin *et al.* (1989) discovered that 38 per cent of males and 7 per cent of females were officially registered for non-traffic offences by age 30. The curves showing the cumulative prevalence up to age 25 of offending by working-class males in London and Stockholm were remarkably similar (Farrington and Wikström, 1994).

The cumulative prevalence of self-reported offences is even higher. In the Cambridge Study, almost all of the males (96 per cent) had committed at least one of ten specified offences (including burglary, theft, assault, vandalism, and drug use) by the age of 32 (Farrington, 1989). Many males commit minor acts, especially in their teenage years, that might, strictly speaking, be classified as offences. In order realistically to compare offenders and non-offenders, it is necessary to set a sufficiently high criterion for 'offending' (e.g. in terms of frequency, seriousness, duration, or in terms of arrests or convictions) so that the vast majority of the male population are not classified as offenders. Alternatively, more and less serious offenders could be compared.

An important focus of criminal career research is the relationship between age and crime. Generally, the 'point prevalence' of offending at each age increases to a peak in the teenage years and then declines. The age–crime curve obtained by following up a cohort of people over time (the same people at different ages) is often different from the cross-sectional curve seen in official statistics (which reflects different people at different ages; see Farrington, 1990*a*).

In the Cambridge Study, the peak age for the prevalence of convictions was 17 (Farrington, 1992a). The median age of conviction for most types of offences (burglary, robbery, theft of and from vehicles, shoplifting) was 17, while it was 20 for violence and 21 for fraud. Mean ages are typically higher than medians and modes (peaks), because of the skewed age–crime curve (Farrington, 1986a: 196). In national English data, the peak age varied from 14 for shoplifting to 20 for fraud/forgery and drug offences (Tarling, 1993). Similarly, in the Philadelphia cohort study of Wolfgang et al. (1987), the arrest rate increased to a peak at age 16 and then declined. In the Cambridge Study, the peak age of increase in the prevalence of offending was 14, while the peak age of decrease was 23. These times of maximum acceleration and deceleration in prevalence draw our attention to times in people's lives when important life events may be occurring that influence offending. They also indicate that the modal age of onset of offending is probably 14 and the modal age of desistance is probably 23.

Self-report studies also show that the most common types of offending decline from the teens to the twenties. In the Cambridge Study, the prevalence of burglary, shoplifting, theft of and from vehicles, theft from automatic machines, and vandalism all decreased from the teens to the twenties, but the same decreases were not seen for theft from work, assault, drug abuse, and fraud (Farrington, 1989). For example, burglary (since the last interview) was admitted by 13 per cent at both 25 and 32. In their American National Youth Survey, Elliott et al. (1989) found that self-reports of the prevalence of offending increased from 11–13 to a peak at 15–17 and then decreased by 19–21.

Individual offending frequency

Since the pioneering research of Blumstein and Cohen (1979), much criminal career research has been concerned to estimate the individual offending frequency of active offenders during their criminal careers (for a review, see Cohen, 1986). For example, based on American research, Blumstein and Cohen concluded that the average active Index (more serious) offender committed about ten Index offences per year free, and that the individual offending frequency essentially did not vary with age. Furthermore, the average active Index offender accumulated about one arrest per year free.

In calculating the individual offending frequency and other criminal career parameters such as onset, duration, and desistance, a major problem is to estimate when careers really begin and when they really end. Tarling (1993: 53) assumed that careers began at the age of criminal responsibility and ended on the date of the last conviction. On this assumption, males in the 1953 birth cohort had a conviction rate of 0.5 per year (one every two years), while the corresponding figure for females was 0.3 per year (one every 3.3 years).

The British and American studies reviewed by Farrington (1986a) indicated that the individual offending frequency did not vary greatly with age or during criminal careers. However, Loeber and Snyder (1990) concluded that it increased during the juvenile years up to age 16, and Haapanen (1990) found that it decreased during the adult years. Furthermore, in the Stockholm Project Metropolitan, Wikström (1990) showed that frequency peaked at 15–17, and in retrospective self-report research with Nebraska prisoners Horney and Marshall (1991) concluded that it varied over time within individuals. Since there are several contrary studies indicating that frequency is stable with age (e.g. Home Office Statistical Bulletin, 1987; LeBlanc and Frechette, 1989), more research is clearly needed to establish the conditions under which it is relatively stable or varying with age.

If periods of acceleration or deceleration in the individual offending frequency could be identified, and if the predictors of acceleration or deceleration could be established (Farrington, 1987), these could have important implications for theory and policy. Barnett and Lofaso (1985) found that the best predictor of the future offending frequency in the Philadelphia cohort study was the past offending frequency.

There are many life events or conditions that might lead to an increase in the individual offending frequency. For example, using retrospective self-reports, Ball et al. (1981) found that Baltimore heroin addicts committed non-drug offences at a higher rate during periods of addiction than during periods when they were off opiates, suggesting that addiction caused an increase in offending. Using official records in the Cambridge Study, London males committed offences at a higher rate during periods of unemployment than during periods of employment (Farrington et al., 1986). This difference was restricted to offences involving material gain, suggesting that unemployment caused a lack of money, which in turn caused an increase in offending to obtain money. However, neither of these studies adequately disentangled differences in prevalence from differences in frequency.

The individual offending frequency cannot be estimated from aggregate date simply by dividing the number of offences at each age by the number of arrested or convicted persons at each age, because some persons who have embarked on a criminal career may not sustain an official record at a particular age. Barnett et al. (1987) tested several mathematical models of the criminal careers of the Cambridge Study males, restricting the analyses to persons with two or more convictions. They found that models assuming that all offenders had the same frequency of offending were inadequate. Hence, they assumed that there were two categories of offenders, 'frequents' and 'occasionals'. The data showed that both categories incurred convictions at a constant (but different) rate during their active criminal careers. Barnett et al. did not suggest that there were in reality only two categories of offenders, but rather that it was possible to fit the actual data with a simple model assuming only two categories. [. . .]

Onset

Criminal career research on onset using official records generally shows a peak age of onset between 13 and 16. For example, in the United States, Blumstein and Graddy (1982) showed that the age of onset curve for arrests of both white and non-white males peaked at age 15, and Stattin et al. (1989) also reported a peak age of 15 for males in a small Swedish city (Örebro). In the Swedish Project Metropolitan, Fry (1985) found that the peak ages of first arrest for Stockholm males and females were both at 13, while the peak age of onset for males in Finland was 16–17 (Pulkkinen, 1988). In the Cambridge Study, the peak age of onset was 14; 5 per cent of the males were first convicted at that age (Farrington, 1992a). The onset curves up to age 25 of working-class males in London and Stockholm were quite similar (Farrington and Wikström, 1994).

Rather than presenting the onset rate, taking all persons in a cohort still alive as the denominator, it might be better to present a 'hazard' rate. This relates the number of first offenders to the number of persons still at risk of a first offence, excluding those with a previous onset. In the Cambridge Study, the hazard rate showed a later peak than the onset rate at age 17; 6 per cent of the males still at risk were first convicted at that age (Farrington *et al.*, 1990). Basically, the peak hazard rate was later and greater than the peak onset rate because of the decreasing number of males still at risk of a first conviction with increasing age (the denominator). McCord (1990) showed how hazard rates varied according to social background variables. In the Cambridge Study, the best childhood predictors of an early versus a later onset of offending were rarely spending leisure time with the father, high troublesomeness, authoritarian parents and high psychomotor impulsivity (Farrington and Hawkins, 1991). [. . .]

In a study of Montreal delinquents, LeBlanc and Frechette (1989) discovered that shoplifting and vandalism tended to occur before adolescence (average age of onset 11), burglary and motor vehicle theft in adolescence (average onset 14–15), and sex offences and drug trafficking in the later teenage years (average onset 17–19). Judging from average ages of onset, the onset of shoplifting or vandalism might provide an early opportunity to detect future serious criminal offenders.

In the Cambridge Study, the average age of the first conviction was 17.5. The males first convicted at the earliest ages (10–13) tended to become the most persistent offenders, committing an average of 8.1 offences leading to convictions in an average criminal career lasting 9.9 years up to age 32 (Farrington, 1992a). Similarly, Farrington and Wikstrom (1994), using official records in Stockholm, and LeBlanc and Frechette (1989) in Montreal, using both self-reports and official records, showed that the duration of criminal careers decreased with increasing age of onset.

Clearly, an early age of onset foreshadows a long criminal career (see also Home Office Statistical Bulletin, 1987; Tracy and Kempf-Leonard, 1996). Whether it also foreshadows a high frequency of offending is less clear. Haapanen *et al.* (1978), in a study of violent juveniles in Ohio, reported that there was a (negative) linear relationship between the age of onset and the number of offences. Neglecting the possibility of desistance, this suggests that the offending frequency may be tolerably constant between onset and the 18th birthday. In agreement with this, Tarling (1993: 57) found no relationship between age of onset and the conviction rate. However, Tolan (1987) showed that the frequency of current self-reported offending was greatest for those with the earliest age of onset.

Aggregate results may hide different types of offenders. For example, Moffitt (1993) distinguished between 'life-course-persistent' offenders, who had an early onset and a long criminal career, and 'adolescence-limited' offenders, who started later and had a short criminal career. These groups were identified using conviction records in the Cambridge Study (Nagin and Moffitt, 1995). However, according to self-reports, the apparent reformation of the 'adolescence-limited' offenders was less than complete. At age 32, they continued to drink heavily, to use drugs, get into fights, and commit criminal acts.

It is important to establish why an early age of onset predicts a long criminal career and a large number of offences. Following Gottfredson and Hirschi (1986), one possibility is that an early age of onset is merely one symptom of a high criminal potential, which later shows itself in persistent and serious offending. On this theory, an early age of onset has no effect on underlying theoretical constructs. Another possibility is that an early age of onset in some way facilitates later offending, perhaps because of the reinforcing effects of successful early offending or the stigmatizing effects of convictions. In other words, an early onset may lead to a change in an underlying theoretical construct such as the probability of persistence. Nagin and Farrington (1992) concluded that the inverse relationship between age of onset and persistence of offending in the Cambridge Study was entirely attributable to the persistence of a previously existing criminal potential, and that an early age of onset had no additional impact on persistence.

An onset offence of a particular type might predict a later frequent or serious criminal career. For example, the Home Office Statistical Bulletin (1987) showed that an onset offence of burglary or theft was particularly predictive of persistence in offending. This type of information might be useful in identifying at first arrest or conviction those at high risk of progressing into a persistent and serious criminal career.

Desistance

The true age of desistance from offending can be determined with certainty only after offenders die. In the Cambridge Study up to age 32, the average age of the last offence was 23.3, according to official records. Since the average age of the first offence was 17.5, the average length of the recorded criminal career was 5.8 years, with an average of 4.5 recorded convictions per offender during this time period (Farrington, 1992a).

In the Philadelphia cohort study, Wolfgang et al. (1972) showed how the probability of reoffending (persistence as opposed to desistance) increased after each successive offence. This probability was .54 after the first offence, .65 after the second, .72 after the third, and it reached an asymptote of .80 after six or more arrests. Assuming a probabilistic process with a probability p of persisting after each offence, and conversely a probability (1–p) of desisting, the expected number of future offences after any given offence is $p/(1-p)$, which at the asymptote (p = .80) is 4.

Several other researchers have replicated these results by showing the growth in the recidivism probability after each successive offence (see Blumstein et al., 1985; Tarling, 1993; Farrington and Wikström, 1994). For example, national English data for males born in 1953 shows that the probability of persistence increased from .45 after the first conviction to .83 after the seventh (Home Office Statistical Bulletin, 1995). The corresponding probabilities for females were from .22 to .78. [. . .]

Several projects have explicitly investigated why offenders desist. For example, in the Cambridge Study, getting married and moving out of London both fostered desistance (Osborn, 1980; West, 1982). Shover (1985) explicitly asked retrospective questions about desistance to older men who had given up offending. The main reasons advanced for desistance focused on the increasing costs of crime (long prison sentences), the importance of intimate relationships with women, increasing satisfaction with jobs, and becoming more mature, responsible, and settled with age. In the Gluecks' follow-up of 500 Boston delinquents, Sampson and Laub (1993) identified job stability and marital attachment in adulthood as crucial factors in desistance. Some policy implications of desistance research are that ex-offenders should be helped to settle down in stable marital relationships and in stable jobs, and helped to break away from their criminal associates.

Chronic offenders

In the Philadelphia cohort study, Wolfgang et al. (1972) showed that 6 per cent of the males (18 per cent of the offenders) accounted for 52 per cent of all the juvenile arrests, and labelled these 6 per cent the 'chronic offenders'. The chronics accounted for even higher proportions of serious offences: 69 per cent of all aggravated assaults, 71 per cent of homicides, 73 per cent of forcible rapes, and 82 per cent of robberies. Frequency and seriousness of offending are generally related. Other researchers have largely replicated these results. For example, in the Cambridge Study, about 6 per cent of the males accounted for about half of all the convictions up to the age of 32 (Farrington and West, 1993). However, the offences of the chronic offenders were not more serious on average than those of the non-chronic offenders. The chronics committed more serious offences largely because they committed more offences.

In Stockholm, Wikström (1987) showed that only 1 per cent of Project Metropolitan cohort members (6 per cent of all offenders) accounted for half of all the crimes, while Pulkkinen (1988) in Finland found that 4 per cent of males and 1 per cent of females accounted for half of all the convictions. It is useful to quantify these disproportionalities using the Lorenz curve and the Gini coefficient (Fox and Tracy, 1988; Wikström, 1991: 29). The chronic offenders who account for a disproportionate number of all offences are clearly prime targets for crime prevention and control. However, a lot depends on how far they can be identified in advance.

Blumstein *et al.* (1985) pointed out that Wolfgang *et al.* (1972) identified the chronics retrospectively. Even if all the arrested boys were truly homogeneous in their underlying criminal potential, chance factors alone would result in some of them having more arrests and others having fewer. Because of these probabilistic processes, those with the most arrests – defined after the fact as the chronics – would account for a disproportionate fraction of the total number of arrests. For example, if an unbiased die was thrown thirty times and the five highest scores were added up, these would account for a dispro- portionate fraction of the total score obtained in all thirty throws (thirty out of 105, on average; 16.7 per cent of the throws accounting for 28.6 per cent of the total score).

The key question is how far the chronic offenders can be predicted in advance, and whether they differ prospectively from the non-chronic offenders in their individual offending frequency. Blumstein *et al.* (1985) investigated this in the Cambridge Study. They used a seven-point scale of variables measured at 8–10, reflecting child anti-social behaviour, family economic deprivation, convicted parents, low intelligence, and poor parental child-rearing behaviour. Of fifty-five boys scoring four or more, fifteen were chronic offenders (out of twenty-three chronics altogether), twenty-two others were convicted, and only eighteen were not convicted. [. . .]

INFLUENCES ON CRIMINAL CAREERS

Risk factors

Risk factors are prior factors that increase the risk of occurrence of events such as the onset, frequency, persistence, or duration of offending. Longitudinal data are required to establish the ordering of risk factors and criminal career features. The focus in this chapter is on risk factors for the onset or prevalence of offending. Few studies have examined risk factors for persistence or duration. [. . .]

It is also difficult to decide if any given risk factor is an indicator (symptom) or a possible cause of offending. . . . It is not unreasonable to argue that some factors may be both indicative and causal. [. . .]

Cross-sectional studies make it impossible to distinguish between indicators and causes, since they can merely demonstrate correlations between high levels of one factor (e.g. unemployment) and high levels of another (e.g. offending). Longitudinal studies can show that offending is greater (within individuals) during some periods (e.g. of unemployment) than during other periods (e.g. of employment). Because within-individual studies have greater control over extraneous influences than between-individual studies, longitudinal studies can demonstrate that changes in unemployment within individuals cause offending with high internal validity in quasi-experimental analyses (Farrington, 1988; Farrington et al., 1986). . . . Implications for prevention and treatment, which require changes within individuals, cannot necessarily be drawn from effects demonstrated only in between-individual (cross-sectional) research.

It is unfortunate that the static model of relationships between independent and dependent variables has dominated research and theories of offending. This model may have a veneer of plausibility in a cross-sectional study, at least if problems of causal order are neglected. However, it is not easily applied to longitudinal or criminal career data, where all presumed explanatory constructs and all measures of offending and criminal career features change continuously within individuals over different ages. Relationships between an explanatory factor in one age range and a measure of offending in another age range may vary a great deal according to the particular age ranges, and this needs to be systematically investigated by researchers.

It is also unfortunate that insufficient attention has been paid in the literature to protective factors as opposed to risk factors. Protective factors predict a low probability of offending, either in a total cohort or in a high-risk sample (Rutter, 1985; Farrington, 1994). For example, Werner and Smith (1982, 1992) in Hawaii studied high-risk children who possessed a number of risk factors such as poverty, perinatal stress, family discord, and parental alcoholism. They found that the resilient children who did not display offending or anti-social behaviour as adults tended to have high intelligence and affectional ties with substitute parents.

The major risk factors for offending that are reviewed in this chapter are the individual difference factors of impulsivity and intelligence, and family, socio-economic, school, and situational factors. These factors often have additive, interactive or sequential effects, but I will consider them one by one.

Impulsivity

In the Cambridge Study, the boys nominated by teachers as lacking in concentration or restless, those nominated by parents, peers, or teachers as the most daring, and those who were the most impulsive on psychomotor tests all tended to be juvenile but not adult offenders (Farrington, 1992b). Later self-report questionnaire measures of impulsivity (including such items as 'I generally do and say things quickly without stopping to think') were related to both juvenile and adult offending. Daring, poor concentration, and restlessness were all related to both official and self-reported delinquency (Farrington, 1992c). [. . .]

Many other investigators have reported a link between the constellation of personality factors termed 'hyperactivity-impulsivity-attention deficit' or HIA (Loeber, 1987) and offending. [. . .]

Lynam (1996) argued that children with both HIA and conduct problems were at greatest risk of chronic offending. In the most extensive research using eleven different impulsivity measures in the Pittsburgh Youth Study, White *et al.* (1994) found that behavioural impulsivity (e.g. restlessness) was more strongly related to delinquency than was cognitive impulsivity (e.g. poor planning), which was more closely linked to intelligence.

It has been suggested that HIA might be a behavioural consequence of a low level of physiological arousal. Offenders have a low level of arousal according to their low alpha (brain) waves on the EEG, or according to autonomic nervous system indicators such as heart rate, blood pressure, or skin conductance, or they show low autonomic reactivity (e.g. Venables and Raine, 1987; Raine, 1993). In the Cambridge Study, a low heart rate was significantly related to convictions for violence, self-reported violence, and teacher-reported violence, independently of all other explanatory variables (Farrington, forthcoming). In several regression analyses, the most important independent risk factors for violence were daring, poor concentration, and a low heart rate. Other researchers (e.g. Wadsworth, 1976; Raine *et al.*, 1990) have also identified a low heart rate as an important predictor and correlate of offending.

Low intelligence

Low intelligence is an important predictor of offending, and it can be measured very early in life. [. . .]

In the Cambridge Study, one-third of the boys scoring ninety or less on a non-verbal intelligence test (Raven's Progressive Matrices) at age 8–10 were convicted as juveniles, twice as many as among the remainder (Farrington, 1992c). Low non-verbal intelligence was highly correlated with low verbal intelligence (vocabulary, word comprehension, verbal reasoning) and with low school attainment at age 11, and all of these measures were associated juvenile convictions to much the same extent. In addition to their poor school performance, delinquents tended to be frequent truants, to leave school at the earliest possible age (which was then 15), and to take no school examinations.

Low non-verbal intelligence was especially characteristic of the juvenile recidivists (who had an average IQ of eighty-nine) and those first convicted at the earliest ages (10–13). Furthermore, low intelligence and attainment predicted self-reported delinquency almost as well as convictions (Farrington, 1992c), suggesting that the link between low intelligence and delinquency was not caused by the less intelligent boys having a greater probability of being caught. . . . Delinquents often do better on non-verbal performance tests, such as object assembly and block design, than on verbal tests (Walsh *et al.*, 1987), suggesting that they find it easier to deal with concrete objects than with abstract concepts. . . . Also, low school attainment predicted chronic offenders (Farrington and West, 1993). [. . .]

Modern research is studying not just intelligence but also detailed patterns of cognitive and neuro-psychological deficit. For example, in a New Zealand longitudinal study of over 1,000 children from birth to age 15, Moffitt and Silva (1988) found that self-reported delinquency was related to verbal, memory and visual-motor integration deficits, independently of low social class and family adversity. Neuro-psychological research might lead to important advances in knowledge about the link between brain functioning and offending. For example, the 'executive functions' of the brain, located in the frontal lobes, include sustaining attention and concentration, abstract reasoning and concept formation, anticipation and planning, self-monitoring of behaviour, and inhibition of inappropriate or impulsive behaviour (Moffitt, 1990). Deficits in these executive functions are conducive to low measured intelligence and to offending. Moffitt and Henry (1989) found deficits in these executive functions especially for delinquents who were both anti-social and hyperactive.

Supervision, discipline, and child abuse

Loeber and Stouthamer-Loeber (1986) completed an exhaustive review of family factors as correlates and predictors of juvenile conduct problems and delinquency. They found that poor parental supervision or monitoring, erratic or harsh parental discipline, parental disharmony, parental rejection of the child, and low parental involvement with the child (as well as anti-social parents and large family size) were all important predictors.

In the Cambridge-Somerville study in Boston, McCord (1979) reported that poor parental supervision was the best predictor of both violent and property offenders. Parental aggressiveness (which included harsh discipline, shading into child abuse at the extreme) and parental conflict were significant precursors of violent offenders, while the mother's attitude (passive or rejecting) was a significant precursor of property offenders. Robins (1979), in her long-term follow-up studies in St Louis, also found that poor supervision and discipline were consistently related to later offending, and Shedler and Block (1990) in San Francisco reported that hostile and rejecting mothers when children were aged 5 predicted their frequent drug use at age 18.

Other studies also show the link between family factors and offending. In a Birmingham survey, Wilson (1980) concluded that poor parental supervision was the most important correlate of convictions, cautions, and self-reported delinquency. In their English national survey of juveniles aged 14–15 and their mothers, Riley and Shaw (1985) found that poor parental supervision was the most important correlate of self-reported delinquency for girls, and that it was the second most important for boys (after delinquent friends).

In the Cambridge Study, harsh or erratic parental discipline, cruel, passive, or neglecting parental attitude, poor supervision, and parental conflict, all measured at age 8, all predicted later juvenile convictions (West and Farrington, 1973). [. . .]

Poor parental child-rearing behaviour was related to early rather than later offending (Farrington, 1986b), and was not characteristic of those first convicted as adults (West and Farrington, 1977). Hence, poor parental child-rearing behaviour may be related to onset but not persistence. Poor parental supervision was related to both juvenile and adult convictions (Farrington, 1992b).

There seems to be significant intergenerational transmission of aggressive and violent behaviour from parents to children, as Widom (1989) found in a retrospective study of over 900 abused children in Indianapolis. Children who were physically abused up to age 11 were significantly likely to become violent offenders in the next fifteen years (Maxfield and Widom, 1996). Also, child sex abuse predicted later adult arrests for sex crimes in this survey (Widom and Ames, 1994). . . . The extensive review by Malinosky-Rummell and Hansen (1993) confirmed that being physically abused as a child predicted later violent and non-violent offending.

Broken homes and family conflict

Broken homes and early separations are also risk factors for offending. . . . McCord (1982) carried out an interesting study of the relationship between homes broken by loss of the natural father and later serious offending. She found that the prevalence of offending was high for boys reared in broken homes without affectionate mothers (62 per cent) and for those reared in united homes characterized by parental conflict (52 per cent), irrespective of whether they had affectionate mothers. The prevalence of offending was low for those reared in united homes without conflict (26 per cent) or in broken homes with affectionate mothers (22 per cent). These results suggest that it is not so much the broken home which is criminogenic as the parental conflict which causes it. [. . .]

The importance of the cause of the broken home is also shown in the British national longitudinal survey of over 5,000 children born in one week of 1946 (Wadsworth, 1979). Boys from homes broken by divorce or separation had an increased likelihood of being convicted or officially cautioned up to the age of 21 in comparison with those from homes broken by death or from unbroken homes. Homes broken before the age of 5 were especially criminogenic, while homes broken after 10 were not. Remarriage (which happened more often after divorce or separation than after death) was also associated with an increased risk of offending. The meta-analysis by Wells and Rankin (1991) confirmed that broken homes were more strongly related to delinquency when they were caused by parental separation or divorce rather than by death. . . . In contrast, in the Cambridge study, homes broken at an early age (under 5) were not unusually criminogenic (West and Farrington, 1973). [. . .]

In the Dunedin Study in New Zealand, single parent families disproportionally tended to have convicted sons; 28 per cent of violent offenders were from single parent families, compared with 17 per cent of non-violent offenders and 9 per cent of unconvicted boys (Henry *et al.*, 1996). Based on analyses of four surveys (including the Cambridge Study), Morash and Rucker (1989) concluded that the combination of teenage child-bearing and a single-parent female-headed household was especially conductive to the development of offending in children. Later analyses of the Cambridge Study showed that teenage child-bearing combined with a large number of children particularly predicted offending by the children (Nagin *et al.*, 1997). [. . .]

Also, both juvenile and adult offenders tended to have a poor relationship with their wives or cohabitees at age 32, or had assaulted them, and they also tended to be divorced and/or separated from their children (Farrington, 1992b). However, getting married was one factor that led to a decrease in offending, just as becoming separated from a wife led to an increase (Farrington and West, 1995).

Convicted parents

Criminal, anti-social, and alcoholic parents also tend to have delinquent sons, as Robins (1979) found. For example, in her follow-up of over 200 African-American males in St Louis (Robins *et al.*, 1975), arrested parents tended to have arrested children, and the juvenile records of the parents and children showed similar rates and types of offences. McCord (1977), in her thirty-year follow-up of about 250 treated boys in the Cambridge-Somerville study, reported that convicted fathers tended to have convicted sons. Whether there is a specific relationship in her study between types of convictions of parents and children is not clear. McCord found that 29 per cent of fathers convicted for violence had sons convicted for violence, in comparison with 12 per cent of other fathers, but this may reflect the general tendency for convicted fathers to have convicted sons rather than any specific tendency for violent fathers to have violent sons. Wilson (1987) in Birmingham also showed that convictions of parents predicted convictions and cautions of sons; more than twice as many sons of convicted parents were themselves convicted.

In the Cambridge Study, the concentration of offending in a small number of families was remarkable. Less than 6 per cent of the families were responsible for half of the criminal convictions of all members (fathers, mothers, sons, and daughters) of all 400 families (Farrington et al., 1996). [. . .]

Unlike most early precursors, a convicted parent was related less to offending of early onset (age 10–13) than to later offending (Farrington, 1986b). . . . Hence, a convicted parent seemed to be a risk factor for persistence rather than onset. [. . .]

These results are concordant with the psychological theory (e.g. Trasler, 1962) that criminal behaviour develops when the normal social learning process, based on rewards and punishments from parents, is disrupted by erratic discipline, poor supervision, parental disharmony, and unsuitable (anti-social or criminal) parental models. [. . .]

Socio-economic deprivation

Most delinquency theories assume that offenders disproportionally come from lower-class social backgrounds, and aim to explain why this is so. For example, Cohen (1955) proposed that lower-class boys found it hard to succeed according to the middle-class standards of the school. . . . Consequently, lower-class boys joined delinquent subcultures by whose standards they could succeed. Cloward and Ohlin (1960) argued that lower-class children could not achieve universal goals of status and material wealth by legitimate means and consequently had to resort to illegitimate means.

Beginning with the pioneering self-report research of Short and Nye (1957), it was common in the United States to argue that low socio-economic status (SES) was related to official offending but not to self-reported offending, and hence that the official processing of offenders was biased against lower-class youth. However, many reviewers (e.g. Hindelang et al., 1981; Thornberry and Farnworth, 1982) were unable to conclude that low SES was related to either self-reported or official offending. British studies have reported more consistent links between low social class and offending. In the British national survey, Douglas et al. (1966) showed that the prevalence of official juvenile delinquency in males varied considerably according to the occupational prestige and educational background of their parents, from 3 per cent in the highest category to 19 per cent in the lowest.

Numerous indicators of SES were measured in the Cambridge Study, both for the male's family of origin and for the male himself as an adult, including occupational prestige, family income, housing, employment instability, and family size. Most of the measures of occupational prestige (based on the Registrar General's scale) were not significantly related to offending. However, in a reversal of the American results, low SES of the family when the male was aged 8–10 significantly predicted his later self-reported but not his official delinquency (Farrington, 1992c).

More consistently, low family income, poor housing, and large family size predicted official and self-reported, juvenile and adult, offending. In the Cambridge Study, if a boy had four or more siblings by his tenth birthday, this doubled his risk of being convicted as a juvenile (West and Farrington, 1973). Large family size predicted self-reported delinquency as well as convictions (Farrington, 1979), and adult as well as juvenile convictions (Farrington, 1992b). [. . .]

For example, in the National Survey of Health and Development, Wadsworth (1979) found that the percentage of boys who were officially delinquent increased from 9 per cent for families containing one child to 24 per cent for families containing four or more children. The Newsons in their Nottingham study also concluded that large family size was one of the most important predictors of offending (Newson et al., 1993). A similar link between family size and anti-social behaviour was reported by Kolvin et al. (1988) in their follow-up of Newcastle children from birth to the age of 33, by Rutter et al. (1970) in the Isle of Wight survey, and by Ouston (1984) in the Inner London survey. The theoretical links between large family size and offending are not entirely clear. Family size could be classified as either a socio-economic or family factor. For example, the key underlying construct could be less attention given to each child or more overcrowded living conditions (Ferguson, 1952).

Socio-economic deprivation of parents is usually compared with offending by sons. However, when the sons grow up, their own socio-economic deprivation can be related to their own offending. In the Cambridge Study, official and self-reported delinquents tended to have unskilled manual jobs and an unstable job record at age 18. . . . Also, as already mentioned, the Study males were convicted at a higher rate when they were unemployed than when they were employed (Farrington et al., 1986), suggesting that unemployment in some way causes crime, and conversely that employment may lead to desistance from offending.

In recent years, there has been more interest in the idea of an emerging underclass in the United States and England than in low social class per se. For example, in England, Murray (1995) argued that life in lower-class communities was degenerating as illegitimacy rose, there was widespread drug and alcohol addiction, fewer marriages, more unemployment, more child neglect, more crime, and so on. He thought that new divisions were opening up in the lower half of the socio-economic distribution, as two-parent working class families increasingly left council estates, which became increasingly populated by an underclass predominantly consisting of single parent families. These ideas are somewhat controversial.

It seems clear that socio-economic deprivation is an important risk factor for offending. . . . Poverty may have an effect on offending indirectly, through its effects on parenting factors such as supervision and discipline, as Sampson and Laub (1994) concluded.

School factors

It is clear that the prevalence of offending varies dramatically between different secondary schools, as Power et al. (1967) showed more than twenty years ago in London. Characteristics of high delinquency-rate schools are well known (Graham, 1988). For example, such schools have high levels of distrust between teachers and students, low commitment to school by students, and uncertain and inconsistently enforced rules.

However, what is far less clear is how much of the variation should be attributed to differences in school climates and practices, and how much to differences in the composition of the student body.

In the Cambridge Study, the effects of secondary schools on offending were investigated by following boys from their primary schools to their secondary schools (Farrington, 1972). The best primary school predictor of offending was the rating of troublesomeness at age 8–10 by peers and teachers. The secondary schools differed dramatically in their official offending rates, from one school with 20.9 court appearances per 100 boys per year to another where the corresponding figure was only 0.3. However, it was very noticeable that the most troublesome boys tended to go to the high delinquency schools, while the least troublesome boys tended to go to the low delinquency schools. It was clear that most of the variation between schools in their delinquency rates could be explained by differences in the intake of trob’esome boys. [. . .]

The most famous study of schools effects on offending was also carried out in London, by Rutter *et al*. (1979). They studied twelve comprehensive schools, and again found big differences in official delinquency rates between them. High delinquency rate schools tended to have high truancy rates, low ability pupils, and low social class parents. However, the differences between the schools in delinquency rates could not be entirely explained by differences in the social class and verbal reasoning scores of the pupils at intake (age 11). Therefore, Rutter *et al*. argued that they must have been caused by some aspect of the schools themselves or by other, unmeasured factors. [. . .]

The main school factors that were related to delinquency were a high amount of punishment and a low amount of praise given by teachers in class. However, it is difficult to know whether much punishment and little praise are causes or consequences of antisocial school behaviour, which in turn is probably linked to offending outside school.

The research of Rutter *et al*. (1979) does not show unambiguously that school factors influence offending. . . . Longitudinal research is needed . . . This might make it possible convincingly to identify school factors that explained differences in offending rates independently of individual-level factors present at intake.

EXPLAINING THE DEVELOPMENT OF OFFENDING

In explaining the development of offending, a major problem is that most risk factors tend to coincide and tend to be inter-related. For example, adolescents living in physically deteriorated and socially disorganized neighbourhoods disproportionately tend also to come from families with poor parental supervision and erratic parental discipline and tend also to have high impulsivity and low intelligence. The concentration and co-occurrence of these kinds of adversities makes it difficult to establish their independent, interactive, and sequential influences on offending and anti-social behaviour. Hence, any theory of the development of offending is inevitably speculative in the present state of knowledge.

A first step is to establish which factors predict offending independently of other factors. In the Cambridge Study, it was generally true that each of six categories of variables (impulsivity, intelligence, parenting, criminal family, socio-economic deprivation, child anti-social behaviour) predicted offending independently of each other category (Farrington, 1990*b*). For example, the independent predictors of convictions between the ages of 10 and 20 included high daring, low school attainment, poor parental child rearing, a convicted parent, poor housing, and troublesomeness (Farrington and Hawkins, 1991). Hence, it might be concluded that impulsivity, low intelligence, poor parenting, a criminal family and socio-economic deprivation, despite their interrelations, all contribute independently to the development of delinquency. Any theory needs to give priority to explaining these results.

Some of the most important theories of delinquency have already been mentioned in this chapter. These include Cohen's (1955) status frustration – delinquent subculture theory, Cloward and Ohlin's (1960) opportunity – strain theory, Trasler's (1962) social learning theory, Wilson and Herrnstein's (1985) discounting future consequences theory, Clarke and Cornish's (1985) situational decision-making theory, and Gottfredson and Hirschi's (1990) self-control theory. The modern trend is to try to achieve increased explanatory power by integrating propositions derived from several earlier theories (e.g. Elliott *et al.*, 1985; Pearson and Weiner, 1985; Catalano and Hawkins, 1996). My own theory of male offending and anti-social behaviour (Farrington, 1986*b*, 1992*b*, 1996) is also integrative, and it distinguishes explicitly between the development of anti-social tendency and the occurrence of anti-social acts. It is an explicit attempt to integrate developmental and situational theories. The theory suggests that offending is the end result of a four-stage process: energizing, directing, inhibiting, and decision-making.

The main long-term energising factors that ultimately lead to variations in anti-social tendency are desires for material goods, status among intimates, and excitement. The main short-term energizing factors that lead to variations in anti-social tendency are boredom, frustration, anger, and alcohol consumption. The desire for excitement may be greater among children from poorer families, perhaps because excitement is more highly valued by lower-class people than by middle-class ones, because poorer children think they lead more boring lives, or because poorer children are less able to postpone immediate gratification in favour of long-term goals. [. . .]

In the directing stage, these motivations produce an increase in anti-social tendency if socially disapproved methods of satisfying them are habitually chosen. The methods chosen depend on maturation and behavioural skills; for example, a 5-year-old would have difficulty stealing a car. Some people (e.g. children from poorer families) are less able to satisfy their desires for material goods, excitement, and social status by legal or socially approved methods, and so tend to choose illegal or socially disapproved methods. The relative inability of poorer children to achieve goals by legitimate methods could be because they tend to fail in school and tend to have erratic, low status employment histories. [. . .]

In the inhibiting stage, anti-social tendencies can be inhibited by internalized beliefs and attitudes that have been built up in a social learning process as a result of a history of rewards and punishments. The belief that offending is wrong, or a strong conscience, tends to be built up if parents are in favour of legal norms, if they exercise close supervision over their children, and if they punish socially disapproved behaviour using love-oriented discipline. Anti-social tendency can also be inhibited by empathy, which may develop as a result of parental warmth and loving relationships. [. . .]

In the decision-making stage, which specifies the interaction between the individual and the environment, whether a person with a certain degree of anti-social tendency commits an anti-social act in a given situation depends on opportunities, costs, and benefits, and on the subjective probabilities of the different outcomes. The costs and benefits include immediate situational factors such as the material goods that can be stolen and the likelihood and consequences of being caught by the police, as perceived by the individual. They also include social factors such as likely disapproval by parents or spouses, and encouragement or reinforcement from peers. In general, people tend to make rational decisions. However, more impulsive people are less likely to consider the possible consequences of their actions, especially consequences that are likely to be long delayed.

The consequences of offending may, as a result of a learning process, lead to changes in anti-social tendency or in the cost-benefit calculation. This is especially likely if the consequences are reinforcing (e.g. gaining material goods or peer approval) or punishing (e.g. legal sanctions or parental disapproval). Also, if the consequences involve labelling or stigmatizing the offender, this may make it more difficult for offenders to achieve their aims legally, and hence there may be an increase in anti-social tendency. In other words, events that occur after offending may lead to changes in energizing, directing, inhibiting or decision-making processes in a dynamic system.

Applying the theory to explain some of the results reviewed here, children from poorer families are likely to offend because they are less able to achieve their goals legally and because they value some goals (e.g. excitement) especially highly. Children with low intelligence are more likely to offend because they tend to fail in school and hence cannot achieve their goals legally. Impulsive children, and those with a poor ability to manipulate abstract concepts, are more likely to offend because they do not give sufficient consideration and weight to the possible consequences of offending. Children who are exposed to poor parental child-rearing behaviour, disharmony, or separation are likely to offend because they do not build up internal controls over socially disapproved behaviour, while children from criminal families and those with delinquent friends tend to build up anti-establishment attitudes and the belief that offending is justifiable. The whole process is self-perpetuating, in that poverty, low intelligence, and early school failure lead to truancy and a lack of educational qualifications, which in turn lead to low status jobs and periods of unemployment, both of which make it harder to achieve goals legitimately.

The onset of offending might be caused by increasing long-term motivation (an increasing need for material goods, status, and excitement), an increasing likelihood of choosing socially disapproved methods (possibly linked to a change in dominant social influences from parents to peers), increasing facilitating influences from peers, increasing opportunities (because of increasing freedom from parental control and increasing time spent with peers) or an increasing expected utility of offending (because of the greater importance of peer approval and lesser importance of parental disapproval). Desistance from offending could be linked to an increasing ability to satisfy desires by legal means (e.g. obtaining material goods through employment, obtaining sexual gratification through marriage), increasing inhibiting influences from spouses and cohabitees, decreasing opportunities (because of decreasing time spent with peers), and a decreasing expected utility of offending (because of the lesser importance of peer approval and the greater importance of disapproval from spouses and cohabitees).

The prevalence of offending may increase to a peak between the ages of 14 and 20 because boys (especially lower class school failures) have high impulsivity, high desires for excitement, material goods, and social status between these ages, little chance of achieving their desires legally, and little to lose (since legal penalties are lenient and their intimates – male peers – often approve of offending). In contrast, after the age of 20, desires become attenuated or more realistic, there is more possibility of achieving these more limited goals legally, and the costs of offending are greater (since legal penalties are harsher and their intimates – wives or girlfriends – disapprove of offending).

CONCLUSIONS

[. . .]

The criminal career approach has important implications for criminological theories: they should address developmental processes. The theory proposed here suggested that offending depended on energizing, directing, inhibiting, and decision-making processes. It aimed to explain the development of criminal potential and the occurrence of criminal acts. In addition to explaining between-individual differences in the prevalence or frequency of offending, theories should explain within-individual changes: why people start offending, why they continue or escalate their offending, and why they stop offending. For example, onset may depend primarily on poor parental child-rearing behaviour, persistence may depend on criminal parents and delinquent peers, and desistance may depend on settling down with spouses and cohabitees.

References

Ball, J. C., Rosen. L., Flueck, J. A., and Nurco, D. N. (1981), 'The Criminality of Heroin Addicts: When Addicted and When Off Opiates', in J. A. Inciardi, ed., *The Drugs-Crime Connection*, 39–65, Beverly Hills, Cal.: Sage.

Barnett, A., and Lofaso, A. J. (1985), 'Selective Incapacitation and the Philadelphia Cohort Data', *Journal of Quantitative Criminology*, 1: 3–36.

Barnett, A., Blumstein, A., and Farrington, D. P. (1987), 'Probabilistic Models of Youthful Criminal Careers', *Criminology*, 25: 83–107.

Blumstein, A., and Cohen, J. (1979), 'Estimation of Individual Crime Rates from Arrest Records', *Journal of Criminal Law and Criminology*, 70: 561–85.

Blumstein, A., and Graddy, E. (1982), 'Prevalence and Recidivism in Index Arrests: A Feedback Model', *Law and Society Review*, 16: 265–90.

Blumstein, A., Farrington, D. P., and Moitra, S. (1985), 'Delinquency Careers: Innocents, Desisters and Persisters', in M. Tonry and N. Morris, eds., *Crime and Justice*, vi, 187–219. Chicago, Ill.: University of Chicago Press.

Catalano, R. F., and Hawkins, J. D. (1996) 'The Social Development Model: A Theory of Antisocial Behaviour', in J. D. Hawkins, ed., *Delinquency and Crime: Current Theories*, 149–97. Cambridge: Cambridge University Press.

Clarke, R. V., and Cornish, D. B. (1985), 'Modelling Offenders' Decisions: A Framework for Research and Policy', in M. Tonry and N. Morris, eds., *Crime and Justice*, vi, 147–85. Chicago, Ill.: University of Chicago Press.

Cloward, R. A., and Ohlin, L. E. (1960), *Delinquency and Opportunity*, New York: Free Press.

Cohen, A. K. (1955), *Delinquent Boys: The Culture of the Gang*. Glencoe, Ill.: Free Press.

Cohen, J. (1986), 'Research on Criminal Careers: Individual Frequency Rates and Offence Seriousness', in A. Blumstein, J. Cohen, J. A. Roth and C. A. Visher, eds., *Criminal Careers and 'Career Criminals'*, i, 292–481. Washington, DC: National Academy Press.

Douglas, J. W. B., Ross, J. M., Hammond, W. A., and Mulligan, D. G. (1966), 'Delinquency and Social Class', *British Journal of Criminology*, 6: 294–302.

Elliott, D. S., Huizinga, D., and Ageton, S. S. (1985), *Explaining Deliquency and Drug Use*. Beverly Hills, Cal.: Sage.

Elliott, D. S., and Menard, S. (1989), *Multiple Problem Youth: Delinquency, Substance Use and Mental Health Problems*. New York: Springer-Verlag.

Farrington, D. P. (1972), 'Delinquency Begins at Home', *New Society*, 21: 495–7.

—— (1979), 'Environmental Stress, Delinquent Behaviour, and Convictions', in I. G. Sarason and C. D. Spielberger, eds., *Stress and Anxiety*, vi, 93–107. Washington, DC: Hemisphere.

—— (1986*a*), 'Age and Crime', in M. Tonry and N. Morris, eds., *Crime and Justice*, vii, 189–250. Chicago, Ill.: University of Chicago Press.

—— (1986*b*), 'Stepping Stones to Adult Criminal Careers', in D. Olweus, J. Block, and M. R. Yarrow, eds., *Development of Antisocial and Prosocial Behaviour: Research, Theories and Issues*, 359–84. New York: Academic Press.

—— (1987), 'Predicting Individual Crime Rates', in D. M. Gottfredson and M. Tonry, eds., *Prediction and Classification: Criminal Justice Decision Making*, 53–101. Chicago, Ill.: University of Chicago Press.

—— (1988), 'Studying Changes Within Individuals: The Causes of Offending', in M. Rutter, ed., *Studies of Psychosocial Risk: The Power of Longitudinal Data*, 158–83. Cambridge: Cambridge University Press.

—— (1989), 'Self-reported and Official Offending from Adolescence to Adulthood', in M. W. Klein, ed., *Cross-national Research in Self-reported Crime and Delinquency*, 399–423. Dordrecht: Kluwer.

—— (1990*a*), 'Age, Period, Cohort, and Offending', in D. M. Gottfredson and R. V. Clarke, eds., *Policy and Theory in Criminal Justice: Contributions in Honour of Leslie T. Wilkins*, 51–75. Aldershot: Avebury.

—— (1990*b*), 'Implications of Criminal Career Research for the Prevention of Offending', *Journal of Adolescence*, 13: 93–113.

—— (1992*a*), 'Criminal Career Research in the United Kingdom', *British Journal of Criminology*, 32: 521–36.

—— (1992*b*), 'Explaining the Beginning, Progress and Ending of Antisocial Behaviour from Birth to Adulthood', in J. McCord, ed., *Facts, Frameworks and Forecasts: Advances in Criminological Theory*, iii, 253–86. New Brunswick, N.J.: Transaction.

—— (1992*c*), 'Juvenile Delinquency'. In J. C. Coleman, ed., *The School Years*, 2nd edn., 123–63. London: Routledge.

—— (1994), 'Interactions between Individual and Contextual Factors in the Development of Offending', in R. K. Silbereisen and E. Todt, eds., *Adolescence in Context: The Interplay of Family, School, Peers and Work in Adjustment*, 366–89. New York: Springer-Verlag.

—— (1995), 'Crime and Physical Health: Illnesses. Injuries, Accidents and Offending in the Camibridge Study', *Criminal Behaviour and Mental Health*, 5: 261–78.

—— (1996), 'The Explanation and Prevention of Youthful Offending', in J. D. Hawkins, ed., *Delinquency and Crime: Current Theories*, 68–148. New York: Cambridge University Press.

—— (forthcoming), 'The Relationship between Low Resting Heart Rate and Violence', in A. Raine, D. P. Farrington, P. A. Brennan, and S. A. Mednick, eds., *Biosocial Bases of Violence*. New York: Plenum.

Farrington, D. P., and Hawkins, J. D. (1991), 'Predicting Participation, Early Onset, and Later Persistence in Officially Recorded Offending', *Criminal Behaviour and Mental Health*, 1: 1–33.

Farrington, D. P., and West, D. J. (1993), 'Criminal, Penal and Life Histories of Chronic Offenders: Risk and Protective Factors and Early Identification', *Criminal Behaviour and Mental Health*, 3: 492–523.

—— (1995), Effects of Marriage, Separation and Children on Offending by Adult Males', in J. Hagan, ed., *Current Perspectives on Aging and the Life Cycle. iv: Delinquency and Disrepute in the Life Course*, 249–81. Greenwich. Conn.: JAI Press.

Farrington, D. P., and Wikström, P.-O. H. (1994), 'Criminal Careers in London and Stockholm: A Cross-national Comparative Study', in E. G. M. Weitekamp and H.-J. Kerner, eds., *Cross-national Longitudinal Research on Human Development and Criminal Behaviour*, 65–89 Dordrecht: Khuwer.

Farrington, D. P., Barnes, G., and Lambert, S. (1996), 'The Concentration of Offending in Families', *Legal and Criminological Psychology*, 1: 47–63.

Farrington, D. P., Gallagher, B., Morley, L., St Ledger, R. J., and West, D. J. (1986), 'Unemployment School Leaving, and Crime', *British Journal of Criminology*, 26: 335–56.

Farrington, D.P., Elliott, D. S., Hawkins, J. D., Kandel, D. B., Klein, M. W., McCord, J., Rowe, D. C., and Tremblay, R. E. (1990), 'Advancing Knowledge about the Onset of Delinquency and Crime', in B. B. Lahey and A. E. Kazdin, eds., *Advances in Clinical Child Psychology*, xiii, 283–342. New York: Plenum.

Ferguson, T. (1952), *The Young Delinquent in his Social Setting* London: Oxford University Press.

Fox, J. A., and Tracy, P. E. (1988), 'A Measure of Skewness in Offence Distributions', *Journal of Quantitative Criminology*, 4: 259–74.

Fry, L. J. (1985), 'Drug Abuse and Crime in a Swedish Birth Cohort', *British Journal of Criminology*, 25: 46–59.

Gottfredson, M., and Hirschi, T. (1986), 'The True Value of Lambda Would Appear to be Zero: An Essay on Career Criminals, Criminal Careers, Selective Incapacitation, Cohort Studies, and Related Topics', *Criminology*, 24: 213–33.

Graham, J. (1988), *Schools, Disruptive Behaviour and Delinquency*, London: HMSO.

Haapanen, R. A. (1990), *Selective Incapacitation and the Serious Offender*. New York: Springer-Verlag.

Haapanen, R. A., Schuster, R., Dinitz, S., and Conrad, J. P. (1978), *The Violent Few*. Lexington, Mass.: Health.

Hamparian, D. M., Schuster, R., Dinitz, S. and Conrad, J. (1978), *The Violent Few*. Lexington, Mass.: Health.

Henry, B., Caspi, A., Moffitt, T. E., and Silva, P. A. (1996), 'Temperamental and Familial Predictors of Violent and Non-violent Criminal Convictions: Age 3 to Age 18', *Developmental Psychology*, 32: 614–23.

Hindelang, M. J., Hirschi, T., and Wets, J. G. (1981), *Measuring Delinquency*. Beverly Hills, Cal.: Sage.

Home Office Statistical Bulletin (1987), *Criminal Careers of Those Born in 1953: Persistent Offenders and Desistance*. London: Home Office.

—— (1995), *Criminal Careers of Those Born Between 1953 and 1973*. London: Home Office.

Horney, J., and Marshall, I. H. (1991), 'Measuring Lambda Through Self-reports', *Criminology*, 29: 471–95.

Kolvin, I., Miller, F. J. W., Fleeting, M., and Kolvin, P. A. (1988), 'Social and Parenting Factors Affecting Criminal-offence Rates: Findings from the Newcastle Thousand Family Study (1947–1980)', *British Journal of Psychiatry*, 152: 80–90.

LeBlanc, M., and Frechette, M. (1989), *Male Criminal Activity from Childhood Through Youth: Multi-level and Developmental Perspectives*. New York: Springer-Verlag.

Loeber, R., and Snyder, H. N. (1990), 'Rate of Offending in Juvenile Careers: Findings of Constancy and Change in Lambda', *Criminology*, 28: 97–109.

Loeber, R., and Stouthamer-Loeber, M. (1986), 'Family Factors as Correlates and Predictors of Juvenile Conduct Problems and Delinquency', in M. Tonry and N. Morris, eds., *Crime and Justice*, vii, 29–149. Chicago Ill.: University of Chicago Press.

Loeber, R., Van Kammen, W. B., and Farrington, D. P. (1991), 'Initiation, Escalation and Desistance in Juvenile Offending and their Correlates', *Journal of Criminal Law and Criminology*, 82: 36–82.

Lynam, D. (1996), 'Early Identification of Chronic Offenders: Who is the Fledgling Psychopath?', *Psychological Bulletin*, 120: 209–234.

Malinosky-Rummell, R., and Hansen, D. J. (1993), 'Long-term Consequences of Childhood Physical Abuse', *Psychological Bulletin*, 114: 68–79.

Maxfield, M. G., and Widom, C. S. (1996), 'The Cycle of Violence Revisited 6 Years Later', *Archives of Pediatrics and Adolescent Medicine*, 150: 390–5.

McCord, J. (1977), 'A Comparative Study of Two Generations of Native American', in R. F. Meier, ed., *Theory in Criminology*, 83–92. Beverly Hills, Cal.: Sage.

—— (1979), 'Some Child-rearing Antecedents of Criminal Behaviour in Adult Men', *Journal of Personality and Social Psychology*, 37: 1477–86.

—— (1982), 'A Longitudinal View of the Relationship Between Paternal Absence and Crime', in J. Gunn and D. P. Farrington, eds., *Abnormal Offenders, Delinquency, and the Criminal Justice System*, 113–28. Chichester: Wiley.

—— (1990), 'Crime in Moral and Social Contexts', *Criminology*, 28: 1–26.

Moffitt, T. E. (1990), 'The Neuropsychology of Juvenile Delinquency: A Critical Review', in M. Tonry and N. Morris eds., *Crime and Justice*, xii, 99–169. Chicago, Ill.: University of Chicago Press.

—— (1993), 'Adolescence-limited and Life-course-persistent Autisocial Behaviour: A Developmental Taxonomy', *Psychological Review*, 100: 674–701.

Moffitt, T. E., and Henry, B. (1989), 'Neuropsychological Assessment of Executive Functions in Self-reported Delinquents', *Development and Psychopathology*, 1: 105–18.

Moffitt, T. E., and Silva, P. A. (1988), 'Neuropsychological Deficit and Self-reported Delinquency in an Unselected Birth Cohort', *Journal of the American Academy of Child and Adolescent Psychiatry*, 27: 233–40.

Morash, M., and Rucker, L. (1989), 'An Exploratory Study of the Connection of Mother's Age at Childbearing to her Children's Delinquency in Four Data Sets', *Crime and Delinquency*, 35: 45–93.

Murray, C. (1995), 'The Next British Revolution', *The Public Interest*, 118: 3–29.

Nagin, D. S., and Farrington, D. P. (1992), 'The Onset and Persistence of Offending', *Criminology*, 30: 501–23.

Nagin, D. S., and Moffitt, T. E. (1995), 'Lifecourse Trajectories of Different Types of Offenders', *Criminology*, 33: 111–39.

Nagin, D. S., Pogarsky, G., and Farrington, D. P. (1997), 'Adolescent Mothers and the Criminal Behaviour of their Children', *Law and Society Review*, 31: 137–62.

Newson, J., Newson, E., and Adams, M. (1993), 'The Social Origins of Delinquency', *Criminal Behaviour and Mental Health*, 3: 19–29.

Osborn, S. C. (1980), 'Moving Home, Leaving London, and Delinquent Trends', *British Journal of Criminology*, 20: 54–61.

Ouston, J. (1984), 'Delinquency, Family Background, and Educational Attainment', *British Journal of Criminology*, 24: 2–26.

Pearson, F. S., and Weiner, N. A. (1985), 'Toward an Integration of Criminological Theories', *Journal of Criminal Law and Criminology*, 76: 116–50.

Power, M. J., Alderson, M. R., Phillipson, C. M., Shoenberg, E., and Morris, J. N. (1967), 'Delinquent Schools?', *New Society*, 10: 542–3.

Pulkkinen, L. (1988), 'Delinquent Development: Theoretical and Empirical Considerations', in M. Rulter, ed., *Studies of Psychosocial Risk: The Power of Longitudinal Data*, 184–199. Cambridge: Cambridge University Press.

Raine, A. (1993), *The Psychopathology of Crime: Criminal Behaviour as a Clinical Disorder*. San Diego: Academic Press.

Raine, A., Venables, P. H., and Williams. M. (1990), 'Relationships Between Central and Autonomic Measures of Arousal at Age 15 Years and Criminality at Age 24 years', *Archives of General Psychiatry*, 47: 1003–7.

Riley, D., and Shaw, M. (1985), *Parental Supervision and Juvenile Delinquency*. London: HMSO.

Robins, L. N. (1979), 'Sturdy Childhood Predictors of Adult Outcomes: Replications from Longitudinal Studies', in J. E. Barrett, R. M. Rose, and G.L. Klerman, eds., *Stress and Mental Disorder*, 219–35. New York: Raven Press.

Robins, L. N., West, P. J., and Herjanic, B. L. (1975), 'Arrests and Delinquency in Two Generations: A Study of Black Urban Families and their Children', *Journal of Child Psychology and Psychiatry*, 16: 125–40.

Rutter, M. (1985), 'Resilience in the Face of Adversity: Protective Factors and Resistance to Psychiatric Disorder', *British Journal of Psychiatry*, 147: 598–611.

Rutter, M., Tizard, J., and Whitmore, K. (1970), *Education, Health and Behaviour*. London: University of London Press.

Rutter, M., Maughan, B., Mortimore, P., and Ouston, J. (1979), *Fifteen Thousand Hours: Secondary Schools and their Effects on Children*. London: Open Books.

Sampson, R. J., and Laub, J. H. (1993), *Crime in the Making: Pathways and Turning Points through Life*. Cambridge, Mass.: Harvard University Press.

—— (1994), 'Urban Poverty and the Family Context of Delinquency: A New Look at Structure and Process in a Classic Study', *Child Development*, 65: 523–40.

Shedler, J., and Block, J. (1990), 'Adolescent Drug Use and Psychological Health', *American Psychologist*, 45: 612–30.

Short, J. F., and Nye, F. I. (1957), 'Reported Behaviour as a Criterion of Deviant Behaviour', *Social Problems*, 5: 207–13.

Shover, N. (1985), *Aging Crimininals*. Beverly Hills, Cal.: Sage.

Stander, J., and Magnusson, D. (1989), 'The Role of Early Aggressive Behaviour in the Frequency, Seriousness and Types of Later Crime', *Journal of Consulting and Clinical Psychology*, 57: 710–18.

Stattin, H., Magnusson, D. and Reichel, H. (1989), 'Criminal Activity at Different Ages: A Study Based on a Swedish Longitudinal Research Population', *British Journal of Criminology*, 29: 368–85.

Tarling, R. (1993), *Analysing Offending: Data, Models and Interpretations*. London: HMSO.

Thornberry, T. P., and Farnworth, M. (1982), 'Social Correlates of Criminal Involvement: Further Evidence on the Relationship Between Social Status and Criminial Behaviour', *American Sociological Review*, 47: 505–18.

Tolan, P. H. (1987), 'Implications of Age of Onset for Delinquency Risk', *Journal of Abnormal Child Psychology*, 15: 47–65.

Tracy, P. E., and Kempf-Leonard, K. (1996), *Continuity and Discontinuity in Criminal Careers*. New York: Plenum.

Trasler, G. B. (1962), *The Explanation of Criminality*. London: Routledge and Kegan Paul.

Venables, P. H., and Raine, A. (1987), 'Biological Theory', in B. J. McGurk, D. M. Thornton, and M. Williams, eds., *Applying Psychology to Imprisonment*, 3–27. London: HMSO.

Visher, C. A., and Roth, J. A. (1986), 'Participation in Criminal Careers', in A. Blumstein, J. Cohen, J. A. Roth, and C. A. Visher, eds., 'Criminal Careers and "Career Criminals," ' i, 211–91. Washington, DC: National Academy Press.

Wadsworth, M. E. J. (1976), 'Delinquency, Pulse Rates, and Early Emotional Deprivation', *British Journal of Criminology*, 16, 245–56.

Wadsworth, M. E. J. (1979), *Roots of Delinquency: Infnacy, Adolescence and Crime*. London: Martin Robertson.

Walsh, A., Petee, T. A., and Beyer, J. A. (1987), 'Intellectual Imbalance and Delinquency: Comparing High Verbal and High Performance IQ Delinquents', *Criminal Justice and Behaviour*, 14: 370–9.

Wells, L. E., and Rankin, J. H. (1991), 'Families and Delinquency: A Meta-analysis of the Impact of Broken Homes', *Social problems*, 38: 71–93.

Werner, E. E., and Smith, R. S. (1982), *Vulnerable but Invincible: A Longitudinal Study of Resilient Children and Youth*. New York: McGraw-Hill.

—— (1992), *Overcoming the Odds: High Risk Children from Birth to Adulthood*. Ithaca, NY: Cornell University Press.

West, D. J. (1982), *Delinquency: Its Roots, Careers and Prospects*. London: Heinemann.

West, D. J., and Farrington, D. P. (1973), *Who Becomes Delinquent?* London: Heinemann.

—— (1977), *The Delinquent Way of Life*. London: Heinemann.

White, J. L., Moffitt, T. E., Caspi, A., Bartusch, D. J., Needles, D. J., and Stouthamer-Loeber, M. (1994), 'Measuring Impulsivity and Examining its Relationship to delinquency', *Journal of Abnormal Psuchology*, 103: 192–205.

Widom, C. S. (1989), 'The Cycle of Violence', *Science*, 244: 160–6.

Widom, C. S., and Ames M. A. (1994), 'Criminal Consequences of Childhood Sexual Victimization', *Child Abuse and Neglect*, 18: 303–18.

Wikström, P. -O. H. (1987), *Patterns of Crime in a Birth Cohort*. Stockholm: University of Stockholm Department of Sociology.

—— (1990), 'Age amd Crime in a Stockholm Cohort', *Journal of Quantitative Criminology*, 6: 61–84.

—— (1991), *Urban Crime, Criminals and Victims: The Swedish Experience in an Anglo-American Comparative Perspective*. New York: Springer-Verlag.

Wilson, H. (1980), 'Parental Supervision: A Neglected Aspect of Delinquency', *British Journal of Criminology*, 20: 203–35.

—— (1987), 'Parental Supervision Reexamined', *British Journal of Criminology*, 27: 275–301.

Wilson, J. Q., and Herrnstein, R. J. (1985), *Crime and Human Nature*, New York: Simon and Schuster.

Wolfgang, M. E., Figlio, R. M., and Sellin, T. (1972), *Delinquency in a Birth Cohort*. Chicago, Ill.: University of Chicago Press.

Wolfgang, M. E., Thornberry, T. P., and Figlio, R. M. (1987), *From Boy to Man, from Deliquency to Crime*. Chicago: University of Chicago Press.

Chapter 14

James Gilligan

SHAME

The emotions and morality of violence

From: James Gilligan (1997), 'Shame', in James Gilligan, *Violence: Reflections on a National Epidemic*, New York: Vintage Books, pp. 103–114.

I think the tragic feeling is evoked in us when we are in the presence of a character who is ready to lay down his life, if need be, to secure one thing – his sense of personal dignity.
(*Arthur Miller, Tragedy and the Common Man*)

WE KNOW FROM PAST experience how effective the public health approach has been in our struggles against epidemics. In the nineteenth century, for example, strategies such as cleaning up the sewer system and the water supply were far more effective in the battle against diseases than all the doctors, medicines, and hospitals in the world. In addition, discovering the specific pathogen in the water supply that was killing people guided our preventive efforts both by clarifying what specifically needed to be removed from the contaminated water, and by enabling us to know when it had been removed. Identifying the causes of the various forms of disease is the first step in prevention.

Using what I have come to think of as a "germ theory" of violence, I will identify the pathogen that causes the most lethal form of pathology of our time, except that the pathogens under the microscope are not microorganisms but emotions. [. . .]

How might we discover what that pathogen is? My own approach to the study of violence has been to sit down and talk with violent people, and ask them why they have been violent. What I have discovered is that many of them tell me. Not all of them do. Some . . . do not tell me in words; and many may not understand why they committed the violence that sent them to prison. With them I have had to decode the symbolic language of their violent acts, like a cryptologist, or an anthropologist who tries to decipher the meaning of a bizarre and gruesome ritual. Still, surprisingly many men do tell me, simply and directly.

For example, the prison inmates I work with have told me repeatedly, when I asked them why they had assaulted someone, that it was because "he disrespected me," or "he disrespected my visit" (meaning "visitor"). The word "disrespect" is so central in the vocabulary, moral value system, and psychodynamics of these chronically violent men that they have abbreviated it into the slang term, "he dis'ed me."

Chester T., a very angry and violent inmate in his thirties, in prison for armed robbery, was referred to me because he had been yelling at, insulting, threatening, and assaulting another inmate. He had been doing this kind of thing for the past several weeks, and, off and on, for years. But he was usually so inarticulate and disorganized that neither I nor anyone else had been able to figure out what he wanted or what was fueling these repetitive acts of violence; nor had I had much success in persuading him to stop his end-lessly self-defeating power struggles with everyone around him, which inevitably resulted in his being punished more and more severely. This very pattern is extremely common among men in prison. In prisons, the more violent people are, the more harshly the prison authorities punish them; and, the more harshly they are punished, the more violent they become, so that both the inmates and the prison authorities are engaged in a constantly repeated, counterproductive power struggle – the ultimate "vicious" cycle.

In an attempt to break through that vicious cycle with this man, I finally asked him "What do you want so badly that you would sacrifice everything else in order to get it?" And he, who was usually so inarticulate, disorganized, and agitated that it was difficult to get a clear answer to any question, stood up to his full height and replied with calm assur-ance, with perfect coherence and even a kind of eloquence: "Pride. Dignity. Self-esteem." And then he went on to say, again more clearly than before: "And I'll kill every mother-fucker in that cell block if I have to in order to get it! My life ain't worth nothin' if I take somebody disrespectin' me and callin' me punk asshole faggot and goin' 'Ha! Ha!' at me. Life ain't worth livin' if there ain't nothin' worth dyin' for. If you ain't got pride, you got nothin'. That's all you got! I've already got my pride." He explained that the other prisoner was "tryin' to take that away from me. I'm not a total idiot. I'm not a coward. There ain't nothin' I can do except snuff him. I'll throw gasoline on him and light him." He went on to say that the other man had challenged him to a fight, and he was afraid not to accept the challenge because he thought "I'll look like a coward and a punk if I don't fight him."

One hears this from violent men in one variation or another again and again. Billy A., a man in his mid-forties, came in to see me because he also had been involved in a run-ning battle with most of the prisoners and correction officers on his cell block. He began his explanation as to why he was doing this by saying that he didn't care if he lived or died, because the screws and the other prisoners had treated him so badly – "worse than ani-mals in zoos are treated" – that they had taken all his property away from him and he had nothing left to lose; but what he couldn't afford to lose was his self-respect, because that was all he had left, and "If you don't have your self-respect, you don't have nothing." One way they took his self-respect was that another man threw water on him, and the officer who saw this happen did nothing to intervene. So the only way Billy A. felt he could regain his self-respect was to throw water on the officer and the other prisoner – as a result of which they sentenced him to solitary confinement. Still, he remained implacable in his expression of defiance: "Death is a positive in this situation, not a negative, because I'm so tired of all this bullshit that death seems thrilling by comparison. I'm not depressed. I don't have any feelings or wants, but I've got to have my self-respect, and I've declared war on the whole world till I get it!"

This man had a very severe paranoid personality, and was extremely dangerous because of it, in prison and before he was sent to prison. Billy A. had attempted – with no provocation or warning – to murder a woman by whom he felt persecuted. Although he, like most of the violent mentally ill, was sentenced to prison rather than a mental hospital, he was clearly in a state of paranoid delusion. A letter he wrote to a judge illustrates how the prison system made this man even more paranoid and more dangerous by systematically humiliating him. He apparently wrote this letter more for the purpose of unburdening himself and clarifying his thoughts than with any intention of mailing it, although he did finally show it to a prison psychiatrist so that she could help get the situation described in it resolved.

He expresses in the letter his desperation, his feeling that the way he was being treated was bringing him closer and closer to his limit, and his sense that he was running out of time. He describes feeling spiritually and mentally defeated, and writes that he had no fear of anyone or anything, including death. Rather, he felt that his life in solitary confinement, subjected to the mental and physical torment of the guards and other inmates, was not worth living.

Billy A. goes on in the letter to describe a specific incident that took place over three days, days that he describes as having been "the most mentally debilitating" of his whole life, worse even than death. To begin with, eight other inmates had insulted him by calling him "all sorts of unmentionable names." When he told an officer that he wished to bring charges against those prisoners for harassing him, he was ordered to go to the visitors' room and strip. He was left there for half an hour, then was marched back to his cell "buck naked." The prisoners who had exposed him to this "humiliation" began "laughing and making catcalls" at him. He discovered that his cell had also been stripped of all his personal possessions, including his toilet articles (toothbrush, soap, washcloth). What especially distressed him about this was its effect on his self-esteem – that he had been unable to take a shower for more than a week, and "the way I keep my self-respect is by keeping my body clean." Finally, in desperation he began banging on his desk because "I really needed cosmetics." In retaliation officers again ordered him to stand naked in the visitors' room for fifteen minutes while they laughed at him and made "snide remarks." He said "the laughter really troubled me because I did not see a damn thing funny." He thought they were "getting some untold pleasure" out of treating him this way. Eventually they gave him a pair of overalls, but no shoes.

He then described how they strapped him to a bench, tightened (too tightly) the handcuffs and leg irons that all inmates are required to wear whenever they leave a solitary confinement cell, opened all the windows, and opened his overalls so that his bare skin was exposed to the cold air. He said "that brought tears to my eyes. Not because he unzipped my jumpsuit but because he looked at the other hoodlums and winked his eye and smiled." They left him shivering there (this was in January) for three hours. Then an officer grinned and said, "I do not want to get mean" – following which he stepped on and off his bare toes with his boots, as the other officers laughed at him as if he were "a freak." He went on to say that perhaps he was as dumb as everyone treated him as being, or as insane as everyone seemed to think he was – he no longer knew or cared. That was when he resolved to "declare war on the whole world" until he was able to restore his self-respect. While his self-esteem was already so damaged that he was already antisocial, it is also true that prison was only rendering someone who was already wounded, and therefore dangerous, even more so.

Some people think armed robbers commit their crimes in order to get money. And of course, sometimes, that is the way they rationalize their behavior. But when you sit down and talk with people who repeatedly commit such crimes, what you hear is,

"I never got so much respect before in my life as I did when I first pointed a gun at somebody," or, "You wouldn't believe how much respect you get when you have a gun pointed at some dude's face." For men who have lived for a lifetime on a diet of contempt and disdain, the temptation to gain instant respect in this way can be worth far more than the cost of going to prison, or even of dying.

Should we really be so surprised at all this? Doesn't the Bible, in describing the first recorded murder in history, tell us that Cain killed Abel because he was treated with disrespect? "The Lord had respect unto Abel and to his offering: But unto Cain . . . he had not respect" (Gen. 4:4–5). In other words, God "dis'ed" Cain! Or rather, Cain was "dis'ed" because of Abel. The inextricable connection between disrespect and shame is emphasized by the anthropologist Julian Pitt-Rivers, who concluded that in all known cultures "the withdrawal of respect dishonors, . . . and this inspires the sentiment of shame."

In maximum security prisons, this is the story of men's lives.

I have yet to see a serious act of violence that was not provoked by the experience of feeling shamed and humiliated, disrespected and ridiculed, and that did not represent the attempt to prevent or undo this "loss of face" – no matter how severe the punishment, even if it includes death. For we misunderstand these men, at our peril, if we do not realize they mean it literally when they say they would rather kill or mutilate others, be killed or mutilated themselves, than live without pride, dignity, and self-respect. They literally prefer death to dishonor. That hunger strikes in prison go on when inmates feel their pride has been irredeemably wounded, and they see refusing to eat as their only way of asserting their dignity and autonomy and protesting the injustices of which they perceive themselves to be the victims, suggests to me that Frantz Fanon was expressing a psychological truth for many when he said "hunger with dignity is preferable to bread eaten in slavery."

Perhaps the lesson of all this for society is that when men feel sufficiently impotent and humiliated, the usual assumptions one makes about human behavior and motivation, such as the wish to eat when starving, the wish to live or stay out of prison at all costs, no longer hold. Einstein taught us that Newton's laws do not hold when objects approach the speed of light; what I have learned about humans is that the "instinct of (physiological) self-preservation" does not hold when one approaches the point of being so overwhelmed by shame that one can only preserve one's self (as a psychological entity) by sacrificing one's body (or those of others).

The emotion of shame is the primary or ultimate cause of all violence, whether toward others or toward the self. Shame is a necessary but not a sufficient cause of violence, just as the tubercle bacillus is necessary but not sufficient for the development of tuberculosis. Several preconditions have to be met before shame can lead to the full pathogenesis of violent behavior. The pathogenic, or violence-inducing, effects of shame can be stimulated, inhibited, or redirected, both by the presence or absence of other feelings, such as guilt or innocence, and by the specific social and psychological circumstances in which shame is experienced.

The different forms of violence, whether toward individuals or entire populations, are motivated (caused) by the feeling of shame. The purpose of violence is to diminish the intensity of shame and replace it as far as possible with its opposite, pride, thus preventing the individual from being overwhelmed by the feeling of shame. Violence toward others, such as homicide, is an attempt to replace shame with pride. It is important to add that men who feel ashamed are not likely to become seriously violent toward others and inflict lethal or life-threatening, mutilating or disabling injuries on others unless several preconditions are met.

The first precondition is probably the most carefully guarded secret held by violent men, which it took me years of working with them to recognize, precisely because they guard it so fiercely. This is a secret that many of them would rather die than reveal; I put it that extremely because many of them, in fact, do die in order not to reveal it. They try so hard to conceal this secret precisely because it is so deeply shameful to them, and of course shame further motivates the need to conceal. The secret is that they feel ashamed – deeply ashamed, chronically ashamed, acutely ashamed, over matters that are so trivial that their very triviality makes it even more shameful to feel ashamed about them, so that they are ashamed even to reveal what shames them. And why are they so ashamed of feeling ashamed? Because nothing is more shameful than to feel ashamed. Often violent men will hide this secret behind a defensive mask of bravado, arrogance, "machismo," self-satisfaction, insouciance, or studied indifference. Many violent men would rather die than let you know what is distressing them, or even that anything is distressing them. Behind the mask of "cool" or self-assurance that many violent men clamp onto their faces – with a desperation born of the certain knowledge that they would "lose face" if they ever let it slip – is a person who feels vulnerable not just to "loss of face" but to the total loss of honor, prestige, respect, and status – the disintegration of identity, especially their adult, masculine, heterosexual identity; their selfhood, personhood, rationality, and sanity.

The assertion that men do not kill for no reason is often truer the more "unprovoked" the killing appears to be. A man only kills another when he is, as he sees it, fighting to save himself, his own self – when he feels he is in danger of experiencing what I referred to earlier as "the death of the self," unless he engages in violence. Murderers see themselves as literally having no other choice; to them, "it's him or me" (or "her or me"). This is what I mean when I say that the degree of shame that a man needs to be experiencing in order to become homicidal is so intense and so painful that it threatens to overwhelm him and bring about the death of the self, cause him to lose his mind, his soul, or his sacred honor (all of which are merely different ways of expressing the same thought).

This should not be confused with the triviality of the incident that provokes or precipitates a man's shame, which is a completely different matter. In fact, it is well known to anyone who reads the newspapers that people often seem to become seriously violent, even homicidal, over what are patently "trivial" events. Paradoxically it is the very triviality of those precipitants that makes them overwhelmingly shameful.

The second precondition for violence is met when these men perceive themselves as having no nonviolent means of warding off or diminishing their feelings of shame or low self-esteem – such as socially rewarded economic or cultural achievement, or high social status, position, and prestige. Violence is a "last resort," a strategy they will use only when no other alternatives appear possible. But that should hardly be surprising; after all, the costs and risks of engaging in violent behavior are extremely high.

The third precondition for engaging in violent behavior is that the person lacks the emotional capacities or the feelings that normally inhibit the violent impulses that are stimulated by shame. The most important are love and guilt toward others, and fear for the self. What is most startling about the most violent people is how incapable they are, at least at the time they commit their violence, of feeling love, guilt, or fear. The psychology of shame explains this. The person who is overwhelmed by feelings of shame is by definition experiencing a psychically life-threatening lack of love, and someone in that condition has no love left over for anyone else.

With respect to guilt, being assaulted, or punished, or humiliated (the conditions that increase the feeling of shame) decreases the degree of guilt. That is why penance, or self-punishment, alleviates the feeling of sinfulness. Guilt, as Freud saw, motivates the need for punishment, since punishment relieves guilt feelings. That is also why the more harshly we punish criminals, or children, the more violent they become; the punishment increases their feelings of shame and simultaneously decreases their capacities for feelings of love for others, and of guilt toward others.

Freud commented that no one feels as guilty as the saints, to which I would add that no one feels as innocent as the criminals; their lack of guilt feelings, even over the most atrocious of crimes, is one of their most prominent characteristics. But, of course, that would have to be true, for if they had the capacity to feel guilty over hurting other people, they would not have the emotional capacity to hurt them.

With respect to fear, as we have seen, when the psyche is in danger, and overwhelmed by feelings of shame, one will readily sacrifice one's body in order to rescue one's psyche, one's self-respect. That is why so-called psychopaths, or sociopaths, or antisocial personalities have always been described as notably lacking in the capacity to experience fear.

A central precondition for committing violence, then, is the presence of over-whelming shame in the absence of feelings of either love or guilt; the shame stimulates rage, and violent impulses, toward the person in whose eyes one feels shamed, and the feelings that would normally inhibit the expression of those feelings and the acting out of those impulses, such as love and or guilt, are absent. [. . .]

Chapter 15

John H. Laub and Robert J. Sampson

TURNING POINTS IN THE LIFE COURSE
Why change matters to the study of crime

From: John H. Laub and Robert J. Sampson (1993), excerpts from 'Turning Points in the Life Course', *Criminology* 31(3): 301–325.

CRIMINOLOGICAL ATTENTION NOW FOCUSES on the importance of childhood. Gottfredson and Hirschi (1990) argue that effective child rearing in the early formative years of a child's development produces high self-control, which in turn is a stable phenomenon that inhibits crime throughout the life course. Wilson and Herrnslein (1985) pushed the explanation of crime back even earlier in life to constitutional differences (e.g., impulsiveness and temperament) in interaction with familial factors (see also Grasmick et al., 1993; Nagin and Paternoster, 1991).

Ironically, then, as we were resurrecting the Gluecks' data, new life was breathed into the primary thesis of the Gluecks – childhood temperament and family socialization matter most, and thus the "past is prologue" (Glueck and Glueck, 1968:167). Although attracted to this renewed emphasis on the importance of children and families to the explanation of delinquency, we were troubled by the profound questions raised by the childhood-stability argument. Are differences in child rearing and temperament all we need to know to understand patterns of adult crime? Are childhood differences in anti-social behavior invariably stable? Why does continuity in deviant behavior exist? Perhaps most important, what about individual change, salient life events, and turning points in adulthood?

Challenged by these and other questions, we set out to examine crime and deviance in childhood, adolescence, and adulthood in a way that recognized the significance of both continuity and change over the life course. To do so we synthesized and integrated the criminological literature on childhood anti-social behavior, adolescent delinquency, and adult crime with theory and research on the life course (Sampson and Laub, 1992). By also rethinking the findings produced by longitudinal research, we were eventually led to develop an age-graded theory of informal social control to explain crime and deviance over the life span. We then tested this theory on the longitudinal data we reconstructed from the Gluecks' study (Sampson and Laub, 1993).

Building on these efforts, we turn to an examination of conceptual issues relating to continuity and change in antisocial behavior over the life course. With respect to continuity, we highlight the distinction between self-selection and cumulative continuity. We then unite the ideas of state dependence (Nagin and Paternoster, 1991) and cumulative continuity (Caspi and Moffitt, 1993a; Moffitt, 1993) in delineating a developmental, sequential model of crime across the life course. With respect to change, we explicate the relevance of the adult life course and the various meanings of change. Our major thesis is that social capital and turning points are important concepts in understanding processes of change in the adult life course. We illustrate these concepts using qualitative life-history data drawn from the Gluecks' study. Overall, our goal is to advance a framework that challenges theories of crime which "presuppose a developmental determinism in which childhood experiences set the course of later development" (Bandura, 1982:747). To set the stage, we briefly highlight the theoretical framework on change from our recent study (Sampson and Laub, 1993).

AN AGE-GRADED THEORY OF INFORMAL SOCIAL CONTROL

The central idea of social control theory – that crime and deviance are more likely when an individual's bond to society is weak or broken – is an organizing principle in our theory of social bonding over the life course. Following Elder (1975, 1985), we differentiate the life course of individuals on the basis of age and argue that the important institutions of both formal and informal social control vary across the life span. However, we emphasize the role of age-graded, *informal* social control as reflected in the structure of interpersonal bonds linking members of society to one another and to wider social institutions (e.g., work, family, school). Unlike formal sanctions that originate in purposeful efforts to control crime, informal social controls "emerge as by-products of role relationships established for other purposes and are components of role reciprocities" (Kornhauser, 1978:24).

Although rejecting the "ontogenetic" approach dominant in developmental psychology (see Dannefer, 1984), our theoretical framework nonetheless follows a developmental strategy (Loeber and LeBlanc, 1990; Patterson et al., 1989). The specific developmental approach we take views causality as "best represented by a developmental network of causal factors" in which dependent variables become independent variables over time (Loeber and LeBlanc, 1990:433). Moreover, developmental criminology recognizes both continuity and within-individual changes over time, focusing on "life transitions and developmental covariates . . . which may mediate the developmental course of offending" (Loeber and LeBlanc, 1990:451). This strategy has also been referred to as a "stepping-stone approach" whereby factors are time ordered by age and assessed with respect to outcome variables (see Farrington, 1986).

A similar orientation can be found in interactional theory as proposed by Thornberry (1987). Interactional theory embraces a developmental approach and argues convincingly that causal influences are reciprocal over the life course and that delinquency may contribute to the weakening of social bonds over time. Thornberry's perspective is also consistent with a person-centered approach to development as propounded by Magnusson and Bergman (1988:47). Namely, by focusing explicitly on "persons" rather than "variables" and examining individual life histories over time (see Magnusson and Bergman, 1988, 1990), this strategy offers insight into the social processes of intra-individual developmental change in criminal behavior over the life course.

Although beyond the scope of this analysis, the first building block in our "sociogenic" developmental theory focuses on the mediating role of informal family and school social bonds in explaining childhood and adolescent delinquency (Sampson and Laub, 1993: Ch. 4–5). As elaborated more below, the second building block incorporates the subsequent continuity in childhood and adolescent antisocial behavior that extends throughout adulthood across a variety of life's domains (e.g., crime, alcohol abuse, divorce, unemployment).

Having provided a role for continuity, we nonetheless believe that salient life events and social ties in adulthood can counteract, at least to some extent, the trajectories of early child development. Hence, a third and major thesis of our work is that social bonds in adulthood – especially *attachment to the labor force* and *cohesive marriage* (or cohabitation) – explain criminal behavior regardless of prior differences in criminal propensity. In other words, we contend that pathways to both crime and conformity are modified by key institutions of social control in the transition to adulthood (e.g., employment, military service, and marriage).

In contrast to many life-course models, we emphasize the quality or strength of social ties in these transitions more than the occurrence or timing of discrete life events (cf. Loeber and LeBlanc, 1990:430–432). For example, marriage per se may not increase social control, but close emotional ties and mutual investment increase the social bond between individuals and, all else equal, should lead to a reduction in criminal behavior (cf. Shover, 1985:94). Employment by itself also does not necessarily increase social control. It is employment coupled with job stability, commitment to work, and mutual ties binding workers and employers that should increase social control and, all else equal, lead to a reduction in criminal behavior.

In short, our theory attempts to unite continuity and change within the context of a sociological understanding of crime in the life course. A major concept in our framework is the dynamic process whereby the interlocking nature of trajectories and transitions generates *turning points* or a change in life course (Elder, 1985:32). Adaptation to life events is crucial because the same event or transition followed by different adaptations can lead to different trajectories (Elder, 1985:35). That is, despite the connection between childhood events and experiences in adulthood, turning points can modify life trajectories – they can "redirect paths." For some individuals, turning points are abrupt – radical "turnarounds" or changes in life history that separate the past from the future (Elder et al., 1991:215). For most individuals, however, we conceptualize turning points as "part of a process over time and not as a dramatic lasting change that takes place at any one time" (Pickles and Rutter, 1991:134; see also Clausen, 1990; McAdam, 1989:745; Rutter, 1989a, 1989b). The process-oriented nature of turning points leads us to focus on incremental change embedded in informal social controls.

To evaluate and refine our theory, we analyzed the natural histories of two groups of boys that differed dramatically in childhood antisocial behavior and delinquency that were followed into adulthood. More specifically, we reconstructed and examined the life histories originally gathered by Glueck and Glueck (1950, 1968) of 500 delinquents and 500 control subjects matched on age, IQ, ethnicity, and neighborhood deprivation. [. . .]

DISTINGUISHING SELF-SELECTION FROM CUMULATIVE CONTINUITY

Critics will argue that individual differences combine with self-selection to account for patterns of behavior across the life course. In brief, this counter-argument goes as follows: Individuals with an early propensity to crime (e.g., low self-control) determined mainly by family socialization and individual differences (e.g., impulsiveness) systematically sort themselves throughout adulthood into states consistent with this latent trail. For instance, Gottfredson and Hirschi (1990:164–167) argue that delinquent and impulsive youths will choose deviant spouses, unstable jobs, and continue their delinquent ways in adulthood. If true, the adult life course is merely a setting within which predetermined lives are played out.

In one sense the self-selection thesis was supported in the Gluecks' study – adolescent delinquents and non-delinquents displayed significant behavioral consistency well into adulthood. Delinquency and other forms of antisocial conduct in childhood were related not only to adult crime, but also to troublesome behaviors across a variety of adult domains (e.g., AWOL in the military, economic dependence, marital discord). This continuity persisted despite the fact that delinquents and controls were originally matched case-by-case on age, intelligence, neighborhood, and ethnicity.

The hypothesis of self-selection, however, leads to a more fundamental methodological implication – correlations among adult behaviors (e.g., job instability and crime) are completely spurious and should disappear once controls are introduced for prior individual-level differences in criminal propensity or low self-control (see Gottfredson and Hirschi, 1990:154–168). Although rarely examined directly, we believe the data do not support this spuriousness hypothesis. In particular, our quantitative analyses revealed independent effects of marital attachment and job stability on adult crime. These results were consistent for a wide variety of outcome measures, control variables (e.g., childhood and adolescent antisocial behavior, individual-difference constructs, such as IQ, self-control, mesomorphy, and personality), and analytic techniques – including methods that account for persistent unobserved heterogeneity in criminal propensity (see Nagin and Patemoster, 1991). Rutter et al. (1990) have also shown the independent explanatory power of adult marital cohesion on adult deviance, self-selection notwithstanding.

At the same time, our theory incorporates the causal role of prior delinquency in facilitating adult crime by integrating the concept of *state dependence* (Nagin and Paternoster, 1991) with that of *cumulative continuity* (Moffitt, 1993). Although this role is potentially direct, we emphasize a developmental model wherein delinquent behavior has a systematic, attenuating effect on the social and institutional bonds linking adults to society (e.g., labor force attachment, marital cohesion). More specifically, the idea of cumulative continuity posits that delinquency incrementally mortgages the future by generating negative consequences for the life chances of stigmatized and institutionalized youths. For example, arrest and incarceration may spark failure in school, unemployment, and weak community bonds, in turn increasing adult crime (Tittle, 1988:80). Serious delinquency in particular leads to the "knifing off" (Caspi and Moffitt, 1993a; Moffitt, 1993) of future opportunities such that participants have fewer options for a conventional life. The cumulative continuity of disadvantage is thus not only a result of stable individual differences in criminal propensity, but a dynamic process whereby childhood antisocial behavior and adolescent delinquency foster adult crime through the severance of adult social bonds. In this view, weak social bonding is a mediating and, hence, causal sequential link in a chain of adversity between childhood delinquency and adult criminal behavior.

The thesis of cumulative continuity was supported in our quantitative analyses. As noted above, job stability and marital attachment in adulthood were significantly related to changes in adult crime – the stronger the adult ties to work and family, the less crime and deviance among delinquents and controls. Moreover, social bonds to employment were directly influenced by state sanctions – incarceration as a juvenile and as a young adult had a negative effect on later job stability, which in turn was negatively related to continued involvement in crime over the life course. Although we found little direct effect of incarceration on subsequent criminality, the indirect "criminogenic" effects through job stability were substantively important. Recent research by Nagin and Waldfogel (1992) also supports the cumulative continuity thesis in showing a destabilizing effect of convictions on the labor market prospects of a cohort of London boys.

Our synthesis of cumulative continuity and state dependence recasts in a structural and developmental framework the original contentions of labeling theory – that official reactions to primary deviance (e.g., arrest) may create problems of adjustment (e.g., unemployment) that foster additional crime in the form of secondary deviance (Becker, 1963; Lernert, 1951; Tittle, 1988). As Becker (1963:24–39) has argued, the concept of a deviant career suggests a stable pattern of deviant behavior, which is sustained by the labeling process. More recently, Hagan and Palloni (1990) suggested that continuity in delinquent behavior may result from a structural imputation process that begins early in childhood (see also Tittle, 1988:78–81). They show that this process may even extend across generations, thereby explaining the effects of parental conviction on sons' delinquency regardless of family background and propensity to crime.

Cumulative disadvantage and structural background

Hagan's (1991) research further suggests that the deleterious effect of adolescent deviance on adult stratification outcomes is greatest among lower-class boys, especially as mediated by police contacts. Middle-class boys who escaped the negative conse- quences of official labeling did not suffer impairment in adult occupational outcomes as a result of their adolescent delinquency. In other words, avoiding the snares of arrest and institutionalization provided opportunities for pro-social attachments among middle-class youths to take firm hold in adulthood. Similarly, Jessor et al. (1991) show that for middle-class youths, delinquency is not a major handicap with respect to adult outcomes. These studies suggest that the concepts of knifing off and cumulative continuity are most salient in explaining the structurally constrained life chances of the disadvantaged urban poor.

In short, there is evidence that cumulative disadvantage, state-dependence, and location in the class structure may interact. Among those in advantaged positions that provide continuity in social resources over time, non-delinquents and delinquents alike are presumably not just more motivated, but better able structurally to establish binding ties to conventional lines of adult activity. If nothing else, incumbency in pro-social middle-class roles provides advantages in maintaining the status quo and counteracting negative life events (e.g., last hired, first fired). Race, class, and crime also pervade the consciousness of American society more generally and employers in particular.

Consider the widespread perceptions of blacks as "dangerous" and "criminal" as rationales by employers for discrimination in hiring (Kirschenman and Neckerman, 1991). We therefore merge the state-dependence thesis that historical time matters with a concern for structural location. Quite simply, the context of where *and* how long one has been in prior states is crucial in understanding later adult development.

Self-selection reconsidered

Our theoretical conceptualization of cumulative continuity and the causal role of the adult life course does not negate the potential direct or unmediated effect of self-selection through individual differences. In other words, by distinguishing self-selection from cumulative continuity, we incorporate the independent effects of early delinquency (or individual propensity) and the dimensions of adult social bonding on adult crime. This distinction is consistent with recent research on homophily in social choices across the life course. For example, Kandel et al. (1990) studied mate selection and found considerable homophily – deviant individuals tend to select deviant marriage or cohabitation partners (see also Caspi et al., 1990). Nevertheless, social causation emerges as a crucial factor even in the face of such social selection. As Kandel et al. (1990:221) state, "Although individual choices are made, in part, as a function of the individual's prior attributes, values, and personality characteristics, involvement in the new relationship has further effects and influences on that individual." Similarly, Rutter et al. (1990) found homophily in the choice of marital partners but also a substantial effect of marital cohesion that held after taking planning of marriage partners into account.

The emergence of significant social causation in tandem with homophily (or self-selection) undermines the theoretical individualism that pervades social scientific thought. We believe that an overemphasis on self-selection stems from a "broadly perpetuated fiction in modern society" (Coleman, 1990:300):

> This fiction is that society consists of a set of independent individuals, each of whom acts to achieve goals that are independently arrived at, and that the functioning of the social system consists of the combinations of the actions of independent individuals.

Consistent with our theory, social interdependence arises from the fact that actors have social investments in events and relationships that are partially under the control of other actors. Hence, the interdependent web of relations characteristic of social collectivities ensures the operation of constraints and opportunities in shaping behavior notwithstanding individual intentions.

WHY CHANGE STILL MATTERS

Whether generated by self-selection or cumulative continuity, a focus on stability is nonetheless insufficient for understanding crime in the adult life course. First, the stability of antisocial behavior is far from perfect. As the literature on prediction shows, childhood variables tend to be rather modest prognostic devices. In fact, a large percentage of false positives and false negatives is a common result (see, e.g., Loeber and Stouthamer-Loeber, 1987; Farrington and Tarling, 1985). The prediction literature thus reinforces the futility of an invariant or deterministic conception of human development (Jessor et al., 1991; Sampson and Laub, 1992).

Second, and equally important, rank-order correlations and other common measures of stability refer to the consistency of between-individual differences over time and consequently rely on an aggregate picture of relative standing. As Huesmann et al. (1984:131) note, what remains stable over time is the position of an individual relative to the population. Stability coefficients do not measure the heterogeneity of individual behaviors over time and, hence, do not capture within-individual change.

Life is dynamic; change is clearly possible. Yet the theoretical conceptualization of change has been surprisingly neglected, not just in criminology (see Farrington, 1988; Sampson and Laub, 1992) but in developmental psychology as well. [. . .]

Social capital and turning points

Much of the confusion regarding change centers on the various meanings the concept conveys. According to the 1992 edition of *The American Heritage Dictionary of the English Language*, one definition of change is "to cause to be different" – to give a completely different form or appearance, to wholly transform or alter. This definition is most closely related to Caspi and Moffitt's (1993b) notion of "deep" or "real" change (e.g., a high-rate offender who suddenly desists and becomes a productive citizen). But change can also mean a modification, reshaping, or transition from one state, condition, or phase to another. For instance, a high-rate offender who begins to commit fewer crimes than expected based on age and prior criminal propensity changes because his or her trajectory has been modified. A third meaning of change is exchange or replacement with another, usually of the same kind or category. An individual may change from use of beer and wine to use of marijuana and cocaine. Or offenders may change from burglary to robbery.

All of this leads us to think of change along a continuum and to investigate the under-lying processes that enable people to change the course of their lives. We believe this may be accomplished by viewing the life course as a probabilistic linkage or chain of events (Rutter et al., 1990) and by unraveling the mechanisms that operate at key turning points (e.g., when a risk trajectory is recast to a more adaptive path [Rutter, 1987:329]).

In our view, "deep" change and "modified" change are of most interest; both are enhanced when changing roles and environments lead to social investment or *social capital* (Coleman, 1988, 1990; Nagin and Paternoster, 1992) in institutional relationships (e.g., family, work, community). As Coleman (1990:302) argues, the distinguishing feature of social capital lies in the structure of interpersonal relations and institutional linkages. Social capital is created when these relations change in ways that facilitate action. In other words, "social capital is productive, making possible the achievements of certain ends that in its absence would not be possible" (Coleman, 1988:98). By contrast, physical capital is wholly tangible, being embodied in observable material form (1990:304), and human capital is embodied in the skills and knowledge acquired by an individual. Social capital is even less tangible, for it is embodied in the relations among persons (1990:304). A core idea, then, is that independent of the forms of physical and human capital available to individuals (e.g., income, occupational skill), social capital is a central factor in facilitating effective ties that bind a person to societal institutions.

Linking Coleman's notion of social capital to social control theory, we have argued that the lack of social capital or investment is one of the primary features of weak social bonds (Sampson and Laub, 1993; see also Coleman, 1990:307; Nagin and Paternoster, 1992). The theoretical task is to identify the characteristics of social relations that facilitate the social capital available to individuals, families, employers, and other social actors. One of the most important factors is the closure (i.e., "connectedness") of networks among actors in a social system (Coleman, 1990:318–320). In a system involving employers and employees, for example, relations characterized by an extensive set of obligations, expectations, and interdependent social networks are better able to facilitate social control than are jobs characterized by purely utilitarian objectives and non-overlapping social networks. Similarly, the mere presence of a relationship (e.g., marriage) among adults is not sufficient to produce social capital, and hence, the idea of social capital goes beyond simple structural notions of role change (i.e., married versus not married) to capture the idea of embeddedness.

Our theory thus maintains that adult social ties are important insofar as they create interdependent systems of obligation and restraint that impose significant costs for translating criminal propensities into action. In this scheme, adults will be inhibited from committing crime to the extent that over time they accumulate social capital in their work and family lives, regardless of delinquent background. By contrast, those subject to weak systems of interdependency (see also Braithwaite, 1989) and informal social control as an adult (e.g., weak attachment to the labor force or noncohesive marriage) are freer to commit deviance – even if non-delinquent as a youth. This dual premise enables us to explain desistance from crime as well as late onset, and it is consistent with Jessor et al.'s (1991:160) argument that change is "as much an outcome of the person's embeddedness in a socially organized and structured context of age-related roles, expectations, demands, and opportunities as it is of internal dispositions and intentions."

We also emphasize the reciprocal nature of social capital invested by employers and spouses. For example, employers often take chances in hiring workers, hoping that their investment will pay off. Similarly, a prospective marriage partner may be aware of a potential spouse's deviant background but may nonetheless invest his or her future in that person. This investment by the employer or spouse may in turn trigger a return invest-ment in social capital by the employee or other spouse. The key theoretical point is that social capital and interdependency are reciprocal and embedded in the social ties that exist between individuals and social institutions. This conception may help explain how change in delinquent behavior is initiated (e.g., an employer's taking a chance on a for-mer delinquent, fostering a return investment in that job, which in turn inhibits the deviant behavior of the employee).

Sullivan's (1989) research on gangs in New York also provides insight into racial, ethnic, and community differences in the influence of social capital on transitions to work. As they entered young adulthood, the men in the low-income white neighborhood that Sullivan studied secured better-quality jobs than men in African–American or Hispanic neighborhoods. Whites were also better able to hold onto these jobs, in part because of their familiarity with the "discipline of the workplace" gained through personal networks and intergenerational ties (1989:100–105). Networks with the adult community thus differentiated the chances of white youths' escaping environmental adversity from those of their minority counterparts. In a similar vein. Anderson's *Streetwise: Race, Class and Change in an Urban Community* (1990) points to the importance of racial differences in intergenerational ties and the salience of those ties in facilitating employment among young males as they enter adulthood. Anderson (1990) focuses in particular on the sharp decrease over time in African–American "old heads," who socialized boys in the world of work and adulthood more generally. These ethnographies underscore variations by race, ethnicity, and structural context in social capital and its role in promoting successful transitions to young adulthood (see also Short, 1990).

Thus, because individual-difference constructs and childhood antisocial behavior are independent of adult social capital and structural context in fundamental respects, another key aspect of our theory is the partial *exogenous* nature of the adult life course. This conceptualization opens the door for turning points that can redirect behavioral trajectories in the transition to adulthood. To be sure, we are not implying that individuals in our study became completely different or that they transformed their total personality as a result of social bonding in adulthood. We do not have the data to assess such trans-formations, nor would we expect that kind of change to occur given what we know about continuities over the life course. But we strongly contend that behavioral changes do occur and that adult life-course patterns are not solely the result of childhood socialization (Bandura, 1982). [. . .]

CONCLUSION

Perhaps the key idea is ultimately a simple one – the adult life course matters, regardless of how one gets there. We do not deny the reality of self-selection or that persons may sometimes "create" their own environment. But once in place, those environments take on a history of their own in a way that invalidates a pure spuriousness or self-selection argument. Moreover, the self-selection view of the world is, in our opinion, much too deterministic and neglects the role of state sanctions, chance, luck, structural location, historical context, and opportunity structure in shaping the life course.

In sum, by redirecting attention to the significance of both pathways and turning points in the life course, we are optimistic about the possibilities for a new research agenda that has the potential to unify heretofore divergent conceptions of stability and change in human development. For example, Gottfredson and Hirschi (1990:177–178; Hirschi and Gottfredson, 1993) explicitly incorporate the role of opportunity in explaining criminal events. If opportunity matters for criminal events, surely it matters for the establishment of strong employment and marital bonds. More important, at one point Gottfredson and Hirschi (1990:115) allow for *social* control in explaining adolescent delinquency. In this sense we see some compatibility between our theory and Gottfredson and Hirschi's theory, especially if one conceptualizes variations in social control as partly influenced by variations in self-control (see also Hirschi, 1992; Hirschi and Gottfredson, 1993; Nagin and Paternoster, 1992). Therefore, while Gottfredson and Hirschi (1990) and Wilson and Herrnstein (1985) start off with a similar premise, they offer quite different possibilities for potential integration with our focus on change and informal social control across the adult life course. Future research is needed to examine these possibilities, especially the relative importance of stability and change throughout lives in varying contexts.

Acknowledgment

An earlier version of this article was presented at the annual meeting of the American Society of Criminology, New Orleans, 1992. We thank the reviewers for constructive criticisms on an earlier draft. Life-history data were derived from the Sheldon and Eleanor Glueck archives of the Harvard Law School Library, currently on long-term loan in the Henry A. Murray Research Center of Radcliffe College.

References

Anderson, Elijah 1990, Streetwise: Race, Class, and Change in an Urban Community. Chicago: University of Chicago Press.

Bandura, Albert 1982, The psychology of chance encounters and life paths. American Psychologist: 747–755.

Becker, Howard 1963, The Outsiders. New York: Free Press.

Braithwaite, John 1989, Crime, Shame, and Reintegration. New York: Cambridge University Press.

Caspi, Avshalom and Terric E. Moffitt 1993a, The continuity of maladaptive behavior: from description to understanding in the study of antisocial behavior. In Dante Cicchetti and Donald Cohco (eds.), Manual of Developmental Psychopathology. New York: John Wiley & Sons, in press.

—— 1993b, Continuity amidst change: A paradoxical theory of personality coherence. Psychological Inquiry, in press.

Caspi, Avshalom, Glen H. Elder, Jr., and Ellen S. Herbeaer 1990, Childhood personality and the prediction of life-course patterns. In Lee Robins and Michael Rutter (eds.), Straight and Devious Pathways from Childhood to Adulthood. New York: Cambridge University Press.

Clausen, John 1990, Turning point as a life course concept: Meaning and measurement. Paper presented at the annual meeting of the American Sociological Association, Washington, D.C.

Coleman, James S. 1988, Social capital in the creation of human capital. American Journal of Sociology 94:95–120.

—— 1990, Foundations of Social Theory. Cambridge, Mass.: Harvard University Press.

Dannefer, Dale 1984, Adult development and social theory: A paradigmatic reappraisal. American Sociological Review 49:100–116.

DiMaggio, Paul and John Mohr 1985, Cultural capital, educational attainment and marital selection. American Journal of Sociology 90:1231–1261.

Ebaugh, Helen Rose Fuchs 1988, Becoming an EX: The Process of Role Exit. Chicago: University of Chicago Press.

Elder, Glen H., Jr. 1975, Age differentiation and the life course. Annual Review of Sociology 1:165–190.

—— 1985, Perspectives on the life course. In Glen H. Elder, Jr. (ed.), Life Course Dynamics. Ithaca, N.Y.: Cornell University Press.

Elder, Glen H., Jr., Cynthia Gimbel, and Rachel Ivie 1991, Turning points in life: The case of military service and war. Military Psychology 3:215–231.

Farrington, David P. 1986, Stepping stones to adult criminal careers. In Dan Olweus, Jack Block, and Marian Rodke–Yarrow (eds.), Development of Antisocial and Prosocial Behavior. New York: Academic Press.

—— 1988, Studying changes within individuals: The causes of offending. In Michael Rutter (ed.), Studies of Psychosocial Risk: The Power of Longitudinal Data. New York: Cambridge University Press.

Farrington, David P. and Roger Tarling 1985, Prediction in Criminology. Albany: State University of New York Press.

Glueck, Sheldon and Eleanor Glueck 1950, Unraveling Juvenile Delinquency. New York: Commonwealth Fund.

—— 1968, Delinquents and Nondelinquents in Perspective. Cambridge, Mass.: Harvard University Press.

Gottfredson, Michael and Travis Hirschi 1990, A General Theory of Crime. Stanford, Calif.: Stanford University Press.

Grasmick, Harold, Charles R. Tittle, Robert J. Bursik, Jr., and Bruce Arneklev 1993, Testing the core empirical implications of Gottfredson and Hirschi's general theory of crime. Journal of Research in Crime and Delinquency 30:5–29.

Hagan, John 1991, Destiny and drift: subcultural preferences, status attainments, and the risks and rewards of Youth. *American Sociological Review* 56: 567–582.

Hagan, John and Alberto Palloni 1990, The social reproduction of a criminal class in working-class London, circa 1950–1980, American Journal of Sociology 96:265–299.

Hirschi, Travis 1992, From social control to self control. Paper presented at the annual meeting of the American Society of Criminology. New Orleans.

Hirschi, Travis and Michael Gottfredson 1993, Commentary. Testing the general theory of crime. Journal of Research in Crime and Delinquency 30:47–54.

Huesmann, Rowell, Leonard Eroa, Monroe Lefkowitz, and Leopold Walder 1984, Stability of aggression over time and generations. Developmental Psychology 20:1120–14.

Jessor, Richard, John E. Donovan, and Frances M. Coste 1991, Beyond Adolescence: Problem Behavior and Young Adult Development. New York: Cambridge University Press.

Kandel, Denise, Mark Davies, and Nazli Baydar 1990, The creation of interpersonal contexts: Homophily in dyadic relationships in adolescence and young adulthood. In Lee Robins and Michael Rutter (eds.), Straight and Devious Pathways from Childhood to Adulthood. New York: Cambridge University Press.

Kirschenman, Joleen and Kathryn Neckerman 1991, "We'd love to hire them, but . . . " The meaning of race for employers. In Christopher Jencks and Paul Peterson (eds.), The Urban Underclass. Washington, D.C.: Brookings Institution.

Kornhauser, Ruth 1978, Social Sources of Delinquency. Chicago: University of Chicago Press.

Lernert, Edwin 1951, Social Pathology. New York: McGraw–Hill.

Loeber, Rolf and Magda Stouthamer–Loeber 1987, Prediction. In Herbert C. Quay (ed.), Handbook of Juvenile Delinquency. New York: John Wiley & Sons.

Loeber, Rolf and Marc LcBlanc 1990, Toward a developmental criminology. In Michael Tonry and Norval Morris (eds.), Crime and Justice. Chicago: University of Chicago Press.

Magnusson, David and Lars R. Bergman 1988, Individual and variable-based approaches to longitudinal research on early risk factors. In Michael Rutter (ed.), Studies of Psychosocial Risk: The Power of Longitudinal Data. New York: Cambridge University Press.

—— 1990, A pattern approach to the study of pathways from childhood to adulthood. In Lee Robins and Michael Rutter (eds.), Straight and Devious Pathways from Childhood to Adulthood. New York: Cambridge University Press.

McAdam, Doug 1989, The biographical consequences of activism. American Sociological Review 54:744–760.

Moffitt, Terrie E. 1993, Adolescence-limited and life-course-persistent antisocial behavior: A developmental taxonomy. Psychological Review, in press.

Nagin, Daniel and Joel Waldfogel 1992, The effects of criminality and conviction on the labour market status of young British offenders. Unpublished manuscript. Carnegie Mellon University, Pittsburgh.

Nagin, Daniel and Raymond Paternoster 1991, On the relationship of past and future participation in delinquency. Criminology 29:163–190.

—— 1992, Social capital and social control: The deterrence implications of a theory of individual differences in criminal offending. Unpublished manuscript. Carnegie Mellon University, Pittsburgh.

Patterson, Gerald R., Barbara D. DeBaryshe, and Elizabeth Ramsey 1989, A developmental perspective on antisocial behavior. American Psychologist 44:329–335.

Pickles, Andrew and Michael Rutter 1991, Statistical and conceptual models of "turning points" in developmental processes. In David Magnusson, Lais Bergman, Georg Rudinger, and Derrill Toresad (eds.), Problems and Methods in Longitudinal Research: Stability and Change. New York: Cambridge University Press.

Rutter, Michael 1987, Psychosocial resilience and protective mechanisms. American Journal of Orthopsychiatry 57:316–333.

—— 1989a, Age as an ambiguous variable in developmental research: Some epidemiological considerations from developmental psychopathology. International Journal of Behavioral Development 12:3–34.

—— 1989b, Pathways from childhood to adult life. Journal of Child Psychology and Psychiatry 30:23–51.

Rutter, Michael, David Quinton, and Jonathan Hill 1990, Adult outcomes of institution-reared children: Males and females compared. In Lee Robins and Michael Rutter (eds.), Straight and Devious Pathways from Childhood to Adulthood. New York: Cambridge University Press.

Sampson, Robert J. and John H. Laub 1992, Crime and deviance in the life course. Annual Review of Sociology 18:63–89.

—— 1993, Crime in the Making: Pathways and Turning Points Through Life. Cambridge, Mass.: Harvard University Press.

Short, James F., Jr. 1990, Gangs, neighborhoods, and youth crime. Criminal Justice Research Bulletin 5:1–11.

Shover, Neal 1985, Aging Criminals. Beverly Hills. Calif.: Sage.

Sullivan, Merces 1989, "Getting Paid:" Youth Crime and Work in the Inner City. Ithaca, N.Y.: Cornell University Press.

Thornberry, Terence P. 1987, Toward an interactional theory of delinquency. Criminology 25:863–891.

Tittle, Charles R. 1988, Two empirical regularities (maybe) in search of an explanation: Commentary on the age-crime debate. Criminology 26:75–86.

Wilson, James Q. and Richard Herrastein 1985, Crime and Human Nature. New York: Simon & Schuster.

Chapter 16

Jack Henry Abbott

STATE RAISED CONVICT

From: Jack Henry Abbott (1981), 'State raised convict', in Jack Henry Abbott, *In the Belly of the Beast*, New York: Random House, pp. 3–14.

I'VE WANTED SOMEHOW TO convey to you the sensations – the atmospheric pressure, you might say – of what it is to be seriously a long-term prisoner in an American prison. That sentence does not adequately say what I mean. I've wanted to convey to you what it means to be in prison after a childhood spent in penal institutions. To be in prison so long, it's difficult to remember exactly what you did to get there. So long, your fantasies of the free world are no longer easily distinguishable from what you "know" the free world is really like. So long, that being free is exactly identical to a free man's dreams of heaven. To die and go to the free world . . .

That part of me which wanders through my mind and never sees or feels *actual* objects, but which lives in and moves through my passions and my emotions, experiences this world as a horrible nightmare. I'm talking now about the *me* in my dreams. The one that appears in my dreams as me. The one that is both the subject and object of all those surreal symbols. The one that journeys within my life, within me, on what St. John of the Cross viewed as a nighttime quest for fulfillment. When they talk of ghosts of the dead who wander in the night with things still undone in life, they approximate my subjective experience of this life.

> . . . I have been desperate to escape for so many years now, it is routine for me to try to escape. My eyes, my brain seek out escape routes wherever I am sent, the way another prisoner's eyes, brain, seek friendliness, refuge or a warm, quiet place to rest and be safe. Too often for my liking those eyes and brains find me.

I escaped one time. In 1971 I was in the free world for six weeks. I was in a hotel room in Montreal, Canada. I was asleep. I had been a fugitive about three weeks. I began waking in the night in a sweat from bad dreams. I had simply been dreaming of prison. When I was *in* prison, I must have pushed all fear aside until not fearing was habitual. But that part of me I call my subjective side *did* feel that fear every minute of every day. Now the loathing and stark terror suppressed within me were coming to the surface in dreams. One morning I woke up and was plunged into psychological shock. I had *forgotten* I was free, I had escaped. I could not grasp where I was. I was in a nice bedroom with fancy furnishings. A window was open and the sunlight was shining in. There were no bars. The walls were papered in rich designs. My bed was large and comfortable. So much more. I must have sat there in bed reeling from shock and numbness for an hour while it all gradually came back to me that I had escaped.

So we can all hold up like good soldiers and harden ourselves in prison. But if you do that for too long, you lose yourself. Because there is something helpless and weak and innocent – something like an infant – deep inside us all that really suffers in ways we would never permit an insect to suffer.

That is how prison is tearing me up inside. It hurts every day. Every day takes me further from my life. And I am not even conscious of how my dissolution is coming about. Therefore, I cannot stop it.

I don't ever talk of these feelings. I never spent much time thinking of them. In fact, I'm only now thinking of them as I write this. I find it painful and angering to look in a mirror. When I walk past a glass window in the corridor and happen to see my reflection, I get angry on impulse. I feel shame and hatred at such times. When I'm forced by circumstances to be in a crowd of prisoners, it's all I can do to refrain from attack. I feel such hostility, such hatred, I can't help this anger. All these years I have felt it. Paranoid. I can control it. I never seek a confrontation. I have to intentionally gauge my voice in conversation to cover up the anger I feel, the chaos and pain just beneath the surface of what we commonly recognize as reality. Paranoia is an illness I contracted in institutions. It is not the reason for my sentences to reform school and prison. It is the effect, not the cause.

How would you like to be forced all the days of your life to sit beside a stinking, stupid wino every morning at breakfast? Or for some loud fool in his infinite ignorance to be at any moment able to say (slur) "Gimme a cigarette, man!" And I just look into his sleazy eyes and want to kill his ass there in front of God and everyone.

. . . Imagine a thousand more such daily intrusions in your life, every hour and minute of every day, and you can grasp the source of this paranoia, this anger that could consume me at any moment if I lost control. [. . .]

I was born January 21, 1944, on a military base in Oscoda, Michigan. I was in and out of foster homes almost from the moment of my birth. My formal education: I never completed the sixth grade. At age nine I began serving long stints in juvenile detention quarters. At age twelve I was sent to the Utah State Industrial School for Boys. I was "paroled" once for about sixty days, then returned there. At age eighteen I was released as an adult. Five or six months later I was sent to the Utah State Penitentiary for the crime of "issuing a check against insufficient funds." I went in with an indeterminate sentence of up to five years. About three years later, having never been released, I killed one inmate and wounded another in a fight in the center hall. I was tried for the capital offense under the old convict statute that requires either *mandatory* death if malice *aforethought* is found, or a sentence of from three to twenty years. I received the latter sentence. An "indeterminate term" is what justifies the concept of *parole*. Your good behavior determines how long you stay in prison. The law merely sets a minimum and a maximum – the underlying assumption being that *no one* serves the maximum. A wrong assumption in my case. At age twenty-six I escaped for about six weeks.

I am at this moment thirty-seven years old. Since age twelve I have been free the sum total of nine and a half months. I have served many terms in solitary. In only three terms I have served over ten years there. I would estimate that I have served a good fourteen or fifteen years in solitary. The only serious crime I have ever committed in free society was bank robbery during the time I was a fugitive.

It was a big red-brick building with two wings. It stood about four stories high. It was constructed by the U.S. Army back when the state was still a territory. It was one of several buildings that had served as disciplinary barracks for the military. These barracks had long ago passed into the hands of the state and were part of a juvenile penal institution.

In the basement of the big red-brick building were rows of solitary confinement cells. The basement was entered from outside the building only.

I am about twelve or thirteen years old. It is winter. I am marching in a long double-file of boys. We are marching to the mess hall. There is a guard watching as we march toward him. There is a guard walking behind us as we march.

My testes shrink and the blood is rushing and my eyes burn, ache. My heart is pounding and I am trying hard to breathe slowly, to control myself.

I keep glancing at the guards: in front and behind the line.

The fields beyond are plowed and covered with an icy blanket of snow. I do not know how far beyond those fields my freedom lies.

Suddenly my confederate at the front of the line whirls and slugs the boy behind him. The front guard, like an attack dog, is on them both — beating them into submission. Seconds later the guard at the back rushes forward, brushing me as he passes.

I break away from the line, and run *for my life*. I stretch my legs as far as I can, and as quickly as I can, but the legs of a boy four feet six inches tall cannot stretch very far.

The fields are before me, a still flatland of ice and snow, and the huge clods of frozen, plowed earth are to me formidable obstacles. The sky is baby-blue, almost white. The air is clear.

I haven't covered fifty yards when I hear the pursuit begin: "You! Stop!" I immediately know I will be caught, but I continue to run.

I do not feel the blow of his fist. I'm in mid-air for a moment, and then I'm rolling in frozen clods of soil. I am pulled to my feet; one of my arms is twisted behind my back; my lungs are burning with the cold air; my nostrils are flared. I am already trying to steel myself for the punishment to come.

The other inmates stand in a long straight line, flanked by guards, and I am dragged past them. I do not respect them, because they will not run — will not try to escape. My legs are too short to keep up with the guard, who is effortlessly holding my arm twisted high up behind my back, so I stumble along, humiliated. I try hard to be dignified.

I see the door to the basement of the red-brick building, and we are approaching it in good time. A snowflake hits my eye and melts. It is beginning, softly, to snow.

At the top of the stairs to the basement, I am flung down against a high black-steel door. I stand beside it at attention as the guard takes out a huge ring of keys and bangs on the door. We are seen through a window. The door yawns open and an old guard appears, gazing at me maliciously.

We enter. We are standing at the top of a number of wide concrete steps that descend to the floor of the basement. I am thrown down the stairs, and I lie on the floor, waiting. My nose is bleeding and my ears are ringing from blows to my skull.

"Get up!"

Immediately I am knocked down again.

"Strip!"

I stand, shakily, and shed my clothing. His hands are pulling my hair, but I dare not move. [. . .]

He orders me to follow him.

We enter a passageway between rows of heavy steel doors. The passage is narrow; it is only four or five feet wide and is dimly lighted. As soon as we enter, I can smell nervous sweat and feel body warmth in the air.

We stop at one of the doors. He unlocks it. I enter. Nothing is said. He closes and locks the door, and I can hear his steps as he walks down the dark passageway. [. . .]

When my light was turned out at night, I would weep uncontrollably. Sixty days in solitary was a long, long time in those days for me.

When the guard's key would hit the lock on my door to signal the serving of a "meal," if I were not standing at attention in the far corner of the cell, facing it, the guard would attack me with a ring of keys on a heavy chain.

I was fed one-third of a regular meal three times a day. Only one day a week I was taken from my cell and ordered to shower while the guard stood in the shower-room doorway and timed me for three minutes.

Locked in our cells, we could not see one another, and if we were caught shouting cell-to-cell, we were beaten. We tapped out messages, but if they heard our taps, we were beaten – the entire row of cells, one child at a time.

I served five years in the big red-brick building, and altogether, two or three in solitary confinement. When I walked out, I was considered an adult, subject to adult laws.

I served so long because I could not adjust to the institution and tried to escape over twenty times. I had been there for the juvenile "crime" of "failure to adjust to foster homes."

. . . He who is state-raised – reared by the state from an early age after he is taken from what the state calls a "broken home" – learns over and over and all the days of his life that people in society can do anything to him and not be punished by the law. Do anything to him with the full force of the state behind them.

As a child, he must march in lock-step to his meals in a huge mess hall. He can own only three shirts and two pair of trousers and one pair of shoes.

People in society come to him through the state and injure him. Everyone in society he comes in contact with is in some capacity employed by the state. He learns to avoid people in society. He evades them at every step.

In *any* state in America someone who is state-raised can be shot down and killed like a dog by anyone, who has no "criminal record," with full impunity. I do not exaggerate this at all. It is a fact so ordinary in the minds of state-raised prisoners that it is a matter of common sense. If a prisoner were to show a skeptical attitude toward things of this nature, the rest of us would conclude that he is losing his mind. He is questioning what is self-evident to us: a practical fact of life.

. . . My mind keeps turning toward one of the main aspects of prison that separates ordinary prisoners who, at some point in their lives, serve a few years and get out never to return – or if they do, it is for another short period and never again – and the convict who is "state-raised," i.e., the prisoner who grows up from boyhood to manhood in penal institutions.

I have referred to it as a form of instability (mental, emotional, etc.). There is no doubt (let us say there is *little* doubt) that this instability is *caused* by a lifetime of incarceration. Long stretches of, say, from ages ten to seventeen or eighteen, and then from seventeen or eighteen to ages thirty and forty.

You hear a lot about "arrested adolescence" nowadays, and I believe this concept touches the nub of the instability in prisoners like myself.

Every society gives its men and women the prerogatives of men and women, of *adults*. Men are given their dues. After a certain age you are regarded as a man by society. You are referred to as "sir"; no one interferes in your affairs, slaps your hands or ignores you. Society is solicitous in general and serves you. You are shown respect. Gradually your judgment is tempered because gradually you see that it has real effects; it impinges on the society, the world. Your experience mellows your emotions because you are free to move about anywhere, work and play at anything. You can pursue any object of love, pleasure, danger, profit, etc. You are taught by the very terms of your social existence, by the objects that come and go from your intentions, the nature of your own emotions – and you learn about yourself, your tastes, your strengths and weaknesses. You, in other words, mature emotionally.

It is not so for the state-raised convict. As a boy in reform school, he is punished for being a little boy. In prison, he is punished for trying to be a man in the sense described above. He is treated as an adolescent in prison. Just as an adolescent is denied the keys to the family car for *any* disobedience, *any* mischief, I am subjected to the hole for *any* disobedience, *any* mischief. I will go to the hole for murder as well as for stealing a packet of sugar. I will get out of the hole in either case, and the length of time I serve for either offense is no different. My object is *solely* to avoid leaving evidence that will leave me open to prosecution out there in the world beyond these walls where a semblance of democracy is practiced.

Prison regimes have prisoners making extreme decisions regarding moderate questions, decisions that only fit the logical choice of either-or. No contradiction is allowed openly. You are not allowed to change. You are only allowed to submit; "agreement" does not exist (it implies equality). You are the rebellious adolescent who must obey and submit to the judgment of "grownups" "*tyrants*" they are called when we speak of men.

A prisoner who is not state-raised tolerates the situation because of his social maturity prior to incarceration. He knows things are different outside prison. But the state-raised convict has no conception of any difference. He lacks experience and, hence, maturity. His judgment is untempered, rash; his emotions are impulsive, raw, unmellowed.

There are emotions – a whole spectrum of them – that I know of only through words, through reading and my immature imagination. I can *imagine* I feel those emotions (know, therefore, what they are), but *I do not*. At age thirty-seven I am barely a precocious child. My passions are those of a boy.

This thing I related above about emotions is the hidden, dark side of state-raised convicts. The foul underbelly everyone hides from everyone else. There is something else. It is the other half – which concerns *judgment, reason* (moral, ethical, cultural). It is the mantle of pride, integrity, honor. It is the high esteem we naturally have for violence, force. It is what makes us *effective*, men whose judgment impinges on others, on the world: Dangerous killers who act alone and *without* emotion, who act with calculation and principles, to avenge themselves, establish and defend their principles with acts of murder that usually evade prosecution by law: this is the state-raised convicts' conception of manhood, in the highest sense.

The model we emulate is a fanatically defiant and alienated individual who cannot imagine what forgiveness is, or mercy or tolerance, because he has no *experience* of such values. His emotions do not know what such values are, but he *imagines* them as so many "weaknesses" precisely because the unprincipled offender appears to escape punishment through such "weaknesses" on the part of society.

But if you behave like a man (a man such as yourself) you are doomed; you are feared and hated. You are "crazy" by the standards of the authorities – by their prejudices against prison-behavior.

Can you imagine how I feel – to be treated as a little boy and not as a man? And when I was a little boy, I was treated as a man – and can you imagine what that does to a boy? (I keep waiting for the years to give me a sense of humor, but so far that has evaded me completely.)

So. A guard frowns at me and says: "Why are you not at work?" Or: "Tuck in your shirttail!" Do this and do that. The way a little boy is spoken to. This is something I have had to deal with not for a year or two – nor even ten years – but for, so far, eighteen years. And when I explode, then I have burnt myself by behaving like a contrite and unruly little boy. So I have, in order to avoid that deeper humiliation, developed a method of reversing the whole situation–and I become the man chastising the little boy. (Poor kid!) It has cost me dearly, and not just in terms of years in prison or in the hole.

I cannot adjust to daily life in prison. For almost twenty years this has been true. I have never gone a month in prison without incurring disciplinary action for violating "rules." Not in all these years.

Does this mean I must die in prison? Does this mean I cannot "adjust" to society outside prison?

The government answers *yes* – but I *remember* society, and it is not like prison. I feel that if I ever did *adjust to prison*, I could by that alone never adjust to society. I would be back in prison within months.

Now, I care about myself and I cannot let it happen that I cannot adjust to freedom. Even if it means spending my life in prison – because to me prison is nothing but mutiny and revolt. [. . .]

A round peg will not fit into a square slot. I don't think they'll ever let me out of prison so long as my release depends upon my "good adjustment to prison." [. . .]

PART FOUR

Social and spatial structure of community

INTRODUCTION

AT THE CORE OF criminological research lies the challenge of determining what gives rise to and shapes criminal offending. Some of the most interesting new work focuses on the social and spatial structure of community. These works fall into two main groups. The first, social control theories, highlights the power of social control against universal human tendencies to crime. This is exerted by social bonds and webs of community relationships in curtailing offending. The second, situational crime prevention and routine activity theories, depict crime as a rational choice in response to promising opportunities presented through scheduling, lack of protection or proximity.

In recent years, much attention has refocused on the role of community social disorganization for crime. Arguments, primarily from strain theory, about the criminogenic effects of economic disadvantage were challenged by a return of attention to social disorganization and the weakening of the control afforded by families, their cultural practices and neighborhood institutions. Deprivation, after initially being softpedalled, was then to be shown to be working through cultural and institutional mechanisms, such as parenting, which incorporated those socio-economic effects. Thus, it became clear that disadvantage was working through micro-processes of control to influence the propensity for crime.

Not all scholars agreed that this was the entire story, though there was broad agreement that these conclusions were a major advance. Some scholars, especially Elliott Currie, argued that economic deprivation exerted an independent effect on the propensity for criminal offending. In important related work, Kenneth Land and his colleagues sharpened that claim to focus it on extreme poverty which he and his associates showed in a methodologically sophisticated analysis to be directly related to crime. In England, Box and also Taylor have shown that unemployment, which can produce harsh relative deprivation, is strongly associated with crime. Bursik and Grasmick confirm an independent effect of extreme economic deprivation. They suggest that this may be due to intervening factors such as ability to connect with networks of power and funding. Recently, Claude Fischer and his colleagues at the University of California at Berkely have pointed to the consequences of public policies in actively perpetuating or, in some actually creating "structured inequality" that could be a source of such deprivation.

From a social control and social bond perspective, both the experience of relationships and their socializing effects importantly shape behavior. Robert Sampson and John Laub have shown that for youth at risk, parenting, peers and schools emerge as especially powerful influences. Their presence and expectations, the responsibilities they bring, the sense of attachment and belonging they create, the involvement in groups and their norms, and the contribution to ego development and self control that relationships foster all work to constrain potentially delinquent behavior. From a social control perspective, we are all potential delinquents.

Community social disorganization can, as Robert Sampson and William Julius Wilson also demonstrate, produce concentrations of families with weak parenting and unconstructive family processes – especially due to stress, harsh and erratic discipline, alcoholism and abuse. The nature of these effects are controversial. Growing up in such an environment also can weaken one's sense of self, ego strength and inner control as well as limiting one's scripts for reading situations and responding. These problems of one's inner world can be further exacerbated by subsequent labelling.

Peer groups are another primary formative influence though here the influence of social relationships may reinforce rather than inhibit crime. Peers may coalesce in gangs either due to threats and losses, as in some of the groups that Scott Decker and Barrik Van Winkle study, or on a basis of attachment and easy sociability. Though often thought of as urban, comparable groups of punks, skinheads and others are now forming in suburbs too.

Situational and routine activity theories, which depict crime as a rational choice, examine why, when and where crime happens. Returning to a focus on the criminal act rather than the "career" or "life course" of the offender, this work explores the conditions that shift the balance of decision on the part of a prospective offender in favour of crime.

Recent elegant research in Britain by Bottoms and Wiles (2002) has analyzed neighborhood and housing market structure in terms of their implications for patterns of crime under a rational choice paradigm. Not surprisingly, proximity to major arteries, council estates, magnet shopping centres and commercial areas were associated with higher frequency of crime. Thus, they combine spatial and social structure within an environmental analysis that promises to be helpful in clarifying the extent to which crime is a choice.

While social control and rational choice theories have highlighted the role of social relationships, institutions and the spatial environment as contextual factors giving rise to or inhibiting crime, both perspectives have tended to downplay an independent direct effect of economic deprivation on crime. That does appear to be changing now. Increasingly, attention has refocused on how disadvantage may work through these cultural and spatial features of community life to shape the propensity for offending. While crime always involves an element of choice, the question is whether everyone faces the same choices and, in light of the palette from which he or she works, is really being held accountable to the same standards? It is fashionable among policymakers, who are committed to "responsibilizing" the individual, to exhort that crime is always a choice. Yet, is this not a bit like a parent sending their teenage daughter off on an unchaperoned co-ed sleepover with advice to "be good." This research challenges the notion of the individual as the focus of criminological analyses. It directs our attention to the spatial, social and institutional structure of our communities and society as a whole.

Chapter 17

Anthony E. Bottoms and Paul Wiles

ENVIRONMENTAL CRIMINOLOGY

From: Anthony E. Bottoms and Paul Wiles (1997), excerpts from 'Environmental criminology', in Mike Maguire et al., *Oxford Handbook of Criminology*, 2nd edn, Oxford: Oxford University Press, pp. 305–359.

ENVIRONMENTAL CRIMINOLOGY IS THE study of crime, criminality, and victimization as they relate, first, to particular places, and secondly, to the way that individuals and organizations shape their activities spatially, and in so doing are in turn influenced by place-based or spatial factors.

Environmental criminology would be of little interest – either to scholars or those concerned with criminal policy – if the geographical distribution of offences, or of offender residence, were random. In fact this is (as we shall shortly see) very far from being the case. Indeed, in recent criminology there has been an increasing interest in the geographical 'hotspots' of crime and criminality which matches the parallel interest in other 'skews' in criminological data (for example, the fact that relatively few persistent offenders commit a very disproportionate proportion of all street crimes). [. . .]

Traditionally, the two central concerns of environmental criminology have been *explaining the spatial distribution of offences* and *explaining the spatial distribution of offenders*. Hence, sections on these topics will form the core of this chapter. [. . .]

ENVIRONMENTAL CRIMINOLOGY: A BRIEF HISTORY

[. . .]

Because of its major subsequent influence, considerable attention must be paid to the criminological work carried out between the two world wars from within the Chicago School of Sociology (for general accounts of this group of sociologists, see Bulmer, 1984 and Kurtz, 1984).

The main Chicagoan criminological contribution came from Clifford Shaw and Henry McKay, whose *magnum opus* on juvenile delinquency in urban areas is still read, half a century on (Shaw and McKay, 1942). As well as making a theoretical contribution themselves – notably through the theory of 'social disorganisation' (see below) – Shaw and

McKay's research heavily influenced much other criminological theory in the 1930s, notably Thorsten Sellin's (1938) 'culture conflict' theory and Edwin Sutherland's theory of differential association (see Cressey, 1964). But Shaw and McKay's main contribution to criminology was empirical, and here their research embraced two very different styles, always seen by the authors as complementary: first mapping the residences of juvenile delinquents in Chicago and then in other American cities, . . . and, second . . . histories of offenders and low life in the city (see for example Shaw, 1930). For present purposes, we can concentrate mainly on the first. [. . .]

In developing this research, they drew upon the work in urban sociology of the Chicago School, notably that of Robert E. Park and Ernest W. Burgess, the dominant concept of which was 'human ecology'. Human ecology [is . . .] the study of the spatial and temporal relations of human beings as affected by the selective, distributive, and accommodative forces of the environment: the concept was derived, by analogy, from the botanical sub-discipline of plant ecology. Shaw and McKay drew only to a limited extent upon the most explicitly quasi-biological elements of Park's urban sociology (see Alihan, 1938: 83), but they made quite central use of Burgess's zonal theory of city development. According to this theory, the typical city could be conceptualized as consisting of five main concentric zones (see Figure 17.1), the innermost of which was described as the non-residential central business district (or 'loop'), which was then circled by a 'zone in transition' where factories and poorer residences were intermingled, and finally by three residential zones of increasing affluence and social status. New immigrants, it was postulated, would move into the cheapest residential areas of the city (in the 'zone in transition') and then, as they became economically established, migrate outwards. This would be a continuous process, so that the 'zone in transition' would (as its name implies) have a high residential mobility rate and, by implication, a rather heterogeneous population. In the case of a rapidly expanding city, particular districts

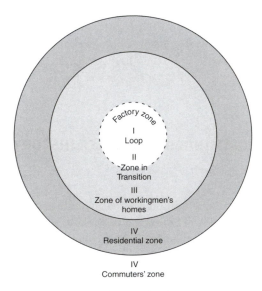

Figure 17.1 E. W. Burgess's zone model of urban development
Source: Burgess (1925).

which had once been peripheral and affluent might become, in time, part of the zone in transition within the larger metropolis (see e.g. Rex and Moore, 1967, on Sparkbrook, Birmingham).

Applying this zonal model to their empirical data, Shaw and McKay made the following three central discoveries:

> *First*, the rates of juvenile delinquency residence conformed to a regular spatial pattern. They were highest in the inner-city zones and tended to decline with distance from the centre of the city; and this was so not only in Chicago but in other cities as well (see Table 17.1).
>
> *Secondly*, the same spatial pattern was shown by many other indices of social problems in the city.
>
> *Thirdly*, the spatial pattern of rates of delinquency showed considerable long-term stability, even though the nationality make-up of the population in the inner-city areas changed greatly from decade to decade (with successive waves of migration to American cities in the early twentieth century).

In seeking to explain these striking findings, Shaw and McKay focused especially upon the observed *cultural heterogeneity* and the *constant population movements* in the 'zone in transition'. As Robert Bursik (1986: 38) has pointed out, economic mobility lay at the heart of the process they described, but they did not posit a direct relationship between economic factors and rates of delinquency – rather, areas characterized by economic deprivation and physical deterioration were seen also as having population instability and cultural fragmentation, and it was these factors which especially influenced delinquency through a process which they called 'social disorganization'. . . . This process, as seen by Shaw and McKay, was later well summarized by Finestone (1976: 28–9) in a passage that is worth quoting in full:

> The same selective processes which made it relatively easy for the first generation of newcomers to the city to become aggregated in inner-city areas also permitted the location there of many illegitimate enterprises and deviant moral worlds. . . . In the face of many centrifugal pulls, the traditional

Table 17.1 Delinquency residence rates for the concentric zones of seven American cities, *c.* 1930

	Zone 1	Zone 2	Zone 3	Zone 4	Zone 5
Chicago	10.3	7.3	4.4	3.3	—
Philadelphia	11.6	6.8	4.4	3.5	3.4
Richmond	19.7	12.2	6.4	—	—
Cleveland	18.3	10.2	7.8	7.0	5.1
Birmingham	14.1	6.9	6.4	—	—
Denver	9.4	7.1	4.2	3.7	3.2
Seattle	19.1	9.7	7.6	6.1	—

Source: Brantingham and Brantingham (1981: 14), collating data from various tables in Shaw and McKay (1931).

institutions, the family, the church, and the local community, became incapable of maintaining their solidarity. . . . Continued high rates of delinquents in inner-city areas were a product of the joint operation of locational and cultural processes which maximised the moral diversity of population types at the same time as they weakened the collective efforts of conventional groups and institutions to protect their own integrity.

Hence in Shaw and McKay's thinking, 'social disorganization exists in the first instance when the structure and culture of a community are incapable of implementing and expressing the values of its own residents' (Kornhauser, 1978: 63); and this was seen as strongly related to the genesis of juvenile delinquency because the community did not provide common and clear non-delinquent values and control.

The subsequent history of the social disorganization concept is complex, and there have been a number of criticisms such as [the theory's underemphasis on criminal...] subcultures, . . . insufficient attention to the distribution of power in society (see Snodgrass, 1976; cf. Bursik, 1986: 61); . . . and [sometimes uses . . .] a single indicator (such as a delinquency rate) both as an example of disorganization and as an effect allegedly caused [by . . .] disorganization. Finally, like a number of other early socio-logical theories of crime, it has been argued that social disorganization theory is over-deterministic and therefore over-predictive of crime (see e.g. Matza, 1964). Despite these criticisms, the concept of social disorganization remains a live one today. [. . .]

But the 1970s were to see environmental criminology given fresh impetus; and in this respect two main developments were of particular importance.

The first of these might be described as the *rediscovery of the offence*. Shaw and McKay's work had been all about *areas of delinquent residence*, i.e. the areas where the juvenile delinquents lived. But these *high offender rate areas* are in fact not necessarily the same as *high offence rate areas* since offenders do not necessarily commit offences close to their homes. [. . .]

This 'rediscovery of the offence' in environmental criminology has been of major importance. Moreover, the careful synthesis of work on the explanation of *who commits offences* (offender-based theory) with work on the explanation of *where and why offences are committed* (offence-based theory) can be regarded as an issue of central significance in contemporary criminology.

The second major development of the 1970s came more in the field of explaining offender rates. Once again, it had its precursors. In his pioneering book, Terence Morris (1957) carried out an empirical study of Croydon, and showed that the areal rates of offender residence in that borough did not conform particularly well to the Chicago zonal hypothesis, not least because of the existence of high offender rate council estates located at a considerable distance from the urban centre . . . Morris (1957: 130) shrewdly observed that:

> where the provision of housing is not solely within the province of the market, and the local authority has stepped in to provide housing as a social amenity for a not inconsiderable proportion of the population, then the natural ecological processes of selection manifesting themselves in the cycle of 'invasion-dominance-succession' are likely to be severely modified by social policy, with strikingly different results.

All these points were to be confirmed and strengthened in work in the city of Sheffield, published in the 1970s (Baldwin and Bottoms 1976). . . .

These considerations have taken some researchers working on crime-related topics deep into analyses of the complex housing market contexts of particular local areas (see for example Taub et al., 1984; Bottoms et al., 1989).

The *rediscovery of the offence* and the *discovery of the significance of housing markets* have, between them, done much to revivify environmental criminology in the last quarter of a century. [. . .]

EXPLAINING THE LOCATION OF OFFENCES

We begin with the explanation of the location of offences. . . . Wikström's study provides one of the best illustrations of the way in which police recorded offences are locationally distributed in a major city. Previous research work in Sheffield (Baldwin and Bottoms, 1976) and elsewhere had shown that offences in general tend, in traditional cities, to be very much clustered around the city centre; and the offence rates in Wikström's study (see Figure 17.2 (a), (b), and (c)) show this to be especially the case for violence in public, vandalism in public, and theft of and from cars. [. . .]

Turning to offences in residential areas, the distributions of family violence and residential burglaries in Wikström's study are shown in Figure 17.2 (d) and (e). The highest rates of family violence were found in certain outer-city wards, and further analysis showed that there was a strong positive correlation (at an area level) between (i) an area's rates of recorded family violence and (ii) its score on a factor (derived from a factor analysis of social areas in Stockholm) which was labelled by Wikström as 'problem residential areas' (Wikström, 1991: 226). [Hence, p]olice-recorded family violence was heavily concentrated in poorer public housing areas. A further inspection of the maps at Figure 17.2 (d) and (e), indicates however that the distribution of offences of residential burglary was substantially different from that of family violence, and additional analysis by Wikström (1991: 226–7) showed that residential burglaries in fact tended to occur in areas of high socio-economic status, and especially in districts where there were nearby high offender-rate areas. This finding, while not unique in the literature, conflicts with the results of some other research studies, which suggest that rates of residential burglary are greatest in, or in areas close to, socially disadvantaged housing areas (for a summary, see Maguire and Bennett, 1982: 20–1). Possible reasons for these conflicting results will become apparent as the discussion proceeds.

Wikström's study fairly conclusively demonstrates, at any rate as regards crimes as measured by official data, *first* that there are marked geographical skews in the patterning of offence locations, and *secondly* that these can vary significantly by type of offence. This general message has been heavily reinforced, at a micro level of analysis, by research on so-called 'hotspots' of crime. For example, Lawrence Sherman et al. (1989) used 'police call data' for the city of Minneapolis for 1985–6, and found, *inter alia*, (i) that just 3.3 percent of specific addresses or intersections in the city generated 50 per cent of crime-related calls to the police to which cars were despatched, and (ii) that there was considerable variation in the victimization rate (as measured by call data) of specific micro-locations even *within* high crime rate areas – that is, even high-crime areas have their relatively safe specific locations, as well as their 'hotspots' where the public are likely to be especially vulnerable. [. . .]

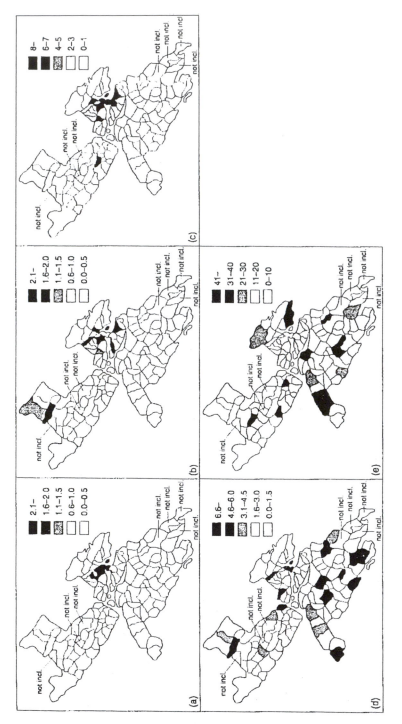

Figure 17.2 Areal offence rates for selected types of crime. Stockholm, 1982: (a) violence in public per hectare; (b) vandalism in public per hectare; (c) thefts of and from cars per hectare; (d) family violence per 1,000 households; (e) residential burglaries per 1,000 residences

Source: Wikström (1991: 203–6).

Opportunity theory and routine activities theory

As Clarke (1995) has shown in some detail, the concept of opportunity is a multifaceted one. In the context of environmental criminology, two aspects of opportunity are especially important (Bursik and Grasmick, 1993: 70). The first of these can be described as *target attractiveness*, a concept which includes both value (monetary and/or symbolic) and portability. [. . .]

The second main dimension of opportunity might be described as *accessibility*, a concept that includes visibility, ease of physical access, and the absence of adequate surveillance. [. . .]

The 'opportunity' approach to the explanation of crime patterns, as outlined above, is very closely related to so-called 'routine activities theory', originally developed in an article by Cohen and Felson (1979) and subsequently elaborated mostly by Marcus Felson and others (see e.g. Felson, 1986, 1992, and 1995 and Eck, 1995). The central hypothesis of routine activities theory was originally stated as: 'the probability that a violation will occur at any specific time and place might be taken as a function of the convergence of likely offenders and suitable targets in the absence of capable guardians' (Cohen and Felson, 1979, 590).

However, of the three elements identified in the above quotation, routine activities theory (as developed by its advocates) has in practice concentrated very heavily on the second and third (suitable targets and capable guardians). That being so, the link with opportunity theory is self-evident; but there are nevertheless two features of the routine activities approach which develop and in a sense extend the straightforward concept of 'opportunity'. *First*, there is a strong interest within routine activities theory in *the day-to-day activities of potential victims of crime, and of those potentially able to offer 'natural surveillance'*. *Secondly*, routine activities theory has an explicitly spatial dimension which, while implicitly present in simple opportunity theory, has not always been much developed by writers of that school. Routine activities theory because of its interest in the everyday lives of potential victims of crime and of potential 'natural guardians', specifically emphasizes 'the . . . human ecological character of illegal acts as *events* which occur at specific locations in *space* and *time*. . . '. (Cohen and Felson, 1979: 589, emphasis in original).

In sum, routine activities theory in effect embeds the concept of opportunity within the parameters of the day-to-day lives of ordinary people, and in doing so also emphasizes the spatial-temporal features of opportunity. [. . .]

Once one begins – as in Cohen and Felson's approach – to link the opportunity concept to that of routine activities, then other relevant issues in considering the spatial distribution of offences also begin to become apparent. One such issue is that of *self-policing*, as it affects potential offences against the person. Potential victims can respond to possible opportunities for them to be attacked by various kinds of 'avoidance' behaviour. [. . .]

Taking all the evidence of this subsection together, there is not much doubt that the broad concept of 'opportunity' (understood here as incorporating the routine activities approach) powerfully influences crime locations. But is it the *only* relevant variable to be considered in explaining the spatial distribution of offences? [. . .]

Unfortunately, the research literature suggests that matters are more complex than this. To begin to see why that is so, let us first consider an ethnographic study of convicted burglars in a Texas city (Cromwell et al., 1991). These authors found, congruently with opportunity theory, that offenders weighed potential gains, levels of guardianship (e.g. signs of occupancy) and risks of detection at possible sites of residential burglary (see also Bennett and Wright 1984). Hence, it appeared that *active weighing of the opportunity factor at the potential crime site* was a significant factor in the ultimate decision whether or not to commit a particular crime. On the other hand, Cromwell et al. also found that there was individual variation in the degree of planning between burglars (see also Bennett and Wright, 1984); complex interactive effects within groups of burglars; differences related to whether illicit drugs were used by the offenders; and that interactions with fences could affect the decision processes.

Opportunity theory uses a rational model of decision-making, but all too often its exponents have assumed both that the form of rationality is instrumental and that the actual behaviour mirrors the model. . . . Cromwell et al.'s (1991) research suggests a less straightforward empirical reality, and this view has been strongly reinforced by the most recent research on burglars' decision-making, by Wright and Decker (1994), which shows that decisions to offend can be irrational, arational, or rational, and, when rational, are more likely to be affectually rather than instrumentally rational and be driven by short-term, immediate emotional needs. Insofar as targets were instrumentally assessed for degree of risk, Wright and Decker found that because most crimes were committed to satisfy an immediate need (for money, drugs etc.) this was more often based on existing routine knowledge rather than a calculated process of crime planning prior to the act. [. . .]

Offenders' use of space

It is a commonplace of criminological textbooks that much crime is committed close to offenders' homes, though, not surprisingly, that is more likely to be true for juvenile delinquents than for adult offenders (see e.g. Baldwin and Bottoms, 1976). However, while a number of so-called 'crime and distance' studies may be found in the literature, empirically exploring the data on detected offenders' distance from home when committing offences, it can plausibly be argued that this issue is in fact rather less interesting than is the related question of *the relationship of the place of the offence to the offender's habitual use of space*. [. . .]

In preliminary exploration of this issue, let us first note that there are some purely *opportunist* crimes, where a person responds 'there and then' to a set of attractive environmental cues . . . and also some *affectively spontaneous* crimes. These offences, by definition, must occur in the place where the offender happens to be, as a result of his/ her daily life-choices. More than a decade ago, however, Patricia and Paul Brantingham (1981) proposed, in a very interesting hypothetical paper, that the offender's daily life patterns might influence the location of offending behaviour even where the offender was engaging, to some degree, in a search pattern for a suitable target, having already decided in principle to commit an offence (as, perhaps, in burglary). All of us, it was argued by these authors, carry in our heads 'cognitive maps' of cities where we live. . . . The Brantinghams innovatively postulated that most offenders will not commit offences in poorly known areas; hence offences, even 'search pattern' offences, were, they argued, most likely to occur where *criminal opportunities* intersected with *cognitively known areas* – a hypothesis schematically illustrated in Figure 17.3.

Figure 17.3 The Brantinghams' hypothetical model of intersection of criminal opportunities with offenders' cognitive awareness space
Source: Brantingham and Brantingham (1984: 362).

Whilst the degree of empirical testing of this hypothetical model has not been extensive, what evidence we have tends clearly to support it, at least for many crimes (see for example Rhodes and Conly, 1981; Brantingham and Brantingham, 1991: 1–5, 239–51; Figlio et al., 1986: Part 2). [. . .]

These results and suggestions provide a plausible reason why so much offending takes place near offender's homes or other areas in which they routinely and regularly move.

Multiple victimization

At this point, we must further complicate the emerging picture by drawing attention to a topic that has, until recently, been systematically neglected in criminological explanation, namely the issue of *multiple victimization*. [. . .]

First, multiple victimization is not uncommon and the rate of multiple victimization varies by offence. For example, of those who reported being victimized in the 1996 British Crime Survey, 19 per cent of burglary victims had been victimized more than once; 28 per cent of car theft victims and 37 per cent of contact crime victims (Mirlees-Black et al., 1996 – see also Farrell, 1995).

Secondly, even more interesting is that multiple victimization not only varies by offence type but its geographical distribution is also skewed. In particular multiple victimization is more common in high crime areas. Analysis by the Quantitative Criminology Group at Manchester University of the 1982 BCS data showed that 'the number of victimisations per victim rises markedly as area crime rates increase' (Trickett et al., 1992) and, furthermore, between 1982 and 1988 the whole of the increased inequality in crime incidence as between different geographical areas in England and Wales was attributable to multiple victimization (Pease, 1993).

Thirdly, although multiple victimization is more common in high crime areas not everyone living in such areas is necessarily victimized, let alone multiply victimized. This is because multiple victimization is also very unevenly distributed between individuals and households, and therefore geographically skewed even within high crime areas. . . . This skewed pattern mirrors, in a general sense, the skewed distribution of offence locations found by the hot spots analysis discussed earlier. [. . .]

Wikström's tentative model for explaining offence locations

So far, in this major section on explaining the location of offences, we have discussed opportunities, the routine activities of the general population, the routine activities of offenders, and the role of multiple victimization. It is now time to try to draw some threads together, and seek to develop, if possible, some overall framework for understanding the way in which offences are geographically distributed.

Such a task was attempted by the Swedish criminologist Per-Olof Wikström (1990), as a prelude to a major study of crime in Stockholm. Wikström's 'tentative model', as he calls it, for the explanation of variations in crime rates and types of crime in the urban environment is set out in Figure 17.4. This model begins (see left-hand box) by emphasizing basic *variations in land use* within the urban environment. This feature has two aspects: first, the types of activities which take place in the area (e.g. is the area . . . residential, shopping, industrial, leisure area, etc.); and secondly, the composition of the population at any given time (including both residents and visitors). In drawing attention to these matters, Wikström also rightly emphasizes that particular areas may be the host to different kinds of activities (and/or populations) on different days of the week, or at different times of the day. [. . .]

Wikström's model then postulates that the *variations in land use* of the left-hand box will directly influence a number of criminologically relevant social interactions (see central box). The first of these is intended to embrace not only Cohen and Felson's emphasis on the routine activities of the general population, but also the Brantinghams' (1981) work on the cognitive spatial awareness of offenders (see Wikström, 1990: 21). Wikström goes on to point out, however, that Cohen and Felson's concept of 'suitable targets' focuses principally upon theft and theft-related offences and upon instrumental personal crimes (e.g. robbery, stranger rape), and is less easily applied to expressive crimes (the majority of assaults or malicious damage). Wikström therefore adds to the central box both 'encounters and environments liable to promote friction' and

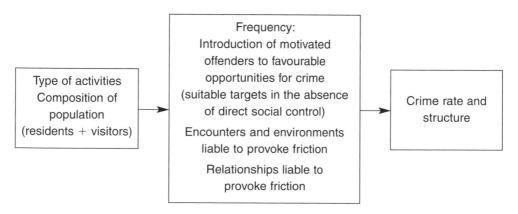

Figure 17.4 Wikström's tentative model for explaining variation in crime rate and types of crime in the urban environment
Source: Wikström (1990: 24).

'relationships liable to promote friction' (Wikström, 1990: 22–3). . . . Addition of these dimensions re-enforces the overall emphasis on routine activities. [. . .]

Wikström's 'tentative model' for explaining the location of offences is of very great interest and value. However, a number of points perhaps need to be made in elaboration and modification of the model.

In the first place, we should note that Wikström's model effectively begins with *variations in land use* in the city, taking this as essentially given. . . . Conceptually, however, it is perhaps worth taking this process a stage further by trying to set urban sub-areas within a wider sociological and geographical framework, in an attempt to explain more fully the types of activities and population composition found within specific areas. . . . A useful framework for this kind of exercise has been suggested by the geographer David Herbert (1982: 26). . . . His analysis very helpfully draws attention to the importance of three different levels of analysis. First, there are the *macro-level material, political, and ideological factors* (of both political economy and ideology) – what Giddens (1984: 283) calls the 'structural principles' of a given society. Secondly, meso level *allocative processes*, within a given society, have considerable importance. Thirdly, both *spatial behaviour/processes* and the *meaning of place* are important at an individual or micro level – the latter being a specially significant issue, which has not always been given adequate attention by environmental criminologists. [. . .]

With such modifications and developments, Wikström's outline model is of very considerable value in the explanation of offence locations.

EXPLAINING THE LOCATION OF OFFENDER RESIDENCE

We turn now to the problem of explaining the observed area distribution of offender residence. As seen in an earlier section, traditionally this subject was heavily dominated by the conceptualizations of the Chicago School; and the explanations of the Chicago School were themselves strongly influenced by the facts of *stability over time* in the distribution of area offender rates, and (essentially) to the nature of land use in different zones of the city as an outcome of the operation of the market (Bursik, 1986: 61).

Post-World War II evidence, however, dealt a mortal blow to these under-pinning assumptions. As we saw earlier, . . . offender rates in post-war British cities have borne little resemblance to the Chicagoan concentric ring pattern. Even in Chicago, careful analysis by Bursik (1986) has shown that the old areal regularities have broken down, and that while the areas of the city that underwent the most rapid social change generally experienced considerable increases in delinquency, nevertheless, there were some atypical areas where this relationship did not hold (Taub et al., 1984). Hence, while Shaw and McKay's social disorganization theory is still being supported and developed, noone would now defend – at least in any generalized fashion – the Chicago concentric ring theory and the formulation of urban process that went with it.

In order to see what might replace this approach, we shall look first at some statistical studies of the distribution of offender rates, and secondly at some more focused field research in local communities. Before turning to this evidence, however, let us consider how, in principle, area of residence and offender rates might be statistically related (this discussion develops that of Wikström, 1991: 130).

First, area of residence and offender rates might be related because more or less crime-prone individuals or groups are distributed (by the dynamics of the local housing market) to certain areas. In this kind of correlation, however, the social life of the area itself does not affect the criminality levels of the residents. To take an extreme example . . . some small council estates in British cities are reserved for elderly tenants; obviously, one would expect such areas to have low offender rates, for reasons unconnected with social processes within the area.

Secondly, however, in principle *the social life of the area might itself influence criminal motivation*; and this possible influence is itself of two types. First, friendship patterns among local residents may lead to one being influenced by others to commit an offence. In such cases, it can be assumed (for the sake of argument) that the transaction is a one-off affair not necessarily affecting the person's general way of living. Secondly, however, the social life of an area might have longer-term effects on a person's daily routines, social activities, thought processes, and even personality, such that his/her overall propensity to commit crime in certain situations is intrinsically affected. This kind of longer-term effect is obviously most likely to be manifested among young residents of an area. . . .

In describing the first of the above possibilities, we referred to the operations of the local housing market as obviously relevant to the distribution of more or less crime-prone individuals to different areas. One of our own central contentions is that the housing market is also the key to understanding the kinds of processes described in the second paragraph, but in order to see why this is so, we must examine some research studies.

Statistical studies of offender-rate distribution

When the study of criminology at the University of Sheffield began, in the late 1960s, it was decided that it would be sensible to attempt, as a first major research project, a statistical study of recorded crime and offending in the city. Shortly before this project was begun, Rex and Moore (1967) had published an influential sociological analysis of Commonwealth migration to Birmingham, which emphasized how the detailed rules and social practices concerning access to particular kinds of housing were of *general* sociological importance in shaping the population composition of different geographical areas, and had significant subsequent effects on the kind of social community and social life developed in various districts. These observations seemed to the Sheffield researchers to be of some importance. Hence, in the statistical study of offender data and Census data that was then undertaken, it was decided to operationalize Rex and Moore's insights by classifying each Census enumeration district in terms of its predominant housing type, and then seeing whether these were of importance in 'explaining' (statistically) the offender rates of urban sub-areas, when population data were also considered. The answer proved to be emphatically in the affirmative (Baldwin and Bottoms, 1976: chapter 4). It was also found, however, that there were major variations in offender rates *within* the range of areas that shared a predominant housing type – for example, some council housing areas had very high offender rates, and some very low rates – and some preliminary more detailed exploration of the council sector revealed, *inter alia*, that there was no statistically significant relationship between the rate of tenant turnover on council estates and the offender rate (Baldwin and Bottoms 1976: 149–51, 169–71). These findings clearly suggested a potential importance for the housing market in explaining offender rates, but also . . . indicated that one would have to look beyond the conceptualizations of the Chicago School – which, as we have seen, placed a special emphasis on residential mobility – if adequate sense were to be made of the data. [. . .]

Following on from the Sheffield statistical analysis of offender rates, Wikström (1991) conducted a similar analysis for Stockholm. He adopted a path model approach, hypothesizing that housing tenure variables would feed through to population composition variables, with the whole providing some statistical explanation of the varying offender rates in different districts. The final path model found that the housing type and social composition of areas explained about half the area variation in the total offender rates. [. . .]

Detailed studies of particular areas

Whilst the statistical studies of offender rates on a whole-city basis (in Sheffield and Stockholm) seem to suggest that one must go beyond social class and social status in explaining differential offender rates, and seem further to suggest that the housing market is likely to be important, . . . they cannot address the qualitative aspects of social processes in particular areas.

Work in Sheffield subsequent to Baldwin and Bottoms's (1976) statistical analysis did, however, attempt this. In particular, three pairs of small areas with contrasting offender rates were selected on the basis of the prior statistical analysis, with each pair being (in the mid-1970s) of a different housing type, as follows:

> *Pair 1: Low-rise council housing*
> Two adjacent areas, one with a high offender rate, one with a lower rate.
> *Pair 2: High-rise council dwellings*
> Two adjacent areas, one with a high offender rate, one with a lower rate.
> *Pair 3: Privately rented areas*
> Two non-adjacent areas, one with a high offender rate, one with a lower rate. The high-rate area was also, in the mid-1970s, Sheffield's principal prostitution area.

We will concentrate attention here on the first of these pairs, as it was in the mid-1970s (the following account draws principally upon Bottoms, Mawby, and Xanthos, 1989; for a follow-up study of the same areas in the 1980s see Bottoms, Claytor, and Wiles, 1992). Briefly, the original problem for explanation . . . was that these two small areas (population 2,500–3,000 each, and separated only by a main road), had (i) a 300 per cent difference in recorded offender rates, and a 350 per cent difference in recorded offence rates against individual residents and households, but (ii) no statistically significant differences at all on a set of key demographic variables (namely, sex; age; social class; ethnic origin; mean household size; percentage single; percentage male unemployment; age of termination of full-time education; and length of stay in current dwelling). Preliminary research (adult victim and juvenile self-report studies) established that the crime rate differences could not, for the most part, be regarded as artefactual. A further point of interest was that both areas had been built at approximately the same time (in the first quarter of the twentieth century), and both had, it seemed clear, begun as 'good', crime-free council areas. One of the estates (Stonewall) had retained this characteristic, but its neighbour (Gardenia) had 'tipped' sometime in the 1940s. Neither, however, was in any serious sense an 'area in transition'; rather, they were extremely settled, with 60 per cent of the adult residents in both areas having lived in their current dwelling for ten years or more.

The research team was unable to discover retrospectively exactly why Gardenia had tipped. . . . But through detailed analysis of records in the local authority's housing department, plus ethnographic work, we were able to show that, once Gardenia had tipped, the local authority's rules of housing allocation had the unintended effects of maintaining the difference between the two areas, and of ensuring that Gardenia attracted, as new tenants, predominantly (i) those in severe housing need, and (ii) those who had prior affective links with the area (relatives living on the estate etc.). To some extent, therefore, housing allocative processes were drawing to the two estates new residents with a differential propensity to offend (i.e. the first possible explanation for differential offender rates discussed earlier). On the other hand, ethnographic work also showed that the second likely explanation also applied: the factors involved were very complex, and interactive, but included (in addition to the housing market context) certain physical geographical features: a mild criminal sub-culture in one part of the more criminal estate (Gardenia); the effects of the negative reputation of Gardenia on its residents and on potential residents: possibly a difference relating to the main schools serving the two areas; and some important differences in parental and peer socialization processes (see Bottoms, Mawby, and Xanthos, 1989: 67–75, especially 74). [. . .]

The operation of the local housing market, however, does not work in a stand-alone fashion, nor only in relation to the population composition of an area. Rather, the Sheffield researchers stressed that the housing market could have crucial secondary social effects – in terms of, for example, the nature of the relationships which subsequently developed in an area, or responses by outsiders (including social control agents, potential residents, etc.). Subsequently, some of these effects might themselves have the potential to influence the housing market context of the area, e.g. by altering the area's perceived desirability, or perhaps escalating the number of residents wishing to leave. [. . .]

Without discussing the other Sheffield areas in detail here, it is of note that the three high offender rate areas studied were (in the 1970s) very different in social terms. Both the other two high rate areas had higher proportions of recent move-ins than Gardenia (indicative of greater overall residential mobility). Alone of the three high rate areas, fewer than half of those living in the high-rise high-crime area (Skyhigh) said they felt they belonged to the area, and a higher proportion than in any other area said they would like to move elsewhere. . . . Meanwhile, the privately rented high-crime area was the only one of the three with substantial prostitution and drugs problems, and the only one with a sizeable ethnic minority population. These various points of difference between high offender-rate areas are of importance, because Chicago theorization would lead one to suppose that all high offender rate areas would tend to share broadly similar social characteristics, yet here were three that were very varied. Moreover, more detailed analysis of these areas showed that their high offender rate status, and the social and crime-type differences of each of them from the other two, could in every case be explained through the direct and indirect consequences of the housing market. [. . .]

Socialization processes and area offender rate differences

One point in the preceding discussion now needs to be developed. When discussing Gardenia and Stonewall, it was noted that there were some important differences in peer and parental socialization processes as between the two estates. Since it is well known in the criminological literature that socialization processes can affect delinquency rates (the concentration here being upon parental socialization), it is not difficult to imagine some critics wishing to argue that much of the observed Gardenia–Stonewall area difference in criminality might be attributable to differential child socialization; the critics might then wish to pursue the case further by suggesting that the socialization difference was an individual effect, and hence that the extent to which there really were additional 'area contextual effects' in operation might be very doubtful (cf. Rutter and Giller, 1983: 204–6).

This line of argument is, however, in our view ultimately flawed, because it fails to take account of the possibility that parental socialization processes might themselves be affected by area contextual characteristics. Yet exactly that possibility has been elaborated – in contradistinction to more traditional socialization theories – in Bronfenbrenner's (1979) so-called 'ecology of human development' frame of reference; and the Swedish criminologist Peter Martens (1990, 1993) has in recent years argued the case for the relevance of Bronfenbrenner's approach in criminological studies.

Bronfenbrenner particularly emphasizes that the child's development has to be seen in its *everyday context*; hence, he focuses less strongly than would some psychologists on purely psychological processes during the child's development, and more strongly on, as Martens (1993) puts it:

> with *whom* the child *interacts* in day-to-day situations, the character of these interactions and in what ways persons outside the family can enhance or inhibit the quality of parent–child interaction. Hence, the focus is on . . . in Bronfenbrenner's own words, 'the actual environments in which human beings live and grow' (Bronfenbrenner, 1979, p. xiv).
>
> (Martens, 1993)

[. . .]

Among the consequences of all this, as Martens (1993) puts it, is that:

> the success of parenting can depend on the support parents receive in their community in the form of social networks (relatives, neighbours, friends, etc.) or social services such as day nurseries and leisure centres. Parents living in a socially stable community have better outward conditions for their role than [other] parents.

At this point in the argument, one can begin to see some very interesting convergences between the way in which criminological understandings of *differential area offence rates* and of *differential area offender rates* have been developing. We saw in an earlier section that explanations of the location of offences now rely substantially, in various ways, on the concept of routine activities; but it was argued (via Herbert's framework) that such explanations needed to be set within a context of macro-social developments, and of meso-level allocative decisions by urban planners and others. As regards offender rates, it has been argued that the housing market (a crucial meso-level allocative mechanism) is of central importance, but that it has to be understood as operating in interaction with other social processes in the production of offender rates. Among those potential social processes is child socialization, and we have argued, via Bronfenbrenner and Martens, that child socialization should be seen not in purely psychological terms, but as influenced by the area context. In understanding that area context, however, not only are the everyday and routine activities of parents and others crucial to the child's socialization, but those processes themselves have to be set within meso-level and macro-level aspects of the organization of the wider society.

THE NEW CHICAGOANS

This chapter began with a fairly full explication of the work of Shaw and McKay, because it has remained a central reference point for much of the subsequent research. The city of Chicago has continued to be used as a vast laboratory for new generations of criminological researchers, and recently Robert Bursik and Harold Grasmick have laid claim to a re-flowering of the Chicago tradition of criminological explanation, and have given fresh prominence (within the context of contemporary criminology) to the study of high offender rate areas (Bursik and Grasmick, 1993). Bursik and Grasmick present two main claims. They argue, first, that continuing research in Chicago (especially that by Bursik himself) supports Shaw and McKay's explanation of differential residential area offender rates: 'the most fully developed aspects of [Shaw and McKay's] model, which focused on the internal dynamics of local communities and the capacity of local residents to regulate the behavior of their fellow neighbors, continue to be significantly related to neighborhood variations in crime rates' (Bursik and Grasmick, 1993: p. x). But, secondly, Bursik and Grasmick argue that although Shaw and McKay saw the city as a set of inter-related neighbourhoods, they failed to take account of each neighbourhood's relations with the external world, and particularly the external world of politically organized social control. This lack, Bursik and Grasmick argue, can be corrected by linking social disorganization theory with control theory, as explicated by Ruth Kornhauser (1978):

> this shortcoming of the social disorganisation perspective can be addressed by reformulating it within a broader systematic theory of community, which emphasises how neighborhood life is shaped by the structure of formal and informal networks of association. Not only is the orientation of a systematic model consistent with social disorganisation in its discussion of the regulatory capacities of networks embedded within the neighborhood, but it also formally addresses two aspects of community structure that Shaw and McKay virtually ignored: the networks amongst residents and local institutions, and the networks amongst local representatives of the neighborhood and external actors, institutions, and agencies.
>
> (Bursik and Grasmick, 1993, p. x)

Bursik and Grasmick argue that much recent research provides empirical evidence for such a re-formulation, or what they refer to as the 'systemic theory of neighbourhood organisation'. Their systemic theory is that social control in neighbourhoods operates at three levels (following Hunter, 1985). The first is the *primary level* by which informal primary groups (such as families or friendship groups) socialize their members against deviance and sanction deviant acts. The second is the *parochial level* at which local networks and organizations (such as schools, businesses, or voluntary groups) exercise control. Finally, there is the *public level* at which agencies external to a neighbourhood either provide the resources to support primary and parochial level control (e.g. by adequately supporting schools or youth groups), or exercise external control, primarily by public policing. Basically, Bursik and Grasmick argue that the development and successful integration of these three levels of control takes time and can, therefore, only properly occur in neighbourhoods which are stable over time. Instability or, to use the concept of the original Chicago School, 'social disorganization' will, therefore, militate against the development of successful neighbourhood control over crime. [. . .]

Bursik and Grasmick reference various studies which they believe have successfully tested at least parts of their systemic theory of offender rates, but in particular they point to the re-analysis of the 1982 British Crime Survey data by Robert Sampson and Byron Groves (1989). Sampson and Groves used the BCS data set because, unlike its American equivalent, it provided sufficient respondents in small areas for analysis and survey data both about crime *and* about social behaviour and networks in areas. Their analysis demonstrates a link between their constructed measures of general area instability and intermediate community level behaviour (especially unsupervised groups of youths on the streets), which in turn are related to self-reported offending rates, and to victimization rates. Their conclusion is that:

> our empirical analysis established that communities characterised by sparse friendship networks, unsupervised teenage peer groups, and low organizational participation had disproportionately high rates of crime and delinquency. Moreover, variations in these dimensions of community social disorganisation were shown to mediate in large part the effects of community structural characteristics (i.e. low socio-economic status, residential mobility, ethnic heterogeneity, and family disruption) in the manner predicted by our theoretical model. We have thus demonstrated that social-disorganisation theory has vitality and renewed relevance for explaining macro-level variations in crime rates.
>
> (Sampson and Groves, 1989: 799)

Overall, however, Sampson and Groves are modest about their analysis and recognize both the problems of the data sets they used and the sometimes modest degree of variance in crime explained by their model. Nevertheless, their testing of the revised theory offers a possible explanation for variations in offender rates in demographically similar areas, as found in the Sheffield work, which is logically compatible with the role of housing markets in generating or sustaining such areal differences.

The revised theory certainly has a logical elegance – crime in neighbourhoods, it is argued, depends on a community's ability to organize control at three levels, and this depends on neighbourhood stability. Moreover, the theory overcomes some of the objections to the original theory of social disorganization by taking account of the political processes beyond the neighbourhood. However, we have seen how the Sheffield research identified a neighbourhood (Gardenia) which was residentially stable, and indeed scored well on some of the kind of measures which Sampson and Groves used to instantiate the capacity for social organization, and yet had high offender and victimization rates. This was an area whose life was organized around a mild criminal subculture, within which both youths and adults coped with their financially disadvantaged position by involvement in the black economy. This contra example raises two issues. First, it reintroduces a traditional objection to the theory of social disorganization discussed earlier, namely that the theory assumes a normative homogeneity across the society which may not exist, and Bursik and Grasmick (1993: 15) recognize that their theory does make such an assumption. . . . Secondly, empirically the apparent conflict between Sampson and Groves' analysis and the Sheffield example may simply be an artefact of the level of analysis. In the end how well the revised theory explains variations in residential area crime rates is an empirical question, and as we write the New Chicagoans are conducting further research to test the theory.

The most recent empirical study of the black ghettos of Chicago by William Julius Wilson, however, suggests that a straightforward notion of 'social disorganization' does not adequately conceptualize the social processes in such neighbourhoods. Instead it is argued that:

> what many impoverished and dangerous neighborhoods have in common is a relatively high degree of social integration (high levels of local neighboring while being relatively isolated from contacts in the broader mainstream society) and low levels of informal social control (feelings that they have little control over their immediate environment, including the environment's negative influence on their children). In such areas, not only are children at risk because of the lack of informal social controls, they are also disadvantaged because social interaction among neighbors tends to be confined to those whose skills, styles, orientations, and habits are not as conducive to positive social outcomes (academic success, pro-social behavior, etc.) as are those in more stable neighborhoods. . . . Despite being socially integrated, the residents of Chicago's ghetto neighborhoods shared a feeling that they had little informal social control over their children in their environment. A primary reason is the absence of a strong organizational capacity or an institutional resource base that would provide an extra layer of social organization in their neighborhood.
>
> (Wilson, 1996: 63–4)

This description is more complex and subtle than Bursick and Grasmick's theorization, and suggests that, instead of an area being characterized either by the presence or absence of 'social disorganization' *different types of social organization and disorganization can coexist in a neighbourhood*, some combinations of which may be conducive to different kinds of crime or lawlessness. This picture, in our view, fits much more closely to the evidence from the Sheffield research, and the existence of different types of high offender rate residential areas [. . .]

References

Alihan, M. (1938), *Social Ecology*. New York: Columbia University Press.
Baldwin, J. and Bottoms, A. E. (1976), *The Urban Criminal*. London: Tavistock.
Bennett, T, and Wright, R. (1984), *Burglars on Burglary*. Aldershot: Gower.

Block, R. L. and Block, C. R. (1995), 'Space, Place and Crime: Hot Spots Areas and Hot Places of Liquor-related Crime' in J. E. Eck and D. Weisburd, eds., *Crime and Place*. New York: Criminal Justice Press.

Bottoms, A. E., Claytor, A. and Wiles, P. (1992), 'Housing Markets and Residential Community Crime Careers: a Case Study from Sheffield', in D. J. Evans, N. R. Fyfe and D. T. Herbert, eds., *Crime, Policing and Place: Essays in Environmental Criminology*. London: Routledge.

Bottoms, A. E., Mawby, R. I. and Xanthos, P. (1989), 'A tale of two estates', in D. Downes, ed., *Crime and the City*. London: Macmillan.

Brantingham, P. J. and Brantingham, P. L. (1981), *Environmental Criminology*. Beverly Hills, Cal.: Sage Publications.

—— (1984), *Patters in Crime*. New York: Macmillan.

—— (1991), *Environmental Criminology*. (revised edition). Prospect Heights, Ill.: Waveland Press.

Brantingham, P. L. and Brantigham, P. J. (1981), 'Notes on the Geometry of Crime', in P. J. Brantingham and P. L., Brantingham, eds., *Environmental Criminology*. Beverly Hills, Cal.: Sage Publications.

Bronfenbrenner, U. (1979), *The Ecology of Human Development*. Cambridge, Mass.: Harvard University Press.

Bulmer, M. (1984), *The Chicago School of Sociology*. Chicago, Ill.: University of Chicago Press.

Burgess, E. W. (1925), 'The Growth of the City' in R. E. Park, E. W. Burgess, and R. D. McKenzie, eds., *The City*. Chicago: University of Chicago Press.

Bursik, R. J. (1986), 'Ecological Stability and the Dynamics of Delinquency' in A. J. Reiss and M. Tonry, eds., *Communities and Crime*. Chicago, Ill.: University of Chicago Press.

Bursik, R. J. and Grasmick, H. G. (1993), *Neighborhoods and Crime*. New York: Lexington.

Clarke, R. V. G. (1995), 'Situational Crime Prevention', in M. Tonry and D. Farrington, eds., *Building a Safer Society*. Chicago. Ill.: University of Chicago Press.

Cohen, L. E. and Felson, M. (1979), 'Social Change and Crime Rate Trends: A Routine Activities Approach', *American Sociological Review*, 44: 588–608.

Cressey, D. (1964), *Delinquency, Crime and Differential Association*. The Hague: Martinus Nijhoff.

Cromwell, P. F., Olson, J. N. and Avary, D. A. W. (1991), *Breaking and Entering: An Ethnographic Analysis of Burglary*. Newbury Park, California: Sage.

Damier, S. (1974), 'Wine Alley: The Sociology of a Dreadful Enclosure'. *Sociological Review*, 22: 221–48.

Eck, J. E. (1995), 'A General Model of the Geography of Illicit Retail Marketplaces', in J. E. Eck and D. Weisburd, eds., *Crime and Place*. New York: Criminal Justice Press.

Farrell, G. (1995), 'Preventing Repeat Victimisation', in M. Tonry and D. Farrington, eds., *Building a Safer Society*. Chicago. Ill.: Chicago University Press.

Felson, M. (1986), 'Linking Criminal Choices, Routine Activities, Informal Control and Criminal Outcomes', in D. B. Cornish and R. V. G. Clarke, eds., *The Reasoning Criminal*. New York: Springer-Verlag.

—— (1992), 'Routine Activities and Crime Prevention', *Studies on Crime and Crime Prevention: Annual Review*, 1: 30–4.

—— (1995), 'Those who Discourage Crime', in J. E. Eck and D. Weisburd, eds., *Crime and Place*. New York: Criminal Justice Press.

Figlio, R. M., Hakim, S. and Rengert, G. F., eds. (1986), *Metropolitan Crime Patterns*. Monsey, NY: Willow Tree Press.

Finestone, H. (1976), 'The Delinquent and Society: The Shaw and McKay Tradition', in J. F. Short, Jr., ed., *Delinquency, Crime and Society*. Chicago, Ill.: University of Chicago Press.

Giddens, A. ed. (1984), *The Constitution of Society*, Cambridge: Polity Press.

Herbert, D. (1982), *The Geography of Urban Crime*. London: Longman.

Hunter, A. J. (1985), 'Private, Parochial and Public School Orders: The Problem of Crime and Incivilities in Urban Communities', in G. D. Suttles and M. N. Zald, eds., *The Challenge of Social Control: Citizenship and Institution Building in Urban Society*. Norwood NJ: Abex Publishing.

Kornhauser, R. R. (1978), *Social Sources of Delinquency*. Chicago. Ill.: University of Chicago Press.

Kurtz, L. R. (1984), *Evaluating Chicago Sociology*. Chicago Ill.: University of Chicago Press.

Maguire, M. and Bennett, T. (1982), *Burglary in a Dwelling*. London: Heinemann.

Martens, P. L. (1990), 'Family, Neighbourhood and Socialization', in P.-O. H. Wikström, ed., *Crime and Measures Against Crime in The City*. Stockholm: National Council for Crime Prevention.

—— (1993), 'An Ecological Model of Socialisation in Explaining Offending', in D. P. Farrington, R. J. Sampson and P.-O. H. Wikström, eds., *Integrating Individual and Ecological Aspects of Crime*. Stockholm: National Council for Crime Prevention.

Matza, D. (1964), *Delinquency and Drift*. New York: John Wiley.

Mayhew, P. and Hough, M. (1982), 'The British Crime Survey', *Home office Research Bulletin*. No 14, 24–7.

McIver, J. P. (1981), 'Criminal Mobility: A Review of Empirical Studies', in S. Hakin and G. Rengert, eds., *Crime spillover*. Beverly Hills, Cal.: Sage.

Mirlees-Black, C. Mayhew, P. and Percy, A (1996), *The 1996 British Crime Survey: England and Wales*. London: Home Office Statistical Bulletin 19/96.

Morris, T. P. (1957), *The Criminal Area. A Study in Social Ecology*. London: Routledge and Kegan Paul.

Pease, K. (1993), 'Individual and Community Influences on Victimisation and their Implications for Crime Prevention', in D. P. Farrington, R. J. Sampson and P.-O. H. Wikström, eds., *Integrating Individual and Ecological Aspects of Crime*. Stockholm: National Council for Crime Prevention.

Reiss, A. J. (1986), 'Why are Communities Important in Understanding Crime?', in A. J. Reiss and M. Tonry, eds., *Communities and Crime*. Chicago, Ill.: University of Chicago Press.

Rex, J. and Moore, R. (1967), *Race, Community and Conflict: A Study of Sparkbrook*. London: Oxford University Press.

Reynolds, F. (1986), *The Problem Housing Estate*. Aldershot: Gower.

Rhodes, W. M. and Conly, C. (1981), 'Crime and Mobility: an Empirical Study', in P. J. Brantingham and P. L. Brantingham, eds., *Environmental Criminology*. Beverly Hills, Cal.: Sage Publications.

Rutter, M. and Giller, H. (1983), *Juvenile Delinquency: Trends and Prospects*. Harmondsworth: Penguin Books.

Sampson, R. J. (1995), 'The Community', in J. Q. Wilson and J. Petersilia, eds., *Crime*. San Francisco, Cal.: Institute for Contemporary Studies.

Sampson, R. J. and Groves, W. B. (1989), 'Community Structure and Crime: Testing Social Disorganisation Theory', *American Journal of Sociology*, 94: 774–802.

Sellin, T. (1938), *Culture Conflict and Crime*. New York. Social Science Research Council.

Shaw, C. R. (1930), *The Jack Roller*. Chicago, Ill.: University of Chicago Press.

Shaw, C. R. and McKay, H. D. (1931), *Social Factors in Juvenile Delinquency*. Washington, DC: Government Printing Office.

—— (1942), *Juvenile Delinquency and Urban Areas*. Chicago, Ill.: University of Chicago Press.

Sherman, L. W. (1995), 'Hot Spots of Crime and Criminal Careers of Places', in J. E. Eck and D. Weisburd, eds., *Crime and Place*. New York: Criminal Justice Press.

Sherman, L. W., Gartin, P. R. and Buerger, M. E. (1989), 'Hot Spots of Predatory Crime: Routine Activities and the Criminology of Place', *Criminology*. 27: 27–55.

Skogan, W. G. (1986), 'Fear of Crime and Neighborhood Change', in A. J. Reiss and M. Tonry, eds., *Communities and Crime*. Chicago, Ill.: University of Chicago Press.

—— (1990), *Disorder and Decline: Crime and the Spiral of Decay in American Neighborhoods*. New York: Free Press.

Snodgrass, J. (1976), 'Clifford R. Shaw and Henry D. McKay: Chicago criminologists', *British Journal of Criminology*, 16: 1–19.

Spelman, W. (1995), 'Criminal Careers of Public Places', in J. E. Eck and D. Weisburd, eds., *Crime and Place*. New York: Criminal Justice Press.

Taub, R., Taylor, D. G. and Dunham, J. D. (1984), *Paths of Neighborhood Change*. Chicago, Ill.: University of Chicago Press.

Trickett, A., Osborn, D. R., Seymour, J. and Pease, K. (1992), 'What is Different About High Crime Areas?', *British Journal of Criminology*, 32: 81–9.

Weber, M. (1949), *The Methodology of the Social Sciences*. Trans. E. A. Shils and H. A. Finch. New York: Free Press.

—— (1968), *Economy and Society: An Outline of Interpretive Sociology*. 3 vols, ed. G. Roth and C. Wittich. New York: Bedminster Press.

Wikström, P.-O. H. (1990), 'Delinquency and the Urban Structure', in P.-O. H. Wikström, ed., *Crime and Measures Against Crime in the City*. Stockholm: National Council for Crime Prevention.

—— (1991), *Urban Crime Criminals and Victims: The Swedish Experience in an Anglo-American Comparative Perspective*. New York: Springer-Verlag.

Wilson, W. J. (1996), *When work Disappears: The World of the New Urban Poor*. New York: Alfred Knopf.

Winchester, S. and Jackson, H. (1982), *Residential Burglary*. Home Office Research Study No. 74, London: Home Office.

Wright, R. T. and Decker, S. H. (1994), *Burglars on the Job: Street Life and Residential Break-Ins*. Boston, Mass.: Northeastern University Press.

Chapter 18

Robert Agnew

FOUNDATION FOR A GENERAL STRAIN THEORY OF CRIME AND DELINQUENCY

From: Robert Agnew (1992), excerpts from 'Foundation for a general strain theory of crime and delinquency', *Criminology* 30(1): 47–87.

AFTER DOMINATING DEVIANCE RESEARCH in the 1960s, strain theory came under heavy attack in the 1970s (Bernard, 1984; Cole, 1975), with several prominent researches suggesting that the theory be abandoned (Hirschi, 1969; Kornhauser, 1978). Strain theory has survived those attacks, but its influence is much diminished (see Agnew, 1985; Bernard, 1984; Farnworth and Leiber, 1989). In particular, variables derived from strain theory now play a very limited role in explanations of crime/delinquency. Several recent causal models of delinquency, in fact, either entirely exclude strain variables or assign them a small role (e.g., Elliott et al., 1985; Johnson, 1979; Massey and Krohn, 1986; Thornberry, 1987; Tonry et al., 1991). Causal models of crime/delinquency are dominated, instead, by variables derived from differential association/social learning theory and social control theory.

This chapter argues that strain theory has a central role to play in explanation of crime/delinquency, but that the theory has to be substantially revised to play this role. Most empirical studies of strain theory continue to rely on the strain models developed by Merton (1938), A. Cohen (1955), and Cloward and Ohlin (1960). In recent years, however, a wealth of research in several fields has questioned certain of the assumptions underlying those theories and pointed to new directions for the development of strain theory. Most notable in this area is the research on stress in medical sociology and psychology, on equity/justice in social psychology, and on aggression in psychology – particularly recent versions of frustration-aggression and social learning theory. Also important is recent research in such areas as the legitimation of stratification, the sociology of emotions, and the urban underclass. Certain researches have drawn on segments of the above research to suggest new directions for strain theory (Agnew, 1985; Bernard, 1987; Elliott et al., 1979; Greenberg, 1977), but the revisions suggested have not taken full advantage of this research and, at best, provide only incomplete models of strain and delinquency. . . . This chapter draws on the above literatures, as well as the recent revisions in strain theory, to present the outlines of a general strain theory of crime/delinquency. [. . .]

STRAIN THEORY AS DISTINGUISHED FROM CONTROL AND DIFFERENTIAL ASSOCIATION/SOCIAL LEARING THEORY

Strain, social control, and differential association theory are all sociological theories: They explain delinquency in terms of the individual's social relationships. Strain theory is distinguished from social control and social learning theory in its specification of (1) the type of social relationship that leads to delinquency and (2) the motivation for delinquency. First, strain theory focuses explicitly on *negative relationships with others*: relationships in which the individual is not treated as he or she wants to be treated. Strain theory has typically focused on relationships in which others prevent the individual from achieving positively valued goals. Agnew (1985), however, broadened the focus of strain theory to include relationships in which others present the individual with noxious or negative stimuli. Social control theory, by contrast, focuses on the *absence of significant relationships with conventional others and institutions*. In particular, delinquency is most likely when (1) the adolescent is not attached to parents, school, or other institutions; (2) parents and others fail to monitor and effectively sanction deviance; (3) the adolescent's actual or anticipated investment in conventional society is minimal; and (4) the adolescent has not internalized conventional beliefs. Social learning theory is distinguished from strain and control theory by its focus on *positive relationships with deviant others*. In particular, delinquency results from association with others who (1) differentially reinforce the adolescent's delinquency, (2) model delinquent behavior, and/or (3) transmit delinquent values.

Second, strain theory argues that adolescents are *pressured into delinquency by the negative affective states — most notably anger and related emotions — that often result from negative relationships* (see Kemper, 1978, and Morgan and Heise, 1988, for typologies of negative affective states). This negative affect creates pressure for corrective action and *may* lead adolescents to (1) make use of illegitimate channels of goal achievement, (2) attack or escape from the source of their adversity, and/or (3) manage their negative affect through the use of illicit drugs. Control theory, by contrast, denies that outside forces pressure the adolescent into delinquency. Rather, the absence of significant relationships with other individuals and groups *frees the adolescent to engage in delinquency*. The freed adolescent either drifts into delinquency or, in some versions of control theory, turns to delinquency in response to inner forces or situational inducements (see Hirschi, 1969:31–34). In differential association/social learning theory, the adolescent commits delinquent acts because group forces lead the adolescent to *view delinquency as a desirable or at least justifiable form of behavior* under certain circumstances. [. . .]

Phrased in the above manner, it is easy to see that strain theory complements the other major theories of delinquency in a fundamental way. While these other theories focus on the absence of relationships or on positive relationships, strain theory is the only theory to focus explicitly on negative relationships. And while these other theories view delinquency as the result of drift or of desire, strain theory views it as the result of pressure.

THE MAJOR TYPES OF STRAIN

[. . .]

The classic strain theories of Merton (1938), A. Cohen (1955), and Cloward and Ohlin (1960) focus on only one type of negative relationship: relationships in which others prevent the individual from achieving positively valued goals. In particular, they focus on the goal blockage experienced by lower-class individuals trying to achieve monetary success or middle-class status. More recent versions of strain theory have argued that adolescents are not only concerned about the future goals of monetary success/middle-class status, but are also concerned about the achievement or more immediate goals – such as good grades, popularity with the opposite sex, and doing well in athletics (Agnew, 1984; Elliott and Voss, 1974; Elliott et al., 1985; Empey, 1982; Greenberg, 1977; Quicker, 1974). The focus, however, is still on the achievement of positively valued goals. Most recently, Agnew (1985) has argued that strain may result not only from the failure to achieve positively valued goals, but also from the inability to escape legally from painful situations. If one draws on the above theories – as well as the stress, equity/justice, and aggression literatures – one can begin to develop a more complete classification of the types of strain.

Three major types of strain are described – each referring to a different type of negative relationship with others. Other individuals may (1) prevent one from achieving positively valued goals, (2) remove or threaten to remove positively valued stimuli that one possesses, or (3) present or threaten to present one with noxious or negatively valued stimuli. [. . .]

STRAIN AS THE FAILURE TO ACHIEVE POSITIVELY VALUED GOALS

At least three types of strain fall under this category. The first type encompasses most of the major strain theories in criminology, including the classic strain theories of Merton, A. Cohen, and Cloward and Ohlin, as well as those modern strain theories focusing on the achievement of immediate goals. The other two types of strain in this category are derived from the justice/equity literature and have not been examined in criminology.

Strain as the disjunction between aspirations and expectations/actual achievements

The classic strain theories of Merton, A. Cohen, and Cloward and Ohlin argue that the cultural system encourages everyone to pursue the ideal goals of monetary success and/or middle-class status. Lower-class individuals, however, are often prevented from achieving such goals through legitimate channels. In line with such theories, adolescent strain is typically measured in terms of the disjunction between *aspirations* (or ideal goals) and *expectations* (or expected levels of goal achievement). These theories, however, have been criticized for several reasons (see Agnew, 1986, 1991b; Clinard, 1964; Hirschi, 1969; Kornhauser, 1978; Liska, 1987; also see Bernard, 1984; Farnworth and Leiber, 1989). Among other things, it has been charged that these theories (1) are unable to explain the extensive nature of middle-class delinquency, (2) neglect goals other than monetary success/middle-class status, (3) neglect barriers to goal achievement other than social class, and (4) do not fully specify why only *some* strained individuals turn to delinquency. The most damaging criticism, however, stems from the limited empirical support provided by studies focusing on the disjunction between aspirations and expectations (see Kornhauser, 1978, as well the arguments of Bernard, 1984; Elliott et al., 1985; and Jensen, 1986).

As a consequence of these criticisms, several researchers have revised the above theories. The most popular revision argues that there is a youth subculture that emphasizes a variety of immediate goals. The achievement of these goals is further said to depend on a variety of factors besides social class: factors such as intelligence, physical attractiveness, personality, and athletic ability. As a result, many middle-class individuals find that they lack the traits or skills necessary to achieve their goals through legitimate channels. This version of strain theory, however, continues to argue that strain stems from the inability to achieve certain ideal goals emphasized by the (sub)cultural system. As a consequence, strain continues to be measured in terms of the disjunction between *aspiration* and *actual achievements* (since we are dealing with immediate rather than future goals, actual achievements rather than expected achievements may be examined).

Strain as the disjunction between expectations and actual achievements

As indicated above, strain theories in criminology focus on the inability to achieve *ideal* goals derived from the cultural system. This approach stands in contrast to certain of the research on justice in social psychology. Here the focus is on the disjunction between *expectations* and *actual achievements* (rewards), and it is commonly argued that such expectations are existentially based. In particular, it has been argued that such expectations derive from the individual's past experience and/or from comparisons with referential (or generalized) others who are similar to the individual (see Berger et al., 1972, 1983; Blau, 1964; Homans, 1961; Jasso and Rossi, 1977; Mickelson, 1990; Ross et al., 1971; Thibaut and Kelley, 1959). Much of the research in this area has focused on income expectations, although the above theories apply to expectations regarding all manner of positive stimuli. The justice literature argues that the failure to achieve such expectations may lead to such emotions as anger, resentment, rage, dissatisfaction, disappointment, and unhappiness – that is, all the emotions customarily associated with strain in criminology. Further, it is argued that individuals will be strongly motivated to reduce the gap between expectations and achievements – with deviance being commonly mentioned as one possible option. This literature has not devoted much empirical research to deviance, although limited data suggest that the expectations-achievement gap is related to anger/hostility (Ross et al., 1971).

This alternative conception of strain has been largely neglected in criminology. This is unfortunate because it has the potential to overcome certain of the problems of current strain theories. First, one would expect the disjunction between expectations and actual achievements to be more emotionally distressing than that between aspirations and achievements. Aspirations, by definition, are *ideal* goals. They have something of the utopian in them, and for that reason, the failure to achieve aspirations may not be taken seriously. The failure to achieve expected goals, however, is likely to be taken seriously since such goals are rooted in reality – the individual has previously experienced such goals or has seen similar others experience such goals. [. . .]

Strain as the disjunction between just/fair outcomes and actual outcomes

The above models of strain assume that individual goals focus on the achievement of specific outcomes. Individual goals, for example, focus on the achievement of a certain amount of money or a certain grade-point average. A third conception of strain, also derived from the justice/equity literature, makes a rather different argument. It claims that individuals do not necessarily enter interactions with specific outcomes in mind. Rather, they enter interactions expecting that certain distributive justice rules will be followed, rules specifying how resources should be allocated. The rule that has received the most attention in the literature is that of equity. An equitable relationship is one in which the outcome/input ratios of the actors involved in an exchange/allocation relationship are equivalent (see Adams, 1963, 1965; Cook and Hegtvedt, 1983; Walster et al., 1978). Outcomes encompass a broad range of positive and negative consequences, while inputs encompass the individual's positive and negative contributions to the exchange. Individuals in a relationship will compare the ratio of their outcomes and inputs to the ratio(s) of specific others in the relationship. If the ratios are equal to one another, they feel that the outcomes are fair or just. This is true, according to equity theorists, even if the outcomes are low. If outcome/input ratios are not equal, actors will feel that the outcomes are unjust and they will experience distress as a result. Such distress is especially likely when individuals feel they have been underrewarded rather than overrewarded (Hegtvedt, 1990).

The equity literature has described the possible reactions to this distress, some of which involve deviance (see Adams, 1963, 1965; Austin, 1977; Walster et al., 1973; 1978; see Stephenson and White, 1968, for an attempt to recast A. Cohen's strain theory in terms of equity theory). In particular, inequity may lead to delinquency for several reasons – all having to do with the restoration of equity. Individuals in inequitable relationships may engage in delinquency in order to (1) increase their outcomes (e.g., by theft); (2) lower their inputs (e.g., truancy from school); (3) lower the outcomes of others (e.g., vandalism, theft, assault); and/or (4) increase the inputs of others (e.g., by being incorrigible or disorderly). In highly inequitable situations, individuals may leave the field (e.g., run away from home) or force others to leave the field.[1] There has not been any empirical research on the relationship between equity and delinquency, although much data suggest that inequity leads to anger and frustration. A few studies also suggest that insulting and vengeful behaviors may result from inequity (see Cook and Hegtvedt, 1991; Donnerstein and Hatfield, 1982; Hegtvedt, 1990; Mikula, 1986; Sprecher, 1986; Walster et al., 1973, 1978).

It is not difficult to measure equity. Walster et al. (1978:234–242) provide the most complete guide to measurement. Sprecher (1986) illustrates how equity may be measured in social surveys; respondents are asked who contributes more to a particular relationship and/or who "gets the best deal" out of a relationship. A still simpler strategy might be to ask respondents how fair or just their interactions with others, such as parents or teachers, are. One would then predict that those involved in unfair relations will be more likely to engage in current and future delinquency.

The literature on equity builds on the strain theory literature in criminology in several ways. First, all of the strain literature assumes that individuals are pursuing some specific outcome, such as a certain amount of money or prestige. The equity literature points out that individuals do not necessarily enter into interactions with specific outcomes in mind, but rather with the expectation that a particular distributive justice rule will be followed. Their goal is that the interaction conform to the justice principle. This perspective, then, points to a new source of strain not considered in the criminology literature. Second, the strain literature in criminology focuses largely on the individual's outcomes. Individuals are assumed to be pursuing a specific goal, and strain is judged in terms of the disjunction between the goal and the actual outcome. The equity literature suggests that this may be an oversimplified conception and that the individual's *inputs* may also have to be considered. In particular, an equity theorist would argue that inputs will condition the individual's evaluation of outcomes. That is, individuals who view their inputs as limited will be more likely to accept limited outcomes as fair. [. . .]

Summary: strain as the failure to achieve positively valued goals

Three types of strain in this category have been listed: strain as the disjunction between (1) aspirations and expectations/actual achievements, (2) expectations and actual achievements, and (3) just/fair outcomes and actual outcomes. Strain theory in criminology has focused on the first type of strain, arguing that it is most responsible for the delinquency in our society. Major research traditions in the justice/equity field, however, argue that anger and frustration derive primarily from the second two types of strain. [. . .]

STRAIN AS THE REMOVAL OF POSITIVELY VALUED STIMULI FROM THE INDIVIDUAL

The psychological literature on aggression and the stress literature suggest that strain may involve more than the pursuit of positively valued goals. Certain of the aggression literature, in fact, has come to de-emphasize the pursuit of positively valued goals, pointing out that the blockage of goal-seeking behavior is a relatively weak predictor of aggression, particularly when the goal has never been experienced before (Bandura, 1973; Zillman, 1979). The stress literature has largely neglected the pursuit of positively valued goals as a source of stress. Rather, if one looks at the stressful life events examined in this literature, one finds a focus on (1) events involving the loss of positively valued stimuli and (2) events involving the presentation of noxious or negative stimuli (see Pearlin, 1983, for other typologies of stressful life events/conditions). So, for example, one recent study of adolescent stress employs a life-events list that focuses on such items as the loss of a boyfriend/girlfriend, the death or serious illness of a friend, moving to a new school district, the divorce/separation of one's parents, suspension from school, and the presence of a variety of adverse conditions at work (see Williams and Uchiyama, 1989, for an overview of life-events scales for adolescents; see Compas, 1987, and Compas and Phares, 1991, for overviews of research on adolescent stress).

Drawing on the stress literature, then, one may state that a second type of strain or negative relationship involves the actual or anticipated removal (loss) of positively valued stimuli from the individual. As indicated above, numerous examples of such loss can be found in the inventories of stressful life events. The actual or anticipated loss of positively valued stimuli may lead to delinquency as the individual tries to prevent the loss of the positive stimuli, retrieve the lost stimuli or obtain substitute stimuli, seek revenge against those responsible for the loss, or manage the negative affect caused by the loss by taking illicit drugs. While there are no data bearing directly on this type of strain, experimental data indicate that aggression often occurs when positive reinforcement previously administered to an individual is withheld or reduced (Bandura, 1973; Van Houten, 1983).

And as discussed below, inventories of stressful life events, which include the loss of positive stimuli, are related to delinquency.

STRAIN AS THE PRESENTATION OF NEGATIVE STIMULI

The literature on stress and the recent psychological literature on aggression also focus on the actual or anticipated presentation of negative or noxious stimuli. Except for the work of Agnew (1985), however, this category of strain has been neglected in criminology. And even Agnew does not focus on the presentation of noxious stimuli per se, but on the inability of adolescents to escape legally from noxious stimuli. Much data, however, suggest that the presentation of noxious stimuli may lead to aggression and other negative outcomes in certain conditions, even when legal escape from such stimuli is possible (Bandura, 1973; Zillman, 1979). Noxious stimuli may lead to delinquency as the adolescent tries to (1) escape from or avoid the negative stimuli; (2) terminate or alleviate the negative stimuli; (3) seek revenge against the source of the negative stimuli or related targets, although the evidence on displaced aggression is somewhat mixed (see Berkowitz, 1982; Bernard, 1990; Van Houten, 1983; Zillman, 1979); and/or (4) manage the resultant negative affect by taking illicit drugs.

A wide range of noxious stimuli have been examined in the literature, and experimental, survey, and participant observation studies have linked such stimuli to both general and specific measures of delinquency – with the experimental studies focusing on aggression. Delinquency/aggression, in particular, has been linked to such noxious stimuli as child abuse and neglect (Rivera and Widom, 1990), criminal victimization (Lauritsen et al., 1991), physical punishment (Straus, 1991), negative relations with parents (Healy and Bonner, 1969), negative relations with peers (Short and Strodtbeck, 1965), adverse or negative school experiences (Hawkins and Lishner, 1987), a wide range of stressful life events (Gersten et al., 1974; Kaplan et al., 1983; Linsky and Straus, 1986; Mawson, 1987; Novy and Donohue, 1985; Vaux and Ruggiero, 1983), verbal threats and insults, physical pain, unpleasant odors, disgusting scenes, noise, heat, air pollution, personal space violations, and high density (see Anderson and Anderson, 1984; Bandura, 1973, 1983; Berkowitz, 1982, 1986; Mueller, 1983). In one of the few studies in criminology to focus specifically on the presentation of negative stimuli, Agnew (1985) found that delinquency was related to three scales measuring negative relations at home and school. The effect of the scales on delinquency was partially mediated through a measure of anger, and the effect held when measures of social control and deviant beliefs were controlled. And in a recent study employing longitudinal data, Agnew (1989) found evidence suggesting that the relationship between negative stimuli and delinquency was due to the *causal* effect of the negative stimuli on delinquency (rather than the effect of delinquency on the negative stimuli). Much evidence, then, suggests that the presentation of negative or noxious stimuli constitutes a third major source of strain.

Certain of the negative stimuli listed above, such as physical pain, heat, noise, and pollution, may be experienced as noxious largely for biological reasons (i.e., they may be unconditioned negative stimuli). Others may be conditioned negative stimuli, experienced as noxious largely because of their association with unconditioned negative stimuli (see Berkowitz, 1982). Whatever the case, it is assumed that such stimuli are experienced as noxious regardless of the goals that the individual is pursuing.

THE LINKS BETWEEN STRAIN AND DELINQUENCY

Three sources of strain have been presented: strain as the actual or anticipated failure to achieve positively valued goals, strain as the actual or anticipated removal of positively valued stimuli, and strain as the actual or anticipated presentation of negative stimuli. While these types are theoretically distinct from one another, they may sometimes overlap in practice. So, for example, the insults of a teacher may be experienced as adverse because they (1) interfere with the adolescent's aspirations for academic success, (2) result in the violation of a distributive justice rule such as equity, and (3) are conditioned negative stimuli and so are experienced as noxious in and of themselves. Other examples of overlap can be given, and it may sometimes be difficult to disentangle the different types of strain in practice. Once again, however, these categories are ideal types and are presented only to ensure that all events with the potential for creating strain are considered in empirical research.

Each type of strain increases the likelihood that individuals will experience one or more of a range of negative emotions. Those emotions include disappointment, depression, and fear. Anger, however, is the most critical emotional reaction for the purposes of the general strain theory. Anger results when individuals blame their adversity on others, and anger is a key emotion because it increases the individual's level of felt injury, creates a desire for retaliation/revenge, energizes the individual for action, and lowers inhibitions, in part because individuals believe that others will feel their aggression is justified (see Averill, 1982; Berkowitz, 1982; Kemper, 1978; Kluegel and Smith, 1986: Ch. 10; Zillman, 1979). Anger, then, affects the individual in several ways that are conducive to delinquency. Anger is distinct from many of the other types of negative affect in this respect, and this is the reason that anger occupies a special place in the general strain theory. It is important to note, however, that delinquency may still occur in response to other types of negative affect – such as despair, although delinquency is less likely in such cases. The experience of negative affect, especially anger, typically creates a desire to take corrective steps, with delinquency being one possible response. Delinquency may be a method for alleviating strain, that is, for achieving positively valued goals, for protecting or retrieving positive stimuli, or for terminating or escaping from negative stimuli. Delinquency may be used to seek revenge; data suggest that vengeful behavior often occurs even when there is no possibility of eliminating the adversity that stimulated it (Berkowitz, 1982). And delinquency may occur as adolescents try to manage their negative affect through illicit drug use (see Newcomb and Harlow, 1986). The general strain theory, then, has the potential to explain a broad range of delinquency, including theft, aggression, and drug use.

Each type of strain may create a *predisposition* for delinquency or function as a *situational event* that instigates a particular delinquent act. In the words of Hirschi and Gottfredson (1986), then, the strain theory presented in this paper is a theory of both "criminality" and "crime" (or to use the words of Clarke and Cornish [1985], it is a theory of both "criminal involvement" and "criminal events"). Strain creates a predisposition for delinquency in those cases in which it is chronic or repetitive. Examples include a continuing gap between expectations and achievements and a continuing pattern of ridicule and insults from teachers. Adolescents subject to such strain are predisposed to delinquency because (1) nondelinquent strategies for coping with strain are likely to be taxed; (2) the threshold for adversity may be lowered by chronic strains (see Averill, 1982:289);

(3) repeated or chronic strain may lead to a hostile attitude – a general dislike and suspicion of others and an associated tendency to respond in an aggressive manner (see Edmunds and Kendrick, 1980:21); and (4) chronic strains increase the likelihood that individuals will be high in negative affect/arousal at any given time (see Bandura, 1983; Bernard, 1990). A particular instance of strain may also function as the situational event that ignites a delinquent act, especially among adolescents predisposed to delinquency. Qualitative and survey data, in particular, suggest that particular instances of delinquency are often instigated by one of the three types of strain listed above (see Agnew, 1990; also see Averill, 1982, for data on the instigations to anger). [. . .]

ADAPTATIONS TO (COPING STRATEGIES FOR) STRAIN

The discussion thus far has focused on the types of strain that might promote delinquency. Virtually all strain theories, however, acknowledge that only *some* strained individuals turn to delinquency. Some effort has been made to identify those factors that determine whether one adapts to strain through delinquency. The most attention has been focused on the adolescent's commitment to legitimate means and association with other strained/delinquent individuals (see Agnew, 1991b). [. . .]

PREDICTING THE USE OF DELINQUENT VERSUS NONDELINQUENT ADAPTATIONS

[. . .]

Factors affect the choice of coping strategies by affecting (1) the constraints to nondelinquent and delinquent coping and (2) the disposition to engage in nondelinquent versus delinquent coping.

Constraints to nondelinquent and delinquent coping

While there are many adaptations to objective strain, those adaptations are not equally available to everyone. Individuals are constrained in their choice of adaptation(s) by a variety of internal and external factors. The following is a partial list of such factors.

Initial goals/values/identities of the individual

If the objective strain affects goals/values/identities that are high in absolute and relative importance, and if the individual has few alternative goals/values/identities in which to seek refuge, it will be more difficult to relegate strain to an unimportant area of one's life (see Agnew, 1986; Thoits, 1991a). This is especially the case if the goals/values/identities receive strong social and cultural support (see below). As a result, strain will be more likely to lead to delinquency in such cases.

Individual coping resources

A wide range of traits can be listed in this area, including temperament, intelligence, creativity, problem-solving skills, interpersonal skills, self-efficacy, and self-esteem. These traits affect the selection of coping strategies by influencing the individual's sensitivity to objective strains and ability to engage in . . . coping (Agnew, 1991a; Averill, 1982; Bernard, 1990; Compas, 1987; Edmunds and Kendrick, 1980; Slaby and Guerra, 1988; Tavris, 1984). Data, for example, suggest that individuals with high self-esteem are more resistant to stress (Averill, 1982; Compas, 1987; Kaplan, 1980; Pearlin and Schooler, 1978; Rosenberg, 1990; Thoits, 1983). Such individuals, therefore, should be less likely to respond to a given objective strain with delinquency. Individuals high in self-efficacy are more likely to feel that their strain can be alleviated by behavioral coping of a nondelinquent nature, and so they too should be less likely to respond to strain with delinquency (see Bandura, 1989, and Wang and Richarde, 1988, on self-efficacy; see Thoits, 1991b, on perceived control).

Conventional social support

Vaux (1988) provides an extended discussion of the different types of social support, their measurement, and their effect on outcome variables. . . . There is informational support, instrumental support, and emotional support (House, 1981). Adolescents with conventional social supports should be better able to respond to objective strains in a nondelinquent manner.

Constraints to delinquent coping

The crime/delinquency literature has focused on certain variables that constrain delinquent coping. They include (1) the costs and benefits of engaging in delinquency in a particular situation (Clarke and Cornish, 1985), (2) the individual's level of social control (see Hirschi, 1969), and (3) the possession of those "illegitimate means" necessary for many delinquent acts (see Agnew, 1991a, for a full discussion).

Macro-level variables

The larger social environment may affect the probability of delinquent versus nondelinquent coping by affecting all of the above factors. First, the social environment may affect coping by influencing the importance attached to selected goals/values/identities. For example, certain ethnographic accounts suggest that there is a strong social and cultural emphasis on the goals of money/status among certain segments of the urban poor. Many poor individuals, in particular, are in a situation in which (1) they face strong economic/status demands, (2) people around them stress the importance of money/ status on a regular basis, and (3) few alternative goals are given cultural support (Anderson, 1978; MacLeod, 1987; Sullivan, 1989). As such, these individuals should face more difficulty in cognitively minimizing the importance of money and status.

    Second, the larger social environment may affect the individual's sensitivity to particular strains by influencing the individual's beliefs regarding what is and is not adverse. The subculture of violence thesis, for example, is predicated on the assumption that young black males in urban slums are taught that a wide range of provocations and insults are highly adverse. Third, the social environment may influence the individual's ability to minimize cognitively the severity of objective strain. Individuals in some environments are regularly provided with external information about their accomplishments and failings (see Faunce, 1989), and their attempts at cognitively distorting such information are quickly challenged. Such a situation may exist among many adolescents and among those who inhabit the "street-corner world" of the urban poor. Adolescents and those on the street corner live in a very "public world"; one's accomplishments and failings typically occur before a large audience or they quickly become known to such an audience. Further, accounts suggest that this audience regularly reminds individuals of their accomplishments and failings and challenges attempts at cognitive distortion.

Fourth, certain social environments may make it difficult to engage in behavioral coping of a non-delinquent nature. Agnew (1985) has argued that adolescents often find it difficult to escape legally from negative stimuli, especially negative stimuli encountered in the school, family, and neighborhood. Also, adolescents often lack the resources to negotiate successfully with adults, such as parents and teachers (although see Agnew, 1991a). Similar arguments might be made for the urban underclass. They often lack the resources to negotiate successfully with many others, and they often find it difficult to escape legally from adverse environments – by, for example, quitting their job (if they have a job) or moving to another neighborhood.

The larger social environment, then, may affect individual coping in a variety of ways. And certain groups, such as adolescents and the urban underclass, may face special constraints that make non-delinquent coping more difficult. This may explain the higher rate of deviance among these groups.

Factors affecting the disposition to delinquency

The selection of delinquent versus non-delinquent coping strategies is not only dependent on the constraints to coping, but also on the adolescent's disposition to engage in delinquent versus non-delinquent coping. This disposition is a function of (1) certain temperamental variables (see Tonry et al., 1991), (2) the prior learning history of the adolescent, particularly the extent to which delinquency was reinforced in the past (Bandura, 1973; Berkowitz, 1982), (3) the adolescent's beliefs, particularly the rules defining the appropriate response to provocations (Bernard's, 1990, "regulative rules"), and (4) the adolescent's attributions regarding the causes of his or her adversity. Adolescents who attribute their adversity to others are much more likely to become angry, and as argued earlier, that anger creates a strong predisposition to delinquency. Data and theory from several areas, in fact, suggest that the experience of adversity is most likely to result in deviance when the adversity is blamed on another. [. . .]

A key variable affecting several of the above factors is association with delinquent peers. It has been argued that adolescents who associate with delinquent peers are more likely to be exposed to delinquent models and beliefs and to receive reinforcement for delinquency (see especially, Akers, 1985). It may also be the case that delinquent peers increase the likelihood that adolescents will attribute their adversity to others.

The individual's disposition to delinquency, then, may condition the impact of adversity on delinquency. At the same time, it is important to note that continued experience with adversity may create a disposition for delinquency. This argument has been made by Bernard (1990), Cloward and Ohlin (1960), A. Cohen (1955), Elliott et al. (1979), and others. In particular, it has been argued that under certain conditions the experience of adversity may lead to beliefs favorable to delinquency, lead adolescents to join or form delinquent peer groups, and lead adolescents to blame others for their misfortune.

Virtually all empirical research on strain theory in criminology has neglected the constraints to coping and the adolescent's disposition to delinquency. Researchers, in particular, have failed to examine whether the effect of adversity on delinquency is conditioned by factors such as self-efficacy and association with delinquent peers. This is likely a major reason for the weak empirical support for strain theory.

CONCLUSION

Much of the recent theoretical work in criminology has focused on the integration of different delinquency theories. This chapter has taken an alternative track and, following Hirschi's (1979) advice, has focused on the refinement of a single theory. The general strain theory builds upon traditional strain theory in criminology in several ways. First, the general strain theory points to several new sources of strain. [. . .]

Second, the general strain theory more precisely specifies the relationship between strain and delinquency, pointing out that strain is likely to have a cumulative effect on delinquency after a certain threshold level is reached. [. . .]

The general strain theory more fully describes those factors affecting the choice of delinquent versus no delinquent adaptations. The failure to consider such factors is a fundamental reason for the weak empirical support for strain theory. [. . .]

Acknowledgement

I would like to thank Helene Raskin White and Karen Hegtvedt for their comments.

References

Adams, J. Stacy 1963, Toward an understanding of inequity. Journal of Abnormal and Social Psychology 67:422–436.
—— 1965, Inequity in social exchange. In Leonard Berkowitz (ed.), Advances in Experimental Social Psychology. New York: Academic Press.
Agnew, Robert 1984, Goal achievement and delinquency. Sociology and Social Research 68:435–451.
—— 1985, A revised strain theory of delinquency. Social Forces 64:151–167.
—— 1986, Challenging strain theory: An examination of goals and goal-blockage. Paper presented at the annual meeting of the American Society of Criminology, Atlanta.
—— 1989, A longitudinal test of the revised strain theory. Journal of Quantitative Criminology 5:373–387.

Agnew, Robert 1990, The origins of delinquent events: An examination of offender accounts. Journal of Research in Crime and Delinquency 27:267–294.

—— 1991a, Adolescent resources and delinquency. Criminology 28:535–566.

—— 1991b, Strain and subcultural crime theory. In Joseph Sheley (ed.), Criminology: A Contemporary Handbook. Belmont, Calif.: Wadsworth.

Akers, Ronald L. 1985, Deviant Behaviour: A Social Learning Approach. Belmont, Calif: Wadsworth.

Alves, Wayne M. and Peter H. Rossi 1978, Who should get what? Fairness judgments of the distribution of earnings. American Journal of Sociology 84:541–564.

Anderson, Elijah 1978, A Place on the Corner. Chicago: University of Chicago Press.

Anderson, Craig A. and Dona C. Anderson 1984, Ambient temperature and violent crime: Tests of the linear and curvilinear hypotheses. Journal of Personality and Social Psychology 46:91–97.

Austin, William 1977, Equity theory and social comparison processes. In Jerry M. Suls and Richard L. Miller (eds.), Social Comparison Processes. New York: Hemisphere.

Averill, James R. 1982, Anger and Aggression. New York: Springer-Verlag.

Bandura, Albert 1973, Aggression: A Social Learning Analysis. Englewood Cliffs, N.J.: Prentice-Hall.

—— 1983, Psychological mechanisms of aggression. In Russell G. Geen and Edward Donnerstein (eds.), Aggression: Theoretical and Empirical Reviews. New York: Academic Press.

—— 1989, Human agency and social cognitive theory. American Psychologist 44:1175–1184.

Berger, Joseph, Morris Zelditch, Jr., Bo Anderson, and Bernard Cohen 1972, Structural aspects of distributive justice: A status-value formulation. In Joseph Berger, Morris Zelditch, Jr., and Bo Anderson (eds.), Sociological Theories in Progress. New York: Houghton Mifflin.

Berger, Joseph, M. Hamit Fisck, Robert Z. Norman, and David G. Wagner 1983, The formation of reward expectations in status situations. In David M. Messick and Karen S. Cook (eds.), Equity Theory: Psychological and Sociological Perspectives. New York: Praeger.

Berkowitz, Leonard 1982, Aversive conditions as stimuli to aggression. In Leonard Berkowitz (ed.), Advances in Experimental Social Psychology. Vol. 15. New York: Academic Press.

—— 1986, A Survey of Social Psychology. New York: Holt, Rinehart & Winston.

Bernard, Thomas J. 1984, Control criticisms of strain theories: An assessment of theoretical and empirical adequacy. Journal of Research in Crime and Delinquency 21:353–372.

—— 1987, Testing structural strain theories. Journal of Research in Crime and Delinquency 24:262–280.

—— 1990, Angry aggression among the "truly disadvantaged." Criminology 28:73–96.

Blau, Peter 1964, Exchange and Power in Social Life. New York: John Wiley & Sons.

Clarke, Ronald V. and Derek B. Cornish 1985, Modeling offenders' decisions: A framework for research and policy. In Michael Tonry and Norval Morris (eds.), Crime and Justice: An Annual Review of Research. Vol. 6. Chicago: University of Chicago Press.

Clinard, Marshall B. 1964, Anomie and Deviant Behavior. New York: Free Press.

Cloward, Richard A. and Lloyd E. Ohlin 1960 Delinquency and Opportunity. New York: Free Press.

Cohen, Albert K. 1955 Delinquent Boys. New York: Free Press.

Cohen, Ronald L. 1982 Perceiving justice: An attributional perspective. In Jerald Greenberg and Ronald L. Cohen (eds.), Equity and Justice in Social Behavior. New York: Academic Press.

Cole, Stephen 1975 The growth of scientific knowledge: Theories of deviance as a case study. In Lewis A. Coser (ed.), The Idea of Social Structure: Papers in Honor of Robert K. Merton. New York: Harcourt Brace Jovanovich.

Compas, Bruce E. 1987, Coping with stress during childhood and adolescence. Psychological Bulletin 101:393–403.

Compas, Bruce E. and Vicky Phares 1991, Stress during childhood and adolescence: Sources of risk and vulnerability. In E. Mark Cummings, Anita L. Greene, and Katherine H. Karraker (eds.), Life-Span Developmental Psychology: Perspectives on Stress and Coping. Hillsdale, N.J.: Lawrence Erlbaum.

Cook, Karen S. and Karen A. Hegtvedt 1983, Distributive justice, equity, and equality. Annual Review of Sociology 9:217–241.

—— 1991, Empirical evidence of the sense of justice. In Margaret Gruter, Roger D. Masters, Michael T. McGuire (eds.), The Sense of Justice: An Inquiry into the Biological Foundations of Law. New York: Greenwood Press.

Crosby, Faye and A. Miren Gonzales-Intal 1984, Relative deprivation and equity theories: Felt injustice and the undeserved benefits of others. In Robert Folger (ed.), The Sense on Injustice: Social Psychological Perspectives. New York: Plenum.

Deutsch, Morton 1975, Equity, equality, and need: What determines which value will be used as the basis of distributive justice. Journal of Social Issues 31:137–149.

Dohrenwend, Barbara Snell and Bruce P. Dohrenwend 1974, Overview and prospects for research on stressful life events. In Barbara Snell Dohrenwend and Bruce P. Dohrenwend (eds.), Stressful Life Events: Their Nature and Effects. New York: John Wiley & Sons.

Donnerstein, Edward and Elaine Hatfield 1982, Aggression and equity. In Jerald Greenberg and Ronald L. Cohen (eds.), Equity and Justice in Social Behavior. New York: Academic Press.

Edmunds, G. and D. C. Kendrick 1980, The Measurement of Human Aggressiveness. New York: John Wiley & Sons.

Elliott, Delbert and Harwin Voss 1974, Delinquency and Dropout. Lexington, Mass.: Lexington Books.

Elliott, Delbert, Suzanne Ageton, and Rachel Canter 1979, An integrated theoretical perspective on delinquent behavior. Journal of Research in Crime and Delinquency 16:3–27.

Elliott, Delbert, David Huizinga, and Suzanne Ageton 1985, Explaining Delinquency and Drug Use. Beverly Hills, Calif.: Sage.

Empey, LaMar 1982, American Delinquency: Its Meaning and Construction. Homewood, Ill.: Dorsey.

Farnworth, Margaret and Michael J. Leiber 1989, Strain theory revisited: Economic goals, educational means, and delinquency. American Sociological Review 54:263–274.

Faunce, William A. 1989, Occupational status-assignment systems: The effect of status on self-esteem. American Journal of Sociology 95:378–400.

Folger, Robert 1984, Emerging issues in the social psychology of justice. In Robert Folger (ed.), The Sense of Injustice: Social Psychological Perspectives. New York: Plenum.

Garrett, James and William L. Libby, Jr. 1973, Role of intentionality in mediating responses to inequity in the dyad. Journal of Personality and Social Psychology 28:21–27.

Gersten, Joanne C., Thomas S. Langer, Jeanne G. Eisenberg, and Lida Ozek 1974, Child behavior and life events: Undesirable change or change per se. In Barbara Snell Dohrenwend and Bruce P. Dohrenwend (eds.), Stressful Life Events: Their Nature and Effects. New York: John Wiley & Sons.

Greenberg, David F. 1977, Delinquency and the age structure of society. Contemporary Crises 1:189–223.

Hawkins, J. David and Denise M. Lishner 1987, Schooling and delinquency. In Elmer H. Johnson (ed.), Handbook on Crime and Delinquency Prevention. New York: Greenwood.

Healy, William and Augusta F. Bonner 1969, New Light on Delinquency and Its Treatment. New Haven, Conn.: Yale University Press.

Hegtvedt, Karen A. 1987, When rewards are scarce: Equal or equitable distributions. Social Forces 66:183–207.

—— 1990, The effects of relationship structure on emotional responses to inequity. Social Psychology Quarterly 53:214–228.

—— 1991a, Justice processes. In Martha Foschi and Edward J. Lawler (eds.), Group Processes: Sociological Analyses. Chicago: Nelson-Hall.

—— 1991b, Social comparison processes. In Edgar F. Borgotta and Marie E. Borgotta (eds.), Encyclopedia of Sociology. New York: Macmillan.

Hirschi, Travis 1969, Causes of Delinquency. Berkeley: University of California Press.

—— 1979, Separate and unequal is better. Journal of Research in Crime and Delinquency 16:34–38.

Hirschi, Travis and Michael Gottfredson 1986, The distinction between crime and criminality. In Timothy F. Hartnagel and Robert A. Silverman (eds.), Critique and Explanation. New Brunswick, N.J.: Transaction Books.

Hochschild, Jennifer L. 1981, What's Fair: American Beliefs about Distributive Justice. Cambridge, Mass.: Harvard University Press.

Homans, George C. 1961, Social Behavior: Its Elementary Forms. New York: Harcourt, Brace and World.

House, James S. 1981, Work Stress and Social Support. Reading, Mass.: Addison-Wesley.

Jasso, Guillermina and Peter H. Rossi 1977, Distributive justice and earned income. American Sociological Review 42:639–651.

Jensen, Gary 1986, Dis-integrating integrated theory: A critical analysis of attempts to save strain theory. Paper presented at the annual meeting of the American Society of Criminology, Atlanta.

Johnson, Richard E. 1979, Juvenile Delinquency and Its Origins. London: Cambridge University Press.

Kaplan, Howard B. 1980, Deviant Behavior in Defense of Self. New York: Academic Press.

Kaplan, Howard B., Cynthia Robbins, and Steven S. Martin 1983, Toward the testing of a general theory of deviant behavior in longitudinal perspective: Patterns of psychopathology. In James R. Greenley and Roberta G. Simmons (eds.), Research in Community and Mental Health. Greenwich, Conn.: Jai Press.

Kemper, Theodore D. 1978, A Social Interactional Theory of Emotions. New York: John Wiley & Sons.

Kluegel, James R. and Eliot R. Smith 1986, Beliefs about Inequality. New York: Aldine De Gruyter.

Kornhauser, Ruth Rosner 1978, Social Sources of Delinquency. Chicago: University of Chicago Press.

Lauritsen, Janet L., Robert J. Sampson, and John Laub 1991, The link between offending and victimization among adolescents. Criminology 29:265–292.

Lerner, Melvin J. 1977, The justice motive: Some hypotheses as to its origins and forms. Journal of Personality 45:1–52.

Leventhal, Gerald S. 1976, The distribution of rewards and resources in groups and organizations. In Leonard Berkowitz and Elaine Walster (eds.), Advances in

Experimental Social Psychology: Equity Theory: Toward a General Theory of Social Interaction. New York: Academic Press.

Leventhal, Gerald S., Jurgis Karuzajr, and William Rick Fry 1980, Beyond fairness: A theory of allocation preferences. In Gerald Mikula (ed.), Justice and Social Interaction. New York: Springer-Verlag.

Linsky, Arnold S. and Murray A. Straus 1986, Social Stress in the United States. Dover, Mass.: Auburn House.

Liska, Allen E. 1987, Perspectives on Deviance. Englewood Cliffs, N.J.: Prentice-Hall.

MacLeod, Jay 1987, Ain't No Makin' It. Boulder, Colo.: Westview Press.

Mark, Melvin M. and Robert Folger 1984, Responses to relative deprivation: A conceptual framework. In Philip Shaver (ed.), Review of Personality and Social Psychology. Vol. 5. Beverly Hills, Calif.: Sage.

Martin, Joanne and Alan Murray 1983, Distributive injustice and unfair exchange. In David M. Messick and Karen S. Cook (eds.), Equity Theory: Psychological and Social Perspectives. New York: Praeger.

—— 1984, Catalysts for collective violence: The importance of a psychological approach. In Robert Folger (ed.), The Sense of Injustice: Social Psychological Perspectives. New York: Plenum.

Massey, James L. and Marvin Krohn 1986, A longitudinal examination of an integrated social process model of deviant behavior. Social Forces 65:106–134.

Mawson, Anthony R. 1987, Criminality: A Model of Stress-Induced Crime. New York: Praeger.

Merton, Robert 1938, Social structure and anomie. American Sociological Review 3:672–682.

Messick, David M. and Keith Sentis 1979, Fairness and preference. Journal of Experimental Social Psychology 15:418–434.

—— 1983, Fairness, preference, and fairness biases. In David M. Messick and Karen S. Cook (eds.), Equity Theory: Psychological and Sociological Perspectives. New York: Praeger.

Michael, Jack 1973, Positive and negative reinforcement, a distinction that is no longer necessary; or a better way to talk about bad things. In Eugene Ramp and George Semb (eds.), Behavior Analysis: Areas of Research and Application. Englewood Cliffs, N.J.: Prentice-Hall.

Mickelson, Roslyn Arlin 1990, The attitude-achievement paradox among black adolescents. Sociology of Education 63:44–61.

Mikula, Gerold 1980, Justice and Social Interaction. New York: Springer-Verlag.

—— 1986, The experience of injustice: Toward a better understanding of its phenomenology. In Hans Werner Bierhoff, Ronald L. Cohen, and Jerald Greenberg (eds.), Justice in Social Relations. New York: Plenum.

Morgan, Rick L. and David Heise 1988, Structure of emotions. Social Psychology Quarterly 51:19–31.

Mueller, Charles W. 1983, Environmental stressors and aggressive behavior. In Russell G. Geen and Edward I. Donnerstein (eds.), Aggression: Theoretical and Empirical Reviews. Vol. 2. New York: Academic Press.

Newcomb, Michael D. and L. L. Harlow 1986, Life events and substance use among adolescents: Mediating effects of peceived loss of control and meaninglessness in life. Journal Personality and Social Psychology 51:564–577.

Novy, Diane M. and Stephen Donohue 1985, The relationship between adolescent life stress events and delinquent conduct including conduct indicating a need for supervision. Adolescence 78:313–321.

Pearlin, Leonard I. 1983, Role strains and personal stress. In Howard Kaplan (ed.), Psychosocial Stress: Trends in Theory and Research. New York: Academic Press.

Pearlin, Leonard I. and Carmi Schooler 1978, The structure of coping. Journal of Health and Social Behavior 19:2–21.

Pearlin, Leonard I., Elizabeth G. Menaghan, Morton A. Lieberman, and Joseph T. Mullan 1981, The stress process. Journal of Health and Social Behavior 22:337–356.

Quicker, John 1974, The effect of goal discrepancy on delinquency. Social Problems 22:76–86.

Rivera, Beverly and Cathy Spatz Widom 1990, Childhood victimization and violent offending. Violence and Victims 5:19–35.

Rosenberg, Morris 1990, Reflexivity and emotions. Social Psychology Quarterly 53:3–12.

Ross, Michael, John Thibaut, and Scott Evenback 1971, Some determinants of the intensity of social protest. Journal of Experimental Social Psychology 7:401–418.

Schwinger, Thomas 1980, Just allocations of goods: Decisions among three principles. In Gerald Mikula (ed.), Justice and Social Interaction. New York: Springer-Verlag.

Short, James F. and Fred L. Strodtbeck 1965, Group Process and Gang Delinquency. Chicago: University of Chicago Press.

Slaby, Ronald G. and Nancy G. Guerra 1988, Cognitive mediators of aggression in adolescent offenders: 1. Developmental Psychology 24:580–588.

Sprecher, Susan 1986, The relationship between inequity and emotions in close relationships. Social Psychology Quarterly 49:309–321.

Stephenson, G.M. and J.H. White 1968, An experimental study of some effects of injustice on children's moral behavior. Journal of Experimental Social Psychology 4:460–469.

Straus, Murray 1991, Discipline and deviance: Physical punishment of children and violence and other crimes in adulthood. Social Problems 38:133–154.

Sullivan, Mercer L. 1989, Getting Paid. Ithaca, N.Y.: Cornell University Press.

Suls, Jerry M. and Thomas Ashby Wills 1991 Social Comparison: Contemporary Theory and Research. Hillsdale, N.J.: Lawrence Erlbaum.

Tavris, Carol 1984, On the wisdom of counting to ten. In Philip Shaver (ed.), Review of Personality and Social Psychology: 5. Beverly Hills, Calif.: Sage.

Thibaut, John W. and Harold H. Kelley 1959, The Social Psychology of Groups. New York: John Wiley & Sons.

Thoits, Peggy 1983, Dimensions of life events that influence psychological distress: An evaluation and synthesis of the literature. In Howard B. Kaplan (ed.), Psychosocial Stress: Trends in Theory and Research. New York: academic Press.

—— 1991a, On merging identity theory and stress research. Social Psychology Quarterly 54:101–112.

—— 1991b, Patterns of coping with controllable and uncontrollable events. In E. Mark Cummings, Anita L. Greene, and Katherine H. Karraker (eds.), Life-Span Developmental Psychology: Perspectives on Stress and Coping. Hillsdale, N.J.: Lawrence Erlbaum.

Thornberry, Terence P. 1987, Toward an Interactional Theory of Delinquency. Criminology 25:863–891.

Tonry, Michael, Lloyd E. Ohlin, and David P. Farrington 1991, Human Development and Criminal Behavior. New York: Springer-Verlag.

Utne, Mary Kristine and Robert Kidd 1980, Equity and attribution. In Gerald Mikula (ed.), Justice and Social Interaction. New York: Springer-Verlag.

Van Houten, Ron 1983, Punishment: From the animal laboratory to the applied setting. In Saul Axelrod and Jack Apsche (eds.), The Effects of Punishment on Human Behavior. New York: Academic Press.

Vaux, Alan 1988, Social support: Theory, Research, and Intervention. New York: Praeger.

Vaux, Alan and Mary Ruggiero 1983, Stressful life change and delinquent behavior. American Journal of Community Psychology 11:169–183.

Walster, Elaine, Ellen Berscheid, and G. William Walster 1973, New directions in equity research. Journal of Personality and Social Psychology 25:151–176.

Walster, Elaine, G. William Walster, and Ellen Bersheid 1978, Equity: Theory and Research. Boston: Allyn & Bacon.

Wang, Alvin Y. and R. Stephen Richarde 1988, Global versus task-specific measures of self-efficacy. Psychological Record 38:533–541.

Weiner, Bernard 1982, The emotional consequences of causal attributions. In Margaret S. Clark and Susan T. Fiske (eds.), Affect and Cognition: The Seventeenth Annual Carnegie Symposium on Cognition. Hillsdale, N.J.: Lawrence Erlbaum.

Williams, Carolyn L. and Craige Uchiyama 1989, Assessment of life events during adolescence: The use of self-report inventories. Adolescence 24:95–118.

Zillman, Dolf 1979, Hostility and Aggression. Hillsdale, N.J.: Lawrence Erlbaum.

Chapter 19

Robert J. Sampson and William J. Wilson

TOWARD A THEORY OF RACE, CRIME, AND URBAN INEQUALITY

From: Robert J. Sampson and William J. Wilson (1990), excerpts from 'Toward a theory of race, crime, and urban inequality', in John Hagan and Ruth D. Peterson (eds), *Crime and Inequality*, Stanford, CA: Stanford University Press, pp. 37–54.

O**UR PURPOSE IN THIS** chapter is to address one of the central yet difficult issues facing criminology – race and violent crime. The centrality of the issue is seen on several fronts: the leading cause of death among young black males is homicide (Fingerhut and Kleinman 1990: 3292), and the lifetime risk of being murdered is as high as 1 in 21 for black males, compared with only 1 in 131 for white males (U.S. Department of Justice 1985). Although rates of violence have been higher for blacks than whites at least since the 1950s (Jencks 1991), record increases in homicide since the mid-1980s in cities such as New York, Chicago, and Philadelphia also appear racially selective (Hinds 1990; James 1991; Recktenwald and Morrison 1990). For example, while white rates remained stable, the rate of death from firearms among young black males more than doubled from 1984 to 1988 alone (Fingerhut et al. 1991). These differentials help explain recent estimates that a resident of rural Bangladesh has a greater chance of surviving to age 40 than does a black male in Harlem (McCord and Freeman 1990). Moreover, the so-called drug war and the resulting surge in prison populations in the past decade have taken their toll disproportionately on the minority community (Mauer 1990). Overall, the evidence is clear that African-Americans face dismal and worsening odds when it comes to crime in the streets and the risk of incarceration.

Despite these facts, the discussion of race and crime is mired in an unproductive mix of controversy and silence. At the same time that articles on age and gender abound, criminologists are loath to speak openly on race and crime for fear of being misunderstood or labeled racist. This situation is not unique, for until recently scholars of urban poverty also consciously avoided discussion of race and social dislocations in the inner city lest they be accused of blaming the victim (see W. J. Wilson 1987). And when the topic is broached, criminologists have reduced the race-crime debate to simplistic arguments about culture versus social structure. On the one side, structuralists argue for the primacy of "relative deprivation" to understand black crime (e.g., Blau and Blau 1982), even though the evidence on social class and crime is weak at best. On the other side, cultural theorists tend to focus on an indigenous culture of violence in black ghettos (e.g., Wolfgang and Ferracuti 1967), even though the evidence there is weak too.

Still others engage in subterfuge, denying race-related differentials in violence and focusing instead on police bias and the alleged invalidity of official crime statistics (e.g., Stark 1990). This in spite of evidence not only from death records but also from survey reports showing that blacks are disproportionately victimized by, and involved in, criminal violence (Hindelang 1976, 1978). Hence, much like the silence on race and inner-city social dislocations engendered by the vociferous attacks on the Moynihan Report in the 1960s, criminologists have, with few exceptions (e.g., Hawkins 1986; Hindelang 1978; Katz 1988), abdicated serious scholarly debate on race and crime.

In an attempt to break this stalemate we advance in this chapter a theoretical strategy that incorporates both structural and cultural arguments regarding race, crime, and inequality in American cities. In contrast to psychologically based relative deprivation theories and the subculture of violence, we view the race and crime linkage from contextual lenses that highlight the very different ecological contexts that blacks and whites reside in – regardless of individual characteristics. The basic thesis is that macrosocial patterns of residential inequality give rise to the social isolation and ecological concentration of the truly disadvantaged, which in turn leads to structural barriers and cultural adaptations that undermine social organization and hence the control of crime. This thesis is grounded in what is actually an old idea in criminology that has been overlooked in the race and crime debate – the importance of communities.

THE COMMUNITY STRUCTURE OF RACE AND CRIME

Unlike the dominant tradition in criminology that seeks to distinguish offenders from non-offenders, the macrosocial or community level of explanation asks what it is about community structures and cultures that produces differential rates of crime (Bursik 1988; Byrne and Sampson 1986; Short 1985). As such, the goal of macrolevel research is not to explain individual involvement in criminal behavior but to isolate characteristics of communities, cities, or even societies that lead to high rates of criminality (Byrne and Sampson 1986; Short 1985). From this viewpoint the "ecological fallacy" – inferring individual-level relations based on aggregate data – is not at issue because the unit of explanation and analysis is the community.

The Chicago School research of Clifford Shaw and Henry McKay spearheaded the community-level approach of modern American studies of ecology and crime. In their classic work *Juvenile Delinquency and Urban Areas*, Shaw and McKay (1942) argued that three structural factors – low economic status, ethnic heterogeneity, and residential mobility – led to the disruption of local community social organization, which in turn accounted for variations in crime and delinquency rates (for more details see Kornhauser 1978).

Arguably the most significant aspect of Shaw and McKay's research, however, was their demonstration that high rates of delinquency persisted in certain areas over many years, regardless of population turnover. More than any other, this finding led them to reject individualistic explanations of delinquency and focus instead on the processes by which delinquent and criminal patterns of behavior were transmitted across generations in areas of social disorganization and weak social controls (1942, 1969: 320). This community-level orientation led them to an explicit contextual interpretation of correlations between race/ethnicity and delinquency rates. Their logic was set forth in a rejoinder to a critique in 1949 by Jonassen, who had argued that ethnicity had direct effects on delinquency. Shaw and McKay countered:

> The important fact about rates of delinquency for Negro boys is that they, too, vary by type of area. They are higher than the rates for white boys, but it cannot be said that they are higher than rates for white boys in comparable areas, since it is impossible to reproduce in white communities the circumstances under which Negro children live. Even if it were possible to parallel the low economic status and the inadequacy of institutions in the white community, it would not be possible to reproduce the effects of segregation and the barriers to upward mobility.
>
> (1949: 614)

Shaw and McKay's insight almost a half century ago raises two interesting questions still relevant today. First, to what extent do black rates of crime vary by type of ecological area? Second, is it possible to reproduce in white communities the structural circumstances in which many blacks live? The first questions is crucial, for it signals that blacks are not a homogeneous group any more than whites are. Indeed, it is racial stereotyping that assigns to blacks a distinct or homogeneous character, allowing simplistic comparisons of black-white group differences in crime. As Shaw and McKay recognized, the key point is that there is heterogeneity among blacks in crime rates that correspond to community context. To the extent that the causes of black crime are not unique, its rate should thus vary with specific ecological conditions in the same way that the white crime rate does. As we shall now see, recent evidence weighs in Shaw and McKay's favor.

Are the causes of black crime unique?

Disentangling the contextual basis for race and crime requires racial disaggregation of both the crime rate and the explanatory variables of theoretical interest. This approach was used in recent research that examined racially disaggregated rates of homicide and robbery by juveniles and adults in over 150 U.S. cities in 1980 (Sampson 1987). Substantively, the theory explored the effects of black male joblessness and economic deprivation on violent crime as mediated by black family disruption. The results supported the main hypothesis and showed that the scarcity of employed black males relative to black females was directly related to the prevalence of families headed by women in black communities (W. J. Wilson 1987). In turn, black family disruption was substantially related to rates of black murder and robbery, especially by juveniles (see also Messner and Sampson 1991). These effects were independent of income, region, density, city size, and welfare benefits.

The finding that family disruption had stronger effects on juvenile violence than on adult violence, in conjunction with the inconsistent findings of previous research on individual-level delinquency and broken homes, supports the idea that the effects of family structure are related to macro-level patterns of social control and guardianship, especially for youth and their peers (Sampson and Groves 1989). Moreover, the results suggest why unemployment and economic deprivation have had weak or inconsistent direct effects on violence rates in past research – joblessness and poverty appear to exert much of their influence indirectly through family disruption.

Despite a tremendous difference in mean levels of family disruption among black and white communities, the percentage of white families headed by a female also had a large positive effect on white juvenile and white adult violence. In fact, the predictors of white robbery were shown to be in large part identical in sign and magnitude to those for blacks. Therefore, the effect of black family disruption on black crime was independent of commonly cited alternative explanations (e.g., region, density, age composition) and could not be attributed to unique cultural factors within the black community given the similar effect of white family disruption on white crime.

To be clear, we are not dismissing the relevance of culture. As discussed more below, our argument is that if cultural influences exist, they vary systematically with structural features of the urban environment. How else can we make sense of the systematic varia-tions *within* race – for example, if a uniform subculture of violence explains black crime, are we to assume that this subculture is three times as potent in, say, New York as in Chicago (where black homicide differs by a factor of three)? In San Francisco as in Baltimore (3:1 ratio)? These distinct variations exist even at the state level. For example, rates of black homicide in California are triple those in Maryland (Wellbanks 1986). Must whites then be part of the black subculture of violence in California, given that white homicide rates are also more than triple the rates for whites in Maryland? We think not. The sources of violent crime appear to be remarkably invariant across race and rooted instead in the structural differences among communities, cities, and states in economic and family organization.

The ecological concentration of race and social dislocations

Having demonstrated the similarity of black-white variations by ecological context, we turn to the second logical question. To what extent are blacks as a group differentially exposed to criminogenic structural conditions? More than 40 years after Shaw and McKay's assessment of race and urban ecology, we still cannot say that blacks and whites share a similar environment – especially with regard to concentrated urban poverty. Consider the following. Although approximately 70 percent of all poor non-Hispanic whites lived in nonpoverty areas in the ten largest U.S. central cities (as determined by the 1970 census) in 1980, only 16 percent of poor blacks did. Moreover, whereas less than 7 percent of poor whites lived in extreme poverty or ghetto areas, 38 percent of poor blacks lived in such areas (W. J. Wilson et al. 1988: 130). In the nation's largest city, New York, 70 percent of poor blacks live in poverty neighborhoods; by contrast, 70 percent of poor whites live in non-poverty neighborhoods (Sullivan 1989: 230). Potentially even more important, the majority of poor blacks live in communities characterized by high rates of family disruption. Poor whites, even those from "broken homes," live in areas of relative family stability (Sampson 1987; Sullivan 1989).

The combination of urban poverty and family disruption concentrated by race is particularly severe. As an example, we examined race-specific census data on the 171 largest cities in the United States as of 1980. To get some idea of concentrated social dislocations by race, we selected cities where the proportion of blacks living in poverty was equal to or less than the proportion of whites, *and* where the proportion of black families with children headed by a single parent was equal to or less than that for white families. Although we knew that the average national rate of family disruption and poverty among blacks was two to four times higher than among whites, the number of distinct ecological contexts in which blacks achieve equality to whites is striking. In not one city over 100,000 in the United States do blacks live in ecological equality with whites when it comes to these basic features of economic and family organization. Accordingly, racial differences in poverty and family disruption are so strong that the "worst" urban contexts in which whites reside are considerably better than the average context of black communities (Sampson 1987: 354).

Taken as a whole, these patterns underscore what W. J. Wilson (1987) has labeled "concentration effects," that is, the effects of living in a neighborhood that is overwhelmingly impoverished. These concentration effects, reflected in a range of outcomes from degree of labor force attachment to social deviance, are created by the constraints and opportunities that the residents of inner-city neighborhoods face in terms of access to jobs and job networks, involvement in quality schools, availability of marriageable partners, and exposure to conventional role models.

The social transformation of the inner city in recent decades has resulted in an increased concentration of the most disadvantaged segments of the urban black population – especially poor, female-headed families with children. Whereas one of every five poor blacks resided in ghetto or extreme poverty areas in 1970, by 1980 nearly two out of every five did so (W. J. Wilson et al. 1988: 131). This change has been fueled by several macrostructural forces. In particular, urban minorities have been vulnerable to structural economic changes related to the deindustrialization of central cities (e.g., the shift from goods-producing to service-producing industries; increasing polarization of the labor market into low-wage and high-wage sectors; and relocation of manufacturing out of the inner city). The exodus of middle and upper-income black families from the inner city has also removed an important social buffer that could potentially deflect the full impact of prolonged joblessness and industrial transformation. This thesis is based on the assumption that the basic institutions of an area (churches, schools, stores, recreational facilities, etc.) are more likely to remain viable if the core of their support comes from more economically stable families in inner-city neighborhoods (W. J. Wilson 1987: 56). The social milieu of increasing stratification among blacks differs significantly from the environment that existed in inner cities in previous decades (see also Hagedorn 1988).

Black inner-city neighborhoods have also disproportionately suffered severe population and housing loss of the sort identified by Shaw and McKay (1942) as disrupting the social and institutional order. Skogan (1986: 206) has noted how urban renewal and forced migration contributed to the wholesale uprooting of many urban black communities, especially the extent to which freeway networks driven through the hearts of many cities in the 1950s destroyed viable, low-income communities. For example, in Atlanta one in six residents was dislocated by urban renewal; the great majority of those dislocated were poor blacks (Logan and Molotch 1987: 114). Nationwide, fully 20 percent of all central-city housing units occupied by blacks were lost in the period 1960–70 alone. As Logan and Molotch (1987: 114) observe, this displacement does not even include that brought about by more routine market forces (evictions, rent increases, commercial development).

Of course, no discussion of concentration effects is complete without recognizing the negative consequences of deliberate policy decisions to concentrate minorities and the poor in public housing. Opposition from organized community groups to the building of public housing in their neighborhoods, de facto federal policy to tolerate extensive segregation against blacks in urban housing markets, and the decision by local governments to neglect the rehabilitation of existing residential units (many of them single-family homes), have led to massive, segregated housing projects that have become ghettos for the minorities and disadvantaged (see also Sampson 1990). The cumulative result is that, even given the same objective socioeconomic status, blacks and whites face vastly different environments in which to live, work, and raise their children. As Bickford and Massey (1991: 1035) have argued, public housing is a federally funded, physically permanent institution for the isolation of black families by race and class and must therefore be considered an important structural constraint on ecological area of residence.

In short, the foregoing discussion suggests that macrostructural factors – both historic and contemporary – have combined to concentrate urban black poverty and family disruption in the inner city. These factors include but are not limited to racial segregation, structural economic transformation and black male joblessness, class-linked out-migration from the inner city, and housing discrimination. It is important to emphasize that when segregation and concentrated poverty represent structural constraints embodied in public policy and historical patterns of racial subjugation, notions that individual differences (or self-selection) explain community-level effects on violence are considerably weakened (see Sampson and Lauritsen 1994).

Implications

The consequences of these differential ecological distributions by race raise the substantively plausible hypothesis that correlations of race and crime may be systematically confounded with important differences in community contexts. As Testa has argued with respect to escape from poverty:

> Simple comparisons between poor whites and poor blacks would be confounded with the fact that poor whites reside in areas which are ecologically and economically very different from poor blacks. Any observed relationships involving race would reflect, to some unknown degree, the relatively superior ecological niche many poor whites occupy with respect to jobs, marriage opportunities, and exposure to conventional role models.
> (quoted in W. J. Wilson 1987: 58–60)

Regardless of a black's individual-level family or economic situation, the average community of residence thus differs dramatically from that of a similarly situated white (Sampson 1987). For example, regardless of whether a black juvenile is raised in an intact or single-parent family, or a rich or poor home, he or she will not likely grow up in a community context similar to that of whites with regard to family structure and income. Reductionist interpretations of race and social class camouflage this key point.

In fact, a community conceptualization exposes the "individualistic fallacy" – the often-involved assumption that individual-level causal relations necessarily generate individual-level correlations. Research conducted at the individual level rarely questions whether obtained results might be spurious and confounded with community-level processes. In the present case, it is commonplace to search for individual-level (e.g., constitutional) or group-level (e.g., social class) explanations for the link between race and violence. In our opinion these efforts have largely failed, and so we highlight contextual sources of the race-violence link among individuals. More specifically, we posit that the most important determinant of the relationship between race and crime is the differential distribution of blacks in communities characterized by (1) *structural social disorganization* and (2) *cultural social isolation*, both of which stem from the concentration of poverty, family disruption, and residential instability.

Before explicating the theoretical dimensions of social disorganization, we must also expose what may be termed the "materialist fallacy" – that economic (or materialist) causes necessarily produce economic motivations. Owing largely to Merton's (1938) famous dictum about social structure and anomie, criminologists have assumed that if economic structural factors (e.g., poverty) are causally relevant it must be through the motivation to commit acquisitive crimes. Indeed, "strain" theory was so named to capture the hypothesized pressure on members of the lower classes to commit crime in their pursuit of the American dream. But as is well known, strain or materialist theories have not fared well empirically (Kornhauser 1978). The image of the offender stealing to survive flourishes only as a straw man, knocked down most recently by Jack Katz, who argues that materialist theory is nothing more than "twentieth-century sentimentality about crime" (1988: 314). Assuming, however, that those who posit the relevance of economic structure for crime rely on motivational pressure as an explanatory concept, is itself a fallacy. The theory of social disorganization *does* see relevance in the ecological concentration of poverty, but not for the materialist reasons Katz (1988) presupposes. Rather, the conceptualization we now explicate rests on the fundamental properties of structural and cultural organization.

THE STRUCTURE OF SOCIAL (DIS)ORGANIZATION

In their original formulation Shaw and McKay held that low economic status, ethnic heterogeneity, and residential mobility led to the disruption of community social organization, which in turn accounted for variations in crime and delinquency rates (1942; 1969). As recently extended by Kornhauser (1978), Bursik (1988), and Sampson and Groves (1989), the concept of social disorganization may be seen as the inability of a community structure to realize the common values of its residents and maintain effective social controls. The *structural* dimensions of community social disorganization refer to the prevalence and interdependence of social networks in a community – both informal (e.g., the density of acquaintanceship; intergenerational kinship ties; level of anonymity) and formal (e.g., organizational participation; institutional stability) – and in the span of collective supervision that the community directs toward local problems.

This social-disorganization approach is grounded in what Kasarda and Janowitz (1974: 329) call the "systemic" model, where the local community is viewed as a complex system of friendship and kinship networks, and formal and informal associational ties are rooted in family life and ongoing socialization processes (see also Sampson 1991). From this view social organization and social *disorganization* are seen as different ends of the same continuum of systemic networks of community social control As Bursik (1988) notes, when formulated in this way, social disorganization is clearly separable not only from the processes that may lead to it (e.g., poverty, residential mobility), but also from the degree of criminal behavior that may be a result. This conceptualization also goes beyond the traditional account of community as a strictly geographical or spatial phenomenon by focusing on the social and organizational networks of local residents (see Leighton 1988).

Evidence favoring social disorganization theory is available with respect both to its structural antecedents and to mediating processes. In a recent paper, Sampson and Lauritsen (1994) reviewed in depth the empirical literature on individual, situational, and community-level sources of interpersonal violence (i.e., assault, homicide, robbery, and rape). This assessment revealed that community-level research conducted in the past twenty years has largely supported the original Shaw and McKay model in terms of the exogenous correlates of poverty, residential mobility, and heterogeneity. What appears to be especially salient is the *interaction* of poverty and mobility. As anticipated by Shaw and McKay (1942) and Kornhauser (1978), several studies indicate that the effect of poverty is most pronounced in neighborhoods of high residential instability (see Sampson and Lauritsen 1994).

In addition, recent research has established that crime rates are positively linked to community-level variations in urbanization (e.g., population and housing density), family disruption (e.g., percentage of single-parent households), opportunity structures for predatory crime (e.g., density of convenience stores), and rates of community change and population turnover (see also Bursik 1988; Byrne and Sampson 1986; Reiss 1986). As hypothesized by Sampson and Groves (1989), family disruption, urbanization, and the anonymity accompanying rapid population change all undercut the capacity of a community to exercise informal social control, especially of teenage peer groups in public spaces.

Land et al. (1990) have also shown the relevance of *resource deprivation*, *family dissolution*, and *urbanization* (density, population size) for explaining homicide rates across cities, metropolitan areas, and states from 1960 to 1980. In particular, their factor of resource deprivation/affluence included three income variables – median income, the percentage of families below the poverty line, and the Gini index of income inequality – in addition to the percentage of population that is black and the percentage of children not living with both parents. This coalescence of structural conditions with race supports the concept of concentration effects (W. J. Wilson 1987) and is consistent with Taylor and Covington's finding (1988) that increasing entrenchment of ghetto poverty was associated with large increases in violence. In these two studies the correlation among structural indices was not seen merely as a statistical nuisance (i.e., as multicollinearity), but as a predictable substantive outcome. Moreover, the Land et al. (1990) results support Wilson's argument that concentration effects grew more severe from 1970 to 1980 in large cities. Urban disadvantage thus appears to be increasing in ecological concentration.

It is much more difficult to study the intervening mechanisms of social disorganization directly, but at least two recent studies provide empirical support for the theory's structural dimensions. First, Taylor et al. (1984) examined variations in violent crime (e.g., mugging, assault, murder, rape) across 63 street blocks in Baltimore in 1978.

Based on interviews with 687 household respondents, Taylor et al. (1984: 316) constructed block-level measures of the proportion of respondents who belonged to an organization to which co-residents also belonged, and the proportion of respondents who felt responsible for what happened in the area surrounding their home. Both of these dimensions of informal social control were significantly and negatively related to community-level variations in crime, exclusive of other ecological factors (1984: 320). These results support the social disorganization hypothesis that levels of organizational participation and informal social control – especially of public activities by neighborhood youth – inhibit community-level rates of violence.

Second, Sampson and Groves's analysis of the British Crime Survey in 1982 and 1984 showed that the prevalence of unsupervised teenage peer groups in a community had the largest effects on rates of robbery and violence by strangers. The density of local friend-ship networks – measured by the proportion of residents with half or more of their friends living in the neighbourhood – also had a significant negative effect on robbery rates. Further, the level of organizational participation by residents had significant inverse effects on both robbery and stranger violence (Sampson and Groves 1989: 789). These results suggest that communities characterized by sparse friendship networks, unsuper-vised teenage peer groups, and low organizational participation foster increased crime rates (see also Anderson 1990).

Variations in these structural dimensions of community social disorganization also transmitted in large part the effects of community socioeconomic status, residential mobility, ethnic heterogeneity, and family disruption in a theoretically consistent manner. For example, mobility had significant inverse effects on friendship networks, family disruption was the largest predictor of unsupervised peer groups, and socioeconomic sta-tus had a significant positive effect on organizational participation in 1982. When combined with the results of research on gang delinquency, which point to the salience of informal and formal community structures in controlling the formation of gangs (Short and Strodtbeck 1965; Sullivan 1989; Thrasher 1963), the empirical data suggest that the structural elements of social disorganization have relevance for explaining macrolevel variations in crime.

Further modifications

To be sure, social-disorganization theory *as traditionally conceptualized* is hampered by a restricted view of community that fails to account for the larger political and structural forces shaping communities. As suggested earlier, many community characteristics hypothesized to underlic crime rates, such as residential instability, concentration of poor, female-headed families with children, multi-unit housing projects, and disrupted social networks, appear to stem directly from planned governmental policies at local, state, and federal levels. We thus depart from the natural market assumptions of the Chicago School ecologists by incorporating the political economy of place (Logan and Molotch 1987), along with macrostructural transformations and historical forces, into our conceptualization of community-level social organization.

Take, for example, municipal code enforcement and local governmental policies toward neighborhood deterioration. In *Making the Second Ghettos: Race and Housing in Chicago, 1940–1960*, Hirsch (1983) documents in great detail how lax enforcement of city housing codes played a major role in accelerating the deterioration of inner-city

Chicago neighborhoods. More recently, Daley and Mieslin (1988) have argued that inadequate city policies on code enforcement and repair of city properties contributed to the systematic decline of New York City's housing stock, and consequently, entire neighborhoods. When considered with the practices of redlining and disinvestment by banks and "block-busting" by real estate agents (Skogan 1986), local policies toward code enforcement – that on the surface are far removed from crime – have in all likelihood contributed to crime through neighborhood deterioration, forced migration, and instability.

Decisions to withdraw city municipal services for public health and fire safety – presumably made with little if any thought to crime and violence – also appear to have been salient in the social disintegration of poor communities. As Wallace and Wallace (1990) argue based on an analysis of the "planned shrinkage" of New York City fire and health services in recent decades: "The consequences of withdrawing municipal services from poor neighborhoods, the resulting outbreaks of contagious urban decay and forced migration which shred essential social networks and cause social disintegration, have become a highly significant contributor to decline in public health among the poor" (1990: 427). The loss of social integration and networks from planned shrinkage of services may increase behavioral patterns of violence that may themselves become "convoluted with processes of urban decay likely to further disrupt social networks and cause further social disintegration" (1990: 427). . . . . As Wacquant has recently argued, federal U.S. policy seems to favor "the institutional desertification of the urban core" (1991: 36).

Decisions by government to provide public housing paint a similar picture. Bursik (1989) has shown that the planned construction of new public housing projects in Chicago in the 1970s was associated with increased rates of population turnover, which in turn were related to increases in crime. More generally, we have already noted how the disruption of urban renewal contributed disproportionately to housing loss among poor blacks.

Boiled down to its essentials, then, our theoretical framework linking social-disorganization theory with research on urban poverty and political economy suggests that macrosocial forces (e.g., segregation, migration, housing discrimination, structural transformation of the economy) interact with local community-level factors (e.g., residential turnover, concentrated poverty, family disruption) to impede social organization. [. . .]

SOCIAL ISOLATION AND COMMUNITY CULTURE

Although social disorganization theory is primarily structural in nature, it also focuses on how the ecological segregation of communities gives rise to what Kornhauser (1978: 75) terms *cultural* disorganization – the attenuation of societal cultural values. Poverty, heterogeneity, anonymity, mutual distrust, institutional instability, and other structural features of urban communities are hypothesized to impede communication and obstruct the quest for common values, thereby fostering cultural diversity with respect to non-delinquent values. For example, an important component of Shaw and McKay's theory was that disorganized communities spawned delinquent gangs with their own subcultures and norms perpetuated through cultural transmission.

Despite their relative infrequency, ethnographic studies generally support the notion that structurally disorganized communities are conducive to the emergence of cultural value systems and attitudes that seem to legitimate, or at least provide a basis of tolerance for, crime and deviance. [. . .]

Whether community subcultures are authentic or merely "shadow cultures" (Liebow 1967) cannot be resolved here (see also Kornhauser 1978). But that seems less important than acknowledging that community contexts seem to shape what can be termed *cognitive landscapes* or ecologically structured norms (e.g., normative ecologies) regarding appropriate standards and expectations of conduct. That is, in structurally disorganized slum communities, it appears that a system of values emerges in which crime, disorder, and drug use are less than fervently condemned and hence expected as part of everyday life. These ecologically structured social perceptions and tolerances in turn appear to influence the probability of criminal outcomes and harmful deviant behavior (e.g., drug use by pregnant women). In this regard Kornhauser's attack on subcultural theories misses the point. By attempting to assess whether subcultural values are authentic in some deep, almost quasi-religious sense (1978: 1–20), she loses sight of the processes by which cognitive landscapes rooted in social ecology may influence everyday behavior. Indeed, the idea that dominant values become existentially irrelevant in certain community contexts is a powerful one, albeit one that has not had the research exploitation it deserves (cf. Katz 1988).

A renewed appreciation for the role of cultural adaptations is congruent with the notion of *social isolation* – defined as the lack of contact or of sustained interaction with individuals and institutions that represent mainstream society (W. J. Wilson 1987: 60). According to this line of reasoning, the social isolation fostered by the ecological concentration of urban poverty deprives residents not only of resources and conventional role models, but also of cultural learning from mainstream social networks that facilitate social and economic advancement in modern industrial society (W. J. Wilson 1991). Social isolation is specifically distinguished from the culture of poverty by virtue of its focus on adaptations to constraints and opportunities rather than internalization of norms. [. . .]

CONCLUSION

By recasting traditional race and poverty arguments in a contextual framework that incorporates both structural and cultural concepts, we seek to generate empirical and theoretical ideas that may guide further research. The unique value of a community-level perspective is that it leads away from a simple "kinds of people" analysis to a focus on how social characteristics of collectivities foster violence. On the basis of our theoretical framework, we conclude that community-level factors such as the *ecological concentration of ghetto poverty*, *racial segregation*, *residential mobility* and population turnover, *family disruption*, and the dimensions of local *social organization* (e.g., density of friendship/ acquaintanceship, social resources, intergenerational links, control of street-corner peer groups, organizational participation) are fruitful areas of future inquiry, especially as they are affected by macrolevel public policies regarding housing, municipal services, and employment. In other words, our framework suggests the need to take a renewed look at social policies that focus on prevention. We do not need more after-the-fact (reactive) approaches that ignore the structural context of crime and the social organization of inner cities.

References

Anderson, E. 1978. *A Place on the Corner*. Chicago, IL: University of Chicago Press.

———. 1990. *Streetwise: Race, Class, and Change in an Urban Community*. Chicago, IL: University of Chicago Press.

Bickford, A. and D. Massey. 1991. "Segregation in the second ghetto: Racial and ethnic segregation in American public housing, 1977." *Social Forces* 69: 1011–36.

Blau, J. and P.M. Blau. 1982. "The cost of inequality: Metropolitan structure and violent crime." *American Sociological Review* 47: 114–29.

Bursik, R.J., Jr. 1998. "Social disorganization and theories of crime and delinquency: Problems and prospects." *Criminology* 26: 519–52.

———. 1989. "Political decision-making and ecological models of delinquency: Conflict and consensus." In S. Messner, M. Krohn, and A. Liska (eds) *Theoretical Integration in the Study of Deviance and Crime*. Albany, NY: State University of New York at Albany Press.

Byrne, J. and R.J. Sampson. 1986. "Key issues in the social ecology of crime." In J. Byrne and R.J. Sampson (eds) *The Social Ecology of Crime*. New York: Springer-Verlag, pp. 1–22.

Daley, S. and R. Meislin. 1988. "New York City, the landlord: A decade of housing decay." *New York Times*, February 8.

Fingerhut, L. and J. Kleinman. 1990. "International and interstate comparisons of homicide among young males." *Journal of the American Medical Association* 263: 3292–95.

Fingerhut, L., J. Kleinman, E. Godfrey, and H. Rosenberg. 1991. "Firearms mortality among children, youth, and young adults 1–34 years of age, trends and current status: United States, 1979–88." *Monthly Vital Statistics Report* 39(11): 1–16.

Hagedorn, J. 1988. *Gangs, Crime and the Underclass in a Rustbelt City*. Chicago, IL: Lake View Press.

Hannerz, Ulf. 1969. *Soulside: Inquiries into Ghetto Culture and Community*. New York: Columbia University Press.

Hawkins, D. (ed.). 1986. *Homicide Among Black Americans*. Lanham, MD: University Press of America.

Hindelang, M. 1976. *Criminal Victimization in Eight American Cities*. Cambridge: Ballinger.

———. 1978. "Race and involvement in common-law personal crimes." *American Sociological Review* 43: 93–109.

Hinds, M. 1990. "Number of killings soars in big cities across U.S." *New York Times*, July 18, p. 1.

Hirsch, A. 1983. *Making the Second Ghetto: Race and Housing in Chicago 1940–1960*. Chicago, IL: University of Chicago Press.

Horowitz, R. 1987. "Community tolerance of gang violence." *Social Problems* 34: 437–50.

James, G. 1991. "New York killings set record in 1990." *New York Times*, p. A14.

Jencks, C. 1991. "Is violent crime increasing?" *The American Prospect* Winter: 98–109.

Jonassen, C. 1949. "A reevaluation and critique of the logic and some methods of Shaw and McKay." *American Sociological Review* 14: 608–14.

Kasarda, J. and M. Janowitz. 1974. "Community attachment in mass society." *American Sociological Review* 39: 328–39.

Katz, J. 1988. *Seductions of Crime: The Sensual and Moral Attractions of Doing Evil*. New York: Basic.

Kornhauser, R. 1978. *Social Sources of Delinquency*. Chicago, IL: University of Chicago Press.

Land, K., P. McCall, and L. Cohen. 1990. "Structural covariates of homicide rates: Are there any invariances across time and space?" *American Journal of Sociology* 95: 922–63.

Leighton, B. 1988. "The community concept in criminology: Toward a social network approach." *Journal of Research in Crime and Delinquency* 25: 351–74.

Liebow, E. 1967. *Tally's Corner*. Boston, MA: Little Brown.

Logan, J. and H. Molotch. 1987. *Urban Fortunes: The Political Economy of Place*. Berkeley, CA: University of California Press.

McCord, M. and H. Freeman. 1990. "Excess mortality in Harlem." *New England Journal of Medicine* 322: 173–75.

Mauer, M. 1990. *Young Black Men and the Criminal Justice System: A Growing National Problem*. Washington, DC: The Sentencing Project.

Merton, R. 1938. "Social structure and anomie." *American Sociological Review* 3: 672–82.

Messner, S. and R. Sampson. 1991. "The sex ratio, family disruption, and rates of violent crime: The paradox of demographic structure." *Social Forces* 69: 693–714.

Prothrow-Stith, D. 1991. *Deadly Consequences*. New York: Harper Collins.

Recktenwald, W. and B. Morrison. 1990. "Guns, gangs, drugs make a deadly combination." *Chicago Tribune*, July 1, section 2, p. 1.

Reiss, A.J., Jr. 1986. "Why are communities important in understanding crime?" In A.J. Reiss, Jr and M. Tonry (eds) *Communities and Crime*. Chicago, IL: University of Chicago Press, pp. 1–33.

Sampson, R.J. 1987. "Urban black violence: The effect of male joblessness and family disruption." *American Journal of Sociology* 93: 348–82.

——. 1990. "The impact of housing policies on community social disorganization and crime." *Bulletin of the New York Academy of Medicine* 66: 526–33.

——. 1991. "Linking the micro and macrolevel dimensions of community social organization." *Social Forces* 70: 43–64.

Sampson, R.J. and W.B. Groves. 1989. "Community structure and crime: Testing social-disorganization theory." *American Journal of Sociology* 94: 774–802.

Sampson, R.J. and J. Lauritsen. 1994. "Violent victimization and offending: Individual-, situational-, and community-level risk factors." In Albert J. Reiss, Jr and Jeffrey Roth (eds) *Understanding and Preventing Violence: Social Influences*, Volume 3. Washington, DC: National Academy Press (National Research Council), pp. 1–114.

Shaw, C. and H. McKay. 1942. *Juvenile Delinquency and Urban Areas*. Chicago, IL: University of Chicago Press.

——. 1949. "Rejoinder." *American Sociological Review* 14: 614–17.

——. 1969. *Juvenile Delinquency and Urban Areas,* revised edition. Chicago, IL: University of Chicago Press.

Short, J.F., Jr. 1963. "Introduction to the abridged edition." In F. Thrasher (ed.) *The Gang: A Study of 1,313 Gangs in Chicago*, revised edition. Chicago, IL: University of Chicago Press, pp. xv–liii.

——. 1985. "The level of explanation problem in criminology." In R. Meier (ed.) *Theoretical Methods in Criminology*. Beverley Hills, CA: Sage, pp. 51–74.

Short, J.F., Jr and F. Strodtbeck. 1965. *Group Process and Gang Delinquency*. Chicago, IL: University of Chicago Press.

Skogan, W. 1986. "Fear of crime and neighborhood change." In A.J. Reiss, Jr and M. Tonry (eds) *Communities and Crime*. Chicago, IL: University of Chicago Press, pp. 203–29.

Stark, Evan. 1990. "The myth of black violence." *New York Times*.

Sullivan, M. 1989. *Getting Paid: Youth Crime and Work in the Inner City*. Ithaca, NY: Cornell University Press.

Suttles, G. 1968. *The Social Order of the Slum*. Chicago, IL: University of Chicago Press.

Taylor, R. and J. Covington. 1988. "Neighborhood changes in ecology and violence." *Criminology* 26: 553–90.

Taylor, R., S. Gottfredson, and S. Brower. 1984. "Block crime and fear: Defensible space, local social ties, and territorial functioning." *Journal of Research in Crime and Delinquency* 21: 303–31.

Thrasher, F. 1963. *The Gang: A Study of 1,313 Gangs in Chicago*, revised edition. Chicago, IL: University of Chicago Press.

US Department of Justice. 1985. *The Risk of Violent Crime.* Washington, DC: US Government Printing Office.

Wacquant, Loic. 1991. "The specificity of ghetto poverty: A comparative analysis of race, class, and urban exclusion in Chicago's Black Belt and the Parisian Red Belt." Paper prepared for presentation at the Chicago Urban Poverty and Family Life Conference, University of Chicago.

Wallace, R. and D. Wallace. 1990. "Origins of public health collapse in New York City: The dynamics of planned shrinkage, contagious urban decay and social disintegration" *Bulletin of the New York Academy of Medicine* 66: 391–434.

Wilbanks, W. 1986. "Criminal homicide offenders in the U.S.: Black vs. white." In D. Hawkins (ed.) *Homicide Among Black Americans*. Lanham, MD: University Press of America, pp. 43–56.

Wilson, W.J. 1987. *The Truly Disadvantaged: The Inner City, the Underclass, and Public Policy*. Chicago, IL: University of Chicago Press.

——. 1991. "Studying inner-city social dislocations: The challenge of public agenda research." *American Sociological Review* 56: 1–14.

Wilson, W.J., R. Aponte, J. Kirschenman, and L. Wacquant. 1988. "The ghetto underclass and the changing structure of American Poverty." In F. Harris and R.W. Wilkins (eds) *Quiet Riots: Race and Poverty in the United States*. New York: Pantheon, pp. 123–54.

Wolfgang, M. and F. Ferracuti. 1967. *The Subculture of Violence*. London: Tavistock.

Chapter 20

Elliott Currie

SOCIAL ACTION

From: Elliott Currie (1998), excerpts from 'Social action', in Elliott Currie, *Crime and Punishment in America: Why the Solutions to America's Most Stubborn Social Crisis have not Worked – and What Will*, New York: Henry Holt, pp. 110–148.

BEGINNING AS FAR BACK as the 1920s, and continuing for fifty years thereafter, most serious students of crime in America agreed that our unusually high levels of violence were related to our equally unusual extremes of economic deprivation and inequality. Exactly how these adversities translated into higher rates of serious crime was the subject of considerable debate. But few doubted that if we wanted to make enduring changes in the level of violent crime that distinguished us from the rest of the industrial world, we would need to attack those social deficits head on. The President's Commission on Law Enforcement and the Administration of Justice put it simply and forcefully in 1967: "Crime flourishes where the conditions of life are the worst." The "foundation of a national strategy against crime," therefore, had to be "an unremitting national effort for social justice." [. . .]

The consensus started to unravel in the 1970s, when conservative critics began to argue that the link between crime and social exclusion was a figment of the liberal imagination – in the most extreme version, that there were no "root causes" of crime at all. By the 1980s, what had begun as a trickle of ideas on the margins of public discourse had become a flood. Today, the idea that taking action against the social roots of crime is either unworkable, ill advised, or irrelevant has become the most pervasive myth of all.

Nowadays, even many conservatives acknowledge, if grudgingly, that at least *some* good may be accomplished by modest programs that deal, early on, with high-risk children and families. But the same is not true of broader efforts to attack the social roots of crime. . . . And among conservatives, suspicion of attempts to attack the social roots of crime is almost an article of faith. James Q. Wilson, for example, while skeptical about the impact of panaceas like three-strikes laws and boosting prison populations, also insists that there is little else that we "know how to do," at least within the constraints of a "free society." Wilson acknowledges, for example, that crime is disproportionately committed by impoverished young black men in the inner cities, but he also insists that there is not much we can do about the problem. . . . Though they "face a bleak life," he argues, "we don't know how to intervene effectively to prevent it."

The implication is clear: since we can't do much to stem the flow of violent criminals, we must redouble efforts to "contain" them. . . . But what is the evidence for this assertion that we are powerless to deal with the roots of crime? In the most simplistic versions of the argument, there is no attempt to offer evidence at all. [. . .]

Some conservative writers offer more elaborate arguments . . . purporting to show that a variety of social and economic factors often implicated in crime – poverty and inequality, joblessness, a harsh and depriving social order – aren't very important after all. The "real" causes of crime are to be found either within the flawed character of individuals or in small-scale settings like the family, into which free governments cannot or should not intrude. . . . Others make a distinction between moral or cultural causes – which are real – and economic ones, which are not. The cover of Bennett et al.'s *Body Count* informs us that the book "demolishes the myth [that] economic poverty" causes crime; something called "moral poverty," on the other hand, is the main explanation for the frightening levels of violence in America. Since these writers usually argue that moral decline is relatively impervious to government intervention, the emphasis on moral causes implies that not much can be done about crime through public action. [. . .]

Virtually by definition, violent crime represents a breakdown of morality, and the family practices that often breed it may, by anyone's measure, reflect a kind of moral impoverishment. . . . What's wrong in the conservative view is not the belief that the moral and cultural condition of American families and communities is important in understanding crime, but the denial that those conditions are themselves strongly affected by larger social and economic forces.

For there is now overwhelming evidence that inequality, extreme poverty, and social exclusion matter profoundly in shaping a society's experience of violent crime. And they matter, in good part, precisely because of their impact on the close-in institutions of family and community. [. . .]

I

One way to disparage the role of social and economic factors in crime is to downplay the differences in the seriousness of crime across different societies. If crime is pretty much the same everywhere, then, by implication, differences in social structure or economic policies can't have much to do with it. This is a central feature, for example, of James Q. Wilson's argument about the folly of government efforts to deal with the root causes of crime. In its most recent versions, the argument goes something like this: crime has risen throughout the industrial world in the past thirty years, just as those nations have become richer, freer, and more prosperous. Accordingly, the real root cause of crime is "prosperity, freedom, and democracy": crime, in other words, is a "cost of prosperity." [. . .]

Wilson's view is simply wrong. Around the world, the countries with relatively *low* levels of violent crime tend to be not only among the most prosperous but also those where prosperity has become most *general*, most evenly distributed throughout the population. The countries where violent crime is an endemic problem are those in which prosperity, to the extent that it is achieved at all, is confined to some sectors of the population and denied to others. That includes a number of less developed countries in Latin America, Africa, and the Caribbean (and parts of the former Soviet bloc) and one country in the developed world – the United States.

America's dominance in violent crime is sometimes masked by statistics suggesting that for *less* serious crimes – including most property crimes and lesser forms of assault – the industrial democracies are more alike than different. Even for these crimes, however, the similarities may be exaggerated, for lesser crimes are even more difficult to measure than more serious ones, and the instruments used to count them are more than usually imperfect, especially when we try to compare the extent of these offenses across national borders. And more important, there is no real disagreement that the United States stands out from all other advanced industrial nations in its level of serious violence. Whatever may be said about burglary, bicycle theft, or schoolyard fights, what *most* distinguishes America from other developed countries is the extent to which Americans are willing to rob, maim, kill, and rape one another. Even Wilson acknowledges that we have "two crime problems" in America: lesser crimes, mostly property offenses, a problem that we share with other countries; and serious violence, a problem that he admits we do not. [. . .]

Let's consider, in more detail, some of the dimensions of this difference. In recent years our national homicide rate has ranged from about three or four to more than twenty times that of other advanced industrial nations. The biggest differences are for young men – among whom the enormous increases in lethal violence took place in the United States after the mid-1980s. But such is the magnitude of the national differences in the risks of homicide that they transcend other usually powerful predictors, like age and gender. American men in their forties are far more likely to die of deliberate violence than are *youths* in every western European society. [. . .]

These differences are not confined to homicide, although it's there that our statistics are most reliable and, probably not coincidentally, that the international differences are sharpest. Take robbery: although even minor robberies are apparently more likely to be reported and recorded in many other developed countries (because their citizens are less resigned to being robbed and less fearful of reporting crime to the police), reported robbery rates are much higher here than in comparable countries. Thus, despite the several-year decline in crime in New York City, it was only in 1995 that the number of robberies there fell below that in *all* of England and Wales, with seven times the population. [. . .]

Compared with the British, the American pattern is distinctive at every level: Americans are far more likely to commit robbery in the first place, more likely to use a gun and thus risk the death or serious injury of their victim if they do, and more likely to inflict deadly force on their victim *whether or not* they use a gun. Among other things, this suggests that reducing the use of guns in predatory crimes could go a very long way toward reducing the worst American violence. [. . .]

Let me be clear: I do not mean to romanticize the state of crime in other advanced western European or Asian countries. Some kinds of violent crime have risen significantly in most of them. Most also share, if not the magnitude of our violent crime problem, a similar social *distribution* of violence: though serious violence remains infrequent on a national level, it is concentrated in relatively impoverished and disorganized communities, often those heavily populated by ethnic or racial minorities, who are disproportionately likely to suffer repeated victimization. And what's particularly troubling is that many of these countries are now adopting social policies that may indeed, over the long run, narrow the gap in violence that now separates them from us. But the stark differences in serious criminal violence among the wealthy industrial democracies make it clear that neither democracy nor freedom nor prosperity can explain these patterns – and that something that *distinguishes* the United States from most other industrial countries must be an important part of that explanation.

II

[. . .]

We can begin to trace some of these differences in the findings of the Luxembourg Income Study (LIS), an international survey of poverty, inequality, and government spending in industrial countries, directed by Lee Rainwater of Harvard University and Timothy Smeeding of Syracuse University. With carefully assembled data and in cautious, understated language, the LIS paints a troubling portrait of the United States – a country that, though generally quite wealthy, is also far more unequal and far less committed to including the vulnerable into a common level of social life than are other developed nations.

To begin with, children and families in the United States are far more likely to be poor than are their counterparts in other industrial democracies – and, if they are poor, are more likely to be *extremely* poor. Our overall child poverty rate in the early 1990s was about 22 percent; Australia and Canada, our closest "competitors" in the industrial world, had rates of about 14 percent. Most of Europe was far behind, with France and Germany at around 6 percent and Sweden, Norway, and Denmark, among others, below 4 percent. [. . .]

But the . . . United States also does less to offset the problem of poor earnings through government benefits. The United Kingdom, for example, also has a high rate of family poverty before government transfers, but a moderate (though recently increasing) rate after the government steps in with income assistance (again, this is true even without factoring in the value of free health care under the British national health system). [. . .]

A similar picture of America's distinctive pattern of high inequality and low social support emerges if we calculate how much various countries spend on what Europeans call "social protection" as a proportion of their overall economic wealth. Thus, counting not only what we normally think of as "welfare" but also family allowances, unemployment compensation, and disability benefits, the United States spends less than 4 percent of its Gross Domestic Product (GDP) on such programs, and the proportion has fallen steadily since 1980. . . . Even after years of conservative rule, Britain spends twice what the United States does, proportionately, on social protection. [. . .]

The bottom line, then, is that American children and their families are forced to make do in the vicissitudes of a volatile market economy with unusually little public support. They are far more likely to suffer a kind and degree of social exclusion that is no longer tolerated in other industrial societies – even ones that in sheer material terms are considerably poorer than the United States. . . . And these differences are becoming more pronounced, for both inequality and poverty have recently increased more rapidly in the United States than in most other developed countries. [. . .]

It is sometimes said that these adverse changes mostly reflect rising numbers of single-parent families on welfare, but though that is part of the explanation, it is *only* a part. The declining economic fortunes of intact families and of workers at the lower end of the pay scale also play a role. [. . .]

III

The depths of social exclusion and deprivation in the United States has ramifications for virtually every aspect of our common life – including our level of violent crime. As we'll see, the relationship is complex and sometimes indirect. But it is critically important in understanding America's affliction with violence.

Studies of the correlates of international differences in violent crime offer one kind of evidence. Countries where there is a wide gap between rich and poor routinely show higher levels of violent crime. . . . Look closer, and it becomes apparent that violence is worse in neglectful or mean-spirited societies than in more generous ones – even if they are poorer. Societies with weak "safety nets" for the poor and economically insecure are more likely than others at a comparable level of development to be wracked by violence.

That is one conclusion, for example, of a study by Rosemary Gartner of the University of Toronto, who examined homicide rates in eighteen developed countries from 1950 to 1980. Even in the earlier part of the period, the United States already suffered considerably higher rates of homicide than the other countries, and the *composition* of American homicide was different as well: Americans homicide victims were more likely to have been murdered by strangers, as opposed to intimates, than were murder victims in other countries. And though homicide increased somewhat for the eighteen countries as a whole over the thirty-year period, the extraordinary dominance of the United States remained unchanged. [. . .]

What accounted for these differences? Gartner's study points to several factors. Economic inequality had a powerful effect on the countries' homicide levels. A measure of "social security" expenditure as a proportion of GNP – including cash benefits for social welfare and family allowances, along with unemployment insurance, public health spending, and other ameliorative programs – likewise had a strong effect on the risks of homicide for every age group. High divorce rates, ethnic and cultural heterogeneity, and a cultural leaning toward violence generally (as measured by support for the death penalty and frequent wars) also seemed to promote homicide. But the effects of both inequality and the relative absence of social provision remained powerful even when all else was accounted for. . . . Being poor in America *means* being at the bottom of an exceptionally harsh system of inequality; being black greatly increases the chances of being impoverished and, therefore, trapped at the lower end of the social ladder.

Recent studies . . . have given us powerful evidence of the close connection between violence and social disadvantage. In a seminal analysis of the covariates of homicide in the United States, for example, Kenneth Land, Patricia McCall, and Lawrence Cohen found that a measure of "resource deprivation" – which includes the proportion of families in poverty, the median income, the degree of income inequality, the percentage of the population that is black, and the percentage of children not living with both parents – had "by far the strongest and most invariant effect" on the rate of homicide. That effect held true for cities, metropolitan areas, and states, and prevailed across three different years – 1960, 1970, and 1980. "Resource deprivation" was not the *only* explanation for the wide differences in homicide rates among American cities and states – the proportion of the population that was divorced, in particular, also played an important role – but it was the biggest.

Moreover, we also know that the links between disadvantage and violence are strongest for the poorest and most neglected of the poor. If we simply divide the population into broad categories by social class, or what sociologists often call "socioeconomic status" (SES), the group differences in violent crime are less stark. It is when we focus more narrowly on people locked into the most permanent forms of economic marginality in the most impoverished and disrupted communities that we see the highest concentrations of serious violent crime. [. . .]

The finding that even within a generally deprived population it is the *most* deprived children who face the greatest risks of delinquency and crime also stands out in another often-cited longitudinal study, this one done in South London, England, by Donald West and David Farrington of Cambridge University. The Cambridge Study of Delinquent Development followed over four hundred boys who were between eight and nine years old in the early 1960s – "a traditional white, urban, working class sample of British origin" – up to about age thirty-two. The study shows that a wide range of factors, including family problems like poor child-rearing techniques, poor supervision, erratic or harsh discipline, and parental conflict or criminality, influence the likelihood of later delinquency, violence, and adult crime. But it also found that "the major risk factors for delinquency include poverty, poor housing, and living in public housing in inner-city, socially disorganized communities." As in many other studies, delinquency was not strongly correlated with a general measure of the boys' "social class" based on their parents' occupation. But *poverty* was another matter. *Within* this basically working-class and decidedly unaffluent group, ninety-three of the boys, at age eight, lived in families defined as having "low income" compared with the sample as a whole. Of those ninety-three, about 42 percent became involved in violence as teenagers, versus 26 percent of the others. Even more significantly, 24 percent of the "low-income" boys – but less than 9 percent of the rest – were *convicted* of violent offenses as adults. "In the light of the clear link between poverty and antisocial behaviour," writes David Farrington, "it is surprising that more prevention experiments targeting this factor have not been conducted." [. . .]

Krivo and Peterson's (1996) research suggests that it is this strong link between extreme disadvantage and violence which underlies much of the association between *race* and violent crime in the United States. Columbus was a particularly fruitful place to study this issue, because it is one of the relatively few major American cities that have several neighborhoods with high concentrations of the *white* poor. And the same strong connection between extreme disadvantage and violence appeared in neighborhoods that were mostly or entirely white as in those that were mostly black. [. . . .]

IV

The links between extreme deprivation, delinquency, and violence, then, are strong, consistent, and compelling. There is little question that growing up in extreme poverty exerts powerful pressures toward crime. The fact that those pressures are overcome by some individuals is testimony to human strength and resiliency, but does not diminish the importance of the link between social exclusion and violence. The effects are compounded by the absence of public supports to buffer economic insecurity and deprivation, and they are even more potent when racial subordination is added to the mix. [. . .]

These conclusions fly in the face of the common conservative argument that government efforts to reduce poverty and disadvantage have no effect on crime – or, in a more extreme version, that the expansion of the "welfare state" is itself to blame for high crime rates. [. . .]

Most crucially, of course, the argument that the welfare state causes crime founders against the reality that those countries with the most developed welfare states have far less violence than the United States, the industrial nation with the *least* developed welfare state.

The cross-national research conducted by Rosemary Gartner and her colleagues sheds more light on this issue. In one study, Gartner and Fred C. Pampel of the University of Colorado explored the implications of a peculiar difference in the pattern of youth violence between the United States and other high-income countries. One of the most consistent findings about the homicide rate in this country is that it tends to be higher when there is a higher proportion of youths in the population. (A rising proportion of young people is one key reason, for example, why homicide rates rose sharply in the United States during the late 1960s.) Some criminologists have taken this to mean that there is an ironclad connection between youth and violence. But when we look overseas, the connection evaporates.

Rejecting what they call a "naive demographic determinism," Gartner and Pampel found that what matters more than the sheer number of youths are the social protections a society provides for young people and their families. In societies sharing what they call a "collectivist" orientation – societies that, among other things, provide universal and relatively generous social benefits (including health care, income support, disability, unemployment insurance, and family allowances) – there is only a weak connection between the size of the youth population and the rate of homicide. In Norway, for example, a classic "social democracy," changes in the age structure have no effect on the level of homicide; in the U.S., an equally classic example of an "individualistic" political culture, rises in the proportion of youths in the population translate directly into higher homicide rates.

Similarly, the few studies that look specifically at the impact of welfare benefits on rates of crime *within* the United States show that welfare actually tends to *lower* crime rates, not raise them. The University of Connecticut sociologist James DeFronzo, for example, has found that higher welfare payments appear to reduce rates of burglary. DeFronzo looked at Aid to Families with Dependent Children (AFDC) benefits per person, adjusted for differences in the cost of living, in 140 metropolitan areas across the United States. He also included, as "control" variables, the cities' level of poverty and unemployment, the number of households headed by women, the percentage that was black or Hispanic, the proportion of young males in the population, the per capita income, and the city population. With all of these other factors controlled, AFDC payments had a strong *negative* relationship to burglary rates – that is, the higher the average welfare benefit, the lower the burglary rate.

DeFronzo has found a similar pattern for homicide; once other social and economic factors are controlled, high homicide rates are strongly correlated with *low* AFDC payments . . . "Welfare as we know it" was surely not the best system for supporting families and children in America, but at the very least it offered enough support – in some states, in any case – to soften the impact of extreme deprivation and, if DeFronzo is right, to reduce some kinds of crime. [. . .]

V

[. . .]

To give the skeptics their due, it's true that the connections between poverty, inequality, and violence aren't always either simple or direct. It isn't the lack of money alone that breeds violence; if that were the case, then graduate students would be very dangerous people indeed. It's rather that the experience of life year in, year out at the bottom of a harsh, depriving, and excluding social system wears away at the psychological and communal conditions that sustain healthy human development. It stunts children's intellectual and emotional growth, undercuts parents' ability to raise children caringly and effectively, increases the risks of child abuse and neglect, and diminishes the capacity of adults to supervise the young. It creates neighborhoods that are both dangerous and bereft of legitimate opportunities and role models, makes forming and maintaining families more difficult, and makes illicit activities far more alluring for teenagers and adults. Life, in short, is harder, bleaker, less supportive, and more volatile at the bottom – especially when the bottom is as far down as it is in the United States. And those conditions, in ways both direct and indirect, both obvious and subtle, breed violent crime.

Consider just a few of the findings from what is by now a large and impressively consistent body of research.

First, *extreme deprivation inhibits children's intellectual development* – which may ultimately lead to crime by crippling children's ability to "make it" in the conventional worlds of school and work. The most revealing evidence on the connection between poverty and cognitive development comes from a study by Greg Duncan, Jeanne Brooks-Gunn, and Pamela Kato Klebanov, of the University of Michigan and Columbia University. Looking at data from two long-term studies of family income and child development, they found that "family income and poverty status are powerful determinants of the cognitive development of children" – even after accounting for other differences between affluent and poor families, like education and family structure. And the longer children remained in poverty, the worse the impact was. At age five, "persistently poor" children – those whose families had been in poverty for all of their short lives – averaged nine points lower on standard IQ tests than those who had never been poor. [. . .]

How, exactly, does low income translate into lower IQ? The researchers concluded that it does so mainly through its effect on the home environment. The amount and quality of intellectual stimulation and the warmth of the relationship between parents and children turned out to be important "mediators" that helped explain a significant portion of the IQ differences among children at different levels of income. "Persistently poor" parents were less able to provide these forms of attention.

Second, *extreme deprivation breeds violence by encouraging child abuse and neglect*. The connection between child maltreatment and later violence is widely accepted across the political spectrum: the authors of *Body Count*, for example, correctly point to child abuse as a critical part of the problem of American violence. But many observers tend to detach child abuse from its social context – to think of it as a "classless" problem.

The reality is very different. Serious violence against children, though it *can* be found throughout society, is heavily concentrated in the poorest and most vulnerable parts of the population. The developmental psychologist Jay Belsky, summarizing a profusion of research, argues that poverty is "undoubtedly the major risk for child abuse and neglect." And it is increasingly clear that the *worst* conditions of extreme poverty and social isolation create the highest risks. [. . .]

Third, even when it does not lead to abuse or neglect, *extreme poverty creates multiple stresses that undermine parents' ability to raise children caringly and effectively.*

Duncan, Brooks-Gunn, and Klebanov's study of the impact of persistent poverty on early childhood development suggests one way in which this happens. We've seen that the study found that poverty inhibited children's intellectual development; it also found that persistent poverty increased children's behavioral problems. Once again, the effects of poverty proved to be stronger than those of family structure, a factor often blamed for childhood misbehavior. On the surface, children in single-parent families appeared to have more problems, but the difference washed away once the family's income was controlled for. But why, exactly, would poverty cause early behavior problems? The researchers argue that it did so, in good part, by undermining the mental health of the mothers. Poor mothers were especially likely to suffer depression, which in turn undercut their capacity to provide nurturance and stimulation for their children. [. . .]

What distinguished the mothers of the more troubled children from the others? Again, depression played a key role, and depression, in turn, was related to a broader problem: the mothers of the more troubled children faced a heavier onslaught of "stressful events" in their social environment – including unemployment, frequent moves, inadequate housing, and deaths of close family members or friends. The children of mothers who were able to rely on other family members and friends for support, on the other hand, were less likely to have serious behavioral problems. Again, this suggests that it is a particular *kind* of poverty, and the constellation of problems that go along with it, that carries the most risks for early childhood development. Being poor *and* trapped in a chaotic and stressful community, isolated from extended family and friends, is a particularly toxic condition – and, unfortunately, one that is all too common in America (Bishop and Leadbeater).

Fourth, *poverty breeds crime by undermining parents' ability to monitor and supervise their children.* Most criminologists would agree that a lack of effective parental supervision often means trouble. But how capably parents can carry out this job depends, in part, on forces operating outside the family. The link between poverty and poor parenting comes out clearly in an innovative study by Robert Sampson of the University of Chicago and John Laub of Northeastern University. In the late 1980s, Sampson and Laub re-examined a wealth of data that had been collected in the 1940s as part of a well-known research project on the roots of juvenile delinquency. In the original research, Sheldon and Eleanor Glueck at Harvard Law School had matched five hundred delinquents from reform schools in Massachusetts with five hundred non-delinquent "controls." Both groups were drawn from disadvantaged neighborhoods in Boston. The Gluecks gathered a vast amount of interview data on the boys' lives, including extensive information on their early family experiences, and concluded that what they called "under-the-roof culture" – the inner character of family life – was the most important influence on whether the children turned out to be delinquent or not.

Sampson and Laub, looking at the same evidence, took the analysis one important step further. Their reanalysis confirmed that harsh or erratic discipline and poor maternal supervision often distinguished the family lives of the delinquents. But those practices were found much more often among poorer parents. Poverty, in other words, exerted a strong pressure toward delinquency among disadvantaged Boston children born in the 1920s and 1930s – just as it does with their counterparts in Chicago or Los Angeles today – because it inhibited "the capacity of families to achieve informal social control" of their children. What makes this finding all the more significant is that it showed up so plainly despite the fact that *all* of the families in this study came from relatively disadvantaged communities. Thus even *within* a sample of generally low-income families, those with lower income had the most difficulty with parenting – and the highest rates of delinquency. [. . .]

VI

The most crucial lesson of these studies is that what goes on in families cannot be understood apart from what goes on outside them. Conservative writers in particular often argue that it is the family *rather than* poverty or inequality that shapes patterns of violence or juvenile delinquency. That perspective lends itself to strategies that seek to control crime through moral exhortation, or punishment of parents who do a poor job of child rearing. But the research increasingly tells us that the family's role is so powerful precisely because it is the place where the strains and pressures of the larger society converge to influence individual development. [. . .]

As with poverty and violence, the connections between unemployment and violence are neither simple nor, necessarily, direct. Whether joblessness breeds violent crime depends on what kind of joblessness it is and what consequences it has for individuals, families, and communities. Criminologists who study this issue have long argued that it isn't the short-term loss of a job by someone who is otherwise steadily employed that is most linked to violence. but the experience of being confined to parts of the economy where the long-term prospects for stable and rewarding work are minimal or nonexistent. . . . Even more important is the corrosive effect of economic marginality on family stability and on the capacity of local communities to provide opportunity, support, and social control.

More recent research confirms these findings. In their long-term studies of delinquency, for example, Delbert Elliott of the University of Colorado and his colleagues found that white youths, measured by their own self-reports, had rates of violence that were not very different from those of blacks – while they were adolescents. But the rates began to diverge widely as the two groups moved out of adolescence and into young adulthood. What seemed to happen was that as white youths entered into stable and responsible jobs, most of them "desisted" from serious crime. But the black youths desisted far less often; their rates of offending remained high even into their twenties, a reflection of their inability to move into stable adult economic roles. . . . Robert Sampson and John Laub likewise found stable work to be critically important in the lives of the Boston men the Gluecks began studying before World War II, most of whom were white. Among the men who had been seriously delinquent in adolescence, two factors – two "turning points" – most influenced whether they stopped committing crimes as they grew into adulthood: getting married and getting a stable job. Furthermore, even among the men who had had *no* trouble with the law in their teen years, the *lack* of a steady job as a young adult often precipitated a turn to crime. . . . But it also shows that the presence or absence of strong "social bonds in adulthood" – especially a good job and a supportive family – can alter that childhood trajectory, for better or worse.

Stable work, then, prevents violent crime by making it possible for the young to successfully complete the transition into respected and supported adulthood. It also inhibits violence in another way: by creating the material and emotional infrastructure to support healthy families – families that are capable of providing the attention, nurturance, and care that ensure that children can develop into competent and compassionate people. [. . .]

Chronic joblessness, then, breeds violent crime in part because of its impact on family *structure*. But, even more importantly, it also breeds violence by undermining family *functioning*. Again, the findings are hardly surprising. Anyone who has been involuntarily unemployed, even for a short time, knows that it is a psychologically jolting experience, and one that can dramatically affect relationships with other people. Translated to the experience of long-term, chronic joblessness, the effects are enormously magnified. Some of the most suggestive work on the impact of joblessness on family life has been done by the sociologist Glen Elder and his colleagues. During the Depression, Elder found, widespread economic hardship often had adverse psychological effects on children – but the effects were indirect, operating through changes in their parents' behavior. Specifically, unemployment and loss of income made fathers angry, tense, and explosive, and therefore punitive and arbitrary in disciplining their children. The children, in turn, responded with tantrums, negativism, lowered aspirations, and feelings of inadequacy. More recently, Elder and his coworkers found similar processes at work in a sample of over four hundred inner-city families in Philadelphia, most of them headed by single women. For many of these families, financial strain was "virtually a way of life." But even within this generally low-income group, those who were experiencing a heavy dose of what the researchers called "economic pressure" – who were worried that they couldn't pay the bills – were far more likely to be depressed and to feel powerless to make "a positive difference in their children's lives." [. . .]

The lack of opportunities for good jobs also increases the likelihood of violence within the family itself, for several reasons. Men who are unemployed or working in poorly paying, marginal jobs are far more likely to commit serious violence against their female partners (or their children) and less likely to be deterred from repeated violence by the experience of arrest. In a study of female victims of homicide in Detroit, Ann Goetting describes the typical offender in these cases as "disadvantaged along multiple dimensions" and "poorly equipped to overcome their daily struggles to just get by." At the same time, the lack of marketable skills and tangible job opportunities often traps disadvantaged women in potentially life-threatening relationships with abusive men. Some findings from a recent study of battered women's shelters in Kentucky illustrate the problem: 87 percent of sheltered women reported an income of less than $10,000 a year, and about half said they earned less than $3,000. "With few options for independent economic survival," write Neil Websdale and Byron Johnson, these women "return to the shelter between seven and nine times before leaving a violent spouse. . . . A large percentage return to their abusers and the communities they are part of."

But the effect of nonexistent or inadequate work on individual families is only part of the picture. Mass joblessness also profoundly shapes the local culture and the structure of rewards and incentives in entire communities – changing, in complex and devastating ways, the environment in which children and adolescents grow up. For one thing, illegitimate means of earning a living – especially drug dealing – become more appealing, which in turn generates violence in several ways at once. It floods the community with large numbers of people whose addiction leads them to violent crime to get money to support their habits. If the drug is crack or methamphetamine, its pharmacological effects may lead directly to violent behavior; and street drug markets, especially for crack cocaine, breed violence, which spills well beyond the boundaries of the drug trade itself. [. . .]

A more complex analysis of the connections between violence and the massive loss of jobs is offered in a study of the effects of deindustrialization on crime in several U.S. cities in the 1980s, by Jeffrey Fagan of Rutgers University and his colleagues. They describe a cascading series of adverse changes in local community life that are set in motion by the massive loss of traditional blue-collar jobs. The flight of jobs not only eliminated traditional ladders of economic opportunity but also took away the stabilizing influence that steadily employed people provide. As the more capable men moved out of the community in search of work, the researchers found, "collective supervision of youths suffered" and "informal social controls weakened." As legitimate opportunities withered, drug markets flourished, overwhelming the fragile social controls that remained in these communities and flooding the neighborhood with guns. The loss of steadily employed people to better-off areas simultaneously weakened the political power of the hard-hit neighborhoods, which in turn accelerated the decline of the social services that might have helped cushion the effects of economic decline. Traditional norms about work and achievement were pushed aside, meanwhile, by a pervasive materialism – even, in some places, what the researchers describe as "hypermaterialism." What began as an economic change, in short, quickly rippled through virtually every institution, public and private, in the inner cities, radically transforming the culture of poor communities and precipitating a rise in violent crime.

VII

These findings are only a sample of what we've learned about the connections among poverty, inequality, and violent crime. But they help us understand why violence is so much worse in America than in otherwise comparable countries, and why it has remained intolerably high despite our massive investment in imprisonment.

The diagnosis points toward enduring solutions. For beneath the grim findings there is a pragmatic and even hopeful message. The concentration of violence among the most deprived tells us that to reduce it doesn't require the abolition of poverty or inequality (much less the end of "prosperity"); a great deal can be accomplished simply by raising the floor of social inclusion to a level more in line with virtually every other advanced society. Those countries have not eliminated violence, but they have kept it within more tolerable bounds. If we brought our homicide rate down to the level in Germany or France, we would save more than fifteen thousand American lives every year. Relatively low levels of violence, in short, represent one of the great successes of more egalitarian and generous countries. [. . .]

Chapter 21

Scott H. Decker and Barrik Van Winkle

LIFE IN THE GANG
Family, friends, and violence

From: Scott H. Decker and Barrik Van Winkle (1996), excerpts from *Life in the Gang*: *Family, Friends, and Violence*, Cambridge: Cambridge University Press, pp. 1–3, 20–25, 56–83, 144–186.

I'm a die for my colors, that's the first thing they say, I'm a die for my colors. What a color? A color that somebody done painted, red and blue. [. . .]

THE COLORS RED AND blue are the symbols of street gangs, especially the Bloods and Crips. And as . . . [the quote above] from a leader of the "Thundercats" illustrates, colors can have lethal consequences. [. . .]

Interest in gangs is not new. They have been an object of study for at least the last century, and their consideration by journalists and novelists extends well beyond that. Surges of academic and public interest in gangs occurred in the 1890s, 1920s, 1960s and late 1980s into the 1990s. Changes in four social and demographic characteristics link interest in gangs in each of these periods: (1) immigration, (2) urbanization, (3) ethnicity, and (4) poverty. . . . Yet economic and population variables alone cannot explain the growth of gangs or the nature of gang activities. [. . .]

There is controversy about the first use of the term "gang" to refer to an aggregation of relatively organized offenders. Sanchez-Jankowski argues that the term was first applied to "outlaws" in the 1800s. However, Bursik (1993) cites evidence from Johnson regarding groups in Philadelphia and from Haskins for New York City that gangs existed in cities before they did in more rural Western outposts. Sheldon (1898) is generally credited with the first academic use of the term "gang" (see Yablonsky 1962, 73). His description of gangs stems from a broader interest in the group activities of children, particularly games. In observing youthful social associations, he found that "spontaneous societies" seemed to emerge from the everyday activities of young people. Of particular interest were the predatory organizations involved in violent and property crimes, which he labeled gangs. [. . .]

In this study, we present the results of three years of studying gangs in a declining Midwestern rust belt city, St. Louis, Missouri. Working the street, we recruited, interviewed, and observed active gang members and their families. Our study corresponded to a period of rapid growth in both the number of gangs and gang members in St. Louis. [. . .]

A theoretical framework: the role of threat

. . .The framework we use to explain both the origin of gangs and the decisions of individuals to join a gang focuses on the role of *threat*. Threats of physical violence, whether real or perceived, have important consequences for these questions.

Threat describes a process in which perceptions and interactions work together to produce behavior. But this process does not occur in a vacuum; indeed, it takes place in a context shaped by the labor market, political forces, and other neighborhood opportunity structures. These structural forces, working together, produce external constraints that limit the options and opportunities available to young men and women in the neighborhood. It is within this context that threats emerge and flourish. As Anderson (1994) observed, street culture is a response to the underclass conditions within which gangs operate. This culture has produced a "code of the streets" (86) in which "nerve," "retaliation," and opposition to mainstream social institutions have become the norm. The sources of such a culture are largely institutional: the evaporation of factory jobs, increasing residential segregation, disinvestment in and by neighborhood social institutions such as schools and neighborhood groups, and the resultant alienation and disenfranchisement of young people. Taken together, these forces create a neighborhood context within which threats are not effectively controlled, either by formal or informal social control processes.

The key element in this process is violence. Violence and fighting have been integral to gangs since their origins. Thrasher observed that gangs developed through strife and flourished on conflict. According to Klein (1971, 85) violence provides a "predominant 'myth system' " among gang members and is constantly present. For these reasons, we emphasize the role of physical threat in gang formation, individual decisions to join the gang, and gang activities.

Threat plays an important role in accounting for the origins of gangs. Within many neighborhoods, groups form for protection against outside groups. Sometimes these groups are formed around ethnic lines, though it is often the case that territorial concerns guide their formation, providing support for Katz' notion that gangs seek to "own the street" through a variety of actions. Hagedorn (1988) found that conflicts between the police and young men "hanging out" on the corner led to more formalized structures that ultimately became gangs. [. . .]

Another area in which threat accounts for gang process is in stimulating the growth of such groups. First, threats of physical violence, whether real or perceived, increase the solidarity or cohesiveness of gangs within neighborhoods as well as across neighborhoods. Klein (1971) identified the source of gang cohesion as primarily external to the gang, an observation also made by Hagedorn. . . . Padilla (1992) also underscored this notion, noting the role of threat in maintaining boundaries between the gang and other groups. [. . .]

A second part of the growth in gangs and gang violence contains an element of what Loftin (1984) calls "contagion." Violence, or its threat, is the mechanism that drives the spread of gangs from one neighborhood to another, as well as causes them to grow in size. From Loftin's perspective, the concept of contagion can be used to explain the rapid growth or "spikes" that occur in violent crime. Three conditions must be present for contagion to occur: (1) a spatial concentration of assaultive violence, (2) a reciprocal nature to assaultive violence, and (3) escalations in assaultive violence. These conditions also apply to our use of the concept of threat. Gangs have a strong spatial structure; they claim particular turf as their own and are committed to its "defense" against outsiders. The specter of a rival gang "invading" their turf to violate its sanctity is likely to evoke a violent response from a gang. . . . The reciprocal nature of gang violence, in part, accounts for the initial formation of gangs, as well as how they increase in size and how ties are strengthened among members. The need to engage in retaliatory violence also helps us understand the demand for increasingly sophisticated weapons on the part of gang members. [. . .]

Threat has a third function. Because gangs and gang members are perceived as engaging in acts of violence that defy rational explanation (such as drive-by shootings), they are viewed as threatening by other (non-gang) groups and individuals in society. Eventually, because of the threats they face (and pose), gang members become increasingly isolated from legitimate social institutions such as schools and the labor market. As gang members are involved in violent events, both as perpetrators and victims, members of the community attempt to distance themselves from relationships and contacts with gang members. It is within this context that life in the gang must be understood. Life in the gang is an existence characterized by estrangement from social institutions, many neighborhood groups, and, ultimately, conforming peers and adults. [. . .]

This makes it particularly difficult to leave the gang, because even after doing so, many individuals continue to be treated as if they were still members and often are blocked from desirable conventional roles. [. . .]

It is important to emphasize that gang members are not merely reactive. While it is clear that much gang violence occurs in response to threats from rival gangs, gangs also act proactively to create threats. [. . .]

"I'M DOWN WITH THE BLOODS, WHAT'S UP CUZ?" MEMBERSHIP ISSUES

> I don't know Shit man, there wasn't no joinin' in it and it was a little neighborhood thang you know, just somethin you know, we just grew up like that. We grew up fightin, we just grew up fightin and everybody hangin around so they decided to call they self somethin since we hung around like that, went out doin things and stuff.
>
> (Male #002, "Eric," sixteen-year-old Thundercat)

[. . .]

Background characteristics

[. . .]

The members of our sample were primarily young African American males. The average age of gang members we interviewed was 16.9 years, with the youngest member being 13, and the oldest 29. Seven of our subjects were females, often recruited in groups of two . . . or through their boyfriends. Four of our subjects were white; the remainder were black. The racial composition of our sample merits some comment. We are aware of white and Asian gangs . . . but were not able to gain access to members of these gangs through our street contacts. . . . The nature of our sample, therefore, is not strictly representative of gang members in St. Louis; however, we are confident that we have interviewed within the modal category. [. . .]

Our subjects represented twenty-nine different gangs. Sixteen of the gangs were affiliated with Crips and include sixty-seven of the ninety-nine members of our sample. The remaining thirteen gangs included thirty-two different members and were affiliated with Bloods. [. . .]

How do you define a gang?

There is considerable debate about what constitutes a gang and who qualifies as a gang member. Bursik and Grasmick (1993) identify two main approaches to defining gang membership; definitions that focus on gang processes (such as formation, recruitment, evolution, transmission) and those that focus on behavior (especially participation in illegal activities). [. . .]

Finally, there were those who simply defined a gang in terms of its criminal activities. Seventy-four percent of our respondents indicated that this was a reason to define their group as a gang. While violence was primary among these activities, drug sales and other crimes often were mentioned as well.

> INT: So the reason you call it a gang basically is why? [. . .]

> A bunch of thugs doing bad stuff. Some people good but they get in trouble and take it out on somebody else. Cause they devilish. They don't think before they do things, they just do things, they don't think. Regular people think.
> (Male #015, "Karry," fifteen-year-old Crenshaw Gangster Blood)

> INT: What makes you all a gang?
> WHITE MALE #091, "Paul," eighteen-year-old 107 Hoover Crip: The things we do. Fighting, shooting, selling drugs.

[. . .]

The group nature and cohesive aspects of gangs were consistent aspects of their responses. Regardless of how they initially characterized gangs, most subjects (74 percent) quickly focused on criminal activities – especially violence – as the defining feature of their gang. . . .

Pushed or pulled into membership

[. . .]

In every instance, joining the gang was the result of a process that evolved over a period of time, typically less than a year. In some cases, the process more closely resembled recruitment, whereby members of a gang would identify a particular individual and "convince" them to join the gang. This, however, accounted for very few of the individuals in our sample, fourteen out of ninety-nine. For the most part, the process of joining the gang was consistent with the formation of neighborhood friendship groups. Twenty of our respondents specifically mentioned that they had grown up in the same neighborhood as other gang members and had done things with them over a lengthy period of time. For these individuals, their gang evolved from these playgroups into a more formal association, in much the same way Thrasher (1927) described gangs in Chicago.

The process of joining the gang has two elements; the first is a series of "pulls" that attract individuals to the gang, the second are the "pushes" that compel individuals to join the gang. The pull or lure of gangs was an opportunity to make money selling drugs (a response offered by 84 percent of our subjects), to increase one's status in the neighborhood (indicated by 60 percent), or both. The primary factor that pushes individuals into gangs is their perceived need for protection. . . . A number of gang members (84 percent) found it impossible to live without some form of protection, typically finding such protection through their association with a gang. It is our argument that, for most members, both pushes and pulls play a role in the decision to join the gang. Four specific reasons were cited for joining the gang. In declining order of importance, they were: (1) protection, (2) the prompting of friends and/or relatives, (3) the desire to make money through drug sales, and (4) the status associated with being a gang member. The desire for protection is an example of a "push" – an external force compelling gang membership. The efforts of friends or relatives to encourage gang membership also represent a push toward gang membership. The other two reasons, desire for money and status, are clearly "pulls," or forces that attract individuals to gangs. [. . .]

Reasons to be in a gang

We now consider what gang members regard as the positive features or advantages of gang membership. We presented subjects with twelve features of gang life, asking them to specify whether they represented a good reason to be in their gang. [. . .]

Protection was identified as a positive feature of gang membership by 86 percent of the subjects, more than any other category. However, selling drugs and opportunities to make money were seen as advantages of gang membership by 84 percent and 82 percent of subjects respectively. Defending the neighborhood also was viewed as an important reason to belong, as 81 percent of gang members responded in the affirmative when asked if this activity was a positive feature of gang membership. Interestingly, impressing people in the neighborhood, impressing friends, and impressing girls, all measures of status, received lower levels of support from gang members than did the categories just reviewed. In general, status concerns were endorsed as advantages to being in the gang by fewer members (thirty-eight) than were more instrumental aspects of gang life such as protection (eighty-three) or making money (seventy-nine). These responses reflect a preference for instrumental benefits of a more tangible nature than status concerns.

It is interesting to compare the responses to this series of questions to the answers gang members gave us about their reasons to join the gang. The desire for protection was the overwhelming motivation cited by gang members in their decision to join the gang.

Their experiences in the gang had done little to change this. However, two notable differences can be observed between the reasons to join the gang and, once having joined, the advantages of membership. The second and third most frequent responses to the question "Why did you join your gang?" were the chance to sell drugs and make money. However, these categories received far stronger endorsements from currently active gang members as reasons to belong to their gang. At the same time, status concerns (ranked as the fourth most important reason to join) fell farther down the list as advantages to membership. This pattern suggests that once in the gang, instrumental concerns like protection and money assume even greater importance. In addition, it is no surprise that drug sales and defending the neighborhood received similar high levels of support. [. . .]

Despite these instrumental concerns (protection and making money), a number of members indicated that their gang fulfilled a variety of more typical adolescent needs – especially companionship and support. [. . .]

Who belongs to the gang?

Race and gang membership

Race is an important element of the composition of gangs. The growth of the underclass, especially in predominantly minority neighborhoods, is clearly related to the high numbers of minority gang members (Hagedorn 1988; Jackson 1991). While the majority of individuals we interviewed were black (96 percent), not all gang members in St. Louis are black. However, nearly half (45 percent) of our gang members said their gang would accept white members, and an equal proportion told us that there were white members of their gang. Only one-fifth of respondents said they were "dead set" against having whites in their gang.

Gang members who told us they would have whites in their gang said that, for the most part, color doesn't matter. For a number of gangs, the proof of this assertion could be seen in the racial composition of their membership; a large number of the gangs whose members we interviewed had mixed-race membership. Typically members of such gangs informed us that the gang transcended race.

> We feel that color ain't nothing about gang banging, they can be any color.
> (Male #101, "Money Love," twenty-year-old
> Insane Gangster Disciple)

> INT: How did white guys get in?
> MALE #015, "Karry," fifteen-year-old Crenshaw Gangster Blood: The same way a black man does. They was just real cool. We don't care about they skin color as long as they was cool. There's some white guys in our group in St. Louis.

The majority of whites (3/5) who joined the gang did so as a consequence of living in the neighborhood where a black gang was operating. This underscores the importance of neighborhoods as a setting for gangs. [. . .]

Other black gang members told us that having white members provided their gang with access to either drugs or guns. In this sense, having a mixed-race gang provided instrumental advantages to the gang. These advantages were strong enough to transcend parochial concerns over race.

[. . .]

INT: Why do you have white people in your gang?

MALE #092, "Derone," twenty-one-year-old Rolling 60's Crip: Easier to hook up with guns. They know how to get to the guns, they know how to get to anything really.

The majority of subjects (55 percent) came from gangs with only black members. However, slightly more than half (52 percent) of this group told us that their gang was open to the possibility of having white members. A major impediment to expanding the racial diversity of gangs stemmed from the rigid racial segregation in most St. Louis neighborhoods. [. . .]

Twenty gang members told us they were opposed to whites joining their gang. Some of the opposition centered on what was referred to as the "Three K Posse" (the Ku Klux Klan). Others simply stated that they didn't like whites. Some of the dislike was linked to the belief that whites would readily "snake out" black members. [. . .]

Women

Despite notable exceptions (Bowker and Klein 1983; Campbell 1984; Taylor 1993) female gang members and female gangs have received little explicit attention. In some ways, this makes sense, because males dominate gang membership and are arrested with much higher frequency for violent offenses. On the other hand, female gang membership may be a more significant problem than their numerical representation in gangs suggests. . . . Female gang membership seems to accelerate several years after males begin to form gangs and expand membership. Thus the growth in female gang members may be a sign of the increased formalization and expansion of gangs. In addition, many reports of female gang activities indicate that they engage in considerable amounts of violence (Curry, Ball, and Fox 1994). The consequences of female gang membership also are magnified, because women in gangs often attract males to gang membership. Finally, because women tend to play the primary role in raising children in poor communities, the consequences of increased female gang member-ship may have profound effects for intergenerational transmission of gang membership. [. . .]

In general, we found few differences between the roles and activities of women regardless of whether they were in an all female gang or a male dominated gang. . . . Over the course of our study, we observed an increase in female gang members as well as in their activities.

Gang members in St. Louis reported that women were integrated into their gangs, even though those gangs were dominated by males. Indeed, 70 percent of our respon-dents said that the roles of women were indistinguishable from those of men. A high value was placed on being able to get the job done, and women who could be counted on to achieve this goal were held in high regard.

INT: Are they a separate part or are they mixed in with the guys?

MALE #001, "Mike Mike," twenty-year-old Thundercat: Mixed in with the guys. B-Dogs and C-Dogs.

INT: Do they sell drugs too?

001:    Yes they does.

INT: And how about, uh, guns and stuff? Are they involved in that?

001:    Yeah, they shoot them pistols. [. . .]

Other accounts of the female gang members' activities placed women in a role secondary to males. This group represented one-third of the sample. From this perspective, women joined the gang because they were following their boyfriends or were just hanging around with the boys. [. . .]

These secondary roles often involved the use of women to "set up" rival gang members. Women gang members were used to attract rival gang members making them vulnerable to attacks. [. . .]

The diversity of female involvement in gangs was reinforced by the comments of the female gang members we interviewed. Two women indicated that their gangs were separate from males, while the others told us they played subservient roles within male gangs. One woman reported that most female gang members were affiliated with male gangs. [. . .]

"I LOVE TO BANG": SERIOUS CRIME BY GANG MEMBERS

> Bang, drive-by and shoot shit up. It just feels good. Like [unclear] says, damn it feels good to be a gangster. I love to do it. I love to bang, I love to shoot shit up, we all do it together.
>
> (White male #099, "Joe L.," eighteen-year-old
> Insane Gangster Disciple)

Popular stereotypes of gangs and gang members – reflected in news and entertainment media, in public opinions, in officials' statements, and in some scholarly works – consider them to be organized, violent predators on society. . . . Some of this may be true, as the statement by "Joe L." implies. What is not true, at least from talking with our subjects, is the intensity of this stereotype, the well organized nature of their group activities, and the delight in violence shown above (a more common attitude towards violence was fatalism – "you gotta do what you gotta do"; "we don't go looking for trouble"; "we use violence when it comes to us"). Serious crimes – both non-violent and violent – are a defining feature of gangs, but gang crimes seem neither as purposive, organized, or frequent as the popular (and official) mind imagines. Often, violence is a response to the threat of violence from the presence of other gangs. . . .

"I Was Robbing and Steal and This, That, and The Other": Felony property crime

St. Louis gangs and individual members routinely steal things, both together and on their own. Sixty-seven subjects, for example, said that their gang steals things together. Although much of this theft may be no more harmful than minor shoplifting – sodas, candy, beer, cigarettes – gangs still are involved in a lot of serious property crime. Our subjects' self-reports of their most recent arrests, for example, included two for possession of stolen property, two for burglary, four for robbery, and eight for possession of a stolen vehicle. Property crimes also occur frequently: fourteen subjects said that the gang stole things together every day, seven said that they stole weekly, and eight said monthly.

> They beat up people and take their stuff. About every now and then . . . Five times [in a month].
>> (Male #010, "Jason C.," fifteen-year-old Compton Gangster)

> Some of them do and some of them don't. they do it mostly everyday.
>> (Male #052, "Jonathan," fifteen-year-old 107 Hoover Crip)

[. . .]

Forty-three subjects said that the gang planned property crimes, although very few could or would elaborate on such assertions. Two examples of somewhat rational planning include:

> Well, first we won't do no robbery, we do a burglary to get some quick money. We might creep around the neighborhood, we don't do it in our neighborhood, not downtown we go somewhere like across the street you know and see a open house you know, we go in there and hit it, boom, you know come on out with a VCR, nineteen-inch TV, jewelry. We go over there on the lane, the guy selling drugs he buy all this kind of stuff.
>> (Male #003, "Jerry," eighteen-year-old Thundercat)

[. . .]

But other subjects pointed out that much "planning" was remarkably spontaneous and haphazard.

> [. . .]
>
> INT: How often do you do [robberies]?
> MALE #035, "Edward," twenty-year-old Hoover Gangster Crip: Whenever we get drunk and somebody mention it. People walking downtown. They be drunk as a skunk.
> INT: So you do it mainly at night when people are walking around drunk?
> 035:   Yeah. [. . .]

The relative absence of planned, organized, and gang-motivated property crimes is also apparent in the division and use of criminal proceeds. Although forty-seven subjects said that illegally obtained profits (chiefly from drug sales) went for gang-related acts or needs, the actual percentages and items were usually inconsequential.

> We'll rob somebody and everybody will go buy some drinks or something.
>> (Male #087, "Blue Jay," eighteen-year-old Rolling 60's Crip)

> Sometimes they might go out and buy ski masks or stuff that will get us in some more trouble.
>> (Male #031, "John Doe," sixteen-year-old Thundercat)

MALE #083, "Winchester," fourteen-year-old Rolling 60's Crip: Yeah, we
    have to give it [money to the gang].
INT: Half the money go to the gang? If you got a burglary where you got
    $100, how much would go to the gang?
083:   About $5.00.

Many subjects denied that they, or other gang members, currently engaged in property
crimes; they were bringing in more money selling drugs.

I don't steal no more, I got whatever I need. I don't steal no more. If I ever catch
anybody in my group stealing, I'm going to get down on them cause they know
they can come to me and ask anybody in the posse you know what I'm saying,
that they want this or they want that. They know they will get it. Ain't no sense
in stealing it. What you steal it for?
(Male #033, "Larry," eighteen-year-old Thundercat)

We don't take nothing. We pay for ours. We make money.
(Male #037, "Big Money," twenty-two-year-old
Compton Gangster)

[. . .]

"I'm In This For Myself": Drug sales

Gang involvement in illegal drug sales is a major concern of the public, media, and law
enforcement agencies. Many observers have drawn a causal link between the rise and
growth of street gang involvement in drug sales as well organized at both local and
national levels (National Institute of Justice 1993; Skolnick et al. 1988; Sanchez-
Jankowski 1991). But St. Louis gangs contradict these stereotypical notions in many
ways. Although every gang in our sample had some members who sold drugs (crack
cocaine, in the main), gang involvement was generally poorly organized, episodic, non-
monopolistic, carried out by individuals or cliques on their own, and was not a rational
for the gang's existence and continuance. [. . .]
Because drug money is such an important reason for belonging to a gang, we might
have expected subjects to wax eloquent about their earnings and expenditures.
But many subjects seemed reluctant, hesitant, or confused about their income from
drug sales.

[. . .]

INT: About how much do you make per week?
092:   How much do I make per week?
INT: Yeah.
092:   Just my check plus like if I need some money for something, on my
    own I can go over there and hook up with $500.
INT: So you make about $500 a week selling drugs?
092:   If I want to.

Reported weekly compensation from drug sales ranges from the ridiculous of zero to the absurd of $15,000. The median and modal category was $500, with eleven subjects reporting that amount. Interestingly, this is approximately the figure reported by Peter Reuter and his associates in their study of the earning of street drug dealers (1990). But we suspect an enormous amount of braggadocio and income inflation in these answers. [. . .]

Instead of collective uses, the money made from drugs was usually kept by individual sellers, reflecting the fact that gang members rarely sell drugs in groups larger than pairs or trios as well as the fact that gangs in St. Louis exist primarily for non-economic reasons. Members of the gangs we interviewed generally lacked the skills or commitment to organize for a long-range profit-making venture. [. . .]

While most of the gang members we interviewed sell drugs, there is little indication that much pressure was put on members to sell. Only eighteen subjects said that everyone was expected to meet a sales quota. . . . Two subjects described how much their drug sales resembled a business:

> Records, salesmen, muscles, same as a legal business.
> (Male #019, "Anthony," twenty-two-year-old Crip)

[. . .]

Heroin was mentioned twenty-nine times, although it appears that few, if any, of our subjects sell heroin and many are unfamiliar with the drug. One mention, for example, was made of "capsules" (not the form in which the drug is sold) of black tar being sold on the street. PCP was mentioned eighteen times – it seems most frequently to have been sold mixed with cocaine or weed. [. . .]

"Piling on Crabs and Shooting Slobs": Violence and gangs

> Beating Crabs. If it wasn't for beating Crabs I don't think that I would be in a gang right now.
> (Male #057, "Smith & Wesson," fifteen-year-old
> Neighborhood Posse Blood)

> [Our] group is the Rolling 60's. Basically we're just a fighting crew. What we do is to fight and make money. . . .
> (Male #092, "Derone," twenty-one-year-old Rolling 60's Crip)

Violence and violent crime is a central part of our subjects' lives in manifold ways. The "violence of everyday life," for example, is excessively high in their neighborhoods and families. City rates of child abuse, forcible theft, rape, assaults, and homicide are well above those for the St. Louis metropolitan area and the nation. . . . Eight of our subjects mentioned having a relative who died from gunshot wounds or some other form of homicide; *more than half knew another gang member who had been shot*. Eleven of our subjects are now dead. [. . .]

"We Just Grew Up Fightin"

Violence is an ordinary part of most of our subjects lives, although it obviously intensifies once they joined a gang and become more involved in gang activities. One subject described why he joined the gang in this way.

> We just grew up like that. We grew up fightin, if, I don't know, we just grew up fightin and everybody hangin around so they decided to call they self somethin since we hung around like that went out doin things and stuff.
>
> (Male #002, "Eric," sixteen-year-old Thundercat)

Violence in and by the gang starts early for our subjects: seventy subjects said they were "jumped in" for their initiation. . . . Eight subjects said they had to shoot someone for their initiation. . . . And several subjects mentioned other kinds of violence involved in joining a gang. . . . These acts at initiation serve to legitimate and normalize violence within the gang. . . . Eighty-four subjects mentioned "fighting" as "something they did with their gang," while nineteen said it was what they did the most with their fellow members. . . . Seventy-eight subjects said there were gang fights at their schools, eighty-three said that weapons (usually guns) were brought to school, and thirty-eight said that weapons were used at school.

Gun possession and use is another window into our subjects' violent propensities and opportunities. Guns were the overwhelming weapon of choice for gang-motivated and gang-related violence. Eighty subjects said they owned guns (two subjects reported they owned over one hundred guns), and the mean number of guns reported was four and a half (the mode was one). Only 192 guns were specifically identified by our subjects, and 75 percent of those were handguns of one sort or another. Subjects also mentioned owning other kinds of weapons besides firearms.

> Hand grenades? I got about fifty of them.
>
> (Male #001, "Mike-Mike," twenty-year-old Thundercat)

[. . .]

Our subjects most recent arrests also show how commonplace violence is: Seventeen were for assault, six for peace disturbances, three for weapons violations, two for obstructing police, and one was for homicide. Nine subjects had an assault conviction; six had weapons violations convictions; one had a manslaughter conviction. Ten subjects had done time for assault, four for weapons violations, and one for manslaughter.

"We Be Fighting All the Time": Causes and kinds of violence

While we would like to report that our subjects sharply differentiate their use of lethal versus nonlethal violence according to targets, too many subjects' descriptions invalidate the distinction. It is our impression that violence that lacks a gang motive or is unrelated to the gang is less likely to be lethal. [. . .]

Violence by and towards gang members seems to lurk around every corner. Sometimes it is a sudden unexpected eruption, sometimes the result of long simmering feuds or disagreements that are not seemingly gang motivated or related. [. . .]

Disrespect has to be corrected and answered – physically. And drug turfs are defended; customers who cheat you are violently punished.

> A guy came in, he had the wrong colors on, he got to move out. He got his head split open with a sledgehammer, he got two ribs broken, he got his face torn up. We dropped him off on the other side of town. If he did die, it was on the other side of town.
>
>   (Male #013, "Darryl," twenty-nine-year-old Blood)

> I had to pistol whip a guy, I shot him in the knee. Since then he never came back.
>
>   (Male #017, "Billy," twenty-one-year-old North Side Crip)

[. . .]

Getting out of this violent cycle is not easy. One subject told this story of how his brother left a gang.

> My big brother. He was in the 38s. They say to get out of the 38s you got to kill your parents, kill one of your parents. My brother was making good grades, got him a scholarship and everything and he was like I'm leaving this alone. They tried to make him kill my mother. He was like, you must be crazy and I was on his side. So the leader, _____, big husky dude, him and my brother got into it. They was fighting and he pulled a gun out so I stabbed him in the back. I thought he was going to shoot my brother, which he was, so I stabbed him in the back. He paralyzed now.
>
>   (Male #037, "Big Money," twenty-two-year-old Compton Gangster)

Cowardice is highly disapproved, since standing up for your friends and fellow members is almost a sacred duty (and a raison d'être for being in a gang). [. . .]

"We Don't Go Looking for It; If It Happens, It Happens": Attitudes on violence

Although we began this chapter with a statement reflecting a "love" of violence, most of our subjects do not revel in confrontation to quite the degree that subject boasted of (to be fair, he was probably bragging and exaggerating both his love of violence and his involvement in it). The most common attitude toward the possibility of violence and actually initiating it was more fatalistic and commonplace.

> INT: When do members of your gang use violence?
> MALE #092, "Derone," twenty-one-year-old Rolling 60's Crip: Only when violence is necessary. Like at a confrontation or somebody talk crap or if somebody throw up the wrong sign then we fuck they ass up.

> If a Blood would shoot me and I happen to get hit, I get hit. Then I be dead.
>
>   (Male #025, "Tony," seventeen-year-old Hoover Gangster Crip)

There is, in fact, something of "a man's gotta do what a man's gotta do" about our subjects' responses to violence, perhaps because it is a normal and expected part of their lives. At times there was also a rather chilling, matter-of-fact attitude in our subjects' descriptions of violence and killing.

> Oh man, you shoot somebody and they don't die they shoot you and you be feuding until one of you all dead. A dude named Scotty and Kevin. Every time they see each other. They done shot a pregnant girl at Saints a few months ago. Kevin was trying to hit him. They will go on with it.
>
> (Male #012, "Lance," twenty-year-old West Side Mob member)

[. . .]

Other subjects seem also bored with violence, or talking about violence, and some gave the impression of being tired with that whole scene. [. . .]

And a sufficient number of subjects mentioned fear or the psychological effects of being on the receiving or giving end of violence. [. . .]

> When, when you shoot a person it seem like everybody watching you. I always thought somebody was after me. Everytime I'd hear a police car I'd jump. Every time my mother call me I say WHAT! cause the cops was bothering me but it was an accident. I shot him though.
>
> (Male #003, "Jerry," eighteen-year-old Thundercat)

[. . .]

"It Don't Hurt, It Don't Faze Me No More"

[. . .]

Though it contains elements of self protection, the expressive character is evident in efforts to establish dominance or identity. Viewed in this light, violence that erupts over what appear to be petty acts – disrespecting a color, stepping in front of another person, flashing hand signs, driving through a rival neighborhood – takes on a deeper and more serious meaning. [. . .]

Fundamental personal identity is also involved. Most of the gang members portrayed in our study are proud, insecure, tough teenagers and young adults whose self-esteem, self-worth, and identity appear to be constantly at risk. Toughness, manliness, not backing down, are important values of their world and their psyches – to be upheld even at the cost of their own or others' lives.

Postscript

Life in the Gang was published in 1996, based on fieldwork conducted between 1992 and 1994.

The research for the book included 99 primary subjects. By 2004, 28 members of the 99 primary subjects were dead.

This includes only those members of the sample that we were able to stay in touch with or learned about, roughly half of the total sample.

This sobering figure underscores one of the central premises of *Life in the Gang*, that violence is an ever-present feature of the lives of gang members.

Ironically, many gang members told us they joined their gang for protection. Gang membership put them at imminent risk for being a victim of violence and imprisonment. Gang membership itself is a primary risk factor for becoming a victim of violence.

Bibliography

Anderson, Elijah. 1994. *The Code of the Street: Decency, Violence and the Moral Life of the Inner City*. New York: W. W. Norton.

Block, Carolyn R. and Block, Richard. 1993. *Street Gang Crime in Chicago*. National Institute of Justice Research in Brief. Washington, DC: U.S. Department of Justice.

Bowker, Lee H. and Klein, Malcolm W. 1983. "The Etiology of Female Juvenile Delinquency and Gang Membership: A Test of Psychological and Social Structural Explanations." *Adolescence* 18: 739–51.

Bursik, Robert J. and Grasmick, Harold G. 1993. *Neighborhoods and Crime: The Dimensions of Effective Community Control*. Boston, MA: Lexington Books.

Campbell, A. 1984. *The Girls in the Gang*. Cambridge, MA: Basil Blackwell.

Curry, G. David, Ball, Richard A., and Fox, Robert J. 1994. *Gang Crime and Law Enforcement Recordkeeping*. National Institute of Justice Research in Brief. Washington, DC: U.S. Department of Justice.

Hagedorn, John. 1988. *People and Folks*. Chicago, IL: Lakeview Press.

Jackson, Pamela Irving. 1991. "Crime, Youth Gangs and Urban Transition: The Social Dislocations of Postindustrial Economic Development." *Justice Quarterly* 6: 379–97.

Katz, Jack. 1988. *The Seductions of Crime: The Moral and Sensual Attractions in Doing Evil*. New York: Basic Books.

Klein, Malcolm W. 1971. *Street Gangs and Street Workers*. Englewood Cliffs, NJ: Prentice-Hall.

Loftin, Colin. 1984. "Assaultive Violence as Contagious Process." *Bulletin of the New York Academy of Medicine* 62: 550–55.

Padilla, Felix. 1992. *The Gang as an American Enterprise*. New Brunswick, NJ: Rutgers University Press.

Sanchez-Jankowski, Martin. 1991. *Islands in the Street: Gangs in American Society*. Berkeley, CA: University of California Press.

Scheper-Hughes, Nancy. 1992. *Death Without Weeping: The Violence of Everyday Life*. Berkeley, CA: University of California Press.

Sheldon, H.D. 1898. "The Institutional Activities of American Children." *The American Journal of Psychology* 9: 424–48.

Skolnick, Jerome, Correl, T., Navarro, E., and Robb, R. 1988. *The Social Structure of Street Drug Dealing*. BSC Forum. Office of the Attorney General, State of California.

Taylor, Carl. 1993 [1990]. *Girls, Gangs, Women and Drugs*. East Lansing, MI: Michigan State University Press.

Thrasher, Frederic M. 1927. *The Gang*. Chicago, IL: University of Chicago Press.

Yablonsky, Lewis. 1966. *The Violent Gang*. Baltimore, MD: Penguin.

Chapter 22

Ian Taylor

THE POLITICAL ECONOMY OF CRIME

From: Ian Taylor (1997), excerpts from 'The political economy of crime', in Mike Maguire et al., *Oxford Handbook of Criminology*, 2nd edn, Oxford: Oxford University Press, pp. 265–359.

INTRODUCTION

[. . .]

IN THIS CHAPTER, MY concern is to survey the literature of nineteenth- and twentieth-century criminology, and associated social scientific fields, in respect of the issue of 'political economy' and crime. What will very rapidly be apparent is that much of this literature works from within what was essentially a simplified and uncritical version of earlier forms of political-economic thinking. [. . .]

THE BUSINESS CYCLE AND CRIME

[. . .]

In twentieth-century criminology, probably the best-known attempt at exploring the impact of the economic cycle on crime has been Georg Rusche and Otto Kirchheimer's examination of the relation between unemployment and *imprisonment* (1939). Rusche and Kirchheimer's analysis of these relationships in England, France, Germany, and Italy in the period between 1911 and 1928, and in Italy and Germany in the first years of fascism (1928–36), is actually quite complex in its various conclusions, but the most usual interpretation of their overall argument is 'that prisons help to control the labour supply by jettisoning inmates when labour is scarce and filling up when labour is abundant' (Box and Hale, 1982: 21). Similar findings have been reported in two separate studies of the relationship between unemployment and imprisonment in Canada (Greenberg, 1977; Kellough *et al.*, 1980) and by Jankovic (1977) in an analysis of Californian imprisonment in the early 1970s. A further study by Lessan (1991) uses American time-series data drawn from the period 1948–85 to examine the relationship between unemployment and imprisonment, with the addition of *inflation*, which is seen as a constraint on the state's ability to fund what Lessan calls 'placatory' measures: this study generally confirms the influence of unemployment on imprisonment, especially for males.

The theoretical argument embedded in Rusche and Kirchheimer is clear. It is not simply that capitalist economies experience continual cycles of boom and slump and that slumps tend to produce significant increases in crime: it is also, quite specifically, that capitalist economies systematically give rise to *or even require* instability in the employment chances of a section of the working population (a 'reserve army' of labour). When the business cycle throws this reserve army out of work, prisons fill up with unemployed workers attempting to maintain themselves through theft and other crime. In this respect, the political economy of capitalist societies is itself a determining factor in the cyclical production of crime and also the 'workload' of the criminal justice system itself. *Punishment and Social Structure* was first published in 1938. It could not have predicted the explosion of the prison populations that has been occurring in the majority of western societies in the 1980s and 1990s with the prison population in the United States nearly tripling since the election of Ronald Reagan in 1981. . . . There is no doubt, however, that Rusche and Kircheimer's analysis seems highly pertinent to the explanation of the 'explosion of penality' that has emerged in the context of deep crisis in the Fordist system of mass manufacturing, and the return of mass unemployment in current post-Fordist circumstances.

A criminological wisdom of this kind, focused on the close and essentially determinate relationship between crime, imprisonment, and economic distress, lies at the core of nearly all the Marxist criminological texts that emerged in North America (Platt and Takagi, 1968; Quinney, 1974) and in Europe (Melossi and Pavarini, 1981) in the 1970s. But an interest in the social effects of 'market failure' in otherwise healthy and dynamic capitalist societies has been at the heart of much social-democratic scholarship in the field—for example, in the 1970s, in the work of Harvey Brenner.

Harvey Brenner was widely known among sociologists of health and illness, epidemiologists, social work lobby groups, and others in the United States and in England for a number of published studies which purported to demonstrate the existence of a close causal relationship between unemployment and mortality and morbidity rates. His work was distinctive for its adoption of 'time series regression analysis', wherein the analyst 'lagged' the effects of unemployment over a period of years and thereby avoided the necessity of demonstrating the immediate, temporal coincidence of unemployment and its hypothesized effects. One of the most widely quoted of Brenner's findings in the United States was a study published in 1977, concluding that 'the 1.4 per cent rise in unemployment during 1970 [was] directly responsible for some 51,570 total deaths, including 1,740 additional homicides, 1,540 additional suicides, and for 5,520 additional state mental hospitalizations' (Brenner, 1977: 4).

Earlier, in evidence presented to the Joint Economic Committee of the US Congress, Brenner had argued that every 1 per cent increase in unemployment in that country had meant that 4.3 per cent more men and 2.3 per cent more women were introduced into state mental hospitals for the first time; that 4.1 per cent more people committed suicide; that 5.7 per cent more were murdered; and that 4 per cent more entered state prisons. In the next six years, in addition, 1.9 per cent would die from heart disease, cirrhosis of the liver, and other stress-related chronic ailments (Brenner, 1971). [. . .]

Attempts to relate economic conditions to crime rate gained popularity in the late 1980s and early 1990s in both Britain and North America, consequent on the continuing and severe recessions in the economics of those two societies. Cantor and Lund's study of 1985 was notable for the argument it marshalled – against the established conventional wisdom within the literature on the economics of crime – suggesting that 'unemployment' could act in some circumstances to *suppress* crime, in the sense of reducing the amount of criminal opportunity available. In areas of high unemployment, there are more people at home acting, in effect, as guardians of private property and private homes. In addition, they averred, unemployment can sometimes involve a number of domestic economies of scale (lower transport costs, savings on meals and subsistence, etc.) which offset the impact of wage loss. Over time, however – Cantor and Lund recognize – these compensations are likely to reduce in importance and to mitigate the economic effects of long-term unemployment, . . . so that the 'suppressor effect' of unemployment was likely to be short term and the negative consequences (in terms of personal dislocation and attraction into careers of property crime) visible after a lag.

Allan and Steffensmeier's objective, in a study published in 1989, was to try and advance beyond straightforward analysis of the relationship between 'unemployment' and 'crime', as brute unqualified concepts, in order to examine whether the *quality* of work available in particular regions had an independent effect on levels of criminal activity in that locality. The theoretical focus of this work – important in all post-Fordist societies – was on what Allan and Steffesmeier call 'the labour market climate of a region' (1989: 110), and this was conceived by them as involving four different dimensions – *unemployment* itself (the proportion of the labour force without work but looking for work); *sub-unemployment* (the numbers and percentage of people without work for a lengthy period of time who have given up looking, i.e. those who are often identified as 'discouraged workers'); *low hours* (the percentage of the labour force employed only on a part-time basis by virtue of being unable to find fulltime work) and *low wages* (the proportion of the labour force on sub-poverty level wages). From US census sources, Allan and Steffensmeier constructed two 100 per cent samples of males between 13 and 17 years of age and 18 and 24, identified their status on their four dimensions of unemployment, and then regressed these data against the four property crimes in the Uniform Crime Reports index (robbery, burglary, larceny, and auto theft). Their findings were, first, that full employment was, indeed, associated with low arrest rates, whilst 'unemployment'; as a brute category, was generally associated with high arrest rates. But their analysis also suggested that poorly paid and part time work, in the case of young adults (18–24-year-olds) tended to be associated with high arrest rates, but that this association did not hold in the case of the younger age group of adolescent males. Allan and Steffensmeier observe themselves that they were not surprised by this finding, since, they argued, most 'juveniles' in the labour market are only working on what they called a 'voluntary, part time basis'.

In Britain, where there were 5.3 million offences known to the police in 1991 (compared to 2.4 million in 1979) and a record annual increase of 19 per cent in the twelve months to September 1991, a study by Simon Field suggested that the increases of the previous twelve years were most marked in respect of property crime (theft, burglary, and car crime) in the years where spending power decreased, and that in contrast the increases in crimes of violence (assault, armed robbery, and sex offences) were more marked in the years of relative economic boom. Field particularly noted a close correlation between economic boom, consumption of beer, and violent offences

(Field, 1991). More recently, Eisner has released some early data on a large-scale investigation of the relationship between crime rates and economic conditions over ten-year time periods, as revealed in the available official statistics of seven different European societies, relating the growth rate in economic activity in those societies to crime (Eisner, 1995).

THE POLITICAL ECONOMY OF INEQUALITY AND CRIME

The last section was concerned with reviewing the criminological literature focusing on the determinate effects of the economic cycle on crime (and on incarceration) and dealing therefore with the relation between absolute levels of economic distress or deprivation and levels of crime and delinquency. There is also a distinct body of (usually quite specifically sociological) literature, which has been more interested in thinking about *inequalities in the distribution of economic return or economic well-being*, and the broad social effects of such inequalities, e.g. in respect of crime. In this approach it is not so much the 'volatility' of political economy which is at issue but the systematic or ongoing production of and trends in unequal opportunity and/or poverty. [. . .]

The polarization of the labour market in the United States, Britain, and other western industrial societies that was produced by technological advances in the 1950s and 1960s was relatively insignificant, by comparison with the convulsions that occurred in the 1980s. Taking the official unemployment rate as the most immediate expression of these changes, there was a calamitous increase in unemployment in Britain. On official figures which quite notoriously have been subjected to a series of definitional changes, all of which have had the effect of deflating the overall official figure, unemployment increased from 4.1 per cent of the labour force in 1972 to 10.3 per cent in 1981. Official figures suggest that the highest level of unemployment in the 1980s in Britain was 12.4 per cent in 1983, declining to 6.8 per cent in 1990, returning to 11 per cent (three million) in 1992, and declining again to 8 per cent in 1996. At each of these moments of 'slump', the absolute numbers of unemployed people exceeded the totals at the previous low point. Economic commentators began to speak not only of 'the end of full employment' as a social and political project, but also of the fearful prospect of 'jobless growth' – i.e. a period of economic recovery that involves no *net* creation of new employment (Aronowitz and DiFazio, 1995). In Western Europe as a whole, in 1993, the annual average of unemployment was calculated officially at 11 per cent, in comparison to an average of only 1.6 per cent in the 1960s (Judt, 1996). Long-term unemployment (lasting over a year) was calculated at about one-third of the total of those still registering for work (*ibid.*).

Rehearsing some of the evidence about the increases in the size of the 'reserve army of labour' or unemployment from the 1960s to the present redirects attention to one of the themes of classical political economy: namely, the consequences of social exclusion in societies in which citizenship and individual worth and merit are in part a matter of 'work' and, indeed, employment. From this perspective, the explosive growth of recorded rates of crime is a measure, precisely, of the deep logic of exclusion unleashed by free market forces. This is, of course, an association which is challenged by philosophers of the right and by Conservative politicians, most famously by Prime Minister Margaret Thatcher, during the riots in England's inner cities in the summer of 1981, in her resounding declaration that 'unemployment was no excuse'. There may be some basis on which one could attribute moral blame to rioters; but we should not be blind to the truth that the riots of 1981, like those that followed on intermittently throughout the 1980s and early 1990s, occurred in areas of extraordinarily high unemployment (such as the north-east of England) – much of it spread over long periods of time. It is clear that unemployment in and of itself would not be a sufficient explanation of the occurrence of these riots (or, indeed, of the very high rates of theft, car crime, and assaults – the 'long slow riot of crime', as Jock Young has called it, which characterizes many of these areas): unemployment was just as high, on official measures, in many of these self-same areas in the 1920s without there being anything like the same rate of interpersonal and property crime reported to the police that was being reported in the 1980s and 1990s (Lea and Young, 1984: 90–3).

It is also true that the continuing outbreaks of crime and riot in America's ghetto areas, as well as in the inner cities of Britain, have been subject to an alternative cultural and sociological explanation, namely the theory of the underclass, particularly in the works of the American conservative commentator, Charles Murray (1990). Murray's approach is behavioural, in the sense that he wants to identify the emergence of a pathological type of behaviour and then explain that pathological behaviour in terms of its most immediate conditions of existence. For him, the source of much of the crime and dislocation in the inner city and the ghetto lies in the welfare policies that have been adopted by successive governments in Britain and the United States towards ghetto populations – policies, which have made it possible for deprived or disadvantaged people to survive outside the labour force. Such welfare policies have not provided the support for further initiative and personal development on the part of their clients (which may have been thought to be their original rationale). The argument instead is that these policies have encouraged a form of welfare state dependency in which the recipients of welfare remain content with their minimal conditions of life and do not take responsibility for improving on those conditions. But the second, associated alleged development, which gives cause for further concern, is the way in which young women in Britain, in such circumstances, knowingly become pregnant as a means of ensuring access to public housing, staying out of the labour market, and, in both the United States and Britain, obtaining state benefits over and above basic unemployment support. Murray points, for example, to the increase in illegitimate births in Britain from 10.6 per cent of all live births in 1979 to 25.6 per cent in 1988. The consequence of this, in Britain as in America, is a rather rapid increase in the number of single-parent female-headed households, with what Murray argues are dis-astrous effects in terms of the routine socialization of the children. The third element in Murray's definition of the underclass is its disproportionate involvement in crime, and especially violent crime. For Murray, the bulk of the 60 per cent increase in crimes of violence reported in the English criminal statistics between 1980 and 1988 was attributable to the activities of young men from the underclass, who, deprived of the dignity and the life-project of work in support of a family, tended to engage in other means of self-expression:

> when large numbers of young men don't work, the communities around them break down, just as they break down when large numbers of young women have babies. The two phenomena are intimately related. Just as work is more important than merely making a living, getting married and raising a family are

more than a way to pass the time. Supporting a family is a central means for a man to prove to himself that he is a 'mensch'. Men who do not support families find other ways to prove that they are men, which tend to take various destructive forms. As many have commented through the centuries, young males are essentially barbarians for whom marriage – meaning not just the wedding-vows, but the act of taking responsibility for a wife and children – is an indispensable civilising force.

(Murray, 1990: 22–3)

Murray's theses about the underclass in America and Britain have found many critics in both countries, not least because the policy sub-text of his writing is always the with-drawal of benefits from populations who are already officially in poverty in the context of recession and deindustrialization. Writers in Britain like Alan Walker accuse Murray of inventing an essentially ideological category (i.e. of lower-class people who are to be differentiated in terms of their conditioned behaviour from the rest of the working class – a resurrection of the Victorian distinction between the 'deserving' and 'undeserving' poor), for which there is no widespread evidence, and then ignoring the broad patterns of government policies that generate poverty among pensioners and the elderly, single parents in general, and the disabled. Curiously enough, however, Murray's earlier concern to recognize the differential responses of sections of the lower class in America (now translated to his work on the underclass in Britain) to the collapse of the industrial labour market and other developments in the 1980s do find some support in the work of the pioneering black scholar in America working on such issues. William Julius Wilson (1987).

In contrast to many liberal scholars, Wilson squarely confronts the data on the disproportionate involvement of the black population of America in violent crime, and also recognizes the extraordinary increase in illegitimate births and in female-headed households in the black community in America. But where Murray would want to claim that these developments must be an expression of generous and self-defeating welfare programmes, especially for the single mother, Wilson shows that the real value of such benefits declined throughout the 1980s. Where liberal scholars have pointed to racism as an explanation of blacks' involvement in violent crime and other dysfunctional, anti-social behaviour, Wilson insists that such racism was far worse in earlier periods than it was in the 1980s. For Wilson, explanation of these contemporary phenomena of violent crime and 'labour force drop-out' among large sections of the black lower class in America must lie in an understanding of what he calls *historic discrimination*, a long-term systemic process of subordination and subjugation, as distinct from the immediate presenting symptoms involved in individual acts of discrimination or prejudice. To think that these long-term processes can have evolved without real structural effects in cutting whole sections of the black population off, over generations, from adequate training and education, and also imprisoning such people into tightly bounded ethnic ghettos in which maladaptive individual behaviours were common, is merely naïve.

Wilson points up not the 'culture of poverty' so beloved of earlier critics of the poor but rather a culture of exclusion and subordination which has had long-term, crippling cultural effects, which are not accessible to a quick policy fix, especially in competitive free market conditions. In Britain, throughout the 1980s and in the early 1990s, these processes of deindustrialization had quite extraordinary sudden and fundamental effects. When measured in the same terms as it was before 1979 unemployment reached about four million in November 1992 (in contrast to the 'official' measure, resulting from over a dozen modifications since 1979, of 2.8 million), and adult male unemployment became firmly stuck at a level not seen since the 1930s (Hutton, 1992). On every available measure, inequality continued, until 1996, to show ever-widening gaps between the richest and poorest sections of the society, and, in the meantime, levels of crime known to the police continued to escalate until 1993, nearly doubling in the decade from 1981 to 1991. There were particularly steep increases in the numbers of attempted thefts reported to the police over this period (336 per cent) and in vehicle thefts. Burglaries increased by about 75 per cent, an increase apparent in British Crime Survey findings as well as in police statistics (Mayhew and Maung, 1992; Maguire [1997]).

It matters enormously, in conditions of increasing economic polarization and crime, how analysts attempt to explain the relationship between these developments. Murray lays himself open to accusations of 'blaming the victim', particularly in his strictures on the problems posed by unmarried mothers in respect of the socialization they provide for their offspring and the overall character of 'family life' in such households. In complete contrast to Murray, however, analysis derived from political economy throws up an awareness of unemployment as a structural problem rather than a personal default, and also shows some understanding of the absolutely destructive effects that the acceleration of structural unemployment resulting from deindustrialization in the 1980s and 1990s have had on the lives of individuals and on communities in Europe and North America. It also recognizes that these destructive processes have been magnified, rather than modified, throughout the 1980s and 1990s by the dogged and unyielding pursuit by governments, especially in Britain and the United States, of free-market economic policies as a matter of faith, without any real care for the human consequences of this particular experiment in social engineering. The human effects of the free market experiment are clear and inescapable on the streets of Los Angeles and other parts of southern California (Currie, 1990a, 1990b) and in the 'Rust Belt' of the northern industrial cities of the United States (Henry and Brown, 1990).

These effects included all the well-known expressions of economic deprivation, from poor housing, ill-health, to interpersonal violence, but often in highly concentrated locations – most usually, the areas of settlement of different minority ethnic groups. So, for example, in New York City 70 per cent of blacks live in areas officially designated as areas of 'extreme poverty' (Sampson and Wilson, 1995: 41). This concentration of deprivation, as identified by Wilson and many other scholars, is reflected in similarly concentrated high rates of violent interpersonal crime and property crime. In the early 1990s, Afro-Americans accounted for 40–50 per cent of all homicides, forcible rapes, armed robberies, and aggravated assaults in the United States (Hagan and Peterson, 1995: 19) but they were also much more frequently victimized by such crimes than were whites, by a factor of about 25 per cent (ibid.: 23). The 'life-time risk' of being murdered in the United States in the mid-1980s had already been measured at 1:21 for black American males as compared with 1:131 for whites (Sampson and Wilson, 1995: 37, quoting a US Justice Department study of 1985).

Many of the older industrial areas of England, Scotland, and Wales, over the same period, began to be plagued by what would previously have been quite unknown levels of theft and burglary, car stealing, interpersonal violence, and also by a crippling sense of fear and insecurity, which cuts thousands of their residents off from the pleasures of the broader consumer society and the compensations of friendship and neighbourhood. So also, to repeat our earlier point, were they plagued by quite extraordinary levels of personal and family poverty, by poor physical health resulting from bad diet, and by the increasing levels of suicide and early death associated with loss of a personal sense of morale and self-regard. In Britain, as in the United States, an understanding of the pattern of crime is inextricably connected to an understanding of the political economy, not simply of unemployment, but more broadly of the new inequality characteristic of free market societies. Analysis is particularly urgent now into the *long-term* effects of this inequality and subordination in England, in respect of the unskilled working class in general, but, in particular, amongst young white working-class males left behind in the deindustrialization of the 1980s (the new 'poor whites') (cf. Taylor and Jamieson, 1996). [. . .]

THE COSTS OF CRIME AND THE ENTRY OF NEO-CLASSICAL ECONOMICS

Standing in complete contrast to the kind of political-economic analyses of crime undertaken by critically minded social scientists discussed in the previous section are the approaches to the analysis of crime adopted by economists working within the neo-classical perspective. This approach first came to be applied to crime in an influential fashion in the United States as in a famous essay by the economist Gary Becker in 1968. Isaac Ehrlich (1973) subsequently extended the economic approach to the study of punishment and deterrence, and Kenneth Avio and Scott Clark (1976) reworked these studies using Canadian economic and crime data.

Much of this early North American literature on the political economy of crime is informed by a generalized political concern at the extraordinary costs to the state (and, therefore, to taxpayers) of the continuing post-war expansion in the criminal justice system (provoked, according to a common-sense view, by the rapid and accelerating increases in crime). The defining feature of the literature is the use of the analytic techniques of neo-classical economics (and, specifically, econometrics) in the investigation of crime. The particular objective is to try to evaluate the *effectiveness* of particular forms of social control in the reduction of the incidence of humanly and economically costly crime. A large number of studies in this tradition try to measure the *differential* costs and benefits of different social control interventions on crime, and the cost of achieving a radical reduction – even to an outcome 'no crime' – of certain crimes. In the work of Lehtinen (1977), for instance, cost–benefit analysis is applied, more or less without qualification, to the disposition of convicted murderers in the United States; this analysis of the differential costs of long-term imprisonment versus execution results in firm support for the economic benefits of execution. This economic analysis of punishment began to find an echo among certain applied criminologists and social scientists in the 1980s. In Britain, the application of 'rational choice theory' was first undertaken by Derek Cornish and Ron Clarke, most notably in a monograph entitled *The Reasoning Criminal: Rational Choice Perspectives on Offending* (1986). The central argument advanced, quite straightforwardly, was that people engage in crime primarily because a good opportunity presents itself so to do. The situational decision to engage in an act of theft, for example, is taken in circumstances when people think the risk is worth taking that is, when the opportunity is clear and the chances of being observed and caught are small. This notion of the exercise of reasoned choice is a diluted version of the famous Benthamite calculus of human action being simultaneously deterred by pain and driven by pleasure. What Cornish and Clarke tried to do in *The Reasoning Criminal*, as well as in an earlier paper of 1985, to model the kinds of choices that people will make in different situations of opportunity, in relation to particular forms of crime.

The rational choice theorists have in common with early twentieth-century exponents of utilitarian economics – from whom their work derives – an indifference with respect to the larger questions of classical political economy discussed by Ferguson, Hume, and others in the eighteenth century, namely, the range of choices which are presented to people in respect of conformity and crime and the moral or social organization of the broad society (for example, in respect of equality of life chances). This indifference means that rational choice theorists effectively abstain from examining the ability of particular forms of economic organization to generate *productive work* or *paid employment* for the mass of citizens. Where neo-classical economists speak of the issue of unemployment, it is usually in an idealist rather than analytical fashion, that is to say, they bemoan the underdevelopment of the free market or of the enterprise culture (which has in some way been prevented from working its magic) as the self-evident source of the unemployment problem of the 1980s and 1990s (cf. *inter alia*, Pyle, 1983, 1993). So, for example, mass unemployment cannot be admitted as an empirical demonstration of the failure of free market arrangements (cf. Taylor, 1991).

Rational choice theorists in criminology also seem largely indifferent, unlike the control theorists with whom they are sometimes confused (cf. Hirschi and Gottfredson, 1986) to the processes that might be thought to produce the personal quality of 'criminality' (or 'criminal propensity') in individuals or in particular neighbourhoods. The overwhelming interest of rational choice criminologists is in the *situations of opportunity* that can be analysed to arrive at the way in which they produce crime as an outcome. In fact, one of the first published studies in Britain making use of rational choice-type analysis was Cornish and Clarke's Home Office Research Unit study of the deterrent effects of steering-column locks in cars (Mayhew *et al.*, 1976). Subsequent work ranged widely across the newly established field of 'situational crime prevention', attempting to measure the consequences of different crime-prevention measures (for example, in the redesign of car parks, entrances to buildings in residential areas, lighting and security systems) on the level of crime. There has been a rediscovery of interest (inspired to some extent by the earlier work of Isaac Ehrlich) in the deterrent effects of punishment, and specifically the proposition that an increase in the level of sanction could have effects on the calculations engaged in by the offender at the key situational moment of opportunity (Silberman, 1976; Tittle, 1977, 1980).

In one subsequent study working within this overall framework, Piliavin *et al.* conducted a sophisticated empirical test in order to question this proposition. Their conclusion was that increases in sanctions do *not* feed through to potential offenders' perceptions, but they nonetheless argued that there was support for what they called 'the reward component of the rational choice model' – namely, the idea that when the rewards for engaging in a criminal act are significant, this will substantially outweigh most of the reasons for abstaining (Piliavin *et al.*, 1986). It surely is no surprise . . . to find that young people in low-paid employment in the service industries or on welfare in the United States during the 1980s (the golden era of 'feel-good' Reaganomics, and the unleashing of free market policies in that country) were often persuaded that the rewards accruing from some forms of property crime were more compelling than the benefits which they were receiving from legitimate employment or the weekly welfare cheque. [. . .]

Application of this kind of cost–benefit analysis to crime and to crime control is replete with methodological and theoretical problems, not the least of which is the continuing lack of interest among utilitarian economists in models of human action other than those of the 'rational' Economic Man. Sociologists in general, and most sociologically informed criminologists, would see any such model as too one-dimensional and as far too inattentive to the symbolic and cultural dimensions of social life. Nevertheless, to note the interest in rational choice theory shown by such an influential social thinker as Anthony Giddens. For Giddens:

> situational interpretations of crime can quite easily be connected to the labelling approach, because they clarify one feature of criminality about which labelling theory is silent: why many people who are in no way 'abnormal' choose to engage in acts which they know could be followed by criminal sanctions.
>
> (1989: 133)

Closely associated with this difficulty is the problem of the continuing insistence of economic analysts on extraordinarily restrictive and essentially quite ideological notions of 'social costs' – usually referring to the 'costs' of crime (or other socially problematic human activities) on propertied individuals or institutions within societies as currently and unequally constituted. In the later 1980s, however, there was a perceptible shift in the debate around the social costs of crime and crime control. Both in the United States and in Britain, there was an increasingly widespread recognition that the extraordinary level of state investment in crime control was an ineffective kind of investment, inappropriate in a political culture in which all other forms of public expenditure were subject to increasingly stringent scrutiny.

In Britain these concerns were first voiced, ironically enough, by the so-called left realist school in respect of the declining efficiency of a police force which had been in receipt, from the early 1980s, of increasingly generous state support particularly as measured by the paltry clear-up rates in offences reported by the public (the consumer) to the police (the service-provider) (Kinsey et al., 1986). In the United States, particular attention was paid to the continuing contradiction between the massive increase in the prison population that occurred in the 1980s, with 673,565 sentenced prisoners in state and federal institutions in June 1989, compared to 128,466 in 1974 (Greenberg, 1990: 40) and the continuing escalation in crimes of violence, robberies, and other disruptive and disorderly behaviours on American streets. Edwin Zedlewski, an economist based at the National Institute of Justice, published two studies (1985, 1987) arguing that these increases in numbers imprisoned were actually 'cost-effective'. But these studies were subsequently subjected to close critical examination by Greenberg, who showed that Zedlewski's computations of both costs and benefits were highly ideological (Greenberg, 1990). In particular, Zedlewski's computation of costs did not include any measure of the costs of imprisonment to the imprisoned, and no normative argument is advanced to justify this exclusion. Nor is his computation of the benefits accruing to 'society' from imprisonment placed within any *comparative evaluation* of the benefits in terms of reduction in crime and in public anxieties, and an increased sense of well-being that might result from state expenditures in respect of health, education, transportation, or other areas of the 'public good'. [. . .]

References

Allan, E.A. and Steffensmeier, D.J. (1989), 'Youth Unemployment and Property Crime: Differential Effects of Job Availability and Job Quality on Juvenile and Youth Adult Arrest Rates', *American Sociological Review*, 50: 317–32.

Aronowitz, S. and DiFazio, W. (1995), *The Jobless Future*. Minneapolis, Minn.: University of Minnesota.

Avio, K. and Clark, S. (1976), *Property Crime in Canada: An Econometric Study*. Toronto: University of Toronto Press.

Becker, G. S. (1968), 'Crime and Punishment: An Economic Approach', *Journal of Political Economy*, 76: 169–217.

Beyleveld, D. (1980), *A Bibliography on General Deterrence Research*. Farnborough: Saxon House.

Box, S. (1987), *Recession, Crime and Punishment*. London: Macmillan.

Box, S. and Hale, C. (1982), 'Economic Crisis and the Rising Prisoner Population in England and Wales', *Crime and Social Justice*, 17: 20–35.

—— (1985), 'Unemployment, Imprisonment and Prison Over-crowding', *Contemporary Crises*, 9: 209–28.

Brenner, H. (1971), *Time Series Analysis of Relationships Between Selected Economic and Social Indicators, vol. 1: Texts and Appendices*. Washington, DC: US Government Printing Office.

—— (1977), 'Health Costs and Benefits of Economic Policy', *International Journal of Health Services*, 7: 581–623.

Cornish, D. B. and Clarke, R. V. G. (1986), *The Reasoning Criminal: Rational Choice Perspectives on Offending*. New York: Springer-Verlag.

Currie, Elliott (1990a), 'Crime and Free Market Society: Lessons from the United States', unpublished lecture given to international conference on 'Crime and Policing 1992: A Global Perspective', Islington, London, November.

—— (1990b), 'Heavy with Human Tears: Free Market Policy, Inequality and Social Provision in the United States', in Ian Taylor, ed., *The Social Effects of Free Market Policies*, 299–318. Hemel Hempstead: Harvester Wheatsheaf.

Ehrlich, I. (1973), 'Participation in Illegitimate Activities: A Theoretical and Empirical Investigation', *Journal of Political Economy*, 81: 531–67.

Eisner, M. (1995), 'Socio-Economic Modernization and Long-term Developments of Crime Theories and Empirical Evidence in Europe', paper presented to American Society of Criminology, Boston, 15–19 November.

Field, S. (1991), *Trends in Crime and their Interpretation: A Study of Recorded Crime in Post-war England and Wales*, Home Office Research Study no. 119. London: HMSO.

Giddens, A. (1989), *Sociology*. Cambridge: Polity Press.

Greenberg, D. (1977), 'The Dynamics of Oscillatory Punishment Processes', *Journal of Criminal Law and Criminology*, 68: 643–51.

—— (1990), 'The Cost Benefit Analysis of Imprisonment', *Social Justice*, 17: 49–75.

Hagan, J., and Peterson, R., eds. (1995), *Crime and Inequality*. Stanford, Cal.: Stanford University Press.

Henry, S. and Brown, J. (1990), 'Something for Nothing: The Informal Outcomes of Free Market Policies', in Ian Taylor, ed., *The Social Effects of Free Market Policies*, 319–48. Hemel Hempstead: Harvester Wheatsheaf.

Hirschi, T. and Gottfredson, M. (1986), 'The Distinction between Crime and Criminality', in T.F. Hartnagel and R. A. Silverman, eds., *Critique and Explanation: Essays in Honour of Gwynn Nettler*. New Brunswick, NJ: Transaction.

Hutton, W. (1992), 'How Whitehall Cut the Dole Queues', *Guardian*, 11 November.

James, O. (1995), *Juvenile Violence in a Winner Loser Culture*. London: Free Association Books.

Jankovic, I. (1977), 'Labour Market and Imprisonment', *Crime and Social Justice*, 9: 17–31.

Jankowski, Martin Sanchez (1991), *Islands in the Street: Gangs and American Urban Society*. Berkeley, Cal.: University of California Press.

Judt, T. (1996), 'Europe: The Grand Illusion' *New York Review of Books*, 42, 2: 6–9.

Kellough, D. G., Brickney, S. L. and Greenaway, W. K. (1980), 'The Politics of Incarceration: Manitoba 1918–1939', *Canadian Journal of Sociology*, 5: 253–71.

Kinsey, R., Lea, J. and Young, J. (1986), *Losing the Fight against Crime*. Oxford: Blackwell.

Lea, J., and Young, J. (1984), *What is to be Done about Law and Order?* London: Penguin.

Lehtinen, M. (1977), 'The Value of Life: An Argument for the Death Penalty', *Crime and Delinquency*, 23: 237–52.

Lessan, G. T. (1991), 'Micro-Economic Determinants of Penal Policy: Estimating the Unemployment and Inflation Influences on Imprisonment Rate Changes in the United States 1948–1985', *Crime, Law and Social Change*, 16: 177–98.

MacLeod, J. (1987, 1995), *Ain't No Making It: Aspirations and Attainment in a Low Income Neighbourhood*. Boulder, Colo.: Westview Press.

Mayhew, P. M., Clarke, R. V. G., Sturman, A. and Hough, J. M. (1976), *Crime as Opportunity*, Home Office Research Paper No. 34. London: HMSO.

Mayhew, P. M. and Maung, N. A. (1992), *Surveying Crime: Findings from the 1992 Crime Survey*. London: Home Office Research and Statistics Department.

Melossi, D. (1985), 'Punishment and Social Action: Changing Vocabularies of Motive Within a Political Business Cycle', *Current Perspectives in Social Theory*, 6: 169–97.

Melossi, D. and Pavarini M. (1981), *The Prison and the Factory*. London: Macmillan (originally published in Italian as *Carcere e fabbrica. Bologna*: Società Editrice il Mulino, 1977).

Murray, C. (1990), *The Emerging British Underclass* (with responses by Frank Field, Joan C. Brown, Nicholas Deakin, and Alan Walker). London: IEA Health and Welfare Unit.

Piliavin, I., Gartner, R., Thornton, C. and Matsueda, R. L. (1986), 'Crime, Deterrence and Rational Choice', *American Sociological Review*, 51: 101–19.

Platt, T. and Takagi, P. (1968), *The Iron Fist and the Velvet Glove*. Berkeley, Cal.: Social Justice Associates.

Pyle, D. (1983), *The Economics of Crime and Law Enforcement*. London: Macmillan.

—— (1993), *Crime in Britain*. London: Social Market Forum Discussion Paper (May).

Quinney, R. (1974), *Critique of Legal Order: Crime Control in Capitalist Society*. Boston, Mass.: Little, Brown.

Reiman, J. (1979), *The Rich get Richer and the Poor get Prison: Ideology, Class and Criminal Justice*. 2nd edn., 1984. New York: Wiley.

Sampson, R. J. and Wilson, W. J. (1995), 'Towards a Theory of Race, Crime and Urban Inequality' in J. Hagan and R. Peterson, eds., *Crime and Inequality*. Stanford, Cal.: Stanford University Press.

Scull, A. (1977), *Decarceration*. Englewood Cliffs, NJ: Prentice-Hall.

Silberman, M. (1976), 'Towards a Theory of Criminal Deterrence', *American Sociological Review*, 41: 442–61.

Spitzer, S. (1983), 'The Rationalization of Crime Control in Capitalist Society', in. S. Cohen and A. Scull, eds., *Social Control and the State*, 312–34. Oxford: Martin Robertson.

Taylor, I. (1991), 'The Concept of Social Cost in Free Market Theory and the Social Costs of Free Market Policies', in Ian Taylor, ed., *The Social Effects of Free Market Policies*', 1–26. Hemel Hempstead: Harvester Wheatsheaf.

—— (1992), 'The International Drug Trade and Money-Laundering: Border Controls and Other Issues' *European Sociological Review*, 8, 2: 181–93.

Taylor, I. and Jamieson R. (1996), ' "Proper Little Mesters": Nostalgia and Protest Masculinity in Deindustrialized Sheffield', in Sallie Westwood and John Williams, eds., *Imagining Cities*. London: Routledge.

Tittle, C. (1977), 'Sanctions, Fear and the Maintenance of Social Order', *Social Forces*, 55: 579–96.

—— (1980), *Sanctions and Social Deviance: The Question of Deterrence*. New York: Praeger.

Wilson, W. J. (1987), *The Truly Disadvantaged: The Inner City, the Underclass and Public Policy*. Chicago, Ill.: University of Chicago Press.

Zedlewski, E. W. (1985), 'When Have We Punished Enough?', *Public Administration Review*, 45: 771–9.

—— (1987), *Making Confinement Decisions*. Washington, DC: US Department of Justice.

PART FIVE

Race, class and gender in a deindustrializing society

DISPROPORTIONATE NUMBERS OF THE poor, uneducated, minorities and the disadvantaged have long been evident among those arrested and convicted in both the United States and Britain. Despite this, many still debate whether it is due primarily to higher rates of offending or to conscious or inadvertent bias on the part of the police and the criminal justice system. Certainly bias in law enforcement has been shown to play a part.

Approaches to the role of difference and disadvantage in crime have been many but here I highlight four: social disorganization/social control theories; strain and differential opportunity theories; labelling and conflict theories; and theories of gender and identity. Social disorganization theory, first articulated by Clifford Shaw and William McKay at the University of Chicago, explored the effects of several neighborhood conditions, including turnover and mobility, influx of immigrants, and poverty, in fostering juvenile delinquency. Research in this Chicago tradition argued that, in inner city zones of transition where immigrants have historically clustered, networks of social control are weakened and delinquency rises. The intriguing consequence is that, in such areas, every group that has lived there has had a high crime rate until they moved elsewhere.

Recently, researchers have drawn on this theory to explain high arrest rates among ethnic minorities and the disadvantaged. Focusing on these inner city zones, Robert Sampson and William Julius Wilson have demonstrated the presence there of concentrations of African–American minority families and the poor. Arguing that whomever lived there had historically shown a high propensity for crime, Sampson and Wilson argue that high rates of offending and reoffending among minorities and the very poor has an ecological basis. However, housing and job discrimination make relocation to other neighborhoods particularly difficult so that movement elsewhere is blocked for them. Sampson and Wilson do not reject the possibility of bias in the criminal justice system. In fact, later work by Sampson and Laub has explored structural variation in juvenile court processing that has uncovered such differences.

William Wilson has also shown that the point in time at which African–Americans, historically, have occupied these transient and impoverished inner city neighborhoods has created an additional obstacle that makes movement out harder than it was for earlier immigrant groups. In *The Declining Significance of Race*, Wilson shows that two historical dynamics have profoundly shaped the black urban experience. First, African–Americans have been caught in an historic technological twist in the labor market. They have, thus, attempted to climb the ladder of socio-economic mobility just when manufacturing jobs, traditionally the first rung, are disappearing due to automation or movement by multinationals nearer to low priced labor overseas. Second, African–Americans have gained political control of the cities at a point when the ethnic "political machines" that supported the improving life chances of earlier groups through patronage have been dismantled in the name of "good government" reform. Along with discrimination, these features of historical timing have worked to inhibit movement by African–Americans out of these crime prone neighborhoods longer than might otherwise have been so. In some cities, high crime, especially the threat of violence on the streets, and absence of police protection appears to have produced subcultural adaptations. One is the "code of the streets." Its stylized emphasis on ways of both demanding and according street-wise "respect" to avert as well as deter violence has been richly portrayed by Eli Anderson.

Strain theory offers a second explanation of the causes of crime. In contrast to Chicagoans' claim that poor areas may experience weakened bonds of social control, strain theory contends that poverty limits opportunity directly. Originating from work by Robert Merton in the 1940s, this approach is more individualistic than control theory. Strain theorists assert that for many youth, who hold socially approved goals, the means to achieve them legitimately are blocked. This creates "strain" which leads youth to innovate in ways that can include crime. Richard Cloward and Lloyd Ohlin built on this to argue that what determines whether innovation takes a legal or illegal path is the relative balance of legitimate to illegitimate opportunities to which a youth has access. Where the illegitimate options predominate, they argue, delinquency rises. Yet, critics counter that delinquents are plentiful among many groups and not only the most deprived. Robert Agnew subsequently refined strain theory to include not just innovative responses to blocked opportunity but also activities to avert loss or to alleviate exposure to a noxious stimulus. Piri Thomas' poignant autobiographical account in *Down These Mean Streets* shows starkly the feelings of frustration, shame and anger that the obstacles Agnew points to can produce. Agnew's work overcame some critics but empirical challenges persisted.

Subsequently, both Kenneth Land and his colleagues as well as Elliott Currie began to reanalyze the empirical evidence cited by the critics of strain theory. They show that though socio-economic status generally have not exhibited a strong and consistent effect on crime in the United States, extremes of poverty did. Further, the most deprived families living in impoverished areas were those most likely to offend. In Britain, where public social welfare support is stronger, evidence pointed to a slightly different dynamic of relative deprivation, including unemployment, especially during times of growing prosperity. Currie's work began to suggest ways in which poverty worked indirectly too through institutions of family, prenatal care and schooling to heighten propensity for crime.

Agnew's work and that of Land et al. and Currie all offered new ways of conceptualising an independent effect of disadvantage on offending behavior beyond those influences working through social bonds. Thus, they took new steps to explain high rates of arrest and imprisonment among the disadvantaged. What, these studies left relatively untouched was whether processes of criminalization and the operation of the criminal justice system place ethnic minorities and the disadvantaged at greater risk both of breaching laws and of being apprehended, convicted and imprisoned.

A third approach queries what role social structures and institutions, specifically law and the criminal justice system, play in constructing crime. Initially, labelling theory asked whether state intervention in the lives of deviant youth reduced or amplified their chances of reoffending due to the stigma that detention imposes and its tendancy to be internalized as the basis for a deviant identity. Dario Melossi has advanced a grounded labelling theory that situates the process of identity creation within the context of social class. Melossi shows that not only can early intervention create deviance and reoffending, but that the chances of such stigma being imposed varies with the youth's power to resist, which is to a large extent a product of her or his socio-economic circumstances.

Conflict theory went farther to focus on the roots of crime in social structure and the contours of societal power. Conflict theorists, such as Chambliss, Turk and Quinney claimed that both criminalization and also arrest, prosecution and sentencing targeted the less powerful. Later "left realists" highlighted the fact that the disadvantaged also tend to be primary victims of crime. Only gradually was the experience of disadvantage at the intersection of race, class and gender brought forward in the discourse on causes of crime by scholars such as Meda Chesney-Lind, Patricia Tuitt, and Kathleen Daly.

Gradually, the late twentieth century began to see a fourth series of analyses of crime and criminal "justice" that were developed from the standpoint of its disadvantaged and culturally diverse groups. Feminists, such as Lorraine Gelsthorpe, moved to interpret rising rates of female arrests and relatively longer terms of imprisonment. Masculinities theorists, such as Tony Jefferson, attempted to account for high rates of young male minority violence by theorizing the frustration of high unemployment among "subordinated masculinities" of urban youth. Studies both in America and in Britain, first focused on direct and indirect discrimination and, gradually, moved to query whether a deeper institutional bias was at work in the criminal justice system.

Critical criminologists, feminist criminologists, masculinities theorists and critical race theorists problematize identity and study crime and its causes from the standpoint of the poor, women and racial and ethnic minorities. Critique has been increasingly non-essentialized by scholars such as Sarah Fenstermaker, James Messerschimdt and Tony Jefferson, and creatively embedded in language and consciousness at the intersection of race, class and gender. The sense of "performativity" and of fluidity in identity that occludes the boundaries that constitute the very basis of discrimination has, as Judith Bulter has shown, also gained support in some quarters. It promises a liberating potential. Yet, differences, such as extreme poverty and the visually apparent status of race, lack some of the maneuverability at the boundary that characterizes postmodern feminism or queer theory. In a particularly cruel twist, it appears that society may be nonetheless justifying its carceral turn precisely by responsibilizing the poor and visually distinct ethnic groups for not exercising their "performative" option to "reinvent" their lives.

Not only does law, in practice, continue to impinge powerfully on the lives of the disadvantaged and those who are culturally "the other," but the very norms underpinning law itself appear to be diverging from the norms and way of life of culturally diverse communities. Though procedural fairness may, as Tom Tyler has shown, boost popular acceptance of laws that are perceived as biased, this divergence has gradually brought the criminal justice process as well as the laws themselves openly into question.

Increasingly, it appears to be an open question as to whether politics that remain rooted in traditional nation states can ever be genuinely responsive to difference. As challenge to the fairness of law has mounted, the legal base of legitimation of democratic authority in law has meant that political authority itself has, as Habermas has shown, been brought into question. Whether this contribution to the "hollowing out" of the state has been inadvertent or not is beyond the scope of this book to resolve. Perhaps no genre more vividly conveys a recognition of the scope of the sea change afoot, as Robin Kelley shows, than do the controversial lyrics of "gangsta rap" music as it conveys the outlook of minority youth in the streets today.

Chapter 23

Piri Thomas

HOW TO BE A NEGRO WITHOUT REALLY TRYING

From: Piri Thomas (1967), 'How to be a negro without really trying', in Piri Thomas, *Down These Mean Streets*, New York: Vintage Books, pp. 95–104.

I HAD BEEN AWAY from home maybe three months, knocking around, sleeping in cold hallways, hungry a lot of the time. The fucking heart was going out of me. Maybe I should make it down to the Bowery, I thought, and lap up some sneaky pete with the rest of the bums.

No, I decided, one thing still stood out clear; one thing still made sense and counted – me. Nothing else but me – and I hadda pull outta this shit kick.

It was winter, and all I had on was a paper-weight sports jacket. The cold winds were blowing my skin against my chest. I walked into a bar at 103rd Street and Third Avenue, trying to look like I had a pound on me and was warm. In front of the jukebox was a colored guy and a big, chunky broad. The guy was beating out time and the girl was digging. Not all of her moved, just the right parts.

I smiled. "Cold, eh?" I said, and added, "My name is Piri."

"Sure is, kid," he said. "Mine's Pane, and that's my sistuh, Lorry." I followed his finger as he pointed to her.

"It's cold," I mumbled to no one in particular.

"Want a drink, kid?"

I tried not to act too anxious. "Yeah, cool man," I said casually. Pane took a bottle from his back pocket and handed it to me. "How strong can I hit it?" I asked, holding the bottle to my lips.

"Roll," he said, and I put inside me the warmth and affection of my new friends.

After half an hour a new bottle popped out and I got another long taste, and home was with me, I wasn't so lonely. The hours slipped by. I talked and Pane and his sister were one with me. Then the place was gonna close and I knew it was going to get cold again. Pane was high but not plastered. He nudged Lorry and said, "Let's go." I just sat there.

They got up and walked away. As they reached the door I saw Lorry nudge her brother and whisper something. He shook his head and looked back at me. I waved at him, hoping that the look on his face meant what I thought it did.

"Hey, kid, what's your name again?"

"Piri — some guys call me Johnny."

"Have you got a place to sleep?"

"Uh-uh," I said. I made a mental list of the places I had slept since I had left home — friends' pads at the beginning, with relatives until the welcome was overdrawn, then rooftops, under the stairs, basements, stoops, parked cars.

"Well, we ain't got much room, but you're welcome to share it," Pane said. "You gotta sleep on the floor, 'cause all we got is one room for Lorry, her two kids, and me."

"Crazy, man. Thanks a lot," I said. I almost felt my luck was going to change. I tightened up against the cold and hustled down the street. A couple of blocks over, between Park and Madison, we went down the stairs into a basement. I felt the warmth from the furnace greet me and I welcomed it like a two-days-late home-relief check. Pane fumbled with the key and opened the door into a small room. I noticed that the cellar had been partitioned into several rooms and one kitchen for sharing. Lorry smiled at me and said, "Honey, it ain't much, but it beats a blank."

"*Gracias.*" I smiled, and it was for real. "Thanks, Lorry."

She spread a quilt on the floor between the big bed where she and the two kids slept and a couch where Pane slept. I lay down on my back, my hands behind my head. The room was so small I could touch both the bed and the couch. I felt almost safe.

Soon Pane was sleeping hard on his whisky. In the dim darkness I saw Lorry looking down at me. "You asleep, honey?" she asked.

"No, I ain't," I answered.

She slowly made room in her big warm bed, and just like that I climbed in and made love to her — "love" because I was grateful to her, because I wanted her body as much as she wanted mine. It was all natural, all good, all as innocent and pure as anything could be in Home, Sweet Harlem. That was that — she was my woman. No matter that I was sixteen and she was thirty-three. Her caring, her loving were as young or as old as I wanted it to be.

Months passed. I got a job — Lorry inspired that with carfare and lunch. Every week I gave her a few bucks and loved her as much as I could. Still, I had the feeling that I was in a deep nothing and had to get on. Then I lost the lousy job.

I decided I couldn't stay with Lorry any more. I had been playing around with this Puerto Rican girl who lived in one of the basement rooms. She was sure a pretty bitch, with a kid and no husband. I didn't want Lorry to cop a complex, but I couldn't dig her the way she wanted me to. One night I cut out. The Puerto Rican girl had just hustled ten bucks, and she was talking about all the things it would buy for the kid. They needed food and clothes real bad. I saw where she put her pocketbook and waited till she was in the kitchen getting some grits for her kid. Then I went to her room and copped the ten bucks and made it up to the Bronx. I had a hangout up there. I gave a street buddy five bucks and he let me share his pad for a couple of weeks till I could cop a job.

A few days after I'd copped the ten dollars I ran into the girl. She knew it had been me. She made a plea for her bread back, for her kid. I said I didn't take it and brushed past her. I didn't have to look into her eyes to know the hate she bore me. But it was her or me, and as always, it had to be me. Besides, I had bought some pot with the five left over and rolled some good-size bombers that immediately put me in business. I had a good thought: soon as I was straight, I'd lay her ten *bolos* back on her.

I looked for work, but not too hard. Then I saw this ad in a newspaper:

YOUNG MEN, 17–30
GREAT OPPORTUNITY
LEARN WHILE WORKING
EARN WHILE TRAINING
Door-to-door salesmen in household wares.
Guaranteed by Good Housekeeping. Salary
and commission.
603 E. 73 St. 2nd fl. – 9 a.m.

"Dig, Louie, this sounds good," I said to my boy. "Let's go over in the morning. Hell, with our gift of *labia* we're a mother-hopping cinch to cop a slave."

"*Chevere*, Piri, man, we got all Harlem and we know plenty people. Bet we can earn a hundred bucks or more on commissions alone."

We went down the next day and walked into the office and a girl handed me and Louie each a paper with a number on it and told us to please have a seat. My number was 16 and Louie's was 17. Man, me and Louie were sparklin'. We had our best togs on; they were pressed like a razor and our shoes shone like a bald head with a pound of grease on it.

"Number 16, please?" the girl called out.

I winked at Louie and he gave me the V-for-victory sign.

"Right this way, sir, through the door on your left," the girl said.

I walked into the office and there was this paddy sitting there. He looked up at me and broke out into the friendliest smile I ever saw, like I was a long-lost relative. "Come in, come right in," he said. "Have a chair – that's right, sit right there. Well, sir, you're here bright and early. That's what our organization likes to see. Yes sir, punctuality is the first commandment in a salesman's bible. So you're interested in selling our household wares – guaranteed, of course, by *Good Housekeeping*. Had any experience selling?"

"Well, not exactly, sir, but – er – when I was a kid – I mean, younger, I used to sell shopping bags in the *Marketa*."

"The what?"

"The *Marketa* on 110th Street and Park Avenue. It, er, runs all the way up to 116th Street."

"Ummm, I see."

"And my mom – er, mother, used to knit fancy things called *tapetes*. I think they're called doilies, and I used to sell them door to door, and I made out pretty good. I know how to talk to people, Mr. – er – "

"Mr. Christian, Mr. Harold Christian. See?" and he pointed a skinny finger at a piece of wood with his name carved on it. "Ha, ha, ha," he added, "just like us followers of our Lord Jesus Christ are called. Are you Christian?"

"Yes, sir."

"A good Catholic, I bet. I never miss a Sunday mass; how about you?"

"No, sir, I try not to." *Whee-eoo!* I thought. *Almost said I was Protestant.*

"Fine, fine, now let's see . . . " Good Catholic Mr. Christian took out some forms. "What's your name?"

"Piri Thomas – P-i-r-i."

"Age?"

"Er, seventeen – born September 30,1928."

Mr. Christian counted off on the fingers of one hand . . . "twenty-eight, er, thirty-eight, forty-five – ahum, you were just seventeen this September."

"That's right. Paper said from seventeen to thirty."

"Oh, yes – yes, yes, that's correct. Where do you live?"

I couldn't give him the Long Island address; it was too far away. So I said, "109 East 104th Street."

"That's way uptown, isn't it?"

"Yes, sir."

"Isn't that, um, Harlem?"

"Yes, sir, it's split up in different sections, like the Italian section and Irish and Negro and the Puerto Rican section. I live in the Puerto Rican section. It's called the *Barrio*."

"The *Bar-ree-o?*"

I smiled. "Yes, sir, it's Spanish for 'the place' – er – like a community."

"Oh, I see. But you're not Puerto Rican, are you? You speak fairly good English even though once in a while you use some slang – of course, it's sort of picturesque."

"My parents are Puerto Ricans."

"Is Thomas a Puerto Rican name?"

"Er – well, my mother's family name is Montañez," I said, wondering if that would help prove I was a Puerto Rican. "There are a lot of Puerto Ricans with American names. My father told me that after Spain turned Puerto Rico over to the United States at the end of the Spanish-American War, a lot of Americans were stationed there and got married to Puerto Rican girls." *Probably fucked 'em and forgot 'em*, I thought.

"Oh, I – er, see. How about your education? High school diploma?"

"No, sir, I quit in my second year . . . "

"Tsh, tsh, that was very foolish of you. Education is a wonderful thing, Mr. Thomas. It's really the only way for one to get ahead, especially when – er, uh – why did you leave school?"

My mind shouted out, *On account of you funny paddies and your funny ideas in this funny world*, but I said, very *cara palo*, "Well, sir, we got a big family and – well, I'm the oldest and I had to help out and – well, I quit." Then, in a sincere fast breath, I added, "But I'm going to study nights. I agree with you that education is the only way to get ahead, especially when – "

"Fine, fine. What's your Social Security number?"

I ran it to him quickly.

"By memory, eh? Good! A good salesman's second commandment should be a good memory. Got a phone?"

"Yes, sir. Lehigh 3–6050, and ask for Mr. Dandy. He's my uncle. He doesn't speak English very well, but you can leave any message for me with him."

"Very, very good, Mr. Thomas. Well, this will be all for now. We will get in touch with you."

"Uh, how soon, about, Mr. Christian? 'Cause I'd like to start work, or rather, training, as soon as possible."

"I can't definitely say, Mr. Thomas, but it will be in the near future. Right now our designated territory is fully capacitated. But we're opening another soon and we'll need good men to work it."

"You can't work the territory you want?" I asked.

"Oh, no! This is scientifically planned," he said.

"I'd like to work in Harlem," I said, "but, uh – I can make it wherever you put me to sell."

"That's the spirit!" Mr. Christian bubbled. "The third commandment of a good salesman is he faces any challenge, wherever it may be."

I took Mr. Christian's friendly outstretched hand and felt the warm, firm grip and thought, *This paddy is gonna be all right to work for*. As I walked out, I turned my head and said, "Thank you very much, sir, for the opportunity."

"Not at all, not at all. We need bright young blood for this growing organization, and those that grow with us will be headed for great things."

"Thank you. So long."

"So long, and don't forget to go to mass."

"No, sir, I sure won't!"

"What church you go to?" he asked suddenly.

"Uh" – I tried to remember the name of the Catholic Church on 106th Street – "Saint Cecilia's!" I finally burst out.

"Oh yes, that's on, er, 106th Street between Park and Lexington. Do you know Father Kresser?"

"Gee, the name sounds sort of familiar," I cooled it. "I can almost place him, but I can't say for sure."

"Well, that's all right. He probably wouldn't remember me, but I was a youngster when he had a parish farther downtown. I used to go there. Well, if you run into him, give him my regards."

"I sure will. So long, and thanks again." I closed the door carefully and walked out to where Louie was still sitting.

"Man, Piri," he said, "you was in there a beau-coup long-ass time."

"Shh, Louie, cool your language."

"Got the job? You were in there long enough for two jobs."

I smiled and made an okay face.

Louie cupped his hand to his mouth and put his head next to mine. "That cat ain't a faggot, is he?" he whispered.

I whispered back with exaggerated disgust, "Man! What a fuckin' dirty mind you got."

"Just asking, man," he said. "Sometimes these guys are *patos* and if you handle them right, you get the best breaks. Well, how'd you make out?"

"In like Flynn, Louie."

"Cool, man, hope I get the same break."

"Number 17," the girl called.

"Here I go," Louie said to me.

"*Suerte*, Louie," I said. I gave him the V-for-victory sign and watched his back disappear and dimly heard Mr. Christian's friendly "Come right in. Have a – " before the door closed behind Louie.

Jesus, I thought. *I hope Louie gets through okay. It'll be great to work in the same job. Maybe we can even work together. He'll cover one side of the street and I'll cover the other. As tight as me and Louie are, we'll pool what we make on commissions and split halfies.*

"Hey Piri," Louie said, "let's go."

"Damn, Louie, you just went in," I said. "You only been in there about five minutes or so. How'd Mr. Christian sound?"

We walked down the stairs.

"Okay, I guess. Real friendly, and he asked me questions, one-two-three."

"And?"

"And I'm in!"

"Cool breeze. What phone did you give?" I asked.

"I ain't got no phone. Hey, there's the bus!"

We started to run. "Fuck running," I said, "let's walk a while and celebrate. Man, you could've gave him Dandy's number like I did. Aw, well, they'll probably send you a telegram or special delivery letter telling you when to start work."

"What for?" Louie asked.

"So's they can tell you when the new territory is opened up and when to come in," I said. " 'Cause the other territory – "

"What new territory?"

I opened my mouth to answer and Louie and I knew what was shakin' at the same fuckin' time. The difference between me and Louie was he was white. "That cat Mr. Christian tell you about calling you when some new territory opens up?" Louie said in a low voice.

I nodded, "Yeah."

"Damn! That motherfucker asked me to come and start that training jazz on Monday. Gave me a whole lotta shit about working in a virgin territory that's so big us future salesmen wouldn't give each other competition or something like that." Louie dug that hate feeling in me. He tried to make me feel good by telling me that maybe they got a different program and Mr. Christian was considering me for a special kinda job.

"Le's go back," I said coldly.

"What for, Piri?"

"You see any colored cats up there?"

"Yeah, *panín*, there's a few. Why?"

"Le's wait here in front of the place."

"*Por qué?*" asked Louie.

I didn't answer. I just watched paddies come down out of that office and make it. "Louie," I said, "ask the next *blanco* that comes down how the job hiring is. There's one now."

Louie walked over to him. "Say, excuse me, Mac," he said. "Are they hiring up there – you know, salesmen?"

"Yes, they are," the guy answered. "I start Monday. Why don't you apply if you're looking for work? It's – "

"Thanks a lot, Mac," Louie said. "I might do that." He came back and started to open his mouth.

"Forget it, *amigo*," I said. "I heard the chump."

We waited some more and a colored cat came down. "Hey, bruh," I called.

"You callin' me?"

"Yeah. I dug the ad in the paper. How's the hiring? Putting guys on?"

"I don't know, man. I mean I got some highly devoted crap about getting in touch with me when a new turf opens up."

"Thanks, man," I said.

"You're welcome. Going up?"

"Naw, I changed my mind." I nodded to Louie, and he came up to me like he was down for whatever I was down for.

"Let's walk," I said. I didn't feel so much angry as I did sick, like throwing-up sick. Later, when I told this story to my buddy, a colored cat, he said, "Hell, Piri, Ah know stuff like that can sure burn a cat up, but a Negro faces that all the time."

"I know that," I said, "but I wasn't a Negro then. I was still only a Puerto Rican."

Chapter 24

Coretta Phillips and Ben Bowling

RACISM, ETHNICITY, CRIME AND CRIMINAL JUSTICE

From: Coretta Phillips and Ben Bowling (2002), excerpts from 'Racism, ethnicity, crime, and criminal justice', in Mike Maguire et al. (eds), *Oxford Handbook of Criminology*, 3rd edn, Oxford: Oxford University Press, pp. 593–607, 614–619.

OFFENDING BY ETHNIC MINORITIES

Deconstructing notions of 'black' and 'Asian' criminality

RACIST BELIEFS AND STEREOTYPES depicting African and Caribbean people as criminals have existed for centuries, and were widely and freely expressed in Britain well into the post-War years. This notwithstanding, in the 1970s, a quarter of a century after the onset of mass migration from the West Indies and Indian subcontinent, there was an official consensus that the settler communities offended at lower rates than the majority population. As the House of Commons Select Committee put it: '[t]he conclusions remain beyond doubt: coloured immigrants are no more involved in crime than others; nor are they generally more concerned in violence, prostitution and drugs. The West Indian crime rate is much the same as that of the indigenous population. The Asian crime rate is very much lower' (House of Commons 1972: 71). This position dramatically altered in the mid-1970s in the face of increased conflict between the police and African/Caribbean communities and the accumulation of police statistics which documented higher arrest rates – particularly for robbery and theft from the person – among African/Caribbean youth in London. Despite methodological weaknesses in these statistical data, views about 'black criminality' and its supposed roots in black culture became entrenched in the public consciousness, and even more so following the media reporting of the disorders of the 1980s (Gilroy 1987b). [. . .]

There is clearly a multitude of difficulties which bedevil attempts to discover the 'real' rate of offending among different ethnic groups. Our major sources of data are all flawed in some way: victim reports are available in only a small minority of incidents; self-report studies rely on the honesty of respondents; and the value of official statistics is diluted by the attrition process, and because they are the product of decisions taken by criminal justice agencies. However, despite their limitations, official statistics provide details of who is detected for particular types of offences, who is processed by the criminal justice system, and who become officially labelled as offenders. Criminal justice statistics feature in discussions of policy and practice, and in the media portrayal of crime in England and Wales. For this reason they need to be carefully scrutinized as they contribute to our understanding of the process of criminalization as it affects ethnic minorities. This process begins with the policing of ethnic minority communities.

THE PROCESS OF CRIMINALIZATION: STAGES IN THE CRIMINAL JUSTICE PROCESS

'Over-policing'

Over the past four decades, the relationship between ethnic minorities and the police has often been adversarial, if not in open conflict. One of the earliest community accounts referred to the practice of 'nigger hunting', whereby junior police officers at some police stations allegedly planned to 'bring in a coloured person at all cost' (Hunte 1966: 12). Hunte highlighted issues that would still be at the heart of policing African/Caribbean people thirty-five years later, including racist abuse and a failure to protect ethnic minority communities. Throughout the 1970s and 1980s, other accounts documented the use of oppressive policing techniques, such as mass stop and search operations, the use of riot squads using semi-military equipment, excessive surveillance, unnecessary armed raids, and police use of racially abusive language, particularly in the centres of Britain's African, Caribbean, and Asian communities. Collectively these practices have been referred to as the 'over-policing' of ethnic minority communities (see Bowling and Phillips 2002: 128–9).

Excessive use of force and deaths in custody continue to be a source of tension. Over the years the numbers of deaths in police custody have been disproportionately high for black people compared to both the general and arrest population (Home Office 2000b). In the most recent figures, however, the number of ethnic minority deaths decreased markedly, perhaps influenced by the adverse reaction to such deaths in ethnic minority communities, highlighted by the Macpherson Inquiry (1999).

Police deployment and targeting

It is clear that targeting people from ethnic minorities and trawling for suspects plays a part in producing the over-representation of African/Caribbeans among those arrested by the police. They are less likely to receive the benefits of under-enforcement by the police than other ethnic groups which, alongside the ongoing targeting and heavy police deployment in African/Caribbean communities, means that their offending behaviour is more likely to come to official attention than that of other ethnic groups. Hood's (1992) research in Crown courts in the West Midlands found that 15 per cent of those dealt with for drugs offences – typically for small trades in cannabis – were black compared with only 3 per cent who were of Asian origin and 2 per cent who were whites. These offences came to official attention following proactive policing. Indeed, the most common reason given by police when searching black and Asian people was suspicion of drugs possession, even though self-report studies challenge the perception that they are more likely to use drugs than white people (Home Office 2000b; Ramsay et al. 2001).

Stop and search

The history of police use of 'stop and search' powers provides a context for the distrust of the police felt by African/Caribbean and, increasingly, Asian communities. These practices are seen by many people as the most glaring example of an abuse of police powers, hostility to which dates back to the time of 'sus' laws when a person could be arrested under the 1824 Vagrancy Act (s 4 and s 6) for frequenting or loitering in a public place with intent to commit an arrestable offence. Now regulated by the Police and Criminal Evidence Act (PACE 1984), a stop and search can be carried out only when there is 'reasonable suspicion' that stolen property or prohibited articles are being carried.

The national police data for 1999/2000 found, with some force variation, the number of PACE searches of black people to be five times higher than of whites. Rates for Asians were almost always higher than for whites (Home Office 2000b). The same pattern has been observed in the use of other stop and search powers, including stops under s 13 of the Prevention of Terrorism Act 1989, designed specifically to combat terrorism from the IRA. In 1997/8, 7 per cent of these stops were of African/Caribbeans and 5 per cent were of Asians, a clear example of direct discrimination (Home Office 1998).

It also seems to be the case that the extent of police intrusion and formal action tends to be greater when the suspect is not white. People from ethnic minority communities are more likely to be stopped repeatedly, stops are more likely to result in a search, and searches tend to be more intrusive, including the use of clothing searches and strip searches (Skogan 1990; Newburn and Hayman 2001). Formal action is also more common in stops involving black people compared with other ethnic groups (Norris et al. 1992; Bucke 1997).

Methods of calculating stop and search rates have been questioned recently, because they are based on outdated census figures and take no account of the likelihood that many stops may be of individuals who do not live in the area where they are stopped. To address this problem, a recent study has examined 'suspect availability' for being stopped. Using CCTV and street observers, MVA and Miller (2000) assessed the pedestrian and vehicle populations in Hounslow, Greenwich, Ipswich, Chapeltown, and central Leicester. Based on these calculations they conclude that white people were over-represented among those stopped and searched by the police, while Asian people were under-represented when rates were calculated on 'available' rather than 'resident' populations. The findings for black people were mixed, with evidence of both over- and under-representation in different localities.

This research emphasizes the need for caution in assessing disproportionality in stop and search, but it also raises important questions about the 'neutrality of availability'. For example, African/Caribbean pupils may be victims of direct discrimination when they are excluded from school, and racism undoubtedly contributes to unemployment patterns among ethnic minorities; therefore, 'being available' to be stopped and searched by the police may in itself be explained by discrimination. It is also problematic that 'lifestyle factors' such as going out more in the evening should lead African/Caribbean people to be more often the subject of proactive policing than other ethnic groups (Modood et al. 1997; Bourne, Bridges, and Searle 1997). Moreover, to the list of factors which arouse police suspicion, Quinton, Bland, and Miller (2000) have added items of clothing (such as baseball caps and hooded jackets), type, make, and cost of cars, and engaging in vaguely defined 'suspicious activity', all of which can be negatively associated with African/Caribbeans and Asians to a lesser extent, and which may contribute to the process of criminalization.

FitzGerald's (1999) study in London has provided an insight into the use of stop and search in the late 1990s. It found that reasonable suspicion was frequently absent in the use of stop and search, and that the power is often not used for the purpose of detection (as justified in PACE) but instead is used for 'intelligence-gathering', 'disruption', and the 'social control' of young people. Until 1997 these practices were institutionalized by the Metropolitan Police who used stop and search as a 'performance indicator' of productivity. Despite a policy shift away from this approach, some operational officers believe it is still used by supervisors to measure performance (see HMIC 2000). In the wake of the Lawrence Inquiry, concerns were expressed about the declining use of stop/search for ethnic minorities. However, Home Office (2000a) statistics show that in 1999/2000 the fall in the number of recorded stops was lower for black people in England and Wales (10 per cent) than it was for other ethnic groups (14 per cent).

Direct discrimination through the negative stereotyping of people of African/Caribbean origin offers one explanation for these patterns consistently observed over time. Additionally, Jefferson (1993) has pointed to the role of sex, age, and class in explaining the criminalizing experiences of black people (see also FitzGerald 1993; Reiner 1993). It is certainly to be expected that the police will conduct more stops of younger people than older groups who are less likely to be involved in offending. This is relevant because the age structure of ethnic minority populations is significantly younger than that of whites (FitzGerald 1993). Until recently, BCS analyses have found, nonetheless, that ethnic origin was a predictor of being stopped by the police, after controlling for age, household income, employment status, occupation, type of housing tenure and area, vehicle access, gender, marital status, and age of leaving school (Skogan 1990). In the 2000 BCS, however, ethnic origin was predictive only of car stops for black people and Pakistanis and Bangladeshis, while ethnic origin no longer predicted foot stops (Clancy et al. 2001). The authors speculate as to whether this is due to a 'Macpherson effect' following the Inquiry team's criticism of police practices in this area.

As FitzGerald and Sibbitt (1997) note, force objectives, the use of 'intelligence' about local 'villains', and victim reports are also likely to influence stop and search patterns, although each of these factors may be influenced by racial bias. There is official acknowledgement that stop and search powers must be regulated to safeguard the individual's right to privacy and unnecessary intrusion by the state (Home Office 1997). The inherent danger lies in the extent of discretion which such powers allow and the limitations of legal regulation, particularly where concepts such as 'reasonable suspicion' and 'consent' are applied. These notions are vague, open to different understanding and interpretation by police officers, and therefore difficult to operationalize (Young 1994; Dixon, Coleman, and Bottomley 1990; Quinton, Bland, and Miller 2000; Sanders and Young, in Chapter 28 of this volume). Moreover, as Young has observed, stop/searches occur outside the police station and, like many aspects of police work, are outside the purview of supervisory officers where 'the norms and working practices of the street level police officer take priority over outside regulation' (Young 1994: 14).

A key question remains concerning the role of stop and search in explaining the over-representation of black people in arrest and imprisonment statistics. However, official statistics (which do not record 'voluntary' stop/searches and which may under-record other statutory stops) show that only a small minority of stop/searches – 8 per cent of all ethnic groups in 1999/2000 – led to an arrest (Home Office 2000b). Although this figure is slightly higher for black and Asian people, it is clear that most arrests result from reactive behaviour by the police following notification of an offence by a member of the public (see Mawby 1979; Steer 1980; Bottomley and Coleman 1976). This means that stop and search makes a modest, but significant, contribution to the over-representation of black people in the arrest population.

Nonetheless, the consequences of the abuse of discretionary police powers (such as stop and search and the use of force) and the poor response to racist victimization are wide-ranging. Confidence in the police and cooperation with investigations, for example, in providing information about crime, have undoubtedly been harmed by these negative interactions over the last four decades. Attitudinal and victimization surveys have provided ample evidence to support this, with lower levels of satisfaction with the police among African/Caribbeans compared with white respondents, with mixed findings among Asian respondents (see Bowling and Phillips 2002: 135–8 for a review). It is more than likely that such negative views of the police influence the decision-making of ethnic minority suspects when in police custody under arrest.

Arrest

Under PACE 1984, the police can arrest an individual when they have reasonable grounds for suspicion that he or she has committed an offence. The national aggregated figures for 1999/2000 show that the number of black people arrested was four times higher than would be expected from their numbers in the general population. The arrest rate for Asians was also higher than it was for whites. The breakdown according to offence type mirrors that observed among those imprisoned. As Figure 24.1 shows, the over-representation of blacks was evident in all offence categories, but was most striking in connection with fraud and forgery arrests and drug arrests (these offences accounted for 6 per cent and 2 per cent respectively of recorded notifiable offences in 1999/2000). For robbery there was a significant over-representation of black people in arrest figures (at 28 per cent); and although this is a crime which causes serious public concern, it accounted for only 2 per cent of notifiable offences in 1999/2000 (Home Office 2000b; Povey, Cotton, and Sisson 2000). Asians were over-represented in fraud and forgery arrests.

Once in police custody, opting for legal advice, exercising their right of silence, and denying the offence for which they have been arrested to a greater extent than their white counterparts, all cumulatively disadvantage ethnic minorities in the criminal justice process (see Phillips and Brown 1998; Bucke and Brown 1997). For example, the least punitive outcome of police action following arrest – a caution or reprimand – can be given only where an offender admits the offence, and this partly explains the lower rates of cautioning for ethnic minorities (Home Office 2000b; Phillips and Brown 1998). There is also some evidence that black juveniles are subtly discriminated against, which contributes to their being 'filtered in' to the criminal justice process rather than being diverted from court. Phillips and Brown (1998) found in their observational survey of

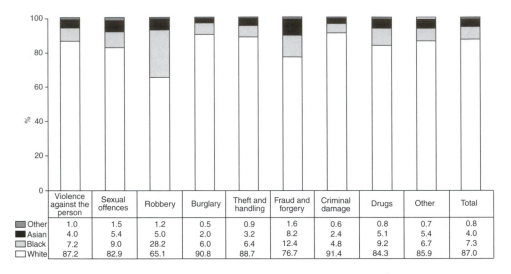

	Violence against the person	Sexual offences	Robbery	Burglary	Theft and handling	Fraud and forgery	Criminal damage	Drugs	Other	Total
Other	1.0	1.5	1.2	0.5	0.9	1.6	0.6	0.8	0.7	0.8
Asian	4.0	5.4	5.0	2.0	3.2	8.2	2.4	5.1	5.4	4.0
Black	7.2	9.0	28.2	6.0	6.4	12.4	4.8	9.2	6.7	7.3
White	87.2	82.9	65.1	90.8	88.7	76.7	91.4	84.3	85.9	87.0

Figure 24.1 Arrest population by ethnic group and notifiable offences, 1999/2000
Source: Home Office 2000b.

over 4,000 police arrests that black juveniles were less likely to have their cases referred to a multi-agency panel which plays a key role in diverting juveniles out of the process, and this held even once admission of the offence had been taken into account. It can be speculated that these decisions derive from ethnic minorities' negative opinions of the police which emerge in attitudinal and victimization surveys, thus further emphasizing the significance of relations between the police and ethnic minorities for how individuals fare in the criminal justice process.

PROSECUTORIAL DECISION-MAKING AND SENTENCING

Following the charge of a suspect by the police, there is a further point at which it is possible for individuals to be diverted from formal action, but this decision-making lies in the hands of the Crown Prosecution Service (CPS). Case files are sent to the CPS who decide whether to proceed to court, or to terminate the case against a suspect so that he or she does not face prosecution. Prosecutors have to consider whether there is a 'realistic prospect of conviction' based on the strength of evidence against the suspect. If the evidence is judged to be strong enough, Crown prosecutors then have to decide whether cases should proceed on public interest grounds (CPS 1994). Factors such as the seriousness of the offence, whether the defendant was central or peripheral to the offence, and the willingness of the victim to participate in the prosecution process are considered by the CPS.

Case termination: a break on criminalization?

There are only two empirical research studies which have examined case termination rates to see if they differ according to the ethnic origin of the defendant. In their study of

1,175 defendants, Phillips and Brown (1998) found that 12 per cent of cases against white defendants were terminated compared with 20 per cent of cases against African/Caribbeans and 27 per cent against Asians. Using multivariate analysis, they found that ethnic origin predicted an increased chance of case termination by the CPS, after controlling for type and seriousness of the offence, and whether the defendant had previous convictions. Higher termination rates for ethnic minorities compared with their white counterparts were also found in more comprehensive research by Mhlanga (1999) with a larger national sample of defendants aged under twenty-two years.

Both studies raise questions about policing practices in relation to ethnic minorities. A presumption of guilt appears to be selectively applied by police officers in the case of some African/Caribbean and Asian suspects, reflecting negative stereotyping and discrimination. The CPS 'break' on criminalizing ethnic minorities might be explained by the fact that case review is a point in the criminal justice process when discretion and subjectivity are at a minimum as Crown prosecutors are guided by the stringent Code for Crown Prosecutors (1994), the reasons for decisions are recorded, and, in most cases, the ethnic origin of the defendant is not known (Phillips and Brown 1998). A second explanation notes the greater ethnic diversity of the CPS compared with other criminal justice agencies such as the police (see Home Office 2000b).

Both studies also highlight the limits to research approaches that study one stage of the criminal justice process in isolation. Phillips and Brown (1998) found that the proportion of white and black suspects charged at the police station was identical at 59 per cent, with slightly fewer Asians (54 per cent) being charged. Differences in outcome became apparent only at the case review stage. This highlights the contingent nature of the criminal justice process which must be taken into account in research in this area.

Pre-sentence processes

The decision to remand a defendant in custody or to bail him or her to appear at court is the next critical decision point in the criminal justice process. Studies have consistently demonstrated that those defendants who are remanded in custody before trial are subsequently more likely to receive a custodial sentence if they are found guilty (Hood 1992), probably because they cannot be presented in a positive light either by demonstrating regular employment, or a smart physical appearance. Commentators such as Hudson (1993) have referred to this as one of the clearest examples of indirect discrimination against ethnic minorities, as research shows that black people are significantly more likely to be remanded in custody before and during their trial, partly because they have an increased risk of being 'of no fixed abode', a key criterion on which courts refuse bail (Walker 1989; Hood 1992; Brown and Hullin 1992). Thus, the apparently neutral legal factor relating to the likelihood of court appearance indirectly discriminates against suspects from ethnic minorities.

Where cases are proceeded with to court, magistrates or juries will consider the guilt of the suspect at trial. A mixed picture emerges in relation to acquittal rates – early studies found little difference in the acquittal rates of white and ethnic minority defendants (Walker 1989; Home Office 1989). However, more recent data, including national ethnic monitoring data for 1999, revealed higher acquittal rates for both black and Asian defendants, which is consistent with the finding of higher levels of case termination by the CPS in cases where ethnic minorities were charged (Home Office 2000b; Barclay and Mhlanga 2000). Rather than indicating the absence of bias, it raises questions about previous actions taken by the police and the CPS in cases involving ethnic minorities (cf. Smith 1997). As the Denman Inquiry (2001: 107) into race discrimination in the CPS concluded, this suggested that the CPS was 'discriminating against ethnic minority defendants by failing to correct the bias in police charging decisions and allowing a disproportionate number of weak cases against ethnic minority defendants to go to trial'.

The writing of pre-sentence reports by probation officers for magistrates to consider before passing sentence presents another opportunity for racial bias to creep in. While much research has been done on this, it is difficult to make definite conclusions because of mixed research findings on the number and quality of reports written and the extent to which specific sentencing recommendations are included when comparing white and ethnic minority defendants (see Bowling and Phillips 2002: 176–9). However, the most recent inspection of the probation service identified 16 per cent of pre-sentence reports written on black offenders and 11 per cent on Asian defendants as reinforcing stereotypical attitudes about race and ethnicity, although the impact on final sentencing was not measured (HMIP 2000).

Statistical and research evidence has consistently documented higher rates of committal to the Crown Court for ethnic minorities, particularly those of African/Caribbean origin. This means that even before sentencing decisions are made, African/Caribbean people face a greater possibility of a more severe sentencing outcome if found guilty than their white counterparts, by virtue of being tried in the Crown Court rather than the magistrates' court. It seems plausible to suggest that the distrust that ethnic minorities have of the police may also affect the prosecution and sentencing process (see Mirrlees-Black 2001). The research is inconclusive as to whether the higher rate of committal to the Crown Court for ethnic minority defendants is because more elect for jury trial, or because magistrates are more likely to decline jurisdiction (Walker 1989; Home Office 1989; Jefferson and Walker 1992; Shallice and Gordon 1990; Brown and Hullin 1992).

SENTENCING

Most studies of sentencing in the magistrates' courts, and the limited statistical evidence that exists, have observed little or no difference in the extent to which white and African/Caribbean defendants have been sentenced to immediate custody, or in custodial sentence lengths (Crow and Cove 1984; Mair 1986; Walker 1989; Home Office 1989; Shallice and Gordon 1990; Brown and Hullin 1992; cf. Hudson 1989). These studies have been limited in their ability to consider a range of legitimate legal factors which influence sentencing decisions. The first study to use more sophisticated techniques in an attempt to isolate the 'independent' effect of ethnic origin on sentencing was Roger Hood's (1992) pioneering research, conducted in five Crown Courts in the West Midlands in 1989. All male black, Asian, and other ethnic minority defendants found guilty and sentenced in 1989 were compared with an equivalent random sample of male white defendants.

The approach taken by Hood (1992) was to construct a 'Probability of Custody Score', using sixteen variables which best predicted the possibility of a custodial sentence, such as offence seriousness and number of previous convictions. This approach, while significantly improving on previous methods, cannot take account of the extent to which legal factors such as seriousness of the offence and previous convictions are themselves the result of discrimination earlier in the process. Since the police 'over-charge' ethnic minority suspects in some cases, seriousness of the offence may be a factor which is itself dependent on ethnic origin. For this reason, Hood's results must be regarded as a conservative estimate of the effect of racial discrimination.

Overall, Hood estimated that only 479 of the 503 male black defendants should have been sentenced to custody on the basis of legally relevant factors. This amounted to a 5 per cent greater probability of black people being sentenced to custody compared with their white counterparts. Where defendants pleaded not guilty, and once all other factors had been controlled for, Asians, on average, were sentenced to nine months longer and blacks three months longer than whites.

The differences in sentencing occurred most often in the middle range of offence seriousness where judicial discretion was high. In these types of cases, black defendants (68 per cent) were significantly more likely to be sentenced to custody than whites (60 per cent). It was also found that the unequal treatment of black defendants occurred mainly at Dudley Crown Court (and Warwick and Stafford courts, although the numbers were much smaller), but not at the more urban Birmingham Crown Court. Using multivariate analysis too, Mhlanga (1997) reported similar findings, with young African/Caribbean defendants having an increased risk of custody being imposed.

For female defendants in Hood's study, the decision to sentence to immediate custody was accounted for by the seriousness of the offence, albeit that this may not be 'racially neutral' in itself. However, as was the case with males, African/Caribbean females at Dudley Crown Court had higher than expected rates of custody. No differences were found in sentence lengths for custody, or in the pattern of non-custodial sentencing (Hood 1992).

Hood's findings represent a clear example of direct discrimination against people of African/Caribbean origin, which has a clear contributory effect to the higher proportion of African/Caribbean people in prison in England and Wales. However, although this section has concluded the review of research on the criminal justice process up to the point of the oft-cited prison statistics, the process does not end there. The treatment of ethnic minorities in prison must also be considered before looking, more generally, at the impact of criminalization processes on the over-representation of African/Caribbean people in prison.

PRISON AND PROBATION

Prison populations

Ethnic monitoring data on Britain's prison population have been available since 1985. The first statistics revealed a marked over-representation of West Indians, Guyanese, and Africans within prisons among both males and females. The over-representation varied by sex of offender and whether they were sentenced or on remand, but the level of over-representation was in the region of seven times as many in prison compared with their representation in the general population. This is partly explained by the inclusion of non-British nationals . . . . The discussion that follows focuses on ethnic minorities of British nationality.

Since the mid-1980s the patterns have largely remained unchanged, although there has been a striking increase in the proportion of African/Caribbeans imprisoned, particularly among female prisoners whose actual numbers in prison are much smaller. As Figures 24.2 and 24.3 indicate, the ethnic minority prison population has fluctuated with the rises and falls of the white prison population, but this masks the overall increase in the ethnic minority prison population. While the white male prison population increased by 31 per cent between 1985 and 1999, the black population grew by 101 per cent, the Asian by 80 per cent, and the 'Chinese/other Asian' population increased 106 per cent. For females, the increase has been even more dramatic, at 217 per cent and 188 per cent for the black and 'Chinese/other Asian' female prison populations respectively. In sharp contrast, the number of Asian women in prison has remained consistently low, with only 34 in 1999. A future area of research should be to shed light on the protective factors which assist Asian women in avoiding criminalization.

The impact of more punitive sentencing policies, the younger age structure of the ethnic minority population contributing proportionately more in the group at risk of offending, and the effects of discrimination in the criminal justice process are all possible explanations for the increase in the ethnic minority prison population.

The most recent Home Office statistics show that on 30 June 1999 there were 12,120 people from ethnic minorities held in custody in Prison Service establishments. This amounted to 18 per cent of the male prison population and 25 per cent of the female population, although one-quarter of the male and one half of the female ethnic minority population were of foreign nationality (Home Office 2000a). Table 24.1 gives the percentages by ethnic origin for British nationals, compared against the census population figures, with the final column presenting incarceration rates – the rate per 100,000 of that ethnic group.

These statistics show that rates of incarceration for the Indian, Bangladeshi, and Chinese communities are very low (fewer than 100 per 100,000). This can be compared

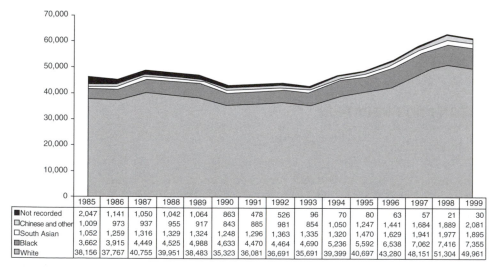

	1985	1986	1987	1988	1989	1990	1991	1992	1993	1994	1995	1996	1997	1998	1999
■Not recorded	2,047	1,141	1,050	1,042	1,064	863	478	526	96	70	80	63	57	21	30
□Chinese and other	1,009	973	937	955	917	843	885	981	854	1,050	1,247	1,441	1,684	1,889	2,081
□South Asian	1,052	1,259	1,316	1,329	1,324	1,248	1,296	1,363	1,335	1,320	1,470	1,629	1,941	1,977	1,895
▦Black	3,662	3,915	4,449	4,525	4,988	4,633	4,470	4,464	4,690	5,236	5,592	6,538	7,062	7,416	7,355
▨White	38,156	37,767	40,755	39,951	38,483	35,323	36,081	36,691	35,691	39,399	40,697	43,280	48,151	51,304	49,961

Figure 24.2 Male prison population by ethnic group, 1985–99
Source: Home Office 2000a.

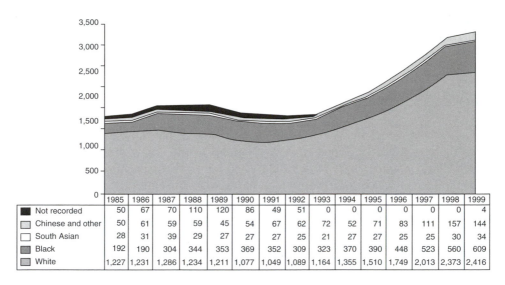

	1985	1986	1987	1988	1989	1990	1991	1992	1993	1994	1995	1996	1997	1998	1999
Not recorded	50	67	70	110	120	86	49	51	0	0	0	0	0	0	4
Chinese and other	50	61	59	59	45	54	67	62	72	52	71	83	111	157	144
South Asian	28	31	39	29	27	27	27	25	21	27	27	25	25	30	34
Black	192	190	304	344	353	369	352	309	323	370	390	448	523	560	609
White	1,227	1,231	1,286	1,234	1,211	1,077	1,049	1,089	1,164	1,355	1,510	1,749	2,013	2,373	2,416

Figure 24.3 Female prison population by ethnic group, 1985–99
Source: Home Office 2000a.

Table 24.1 Prison population by ethnic origin and sex (1999)

Ethnic group	Prison population British Nationals – 1999[1]		Resident population (Age 15–64)[2]	Incarceration rates for 1999[3]
	Males	Females	Males and Females	Males and Females
White	86	85	94	184
Black	10	12	2	1,265
Caribbean	6	6	1	1,395
African	1	1	1	713
Other	3	5	<1	1,399
Asian	2	1	3	147
Indian	1	<1	2	93
Pakistani	1	<1	1	260
Bangladeshi	<1	<1	<1	74
Chinese/Other	2	2	1	424[4]

Notes

1 Source: *Statistics on Race and the Criminal Justice System* (Home Office 2000b).

2 Source: 1991 Census (OPCS 1993).

3 Source: *Prison Statistics 1999* (Home Office 2000a).

4 This figure aggregates incarceration rates for Chinese (44), Other Asian (914), and other ethnic groups (358).

Percentages are rounded to the nearest whole number.

with white people (who make up 97 per cent of the population) imprisoned at a rate of 184 per 100,000 and the strikingly high incarceration rate for black people, of over 1,265, amounting to around 1.25 per cent of the black population. The disparate group of those from other Asian origins experience a similarly high incarceration rate.

Experiences in prison

The historical context for understanding 'race relations' for those in prison is one in which there was staunch support for the National Front among many prison officers in the 1970s, alongside incidents of brutality and harassment by prison officers (Gordon 1983), following which 'race relations' policies were introduced in the early 1980s. The *Alexander v Home Office* case was also pivotal in this development. In December 1987, the Court of Appeal ruled in favour of an African/Caribbean inmate who had been discriminated against in being denied a kitchen job. It was shown that comments based on racial stereotype in his assessment and induction reports at Wandsworth prison had led to him being discriminated against. The report opined that, '[h]e displays the usual traits associated with people of his ethnic background, being arrogant, suspicious of staff, anti-authority, devious and possessing a very large chip on his shoulder, which he will find very difficult to remove if he carries on the way he is doing'.

Genders and Player's (1989) study of five prisons in the mid-1980s revealed similar patterns of direct racial discrimination which disadvantaged African/Caribbean prisoners in particular. African/Caribbean prisoners were stereotyped as arrogant, lazy, noisy, hostile to authority, with values incompatible with British society, and as having 'a chip on their shoulder'. These stereotypes explained patterns of work allocations, with prisoners of African/Caribbean origin most often doing the least favoured jobs. Genders and Player (ibid.: 127) concluded that 'racial bias lies at the root of the racial imbalance evidenced in labour allocation'. Black prisoners were also more likely to be disciplined for misbehaviour in prison, and this appeared to be due to a more stringent application of prison disciplinary rules compared with infractions involving white prisoners. Chigwada-Bailey (1997) has drawn attention to the similar way in which African/Caribbean women are perceived in prison, as troublesome and causing disciplinary problems.

A more recent study by the Race Relations Adviser to HM Prison Service Agency uncovered a climate of victimization, the use of inappropriate language, harassment, abuse, and bullying of both ethnic minority staff and prisoners at Brixton prison (Clements 2000). The 'Reflections' regime – which involved loss of association by prisoners – was used disproportionately against prisoners from minority ethnic groups without due process and without the knowledge of senior managers. In November 2000, the Commission for Racial Equality announced a formal investigation into HM Prison Service, focusing on racial discrimination and racial harassment in HMP Brixton and Parc, and HM Feltham young offenders institution.

It was in the last institution that Zahid Mubarek was murdered by his cellmate, despite evidence that prison authorities were aware of the cellmate's violent racist tendencies. Research by Burnett and Farrell (1994) has suggested that racist victimization in prison is a common occurrence, and deaths in prison custody have raised the same concerns as those occurring in police custody. Again, negative stereotyping of African/ Caribbean people as 'violent' and 'dangerous' appears to legitimize brutality against them, and allows their mental and physical health needs to be overlooked when in the care of the Prison Service.

Probation

Negative stereotyping of ethnic minorities, particularly African/Caribbeans, has also been noted in studies of probation practice, leading to assumptions that there was less possibility for change among African/Caribbean offenders (Green 1989; Denney 1992). A key issue has been the extent to which probation officers have considered the role of racism in explaining the offending of ethnic minorities (Holdaway and Allaker 1990). Claims have been made that the Probation Service operated a 'colour-blind' approach, with all offenders treated in the same way (. . . Mavunga 1993).

In the most recent thematic inspection on racial equality, concerns centred around the quality of supervision of black offenders, particularly in terms of levels of contact during the later stages of probation orders (HMIP 2000). Linked to this has been an acknowledgement that little is known about the needs of ethnic minority probationers, or 'what works' in reducing offending among this group of offenders (Home Office 2001; Lawrence 1996). [. . .]

References

Barclay, G., and Mhlanga, B. (2000), *Ethnic Differences in Decisions on Young Defendants Dealt with by the Crown Prosecution Service*, Home Office Section 95 Findings No. 1, London: Home Office.

Bottomley, A.K., and Coleman, C. (1976), 'Criminal Statistics: the police role in the discovery and detection of crime', *International Journal of Criminology and Penology*, 4: 33–58.

Bourne, J., Bridges, L., and Searle, C. (1997), *Outcast England: How Schools Exclude Black Children*, London: Institute for Race Relations.

Bowling, B., and Phillips, C. (2002), *Racism, Crime and Justice*, London: Longman.

Brown, I., and Hullin, R. (1992), 'A Study of Sentencing in the Leeds Magistrates' Courts', *British Journal of Criminology*, 32, 1: 41–53.

Bucke, T. (1997), *Ethnicity and Contacts with the Police: Latest Findings from the British Crime Survey*, Home Office Research Findings No. 59, London: Home Office.

Bucke, T., and Brown, D. (1997), *In Police Custody: Police Powers and Suspects' Rights Under the Revised PACE Codes of Practice*, Home Office Research Study 174, London: Home Office.

Burnett, R., and Farrell, G. (1994), *Reported and Unreported Racial Incidents in Prisons*, Occasional Paper No. 14, Oxford: University of Oxford Centre for Criminological Research.

Chigwada-Bailey, R. (1997), *Black Women's Experiences of Criminal Justice: Discourse on Disadvantage*, Winchester: Waterside Press.

Clancy, A., Hough, M., Aust, R., and Kershaw, C. (2001), *Crime, Policing and Justice: the Experience of Ethnic Minorities Findings from the 2000 British Crime Survey*, Home Office Research Study 223, London: Home Office.

Clements, J. (2000), *Assessment of Race Relations at HMP Brixton* (www.hmprisonservice. gov.uk/filestore/202_206.pdf).

Crow, I., and Cove, J. (1984), 'Ethnic Minorities in the Courts', *Criminal Law Review*: 413–17.

Crown Prosecution Service (1994), *The Code for Crown Prosecutors*, London: CPS.

Denman, S. (2001), *The Denman Report – Race Discrimination in the Crown Prosecution Service*, London: Crown Prosecution Service.

Denney, D. (1992), *Racism and anti-racism in probation*, London: Routledge.

Dixon, D., Coleman, C., and Bottomley, K. (1990), 'Consent and the Legal Regulation of Policing', *Journal of Law and Society*, 17, 3: 345–59.

FitzGerald, M. (1993), *Ethnic Minorities in the Criminal Justice System*, Research Study No. 20, Royal Commission on Criminal Justice, London: Home Office.

—— (1999), *Searches in London under Section 1 of the Police and Criminal Evidence Act*, London: Metropolitan Police.

FitzGerald, M., and Sibbitt, R. (1997), *Ethnic Monitoring in Police Forces: a Beginning*, Home Office Research Study No. 173, London: Home Office.

Genders, E., and Player, E. (1989), *Race Relations in Prison*, Oxford: Clarendon Press.

Gilroy, P., (1987b), 'The Myth of Black Criminality', in P. Scraton (ed.), *Law, Order and the Authoritarian State: readings in critical criminology*, Milton Keynes: Open University Press.

Gordon, P. (1983), *White Law: Racism in the Police, Courts and Prisons*, London: Pluto.

Green, R. (1989), 'Probation and the Black Offender', *New Community*, 16, 1: 81–91.

Her Majesty's Inspectorate of Constabulary (2000), *Policing London. Winning Consent: A Review of Murder Investigations and Community and Race Relations Issues in the Metropolitan Police Service*, London: Home Office.

Her Majesty's Inspectorate of Probation (2000), *Towards Race Equality. Thematic Inspection*, London: Home Office.

Holdaway, S., and Allaker, J. (1990), *Race Issues in the Probation Service: a Review of Policy*, Wakefield: Association of Chief Officers of Probation.

Home Office (1989), *The Ethnic Group of Those Proceeded Against or Sentenced by the Courts in the Metropolitan District in 1984 and 1985*, Home Office Statistical Bulletin 6/89, London: Home Office Statistical Department.

—— (1997), *Police and Criminal Evidence Act 1984 (s. 66) Code of Practice (A) on Stop and Search*, London: Home Office.

—— (1998), *Statistics on Race and the Criminal Justice System 1998: a Home Office publication under section 95 of the Criminal Justice Act 1991*, London: Home Office.

—— (2000a), *Prison Statistics England and Wales 1999*, Cm 4805, London: The Stationery Office.

—— (2000b), *Statistics on Race and the Criminal Justice System 2000: a Home Office publication under section 95 of the Criminal Justice Act 1991*, London: Home Office.

—— (2001), *What Works Diversity Issues and Race*, Probation Circular 76/2001, London: Home Office.

Hood, R. (1992), *Race and Sentencing*, Oxford: Clarendon Press.

House of Commons (1972), *Select Committee on Race Relations and Immigeation Session 1971–2, Police/Immigration Relations*, 1:471.

Hudson, B. (1989), 'Discrimination and Disparity: the Influence of Race on Sentencing', *New Community*, 16, 1: 23–34.

—— (1993), *Penal Policy and Social Justice*, Basingstoke: Macmillan.

Hunte, J. (1966), *Nigger Hunting in England?*, London: West Indian Standing Conference.

Jefferson, A. (1993), 'The Racism of Criminalization: Police and the Reproduction of the Criminal Other', in L.R. Gelsthorpe (ed.), *Minority Ethnic Groups in the Criminal Justice System*, Cambridge: University of Cambridge Institute of Criminology.

Jefferson, T., and Walker, M.A. (1992), 'Ethnic Minorities in the Criminal Justice System', *Criminal Law Review*, 81, 140: 83–95.

Lawrence, D. (1996), 'Race, Culture and the Probation Service: Groupwork Programme Design', in G. Mclvor (ed.), *Working with Offenders*, Research Highlights in Social Work 26, London: Jessica Kingsley.

Macpherson, W. (1999), *The Stephen Lawrence Inquiry*, Report of an Inquiry by Sir William Macpherson of Cluny, advised by Tom Cook, The Right Reverend Dr John Sentamu and Dr Richard Stone, Cm 4262–1, London: The Stationery Office.

Mair, G. (1986), 'Ethnic Minorities, Probation and the Magistrates' Courts', *British Journal of Criminology*, 26, 2: 147–55.

Mavunga, P. (1993), 'Probation: A Basically Racist Service', in L. Gelsthorpe (ed.), *Minority Groups in the Criminal Justice System*, Cambridge: Cambridge University Institute of Criminology.

Mawby, R. (1979), *Policing the City*, Farnborough: Saxon House.

Mhlanga, B. (1997), *The Colour of English Justice: a Multivariate Analysis*, Aldershot: Avebury.

—— (1999), *Race and Crown Prosecution Service Decisions*, London: The Stationery Office.

Miller, J., Bland, N., and Quinton, P. (2000), *The Impact of Stops and Searches on Crime and the Community*, Police Research Series Paper 127, London: Home Office.

Mirrlees-Black, C. (2001), *Confidence in the Criminal Justice System: findings from the 2000 British Crime Survey*, Research Findings No. 137, London: Home Office.

Modood, T., Berthoud, R., with the assistance of Lakey, J., Nazroo, J., Smith, P., Virdee, S., and Beishon, S. (1997), *Ethnic Minorities in Britain: Diversity and Disadvatage*, London: Policy Studies Institute.

MVA and Miller, J. (2000), *Profiling Populations Available for Stops and Searches*, Police Research Series Paper No. 131, London: Home office.

Norris, C. Fielding, N., Kemp, C., and Fielding, J. (1992), 'Black and Blue: an Analysis of the Influence of Race on Being Stopped by the Police', *British Journal of Sociology*, 43, 2: 207–23.

Newburn, T., and Hayman, S. (2001), *Policing, Surveillance and Social Control: CCTV and Police Monitoring of Suspects*, Cullumpton, Devon: Willan Publishing.

OPCS (1993), *1991 Census: Ethnic Group and Country of Birth (Great Britain)*, London: Office of Population and Censuses Survey.

Phillips, C., and Brown, D. (1998), *Entry into the Criminal Justice System: a Survey of Police Arrests and Their Outcomes*, Home Office Research Study No. 185, London: Home Office.

Povey, D., Cotton, J., and Sisson, S. (2000), *Recorded Crime Statistics: England and Wales, April 1999 to March 2000*, Home Office Statistical Bulletin 12/00, London: Home Office.

Quinton, P., Bland, N., and Miller J. (2000), *Police Stops, Decision-Making and Practice*, Police Research Series Paper No. 130, London: Home Office.

Ramsay, M. Baker, P., Goulden, C., Sharp, C., and Sondhi, A. (2001), *Drug Misuse Declared in 2000: Results from the British Crime Survey*, Home Office Research Study No. 224, London: Home Office.

Reiner, R. (1993), 'Race, Crime and Justice: Models of Interpretation', in L.R. Gelsthorpe (ed.), *Minority Ethnic Groups in the Criminal Justice System*, Cambridge: University of Cambridge Institute of Criminology.

Shallice, A., and Gordon, P. (1990), *Black People, White Justice? Race and the Criminal Justice System*, London: Runnymede Trust.

Skogan, W.G. (1990), *The Police and the Public in England and Wales: A British Crime Survey Report*, Home Office Research Study No. 117, London: HMSO.

Smith, D.J. (1997), 'Ethnic Origins, Crime and Criminal Justice', in M. Maguire, R. Morgan, and R. Reiner (eds), *The Oxford Handbook of Criminology*, 2nd edn, Oxford: Oxford University Press.

Steer, D. (1980), *Uncovering Crime: the police role*, Royal Commission on Criminal Procedure Research Study No. 7, London: HMSO.

Walker, M.A. (1989), 'The Court Disposal and Remands of White, Afro-Caribbean, and Asian Men (London, 1983)', *British Journal of Criminology*, 29, 4: 353–67.

Young, J. (1994), *Policing the Streets: stops and searches in North London*, Middlesex: Centre for Criminology, Middlesex University.

Chapter 25

Elijah Anderson

THE CODE OF THE STREETS
How the inner-city environment fosters a need for respect and a self-image based on violence

From: Elijah Anderson (1994), 'The code of the streets', *The Atlantic Monthly* 273(5): 81–92.

[. . .]

OF ALL THE PROBLEMS besetting the poor inner-city black community, none is more pressing than that of interpersonal violence and aggression. It wreaks havoc daily with the lives of community residents and increasingly spills over into downtown and residential middle-class areas. Muggings, burglaries, carjackings, and drug-related shootings, all of which may leave their victims or innocent bystanders dead, are now common enough to concern all urban and many suburban residents. The inclination to violence springs from the circumstances of life among the ghetto poor – the lack of jobs that pay a living wage, the stigma of race, the fallout from rampant drug use and drug trafficking, and the resulting alienation and lack of hope for the future.

Simply living in such an environment places young people at special risk of falling victim to aggressive behavior. Although there are often forces in the community which can counteract the negative influences, by far the most powerful being a strong, loving, "decent" (as inner-city residents put it) family committed to middle-class values, the despair is pervasive enough to have spawned an oppositional culture, that of "the streets," whose norms are often consciously opposed to those of mainstream society. These two orientations – decent and street – socially organize the community, and their coexistence has important consequences for residents, particularly children growing up in the inner city. Above all, this environment means that even youngsters whose home lives reflect mainstream values – and the majority of homes in the community do – must be able to handle themselves in a street-oriented environment.

This is because the street culture has evolved what may be called a code of the streets, which amounts to a set of informal rules governing interpersonal public behavior, including violence. The rules prescribe both a proper comportment and a proper way to respond if challenged. They regulate the use of violence and so allow those who are inclined to aggression to precipitate violent encounters in an approved way. The rules have been established and are enforced mainly by the street-oriented, but on the streets the distinction between street and decent is often irrelevant; everybody knows that if the rules are violated, there are penalties. Knowledge of the code is thus largely defensive; it is literally necessary for operating in public. Therefore, even though families with a decency orientation are usually opposed to the values of the code, they often reluctantly encourage their children's familiarity with it to enable them to negotiate the inner-city environment.

At the heart of the code is the issue of respect – loosely defined as being treated "right," or granted the deference one deserves. However, in the troublesome public environment of the inner city, as people increasingly feel buffeted by forces beyond their control, what one deserves in the way of respect becomes more and more problematic and uncertain. This in turn further opens the issue of respect to sometimes intense interpersonal negotiation. In the street culture, especially among young people, respect is viewed as almost an external entity that is hard-won but easily lost, and so must constantly be guarded. The rules of the code in fact provide a framework for negotiating respect. The person whose very appearance – including his clothing, demeanor, and way of moving – deters transgressions feels that he possesses, and may be considered by others to possess, a measure of respect. With the right amount of respect, for instance, he can avoid "being bothered" in public. If he is bothered, not only may he be in physical danger but he has been disgraced or "dissed" (disrespected). Many of the forms that "dissing" can take might seem petty to middle-class people (maintaining eye contact for too long, for example), but to those invested in the street code, these actions become serious indications of the other person's intentions. Consequently, such people become very sensitive to advances and slights, which could well serve as warnings of imminent physical confrontation.

This hard reality can be traced to the profound sense of alienation from mainstream society and its institutions felt by many poor inner-city black people, particularly the young. The code of the streets is actually a cultural adaptation to a profound lack of faith in the police and the judicial system. The police are most often seen as representing the dominant white society and not caring to protect inner-city residents. When called, they may not respond, which is one reason many residents feel they must be prepared to take extraordinary measures to defend themselves and their loved ones against those who are inclined to aggression. Lack of police accountability has in fact been incorporated into the status system: the person who is believed capable of "taking care of himself" is accorded a certain deference, which translates into a sense of physical and psychological control. Thus the street code emerges where the influence of the police ends and personal responsibility for one's safety is felt to begin. Exacerbated by the proliferation of drugs and easy access to guns, this volatile situation results in the ability of the street-oriented minority (or those who effectively "go for bad") to dominate the public spaces.

DECENT AND STREET FAMILIES

Although almost everyone in poor inner-city neighborhoods is struggling financially and therefore feels a certain distance from the rest of America, the decent and the street family in a real sense represent two poles of value orientation, two contrasting conceptual categories. The labels "decent" and "street," which the residents themselves use, amount to evaluative judgments that confer status on local residents. The labeling is often the result of a social contest among individuals and families of the neighborhood. Individuals of the two orientations often coexist in the same extended family. Decent residents judge themselves to be so while judging others to be of the street, and street individuals often present themselves as decent, drawing distinctions between themselves and other people. In addition, there is quite a bit of circumstantial behavior – that is, one person may at different times exhibit both decent and street orientations, depending on the circumstances. Although these designations result from so much social jockeying, there do exist concrete features that define each conceptual category.

Generally, so-called decent families tend to accept mainstream values more fully and attempt to instill them in their children. Whether married couples with children or single-parent (usually female) households, they are generally "working poor" and so tend to be better off financially than their street-oriented neighbors. They value hard work and self-reliance and are willing to sacrifice for their children. Because they have a certain amount of faith in mainstream society, they harbor hopes for a better future for their children, if not for themselves. Many of them go to church and take a strong interest in their children's schooling. Rather than dwelling on the real hardships and inequities facing them, many such decent people, particularly the increasing number of grandmothers raising grandchildren, see their difficult situation as a test from God and derive great support from their faith and from the church community.

Extremely aware of the problematic and often dangerous environment in which they reside, decent parents tend to be strict in their child-rearing practices, encouraging children to respect authority and walk a straight moral line. They have an almost obsessive concern about trouble of any kind and remind their children to be on the lookout for people and situations that might lead to it. At the same time, they are themselves polite and considerate of others, and teach their children to be the same way. At home, at work, and in church, they strive hard to maintain a positive mental attitude and a spirit of cooperation.

So-called street parents, in contrast, often show a lack of consideration for other people and have a rather superficial sense of family and community. Though they may love their children, many of them are unable to cope with the physical and emotional demands of parenthood, and find it difficult to reconcile their needs with those of their children. These families, who are more fully invested in the code of the streets than the decent people are, may aggressively socialize their children into it in a normative way. They believe in the code and judge themselves and others according to its values.

In fact the overwhelming majority of families in the inner-city community try to approximate the decent-family model, but there are many others who clearly represent the worst fears of the decent family. Not only are their financial resources extremely limited, but what little they have may easily be misused. The lives of the street-oriented are often marked by disorganization. In the most desperate circumstances people frequently have a limited understanding of priorities and consequences, and so frustrations mount over bills, food, and, at times, drink, cigarettes, and drugs. Some tend toward self-destructive behavior; many street-oriented women are crack-addicted ("on the pipe"), alcoholic, or involved in complicated relationships with men who abuse them. In addition, the seeming intractability of their situation, caused in large part by the lack of well-paying jobs and the persistence of racial discrimination, has engendered deep-seated bitterness and anger in many of the most desperate and poorest blacks, especially young people. The need both to exercise a measure of control and to lash out at somebody is often reflected in the adults' relations with their children. At the least, the frustrations of persistent poverty shorten the fuse in such people – contributing to a lack of patience with anyone, child or adult, who irritates them.

In these circumstances a woman – or a man, although men are less consistently present in children's lives – can be quite aggressive with children, yelling at and striking them for the least little infraction of the rules she has set down. Often little if any serious explanation follows the verbal and physical punishment. This response teaches children a particular lesson. They learn that to solve any kind of interpersonal problem one must quickly resort to hitting or other violent behavior. Actual peace and quiet, and also the appearance of calm, respectful children conveyed to her neighbors and friends, are often what the young mother most desires, but at times she will be very aggressive in trying to get them. Thus she may be quick to beat her children, especially if they defy her law, not because she hates them but because this is the way she knows to control them. In fact, many street-oriented women love their children dearly. Many mothers in the community subscribe to the notion that there is a "devil in the boy" that must be beaten out of him or that socially "fast girls need to be whupped." Thus much of what borders on child abuse in the view of social authorities is acceptable parental punishment in the view of these mothers.

Many street-oriented women are sporadic mothers whose children learn to fend for themselves when necessary, foraging for food and money any way they can get it. The children are sometimes employed by drug dealers or become addicted themselves. These children of the street, growing up with little supervision, are said to "come up hard." They often learn to fight at an early age, sometimes using short-tempered adults around them as role models. The street-oriented home may be fraught with anger, verbal disputes, physical aggression, and even mayhem. The children observe these goings-on, learning the lesson that might makes right. They quickly learn to hit those who cross them, and the dog-eat-dog mentality prevails. In order to survive, to protect oneself, it is necessary to marshal inner resources and be ready to deal with adversity in a hands-on way. In these circumstances physical prowess takes on great significance.

In some of the most desperate cases, a street-oriented mother may simply leave her young children alone and unattended while she goes out. The most irresponsible women can be found at local bars and crack houses, getting high and socializing with other adults. Sometimes a troubled woman will leave very young children alone for days at a time. Reports of crack addicts abandoning their children have become common in drug-infested inner-city communities. Neighbors or relatives discover the abandoned children, often hungry and distraught over the absence of their mother. After repeated absences, a friend or relative, particularly a grandmother, will often step in to care for the young children, sometimes petitioning the authorities to send her, as guardian of the children, the mother's welfare check, if the mother gets one. By this time, however, the children may well have learned the first lesson of the streets: survival itself, let alone respect, cannot be taken for granted; you have to fight for your place in the world.

CAMPAIGNING FOR RESPECT

These realities of inner-city life are largely absorbed on the streets. At an early age, often even before they start school, children from street-oriented homes gravitate to the streets, where they "hang" – socialize with their peers. Children from these generally permissive homes have a great deal of latitude and are allowed to "rip and run" up and down the street. They often come home from school, put their books down, and go right back out the door. On school nights eight- and nine-year-olds remain out until nine or ten o'clock (and teenagers typically come in whenever they want to). On the streets they play in groups that often become the source of their primary social bonds. Children from decent homes tend to be more carefully supervised and are thus likely to have curfews and to be taught how to stay out of trouble.

When decent and street kids come together, a kind of social shuffle occurs in which children have a chance to go either way. Tension builds as a child comes to realize that he must choose an orientation. The kind of home he comes from influences but does not determine the way he will ultimately turn out – although it is unlikely that a child from a thoroughly street-oriented family will easily absorb decent values on the streets. Youths who emerge from street-oriented families but develop a decency orientation almost always learn those values in another setting – in school, in a youth group, in church. Often it is the result of their involvement with a caring "old head" (adult role model).

In the street, through their play, children pour their individual life experiences into a common knowledge pool, affirming, confirming, and elaborating on what they have observed in the home and matching their skills against those of others. And they learn to fight. Even small children test one another, pushing and shoving, and are ready to hit other children over circumstances not to their liking. In turn, they are readily hit by other children, and the child who is toughest prevails. Thus the violent resolution of disputes, the hitting and cursing, gains social reinforcement. The child in effect is initiated into a system that is really a way of campaigning for respect.

In addition, younger children witness the disputes of older children, which are often resolved through cursing and abusive talk, if not aggression or outright violence. They see that one child succumbs to the greater physical and mental abilities of the other. They are also alert and attentive witnesses to the verbal and physical fights of adults, after which they compare notes and share their interpretations of the event. In almost every case the victor is the person who physically won the altercation, and this person often enjoys the esteem and respect of onlookers. These experiences reinforce the lessons the children have learned at home: might makes right, and toughness is a virtue, while humility is not. In effect they learn the social meaning of fighting. When it is left virtually unchallenged, this understanding becomes an ever more important part of the child's working conception of the world. Over time the code of the streets becomes refined.

Those street-oriented adults with whom children come in contact – including mothers, fathers, brothers, sisters, boyfriends, cousins, neighbors, and friends – help them along in forming this understanding by verbalizing the messages they are getting through experience: "Watch your back." "Protect yourself." "Don't punk out." "If somebody messes with you, you got to pay them back." "If someone disses you, you got to straighten them out." Many parents actually impose sanctions if a child is not sufficiently aggressive. For example, if a child loses a fight and comes home upset, the parent might respond, "Don't you come in here crying that somebody beat you up; you better get back out there and whup his ass. I didn't raise no punks! Get back out there and whup his ass. If you don't whup his ass, I'll whup your ass when you come home." Thus the child obtains reinforcement for being tough and showing nerve.

While fighting, some children cry as though they are doing something they are ambivalent about. The fight may be against their wishes, yet they may feel constrained to fight or face the consequences – not just from peers but also from caretakers or parents, who may administer another beating if they back down. Some adults recall receiving such lessons from their own parents and justify repeating them to their children as a way to toughen them up. Looking capable of taking care of oneself as a form of self-defense is a dominant theme among both street-oriented and decent adults who worry about the safety of their children. There is thus at times a convergence in their child-rearing practices, although the rationales behind them may differ.

SELF-IMAGE BASED ON "JUICE"

By the time they are teenagers, most youths have either internalized the code of the streets or at least learned the need to comport themselves in accordance with its rules, which chiefly have to do with interpersonal communication. The code revolves around the presentation of self. Its basic requirement is the display of a certain predisposition to violence. Accordingly, one's bearing must send the unmistakable if sometimes subtle message to "the next person" in public that one is capable of violence and mayhem when the situation requires it, that one can take care of oneself. The nature of this communication is largely determined by the demands of the circumstances but can include facial expressions, gait, and verbal expressions – all of which are geared mainly to deterring aggression. Physical appearance, including clothes, jewelry, and grooming, also plays an important part in how a person is viewed; to be respected, it is important to have the right look.

Even so, there are no guarantees against challenges, because there are always people around looking for a fight to increase their share of respect – or "juice," as it is sometimes called on the street. Moreover, if a person is assaulted, it is important, not only in the eyes of his opponent but also in the eyes of his "running buddies," for him to avenge himself. Otherwise he risks being "tried" (challenged) or "moved on" by any number of others. To maintain his honor he must show he is not someone to be "messed with" or "dissed." In general, the person must "keep himself straight" by managing his position of respect among others; this involves in part his self-image, which is shaped by what he thinks others are thinking of him in relation to his peers.

Objects play an important and complicated role in establishing self-image. Jackets, sneakers, gold jewelry, reflect not just a person's taste, which tends to be tightly regulated among adolescents of all social classes, but also a willingness to possess things that may require defending. A boy wearing a fashionable, expensive jacket, for example, is vulnerable to attack by another who covets the jacket and either cannot afford to buy one or wants the added satisfaction of depriving someone else of his. However, if the boy forgoes the desirable jacket and wears one that isn't "hip," he runs the risk of being teased and possibly even assaulted as an unworthy person. To be allowed to hang with certain prestigious crowds, a boy must wear a different set of expensive clothes – sneakers and athletic suit – every day. Not to be able to do so might make him appear socially deficient. The youth comes to covet such items – especially when he sees easy prey wearing them.

In acquiring valued things, therefore, a person shores up his identity – but since it is an identity based on having things, it is highly precarious. This very precariousness gives a heightened sense of urgency to staying even with peers, with whom the person is actually competing. Young men and women who are able to command respect through their presentation of self – by allowing their possessions and their body language to speak for them — may not have to campaign for regard but may, rather, gain it by the force of their manner. Those who are unable to command respect in this way must actively campaign for it — and are thus particularly alive to slights.

One way of campaigning for status is by taking the possessions of others. In this context, seemingly ordinary objects can become trophies imbued with symbolic value that far exceeds their monetary worth. Possession of the trophy can symbolize the ability to violate somebody — to "get in his face," to take something of value from him, to "dis" him, and thus to enhance one's own worth by stealing someone else's. The trophy does not have to be something material. It can be another person's sense of honor, snatched away with a derogatory remark. It can be the outcome of a fight. It can be the imposition of a certain standard, such as a girl's getting herself recognized as the most beautiful. Material things, however, fit easily into the pattern. Sneakers, a pistol, even somebody else's girlfriend, can become a trophy. When a person can take something from another and then flaunt it, he gains a certain regard by being the owner, or the controller, of that thing. But this display of ownership can then provoke other people to challenge him. This game of who controls what is thus constantly being played out on inner-city streets, and the trophy — extrinsic or intrinsic, tangible or intangible — identifies the current winner.

An important aspect of this often violent give-and-take is its zero-sum quality. That is, the extent to which one person can raise himself up depends on his ability to put another person down. This underscores the alienation that permeates the inner-city ghetto community. There is a generalized sense that very little respect is to be had, and therefore everyone competes to get what affirmation he can of the little that is available. The craving for respect that results gives people thin skins. Shows of deference by others can be highly soothing, contributing to a sense of security, comfort, self-confidence, and self-respect. Transgressions by others which go unanswered diminish these feelings and are believed to encourage further transgressions. Hence one must be ever vigilant against the transgressions of others or even *appearing* as if transgressions will be tolerated. Among young people, whose sense of self-esteem is particularly vulnerable, there is an especially heightened concern with being disrespected. Many inner-city young men in particular crave respect to such a degree that they will risk their lives to attain and maintain it.

The issue of respect is thus closely tied to whether a person has an inclination to be violent, even as a victim. In the wider society people may not feel required to retaliate physically after an attack, even though they are aware that they have been degraded or taken advantage of. They may feel a great need to defend themselves *during* an attack, or to behave in such a way as to deter aggression (middle-class people certainly can and do become victims of street-oriented youths), but they are much more likely than street-oriented people to feel that they can walk away from a possible altercation with their self-esteem intact. Some people may even have the strength of character to flee, without any thought that their self-respect or esteem will be diminished.

In impoverished inner-city black communities, however, particularly among young males and perhaps increasingly among females, such flight would be extremely difficult. To run away would likely leave one's self-esteem in tatters. Hence people often feel constrained not only to stand up and at least attempt to resist during an assault but also to "pay back" — to seek revenge — after a successful assault on their person. This may include going to get a weapon or even getting relatives involved. Their very identity and self-respect, their honor, is often intricately tied up with the way they perform on the streets during and after such encounters. This outlook reflects the circumscribed opportunities of the inner-city poor. Generally people outside the ghetto have other ways of gaining status and regard, and thus do not feel so dependent on such physical displays.

BY TRIAL OF MANHOOD

On the street, among males these concerns about things and identity have come to be expressed in the concept of "manhood." Manhood in the inner city means taking the prerogatives of men with respect to strangers, other men, and women – being distinguished as a man. It implies physicality and a certain ruthlessness. Regard and respect are associated with this concept in large part because of its practical application: if others have little or no regard for a person's manhood, his very life and those of his loved ones could be in jeopardy. But there is a chicken-and-egg aspect to this situation: one's physical safety is more likely to be jeopardized in public *because* manhood is associated with respect. In other words, an existential link has been created between the idea of manhood and one's self-esteem, so that it has become hard to say which is primary. For many inner-city youths, manhood and respect are flip sides of the same coin; physical and psychological well-being are inseparable, and both require a sense of control, of being in charge.

The operating assumption is that a man, especially a real man, knows what other men know – the code of the streets. And if one is not a real man, one is somehow diminished as a person, and there are certain valued things one simply does not deserve. There is thus believed to be a certain justice to the code, since it is considered that everyone has the opportunity to know it. Implicit in this is that everybody is held responsible for being familiar with the code. If the victim of a mugging, for example, does not know the code and so responds "wrong," the perpetrator may feel justified even in killing him and may feel no remorse. He may think, "Too bad, but it's his fault. He should have known better."

So when a person ventures outside, he must adopt the code – a kind of shield, really – to prevent others from "messing with" him. In these circumstances it is easy for people to think they are being tried or tested by others even when this is not the case. For it is sensed that something extremely valuable is at stake in every interaction, and people are encouraged to rise to the occasion, particularly with strangers. For people who are unfamiliar with the code – generally people who live outside the inner city – the concern with respect in the most ordinary interactions can be frightening and incomprehensible. But for those who are invested in the code, the clear object of their demeanor is to discourage strangers from even thinking about testing their manhood. And the sense of power that attends the ability to deter others can be alluring even to those who know the code without being heavily invested in it – the decent inner-city youths. Thus a boy who has been leading a basically decent life can, in trying circumstances, suddenly resort to deadly force.

Central to the issue of manhood is the widespread belief that one of the most effective ways of gaining respect is to manifest "nerve." Nerve is shown when one takes another person's possessions (the more valuable the better), "messes with" someone's woman, throws the first punch, "gets in someone's face," or pulls a trigger. Its proper display helps on the spot to check others who would violate one's person and also helps to build a reputation that works to prevent future challenges. But since such a show of nerve is a forceful expression of disrespect toward the person on the receiving end, the victim may be greatly offended and seek to retaliate with equal or greater force. A display of nerve, therefore, can easily provoke a life-threatening response, and the background knowledge of that possibility has often been incorporated into the concept of nerve.

True nerve exposes a lack of fear of dying. Many feel that it is acceptable to risk dying over the principle of respect. In fact, among the hard-core street-oriented, the clear risk of violent death may be preferable to being "dissed" by another. The youths who have internalized this attitude and convincingly display it in their public bearing are among the most threatening people of all, for it is commonly assumed that they fear no man. As the people of the community say, "They are the baddest dudes on the street." They often lead an existential life that may acquire meaning only when they are faced with the possibility of imminent death. Not to be afraid to die is by implication to have few compunctions about taking another's life. Not to be afraid to die is the quid pro quo of being able to take somebody else's life – for the right reasons, if the situation demands it. When others believe this is one's position, it gives one a real sense of power on the streets. Such credibility is what many inner-city youths strive to achieve, whether they are decent or street-oriented, both because of its practical defensive value and because of the positive way it makes them feel about themselves. The difference between the decent and the street-oriented youth is often that the decent youth makes a conscious decision to appear tough and manly; in another setting – with teachers, say, or at his part-time job – he can be polite and deferential. The street-oriented youth, on the other hand, has made the concept of manhood a part of his very identity; he has difficulty manipulating it – it often controls him.

GIRLS AND BOYS

Increasingly, teenage girls are mimicking the boys and trying to have their own version of "manhood." Their goal is the same – to get respect, to be recognized as capable of setting or maintaining a certain standard. They try to achieve this end in the ways that have been established by the boys, including posturing, abusive language, and the use of violence to resolve disputes, but the issues for the girls are different. Although conflicts over turf and status exist among the girls, the majority of disputes seem rooted in assessments of beauty (which girl in a group is "the cutest"), competition over boyfriends, and attempts to regulate other people's knowledge of and opinions about a girl's behavior or that of someone close to her, especially her mother.

A major cause of conflicts among girls is "he say, she say." This practice begins in the early school years and continues through high school. It occurs when "people," particularly girls, talk about others, thus putting their "business in the streets." Usually one girl will say something negative about another in the group, most often behind the person's back. The remark will then get back to the person talked about. She may retaliate or her friends may feel required to "take up for" her. In essence this is a form of group gossiping in which individuals are negatively assessed and evaluated. As with much gossip, the things said may or may not be true, but the point is that such imputations can cast aspersions on a person's good name. The accused is required to defend herself against the slander, which can result in arguments and fights, often over little of real substance. Here again is the problem of low self-esteem, which encourages youngsters to be highly sensitive to slights and to be vulnerable to feeling easily "dissed." To avenge the dissing, a fight is usually necessary.

Because boys are believed to control violence, girls tend to defer to them in situations of conflict. Often if a girl is attacked or feels slighted, she will get a brother, uncle, or cousin to do her fighting for her. Increasingly, however, girls are doing their own fighting and are even asking their male relatives to teach them how to fight. Some girls form groups that attack other girls or take things from them. A hard-core segment of inner-city girls inclined toward violence seems to be developing. As one thirteen-year-old girl in a detention center for youths who have committed violent acts told me, "To get people to leave you alone, you gotta fight. Talking don't always get you out of stuff." One major difference between girls and boys: girls rarely use guns. Their fights are therefore not life-or-death struggles. Girls are not often willing to put their lives on the line for "manhood." The ultimate form of respect on the male-dominated inner-city street is thus reserved for men.

Chapter 26

Dario Melossi

OVERCOMING THE CRISIS IN CRITICAL CRIMINOLOGY

Toward a grounded labeling theory

From: Dario Melossi (1985), 'Overcoming the crisis in critical criminology',
Criminology 23(2): 193–208.

[. . .]

WHAT HAS BEEN CALLED a "new," "critical," "radical," or "Marxist" criminology is often said to be in a state of crisis (Inciardi, 1980). In a period characterized by a rather sharp shift to the political right, the attacks on this type of criminology are quite understandable. They correspond with the pendulum-like political movement which characterizes issues of law and order and crime and punishment (Melossi, 1985). But if the alleged crisis of critical criminology is something more than a polemical ploy by its political and academic adversaries, then the roots of this situation should be sought within the development of critical criminology itself.

The thesis presented here is that there is indeed a crisis in critical criminology, and that it derives from intellectual stasis and powerlessness vis à vis criminal policies increasingly inspired by right-wing ideological positions. Thus, the *impasse* is fundamentally theoretical, not political.

This situation of theoretical crisis can be identified with a question such as the following: "Has critical criminology really gone beyond the labeling approach's formulations of about 20 years ago?" The beginning of these formulations actually took place in a much earlier period and can be found in developments coming from a Meadian social psychology. First presented by Tannenbaum (1938: 19–20), the notion that societal reaction to primary deviation leads to a more socially significant "secondary deviation" was systematically developed by Lemert (1951) with reference to diverse phenomena such as physical disabilities, political and sexual deviance, crime, alcoholism, and mental illness. A concept of "active" social control, alternative to the homeostatic concept of social control developed by Parsons but very much in line with Mead's idea of social control (1925, reprinted 1964), was identified by Lemert (1942) as actually producing deviance instead of eliminating it. It was this pristine conception which in the early 1960s was developed into what came to be called the labeling perspective on deviance. The leaders were sociologists such as Kitsuse (1962), Cicourel (Kitsuse and Cicourel, 1963), Goffman (1963), Scheff (1963), and Becker (1963). Among these, Becker's was probably the most straightforward and programmatic formulation of the labeling perspective. Becker's version of the labeling approach became indeed the most popular, so much so that he had the honor to be singled out as the primary target of a stinging attack by Gouldner, an attack which became "classical" and the paradigm of subsequent critical/radical/Marxist critiques of the labeling perspective (Gouldner, 1968).

ONCE UPON A TIME THERE WAS A "NEW" CRIMINOLOGY

The Becker–Gouldner exchange loomed large in a book that was published 12 years ago and that is probably the most famous in the still young critical criminological tradition – *The New Criminology* by Taylor, Walton, and Young (1973). This book played a pivotal role in making the American sociology of deviance known to the world and in turning some of its formulations toward Marxism. We shall see, further, that Taylor, Walton, and Young gave the sociology of deviance a twist which made it able to converge intellectually with a rising Marxist "critique of the law" which was developing else-where in Europe and was then reimported into the United States under a different, if somewhat similar, label.

The American sociology of deviance of the 1960s had its roots in two currents of thought. The most important of these was the so-called Chicago School of sociology; the other, complementary, root was the American tradition in sociologically-oriented jurisprudence. The Chicago School, for instance, inspired Sutherland's rejection of the "multifactorial" kinds of explanation of criminal behavior, and his option for a social learning theory in which the actors' "vocabularies of motive" – as Mills was to define them in 1940 – represented the central exogenous variable (Mills, 1963). The step from a social learning theory of criminal behavior to a labeling theory of criminal identity constituted a rather logical progression. Indeed, both kinds of theory relied on that interactionist philosophy which represented the most interesting and lasting heritage of the Chicago School of sociology. The step could easily be taken by anyone who assumed a disenchanted or skeptical attitude toward the legal definition of crime and the activities of the agencies of social control. . . . In the sociology of deviance, it was reinforced by convergence with the realist tradition in jurisprudence. For example, when Chambliss wrote of criminologists turning in the early 1960s from observation of the behavior of "criminals" to that of police, judges, and politicians, and called this process the study of "law in action" (1978: 14), he was not doing anything but expressing the 30- or 40-year-old punch line of the "legal realists." [. . .]

The cultural revolution of the 1960s furnished the new-born sociology of deviance with an extremely favorable environment in which to grow and also with a cross-cultural framework which allowed its diffusion from North America to western Europe and Latin America. . . . The politics of the early years of the British "National Deviance Conference" were nevertheless similar to the original American inspiration. Thus, they showed more sensitivity to an "underdog" perspective than to a "working class" perspective and tended to stress a certain anarchist skepticism rather than a positive political commitment (Cohen, 1974: 25).

But with the onset of more radical and/or more Marxist political and intellectual positions toward the end of the 1960s and the early 1970s, both in the United States and western Europe, a critical/radical criminology developed. It began moving away from the parental figure of the labeling perspective and toward what was called a "Marxist theory of crime and punishment." This was to be the self-assigned task of *The New Criminology*: to settle the issue with the "old" criminology, especially with those interactionist theories which constituted the most recent chapter of that history, and to open the door on the new, undiscovered continent of a Marxist or "materialist" theory of deviance. The book did not, then, properly speaking, present a *new* criminology. Its main contribution was a critique of existing or previous criminological theories, not the presentation of a new theory. . . . If in fact Taylor, Walton, and Young's work was successful in criticizing the criminological positions derived from the legalist and psychiatric presuppositions of the "Classical" and "Positive" schools, it was far less so with respect to sociological criminology.

This is particularly true where *The New Criminology* tried to come to terms with the interactionist positions, from Chicago to labeling theory. . . . This procedure became rather problematic when Taylor, Walton, and Young dealt with the most recent criminological theories, the interactionist ones, because, as a matter of fact, a chronologically following viewpoint from which to criticize them had not yet emerged in sociology. Furthermore, Taylor, Walton, and Young were trying to lay the foundations for a neo-Marxist theory of crime and punishment, but such a theory could only be a product of their critique, not its inspiration.

This is where Gouldner's 1968 article was lowered as a god by the neo-criminological machine (Taylor, Walton, and Young, 1973: 166–171). In turn Taylor, Walton, and Young certified Gouldner's positions. Ever since, the standard "Marxist" critique of the labeling, interactionist and ethnomethodological approaches has been mainly an amplification of Gouldner's criticism. Thereinafter, Gouldner's and/or Taylor, Walton, and Young's critiques will be repeated in a number of European analyses aspiring to critical criminology (Werkentin, Hofferbert, and Baurmann, 1974; Pitch, 1975; Baratta, 1982).

Taylor, Walton, and Young enriched Gouldner's analysis, to be sure. Still, the core of their criticism was represented by Gouldner's fortunate label of a "zookeeping" sociology whose proponents romantically stared at the deviant without really taking sides, theoretically or practically, for the liberation of the ones labeled deviants (Gouldner, 1968: 106–111). [. . .]

Gouldner brilliantly observed a relationship between the ideas of the labeling theorists and the policies of a federal administration which, in the 1960s, was heavily committed to the practice and ideology of welfare. This analysis was not gratuitous, as some have claimed. In retrospect, it can be seen as very foretelling in a society where the structural level of unemployment moved up to 7% of the labor force. Just as Chicago sociologists of the 1920s and 1930s wanted to integrate deviants in the American values of work, family, and the political process, so too, according to Gouldner, the neo-Chicagoans of the 1960s demanded respect for deviants whose only place could be the ghetto, since integration – in an economy whose employment rates in the private sector were rapidly shrinking – was no longer possible (Melossi, 1980: 321–356). [. . .]

LABELING, IDEOLOGY, AND PRACTICE

All this is well and good, but still it can be argued that the most important aspect of labeling theory was really not the fascination with the underdog, or with an abstentionist criminal policy, but its application of the interactionist model to the definition of deviance and crime. By noting that Becker had not paid any attention to the role of "institutions" and "power elites," Gouldner raised the crucial theoretical point but then let it slide (Gouldner, 1968: 111). Taylor, Walton, and Young, on the other hand, criticized labeling theory for not having been able to identify the socio-structural conditioning of the "power to define" (1973: 166–170). [. . .]

Labeling theories are thus criticized because they only point to the study of "mere" linguistic constructs, the labels, and hence fail to analyze a noumenon-like "outside world." The problem is that such a critical standpoint is predicated upon a dualist opposition of the I and the world, of thinking subject and thought world. Such dualism, however, had been the very target of the pragmatist philosophy which was at the roots of the interactionist perspective in sociology. [. . .]

It is then to the discussion of the roots of the interactionist tradition that we must return, namely to the thought of Mead. Mead attempted to provide a description of human behavior in a way that avoided the traditional dualism of the Western intellectual tradition between an internal reflecting Mind and an external reflected World. The symbolic system we usually call "mind" was seen by Mead as an outcome of a process of communication in which the selves of individuals are interactionally shaped within society. It is hard to conceive of a less "idealistically" oriented enterprise than this. [. . .]

According to Mead, "The process of communication is one which is more universal than that of the universal religion or universal economic process in that it is one that serves them both." But "back even of the process of discourse must lie cooperative activity" (Mead, 1934: 259). The Thomasian "definition of the situation," then, was for Mead clearly and inextricably connected with the cooperative social process which presides over the production and reproduction of human life. The set of meanings we call language is a product of this overall process, which is in turn possible only through communication. From this perspective, to name or define something is never merely an "idealistic" procedure. It is instead a consequence of an act. In a typically pragmatist fashion, a name, definition, or label designates something which is the product of a successful conversation of gestures. Instead of drawing our attention away from the world of practice, Mead obliges us to look into this world in order to find our "discourses."

It is certainly true that Mead's theory was – like all great theoretical formulations – only a beginning. His scanty development of the role of the "generalized other," for instance, leaves what is probably the most properly sociological issue quite open. The possibilities of a plurality of meanings and of social innovation must be related to the connection between the hierarchical order of social authorities and the emotional value of an interaction in the process of fixation of meanings. This is a path on which Mead did not travel very far, but that is open to fruitful investigation.

In some of his early writings, Mills attempted a more macrosociological interpretation of Mead's theory. Mills was able to read Mead in a politically relevant way because of his critical appraisal of the pragmatists' experience (Mills, 1941, reprinted 1963) and because of his familiarity with Weber's work (Mills, 1963: 442–443). The most crucial connections between language and social control had already been spelled out by Mead himself (see 1934 and 1964), but Mills's important addition was his emphasis on the concept of a plurality of "audiences" which compete for a successful definition of meanings: "The control of others is not usually direct but rather through manipulations of a field of objects" (Mills, 1963: 445; "objects" must be read here in the Meadian sense). These audiences respond to specific "vocabularies of motive" which are grounded in "sets of collective action" (Mills, 1963: 433). They are treated as a plurality of reference groups by Shibutani (1962), who connected Mead's social psychology to Simmel's concept of social organization according to which individual discursive perspectives depend on the unique combination of social circles in which the person participates (Simmel, 1908, reprinted 1955).

In criminology, Sutherland's "differential association theory" tackled the issue of the emotional value of an interaction by specifying several "modalities of association," and his theory of "differential social organization" developed the idea of a plurality of generalized others (Sutherland, 1947, reprinted 1973). In discussions of the psychology of embezzlers and of so-called "compulsive crimes," Cressey then related Sutherland's theory of differential association to Mill's vocabularies of motive (Cressey, 1953: 93–138; 1954). A more general specification of the ways in which motivational orientations account for delinquent behavior was then given by Sykes and Matza in their discussion of "techniques of neutralization" (1957).

The theoretical problem which seems to be a good candidate for the reason there is a theoretical crisis in critical criminology, then, is the same one implicit in the works of Gouldner and Taylor, Walton, and Young – the problem of the relation between the interactionist model described above and a Marxist model centered in the "ideology" concept. Mills, for instance, was aware of a possible confrontation with Marxism:

> Marxists have not translated their connective terms into sound and unambiguous psychological categories. . . . What is needed is a concept of mind which incorporates social processes as intrinsic to mental operations
>
> (1963: 425)

This concept was to be found, according to Mills, in Meadian psychology. The "mentalistic assumption" that both Mead and Mills saw as a fatal flaw in most of the social psychologies of their times seems to be present in Marx's architectural metaphor of structure/superstructure (Marx and Engels, 1976: 35–37; Marx, 1970). But in *Capital* the categories of political economy are not a mere reflection of reality. They are instead the language of a specific mode of production or, better, of a specific stage of such mode of production. Mills could see that " 'the profit motive' of classical economics may be treated as an ideal-typical vocabulary of motives for delimited economic situations and behaviors" (Mills, 1963: 445, note). The only limits of this language are those determined by the set of collective action within which such language is used.

The critique of ideology and the critique of political economy in *Capital* are the language of a new set of collective action which is, in Marx's terms, industrial capitalism and the creation of a modern working class. The potential members of this class make up the audience for that redefinition of discourse which is the practical work of Marxism and of the organizations which are the vehicles of this new discourse. Such relations, between the sets of collective action and their discourses, between language and the practice within which language is shaped, can be pinned down empirically. For example, they can be shown in the "hunger for new words" of the early attempts at organizing among the working class. They can be shown in the reciprocal adjustments of working masses and intellectuals, class and organizations, followers and leaders. They can be shown in the substitution of a socialistic vocabulary for an earlier religious one during periods of intense social transformation. [. . .]

The critique of ideology cannot possibly be seen, then, as the task of the enlightened theoretician. It is an empirical work, "a sociological work in itself," as Smith puts it. It is the work of deconstructing the ways in which the meanings of events are fixed within the activities of scientific and administrative bureaucracies. [. . .]

TOWARD A GROUNDED LABELING THEORY

To define the kind of sociological work done in studies about "labels" or about participants' accounts in organizations as "idealistic" would be tantamount to defining the very development of contemporary society as idealistic. A "Marxism" which would try to ignore this kind of research would, in the best of cases, be interested in telling its story about the capitalism of 150 years ago and in the worst would represent a variant of some form of economism. By "economism" I mean a specification of a structuralist view that reifies connections between structural variables without questioning the motives and orientations of the actors involved (Maynard and Wilson, 1980). In the early critical criminological literature, such a process of reification consisted essentially in coupling an economic determination of criminal behavior with an acceptance of the legal syllogism which explains punishment with crime. Thus, criminal behavior was seen as individual responses to situations of economic deprivation, and punishment was conceived as the capitalist state's attempt at controlling and repressing such responses (Melossi, 1985).

But after *The New Criminology*, and especially after the second book published by Taylor, Walton, and Young, *Critical Criminology* (1975), the positions *anarchisant* which romanticized crime as a form of individual, pre-political response to oppression, have been criticized very harshly within the ranks of critical criminologists themselves (Young, 1975; Platt, 1978; Baratta, 1982). This more skeptical and critical view of criminal behavior has brought about a positive re-evaluation of the social control function. But in a situation where the societal processes of social control had not been sufficiently investigated theoretically – or had been investigated by that labeling theory that radical criminology pragmatically excluded – a re-evaluation of social control has often meant nothing more than a cosmetic reappraisal of the traditional legal model. Thus, critical and/or Marxist positions in criminology, pressed by political urgency, seem nowadays to be engaged in presenting a left-wing, no-nonsense rhetoric in opposition to the rhetoric of the right. The problem, I submit, is not on which side of the rhetoric we are on. The problem is to further the sociological investigation of the issues at stake and to bracket, at least for the time being, suggestions of criminal policy which are substantially based on an acceptance of the traditional juridical view.

Most of the contemporary liberal or radical attempts at playing the role of the advisor to a (hoped-for) Prince – including those of Platt (1982), Taylor (1981), Lea and Young (1984), and of most of the participants in a debate organized a few years ago by the Italian journal *La Questione Criminale* (1981) – seem to assume that by working with the traditional, but reformed, toolbox of lawmaking, policing, doing justice, and applying some sort of penal sanction, predictable effects on crime and deviance can actually be produced. In order to express this confidence, most of these attempts have, in the tradition of liberalism, taken it for granted that a sociological explanation of "crime," "deviance," and "punishment" already exists and that such explanation is grounded in the traditional modeling of the relationships between the economic conditions of a society, its crime rates, and its punishment rates. Such an explanation is sought, with minor adjustments, in the traditional utilitarian model: economic determinism plus the legal syllogism (Melossi, 1985). In short, the classical, now become neo-classical, tale told by economics and the law.

One is caught by the doubt, therefore, that the Marxist critique of the labeling perspective, which more than ten years ago marked the starting point of a critical criminology, did not constitute much of a step forward. Instead, this critique constituted a classical case of the baby being thrown out with the bath water. By criticizing the lack of practical roots of the labeling approach, a critique which often overlooked the original practical dimension of Mead's formulations, Marxist critique went back to an economistic perspective which saw social actors as utilitarian dopes. This constitutes a fundamental misunderstanding of Marxian theory, because Marx saw his theory as the theory of an *agency*, the working class, engaged in a practical critique of political economy (as the subtitle of *Capital* in fact spells out). Such a non-economistic reading of Marx's work, to which reference is made above and which is not possible to investigate further in this paper, makes it compatible with contributions coming from other intellectual inspirations (for some first tentative attempts in this direction, see Smith, 1976; Maynard and Wilson, 1980; Melossi, 1985). [. . .]

If, as Baratta writes, a critical criminology is characterized by the conjunction of a "dimension of the definition" and a "dimension of power" (1981: 362–363), then what is needed is not a scholastic rejection of the tradition which links the beginnings of the Chicago school of contemporary interactionist theories. What is needed is a process of trial and error, within the practice of research, where concepts deriving from both the interactionist and the Marxist traditions are set free to play their role and to prove themselves or not.

In this encounter, the objective of critical criminology should be to ground the vocabularies of motive on crime and punishment in those sets of collective action within which they are situated. This would amount to putting into practice what might be called a *grounded labeling theory*, that is, a theory of the social discourse about deviance and crime grounded within the social discourse about the economy and the polity. Such theory must have its roots in the principle that social action cannot be made intelligible if it is not set within the specific orientation of the actor, an orientation which can be seen as expressed linguistically in a "vocabulary of motives." This set of linguistic constructs is situated in a sociohistorical context and represents the mediation, so to speak, between society, or a social group, and the individual self. [. . .]

References

Baratta, Alessandro, 1981, Criminologia critica e riforma penale. Osservazioni conclusive sul dibattito 'Il codice Rocco cinquant'anni dopo'e risposta a Marinucci. La Questione Criminale 7: 349–389.

―― 1982, Ciminologia critica e criticia del diritto penale. Bologna: Il mulino.

Becker, Howard S. (ed.), 1963, Outsiders. New York: Free Press.

―― 1971, Culture and Civility in San Francisco. Chicago: Aldine.

Goffman, Erving, 1963, Stigma: Notes on the Management of Spoiled Identity. Englewood Cliffs, NJ: Prentice-Hall.

Gouldner, Alvin W., 1968, The sociologist as partisan: Sociology and the welfare state. The American Sociologist 3: 103–116.

Habermas, Jürgen, 1981, Theorie des Kommunikativen Handelns. Frankfurt: Suhrkamp. Published in English translation as The Theory of Communicative Action. Boston: Beacon. Vol. I, 1983; Vol. II in press.

Joas, Hans, 1981, George Herbert Mead and the 'division of labor': Macrosociological implications of Mead's social psychology. Symbolic Interaction 4: 177–190.

——— 1985, G. H. Mead: A Contemporary Reexamination of His Thought. Cambridge, England: Polity Press.

Kitsuse, John I., 1962, Societal reaction to deviant behavior: Problems of theory and method. Social Problems 9: 247–256.

Kitsuse, John I. and Aaron V. Cicourel, 1963, A note on the uses of official statistics. Social Problems 11: 131–139.

La Questione Criminale, 1981, Dibattito su: Il codice Rocco cinquant'anni dopo. La questione criminale 7: 3–168, 247–322, 349–389, 435–441.

Lea, John and Jock Young, 1984, What Is To Be Done About Law and Order? Harmondsworth, England: Penguin Books.

Lemert, Edwin M., 1951, Social Pathology. A Systematic Approach to the Theory of Sociopathic Behavior. New York: McGraw-Hill.

Marx, Karl, 1970, Preface to A Contribution to the Critique of Political Economy. New York: International Publishers.

Marx, Karl and Frederick Engels, 1976, The German Ideology. In Karl Marx and Frederick Engels, Collected Works. New York: International Publishers.

Maynard, Douglas W. and Thomas P. Wilson, 1980, On the reification of social structure. Current Perspectives in Social Theory 1: 287–322.

Mead, George H., 1934, Mind, Self, and Society. Chicago: University of Chicago Press.

——— 1964, The Genesis of the Self and Social Control. In George H. Mead, Selected Writings. Indianapolis: Bobbs-Merrill.

Melossi, Dario, 1976, The penal question in 'Capital.' Crime and Social Justice 5: 26–33.

——— 1985, Punishment and social action: Changing vocabularies of punitive motive within a political business cycle. Current Perspectives in Social Theory 6: 169–197.

Melossi, Dario and Massimo Pavarini, 1979, The Prison and the Factory: Origins of the Penitentiary System. London: Macmillan.

Mills, C. Wright, 1963, Power, Politics and People. New York: Oxford University.

Platt, Anthony M., 1978, Street crime: A view from the left. Crime and Social Justice 9: 26–48.

——— 1982, Crime and punishment in the United States: Immediate and long-term reforms from a Marxist perspective. Crime and Social Justice 18: 38–45.

Scheff, Thomas J., 1963, The social role of the mentally ill and the dynamics of mental disorder: A research framework. Sociometry 26: 436–453.

Shibutani, Tamotsu, 1962, Reference groups and social control. In Arnold M. Rose (ed.), Human Behavior and Social Processes. Boston: Houghton Mifflin.

Smith, Dorothy E., 1976, The ideological practice of sociology. Catalyst 8: 39–54.

Sutherland, Edwin H., 1973, A statement of the theory. In Edwin H. Sutherland (ed.), On Analyzing Crime. Chicago: University of Chicago.

Tannenbaum, Frank, 1938, Crime and the Community. New York: Ginn.

Taylor, Ian, 1981, Law and Order: Arguments for Socialism. London: Macmillan.

Taylor, Ian, Paul Walton, and Jock Young, 1973, The New Criminology. London: Routledge and Kegan Paul.

—— 1975 (eds.), Critical Criminology. London: Routledge and Kegan Paul.

Werkentin, Falco, Michael Hofferbert, and Michael Baurmann, 1974, Criminology as police science or: How old is the new criminology? Crime and Social Justice 2.

Young, Jock, 1975, Working-class criminology. In Taylor, Walton, and Young (eds.), Critical Criminology. London: Routledge and Kegan Paul.

Chapter 27

Loraine Gelsthorpe

FEMINISM AND CRIMINOLOGY

From: Loraine Gelsthorpe (2002), 'Feminism and criminology', in Mike Maguire, et al. (eds), *Oxford Handbook of Criminology*, 3nd edn, Oxford University Press, pp. 112–143.

INTRODUCTION

FEMINISTS ENGAGING WITH CRIMINOLOGY in the twenty-first century might be forgiven for looking back with a certain envy at the diversity of the projects outlined by their predecessors. These predecessors set out to question some of the gender-blind assumptions within criminology and to create a space for women's voices and experiences. It might be supposed that today there are few silences left to articulate and that the 'classic masculine discourse' of criminology (Collier 1998) has been well and truly (if paradoxically) 'penetrated' by feminism. This is not the case. Doubts are still expressed in conference halls, institutional corridors and class rooms (if not in academic papers) as to whether there *is* such a thing as feminist criminology, let alone its present, past, and future. But reports of its death or non-existence have been greatly exaggerated. The chief aim of this chapter is to alert readers to key precepts and issues which are relevant to an understanding of the importance of feminist contributions to criminology, and to reflect on their overall relationship.

This chapter thus offers an overview of the critical insights provided or prompted by feminism which might be said to have transgressed both the theory and politics of research and action in criminology. But, first, what is meant by 'feminism and criminology'? In 1988, Allison Morris and I attempted to describe something of the relationship between feminism and criminology by reviewing early feminist achievements to address criminologists' 'amnesia' of women, and by giving something of an overview of the impact or potential impact of feminism on the broad parameters of criminology (Gelsthorpe and Morris 1988). But we recorded then, as I reiterate now, that any discussion of the relationship between feminism and criminology would need to recognize complexities in the relationship. For there is no *one* feminism and no *one* criminology. Despite some serious doubts as to whether a single feminist criminology could exist because it could not do justice to the differences and tensions that exist within the field, we acknowledged, however, that it was still possible to talk of feminist criminologies or, better still, of feminist perspectives in criminology.

Yet it is important to speak of different feminist perspectives, and of different criminologies. The chapters in this text provide ample evidence of this. There is no one relationship, but a myriad of relationships between feminism and criminology. Moreover, the criminology of the 1970s, which prompted Carol Smart's 1976 critical text *Women, Crime and Criminology*, one of the first openly feminist critiques of criminology in Britain, is not the criminology of today. The criminology of today seems much more diverse. Whether it is sufficiently diverse or open enough to accommodate some of the critical precepts of feminisms remains a matter for debate. There are feminists who have made a strong case for abandoning criminology (Smart 1990), or who, because of resistance to a feminist transformation of the discipline of criminology, see fundamental incompatibilities between feminism and criminology (Stanko 1993; A. Young 1994). In a percipient conclusion to her 1976 text, Smart commented:

> Criminology and the sociology of deviance must become more than the study of men and crime if it is to play any significant part in the development of our understanding of crime, law and the criminal process and play any role in the transformation of existing social practices.
>
> (Smart 1976: 185)

Her concern was that criminology, even in its more radical form, would be 'unmoved' by feminist critiques. By 1990, she viewed criminology as the 'atavistic man' in intellectual endeavours and wished to abandon it because she could not see what it had to offer feminism. But whereas the abandonment of criminology once seemed a logical response to criminological intransigence, there is arguably good reason to pause before pursuing this option given recent signs of critical thinking in criminology.

There have been several serious explorations of the relationship between feminism and criminology over the years (Daly and Chesney-Lind 1988; Gelsthorpe and Morris 1990; Morris and Gelsthorpe 1991; Heidensohn 1997; A. Young 1994; Rafter and Heidensohn 1995; and Naffine 1995, 1997). A key question which has perplexed some of these writers is whether key substantive and political and epistemological and methodological projects make what might be described as the 'criminological project' untenable in and of itself (see also Heidensohn, 1996). So, what is it about feminist work that might make criminological work untenable?

When we speak of feminism, we are not speaking of something which is obvious or can be taken for granted (Delmar 1986). In a powerful exposition of feminist thinking, Rosemarie Tong (1989) illuminates some of the key differences among feminist perspectives. While her catalogue of feminisms and history of feminist thought is not the only one that might be produced (see Oakley 1981; Evans 1995, for example), Tong (1989) identifies and elaborates six main kinds of feminism: liberal feminism . . . marxist feminism . . . socialist feminism . . . existential feminism . . . psychoanalytical feminism . . . and postmodern feminism. [. . .]

To these types of feminism I would add *Black feminist thought*, which consists of ideas produced by Black women that clarify a standpoint of and for Black women. It is assumed that Black women possess a unique standpoint on, and experiences of, historical and material conditions (Lorde 1984; Hill-Collins 2002). It is further claimed that Black women's experiences uniquely provide an 'outsider-within' perspective on self, family, and society which in turn serves to establish a distinctive standpoint vis-à-vis sociology's paradigmatic facts and theories.

It is also important to acknowledge the notion of 'global' feminisms, by which we must recognize similarities and differences between feminisms in the West, East, North, and South, and the differential attention given to class, racial, ethnic, and imperial tensions in different economic, technological, sexual, reproductive, ecological, and political contexts (Bulbeck 1998; Smith 2000). This is particularly important if we wish to understand something of international feminist perspectives in criminology and accommodate difference and diversity away from westernized concepts of crime and justice.

There are many sophisticated explorations of the different feminist positions, detailed examination of which lies beyond the scope of this chapter (see Carrington 1994; Evans 1995; Daly 1997; and Jackson and Scott 2002). These different positions collectively illustrate men's material interest in the domination of women and the different ways in which men construct a variety of institutional arrangements to sustain this domination. Feminists argue the case for the economy to be fully transformed and aim to 'make visible the invisible' by bringing into focus the gender structure of society (Rowbotham 1973; Mitchell 1984; Mitchell and Oakley 1986; Humm 1992, 1995). Feminists have challenged the political, ontological, and epistemological assumptions that underlie patriarchal discourses as well as their theoretical contents. They have developed both an anti-sexist stance, and a stance which involves the construction of alternative models, methods, procedures, discourses, and so on. Put simply, feminists have a normative commitment to revealing, and attempting to negate, the subordination of women by men.

Such summaries do not do justice to the concepts and theories involved in feminisms, but they do illustrate some of the key challenges to criminology. There are crucial theoretical, conceptual, and methodological distinctions within these feminist perspectives, and such ideas are not mutually exclusive (see, for example, Hirsch and Keller 1990); different theorists subscribe to different strands of thought within each group of theories. Equally, the various feminisms are not always rigorously discrete. But from the summaries it is possible to see how feminist challenges to criminology have been informed in a multiplicity of ways. I will elaborate some of these challenges later in the chapter.

THE INTELLECTUAL INHERITANCE OF CRIMINOLOGY

What does the intellectual endeavour involved in these feminisms mean for criminology? Much of criminology is . . . testament to the dominant intellectual history of . . . the discipline, though it has been the subject of much debate and critique . . . too (Rock 1988, 1994; Cohen 1988; Garland 1992, 1994; J. Young 1994; Naffine 1997, for example). What is beyond dispute, however, is that criminology was traditionally conceived as the scientific study of the causes of crime, and the 'scientific endeavour' involving 'methods, techniques or rules of procedure', more than substantive theory or perspective (Gottfredson and Hirschi 1987: 10), is possibly 'healthier and more self-assured' than hitherto (ibid.: 18). The strident belief in an objective, external reality capable of measurement, and a fascination with causal and correlational factors – whether they be situational opportunities, low self-control, or relative deprivation – is reflected in the pages of new and old textbooks alike.

The essentials are that mainstream criminology has been dominated by a persistent commitment to what Garland (2002) . . . describes as 'the Lombrosian project' and 'the governmental project'. By the former he means a form of inquiry 'which aims to develop an etiological, explanatory science, based on the premise that criminals can somehow be scientifically differentiated from non-criminals' – essentially a 'science of causes'. The 'governmental project' involves a long series of empirical inquiries which 'have sought to enhance the efficient and equitable administration of justice by charting the patterns of crime and monitoring the practice of police and prisons' – essentially what might be described as 'conservative administrative criminology'. In examining developments in criminology, Naffine (1997) describes how the logic of conventional 'scientific criminology' looms large and presses on through the 1980s, 1990s, and into the 2000s.

There have been important intellectual/sociological starts along the way. Sociological insights are evident in the history of the sociology of crime and deviance, though women and 'gender' are absent from analyses (Millman 1975; Smart 1976; Scraton 1990). Picking on one particular 'progressive' criminology as an example, the *New Criminology* (Taylor, Walton, and Young 1973) attempted to eschew the scientific orthodoxy and instead illustrate how crime was socially constructed through the capacity of state institutions to define and confer criminality on others. But the authors do this in an 'ungendered' way (Sumner 1994; Naffine 1997). In this progressive conception of events, crime is not simply an act, but a reflection of a political process. The new criminologists took note of the new deviancy theorists' work on social reaction (see, for example, Becker 1963), seeing the application of a label of deviance as part of a broader context of social, political, economic, and cultural relations. In developing an agenda for a social theory of deviance, they connected the established influences of social interaction with a Marxist perspective which prioritized structural relations. But there was a neglect of gender in their analysis.

Another example concerns Left Realist theoretical propositions (J. Young 1994) which have given attention to the social and political context of crime and crime control and, importantly, to victims. There is 'essentialism' in the thinking (see Brown and Hogg 1992; Carlen 1992, for example) because of the partial or misconceived recognition of gender (women's fear of crime is recognized, but not in a direct way, for women's fear of crime is generally women's fear of men). Left Realism's analytical framework looks at the links between social order and social justice, and its critical stance involves the development of a whole raft of interventionist policies to deal with the realities of crime (including the experiences of victims). But this is inadequate when it comes to women's experiences. Overall, Left Realists do no more than offer a sophisticated version of a scientific paradigm – a paradigm which is largely ungendered.

Foucauldian insights in criminology have also been of crucial importance – this time in directing attention to power and knowledge and to the discursive practices of control. However, as Sumner (1990), for one, has pointed out, while Foucauldian thought addresses issues of discrimination, the deeper, structural condition of hegemonic masculinity is not addressed. The gendered character of disciplinary power is ignored (Diamond and Quinby 1988).

Thus, though these intellectual/sociological challenges to mainstream criminology have offered some exciting critical insights, none has been adequate in conceptualizing gender; there has been no fundamental shift in gear to address feminists' questions about criminological knowledge. Feminists' challenges to criminology have come from different directions – not always in forms that make the theoretical lineage apparent, but in ways that question the epistemological basis and methodological processes of criminology.

FEMINISM WITHIN AND WITHOUT CRIMINOLOGY: A REVIEW OF INTERCONNECTIONS BETWEEN FEMINISM AND CRIMINOLOGY

Eschewing the internecine arguments about who or what is feminist (see Delmar 1986; Morris 1987; Daly and Chesney-Lind 1988; Gelsthorpe and Morris 1988, 1990, for example; and Heidensohn, 2002), we can identify a broad range of feminist work which questions criminology:

1   an early critique of criminological theory and of criminal justice practices: that is, a substantive and political project;
2   a more discursive questioning of the epistemological and methodological contours of the discipline;
3   international feminist perspectives; and
4   theoretical work on gender leading to developments in masculinity theory.

The early critique

Drawing generally from the feminist positions outlined above, one of the first tasks was to develop a comprehensive critique of the discipline. The early critique has been well rehearsed elsewhere (see, for example, Morris 1987); suffice to say here that it has frequently focused on the two main themes of amnesia or neglect and distortion (Smart 1976; Heidensohn 1985). It is indisputable that women account for a very small proportion of all known offenders (cf. Greenwood 1981), despite recently recorded increases (Home Office 2000), and yet there has been relatively little attention given to female offenders. The neglect of women's criminality by a predominantly male profession is one of criminology's determining features. The majority of studies of crime and delinquency prior to the 1980s were of men's crime and delinquency (Leonard 1982; Scraton 1990). The discipline was dominated by men studying other men. A second theme in the critique is that, even when women were recognized, they were depicted in terms of stereotypes based on their supposed biological and psychological nature. While the 'new criminology' challenged the assumptions of positivism in explaining men's crime, it neglected to acknowledge how such assumptions remained most prevalent in academic and popular conceptions of women's crime. Similarly, while analyses of class structure, state control, and the political nature of deviance gained credibility, the study of women's crime remained rooted in notions of biological determinism and an uncritical attitude towards the dominant sexual stereotypes of women as passive, domestic, and maternal (Smart 1976; cf. Brown 1986). Tracing the continuance of sexist assumptions from Lombroso to Pollak and beyond, Smart (1976) examined how assumptions of the abnormality of female offenders came to dominate both theory and criminal justice policy – despite evidence of more critical thinking in relation to men and men's crime. Eileen Leonard usefully summarized mainstream criminological theory by stating:

> Theories that are frequently hailed as explanations of human behaviour are, in fact, discussions of male behaviour and male criminality . . . We cannot simply apply these theories to women, nor can we modify them with a brief addition or subtraction here and there.
>
> (1982: 181)

Women were ignored, or marginalized, or distorted, both in their deviancy and conformity, and the exposure of criminology as the criminology of men marked the starting point of feminists' attempts to find alternative modes of conceptualizing the social worlds of deviance and conformity, punishment and control.

The focus of this general critique, however, was limited. Some writers naively assumed that a remedy to criminological and criminal justice deficiencies could be sought by appropriating existing criminological theories and 'inserting' women: for example, by discovering girl gangs (Velimesis 1975) and considering girls in relation to subcultural theory (McRobbie 1980; Shacklady Smith 1978). Rafter and Natalizia (1981) presented the message in a different way, suggesting that 'women only' studies should strive to produce a body of information as extensive as that which existed for men.

In criminal justice practice there were strivings for 'equality' (that is, for women to be treated like men), though this early, undoubtedly unthinking and limited, liberal feminist position gradually came to be challenged by those who questioned the meaning and nature of equality (e.g., MacKinnon 1987a, 1987b; Fudge 1989; Smart 1990). Some of these feminist claims and assertions now seem naive, but the significance of the critique as a starting point for reflection and for changes in criminal justice practice should not be underestimated. Moreover, feminist contributions soon moved beyond a critique.

Dominant strands in the development of feminist perspectives in criminology have included empirical illuminations about discriminatory practices. For example, imprisoned women have been shown to be likely to experience the promotion and enforcement of a domestic role in penal regimes. Subject to petty and coercive systems of control, they are also more likely to be defined as in need of medical or psychological treatment than as simply criminal (Morris 1987; Carlen and Worrall 1987; Dobash, Dobash, and Gutteridge 1986). The treatment of women in the courts suggests that the widely assumed concept of 'chivalry' is misplaced, and that women who do not occupy the appropriate gender role may be seen by the court as 'doubly deviant' (see, for example, Edwards 1984; Eaton 1986; Gelsthorpe 1989; Gelsthorpe and Loucks 1997; Worrall 1990). New ways of conceptualizing matters – the different ways in which conformity is produced for instance – were also developed. Heidensohn (1985) concluded her review of women, crime, and criminal justice by arguing for a return to the sociology of gender and for the use of insights from other studies of women's oppression. Such a redirection helped to expose the explicit and informal controls exercised over women – in the home and at work – and, above all, focused on the rather peculiar notion of 'normal behaviour'. Smart and Smart (1978), Hutter and Williams (1981), Klein and Kress (1976), and Allen (1987), along with Cain (1989) and Howe (1994), have all made apparent the correspondences between the policing of everyday life and policing through more formal mechanisms of social control. And a large body of empirical work drew attention to the experiences of female victims of crime and to female victims' and offenders' experiences of criminal justice processes (see, for example, Stanko 1985, 1990; Dobash and Dobash 1992; Mawby and Walklate 1994; Lees 1997; Carlen 1998; Walklate 1989, 1992, 2001). Indeed, some of the focus on women and criminal justice developed from important feminist work in this area. Other writers focused on women's role in social control (Zimmer 1986; Jones 1986; Heidensohn 1989, 1992; Brown and Heidensohn 2000). Heidensohn (1992), for example, gave particular attention to gender and policing and the ways in which female police officers survive in a predominantly masculine occupation. Such themes are elaborated upon in Brown and Heidensohn (2000). (For an overview of empirical evidence, see Heidensohn (2002).)

Transforming the discipline?: Discursive questionings of the epistemological and methodological terrain of criminology

In working towards a transformed discipline, feminist perspectives in criminology have moved through stages which resemble a 'Hegelian dialectic' of thesis, antithesis, and synthesis. To translate this into the language of feminism, these stages represent a critique of masculinist criminology, a deconstruction of mainstream portrayals of crime and criminality, and, lastly, steps towards reconstructing adequate theoretical formulations. These three stages do not necessarily follow sequentially throughout the discipline; they are recursive and ongoing. However, the transformation (or need for a transformation) has been depicted in a number of different ways, which are worth repeating here as illustration of the broad body of work which has constituted feminist challenges to criminology.

Daly and Chesney-Lind (1988) raise two key questions in relation to criminological theory. First, can theories generated to describe men's or boys' offending apply to women and girls (what they call the 'generalizability problem')? Secondly, why do women commit less crime than men (what they term the 'gender ratio problem')? In other words, they express concern about *'gender'*, the implication being that theories of crime must be able to take account of both men's and women's (criminal) behaviour, and that they must also be able to highlight factors which operate differently on men and women. But more than this, they draw attention to the crucial problematization of gender in different feminist perspectives. This leads to a sophisticated notion of gender relations in which gender is seen not as a natural fact, but as 'a complex, historical, and cultural product . . . related to, but not simply derived from, biological sex difference and reproductive capacities' (ibid.: 504). Thus complex gender codes are internalized in a myriad of ways to regulate behaviour. In other words, criminologists could learn a great deal from looking at feminist insights in relation to gender. Daly and Chesney-Lind also urge criminologists to read first-hand of women's experiences rather than relying on distorted, received wisdom about women, for these accounts of experience have not only enriched feminist thought, but have also become a central part of feminist analyses and epistemological reflections. There is also encouragement for criminologists to reflect on the ethnocentricity inherent in mainstream criminological thinking: the fact that the questions posed by criminologists are generally those of white, economically privileged men. Lastly, Daly and Chesney-Lind indicate the potentialities of points of congruence between feminist perspectives and social and political theories, and consequently between feminist theories and 'alternative to mainstream' theoretical trajectories in criminology (critical and Marxist criminologies, for example).

In *Feminist Perspectives in Criminology* (Gelsthorpe and Morris 1990), it was similarly noted that creative feminist contributions to criminology go well beyond critique. The contributors to this book both illustrated the hegemonic masculinity of most criminological work and clarified the foundations for future gender-conscious work. To develop this latter point, particular attention was given to the ways in which feminist insights changed the questions relating to violence against women. Whereas conventional theorists focused on the pathological and structural aspects of violent individuals to explain their violence in particular situations, feminists attempted to explain why men *as a group* generally direct their violence towards women. Similarly, while conventional writers focused on the reasons why a woman might stay in an abusive relationship (perhaps signifying that there is something wrong with her), feminist writers asked 'what factors inhibit women's opportunity to leave violent men?'. . . .

Smart's (1990) distinctive contribution is to question whether the focus on female lawbreakers is a proper concern for feminism, and whether a feminist criminology is theoretically possible or politically desirable. She draws attention to the rich variety of feminist scholarship and contrasts it with the limited horizons of criminology. In focusing on the continuing 'marriage' of criminology to (unacknowledged) positivist paradigms and criminologists' pursuit of grand and totalizing theories, she highlights criminology's isolation from some of the major theoretical and political questions which are engaging feminist scholarship in criminology and elsewhere. Indeed, she suggests that feminist criminologists are risking something of a 'marginalized existence – marginal to both criminology and to feminism' (ibid.: 71) – because of their continued engagement with the project of modernism, within which criminology is nurtured and sustained. While feminists outside criminology are increasingly influenced by postmodern reappraisals of knowledge forms and scientific approaches to knowledge (indeed, are leading the way in such appraisals), and are questioning the notion of a universal reality (Weedon 1987; Harding 1986, 1987; Fraser and Nicholson 1988; Gunew 1990; Oakley 2000), many criminologists are perhaps stuck in the conventional mode of seeking 'the truth' through scientific, empirical endeavours – holding fast to the notion of referential finalities. Even critical criminologies such as Left Realism, she argues, are flawed because the work is anchored within positivist paradigms and displays a belief that it is still possible objectively to uncover both the causes of and solutions to 'crime'. Smart claims:

> the core enterprise of criminology is problematic, that feminist attempts to transform criminology have only succeeded in revitalising a problematic enterprise, and that, as feminist theory is increasingly engaging with and generating postmodern ideas, the relevance of criminology to feminist thought diminishes.
>
> (Smart 1990: 70)

As Smart puts it, this gives rise to questions as to whether an association with criminology is desirable:

> . . . for a long time, we have been asking 'what does feminism have to contribute to criminology (or sociology)?'. Feminism has been knocking at the door of established disciplines hoping to be let in on equal terms. These

disciplines have largely looked down their noses (metaphorically speaking) and found feminism wanting. Feminism has been required to become more objective, more substantive, more scientific, more anything before a grudging entry could be granted. . . . It might be that criminology needs feminism more than the converse.

(1990: 83–84)

I want now to give attention to the feminist epistemological and methodological project that I have foreshadowed. In the same volume (*Feminist Perspectives in Criminology*), Kelly (1990), Hudson (1995), and Gelsthorpe (1990) focus on the processes of knowledge production and reflect research experiences and research methodologies – exploring some of the challenges presented by feminism and its core principles of relating research to practice; engaging with 'the researched', recognizing their subjectivity in a non-hierarchical way; and using sensitive research methods which maximize opportunities to reflect more accurately the experiences of 'the researched'. While feminist research practices have been the focus of much debate in recent years (Clegg 1975; Stanley and Wise 1983; Roberts 1981; Cook and Fonow 1986; Cain 1986; Hammersley *et al.* 1992), myths abound. For example, the oft-quoted phrase from sociologists Stanley and Wise that feminist research must be 'on, by and for women' (1983: 17), is often misunderstood. What they actually said indicates that they are *questioning* this dictum, as have a number of feminist writers in criminology (Cain 1986; Gelsthorpe and Morris 1988; Gelsthorpe 1990; Stanko 1993). Close reading of many feminist discussions about research methods (Reinharz 1979; Roberts 1981; Bowles and Duelli Klein 1983; Gelsthorpe 1990; Oakley 1999, for example) ultimately reveals no fixed 'absolutes' beyond the need for sensitivity in the research task, for personal reflexivity – to reflect on the subjectivities of all involved – and commitment to make the research relevant to women.

There is a crucial focus on 'experience' in feminist research, but not in simplistic ways. The focus on women's 'experiences' (with democratic insistence that women should be 'allowed to speak for themselves') has been used both to make women visible and to link feminist ontology (beliefs about the nature of the world) with feminist epistemology (beliefs about what counts as appropriate knowledge). Feminist beliefs about reality, for example, revolve around the idea that reality is constituted by various sets of structural constraints which subordinate and oppress women. From this, appropriate knowledge is that which allows women to speak for themselves, rather than knowledge about men's worlds which so often presumes itself to be about women's worlds too. As Maureen Cain (1990a) puts it, strategies for the transformation of criminology involve reflexivity, de-construction and re-construction, and a clear focus on women – particularly on 'women only' studies. This is not as a corrective to traditional criminology which has excluded or marginalized women, but for 'women's unspeakable "experiences" to be captured, experienced, named and tamed' (ibid.: 9) without using men and their experiences as a yardstick against which women's experiences must be compared. Along with Smart (1990), Cain also exhorts feminists to locate themselves outside the narrow boundaries of criminology. As she reflects:

Only by starting from outside, with the social construction of gender, or with women's experiences of their total lives, or with the structure of the domestic

space, can we begin to make sense of what is going on. Feminist criminology
must now start from outside.

(1990a: 10)

Thus Cain proposes a focus on the construction of gender, on discourses which lie beyond
criminology, and on the sites which are relevant to women. The questions are about
women, she emphasizes, not about crime. This is not to suggest that men are irrelevant
to the task, far from it. Cain's claims for serious consideration of gender include men:
'We shall fall into essentialism if we exclude men from our analyses, even if we may wish
to exclude them from much of our field research' (1990a: 11). Similarly, she encourages
us to learn from the world of women's political struggle:

> We must record those forms of resistance to censure and policing which have
> been effective. This construction of an analytic dossier of women's political
> struggles, repression and resistance will have a moral function, will save us
> from continually having to reinvent the wheel, and will drive the creative
> political enterprise which has brought us this far.

(1990a: 14)

This concern to place women's experiences, viewpoints, and struggles at the centre of
projects has led to the development of what Sandra Harding (1987) has called 'feminist
standpointism': that is, a commitment to try to understand the world from the perspective
of the socially subjugated – to see things through women's eyes. [. . .]

While there are debates about the nature of women's 'shared' experience and different experiences, and about assumptions that women's realities are somehow 'more real'
or produce 'better knowledge' than those discerned from traditional methodologies
(Cain 1986), there are no fixed views. Indeed, there is increasing recognition of ontological complexities which both justifies the focus on women's direct/first-hand 'experiences' and raises questions about the usefulness of standpointism. The implication that
there is perhaps only 'one experience' or one standpoint is clearly very difficult. There
has been a strong tendency to conflate women in feminist theory; different voices (stand-
points) have sometimes assumed a false commonality, a false unity. In particular, race and
class differences have been underplayed and the relational character of identity has been
ignored. At the same time, the notion of 'feminist standpointism' has encouraged both
theoretical and personal reflexivity in relation to knowledge and the processes of knowledge production through research: this can help to overcome some of the problems of
conventional methodologies associated with mainstream criminology.

Feminist writers have reflected long and hard on the research methodologies they
employ and there are methodological preferences within feminist criminology. However,
early dismissals of anything tainted with positivism have (rightly, in my view) given way
to critical reflections on the need to use research methods appropriate to the nature of
the task (Eichler 1980; Kelly 1990; Oakley 1999). There is no longer anything to suggest
that the ideas of feminist writers in criminology are fundamentally antithetical to those
of criminologists, though the former might urge the latter in general to be more reflexive
and to question the epistemological bases of knowledge. In the wake of feminist concerns
to place women's experiences at the centre of research (often exemplified through an exclusively qualitative methodological approach), and criticisms of such feminist concerns, we

have witnessed an expansion of interest in the study of lived experience taking place within the social sciences generally. It would be hard to sustain a claim that some of the challenges to conventional research methodologies are distinctively 'feminist'. The most that might be said is that feminist writers have perhaps reflected on the issues more than conventional criminologists, and can lay claim to a concern with doing 'good' research which is not automatically and unthinkingly driven by positivist paradigms and processes.

If we characterize the first two main developments in feminist criminology as *feminist empiricism* (as evidenced in the wide-ranging criminological research on women, crime, control, and justice to counterbalance the absence of women from conventional work) and *feminist standpointism* (drawing attention to the need to place women's experience at the centre of knowledge), the third is best described as *feminist deconstructionism* (Naffine 1997) since it draws on postmodern insights. Deconstructionism involves the problematizing of language and concepts, with authors in this field coming under the influence of key writers such as Foucault (1970, 1972) and Derrida (1978, 1981), and critical understandings of the constitution of perspective. This is a theme evident in the work of Alison Young (1994) and Adrian Howe (1994).

In counterpoising feminism and criminology, Alison Young (1994) outlines the mismatching of a dominant masculinist culture reflected in criminology along with the insouciant parochialism of criminological practitioners, and the aims of feminism to consciously revindicate representations of the feminine and women by and of women themselves. She argues that postmodern insights empower the feminist critic of criminology to 'resist the master-narratives' of criminology (1994: 71). 'Criminology', she suggests, 'as pre-eminent modernist science, exists in continual suppression of Woman as unpresentable, as Other. Postmodernism, for a feminist critic, can expose this act of suppression and can work to reveal the organisation and self-representation of criminology in binary oppositions' (ibid.: 74). Giving examples of criminology's deployment of binary combinations (the 'normal' and the 'criminal', 'male' and 'female' criminals, for example, thus creating a criminological semantic rectangle), Young suggests that feminist interventions in criminology have hitherto been bound by such a rectangle, and that only a postmodern feminism can effect an escape from such constraints and analytical limitations. Naffine (1997), however, identifies the feminist problem of working both within and without existing frames of reference and the limiting preoccupation with unravelling textual meaning, leaving untouched:

> The economic, political and legal structures that help to keep . . . traditional meaning in place and make it appear natural and inevitable . . . alone it [deconstruction] is insufficient to undo the institutional systems that have been built upon, and that help to sustain, the economic and political power of men over women.
>
> (1997: 89)

Naffine's approach is to build on feminist insights thus gained to argue that we *can* challenge the constitution of meanings in criminological discourse *if* we recognize that meanings can change. In other words, instead of accepting the recalcitrance and intransigence of categories of meaning (woman, crime, rape, and so on), we should realize the 'referential, "relational" and metaphorical nature of meaning' more fully (ibid.: 98). In this way, the fixed, negative categories and tight interpretations of meaning identified through deconstructionist approaches can become fluid – changing their meaning. Naffine acknowledges that such a position bears testament to standpoint feminism (and to its ideas of conscious knowledge production from specific sites and experiences). I would add that we can see traces of Giddensian thinking . . . that social practices comprise both action and structure. Structure is not 'external' to action; it is perhaps more 'internal' to the flow of action which constitutes the practices in question. In the same way, Naffine is promoting the concept of 'agency' – stemming from standpointism – to counteract some of the claims of feminist deconstructionists, and in this way is recognizing a 'duality' in the creation of knowledge.

Thus Naffine (1997) is exploring some creative possibilities for effecting change in the epistemological assumptions that bind conventional criminology. As illustration, she looks at different ways in which understandings of the sexes (and thereby the logic of explanations) within the context of a major crime (rape) can be approached using insights of deconstructionism and feminist standpointism (1997: 98–119).

International feminist perspectives

I now consider the impact of feminist perspectives more broadly. There have been widely published debates about whether a feminist jurisprudence is possible and/or desirable in different parts of the world, for instance. Boyle (1985) in Canada, Dahl (1987) in Norway, MacKinnon (1987a) and Smart (1989) in England, Redcar (1990) in Australia, and Fineman and Thomadsen (1991) in the USA, for example, all contribute to discussions here. One of the first combined attempts to address feminist perspectives regarding criminology on an international basis, however, took place in Quebec in 1991, when Marie-Andrée Bertrand, Kathleen Daly, and Dorie Klein organized an international feminist conference on Women, Law, and Social Control (Bertrand *et al.* 1992). There have been subsequent discussions of global feminist perspectives – particularly at British Society of Criminology and American Society of Criminology conferences (in 1993 and 1994 respectively, for example). But it is Nicole Hahn Rafter's and Frances Heidensohn's (1995) edited collection of essays, *International Feminist Perspectives in Criminology*, which notably first attempted to provide an international picture of developments in feminist thinking in criminology. The contributors collectively question the extent to which the 'macho criminology' (so characterized by Meda Chesney-Lind) can become 'engendered', and they identify a number of themes which reflect feminist interests which are central to theoretical, methodological, and pedagogical developments and policy in criminology. On the positive side, such themes include a unifying focus on the gendered nature of victimhood, and the authors provide evidence of changes in understandings of rape and the abuse of children in theory, policy, and practice. On the negative side, there are stories of the continued marginalization of feminism, feminist scholars, and female students within the academy, and of an intellectual and political backlash against feminism. Individual authors identify tensions too, where feminist concerns seem marginal to broader political concerns. Through Monica Platek's (1995) poignant description of the development of feminism in Poland, we learn that women there in the early 1990s were reluctant to fight for, or take on, any 'rights' that might deplete their energies further. This debate rightly problematizes wider concerns about women's failure to enjoy equal human rights (Bahar 2000).

The authors of *International Feminist Perspectives in Criminology* do not simply celebrate feminist developments and challenges to criminology. They critically reflect on the nature and scope of the intersections between feminism and criminology. . . characterizations of criminology in different countries. There was, in the mid-1990s, a rather depressing picture of a dominant right realist and positivistic criminology in South Africa, a psycho-medical – but fortunately ineffectual – criminology in Italy, and a general sense that criminology is so often detached from central political and practical concerns relating to crime and justice. At the same time, there were pockets of hope. In Australia, for example, we learn from Alder (1995) that feminist scholars in criminology were able to work collaboratively with feminist women in government bureaucracies. In South Africa, Hansson (1995) described that by the mid-1990s there was a new receptivity to a critical criminology which, at that time, was at least partially gendered.

These developments apart, there is certainly evidence of feminist activism in a number of countries (Smith 2000). When apartheid was overthrown in South Africa in the 1990s, for example, women had hard-won political experience and diasporic connections with black activists on other continents. Prompted by warnings from the curtailed women's rights movements that followed on the heels of other national libera-tion movements' success (Mangaliso 1997), South African women were prepared to make demands and ensure their recognition as full citizens by the various parties involved in post-apartheid South Africa. The new constitution of South Africa reflects their insistent efforts. There is also much evidence of transnational feminist activity with regard to racism (Twine and Blee 2001) and legal reform with regard to offences against women (see, for example, Morris 1993; Kelly and Regan 2000). But in other regards, and especially with regard to other forms of crime and criminal justice, the activity of feminist criminologists, as such, remains somewhat unclear or, some would say, parochial. That this may reflect a contemporary detachment of criminology as a whole from such issues, is clearly no answer.

Since the Second World War, the number of people killed globally in wars of liberation or in civil, ethnic, or inter-state wars has, according to various newspaper accounts, passed the fifty million mark. Some have described a twentieth-century descent into 'barbarism' to encapsulate the incidence and ferocity of wars and ethnic conflicts (Mestrovic 1993; Hobsbawm 1994). It is estimated that these wars, and the accompanying rape and violence, have disproportionately impacted on women (Stiglmayer 1994; Nikolic-Ristanovic 1996a, 1996b; Amnesty International 1995; Turpin and Lorentzen 1996). A number of feminist writers in the past twenty-five years have turned their attention to the idea that war crimes such as rape or mass rape are an expression of the gender order or of a militarized masculinity (Enloe 1993; Mackinnon 1994; Nikolic-Ristanovic 1996a, 1996b). Other feminists have focused on the sexual victimization of women in wartime and its relation to pornography (Brownmiller 1975; Mackinnon 1994, for instance). Recent notable exceptions to this include Nikolic-Ristanovic's (1998) concerns with war and crime in the former Yugoslavia, and Pickering's (2000) discussion of women's resistance in Northern Ireland in which she focuses on women's experiences of house raids by security forces. Nevertheless, it is striking how little attention has been given to gender issues in the context of war. Drawing on the important work of Jamieson (1998), there is a need to focus both on women's *and* men's sex-ual victimization in war settings, the impact of the militarization of masculinity on women (and the sexual and other crimes which ensue), and the concomitant sexual regulation and policing of women *by* women in such contexts.

Doing gender: Work on masculinity

Although the 'maleness of crime' has traditionally been acknowledged within mainstream criminology (indeed, sex along with age has long been recognized as one of the most important predictors of crime), it has not, in most mainstream texts, been regarded as problematic. The sociology of masculinity, however, emerged from feminist work on gender, and from men's involvement in feminism, as well as the growing field of gay and lesbian studies. A vital change came in asking what it is about men, 'not as working-class, not as migrants, not as underprivileged individuals but *as men*, [that] induces them to commit crime' (Grosz 1987). Feminist criminologists were interested in this question from the outset. Cain (1990a), for instance, argued that feminist criminology must consider what it was in the social construction of maleness that was so criminogenic.

The literature on masculinity has increased markedly in the last few years (see, for example, Tolson 1977; Connell 1987, 1995; Segal 1990; Hearn and Morgan 1990; Morgan 1992; Messerschmidt 1993; Jefferson 1997; Collier 1998; Hood-Williams 2001). While early feminist work focused on the need to acknowledge women in all areas of criminological debate (see, for example, Heidensohn 1968 and Smart 1976), later work introduced a more critical consideration of the concept of gender (Cain 1990a; Daly 1997; Walklate 2001). There is little doubt that some of the work by feminists in the area of gender therefore contributed to the recognition of masculinities as critical to an understanding of crime and victimization (Newburn and Stanko 1994; Collier 1998). But it is also fair to say that some sociological thinking about gender was prompted by the rather one-dimensional images of men's dominance presented by radical feminist work on gender (for example, the notion that all men are rapists). Some of the problems with the early sociological engagements with masculinity theory have been well documented (Naffine 1997; Walklate 2001). The failure to address the larger issues of social structure in understanding men's power was a major problem – all crime was regarded as an individual phenomenon. This overwhelming focus on men as the 'norm' within criminological discourse served to pathologize the individual 'deviant', obscuring what men (as men) may share. A key shift came with the introduction of a gender paradigm based on the idea that gender was socially constructed, where encultured sex roles were ascribed to bodily difference. Gender became an essential dimension to progressive feminist politics: the idea of the social construction of gender supporting women's rights to claim equality in spite of bodily differences. Connell's (1987) use of the notion of 'categorical theory' (which depends on the key concepts of patriarchy, domination, oppression, and exploitation through which men are deemed the powerful and women the 'other') at once draws together differing feminist perspectives on gender and puts the contestation of power at the centre of his analysis of masculinities. Connell's work has been hugely important for the development of theory into multiple masculinities and in locating different practices of gender within structures of power. The focus on masculinity was thus transformed into an understanding of multiple masculinities which were primarily either 'hegemonic', or 'subordinated'.

Connell's notion of hegemonic masculinity has been used by several scholars to address ways of conceptualizing relations among men, especially where a power differential exists. In fact the concept of 'hegemonic' masculinity is useful in suggesting the power of potential cultural influences. As Connell points out, hegemonic masculinity was not intended to be regarded as corresponding to actual masculinities as they are lived, since 'what most men support is not actually what they are' (1987: 72). It influences, but does not determine what they do. Thorne (1993: 106) elaborates upon this in the following way: 'individuals and groups develop varied forms of accommodation, reinterpretation, and resistance to ideologically hegemonic patterns'. At its core is the Gramscian notion of hegemony, a concept which invokes the constantly contested definition of power. Thus for Connell, the gender structure is always being reproduced and reconstituted. This leads to a more sensitive appreciation of the situational and diverse notions of how the concept of hegemonic masculinity can and should be used.

These intentions, however, have become clouded by varying usage of the term 'hegemonic masculinity'. Collier, for instance, has indicated that the term is used 'on the one hand as referring to a certain set of characteristics or traits, which are then meant to signify "the masculine" in particular contexts; and on the other, as explaining, the *cause* of, the crimes of men' (1998: 19). Hegemonic masculinity is thus expected to explain a vast array of (almost always negative) male behaviours and criminal activities. The concept then becomes overused and potentially tautological (Walklate 1995). For Collier, the use of 'hegemonic masculinity' is untenable since it imposes an 'a priori theoretical/conceptual frame on the psychological complexity of men's behaviour' (1998: 22).

Other commentators have been moved to criticize theoretical developments in a different way. McMahon (1993), for instance, suggests that 'masculinity' is becoming an explanatory cliché in many academic and popular accounts of men, in the same way that sex-role theory did in earlier accounts:

> Masculinity is abstract, fragile, insecure, unemotional, independent, non-nurturant and so on. All the attributes of man discussed in the literature are spoken of as aspects of masculinity. It is remarkable how seldom writers on masculinity explicitly indicate what kind of concept they take masculinity 'to be'.
>
> (1993: 690)

Indeed, recent accounts often leave us with many problems, not least how 'masculine' qualities relate to what men do in concrete and material ways. These analyses also leave unanswered questions of the relationship of masculinity to the individual and the 'embodied social selves' of men. They also fail to help us understand the dimensions of the unities and differences among men. Hood-Williams (2001: 39) proposes that: 'the radical question to be asked here is whether the term "masculinities" adds anything to the analysis of criminal events or is it an empty tautology signifying nothing more than (some of) the things men and boys do'.

Messerschmidt's (1993) analysis has been the most extensive attempt to apply Connell's framework to the study of crime. He draws heavily on Connell's (1987) notions of multiply structured fields of gender relations – those of hegemonic and subordinated masculinities – and on Sylvia Walby's (1990) feminist theory of gender, which revolves around six patriarchal structures. Borrowing also from phenomenological approaches, Messerschmidt develops the idea of gender as a 'situational accomplishment' and of crime as a means of 'doing gender' (West and Zimmerman 1987). Following in Connell's wake, he addresses race and class alongside gender in his theorization of these categories as 'structured action' (1997). The idea is that masculinity can be seen as a crucial point of intersection of different forms of power, stratification, desire, and subjective identity formation. Yet this work is clearly problematic in terms of the way the world is divided up into 'structures' – these 'structures' omit age and disability, for instance (Mac an Ghaill 1994). In short, it is suggested that there is more complexity to these relationships than is presupposed. Hood-Williams (2001) questions whether or not it is actually possible to know and accomplish 'class', for example, in any systematic way.

To add to the complexity, Bob Connell (1995) notes that the concept of masculinity is bound up with modern notions of individuality and self. Although Connell's work is sensitive to the problems of understanding identity, Jefferson (1997) develops these ideas in greater depth. He calls for a more sophisticated understanding of individual identities, and pulls together post-structuralist thinking with psychoanalytic theory to provide a more contextualized account of individuals and crime. He asks:

> How do subjects, for example, come to take up (desire/identify with) one (heterosexual) rather than another (homosexual) subject position within the competing discourses of masculinity? This route makes unavoidable a re-engagement with the split, contradictory subject of psychoanalysis, if Connell's 'practice' is to be fully understood.
>
> (1997: 540)

Following post-structuralist theory, Jefferson (1997) has used a conception of discourse rather than a general notion of 'structures', and has placed the importance of the psyche in the foreground of the investigation.

Needless to say, problems with the notion of 'hegemonic masculinities' have prompted negative attention (in much the same way as there were problems with early feminist theories regarding assumptions about women's shared experiences). Some of the work reveals 'essentializing tendencies' – as did early feminist work (see Hood-Williams 2001; Walklate 2001, for overviews). Neither is it entirely clear where sophisticated theories about masculinity leave us in terms of comprehending crime. In many respects they make the task infinitely more complex, particularly the new 'puzzles' suggested to us by questions of subjectivity (Collier 1998; Hood-Williams 2001). But what should not be underestimated is the importance of feminist work on theorizing about gender relations and expressions of masculinity.

Hood-Williams's (2001: 54) conclusion, that 'criminology knows about gender, confidently goes out to find it and does indeed discover it. Analytic work on the other hand, raises the difficult question of just exactly what is to count as masculinity', lays bare the unresolved difficulties and the relationship between masculinity theory and crime. One of the challenges that Jefferson (1997) throws out at the end of his excellent introduction to masculinity theory is the utility of Jack Katz's (1988) 'seductions of crime' in terms of understanding the lived reality of crime. This is a work, he tells us, that challenges what a gendered dimension of understanding actually contributes. Katz has been admired by critical criminologists as posing an important postmodern challenge to the project of positivistic explanations of crime causation. By focusing on the 'foreground factors' of the exprience of crime and its 'moral emotions', he has perhaps brought us closer to understanding the lived reality of crime. His analysis of 'excitement' and 'seduction' is free from any sustained attempt to perceive or analyse these emotions as masculine elements of identity. What such work suggests is that at the moment of desire, pleasure, and risk-seeking, a specifically masculine identity may not be the most important element in engagement in crime. Thus, crucially, we return to feminist precepts regarding reality as 'lived experience'. The foregrounding of agency goes straight to the heart of the feminist enterprise.

My intention in this section has been to highlight some of the theoretical reasoning regarding masculinity and masculinities studies promoted, at least in part, by feminist insights. It is arguable, though, that neither the work on masculinities nor the work on women, sex, and gender, has yet fully explicated links with crime and victimization. As Walklate indicates, 'a gendered lens certainly helps us see some features of the crime problem more clearly; but how and under what circumstances is that clarity made brighter by gender or distorted by it?' (2001: 186). Moreover, there is much work to be done with regard to recognizing the state as a gendered institution, and identifying how and under what circumstances the state acts as a gendered institution (in combination with considerations of race and class). Yet it is clear that some of the emergent work on masculinities owes a debt to pioneering feminist work on gender theory, and that without it sociological and criminological work would be impoverished. [. . .]

References

Alder, C. (1995), 'Feminist Criminology in Australia', in N.H. Rafter and F. Heidensohn (eds), *International Feminist Perspectives in Criminology*, Buckingham: Open University Press.

Allen, H. (1987), *Justice Unbalanced: Gender, Psychiatry and Judicial Decisions*, Milton Keynes: Open University Press.

Amnesty International (1995), 'Women: "Invisible victims of human rights violations," ' 8 March, new release.

Bahar, S. (2000), 'Human Rights Are Women's Right', originally published in *Hypatia*, 11/1, 1996, reproduced in B. Smith (ed.), *Global Feminisms Since 1945*, London: Routledge.

Becker, H. (1963), *Outsiders*, Glencoe, NY: Free Press.

Belenky, M., Clinchy, B., and Goldberger N. (1986), *Women's Ways of Knowing*, New York: Basic Books.

Bertrand, M. (1969), 'Self-Image and Delinquency: A Contribution to the Study of Female Criminality and Women's Image', in *Acta Criminologica*, II: 71–144.

Bertrand, M., Daly, K., and Klein, D. (eds) (1992), *Proceedings of the International Feminist Conference on Women, Law, and Social Control*, Mont Gabriel, Quebec, 18–21 July 1991.

Bowles, G., and Duelli Klein, R. (eds) (1983), *Theories of Women's Studies*, London: Routledge and Kegan Paul.

Boyle, C. (1985), *A Feminist Review of Criminal Law*, Canada: Ministry of Supply and Services.

Brown, B. (1986), 'Women and crime: the dark figures of criminology', *Economy and Society*, 15/3: 355–402.

Brown, D., and Hogg, R. (1992), 'Law and order politics—left realism and radical criminology: a view from down under', in R. Matthews and J. Young (eds), *Issues in Realist Criminology*, London: Sage.

Brown, J., and Heidensohn, F. (2000), *Gender and Policing*, Basingstoke: Macmillan/Palgrave.

Brownmiller, S. (1975), *Against Our Will*, New York: Simon and Schuster.

Bulbeck, C. (1998), *Re-orienting Western Feminisms: Women's Diversity in a Post Colonial World*, Cambridge: Cambridge University Press.

Cain, M. (1986), 'Realism, feminism, methodology, and law', *International Journal of the Sociology of Law*, 14/3:255–67.

—— (ed.) (1989), *Growing Up Good. Policing the Behaviour of Girls in Europe*, London: Sage.

—— (1990a), 'Towards transgression: new directions in feminist criminology', *International Journal of the Sociology of Law*, 18: 1–18.

—— (1990b), 'Realist philosophy and standpoint epistemologies or feminist criminology as a successor science', in L. Gelsthorpe and A. Morris (eds), *Feminist Perspectives in Criminology*, Buckingham: Open University Press.

Carlen, P. (1992), 'Criminal women and criminal justice: the limits to, and potential of, feminist and left realist perspectives', in R. Matthews and J. Young (eds), *Issues in Realist Criminology*, London: Sage.

—— (1998), *Sledgehammer*, Basingstoke: Macmillan/Palgrave.

Carlen, P., and Worrall, A. (eds) (1987), *Gender, Crime and Justice*, Milton Keynes: Open University Press.

Carrington, K. (1994), 'Postmodernism and Feminist Criminologies: Disconnecting Discourses?', *International Journal of the Sociology of Law*, 22: 261–77.

—— (1998), 'Postmodernism and Feminist Criminologies: Disconnecting Discourses', in K. Daly and L. Maher (eds), *Criminology at the Crossroads*, New York: Oxford University Press.

Chamberlayne, P., Borbat, A., and Wengraf, T. (eds) (2000), *The Turn to Biographical Method in Social Science*, London: Routledge.

Clegg, S. (1975), 'Feminist methodology—fact or fiction?', *Quality and Quantity*, 19: 83–97.

Cohen, S. (1988), *Against Criminology*, New Brunswick, NJ: Transaction Books.

Collier, R. (1998), *Masculinities, Crime and Criminology*, London: Sage.

Connell, P. (1995), 'Black, British and Beaten? Understanding Violence, Agency and Resistance', paper presented to the British Criminology Conference, Loughborough, 1995.

Connell, R. (1987), *Gender and Power*, Cambridge: Polity Press.

—— (1995), *Masculinities*, Cambridge: Polity Press.

Cook, J., and Fonow, M. (1986), 'Knowledge and women's interests: issues of epistemology and methodology in feminist sociological research', *Sociological Inquiry*, 56: 1–29.

Cosslett, T., Lury, C., and Summerfield, P. (eds) (2000), *Feminism and Autobiography. Text, Theories, Methods*, London: Routledge.

Crawford, M., and Gentry, M. (eds) (1989), *Gender and Thought*, New York: Springer Verlag.

Dahl, T. (1987), *Women's Law. An Introduction to Feminist Jurisprudence*, Oslo: Norwegian University Press.

Daly, K. (1997), 'Different Ways of Conceptualising Sex/Gender in Feminist Theory and Their Implications for Criminology', *Theoretical Criminology*, 1/1: 25–51.

Daly, K. and Chesney-Lind, M. (1988), 'Feminism and Criminology', *Justice Quarterly*, 5/4: 498–538.

Delmar, R. (1986), 'What is Feminism?', in J. Mitchell and A. Oakley (eds), *What is Feminism?*, Oxford: Blackwell.

Derrida, J. (1978), 'Structure, Sign and Play in the Discourse of the Human Sciences', in *Writing and Difference*, Chicago: Chicago University Press.

—— (1981), *Positions*, Chicago: University of Chicago Press.

Diamond, I., and Quinby, L. (eds) (1988), *Feminism and Foucault*, Boston: Northeastern University Press.

Dobash, R.E., and Dobash, R.P. (1992), *Women, Violence and Social Change*, London: Routledge.

Dobash, R.E., Dobash, R.P. and Gutteridge, S. (1986), *The Imprisonment of Women*, Oxford: Blackwell.

Eaton, M. (1986), *Justice for Women?*, Milton Keynes: Open University Press.

Edwards, S. (1984), *Women on Trial*, Manchester: Manchester University Press.

Eichler, M. (1980), *The Double Standard: A Feminist Critique of Feminist Social Science*, London: Croom Helm.

Enloe, C. (1993), *Does Khaki Become You? The Militarisation of Women's Lives*, London: Pluto.

Evans, J. (1995), *Feminist Theory Today*, London: Sage.

Fineman, M., and Thomadsen, N. (eds) (1991), *At the Boundaries of Law*, New York: Routledge.

Foucault, M. (1970), *The Order of Things: An Archaeology of the Human Sciences*, London: Tavistock.

—— (1972), *The Archaeology of Knowledge*, London: Tavistock.

Fraser, N., and Nicholson, L. (1988), 'Social criticism without philosophy: an encounter between feminism and postmodernism', *British Journal of Law and Society*, 7: 215–41.

Fudge, J. (1989), 'The effect of entrenching a Bill of Rights upon political discourse: feminist demands and sexual violence in Canada', *International Journal of the Sociology of Law*, 17/4: 445–63.

Garland, D. (1992), 'Criminological Knowledge and its Relation to Power: Foucault's Genealogy and Criminology Today', *British Journal of Criminology*, 32/4: 403–22.

—— (2002), 'Of Crimes and Criminals: The Development of Criminology in Britain', in M. Maguire, R. Morgan, and R. Reiner (eds), *Oxford Handbook of Criminology*, 2nd edn, Oxford: Oxford University Press.

Gelsthorpe, L. (1989), *Sexism and the Female Offender: An Organizational Analysis*, Aldershot: Gower.

—— (1990), 'Feminist methodologies in criminology: a new approach or old wine in new bottles?', in L. Gelsthorpe and A. Morris (eds), *Feminist Perspectives in Criminology*, Bucking ham: Open University Press.

Gelsthorpe, L., and Morris, A. (1988), 'Feminism and Criminology in Britain', *British Journal of Criminology*, 28/2: 93–110.

—— (eds) (1990), *Feminist Perspectives in Criminology*, Buckingham: Open University Press.

Gelsthorpe, L., and Loucks, N. (1997), 'Magistrates' explanations of sentencing decisions', in C. Hedderman and L. Gelsthorpe (eds), *Understanding the Sentencing of Women*, Home Office Research Study 170, London: Home Office.

Gluck, S., and Patai, D. (eds) (1991), *Women's Words: The Feminist Practice of Oral History*, London: Routledge.

Gottfredson, M., and Hirschi, T. (eds) (1987), *Positive Criminology*, Newbury Park: Sage.

Greenwood, V. (1981), 'The myth of female crime', in A. Morris and L. Gelsthorpe (eds), *Women and Crime*, Cambridge: Institute of Criminology.

Grosz, E. (1987), 'Feminist theory and the challenge to knowledge', *Women's Studies International Forum*, 10/5: 208–17.

Gunew, S. (ed.) (1990), *Feminist Knowledge. Critique and Construct*, London: Routledge.

Hammersley, M., Ramazanoglu, C., and Gelsthorpe, L. (1992), 'Debate: Feminist Methodology, Reason and Empowerment', *Sociology*, 26/2: 187–218.

Hansson, D. (1995), 'Agenda-ing gender: feminism and the engendering of academic criminology in South Africa', in N.H. Rafter and F. Heidensohn (eds), *International Feminist Perspectives in Criminology*, Buckingham: Open University Press.

Harding, S. (ed.) (1986), *The Science Question in Feminism*, Milton Keynes: Open University Press.

—— (1987), *Feminism and Methodology*, Milton Keynes: Open University Press.

Hearn, J., and Morgan, D. (eds) (1990), *Men, Masculinities and Social Theory*, London: Unwin Hyman.

Heidensohn, F. (1968), 'The Deviance of Women: A Critique and Enquiry', *British Journal of Sociology*, 19/2: 160–75.

—— (1970), 'Sex, Crime and Society', in G. Harrison (ed.), *Biosocial Aspects of Sex*, Oxford: Blackwell.

—— (1985), *Women and Crime*, London: Macmillan.

—— (1989), *Women and Policing in the USA*, London: Police Foundation.

—— (1992), *Women in Control? The Role of Women in Law Enforcement*, Oxford: Oxford University Press.

—— (1996), *Women and Crime*, 2nd edn, Basingstoke: Macmillan.

—— (1997), 'Gender and Crime', in M. Maguire, R. Morgan, and R. Reiner (eds), *Oxford Handbook of Criminology*, 2nd edn, Oxford: Oxford University Press.

—— (2002), 'Gender and Crime', in M. Maguire, R. Morgan, and R. Reiner (eds), *Oxford Handbook of Criminology*, 3rd edn, Oxford: Oxford University Press.

Hill-Collins, P. (2002), 'Learning From The Outsider Within. The sociological significance of Black feminist thought', in S. Jackson and S. Scott (eds), *Gender. A Sociological Reader*, London: Routledge.

Hirsch, M., and Keller, E. (eds) (1990), *Conflicts in Feminism*, New York: Routledge.

Hobsbawm, E. (1994), 'Barbarism: A User's Guide', *New Left Review*, 206: 44–54.

Hollway, W., and Jefferson, T. (2000). *Doing Qualitative Research Differently*, London: Sage.

Home Office (2000), *Criminal Statistics in England and Wales*, London: HMSO.

Hood-Williams, J. (2001), 'Gender, masculinities and crime: From structures to psyches', *Theoretical Criminology*, 5/1: 37–60.

Howe, A. (1994), *Punish and Critique: Towards a Feminist Analysis of Penality*, London: Routledge.

Hudson, A. (1995), '"Elusive subjects": reseacrhing young women in trouble', in L. Gelsthorpe and A. Morris (eds), *Feminist Perspectives in Criminology*, Buckingham: Open University Press.

Humm, M. (ed.) (1992), *Feminisms: A Reader*, New York: Harvester Wheatsheaf.

—— (1995), *The Dictionary of Feminist Theory*, New York: Prentice Hall.

Hutter, B., and Williams, G. (eds) (1981), *Controlling Women: The Normal and the Deviant*, London: Croom Helm in association with Oxford University Women's Studies Committee.

Jackson, S., and Scott, S. (2002), *Gender. A Sociological Reader*, London: Routledge.

Jamieson, R. (1998), 'Towards a criminology of war in Europe', in V. Ruggiero, N. South, and I. Taylor (eds), *The New European Criminology*, London: Routledge.

Jefferson, T. (1997), 'Masculinities and Crimes', in M. Maguire, R. Morgan, and R. Reiner (eds), *Oxford Handbook of Criminology*, 2nd edn, Oxford: Oxford University Press.

Jones, S. (1986), *Policewomen and Equality*, London: Macmillan.

Katz, J. (1988), *Seductions of Crime: Moral and Sensual Attractions in Doing Evil*, New York: Basic Books.

Keat, R., and Urry, J. (1975), *Social Theory as Science*, London: Routledge and Kegan Paul.

Kelly, L. (1990), 'Journeying in reverse: possibilities and problems in feminist research on sexual violence', in L. Gelsthorpe and A. Morris (eds), *Feminist Perspectives in Criminology*, Buckingham: Open University Press.

Kelly, L., and Regan, L. (2000), *Stopping the Traffic: exploring the extent of, and responses to, trafficking in women for exploitation in the UK*, Home Office: Police Research Series 125.

Klein, D., and Kress, J. (1976), 'Any Woman's blues: a critical overview of women, crime and the criminal justice system', *Crime and Social Justice*, 5: 34–49.

Lees, S. (1997), *Ruling Passions*, London: Sage.

Leonard, E. (1982), *Women, Crime and Society: a Critique of Criminology Theory*, New York: Longman.

Lorde, A. (1984), *Sister Outsider*, Trumansburg, NY: Crossing Press.

Mac an Ghaill, M. (1994), *The Making of Men: Masculinities, Sexualities and Schooling*, Buckingham: Open University Press.

MacKinnon, C. (1987a), *Feminism Unmodified: Discourses on Life and Law*, Cambridge, Mass: Harvard University Press.

—— (1987b), 'Feminism, Marxism, Method and The State: Toward Feminist Jurisprudence', in S. Harding (ed.), *Feminism and Methodology*, Milton Keynes: Open University Press.

—— (1994), 'Rape, Genocide, and Women's Human Rights', in A. Stiglmayer (ed.), *Mass Rape, The War Against Women in Bosnia-Herzegovina*, Lincoln: University of Nebraska Press.

Major, L. (2001), 'Don't count on us', *Guardian*, 6 February.

Mangaliso, Z. (1997), 'Gender and nation-building in South Africa', in L. West (ed.), *Feminist Nationalism*, London: Routledge.

Matthews, R., and Young, J. (1992), 'Questioning left realism', in R. Matthews and J. Young (eds), *Issues in Realist Criminology*, London: Sage.

Mawby, R., and Walklate, S. (1994), *Critical Victimology*, London: Sage.

McMahon, A. (1993), 'Male readings of feminist theory: the psychologisation of sexual politics in the masculinity literature', *Theory and Society*, 22/5: 675–96.

McRobbie, A. (1980), 'Settling accounts with subcultures', in S. Hall and T. Jefferson (eds), *Resistance Through Rituals*, London: Hutchinson.

Messerschmidt, J. (1993), *Masculinities and Crime: Critique and Reconceptualisation of Theory*, Lanham, MD: Rowman and Littlefield.

—— (1997), *Crime As Structured Action. Gender, Race, Class and Crime in the Making*, Thousand Oaks, Cal.: Sage.

Mestrovic, S. (1993), *The Barbarian Temperament*, London: Routledge.

Millman, M. (1975), 'She Did it All for Love: a feminist view of the sociology of deviance', in M. Millman and R.M. Kanter (eds), *Another Voice: Feminist Perspectives on Social Life and Social Science*, New York: Anchor Books.

Mitchell, J. (1984), *Women: The Longest Revolution*, London: Virago.

Mitchell, J., and Oakley, A. (1986), *What is Feminism?*, Oxford: Blackwell.

Morgan, D. (1992), *Discovering Men*, London: Routledge.

Morris, A. (1987), *Women, Crime and Criminal Justice*, Oxford: Blackwell.

—— (1993), 'Law Reform Initiatives on Violence Against Women: successes and pitfalls'. A Paper presented at the International Conference of Women Judges held to celebrate the centenary of women's suffrage in New Zealand. Wellington, NZ: Institute of Criminology, Victoria University of Wellington.

Morris, A. and Gelsthorpe, L. (1991), 'Feminist Perspectives in Criminology: Transforming and Transgressing', *Women & Criminal Justice*, 2/2: 3–26.

Naffine, N. (ed.) (1995), *Gender, Crime and Feminism*, Dartmouth: Aldershot.

—— (1997), *Feminism and Criminology*, Cambridge: Polity.

Nicholson, L. (ed.) (1990), *Feminism/Postmodernism*, New York: Routledge.

Nikolic-Ristanovic, V. (1996a), 'Domestic Violence Against Women in the Conditions of War', in C. Sumner, M. Israel, M. O'Connell, and R. Sarre (eds), *International Victimology*, Canberra: Australian Institute of Criminology.

—— (1996b), 'War and Violence Against Women', in J. Turpin and L. Lorsentzen (eds), *The Gendered New World Order: Militarism, Development and the Environment*, New York: Routledge.

—— (1998), 'War and crime in the former Yugoslavia', in V. Ruggiero, N. South, and I. Taylor (eds), *The New European Criminology*, London: Routledge.

Oakley, A. (1981), *Subject Women*, Oxford: Martin Robertson.

—— (1999), 'People's ways on knowing: gender and methodology', in S. Hood, B. Mayail, and S. Oliver (eds), *Critical Issues in Social Research. Power and Prejudice*, Buckingham: Open University Press.

—— (2000), *Experiments in Knowing. Gender and Method in the Social Sciences*, Cambridge: Polity.

Pickering, S. (2000), 'Women, the Home and Resistance in Northern Ireland', *Women & Criminal Justice*, 11/3: 49–82.

Platek, M. (1995), 'What it's like for women: criminology in Poland and Eastern Europe', in N.H. Rafter and F. Heidemsohn (eds), *International Feminist Perspectives in Criminology*, Bucking ham: Open University Press.

Plummer, K. (2001), *Documents of Life 2*, London: Sage.

Rafter, N.H., and Natalizia, E. (1981), 'Marxist feminism: implications for criminal justice', *Crime and Delinquency*, 27: 81–98.

Rafter, N.H., and Heidensohn, F. (eds) (1995), *International Feminist Perspectives in Criminology*, Buckingham: Open University Press.

Redcar, R. (ed.) (1990), *Dissenting Opinions*, Sydney: Allen & Unwin.

Reinharz, S. (1979), *On Becoming a Social Scientist: From Survey Research and Participant Observation to Experimental Analysis*, San Francisco: Jossey-Bass.

Roberts, B. (2002), *Biographical Research*, Buckingham: Open University Press.

Roberts, H. (ed.) (1981), *Doing Feminist Research*, London: Routledge and Kegan Paul.

Rock, P. (ed.) (1988), *A History of British Criminology*, Oxford: Oxford University Press.

—— (1994), 'The Social Organization of British Criminology', in M. Maguire, R. Morgan, and R. Reiner (eds), *Oxford Handbook of Criminology*, 1st edn, Oxford: Oxford University Press.

Rowbotham, S. (1973), *Women's Consciousness, Man's World*, Harmondsworth: Penguin.

Scraton, P. (1990), 'Scientific knowledge or masculine discourses? Challenging patriarchy in criminology', in L. Gelsthorpe and A. Morris (eds), *Feminist Perspectives in Criminology* Buckingham: Open University Press.

Segal, L. (1990), *Slow Motion: Changing Masculinities, Changing Men*, London: Virago.

Shacklady Smith, L. (1978), 'Sexist assumptions and female delinquency: an empirical investigation', in C. Smart and B. Smart (eds), *Women, Sexuality and Social Control*, London: Routledge and Kegan Paul.

Smart, C. (1976). *Women, Crime and Criminology*, London: Routledge and Kegan Paul.

—— (1989), *Feminism and the Power of Law*, London: Routledge.

—— (1990), 'Feminist approaches to criminology or postmodern woman meets atavistic man', in L. Gelsthorpe and A. Morris (eds), *Feminist Perspectives in Criminology*, Buckingham: Open University Press.

Smart, C., and Smart, B. (eds) (1978), *Women, Sexuality and Social Control*, London: Routledge and Kegan Paul.

Smith, B. (ed.) (2000), *Global Feminisms Since 1945*, London: Routledge.

Stanko, E. (1985), *Intimate Intrusions: Women's Experience of Male Violence*, London: Virago.

—— (1990), *Danger Signals*, London: Pandora.

—— (1993), 'Feminist Criminology: An Oxymoron?', paper presented to the British Criminology Conference, Cardiff, 1993.

Stanley, L., and Wise, S. (1983), *Breaking Out: Feminist Consciousness and Feminist Research*, London: Routledge and Kegan Paul.

Stiglmayer, A. (ed.) (1994), *Mass Rape: The War Against Women in Bosnia-Herzegovina*, Lincoln: University of Nebraska Press.

Sumner, C. (1990), Foucault, gender and the censure of deviance', in L. Gelsthorpe and A. Morris (eds), *Feminist Perspectives in Criminology*, Buckingham: Open University Press.

Sumner, C. (1994), *The Sociology of Deviance: An Obituary, Buckingham*: Open University Press.

Taylor, I., Walton, P. and YOUNG, J. (1973), *The New Criminology* London: Routledge and Kegan Paul.

Thorne, B. (1993), *Gender Play: Girls and Boys in School*, New Brunswick, NJ: Rutgers University Press.

Tolson, A. (1977), *The Limits of Masculinity*, New York: Harper and Row.

Tong, R. (1989), *Feminist Thought*, London: Unwin Hyman.

Turpin, J., and Lorentzen, L. (eds) (1996), *The Gendered New World Order: Militarism, Development and Environment*, New York: Routledge.

Twine, F.W., and Blee, K. (eds) (2001), *Feminism and Antiracism. International Struggles for Justice*, New York: New York University Press.

Velimesis, M. (1975), 'The female offender', *Crime and Delinquency Literature*, 7/1:94–112.

Walby, S. (1990), *Theorizing Patriarchy*, Oxford: Blackwell.

Walklate, S. (1989), *Victimology*, London: Unwin Hyman.

—— (1992), 'Appreciating the Victim: Conventional, Realist or Critical Victimology?', in R. Matthews and J. Young (eds), *Issues in Realist Criminology*, London: Sage.

—— (1995), *Gender & Crime. An Introduction*, Hemel Hempstead, Herts.: Prentice Hall/Harvester Wheatsheaf.

—— (2001), *Gender, Crime and Criminal Justice*, Cullompton, Devon: Willan Publishing.

Weedon, C. (1987), *Feminist Practice and Poststructuralist Theory*, Oxford: Blackwell.

West, C., and Zimmerman, D. (1987), 'Doing Gender', *Gender and Society*, 1/2: 125–51.

Worrall, A. (1990), *Offending Women*, London: Routledge.

Young, A. (1994), 'Feminism and the Body of Criminology', in D. Farrington and S. Walklate (eds), *Offenders and Victims: Theory and Policy*, London: British Society of Criminology and ISTD. (British Criminology Conference Selected Papers, vol. 1.)

Young, J. (1994), 'Incessant Chatter: Recent Paradigms in Criminology', in M. Maguire, R. Morgan, and R. Reiner (eds), *Oxford Handbook of Criminology*, 1st edn, Oxford: Oxford University Press.

Zimmer, L. (1986), *Women Guarding Men*, Chicago: University of Chicago Press.

Chapter 28

Tony Jefferson

MASCULINITIES AND CRIMES

From: Tony Jefferson (1997), 'Masculinities and crimes', in Mike Maguire, et al. (eds), *The Oxford Handbook of Criminology*, 2nd edn, Oxford: Oxford University Press, pp. 535–552.

W̲HAT WE NOTICE SHAPES our understanding of anything. Take a (fictitious) newspaper report about two unemployed Afro-Caribbean teenage males 'mugging' (robbing) an elderly man at knife-point. Do we notice their youthfulness, their unemployed (hence poor) status, their racial origins, their use of violence, the 'mugging' label, how the item came to be regarded as newsworthy, or their 'maleness'? If we notice only their violence and/or their racial origins, our understanding will differ from one based on noticing, for example, their poverty and/or their newsworthiness. Until quite recently, their 'maleness' would have been so taken-for-granted, so unnoticed, as to be totally invisible; Campbell's great *unspoken*. Being unnoticed and unspoken it is unavailable to assist understanding; once noticed, it must change our understanding in some way. What follows is a brief progress report on some of the ways our understanding of crime has been disrupted as a result of some people (not all criminologists it must be said) noticing crime's 'maleness'.

This is not an easy topic to report on for two main reasons. First, masculinity (together with femininity) is both one of the most 'confused' concepts 'that occur in science' (Freud, quoted in Connell, 1995: 3) and, perhaps partly in consequence, highly contentious. Secondly, as everyone reading this should know, there is no single behaviour covered by the term 'crime', only a range of very different activities, from fiddling tax returns to genocide, only some of which, some of the time, attract the 'criminal' label. To meet these difficulties, I propose first to discuss major shifts in thinking about masculinity and then to explore a category of crime where thinking about masculinity has made some impact, namely, sexual violence and 'youth crime', though obviously some crimes straddle categories. Space limitations require certain restrictions. I shall not discuss criminalization/criminal justice matters and shall confine myself to British empirical data, where possible. This restriction does not apply to theoretical and political developments beyond these shores. Far from it. Without these, this review would be seriously impoverished.

The first part of what follows leans on Connell's masterly introductory chapter to *Masculinities* (1995), adopted and adapted with a very broad brush. In this chapter he discusses the three strands – the psycho-analytic, the social psychological, and 'recent developments in anthropology, history and sociology' (*ibid.* 7) – that have, in their different ways, produced knowledge about masculinity in the twentieth century. However, in order to facilitate my later discussion of the relationship of these knowledges to the crime question, my schematic overview will be structured to emphasize the significant theoretical shifts. Thus, I start with what I call 'Orthodox Accounts and the "Normal" Masculine Personality'. Whether of the psycho-analytic or the social psychological kind, their central theoretical production has been that of a relatively fixed and unitary 'normal' masculine personality, the result of a successful oedipal resolution in its psycho-analytic variant, and of successful 'sex-role' learning in its social psychological one. The two subsequent shifts both postdate contemporary feminism. The first of these (Connell's 'recent developments . . . '), I call 'The Social Break with Orthodoxy: Power and Multiple Masculinities'. This is characterized theoretically by the concepts of multiple masculinities, power (since these masculinities are always structured in relations of domination/subordination), and an insistence on the social (or institutional) dimension to masculinities. The second shift is the moment of feminist and poststructuralist engagements with more recent and radical developments in psychoanalytic theorizing. I call this 'The Psychoanalytic Break with Orthodoxy: Contradictory Subjectivities and the Social'. The principal feature of this development is the (re)discovery and reworking of the fragile, contingent and contradictory character of masculinity (and femininity), without losing sight of the social.

ORTHODOX ACCOUNTS AND THE 'NORMAL' MASCULINE PERSONALITY

It was Freud who, as a turn-of-the-century Viennese physician struggling to make sense of his patients' troubled lives, first 'noticed' gender. Their difficulties in living a gendered existence were central to his clinical case-studies. These laid the basis for a new understanding very different from the taken-for-granted one where maleness was a 'natural' product of biological sex. Utilizing his revolutionary ideas about repression and the unconscious, and a variety of novel methods (dream analysis, free association, etc.) for symptomatically 'reading' what had been repressed, he came to see the importance of early parent-child relations, especially the tangled mixture of love and jealousy he found there, to the formation of sexuality and gender in adulthood. The crucial stage in this development he called the œdipal complex, the moment when, for boy children, fear of the potentially castrating father wins out over desire for the mother. This leads, through internalization of his father's prohibitions (the moment of the formation of the super-ego), to identification with the masculine. This is also the moment when the cultural prohibitions of civilization win out over individual desire.

For Freud, this masculinity was built upon a constitutional bisexuality, and a complex mix of pre-œdipal desires and identifications. Hence, it was always multi-layered, consisting of masculine and feminine elements, conflict-ridden, and fragile. Moreover, this 'impure' basis made neurotics of us all. Freud saw no discontinuity between 'normal' and neurotic mental processes. But the history of mainstream psycho-analysis, in its pursuit of acceptance and respectability, was to be one of increasing conservatism, and a concomitant sanitization and simplification of its theory. Thus, by the mid-century, psycho-analytic orthodoxy effectively held that a successful resolution of the œdipal complex paved the way to mental health and the gender 'normality' of adult heterosexuality and marriage; by contrast, an unsuccessful resolution underlay various neuroses and assorted gender 'perversions', including homosexuality.

The social psychological equivalent of the 'normal', post-œdipal masculine personality of mainstream psycho-analysis is the 'normal' man of sex role theory. He is someone who has successfully learned his social script – the cultural norms and expectations of 'being a man' in our society: the male sex role. This idea emerged in the 1950s when 'sex difference' research – the myriad attempts from the 1890s on to measure 'scientifically' how men and women differ psychologically – met up with role theory, the efforts by social scientists from the 1930s to think how positions in social structures get reproduced. This conjunction produced the (now conventional) idea that the psychological differences between men and women (their 'sex differences') result from the learning of the cultural norms and behaviour appropriate to their sex – their 'sex role' (thus reproducing the social categories, men and women). Masculinity is thus the male sex role internalized.

Talcott Parsons saw the origins of the male and female sex roles in the functional requirements of small groups like the family for role differentiation. Thus he produced his influential distinction between 'instrumental' and 'expressive' roles, a distinction which remained within the realm of social explanations (Parsons and Bales, 1956). 'Most often', however, as Connell reminds us, 'sex roles are seen as the cultural elaboration of biological sex differences' (1995: 22). In other words, there is at the heart of most sex role theory a depressing circularity: sex roles are derived from cultural norms which, in turn, are based in innate differences.

Ironically, the early sex difference research, conducted by the first generation of women admitted into North American research universities, found that psychological differences between the sexes are small or non-existent (a finding which echoes Freud's radical findings about the mixture of masculinity and femininity in all of us). But, somewhere along the way, this radical challenge to the doctrine of innate sex differences gets lost, despite the continuing failure in the welter of subsequent research to find many differences. Moreover, though the social nature of the theory allows for change, for new cultural norms to be transmitted, and for the possibility of role-conflict, in practice, and especially before the advent of contemporary feminism, the theory rests largely on highly static, conservative assumptions: that role-expectations are clearly defined, unproblematically internalized, and normative. Consequently, the personalities so produced contribute to the mental health and social stability of society. Mainstream sex role theory thus produces a social parallel to mainstream psycho-analysis: in both, conflict and contradiction are effectively erased, the continuity between normality and pathology is severed, and masculinity and femininity become polarized terms.

THE SOCIAL BREAK WITH ORTHODOXY: POWER AND MULTIPLE MASCULINITIES

Once male social scientists followed the lead of feminist historians, anthropologists, and sociologists in their gendered recasting of women's lives with complementary re-examinations of the lives of men *as men*, a number of important shifts occurred. Historical and anthropological evidence began to show something of the empirical *diversity* in masculinities, cross-culturally and in different historical time periods, though much of the work remains wedded theoretically to the idea of male sex roles. There has, however, also been a stronger focus on the *institutional sites* – labour market, the law, the state, colonialism, etc. – wherein cultural norms pointed up by role theory are embedded. This attention to the dynamic, changing nature of masculinities and to the institutional sites of such transformations has led to a recognition, by some, that masculinity is not simply an external role to be passively internalized, a mere product of socialization, but something constructed in the interactional and institutional struggles of everyday life, an achievement of *practice*. The idea of competing masculinities struggling within institutional settings, and within the broader class, race, and other social relations that constrain these, has rendered this work sensitive to power differences *between men*, as well as the more usual feminist focus on inequalities between men and women.

Diversity, institutions, practice, and power. Of course not all this new work manages to be properly sensitive to all these issues. Linking them up coherently in a single theoretical frame is hard enough, let alone putting them to work on concrete cases. Connell's (1987, 1995) own efforts in this regard are seminal: the centrality of practice and hence of historically constructed gender relations; a constraining, multi-structured field of gender relations comprising three interrelated but irreducible structures of labour, power, and cathexis (roughly, sexuality); the various levels – personality, gender regime (institutional), gender order (societal) – where the historical play of gender relations can be 'read'; and, most famously, his adaptation of Gramsci in coining the idea of hegemonic and subordinate masculinities to make sense of the relation between competing masculinities.

What remains unclear in Connell's work, especially given his obvious interest in psychoanalysis (Connell, 1994), is why he puts an unspecified 'practice' in command? His short definition of masculinity regards it as 'simultaneously a place in gender relations, the practices through which men and women engage that place in gender, and the *effects* of those practices in bodily experience, personality and culture' (1995: 71, my emphasis). To my mind this Sartrean commitment to practice (Sartre was hostile to the psychoanalytic idea of unconscious motivations), of personality as constituted by the practices that collectively define a life, ignores another possibility; one that makes subjectivity and the role of the unconscious central, but without losing a grip on the social. *That* is the contribution of recent developments in psycho-analytic theorizing, to which I now turn.

THE PSYCHO-ANALYTIC BREAK WITH ORTHODOXY: CONTRADICTORY SUBJECTIVITIES AND THE SOCIAL

Ultimately the worth of psychoanalysis in understanding masculinity will depend on our ability to grasp the structuring of personality and the complexities of desire at the same time as the structuring of social relations, with their contradictions and dynamisms.

(Connell, 1995: 20–1)

Why I think Connell has not himself properly realized this aspect of his project has to do with his commitment to what some would now regard as a very modernist notion of structure, when much of the new, radical psycho-analytic theorizing is poststructuralist, and comes at the task heavily influenced by Foucault, discourse, and what has come to be known as the 'turn to language'. Now is not the time to enter the fray on the vexed question of the relation between discourse and the 'real' (see Jefferson, 1994), but the idea of social discourses offering up a range of subject positions (a reversal of Foucault's deterministic idea that discourses position subjects), seems to put the question of motivation/investment/identification/desire (call it what you will for the moment) back at the heart of the matter. How do subjects, for example, come to take up (desire/identify with) one (heterosexual) rather than another (homosexual) subject position within the competing discourses of masculinity? This route makes unavoidable a re-engagement with the split, contradictory subject of psychoanalysis, if Connell's 'practice' is to be fully understood. Where else are the complex and contradictory origins of desire, as Connell (1994) himself has so persuasively argued, taken seriously?

The figures who have been most influential in rendering this subject of psychoanalysis socially literate are Jaques Lacan, Melanie Klein, and other Object Relations theorists. Lacan's linguistically influenced revisions of traditional Freudian theory, principally his notion that it is the child's entry into the social world of language (and hence into Foucault's discursive realm) that founds the unconscious and self-identity, provide a significant opening towards a (non-reductive) social understanding of the psyche. The revisionist work of Melanie Klein and Object Relations theorists, especially their emphases on the importance of relational defence mechanisms (such as 'splitting' off unwanted 'bad' parts of the self and 'projecting' them into others, where they can be disowned) and on early 'object relating', laid a further basis for an understanding of the psyche which is simultaneously social (cf. Rustin, 1991, 1995). Chodorow's object relations-influenced account probably has been the most influential to date in theorizing about masculinity. A Professor of Sociology turned psychoanalyst, she has argued that the emotional dynamics underpinning the process of separation from the mother are different for girls and boys, leaving boys with *the* problem of masculinity, namely, how to relate, and girls with *the* problem of femininity, namely, how to separate (Chodorow, 1978). Its widespread appeal probably had more to do with its recognizable sociology than its psychoanalytic argument, a point she now seems to recognize since she has gone on to criticize this work for giving 'determinist primacy to social relations' (1989: 7; see also Chodorow, 1994). This also goes to show how difficult it is to work seriously with both personality and social relations 'simultaneously'. Nonetheless, in this area we have no other option. Let us see now how my three models can help us understand shifts in approaches to the question of men, masculinities, and particular crimes.

SEXUAL VIOLENCE: RAPE/SEXUAL ABUSE/MURDER

This cluster of crimes in which sex is somewhere implicated is undoubtedly the area where thinking about masculinity has impacted most, not surprisingly perhaps, given the importance of sexuality to constructions of masculinity. Indeed, it was the pathbreaking writings of American radical feminists on rape in the 1970s (Griffin, 1971; Brownmiller, 1976) which, being the first to notice and theorize the 'maleness' of rape, effectively kickstarted the whole current interest in theorizing the relationship between forms of masculinity and certain crimes. The connection with feminist politics, and its location outside criminology, are two enduring features of this work, as we shall see.

Amir's sociological findings based on convicted rapists in Philadelphia (Amir, 1967, 1971) had already begun to challenge the image of the rapist as psychopathic stranger, the 'monster' lurking in the bushes, that has traditionally dominated the common-sense discourse on rape. But its 'maleness' escaped him. Moreover, in characterizing 19 percent of the rapes as 'victim-precipitated' (victim retracting consent after first agreeing, or not reacting strongly enough) he seemed to be blaming the female victim, thus provoking feminist ire. The feminist interventions finally despatched any notion that rape was an activity undertaken only by abnormal or pathological males, most impressively in Brownmiller's monumental historical and cross-cultural cataloguing of the ubiquity of rape. Further, these writings moved beyond the psychological and sociological characteristics of convicted rapists to connect rape to the (patriarchal) organization of society as a whole. In Brownmiller's case (1976: 17), rape was actually the *foundation* of 'the patriarchy'. Finally, and most controversially, *all* men were implicated. As Brownmiller provocatively put it, rape 'is nothing more or less than a conscious process of intimidation by which *all men* keep *all women* in a state of fear' (*ibid.* 15, emphases in original), an idea that produced the feminist slogan, 'all men are potential rapists'. From being a *criminal* act committed by a minority of *deviant* men, rape had become a key tactic in the social control of women and the reproduction of male dominance.

In terms of my three-stage model of theorizing masculinity, these early feminist writings straddle the first two stages. In linking masculinity to patriarchal social relations and thus emphasizing the centrality of power, these move beyond the narrow œdipal and sex-role frames characteristic of orthodox accounts of masculinity. In other ways, though, they fail to surmount orthodox thinking. Masculinity is conceptualized in the singular, effectively *the* ideology underpinning the range of practices and institutions that collectively constitute *the* all-embracing system of male domination that is patriarchal society. Secondly, the notion of how individual men come to acquire patriarchal, masculine values, whether these are seen as rooted in biology (as they were for Brownmiller) or (as became more common) culture, is, like sex-role theory, implicitly deterministic: Weber's 'iron cage'.

One interesting attempt to move beyond these limitations is contained in Box (1983). In recognizing a number of differently motivated types of rape, ranging from the brutally 'sadistic' to the manipulative 'exploitation' rape, and analysing these in relation to a multi-factorial model of causation involving economic inequality, the law, 'techniques of neutralization' as well as what he calls the 'masculine mystique', he takes an important step towards multiplicity without actually breaking with the notion of a singular 'culture of masculinity'. What he does suggest is that men's differential access to socioeconomic resources, and different relationships to cultural stereotypes of masculinity, will affect whether, and how, they rape. Crucially, he took on the (lower) class bias of imprisoned rapists (largely convicted of 'anger' or 'domination' rapes), suggesting that masculine sex-role socialization in the contexts of socio-economic powerlessness and a 'subculture of violence' could begin to account for this class profile (an approach not dissimilar to Polk's more recent attempt (1994) to make sense of both the maleness and the class profile of homicide). Box also makes the important point that, for the sadistic rapist (the rarest category), the 'masculine mystique' factor is all-important. (This, as we shall see below, provides a point of connection with later work on serial killing.) Whereas radical feminism had all men down as 'potential' rapists, thus effectively answering the question of what function rape plays in a patriarchal society, Box was attempting to answer a more traditional criminological question, namely, which men actually become so.

James Messerschmidt's book, *Masculinities and Crime* (1993), offers the most sustained attempt yet by a criminologist to rethink this relationship away from the deterministic reductionism of early feminist theorizing, and thus breaks decisively with orthodox accounts. In so doing, he does for criminology what Connell has done for the study of masculinity more generally. From Giddens (1976, 1981) he takes the idea of a practice-based approach to social structure, and from Acker (1989) the notion that gender, race, and class relations are implicated simultaneously in any given practice. He combines these insights with Connell's (1987) concepts of a multiply structured field of gender relations and hegemonic and subordinated masculinities. Finally, he borrows from phenomenology the idea of the 'situational accomplishment' of gender (West and Zimmerman, 1987; Fenstermaker, West, and Zimmerman, 1991; Goffman, 1979). The result of this creative synthesis sees crime as a resource for the situational accomplishment of gender (1993: 79). It is a form of 'structured action', a way of 'doing gender', which simultaneously accomplishes (or 'does') class and race. Men's resources for accomplishing masculinity, as with those of Box's rapists, will vary, dependent on their positions within class, race, and gender relations. These differences will be reflected in the salience of particular crimes as masculinity-accomplishing resources. For those at the bottom of racial and class hierarchies, with consequently reduced opportunities for the accomplishment of hegemonic masculinity, crime can be particularly salient.

Messerschmidt then proceeds to explain a whole range of crimes, including those of the powerful. Examples include the infamous Central Park rape case where a white woman jogger was repeatedly raped and left near death. At the time of the analysis, four teenage Afro-American youths had been convicted of the crime, accompanied by reports that they had been jubilantly celebrating ('wilding') throughout. Messersschmidt argued that this exemplified his thesis: the rape and 'wilding' were a group resource for accomplishing masculinity in a context of class and race disadvantage where other resources are few. Later, a lone male confessed to the crime and the youths' convictions were quashed. Although this particular case was obviously not group 'wilding', Messerschmidt (personal communication) still feels that the general point about group rape being a resource for accomplishing masculinity in particular contexts is borne out by numerous examples, including group rapes by school and college athletes (cf. Benedict, 1997; Lefkowitz, 1997) and young Puerto Rican crack dealers in New York (Bourgois, 1995 and 1996).

Although Messerschmidt's approach constitutes an advance on the early radical feminist explanations, what it singularly fails to do is to problematize why some young men 'choose' this particular form of behaviour to accomplish their masculinity when other similarly located men, thankfully, do not. In other words, it is a purely sociological theory about which *groups* of men are more or less likely to get involved in particular sorts of crime; it has nothing to say about which *particular man or men* from any given group (usually only a minority) are likely to do so. This requires taking the psychic dimension of subjectivity seriously, especially its contradictoriness; not seeing the self, as Messerschmidt implicitly does, simply as unitary and rational, reflexively monitoring behaviour in the light of the responses of others (*ibid*. 77). This oversocialized, essentially Meadian version of the self (Mead, 1934), helps explain the fact that the examples given of 'doing gender', despite the theoretical importance of practice (doing), all end up explaining the reproduction, not the subversion, of gender/race/class. This emphasis on constraints rather than action explains the ultimately deterministic feel to the analyses, and reveals the limits of a purely social break with orthodoxy.

Another study operating within a broadly similar theoretical framework, but linked to an idea from cultural anthropology that the core properties of hegemonic masculinity in patriarchal societies are 'procreation', 'provision', and 'protection' is that of Kersten (1996). In this, he attempts to explain contemporary (and puzzling) differences in rape rates between Australia, where rates are high, Japan, where they are low, and Germany, which has rates somewhere between the two. The high (and rising) rates in Australia are explained broadly in terms of the effects of the continent's 'deep social, cultural and economic crisis' on the traditional 'national masculinity' built on 'physical prowess and independence'. This, Kersten argues, affects both the newly marginalized, for whom crime, including rape, becomes (following Messerschmidt) a resource for accomplishing masculinity, and those attempting to live up to 'hegemonic masculinity'. In the latter case, the difficulties of rearing and providing for families heighten the salience of the purely protective dimension of 'good' masculinity, and, in consequence, 'the image of the rapist as stranger'. Thus, rising rape rates are connected to increases in rape behaviour *and* to heightened sensitivities, to underlying structural changes, and to their (differential) impact on competing masculinities. In Japan, by contrast, masculinity and assaultive behaviour are not mutually implicated, for a whole host of reasons – cultural, organizational, even architectural – that Kersten attempts to spell out. It is a valiant attempt to think masculinity onto the notoriously difficult terrain of comparative criminology; though, as with Messerschmidt, it remains locked into an exclusively social frame.

What was needed to transcend this 'purely social break' was a better sense of the complexities of men's experiences. One could argue that the return to (a socially literate) psycho-analysis within feminism, my third stage in thinking about masculinities, was prompted, ultimately, by some of the felt disjunctions between personal experience (which had always been a serious object of attention in feminism) and available feminist theory: for many women, for example, their love of and desire for particular men contradicted their theoretical understandings of men-in-general as oppressors, aggressors, potential rapists. Progress in turning a similar spotlight on men's experiences has been slight, but instructive.

Books recounting men's experiences of rape, as rapists, are rare. I know of two (Beneke, 1982; Levine and Koenig, eds., 1983). Reading these, what is striking is the disjunction between how these men experienced themselves ('I had a kind of phobia about women, I just felt I wasn't good enough for them, like really inside'; 'women often made me feel inferior', Levine and Koenig, eds., 1983: 78, 84), and feminism's traditional depiction of the rapist as the personification of power. Here, Frosh's notion of the '*incoherence* of the masculine state, of the way its ideological claims to effectiveness and power are built on a continuing denial of weakness and dependence' (1994: 99, emphasis in original) has telling, concrete purchase.

Where these ideas have been developed most is in two case-studies, both by feminists, one a Professor of English, the other a journalist, of the serial, sexual murderer,

Peter Sutcliffe, the so-called 'Yorkshire Ripper' (Ward Jouve, 1988; Smith, 1989). The question of serial killing has generated a small publishing industry of its own. It may be useful, therefore, to outline the main strands, so as to distinguish clearly my own focus. There is the work on sadistic sexual murder of feminist writers like Cameron and Frazer (1987) and Caputi (1988), and, more generally on women killing, of Radford and Russell (eds., 1992). In this work, the 'maleness' of the violence is certainly central, most thought-provokingly in Cameron and Frazer's idea that the 'common denominator' of sex-murderers is not misogyny, since not all their victims are women, but 'a shared construction of . . . masculinity' in which the 'quest for transcendence' is central (*ibid*. 166–7). However, because masculinity and patriarchy are conceptualized in the singular, theoretically speaking this work is a continuation (along with a whole range of other work on violence against women) of the tradition inaugurated by the work of Brownmiller and Griffin on rape. Then there is the emergent positivistic criminological literature responding to an apparently novel crime phenomenon (Levin and Fox, 1985; Holmes and DeBurger, 1988; Lester, 1995). Definitions, profiles, and typologies are central, based upon the careful assembling of what is known about killers' backgrounds, personalities, motives, methods, victims, and killing locations. Where the 'maleness' of the perpetrators is noticed, it is in a list of factors, conceptualized in the most orthodox terms: a failure to live up to sex-role norms (Levin and Fox, 1985: 53), for example. The understanding of Freud and the unconscious is risible (Holmes and De Burger, 1988: 98). The two final strands are the biographical accounts of particularly heinous killers written by journalists, which now constitute a whole sub-genre of biographical writing, and, what interests us here, certain feminist appropriations of these.

Once Peter Sutcliffe acquired his 'Yorkshire Ripper' tag, and thus became linked in the popular imagination to 'Jack the Ripper', the 'father' to the 'age of sex crime' (Caputi, 1988: 7), the interest of journalists (Beattie, 1981; Burn, 1984; Cross, 1981; Yallop, 1981; Smith, 1989) and academic feminists (Hollway, 1981; Bland, 1984; Ward Jouve, 1988) was assured – with the usual division of labour. The former have done the leg work, attended the trial, conducted the interviews and produced detailed but essentially descriptive accounts of the case; the latter have offered their feminist-inspired theoretical re-readings. Only Smith, a feminist and a journalist who reported on the trial, manages both. Of the re-readings, it is the brilliant discussions of Sutcliffe's fragile and conflicted masculinity, in both Smith and Ward Jouve, that begins to develop the contours of an understanding of masculinity that is both socially literate and psychoanalytically complex.

Connell's notion, that it is in the 'detail of cases' that the deployment of psychoanalytic ideas will greatly assist our understanding of masculinity (Connell, 1995: 34), is superbly exemplified in these two accounts. They reach similar conclusions. Both tell the story of a boy who is painfully torn between the tough, masculine values of father, brother, and working-class neighbourhood, the mantle of masculinity required of him, and the quiet, gentle femininity of his beloved, long-suffering mother, with whom he strongly identified. They show something of the multiple ambivalences that this contradiction produced: the cruel cross-pressures of the socially required versus the psychically desired (but socially punished). And they outline many of the contingencies that, in repeatedly demonstrating his failure to live up to the social expectations of manliness, led him first to blame the feminine in himself, to hate part of himself, and then externalize that hatred and destroy women.

It was a grisly resolution. It was not inevitable. It was in some sense chosen. But it is a resolution and a choice that displays a logic only within the detail of a life observed through a lens of masculinity which is simultaneously social and psychic, alert to the multiple contradictions within and between these dimensions, the anxieties and ambivalences these set up, and the compounding influence of contingencies. It is the strength of the accounts of both Smith and Ward Jouve that they do render Sutcliffe's life comprehensible, at least after a fashion. The fuller, journalistic accounts are drawn on, but transformed by the noticing of, and accounting for, a whole host of apparently inconsequential, overlooked details, thus rendering them theoretically meaningful.

This work has had little impact on the rape debate, which is still heavily influenced by radical feminism. Two decades on, discussions of the various violences against women are still effectively centred on unmasking the many visages of 'male power' (in the singular): for example, the (patriarchal) assumptions and practices in the conduct of rape investigations and trials which produce high 'attrition rates' and low rates of conviction (Adler, 1987; Chambers and Millar, 1983, 1986; Grace, Lloyd, and Smith, 1992; Lees and Gregory, 1995). Some US feminists, however, have changed tack completely and rejected this orthodoxy as a form of 'victim-feminism' (Paglia, 1992; Roiphe, 1993). They regard its picture of woman-as-victim, passively powerless, as one that simply reinforces the conventional stereotype of the weak, helpless woman. These new 'power' (or 'post'?) feminist voices have emerged out of the complex sexual and racial politics on US campuses which engendered the debate about 'political correctness' (Dunant, 1994; Hollway and Jefferson, 1996). In particular, Paglia and Roiphe blame the growth of concern about campus 'date-rape' (Boumil, Friedman, and Taylor, 1993) on feminist extensions of the definition of rape (to include verbal as well as physical coercion, or any sex felt by the victim to be violating; see Roiphe, 1993: 68–70), and generally bemoan the denial of an active female sexuality in the dating scenario (Paglia, 1992: 49–74). Since both Paglia and Roiphe hail from the humanities and not the social sciences, and their purposes were primarily political, it is not surprising that they end up postulating a responsible, choosing' female subject, a simple inversion of radical feminism's passive victim of male power.

But, in putting woman's sexuality back into the picture, by suggesting that she too is a sexual agent, it reconnected with a dimension that had become obscured by radical feminism's preoccupation with power. What was still absent was some more adequate theory of gendered subjectivity. It is this dimension that more recent work on particular date-rape cases is trying to develop (Jefferson, 1997; Hollway and Jefferson, 1998), using a theory of subjectivity derived from combining Foucault's notion of (social) discourses, together with various (psycho-analytically derived) concepts, such as anxiety and the defences of splitting and projection, in order to explain the discursive positions adopted (Jefferson, 1994; Hollway, 1989). Testing this approach on particular cases has involved deconstructions of existing journalistic accounts, highlighting those facts left unexplained, and reconstructions showing how sense can be made of ignored facts, once unconscious motivations and ambivalent feelings, and the anxieties and defensive splittings/ projections these give rise to (for both parties) are recognized. The subjectivities that emerge from such analytical reconstructions turn out to be complexly and contradictorily gendered, a conclusion in line with Ward Jouve and Smith on the 'masculinity' of Sutcliffe. [. . .]

Further support for the idea of ambivalence can be found in Phillips' (2000) interview-based study with young female students in the US exploring their intimate experiences, including coercive sex: the 'women spoke of confusion, of contradictory emotions, of not knowing what to think' (p. 8). Bravely she adds, 'for many of the young women in this study, rape is about sex, as well as about violence. . . Many women report saying yes when they want to say no, and saying no when they want to say yes or maybe' (p. 14).

A further instance of the fruitful rereading of journalistic account . . . is Jackson's pamphlet on the James Bulger case (1995; see also Jefferson, 1996c). Its relevance here is that two year old James' murder by two boys, both aged ten, was preceded by a symbolic rape. It was a shocking case, provoking widespread public revulsion and incomprehension, and, perhaps inevitably, much recourse to demonising discourses. What the journalist David Smith does in his excellent book on the case (1994) is first remind us that killing by children is not new, then meticulously assemble the available evidence, and finally offer an explanation based on the unhappiness, mistreatment and powerlessness of both boys' lives. He . . . [hoped that] explanation . . . [would emerge from the detail] – thus nicely demonstrating the difference between the journalistic and the academic approach. What Jackson does is to take up the neglected issue of masculinity and show how the boys' lives could be understood as attempts to build up a more powerful sense of masculine identity, in the twin contexts of a powerlessness imposed by the frameworks that regulated them (family and school), and the 'idealised fantasy images of hypermasculine toughness, dominance and invulnerability' (p. 22) provided by the media and . . . [their] peer group. . . . The resulting truancy, 'rape' and the killing of . . . James are all rad in this light, with the killing seen as an attempt to master . . . anxieties . . . about their own babyishness by violently projecting them onto James, and destroying them there. . . .

The Bulger killing reignited interest in the case of Mary Bell, the girl . . . convicted of strangling two small children in 1968 when she was eleven (Sereny, 1972–1995). . . . Although Mary Bell was labelled a psychopath by two psychiatrists, thereby securing a conviction for manslaughter on the grounds of diminished responsibility, the similarity between her emotionally impoverished and rejecting background and her troublesome responses, and those of the two boy killers of James is striking. For Sereny, who compares Bell to James' killers, the emotionally impoverished and rejecting background and her troublesome responses, and those (which is never raised). Whether she is right nor not, these cases suggest two things . . . to bear in mind. . . . One is a reminder of the complex fluidity of gender formation, a point being developed most interestingly in the theoretical work of Jessica Benjamin (1995a and b; 1998). How else explain Mary Bell's extremely 'masculine' fearlessness and inability to feel? This would seem to warn against pinning everything on gender difference. . . . Secondly, if masculinity is used over-inclusively . . . , other . . . factors may be obscured.

Lest this focus on individual cases serves to obscure the ultimate object of attention, let me end this section by refocusing on the broadest possible meaning of the social, on what Bob Connell (1993) calls 'the big picture'. Take something like the rise of fascism in inter-war Germany, which, with its genocidal outcome, ought to be of some interest to criminologists. So far as I know, no serious commentator has ever tried to deny fascism's complex social roots. But, in the wake of the Frankfurt School's efforts to understand the psychic underpinnings of its mass appeal, who would now deny the need also to understand the complexities of fascism's and fascist violence's psychological roots . . . (Theweleit, 1987) [. . .]

Authority and the construction of the authoritarian personality were central to the Frankfurt School's understanding of fascism. For Theweleit (1987 and 1989) it is the attraction of violence, and its origins in the construction of the particular masculinities of the . . . Freikorps [men], specifically their fear and hatred of the feminine, which is paramount. His work can thus be seen as a (very rich) case-study in masculinity. In attending to the connections between fantasy life and politics, it is sensitive to both psychic and social levels. The question Theweleit leaves open is how different was the psychic constellation of these men from that of other men. But, in the light of the present 'big picture', in which neither war, genocide nor torture can be consigned safely to the historical past, it would seem madness to leave the question of masculine subjectivities out of account. [. . .]

YOUTH CRIME, UNDERCLASS MALES, AND BLACK MASCULINITY

I want to end with a brief survey of thinking about young 'underclass' men with 'no future', ethnicity and crime, not only because there is relevant work being done here, but also because it is here in particular that we can witness the impact of key transformations in 'the big picture' on a range of subordinate and marginal masculinities across the developed world. But, first, a brief pre-history.

The idea of a connection between a life with 'no future' and crime is not new. Paul Goodman's passionate mid-1950s polemic, *Growing Up Absurd*, saw juvenile delinquency as 'the powerless struggling for life within . . . an unacceptable world' (1956: 197). He even saw this as a problem of 'manliness': 'If there is little interest, honour, or manliness in the working part of our way of life, can we hope for much in the leisure part?' (*ibid*. 235–6). But young men and manliness were assumed categories and not problematized. At around the same time, Albert Cohen (1955), the first of the subcultural theorists, did link male delinquent subcultures partly to anxiety about masculinity, but mostly to the 'status frustration' of growing up working-class in a world dominated by middle-class values (see Walklate, 1995: 166–7). It was only the class basis of youth subcultures that was subsequently taken up by British subcultural theorists and reworked using an admixture of marxist and semiotic concepts (Hall and Jefferson, eds., 1976). These were later to be roundly criticized for ignoring the gender dimension (McRobbie, 1980; Dorn and South, 1982). Paul Willis' classic, *Learning to Labour* (1977), was an early exception to the rule (of gender-blindness). He showed how working-class lads (willingly) take on hard, physical, working-class jobs, partly by rejecting the femininity associated with mental 'pen-pushing' labour (and hence the opportunity to 'get on' in class terms). But, despite Willis' important emphasis on practice, and the superb ethnography of his lads' school-based youth culture, the analytic categories of 'capitalism' and 'patriarchy' remained unidimensional, hence (now) problematic.

The issue of gender was not to resurface properly in the youth debate until the 1990s. When it did reappear, it was feminist writers who once again led the way, this time by drawing attention to the angry and destructive responses of 'underclass' males to their new social and economic marginalization (Campbell, 1991, 1993; Coward, 1994; but see also Jackson, 1992*a* and *b*; Jefferson, 1992). Written partly in response to the conservative 'take' on the underclass debate – that certain young men choose unemployment and crime because both are made easy for them (Murray, 1984, 1989, 1990) – and partly as an attempt to understand the riots of 1991, Bea Campbell's journalistic foray into 'Britain's dangerous places', the new economic 'disaster areas', produced a compelling account of a subordinate masculinity in crisis. Against the background of what she called the 'economic emergency' facing these areas, Campbell talked of how women translate their troubles and anger into 'strategies of survival and solidarity', how men court 'danger and destruction' (1993: 303). It works brilliantly as reportage, and at putting the issue of masculinity and crime on the criminological agenda. But, ultimately, the book succumbs to a kind of victim feminism, with its cast of fearful, long-suffering, somewhat idealized women, preyed upon by criminally predatory, somewhat pathologized young men, and the 'boys in blue' stuck uncomfortably in the middle of this contemporary war between the sexes.

Feminist academic and journalist Ros Coward also takes up this theme of the different responses of men and women to the economic destruction of their neighbourhoods, but adds a further twist, namely, the idea of the 'yob' as the 'classic scapegoat' left 'carrying the weight of masculinity which, for a variety of reasons, middle-class society finds increasingly unacceptable, and rhetorically dumps on the men of the lower class' (1994: 32). We might see this as a contemporary version of Stan Cohen's (1973) 'folk devils' argument, revitalized through the attention given to masculinity.

From within criminology, the late Mike Collison (1996), using interviews with young British male offenders, connected up notions of the 'risk society' and the importance of consumption in detailing how structurally excluded males ('reflexivity losers') accomplish masculinity in creating a street style of spectacular consumption, excessive drug use, and living life on the 'edge', in pursuit of a reputation for being 'mad. Across the Atlantic, Bourgois (1995, 1996) has shown the effect of social and economic marginalization on young Puerto Rican male immigrants. Deprived of jobs and the ability to provide for a family – the culturally traditional avenue to patriarchal respect – their alternative 'search for respect' becomes centred on a misogynistic and parasitic life-style of crack dealing, sexual promiscuity, and interpersonal violence.

All these accounts, journalistic or academic, are about the effects of the global restructuring of the economy on particular, subordinated, or marginalized masculinities. In terms of my three-stage model, these accounts are all at stage two: the world of 'power and multiple masculinities'. This is because, by focusing on the subordinate or marginalized masculinities of socially excluded youths, there is, implicitly anyway, a recognition of a dominant, countervailing, or mainstream masculinity. What would be needed to shift this sort of work into my stage three, where an interest in psychic as well as social dimensions is demanded, would be an analytic interest in particular cases to complement the sociological interest in the group. Until criminologists can believe that 'exceptional' cases can tell us something about the 'rule', indeed ought to be examined in order to alter our understanding of the rule, and need not entail (the much maligned) 'individualistic' explanations, progress will be slow.

Where this debate about subordinate or marginalized masculinities in crisis has proceeded furthest is in relation to the African-American male. It is at the heart of the debate about 'The Crisis of African American Gender Relations', recently featured in *Transition 66* (Summer, 1995). Though undoubtedly stimulated by the Thomas-Hill hearings (Morrison, ed., 1992) and the Tyson rape conviction (Shaw, 1993; Garrison and Roberts, 1994), this debate extends back at least to Wallace's brave critique of the macho politics of Black Power (1990; originally published in 1978). In Britain, the race and crime debate has got itself bogged down trying to assess the degree to which Afro-Caribbean over-representation in official crime statistics can, or cannot, be attributed to discriminatory practices (Smith, 1997). By contrast, the North American debate has had to recognize the role of masculinity much earlier. This has only partly to do with the massive over-representation of Afro-Americans in crime (and punishment) in the United States. More importantly, it has to do with the history of black-white relations since the abolition of slavery, the role of black males in the white imagination, and the response of young ('underclass') black men both to these white fantasies and to their continued (and worsening) social, economic, and political marginalization.

This tortured history has seen black males as the repressed other of the dominant (white) masculinity, a dialectic with a much longer history (see Hoch, 1979: chapter 3). But, in the context of a vicious and continuing history of racist violence and discrimination, the channels for achieving respect as a man have been both narrow and, in consequence, highly salient. Thus, the rise of the Afro-American athlete and entertainer, and 'cool' ghetto hustler, put bodily performance, sexuality, and toughness (the repressed other of 'civilized' white masculinity) at a premium – in line with restricted opportunities and prevailing mythologies.

The civil rights and black liberation movements of the 1960s may not have produced political emancipation, but they did produce a psychic shift (West, 1993: 18). This shift, in combination with the worsening plight of black America (Wacquant, 1995), has fuelled black rage, which, having no legitimate outlets, gets turned inwards, creating both nihilism (West, 1993: chapter 1) and misogyny. This has to do with the limited availability of positive images for black men, and the emasculating effects of continuous and humiliating racism. Together, these made for the profoundly contradictory mix that is contemporary black macho: both an uplifting and unifying form of resistance to (hegemonic) white masculinity (the return of the repressed), *and*, in its misogyny and homophobia, a depressing source of community division (Wallace, 1990). The attempts to theorize all this specifically in relation to masculinity (Staples, 1989), and the problems of 'cool pose' (Majors, 1989; Majors and Billson, 1992) have largely relied on structural and/or sex-role theorizing (in a somewhat problematic combination with psychoanalytic theory in the case of Gibbs and Merighi, 1994) and, to that extent, remain limited. But, once the historical sensitivities of writers like Wallace (1990) and bell hooks (1992: chapter 6) are combined with the theoretical sophistication of Mac an Ghaill (1988; 1994*a* and *b*), an Irishman who has researched black masculinities in a British school informed by an awareness of the psychic dimension of masculinity, the current dominance of this theoretical model should be supplanted.

My own work on Tyson (Jefferson, 1996a and b; 1997), a . . . case-study . . . of a particular form of black masculinity, . . . attempt[s] to shift the theoretical contours to include a psychic as well as a social dimension. That . . . life-history work can be [done] . . . without neglecting the social . . . is demonstrated wonderfully in Wolfenstein's . . . Marxist/psychoanalytic . . . life of Malcolm X (1989). . . . Yet, the petty thief and ordinary burglar rarely leaves the kind of biographical traces necessary for this work. But . . . one could . . . [start] by returning to classic life-histories of ordinary crime, like Shaw's *The Jack Roller* (1930), to see what might be possible – or what future work . . . [is needed]. It seems to me that . . . any real progress on how gender/class/race/age . . . intersect complexly . . . [must build on] particular life-histories. [. . .]

Conclusion

Since this is very much 'work-in-progress', let me end by posing two crucial questions. . . . . In Katz's *Seductions of Crime* (1988), he reverses the usual [criminological] focus . . . on background factors . . . and concentrates instead on 'those aspects in the foreground of criminality that make its various forms sensible, even sensually compelling, ways of being' (p. 3). It is constantly . . . insightful . . . in its pursuit of 'the moral and sensual attractions in doing evil'. Yet, . . . it is (a) thoroughly sociological and (b) only fitfully concerned with . . . gender. When a psychoanalytic, gender . . . dimension is added, as it is, briefly, for example at the end of the chapter on 'Ways of the Badass', it adds little. . . . So, this would seem to present two challenges to the thrust of my argument (both of which I have previously acknowledged). One is the extent to which a psychoanalytic dimension adds a *necessary* explanatory level. The second is the degree to which the question of masculinity aids our understanding. It might be a useful exercise for someone to go back to Katz with these two questions centrally in mind. [. . .]

References

Acker, J. (1989), 'The Problem with Patriarchy', *Sociology*, 23, 2: 235–40.

Adler, A. (1987), *Rape on Trial*. London: Routledge & Kegan Paul.

Amir, M. (1967), 'Victim Precipitated Forcible Rape', *Journal of Criminal Law, Criminology and Police Science*, 58: 493–502.

—— (1971), *Patterns in Forcible Rape*. Chicago, Ill.: University of Chicago Press.

Auletta, K. (1983), *The Underclass*. New York: Vintage.

Beattie, J. (1981), *The Yorkshire Ripper Story*. London: Quartet/Daily Star.

Benedict, J. (1997), Public Heroes, Private Felons: Athletes and Crimes Against Women. Boston: Northeastern University Press.

Beneke T. (1982), *Men on Rape*. New York: St Martin's Press.

Benjamin, J. (1995a), 'Sameness and Difference: Toward an "Over-Inclusive" Theory of Gender Development' in A. Elliot and S. Frosh, eds., *Psychoanalysis in Contexts*, 106–22. London: Routledge.

—— (1995b), *Like Subjects, Love Objects: Essays on Recognition and Sexual Difference*. New Haven: Yale University Press.

—— (1998), *Shadow of the Other: Intersubjectivity and Gender in Psychoanalysis*, New York: Routledge.

Beynon, J. (1995), *The Joy Generation*. Unpublished ESRC Report, ref. No R000233292.

Bland, L. (1984), 'The Case of the Yorkshire Ripper: Mad, Bad, Beast or Male?', in P. Scraton and P. Gordon, eds., *Causes for Concern*, 184–209. Harmondsworth: Penguin.

Boumil, M. M., Friedman, J., and Taylor, B. E. (1993), *Date Rape: The Secret Epidemic*. Deerfield beach, Fla.: Health Communications Inc.

Bourgois, P. (1996), 'In Search of Masculinity: Violence, Respect and Sexuality among Puerto Rican Crack Dealers in East Harlem', in T. Jefferson and P. Carlen, eds., *Masculinities, Social Relations and Crime*, Special Issue of *British Journal of Criminology*, 36, 3: 412–27.

—— (1995), *In Search of Respect: Selling Crack in El Barrio*. Cambridge: Cambridge University Press.

Box, S. (1983), *Power, Crime and Mystification*. London: Tavistock.

Brownmiller, S. (1976), *Against Our Will: Men, Women and Rape*. Harmondsworth: Penguin.

Burn, G. (1984), *Somebody's Husband, Somebody's Son: The Story of Peter Sutcliffe*. London: Heinemann.

Cameron, D., and Frazer, E. (1987), *The Lust to Kill: A Feminist Investigation of Sexual Murder*. Cambridge: Polity.

Campbell, A. (1993), *Out of Control: Men, Women and Aggression*. London: Pandora.

Campbell, B. (1991), 'Kings of the Road', *Marxism Today*, 20–23 December.

—— (1993), *Goliath: Britain's Dangerous Places*. London: Methuen.

Caputi, J. (1988), *The Age of Sex Crime*. London: The Women's Press.

Chambers, G., and Millar, A. (1983), *Investigating Sexual Assault*. Edinburgh: HMSO.

—— (1986), *Prosecuting Sexual Assault*. Edinburgh: HMSO.

Chodorow, N. J. (1978), *The Reproduction of Mothering: Psychoanalysis and the Sociology of Gender*. Berkeley, Cal.: University of California Press.

—— (1989), *Feminism and Psychoanalytic Theory*. London: Yale University Press.

—— (1994), *Femininities, Masculinities, Sexualities: Freud and Beyond*. Lexington, Kentucky: The University Press of Kentucky.

Cohen, A. K. (1955), *Delinquent Boys*. New York: Free Press.

Cohen, S. (1973), *Folk Devils and Moral Panics*. London: Paladin.

Collison, M. (1996), 'In Search of The High Life: Drugs, Crime, Masculinity and Consumption', in T. Jefferson and P. Carlen eds., *Masculinities, Social Relations and Crime*, Special Issue of *British Journal of Criminology*, 36. 3: 428–44.

Connell, R. W. (1987), *Gender and Power: Society, the Person and Sexual Politics*. Cambridge: Polity.

—— (1993), 'The Big Picture: Masculinities in Recent World History', *Theory and Society*, 22, 5: 599–623.

—— (1994), 'Psychoanalysis on Masculinity', in H. Brod and M. Kaufman, eds., *Theorizing Masculinities*, 11–38. London: Sage.

—— (1995), *Masculinities*. Cambridge: Polity.

Coward, R. (1994), 'Whipping Boys', *Guardian Weekend*, 32–5, 3 September.

Craib, I. (1987), 'Masculinity and Male Dominance', *Sociological Review*, 34, 4: 721–43.

Crichton, M. (1994), *Disclosure*. London: Arrow.

Cross, R. (1981), *The Yorkshire Ripper: The In-depth Study of a Mass Killer and His Methods*. London: Granada.

Dahrendorf, R. (1985), *Law and Order*. London: Stevens and Sons.

Dobash, R. E., and Dobash, R. (1979), *Violence Against Wives: A Case Against Patriarchy*. New York: Free Press.

Dorn, N., and South, N. (1982), *Of Males and Markets: A Critical Review of 'Youth Culture' Theory*. Research Paper 1, Centre for Occupational and Community Research. London: Middlesex Polytechnic.

Dunant, S., ed. (1994), *The War of the Worlds: The Political Correctness Debate*. London: Virago.

Elliott, A. (1992), *Social Theory and Psychoanalysis in Transition: Self and Society from Freud to Kristeva*. London: Routledge.

—— (1996), *Subject to Ourselves: Social Theory, Psychoanalysis and Postmodernity*. Cambridge: Polity.

—— and Frosh, S., eds. (1995), *Psychoanalysis in Contexts: Paths between Theory and Modern Culture*. London: Routledge.

Farley, L. (1978), *Sexual Shakedown: the Sexual Harassment of Women on the Job*. New York: McGraw-Hill.

Fenstermaker, S., West, C., and Zimmerman, D. H. (1991), 'Gender Inequality: New Conceptual Terrain', in R. L. Blumberg, ed., *Gender, Family and Economy*, 289–307. Newbury Park, Cal.: Sage.

Frosh, S. (1991), *Identity Crisis: Modernity, Psychoanalysis and the Self*. London: Macmillan.

—— (1994), *Sexual Difference: Masculinity and Psychoanalysis*. London: Routledge.

Garrison, J. G., and Roberts, R. (1994), *Heavy Justice: The State of Indiana v. Michael G. Tyson*. New York: Addison-Wesley.

Gibbs, J. T., and Merighi, J. R. (1994), 'Young Black Males: Marginality, Masculinity and Criminality', in T. Newburn and E. A. Stanko, eds., *Just Boys Doing Business?* 54–80. London: Routledge.

Giddens, A. (1976), *New Rules of Sociological Method*. London: Hutchinson.

—— (1981), 'Agency, Institution and Time-Space Analysis', in K. Knorr-Cetina and A. V. Cicourel, eds., *Advances in Social Theory and Methodology: Toward and Integration of Micro- and Macro-Sociologies*, 161–74. Boston, Mass: Routledge and Kegan Paul.

Goffman, E. (1979), *Gender Advertisements*. New York: Harper and Row.

Goodman, P. (1956), *Growing Up Absurd*. New York: Vintage.

Grace, S., Lloyd, C., and Smith, L. J. F. (1992), *Rape: From Recording to Conviction*. Research and Planning Unit Paper 71 London: Home Office.

Grant, L. (1994), 'Sex and the Single Student: The Story of Date Rape', in S. Dunant, ed., *The War of the Words*, 76–96. London: Virago.

Griffin, S. (1971), 'Rape: The All American Crime', *Ramparts*, 26–35, September.

Grubin, D., and Gunn, J. (1990), *The Imprisoned Rapist and Rape*. London: Dept of Forensic Psychiatry, Institute of Psychiatry.

Hall, S., and Jefferson, T., eds. (1976), *Resistance through Rituals: Youth Subcultures in Post War Britain* London: Hutchinson.

Henriques, J., Hollway, W., Urwin, C., Venn, C., and Walkerdine, V. (1984), *Changing the Subject: Psychology, Social Regulation and Subjectivity*. London: Methuen.

Hoch, P. (1979), *White Hero Black Beast: Recism, Sexism and the Mask of Masculinity*. London: Pluto.

Hollway, W. (1981), ' "I Just Wanted to Kill a Woman." Why?: The Ripper and Male Sexuality', *Feminist Review*, 9, 33–40.

—— (1989), *Subjectivity and Method in Psychology: Gender, Meaning and Science*. London: Sage.

Hollway, W. and Jefferson, T. (1996), 'PC or not PC: Sexual Harassment and The Question of Ambivalence', *Human Relations*, 49, 3: 373–93.

—— (1998), ' "A Kiss is Just a Kiss": Date Rape, Gender and Subjectivity, *Sexualities*, 1(4): 405–23.

Holmes, R. M., and De Burger, J. (1988), Serial Murder. London: Sage.

hooks, B. (1992), 'Reconstructing Black Masculinity', in B. hooks, *Black Looks: Race and Representation*, 87–113. Ontario, Canada: Between the Lines.

Jackson, D. (1992*a*), 'Riding for Joy', *Achilles Heel*, 13: 18–19; 37–8.

—— (1992*b*), 'The Silence of the Wolves', *Achilles Heel*, 13: 25–7.

—— (1995), *Destroying the Baby in Themselves: Why Did the Two Boys Kill James Bulger?* Nottingham: Mushroom Publications.

Jefferson, T. (1992), 'Wheelin and Stealin', *Achilles Hell*, 13: 10–12.

—— (1994), 'Theorising Masculine Subjectivity', in T. Newburn and E. A. Stanko, eds., *Just Boys Doing Business? Men, Masculinities and Crime*, 10–31. London: Routledge.

—— (1996a) 'From "Little Fairy Boy" to "The Complete Destroyer": Subjectivity and Transformation in The Biography of Mike Tyson', in M. Mac an Ghaill, ed.,

Understanding Masculinities: Social Relations and Cultural Arenas, 153–67. Buckingham: Open University Press.

Jefferson, T. (1996b) ' "Tougher Than The Rest": Mike Tyson and the Destructive Desires of Masculinity', *Arena Journal*, 6: 89–105.

—— (1996c) 'The James Bulger Case: A Review Essay', *British Journal of Criminology*, 36, 2: 319–23.

—— (1997), 'The Tyson Rape Trial: The Law, Feminism and Emotional "Truth" ', *Social and Legal Studies*, 6, 2: 281–301.

Katz, J. (1988) *Seductions of crime*. New York: Basic Books.

Kersten, J. (1996), 'Culture, Masculinities and Violence Against Women', in T. Jefferson and P. Carlen, eds., *Masculinities, Social Relations and Crime*, Special Issue of *British Journal of Criminology*, 36, 3: 381–95.

Kovel, J. (1981), *The Age of Desire: Case Histories of a Radical Psychoanalyst*. New York: Basic Books.

—— (1998), *White Racism: A Psycho History*. London: Free Association Books.

Lees, S., and Gregory, J. (1995), *Rape and Sexual Assault: A Study of Attrition*. London: Islington Council.

Lefkovitz, B. (1977), Our Guys: *The Glen Ridge Rape Case and the Secret Life of the Perfect Suburb*. Berkeley: University of California Press.

Lester, D. (1995), *Serial Killers: The Insatiable Passion*. Philadelphia, Penn.: The Charles Press.

Levin, J., and Fox, J. A. (1985), *Mass Murder: America's Growing Menace*. New York: Plenum.

Levine, S., and Koenig, J., eds. (1983), *Why Men Rape*. London: Stag.

Mac an Ghaill, M. (1988), *Young, Gifted and Black: Student-Teacher Relatins in the Schooling of Black Youth*. Milton Keynes: Open University Press.

—— (1994a), *The Making of Men: Masculinities, Sexualities and Schooling*. Buckingham: Open University Press.

—— (1994b), 'The Making of Black English Masculinities', in H. Brod and M. Kaufman, eds., *Theorizing Masculinities*, 183–99. London: Sage.

McRobbie, A. (1980), 'Settling Accounts With Subcultures: A Feminist Critique', *Screen Education*, 39.

Majors, R. (1989), 'Cool Pose: The Proud Signature of Black Survival', in M. S. Kimmel and M. A. Messner, eds., *Men's Lives*, 83–7. New York: Macmillan.

Majors, R. and Billson, J. M. (1992), *Cool Pose: The Dilemmas of Black Manhood in America*. New York: Touchstone.

Mead, G. H. (1934), *Mind, Self and Society*. Chicago, Ill.: University of Chicago Press.

Messerschmidt, J. (1993), *Masculinities and Crime*. Lanham, Md.: Rowman and Littlefield.

Morgan, R. (1982), 'Theory and Practice: Pornography and Rape', in L. Lederer, ed., *Take Back the Night*, 125–40. London: Bantam.

—— (1989), *The Demon Lover*. London: Methuen.

Morris, L, (1994), *Dangerous Classes: The Underclass and Social Citizenship*. London: Routledge.

Morrison, T., ed. (1992), *Race-ing Justice, Engendering Power: Essays on Anita Hill, Clarence Thomas and the Construction of Social Reality, New York:* Pantheon.

Murray, C. (1984), *Losing Ground. New York:* Basic Books

—— (1989), 'Underclass', *Sunday Times Magazine*, 22–46, 26 November.

—— (1990), *The Emerging British Underclass*. Choice in Welfare Series No. 2. London: Health and Welfare Unit, Institute of Economic Affairs.

Paglia, C. (1992), *Sex, Art, and American Culture*. New york: vintage.

Parsons, T., and Bales, R. F. (1956), *Family Socialization and Interdction Process*. London: Routledge and kegan paul.

Phillips, L. M. (2000), *Flirting with Danger: Young Women's Reflections on Sexuality and Domination*. New York: New York University Press.

Polk, K. (1994), *When Men Kill: Scenarios of Masculine Violence*, Combridge: Cambridge University Press.

Radford, Y., and Russel, D. E. H. eds. (1992), *Femicide: The Politice of women killing*. Buckingham: Open University Press.

Richards, B. (1990), 'Masculinity, Identification and Political Culture', in J. Hearn and D. Morgan, eds., *Men, Masculinity and Social Theory*, 160–9. London: Unwin Hyman

—— (1994), *Disciplines of Delight: The Psychoanalytic of popular Culture*. London: Free Association Books.

Roiphe, K. (1993), *The Morning After: Sex Fear and Feminism on Campus*. New York: Little Brown & Co.

Rustin, M. (1991), *The Good Society and the Inner World: Psychoanalysis, Politics and Culture*. London: Verso.

—— (1995), 'Lacan, Klein and Politics: The Positive and Negative in Psychoanalytic Though', in A. Elliott and S. Frosh, eds., *Psychoanalysis in Contexts: Paths between Theory and Modern Culture*, 336–71. London: Routledge.

Scully, D. (1990), *Understanding Sexual Violence: A Study of Convicted Rapists*. Boston Mass: Unwin Hyman.

Sereny, G. (1972), *The Case of Mary Bell*. London: Arrow. Republished 1995, London: Pimlico.

Shaw, C. R. (1930), *The Jack Roller*, Chicago, Ill: Chicago University Press.

Shaw, M. (1993), *Down For The Count: The Shocking Truth Behind the Mike Tyson Rape Trial*. Campaian, Ill.: Sagamore.

Singh, N. P. (1995), 'Black Liberation – the Theater of Nationality: The Black Panthers and "Undeveloped country" of the Left', in C. E. Jones, ed., *The Black Panther Party Reconsidered: Reflections and Scholarship*. Baltimore, Md.: Black Classic Press.

Smart, C. (1989), *Feminism and the Power of Law*. London: rouledge.

Smith, D. J. (1994), *The Sleep of Reason: The James Bulger Case*. London: Century.

Smith, David J. (1997), 'Ethnic Origins, Crime and Criminal Justice', in M. Maguire, R. Morgan and R. Reiner, eds., *The Oxford Handbook of Criminology*, 2nd edn. 703–59, Oxford: Clarendon Press.

Smith, J. (1989), 'There's Only One Yorkshire Ripper', in J. Smith, *Misogynies*, 117–51. London: Faber.

Staples, R. (1989), 'Masculinity and Race: The Dual Dilemma of Black Men'. In M. S. Kimmel and M. A. Messner, eds., *Men's Lives*, 78–83. New York: Macmillan.

Theweleit, K. (1987), *Male Fantasies Volume 1: Women, Floods, Bodies, History*. Cambridge: Polity.

—— (1989), *Male Fantasies Volume 2: Male Bodies: Psychoanalysing the White Terror*. Cambridge: Polity.

Transition (1995), 'Symposium: The Crisis of African American Gender Relations', *Transition*, 66, 5, 2: 91–175.

Wacquant, J. D. (1995), 'The Ghetto, The State and The New Capitalist Economy', in P. Kasinitz, ed., *Metropolis: Centre and Symbol of Our Times*, 418–49. London: Macmillan.

Walklate, S. (1995) *Gender and Crime: An Introduction*. Hemel Hempstead: Prentice Hall/Harvester Wheatsheaf.

Wallace, M. (1990), *Black Macho and the Myth of the superwoman*. London: Verso.

Ward Jouve, N. (1988), 'The Street-Cleaner': The Yorkshire Ripper Case on Trial*. London: Mario Boyars.

West, C. (1993), *Race Matters*. Boston, Mass.: Beacon Press.

West, C., and Zimmerman, D. H. (1987), 'Doing Gender', *Gender and Society*, 1, 2: 125–51.

West, D. (1987), *Sexual Crimes and Confrontations*. Aldershot: Gower.

Willis, P. (1977), *Learning to Labour*. Farnborough: Saxon House.

Wolfenstein, E. V. (1989), *The Victims of Democracy*. London: Free Association.

Wyre, R. (1986), *Women, Men and Rape*. Oxford: Perry Publications.

Wyre, R. and Tate, T. (1995), *The Murder of Childhood: Inside The Mind of One of Britain's Most Notorious Child Murderers*. Harmondsworth: Penguin.

Yallop, D. A. (1981), *Deliver Us From Evil*. London: Macdonald Futura.

PART SIX

Sentencing discretion and inequality in common law

UNDER THE RETRIBUTIVE APPROACH to justice of the Neo-Classical Revival since the 1970s, social policy in America has moved to "get tough" on crime. In Britain, Prime Minister Tony Blair has similarly claimed to "get tough on crime and tough on the causes of crime." What we consider here is why this occurs at a time when crime has been dropping steadily. In practice, this approach has led in both countries to an intensive focus on the individual who is at high risk of reoffending or at high risk of future dangerousness. This has been done in ways that seem ultimately to demand of those targeted a self-generated reduction of the risk they present. Performance based management requires results and the fact that rehabilitative programmes have often produced positive but modest results to an inherently intractable problem matters little. What has been notable is that the move to "get tough" combines both harsher sentences and what ultimately are more, rather than less, discretionary proceedings in the name of a reduced leniency. Yet, in fact, there is growing evidence that both these changes contravene, rather than strengthen, deterrence.

Prime examples of the "tough on crime" approach are the introduction of mandatory sentences such as the "three strikes ('two . . . ' in Britain) and you're out" laws, "truth in sentencing" laws in the United States, longer sentences in Britain, and the American retention of the death penalty. Yet, harsher sentencing practices do little to boost deterrence. Instead, psychological research shows that it is swiftness and certainty, rather than severity, that exerts a capacity to deter. Since relatively few crimes result in arrest and conviction, the ability to achieve certainty is a major problem.

Mandatory pentalies – seemingly the most clearcut and severe of practices – is also problematic in practice to produce no more severe penalties because they are, as Michael Tonry has shown, circumvented by judges and prosecutors. Mandatory penalties are theorized to deter crime because of the certainty of harsh punishment that they introduce.

Tonry demonstrates that when a mandatory penalty is prescribed, the latitude for choice simply shifts elsewhere. Judges, when finding the penalty too excessive, simply dismiss more cases. Today we see that power moves to the prosecutor because the penalties enable her/him to adjust charges and to "bargain" on the basis of guaranteeable outcomes for the offender. Because defendants who go to trial also fight their cases harder, convictions have historically been little changed when mandatory penalties are introduced.

"Getting tough" on crime in the United States has also meant retention of the death penalty. The death penalty was restored in many American states during the 1970s. Its history has been one of recurring policy reversal. At present, the United States is one of the few western countries to preserve the death penalty. This has disrupted extradition arrangements with some countries who refuse to return an accused offender for a trial that could result in death. Evidence overwhelmingly demonstrates that the death penalty is applied almost exclusively in cases involving racial and ethnic minorities, the less educated and the poor. Often horrific in practice, the US Supreme Court this year agreed to consider whether it constitutes cruel and unusual punishment. Justifications of the death penalty as necessary to deter has been powerfully challenged by both Archer and Gartner's and Hood's findings that the preponderance of the evidence shows that the practice produces no reduction in homicide – not in the US now, not in west European countries historically when it operated there, neither concurrently nor as a lagged effect.

Even as "tough," but fraught, sentencing laws have been adopted, procedural changes of great import have also occurred in America and, increasingly, in Britain. These changes are of three sorts: reduced protections for the accused; heightened judicial and/or prosecutorial discretion; and susceptibility of rights to suspension under "states of exception." The cumulative effect of these procedural changes in America has led Charles Ogletree to refer to a "Rehnquist Revolution" in criminal procedure. In Britain, the shift is symptomized by the "shoot to kill" orders recently issued to Metropolitan Police officers if a fleeing suspected terrorist ignores orders to halt. Given the already high incidence of arrests and custody among the disadvantaged and ethnic minorities, these changes further undermine their position.

Increasingly the practices at the core of contemporary prosecution are coming to be recognized for the significant discretion they embody. Discretionary practices, such as the ability to plea bargain, have steadily been gaining greater acceptance and/or prominence. Discretion, which has traditionally permeated the common law, provides openings for inequality. Though evidence as to the existence of differentials in sentences across ethnic groups and social classes is still somewhat contested, the capacity and willingness to seek leniency has consistently varied in England across social groups. Minorities appear less trusting that "bargains" will be honored. As a result, they often receive harsher sentences. Historically, discretionary informality in law has been especially interesting in that it appears to originate and/or gain strength, as Franz Neumann has shown, during times of political reaction. Plea bargaining, for instance, arose in America as part of an elite effort to reconsolidate power in the face of rising popular democratic politics during the Age of Jackson.

Historically, the common law has been structured to provide opportunities for improved behavior. Through forbearance in punishment, which is held in abeyance for use as a last resort, defendants are urged to ameliorate any wrong that has been done. Plea bargaining provides one important mechanism where, traditionally, the favorable testimony of character witnesses prompted grants of leniency to those offenders who had led worthy lives but had, by a misstep, run afoul of the law. Such persons were, upon receipt of such symbolic surety, turned back into the community for re-integration under the watchful eye of those who had testified on their behalf. Historically, this community basis for re-integration empowered established hierarchies of power whose members' intercession was valued as character witnesses.

At present, both the nature of procedures and the capacity of the government to suspend procedural guarantees altogether, either through formal change or by declaring a "state of exception," are changing. Plea bargaining, long established in the United States, is rapidly gaining ground internationally. In Britain, where its existence has long been denied, the practice has been formally embraced in recent years by the Court of Appeal, Lord Woolf, and the new Head of the Crown Prosecution Service. Similarly, plea bargaining has been introduced in France and in China very recently as well. In each of these countries, the power of the executive is also extending relatively unchallenged.

In 1988, the *Harvard Law Review* concluded, in a special issue on the criminal justice system, that minority persons in the United States were being treated more harshly at every stage of the criminal justice process. There is every reason to think that the expansion of discretionary informality may be heightening those differentials both there and elsewhere. Research in Britain arrives at similar conclusions, especially with respect to plea bargaining. In America, social capital appears historically to have played a role in creating the opportunity to bargain. Later, affirmation from the social sorting mechanisms of society's middle level institutions, such as schools, churches, employers or the military, also enhanced one's prospects. Social capital, like trust, thus boosted one's chances of bargaining at all.

While harsh sentencing and mandatory penalties appear to produce little, if any, reduction in offending, increasingly discretionary prosecutorial practices are equally troubling. As these changes have been set in place, their rationale has been unclear. They appear to respond neither to crime trends nor to new knowledge about "what works" in reducing reoffending. Largely abandoning the challenge of rehabilitation, despite mounting evidence that there are options that "work," Anglo-American criminal justice has, as Simon and Feeley have shown, turned to the management of an offender population rather than the rehabilitation and reintegration of offending individuals. The reason these changes in criminal justice policy have been so difficult to explain, I suggest in the Introduction to this book, is that the changes are not about crime but rather a broader political sea change. It is one in which criminal justice is playing a key part.

Chapter 29

Michael Tonry

MANDATORY PENALTIES

From: Michael Tonry (1992), 'Mandatory penalties', in Michael Tonry (ed.), *Crime and Justice: A Review of Research*, Vol. 16, Chicago: University of Chicago Press, pp. 243–265.

MANDATORY PENALTIES DO NOT work. The record is clear from research in the 1950s, the 1970s, the 1980s, and, thanks to the U.S. Sentencing Commission, the 1990s that mandatory penalty laws shift power from judges to prosecutors, meet with widespread circumvention, produce dislocations in case processing, and too often result in imposition of penalties that everyone involved believes to be unduly harsh. From research in the 1970s and 1980s, the weight of the evidence clearly shows that enactment of mandatory penalties has either no demonstrable marginal deterrent effects or short-term effects that rapidly waste away. Why, then, did legislatures in all fifty states enact mandatory penalty laws in the 1970s and 1980s, and why do legislatures continue to enact them?

The reason is that most elected officials who support such laws are only secondarily interested in their effects; officials' primary interests are rhetorical and symbolic. Calling and voting for mandatory penalties, as many state and federal officials repeatedly have done in recent years, is demonstration that officials are "tough on crime." If the laws "work," all the better, but that is hardly crucial. In a time of heightened public anxiety about crime and social unrest, being on the right side of the crime issue is much more important politically than making sound and sensible public policy choices.

This essay retells a story, at least three centuries old, of the political appeal and practical limits of mandatory sentencing laws. The retelling is occasioned by the publication of a U.S. Sentencing Commission report on mandatory penalties in the federal courts and by the possibility that prison crowding, budgetary crises, and a changing professional climate may make more public officials willing to be reminded of what we have long known about mandatory penalties. Officials in some states (there seems little hope at the federal level) may in coming years be more inclined than in the recent past to make policy choices based on knowledge of how mandatory penalties operate in practice. Surprisingly, few published works offer overviews of research on mandatory penalties. This essay is one effort to fill that void.

That mandatory penalties have more costs than benefits does not mean that rational social policies might not incorporate serious penalties for serious crimes. There are more effective, less costly ways than creation of mandatory penalties to achieve that end. In every era, some kinds of crime are regarded as so serious that harsh penalties appear called for. Examples in our time include aggravated forms of stranger violence, non-familial sexual abuse of young children, and flagrant fraudulence in the financial markets. Assuming that legislators will want to provide for severe penalties for especially serious crime, there are ways to avoid or ameliorate the foreseeable dysfunctional effects of mandatory penalties. Here are four examples. First, in order to establish policies calling for severe penalties for serious crimes, while allowing sufficient flexibility to avoid fore-seeable unintended consequences, penalties for especially serious crimes might be made presumptive rather than mandatory. Prosecutors and judges both have powerful voices in sentencing: disregard of the presumption would require that one or both decide either that the penalty would be too severe in a particular case or that the political climate has altered and public sensibilities no longer demand such harsh penalties. Second, as a matter of course, legislators might add "sunset provisions" to mandatory penalty laws. This would assure that laws passed in the passion of the moment will not endure for decades. Legislators can much more comfortably accede to the lapse of a punitive law than vote for its repeal. Third, mandatory (or presumptive) penalties might be limited to serious crimes like armed robbery, aggravated rape, and murder. The most widespread and cynical circumventions of mandatory penalty laws, and the most extreme injustices in individual cases, arise under laws requiring severe penalties for minor crimes like possession or trafficking of small amounts of controlled substances. Fourth, correctional officials might be authorized to reconsider release dates of all offenders receiving prison sentences exceeding a designated length (say three or five years). This would allow eventual release of people receiving unusually long sentences, life sentences without eligibility for parole, and sentences under "habitual offender" fixed-term laws, without requiring extraordinary political decisions like gubernatorial pardons or commutations. [. . .]

MANDATORY PENALTIES IN THE 1970S, 1980S, AND 1990S

Despite earlier generations' understanding of why mandatory penalties are unsound as a matter of policy, mandatory sentencing laws since 1975 have been America's most popular sentencing innovation. By 1983, forty-nine of the fifty states had adopted mandatory sentencing laws for offenses other than murder or drunk driving (Shane-DuBow, Brown, and Olsen 1985, table 30). Most mandatories apply to murder or aggravated rape, drug offenses, felonies involving firearms, or felonies committed by persons who have previous felony convictions. Between 1985 and mid-1991, the U.S. Congress enacted at least twenty new mandatory penalty provisions; by 1991, more than sixty federal statutes defined more than one hundred crimes subject to mandatories (U.S. Sentencing Commission 1991, pp. 8–10). The experience in most states in the late 1980s was similar. In Florida, for example, seven new mandatory sentencing bills were enacted between 1988 and 1990 (Austin 1991, p. 4). In Arizona, for another example, mandatory sentencing laws are so common that 57 percent of felony offenders in fiscal year 1990 were subject to mandatory sentencing enhancements (Knapp 1991, p. 10).

What gave rise to mandatory sentencing laws is not difficult to understand. During the 1980s many political figures of both parties campaigned on "tough on crime" platforms and few elected officials dared risk being seen as "soft". A recent *New York Times* story captures the climate in its title: "Senate's Rule for its Anti-crime Bill: The Tougher the Provision, the Better" (Ifill 1991). Mandatories are often targeted on especially disturbing behaviors, such as large-scale drug sales, murder, or rape, or especially unattractive characters, such as repeat violent offenders or people who use guns in violent crimes. In the case of firearms offenses, mandatory laws allow the state, like Janus, to frown on law-defying villains who use firearms for criminal purposes and to smile on law-abiding citizens who use firearms for legitimate purposes. In a nation in which most approaches to control of gun use are politically impracticable, mandatory sentencing laws are a mechanism for attempting to deter illegal gun use and encourage offenders to use less lethal weapons.

Although the uninitiated citizen might reasonably believe that, under a mandatory sentencing law, anyone who commits the target offense will receive the mandated sentence, the reality is more complicated. Sentencing policy is only as mandatory as police, prosecutors, and judges choose to make it. The people who operate the criminal justice system generally find mandatory sentencing laws too inflexible for their taste and take steps to avoid what they consider unduly harsh, and therefore unjust, sentences in individual cases. And, frequently, the mandatory sentencing law is simply ignored. For example, in Minnesota in 1981, of persons convicted of weapons offenses to which a mandatory minimum applied, only 76.5 percent actually received prison sentences (Knapp 1984, p. 28).

Research on mandatory sentencing laws during the 1970s and 1980s reveals a number of avoidance strategies. Boston police avoided application of a 1975 Massachusetts law calling for mandatory one-year sentences for persons convicted of carrying a gun by decreasing the number of arrests made for that offense and increasing (by 120 percent between 1974 and 1976) the number of weapons seizures without arrest (Carlson 1982). Prosecutors often avoid application of mandatory sentencing laws simply by filing charges for different, but roughly comparable, offenses that are not subject to mandatory sentences. Judges too can circumvent such laws. Detroit judges sidestepped a 1977 law requiring a two-year sentence for persons convicted of possession of a firearm in the commission of a felony by acquitting defendants of the gun charge (even though the evidence would support a conviction) or by decreasing the sentence they would otherwise impose by two years to offset the mandatory two-year term (Heumann and Loftin 1979).

There has been considerable recent research and, taken together, like the work of earlier generations, it supports the following generalizations:

1 lawyers and judges will take steps to avoid application of laws they consider unduly harsh;

2 dismissal rates typically increase at early stages of the criminal justice process after effectuation of a mandatory penalty as practitioners attempt to shield some defendants from the law's reach;

3 defendants whose cases are not dismissed or diverted make more vigorous efforts to avoid conviction and to delay sentencing with the results that trial rates and case processing times increase;

4 defendants who are convicted of the target offense are often sentenced more severely than they would have been in the absence of the mandatory penalty provision; and

5   because declines in conviction rates for those arrested tend to offset increases in imprisonment rates for those convicted, the overall probability that defendants will be incarcerated remains about the same after enactment of a mandatory sentencing law.

The empirical evidence concerning the operation of mandatory sentencing laws comes primarily from five major studies. One is the U.S. Sentencing Commission's recent study of mandatory penalties in the U.S. federal courts (U.S. Sentencing Commission 1991). The second concerns the "Rockefeller Drug Laws," which required mandatory prison sentences for persons convicted of a variety of drug felonies (Joint Committee on New York Drug Law Evaluation 1978). One concerns the operation of a 1977 Michigan law requiring imposition of a two-year mandatory prison sentence on persons convicted of possession of a gun during commission of a felony (Loftin and McDowall 1981; Loftin, Heumann, and McDowall 1983). Two concern a Massachusetts law requiring a one-year prison sentence for persons convicted of carrying a firearm unlawfully (Beha 1977; Rossman et al. 1979).

U.S. Sentencing Commission report

Were federal officials more interested in rational policy-making than in political posturing, the U.S. Sentencing Commission report, "Mandatory Minimum Penalties in the Federal Criminal Justice System," would result in withdrawal of all mandatory sentencing proposals and repeal of those now in effect.

The commission's report demonstrates that mandatory minimum sentencing laws unwarrantedly shift discretion from judges to prosecutors, result in higher trial rates and lengthened case processing times, arbitrarily fail to acknowledge salient differences between cases, and often punish minor offenders much more harshly than anyone involved believes is warranted. Interviews with judges, lawyers, and probation officers at twelve sites showed that heavy majorities of judges, defense counsel, and probation officers dislike mandatory penalties; prosecutors are about evenly divided. Finally, and perhaps not surprisingly given the other findings, the report shows that judges and lawyers not uncommonly circumvent mandatories.

The commission's study was prompted by a congressional mandate. The congressional charge had eight parts, including an assessment of the effects of mandatories on sentencing disparities, a description of the interaction between mandatories and plea bargaining, and "a detailed empirical research study of the effect of mandatory minimum penalties in the Federal system."

The commission's research design effectively combined methods and data sources for investigating charging, bargaining, and sentencing patterns. The combination of quantitative analyses of 1984–90 sentencing patterns, a detailed quantitative analysis of case processing in 1990, and various interviews and surveys aimed at capturing officials' opinions provide complementary sources of information. In presenting and discussing findings, the report carefully notes the limits of the claims it can make and describes alternative interpretations of findings.

The commission analyzed three data sets describing federal sentencing and two sources of data concerning the opinions of judges, assistant U.S. attorneys, and others. The three sentencing data sets were FPSSIS, sentencing commission monitoring data for fiscal year 1990, and a 12.5 percent random sample from the sentencing commission's file of defendants sentenced in fiscal year 1990. Data for the random sample were augmented by examining computerized and paper case files to identify cases (there proved to be 1,165 defendants) that met statutory criteria for receipt of a mandatory minimum drug or weapon sentence.

The two sources of data on practitioners' opinions were structured interviews in twelve sites of 234 practitioners (forty-eight judges, seventy-two assistant U.S. attorneys, forty-eight defense attorneys, sixty-six probation officers), and a May 1991 mail survey of 2,998 practitioners (the same groups as were interviewed; 1,261 had responded by the time the report was written).

1. *Results of the sentencing analyses.* The sentencing data revealed a number of patterns that the commission found disturbing. First, there were clear indications that prosecutors often do not file charges that carry mandatory minimums when the evidence would have supported such charges. For one example, prosecutors failed to file charges for mandatory weapons enhancements against 45 percent of drug defendants for whom they would have been appropriate. For another, prosecutors failed to seek mandatory sentencing enhancements for prior felony convictions in 63 percent of cases in which they could have been sought. For a third, defendants were charged with the offense carrying the highest applicable mandatory minimum in only 74 percent of cases.

Second, there were clear indications that prosecutors used mandatory provisions tactically to induce guilty pleas. For one example, among defendants who were fully charged with applicable mandatory sentence charges and who were convicted at trial, 96 percent received the full mandatory minimum sentence; by contrast, 27 percent of those who pled guilty pled to charges bearing no mandatory minimum or a lower one. For another example, of all defendants who pled guilty (whether or not initially charged with all the applicable mandatory-bearing charges), 32 percent had no mandatory minimum at conviction and 53 percent were sentenced below the minimum that the evidence would have justified. For a third example, among those defendants against whom mandatory weapons enhancements were filed, the weapons charges were later dismissed in 26 percent of cases.

Third, mandatories increased trial rates and presumably also increased workloads and case processing times. Nearly 30 percent of those convicted of offenses bearing mandatory minimums were convicted at trial, a rate two-and-one-half times the overall trial rate for federal criminal defendants.

Fourth, there were indications that judges (often presumably with the assent of prosecutors) imposed sentences less severe than applicable mandatory provisions would appear to require. Before examples are given, it bears mention that the sentencing commission's "modified real offense" policies direct judges, especially in drug cases, to sentence on the basis of actual offense behavior and not simply the offense of conviction.

Here are a couple of the commission's findings that suggest judicial willingness to work around, and under, the mandatories. Forty percent of all defendants whose cases the commission believed warranted specific mandatory minimums received shorter sentences than the applicable statutes would have specified. Another example: mandatory minimum defendants received downward departures 22 percent of the time. The commission observes that "the increased departure rate may reflect a greater tendency to exercise prosecutorial or judicial discretion as the severity of the penalties increases"

(U.S. Sentencing Commission 1991, p. 53). To like effect, "[t]he prosecutors' reasons for reducing or dismissing mandatory charges . . . may be attributable to . . . satisfaction with the punishment received" (U.S. Sentencing Commission 1991, p. 58).

Taken together, these findings suggested to the commission that mandatory minimums are not working. They were shifting too much discretion to the prosecutor. They were provoking judges and prosecutors willfully to circumvent their application (U.S. Sentencing Commission 1991, pp. ii. 76). They were producing high trial rates and unacceptable sentencing disparities.

2. *Results of the opinion surveys*: No category of federal court practitioners, including prosecutors, much likes mandatory minimum sentencing laws (U.S. Sentencing Commission 1991, chap. 6). In one-hour structured interviews, thirty-eight of forty-eight federal district court judges offered unfavorable comments. The most common were that the mandatory sentences are too harsh and that they eliminate judicial discretion. Among forty-eight defense counsel, only one had anything positive to say about guidelines, and he also had negative comments. The most common complaints were that the mandatories are too harsh, that they result in too many trials, and that they eliminate judicial discretion. Probation officers were also overwhelmingly hostile to the mandatories; their most common complaints were that the mandatories are too harsh, result in prison overcrowding, and eliminate judicial discretion. Only among prosecutors was sentiment more favorable to mandatories, and even then thirty-four of sixty-one interviewed who expressed a view were wholly (twenty-three) or partly (eleven) negative.

Consistent with the interview data, the mail survey showed that 62 percent of judges, 52 percent of private counsel, and 89 percent of federal defenders want mandatories for drug crimes eliminated, compared to only 10 percent of prosecutors and 22 percent of probation officers.

The Rockefeller Drug Laws in New York

Perhaps the most exhaustive examination of mandatory sentencing laws before the commission's work was an evaluation of the later repealed Rockefeller Drug Laws in New York. The "Rockefeller Drug Laws" took effect in New York on September 1, 1973. They prescribed severe mandatory prison sentences for narcotics offenses and included selective statutory limits on plea bargaining. A major evaluation (Joint Committee on New York Drug Law Evaluation 1978) focused primarily on the effects of the drug laws on drug use and drug related crime and only to a lesser extent on case processing. The study was based primarily on analyses of official record data routinely collected by public agencies. The key findings were these:

1   drug felony arrests, indictment rates, and conviction rates all declined after the law took effect;
2   for those who were convicted, however, the likelihood of being imprisoned and the average length of prison term increased;
3   the two preceding patterns cancelled each other out and the likelihood that a person arrested for a drug felony would be imprisoned was the same – 11 percent – after the law took effect as before;

4   because defendants struggled to avoid the mandatory sentences, the proportion of
     drug felony dispositions resulting from trials tripled between 1973 and 1976 and the
     average time required for processing of a single case doubled.

Table 29.1 shows case processing patterns for drug felony cases in New York during the
period 1972–76. The percentage of drug felony arrests resulting in indictments declined
steadily from 39.1 percent in 1972, before the law took effect, to 25.4 percent in the first
half of 1976. Similarly, the likelihood of conviction, given indictment, declined from
87.3 percent in 1972 to 79.3 percent in the first half of 1976. Of those defendants, however, who were not winnowed out earlier, the likelihood that a person convicted of a drug
felony would be incarcerated increased from 33.8 percent in 1972 to 54.8 percent in 1976.

The interpretation conventionally put on the proceeding findings is that defense
lawyers, prosecutors, and judges made vigorous efforts to avoid application of the mandatory sentences in cases in which they viewed those sentences as being too harsh and that
the remaining cases were dealt with harshly as the law dictated (Blumstein et al. 1983,
pp. 188–89). Thus, the percentage of drug felonies in New York City disposed of after a
trial rose from 6 percent in 1972 to 17 percent in the first six months of 1976 (Joint
Committee on New York Drug Law Evaluation 1978, p. 104). In other words, many
fewer defendants pled guilty, and the trial rate tripled. No doubt as a consequence of the
increased trial rates, it "took between ten and fifteen times as much court time to dispose
of a case by trial as by plea," and the average case processing time for disposed cases
increased from 172 days in the last four months of 1973 to 351 days in the first six
months of 1976. Backlogs rose commensurately notwithstanding the creation of thirty-
one additional criminal courts in New York City for handling of drug prosecutions (Joint
Committee on New York Drug Law Evaluation 1978, tables 33–35 and p. 105).

Sentencing severity increased substantially for defendants who were eventually convicted. Only 3 percent of sentenced drug felons received minimum sentences of more

Table 29.1 Drug felony processing in New York state

	1972	1973*	1974	1975	1976 (January–June)
Arrests	19,269	15,594	17,670	15,943	8,166
Indictments:					
N	7,528	5,969	5,791	4,283	2,073
Percent of arrests	39.1	38.3	32.8	26.9	25.4
Indictments dispersed	6,911	5,580	3,939	3,989	2,173
Convictions:					
N	6,033	4,739	3,085	3,347	1,724
Percent of dispositions	87.3	84.9	78.3	78.9	79.3
Prison and jail sentences:					
N	2,019	1,555	1,074	1,369	945
Percent of convictions	33.8	32.8	34.8	43.5	54.8
Percent of arrests	10.6	10.0	6.1	8.6	11.6

Source: Joint Committee (1978), tables 19, 24, 27, 29.
Note
* The drug law went into effect September 1, 1973.

than three years between 1972 and 1974 under the old law. Under the new law, the percentage of convicted drug felons receiving sentences of three years or longer increased to 22 percent. The likelihood that a person convicted of a drug felony would receive an incarcerative sentence increased in New York State from 33.8 percent in 1972, before the new law took effect, to 54.8 percent in the first six months of 1976 (Joint Committee on New York Drug Law Evaluation 1978, pp. 99–103).

The broad pattern of findings in the New York study, while more stark in New York than in other mandatory sentencing jurisdictions that have been evaluated, recurs throughout the impact evaluations. The combination of the Rockefeller Drug Laws' effects was more than the system could absorb, and many key features were repealed in mid-1976.

Massachusetts's Bartley-Fox Amendment

Massachusetts's Bartley-Fox Amendment required imposition of a one-year mandatory minimum prison sentence, without suspension, furlough, or parole, for anyone convicted of unlawful carrying of an unlicensed firearm. An offender need not have committed any other crime; the Massachusetts law thus was different from many mandatory sentencing firearms laws that require imposition of a minimum prison sentence for the use or possession of a firearm in the commission of a felony.

Two major evaluations of the Massachusetts gun law were conducted (Beha 1977; Rossman et al. 1979). Some background on the Boston courts may make the following discussion of their findings more intelligible. The Boston Municipal Court is both a trial court and a preliminary hearing court. If a defendant is dissatisfied with either his conviction or his sentence, he may appeal to the Suffolk Country Superior Court where he is entitled to a trial de novo.

The Beha (1977) analysis is based primarily on comparisons of police and court records for the periods six months before and six months after the effective date of the mandatory sentencing law. The Rossman et al. (1979) study dealt with official records from 1974, 1975, and 1976 supplemented by interviews with police, lawyers, and court personnel.

The primary findings:

1   police altered their behavior in a variety of ways aimed at limiting the law's reach: they became more selective about whom to frisk; the absolute number of reports of gun incidents taking place out-of-doors decreased, which meant a concomitant decrease in arrests, and the number of weapons seized without arrest increased by 120 percent from 1974 to 1976 (Carlson 1982, p. 6, relying on Rossman et al. 1979);

2   the number of persons "absconding" increased substantially between the period before the law took effect and the period after (both studies);

3   outcomes favorable to defendants, including both dismissals and acquittals, increased significantly between the before and after periods (both studies);

4   of persons convicted of firearms carrying charges in Boston Municipal Court, appeal rates increased radically (Beha 1977, table 2); in 1974, 21 percent of municipal court convictions were appealed to the Superior Court, and by 1976 that rate had increased to 94 percent (Rossman et al. 1979);

5   the percentage of defendants who entirely avoided a conviction rose from 53.5 percent
     in 1974 to 80 percent in 1976 (Carlson 1982, p. 10, relying on Rossman (Rossman
     et al. 1979));

6   of that residuum of offenders who were finally convicted, the probability of receiving
     an incarcerative sentence increased from 23 percent to 100 percent (Carlson 1982,
     p. 8, relying on Rossman (Rossman et al. 1979)).

Thus the broad patterns of findings for the U.S. Sentencing Commission and
Rockefeller Drug Law evaluations carries over to Massachusetts – more early dismissals,
more protracted proceedings, increased sentencing severity for those finally convicted.
[. . .]

This is not a realm, however, where research counts for much. Policy debates
are likely neither to wait for nor much depend on research results. We now know what
we are likely to know, and what our predecessors knew, about mandatory penalties.
As instruments of public policy, they do little good and much harm. If America does
sometime become a "kinder, gentler place," there will be little need for mandatory
penalties and academics will have no need to propose "reforms" premised on the inability
of elected officials to make decisions that take account of existing knowledge. As yet,
however, America is neither completely kind nor universally gentle, and proposals
such as those offered here might provide mechanisms for reconciling the symbolic and
rhetorical needs of elected officials with the legal system's needs for integrity in process
and justice in punishment.

References

Austin, James. 1991. *The Consequences of Escalating the Use of Imprisonment: The Case Study of
    Florida*. San Francisco: National Council on Crime and Delinquency.

Beha, James A. II. 1977. " 'And Nobody Can Get You Out': The Impact of a Mandatory Prison
    Sentence for the Illegal Carrying of a Firearm on the Use of Firearms and on the
    Administration of Criminal Justice in Boston." *Boston University Law Review* 57:96–146
    (pt. 1), 289–333 (pt. 2).

Blumstein, Alfred, Jacqueline Cohen, and Daniel Nagin. 1978. *Deterrence and Incapacitation:
    Estimating the Effects of Criminal Sanctions on Crime Rates*. Washington, D.C.: National
    Academy of Sciences.

Blumstein, Alfred, Jacqueline Cohen, Susan F. Martin, and Michael Tonry, eds, 1983. *Research
    on Sentencing: The Search for Reform*. Vol. 1. Washington, D.C.: National Academy of
    Sciences.

Carlson, Kenneth. 1982. *Mandatory Sentencing: The Experience of Two States*. National Institute of
    Justice. U.S. Department of Justice. Washington, D.C.: U.S. Government Printing
    Office.

Heumann, Milton, and Colin Loftin. 1979. "Mandatory Sentencing and the Abolition of Plea
    Bargaining: The Michigan Felony Firearms Statute." *Law and Society Review* 13:393–430.

Ifill, Gwen. 1991. "Senate's Rule for Its Anti-Crime Bill: The Tougher the Provision, the
    Better." *New York Times* (July 8, national ed.), p. A6.

Jacobs, James B. 1988. "The Law and Criminology of Drunk Driving." In *Crime and Justice: A
    Review of Research*, vol 10, edited by Michael Tonry and Norval Morris. Chicago:
    University of Chicago Press.

Joint Committee on New York Drug Law Evaluation. 1978. *The Nation's Toughest Drug Law: Evaluating the New York Experience*. A project of the Association of the Bar of the City of New York and the Drug Abuse Council, Inc. Washington, D.C.: U.S. Government Printing Office.

Knapp, Kay A. 1984. *The Impact of the Minnesota Sentencing Guidelines — Three Year Evaluation*. St. Paul, Minn.: Minnesota Sentencing Guidelines Commission.

———. 1991. "Arizona: Unprincipled Sentencing. Mandatory Minimums, and Prison Crowding." *Overcrowded Times* 2(5): 10–12.

Loftin, Colin, and David McDowall. 1981. "One with a Gun Gets You Two: Mandatory Sentencing and Firearms Violence in Detroit." *Annals of the American Academy of Political and Social Science* 455: 150.

Loftin, Colin, Milton Heumann, and David McDowall. 1983. "Mandatory Sentencing and Firearms Violence: Evaluating an Alternative to Gun Control." *Law and Society Review* 17: 287–318.

Moore, Mark I. L. 1990. "Supply Reduction and Drug Law Enforcement." In *Drugs and Crime*, edited by Michael Tonry and James Q. Wilson. Vol. 13 of *Crime and Justice: A Review of Research*, edited by Michael Tonry and Norval Morris. Chicago: University of Chicago Press.

Pierce, Glen L., and William J. Bowers. 1981. "The Bartley-Fox Gun Law's Short-Term Impact on Crime in Boston." *Annals of the American Academy of Political and Social Science* 455: 120–32.

Reuter, Peter, and Mark A. R. Kleiman. 1986. "Risks and Prices: An Economic Analysis of Drug Prices." In *Crime and Justice: A Review of Research*, vol. 7, edited by Michael Tonry and Norval Morris. Chicago: University of Chicago Press.

Rossman, David, Paul Froyd, Glen L. Pierce, John McDevitt, and William J. Bowers. 1979. *The Impact of the Mandatory Gun Law in Massachusetts*. Report to the National Institute of Law Enforcement and Criminal Justice, Law Enforcement Assistance Administration, U.S. Department of Justice, Washington, D.C.

Shane-DuBow, Sandra, Alice P. Brown, and Erik Olsen. 1985. *Sentencing Reform in the United States: History, Content, and Effect*. Washington, D.C.: U.S. Government Printing Office.

U.S. Sentencing Commission. 1991. *Special Report to the Congress: Mandatory Minimum Penalties in the Federal Criminal Justice System*. Washington, D.C.: U.S. Sentencing Commission.

Chapter 30

Dane Archer and Rosemary Gartner

HOMICIDE AND THE DEATH PENALTY
A cross-national test of a deterrence hypothesis

From: Dane Archer and Rosemary Gartner (1984), excerpts from 'Homicide and the death penalty', in Dane Archer and Rosemary Gartner, *Violence and Crime in Cross-national Perspective*, New Haven and London: Yale University Press, pp. 118–139.

D EBATE OVER CAPITAL PUNISHMENT has a long and extensive history. This debate has been complex and confused, partly because support for the death penalty has reflected no single theory but, instead, several different themes. These include a belief in the justice of retribution, the wish to avoid the economic costs of protracted imprisonment, disbelief in the possibility of rehabilitation and, finally, a conception that has come to be called "deterrence theory." While each argument for the death penalty can be considered on its merits, it is deterrence theory that has captured public imagination and scientific attention.

Briefly stated, deterrence theory holds that there is an effective relationship between specific *qualities* of punishment (for example, its certainty, celerity, or severity) and the likelihood that a punishable offense will be committed. A corollary of deterrence theory is that increasing the penalty for an offense will decrease its frequency, while decreasing the penalty will cause infractions to multiply. Deterrence theory therefore conceives of potential offenders as rational actors who weigh the qualities and probabilities of punishment before acting.

Although capital punishment is ancient, the genealogy of deterrence theory is much more recent. Until the past few centuries, the death penalty was imposed often and for many offenses, some of which seem trivial to the modern eye. For most of recorded history, the fate of the executed was regarded as deserved and morally unproblematic. Deterrence theory emerged only two or three centuries ago, when societies for the first time felt obliged to provide rational justifications for using the death penalty. This need reflected a number of historical developments, including a growing distaste for trial by torture, maiming, stoning, burning, and other forms of judicial violence (Archer, in press).

Unique aspects of the death penalty have contributed to abolitionist sentiment. The discovery of judicial errors in capital cases has emphasized the fallibility of determining criminal guilt. This recognition prompted Lafayette to remark, "I shall continue to demand the abolition of the death penalty until I have the infallibility of human judgments demonstrated to me" (Green, 1967). Similarly, violent retribution has become less palatable than it once was. If society's purpose in executions is to exact horrible suffering, it is not clear that contemporary executions maximize this purpose, as Clarence Darrow observed:

> But why not do a good job of it? . . . Why not boil them in oil, as they used to do? Why not burn them at the stake? Why not sew them in a bag with serpents and throw them out to sea? . . . Why not break every bone in their body on the rack, as has often been done for such serious offenses as heresy and witchcraft?
>
> (Green, 1967: 50)

At present, other justifications for the death penalty having become less tenable, deterrence theory occupies center stage in the debate over capital punishment. While deterrence theory may conceal elements of ancient themes (such as the desire for retribution), the theory's manifest justification involves *saving* lives: the killing of convicted offenders is alleged to preserve the lives of future victims of the convicted person and other potential offenders. In this sense, somewhat ironically, deterrence theory is itself a symptom of the increasing sanctity of life, since the theory argues that executions save lives.

While deterrence has been implicit in writings about punishment for centuries, the formal emergence of this theory is often identified with the eighteenth-century criminologist and jurist Cesare Beccaria. In his writings on the control and prevention of crime, Beccaria elaborated the general proposition that human behavior can be influenced by variations in punishments (Sellin, 1967). Deterrence theory also has been prominent in political and parliamentary debates, beginning with the French Constituent Assembly in 1791. It is interesting that the two sides of this 1791 debate over deterrence theory have resurfaced, with little modification, in virtually all subsequent debates:

> There is a class of people with whom the horror of crime counts a great deal less than the fear of punishment: their imagination needs to be shaken, that necessitates something which will resound in their soul, which will move it profoundly, so that the idea of punishment is inseparable from that of crime. . . . The wicked does not fear God, but he does have fear, i.e., the sentiment which the scoundrel feels at the sight of the scaffold.
>
> (Prugnon, 1791, cited in Hornum, 1967)

> It is not the fear of punishment which stops the sacrilegious hand of the assassin. . . . The scoundrel always flatters himself that he will escape the law's surveillance. . . . Also, one cannot believe that the man who is so barbaric that he can soak his hand in the blood of his fellow man will be held back by the distant appearance of a cruel fate.
>
> (Villeneuve, 1791, cited in Hornum, 1967)

The controversy has resurfaced recently in Western societies. In the United States, changes in crime rates and public opinion have both figured in this debate. Support for the death penalty has shown a pattern of long-term decline and, more recently, resurgence. In the 1930s, surveys showed that roughly two-thirds of the American people supported the death penalty, and as late as the 1950s, an average of seventy executions a year were carried out in the United States. This number fell precipitously during the 1960s. Surveys showed that fewer than half the American people approved of the death penalty during the 1960s, and from 1968 until January of 1977 there were no executions in the United States.

Support for capital punishment has since revived. The engine driving this reversal is almost certainly the crime rate. After a monotonic decline since the 1930s, rates of homicide began to increase sharply in the mid-1960s. As a single example, the rate for homicide and non-negligent manslaughter in the United States doubled between 1963 and 1973. Spurred by these increases, the death penalty once again enjoys the support of a majority of the American people. While only a handful of executions have been carried out since 1977, several states that had previously abolished the death penalty have now restored it. As a result, roughly a thousand convicts are now under sentence of death in the United States, and the number grows with each passing week.

It should be noted that there is in this change an interesting non sequitur. The momentary crime rate of course has no bearing on the validity of deterrence theory – executions do not acquire more deterrent value merely because a nation's crime rate has increased. Crime rates and punishment instead have a *political* relationship in that crime rates provide a context which may determine whether or not citizens and politicians are willing to act *as if* the case for criminal deterrence was clear and proven. For this reason, it should be stressed that scientific evidence on the deterrence hypothesis is only one of several factors in the dynamic processes of abolition and restoration.

Finally, the history of this issue is one of cycles; although recent support for the death penalty has mounted rapidly, it could as easily subside. Apart from the seeming impermanence reflected in these changes, the debate between abolitionists and restorationists has centered on a number of enduring questions, and it is to these more durable issues that this chapter is devoted. [. . .]

SELECTED EVIDENCE ON THE EFFECTS OF CAPITAL PUNISHMENT

Debate over capital punishment is anything but new. As early as the 1830s, the death penalty was under attack in several American state legislatures, and a moratorium on public executions was declared. A Massachusetts state legislator named Robert Rantoul, Jr., figured prominently in this debate. In various public meetings, Rantoul presented statistics he had assembled on the deterrence question. Rantoul's efforts were unusually sophisticated and were, in fact, more extensive and detailed than many studies done a century later.

Rantoul examined long-term trends in a number of European countries and found that nations with a low ratio of executions to convictions had recorded declining homicide rates over time – precisely the reverse of what deterrence theory would predict. Rantoul also examined short-term patterns and found that periods with unusually high numbers of executions were followed by increases in the incidence of homicide. Because of its sophistication and breadth, Rantoul's work (see Bowers and Pierce, 1980: 460–61) is a landmark in the history of deterrence research.

The beginning of systematic deterrence research by social scientists coincides with a second "reform" era in the United States early in [the twentieth century]. Over a period of fifty years, social scientists conducted a number of analyses focused primarily on the de jure issue. These studies include Bye (1919), Sutherland (1925), Vold (1932, 1952), Dann (1935), Schuessler (1952), Sellin (1961, 1967), and Reckless (1969). The general conclusion drawn from these studies is captured by Sellin's much-cited statement: "the presence of the death penalty – in law or practice – does not influence homicide death rates" (1967: 138). This body of de jure research has been criticized on several grounds, and by the early 1970s the widely accepted conclusion that the death penalty was not an effective deterrent was under increasing attack. Critics of de jure research have pursued several arguments:

> They have complained (1) that gross homicide rates are not sensitive enough to pick up deterrent effects, specifically, that the proportion of capital to noncapital homicides could be varying even when the overall homicide rate remains unaffected by abolition; (2) that the use of contiguous jurisdictions and before and after comparisons does not fully control for all other factors which could conceivably be masking deterrent effects; and (3) that deterrent effects may not be "jurisdictionally specific" within a nation, that people may not be responsive to the presence of, or changes in, capital statutes in the particular state where they reside, as distinct from neighboring states.
>
> (Bowers, 1974)

These criticisms have prompted new research designs and different approaches. Relying chiefly on the statistical use of multiple regression, a number of studies have tried to control for differences across jurisdictions or over time which could conceivably influence homicide rates. In this way, researchers attempt to determine how much of any observed change in homicide rates is due to nonpunishment variables or, alternatively, to the existence of capital punishment statutes and actual executions.

One of the first of these studies was conducted by Ehrlich (1975). Using aggregate homicide data for the entire United States for the period 1933–1970, Ehrlich analyzed the effect of the probability of execution (given a conviction for a capital offense) on homicide rates. He also controlled for a variety of other factors including unemployment, age, and per capita income. On the basis of this analysis, Ehrlich concluded that executions did have a deterrent effect. Specifically, he claimed that between seven and eight potential homicides were deterred by each execution.

Although Ehrlich's work found an eager audience among many policy-makers, his research has been extensively criticized by a number of researchers using equally sophisticated methods, particularly Bowers and Pierce (1975); Passell and Taylor (1976); Klein, Forst, and Filatov (1978); Loftin (1980); and Brier and Fienberg (1980). Many of these criticisms have been thoroughly summarized elsewhere (e.g., Blumstein, Cohen, and Nagin, 1978) and need not be repeated here. Because Ehrlich's work is one of very few studies to find support for the deterrence hypothesis, it is not surprising that this research garnered widespread popular and scientific interest.

Attempted replications of Ehrlich's work using similar techniques (multivariate analyses and econometric methods) have failed, however, to find a deterrence effect. For example, Loftin (1980) did an elaborate ecological analysis of crime rates and social characteristics in the United States. When social and economic variables such as poverty, education, and family structure were controlled, this study found little or no evidence for the deterrence hypothesis. Similarly, Brier and Fienberg (1980) used econometric models to test for a deterrence effect and concluded that the claims made in Ehrlich's 1975 study were not supported by the evidence. Finally, some of the most interesting longitudinal evidence involves separate time-series analyses of data from five different states on the relationship between execution risk and homicide rates (Bailey, 1978a, 1978b, 1979a, 1979b, and 1979c). In these studies, the evidence ran contrary to deterrence theory in three of the five states examined.

In recent research, there is even some evidence for what might be called the "anti-deterrent" effect of capital punishment. A fine-grained study by Bowers and Pierce (1980) examined monthly homicide rates in New York State between 1907 and 1963 and found an average *increase* of two homicides in the month after an execution. This finding led the authors to postulate a "brutalizing" effect of the death penalty – that is, the possibility that executions might increase violent crimes rather than deter them.

In summary, recent studies of the *de facto* issue do not, as was initially thought, contradict the long-standing conclusion from *de jure* research that the death penalty has no consistent, demonstrable deterrent effect. A number of specific issues, some of which have already been mentioned, continue to bear on new research, *de jure* and *de facto*, on deterrence theory. Two of these are of generic importance, and recent evidence on each can be summarized briefly.

1   *Are gross homicide rates sensitive enough to pick up deterrent effects?* Over fifty years ago, Sutherland stated that "the ordinary practice of drawing conclusions regarding changes in murder rates from changes in homicide rates is logically invalid. But it is the only method that can be used, since we have no other statistics available" (1925: 522). Despite the introduction of the *Uniform Crime Reports* in 1933, the lack of specific, disaggregated statistics has remained a problem:

> In the United States, generally only one type of homicide – murder in the first degree – is punishable by death, with murder in the second degree and voluntary manslaughter usually being punished by imprisonment. Typically, however, investigations of the death penalty have operationally defined premeditated murder as homicide, a much more inclusive offense category. This practice has been necessitated by the fact that no alternative statistics are currently available on a nationwide basis that break down homicide by type and degree. As a result investigators have been forced to make a large and possibly erroneous assumption whether they use police or mortality statistics, that the proportion of first degree murders to total homicides remains constant so that the statistics on the latter provide a reasonably adequate indicator of capital offenses.
>
> (Bailey, 1975: 418)

In order to test this crucial assumption, Bailey collected disaggregated data on first- and second-degree murder convictions from a number of state court systems. He then examined the relationship between capital punishment and murder rates in a manner similar to that used in earlier studies by Schuessler (1952) and Sellin (1959, 1967). Bailey's approach differed from these earlier analyses, however, in that "the murder data examined . . . permit a direct rather than indirect assessment of the relationship between capital homicides and the death penalty" Bailey, 1975: 418). Bailey found that there was no evidence for a deterrent effect whether one examined second-degree, first-degree, or all homicides combined. This research cast doubt on the claim that the deterrent effect has been obscured by the insensitivity of gross homicide rates.

2   *Does the use of contiguous jurisdictions and before and after comparisons fail to control for all factors that could mash deterrent effects?* Van den Haag, a strong critic of much deterrence research, has argued that "homicide rates do not depend exclusively on penalties any more than other crime rates [do]. A number of conditions which influence the propensity to crime (demographic, economic, or social) . . . may influence the homicide rate" (1969: 285). In order to control for these factors, some investigators have compared only similar retentionist and abolitionist jurisdictions such as contiguous states.

Because of differences between even contiguous jurisdictions, critics have claimed that this procedure provides inadequate controls. In response, Bailey (1975) compared states with and without the death penalty while controlling for two socio-economic and five demographic variables. As an additional control, retentionist and abolitionist states with similar rates of aggravated assault were compared to hold constant potentially significant etiological factors. Regardless of which control variables were included, Bailey found that retentionist states had measurably higher homicide rates than abolitionist states. In this instance, again, the evidence runs contrary to the deterrence hypothesis. Therefore, while the inclusion of the suggested control variables would certainly have improved many studies that failed to find a deterrent effect, these controls would not have changed the conclusions these studies reached.

GENERAL AND SPECIFIC DETERRENCE HYPOTHESES

In its de jure form, the general deterrence hypothesis holds that, *ceteris paribus*, jurisdictions which abolish capital punishment will experience increased rates of homicide. As already indicated, there are other forms of the hypothesis, including the focus in de facto research on the fact of executions rather than their legal possibility. While de facto research has an incontestable importance, the de jure issue is inherently interesting and also central to policy decisions that are directly linked to the empirical question of whether and how abolition is likely to affect homicide rates. In addition to what is here called the *general* deterrence hypothesis, a number of more specific hypotheses can be derived.

Offense deterrence

Criminal penalties, and therefore their hypothesized deterrent effects, are offense-specific. Where it exists, the death penalty is prescribed for a society's most grievous offenses, capital crimes. In terms of deterrence theory, the death penalty can be expected to have its most direct effects on the specific offenses for which this punishment can be imposed. A more precise hypothesis can therefore be derived from the theory of general deterrence.

This specific hypothesis, which might be called *offense deterrence*, holds that capital punishment will have its most perceptible effects on capital crimes, the offenses executions are imposed to deter. In terms of offense deterrence, the effect of capital punishment on lesser crimes is less predictable. [. . .]

Residual deterrence

If the general deterrence hypothesis is correct, abolition should be followed by homicide rate increases. That this is a central expectation of deterrence theory is beyond dispute. There is disagreement, however, about the temporal qualities of this relationship, and this is a source of controversy in the interpretation of de jure case studies, the results of which can be summarized as follows:

> Comparative examinations of homicide rates before and after abolition [or] the restoration of the death penalty have . . . . questioned the efficacy of capital punishment. These investigations reveal that states that have abolished the death penalty have generally experienced no unusual increase in homicide. Moreover, the reintroduction of the death penalty (eleven states have abolished the death penalty but later restored it) has not been followed by a significant decrease in homicide.
>
> (Bailey, 1975: 417)

At least for the case studies that have been done, there is little disagreement about this empirical fact: abolition (or restoration) of the death penalty does *not* produce any sudden or dramatic changes in homicide rates. While this null result is frequently cited as evidence against the deterrence hypothesis, some have argued that it may reflect only public ignorance of changes in capital statutes. If citizens are uninformed about such changes, abolition might have no perceptible effect because individuals would continue to be deterred as if capital punishment still existed. [. . .]

Despite their obvious importance, comparative studies of deterrence are relatively rare and large-sample comparisons are almost unknown. In the early 1930s the (British) Royal Commission on Capital Punishment heard extensive testimony from expert witnesses representing European and Commonwealth nations. On the basis of the available evidence, the Commission concluded, "Capital Punishment may be abolished in this country [Britain] without endangering life or property or impairing the security of society" (Calvert, 1931: 48). Almost two decades later, the Commission was reestablished for a more extensive, four-year examination of the question. The new Commission affirmed the earlier conclusion: "There is no clear evidence in any of the figures we have examined that the abolition of capital punishment has led to its an increase in the homicide rate, or that its reintroduction has led to its fall" (1953: 23). This conclusion was supported, once again, by a separate study conducted by the 1962 European Committee on Crime Problems.

The trend toward abolition increased during the 1960s and, although it has since been reversed, there have been no systematic efforts during this period to collect and evaluate data from a large sample of abolitionist nations. The individual case studies that have been done vary greatly in their procedures and use of controlled comparisons. As a result, existing cross-national evidence suffers from a confusing patchwork of results. While a comparative test of the deterrence hypothesis is not without complications, the principal obstacle has been the absence of longitudinal offense data from a large sample of societies.

CROSS-NATIONAL DATA ON FOURTEEN CASES OF ABOLITION

A first step in any cross-national test involves identifying a sample of abolition cases. This task is more complicated than one might imagine. Some societies have abolished capital punishment for mortal offenses generally but retain it for a small number of specific crimes, such as the murder of a prison guard by a prisoner serving a life term. Other nations have eliminated the death penalty but provided for its revival during civil emergencies or martial law. The de jure question is therefore complicated by the need for discrete classification of societies as abolitionist when, in fact, degrees of abolition may be present.

One solution to this classification problem employs a rough working definition: Jurisdictions are considered "abolitionist" if capital punishment is prohibited for civil offenses even if extraordinary crimes – such as murders committeed by individuals serving life sentences – are still punishable by death. It should be emphasized that this is a de jure classification. Nations in which no executions have occurred for long periods of time cannot be considered abolitionist under this definition if capital punishment remains in law. The dates of abolition also include potential ambiguities – for example, one could choose the date on which the penal code is changed or the date on which the change takes effect.

After examining various lists of abolitionist nations and dates, we adopted a modified form of the classifications made by Bowers (1974: 178) and Joyce (1961: 85). This consolidated list was juxtaposed with offense rate data from the Comparative Crime Data File to yield a total of fourteen sets of time-series data for twelve distinct cases of abolition. In two cases (Austria and Finland), separate records for the major cities, Vienna and Helsinki, provided the opportunity to "replicate" national cases with urban data.

Before we present the results of these comparisons, it should be emphasized that most efforts to discern the independent effects of abolition err on the side of simplification. Offense rates are driven by many factors, and single-variable evaluations understate this complexity. For example, a number of abolitions occurred around wartime, and . . . wars frequently elevate postwar rates of violent crime. Similarly, vast demographic changes – such as the coming of age of the post-World War II "baby boom" cohort – can greatly inflate offense rates or otherwise complicate efforts to assess the effects of legal changes. In cross-national studies of deterrence, therefore, the effect of abolition is inevitably muddied somewhat by other changes.

For reasons already discussed, a longitudinal design is preferable to crude cross-sectional comparisons. Because of the infinite number of idiosyncratic national characteristics, it makes little or no sense to compare abolitionist and retentionist countries at a single moment in time. The longitudinal approach, in which the individual experiences of a sample of countries are examined over time, provides a much stronger basis for inferences about the effect of abolition. As will be seen the depth and breadth of data in the Comparative Crime Data File make possible longitudinal comparisons as well as a series of additional control procedures.

CROSS-NATIONAL TESTS OF SPECIFIC DETERRENCE HYPOTHESES

Data from this sample of fourteen cases can be examined in a number of ways. Some of these provide an overall test of the *general deterrence* theory prediction that abolition of the death penalty causes a perceptible increase in homicide rates. As indicated earlier, more specific deterrence hypotheses can be derived from the general theory. *Vicarious deterrence*, the alleged geographic spillover of deterrence from retentionist jurisdictions to abolitionist jurisdictions, is controlled in this design by the examination of sovereign nations. *Residual deterrence*, the alleged temporal spillover of deterrence from retentionist years to abolitionist years, can be tested directly by examining post-abolition time intervals of progressively greater lengths. If the hypothesis of residual deterrence has merit, homicide rate increases should become larger as longer intervals after abolition are examined. *Offense deterrence*, the prediction that post-abolition changes will be most conspicuous in rates of capital offenses, can be tested directly by a contrast between homicide and several noncapital crimes.

General deterrence

An initial comparison of the short-term effects of abolition is presented in Table 30.1. The percentages in this table indicate the increase or decrease in homicide rates from the year prior to abolition to the year following. The homicide rates on which the percentages are based are also included as a cautionary feature. In some cases, such as New Zealand, the homicide rate is so low in absolute terms that the addition of a single homicide can double the national offense rate. The precise indicators in this comparison (offenses known, convictions, etc.) are also shown since these differ for the fourteen cases.

Table 30.1 Homicide rate levels before and after abolition of the death penalty

Jurisdiction (date of abolition, indicator)	One year pre-abolition homicide rate	One year post-abolition homicide rate	% Change
Austria (1968, c)	.72	.71	−1
England and Wales (1965, a)	.36	.35	−3
Finland (1949, a)	1.05	.72	−31
Helsinki (1949, a)	1.96	1.90	−3
Israel (1954, a)	4.00	1.72	−57
Italy (1890, a)	13.30	12.94	−3
Sweden (1921, b)	.43	.15	−65
Switzerland (1942, d)	45.25	35.65	−21
Vienna (1968, e)	.93	.93	0
Canada (1967, a)	1.10	1.52	38
Denmark (1930, c)	33.89	35.68	5
Netherlands Antilles (1957, a)	13.19	20.32	54
New Zealand (1961, b)	.04	.08	100*
Norway (1905, b)	.35	.39	11

Notes
* Because of an extremely low base rate, this 100% increase rellects a change from 1 to 2 cases.
Key to offense indicators:
a homicide offenses known.
b murder, manslaughter, or homicide convictions.
c violent offenses known.
d violent offenses convictions.
e criminal statistics.

With these cautions in mind, the picture in Table 30.1 is one of little change; in fact, eight of the fourteen cases (57%) show a homicide rate decrease in the year following abolition while only five (36%) show an increase. In this crude short-term comparison, therefore, there is no evidence for the deterrence hypothesis. De jure abolition appears to have had little effect. If anything, there appears to be a slight downturn in homicide rates.

Residual deterrence

If one subscribes to the hypothesis of residual deterrence, however, the comparison in Table 30.1 is inconclusive. The effects of deterrence could easily be masked by public ignorance of abolition, particularly in the first year following this change. For this reason, longer intervals are compared in Table 30.2. It seems unlikely that residual deterrence could continue to affect behavior five years following abolition, and this hypothesis becomes even less plausible over longer intervals. The five-year statistics in Table 30.2 compare the five years of homicide data before and after abolition. This comparison does not include all fourteen cases since some entries in the CCDF did not have data for all of these years. The "maximum possible" comparison in this table reflects the longest intervals before and after abolition for which homicide data were available.

This comparison again provides little evidence for the deterrence hypothesis in general or for residual deterrence in particular. In the five-year comparison, half of the ten cases for which the comparison can be made show homicide rate increases following abolition while half show decreases. There is even less support for the deterrence hypothesis when longer intervals are examined. When intervals of maximum possible length are

Table 30.2 Homicide rate changes after abolition: longer trends

Jurisdiction	One year	Five year means[a]	Maximum years possible[b]
Austria	−1%	32%	9% (15,5)
Canada	38	63	67 (5,6)
Denmark	5	—	4 (9,2)
England and Wales	−3	18	27 (14,7)
Finland	−31	−40	−59 (22,18)
Helsinki	−3	−27	−57 (22,18)
Israel	−57	−53	−65 (5,16)
Italy	−3	−5	−30 (10,24)
Netherlands Antilles	54	—	−4 (2,13)
New Zealand	100	117	0 (10,11)
Norway	−11	—	−24 (2,35)
Sweden	−65	—	−63 (1,28)
Switzerland	−21	−36	−46 (13,28)
Vienna	0	94	85 (15,5)

Notes

a Comparison of mean offense levels for five-year periods before and after abolition.

b Comparison of mean offense levels for maximum time periods before and after abolition for which data are available (years indicated in parentheses).

compared, only five of the fourteen cases (36%) show homicide rate increases after abolition while eight (57%) show decreases. This finding runs directly counter to the hypothesis of residual deterrence. Since homicide rate decreases are found most consistently when long intervals are compared, the idea that deterrence progressively erodes in the years following abolition seems untenable.

Offense deterrence

A final comparison addresses the question of whether capital punishment has any specific offense deterrence. The breadth of data in the CCDF makes it possible to contrast changes in capital offenses with changes in noncapital crimes. A deterrence theorist could conceivably argue that Tables 30.1 and 30.2 conceal massive downward trends in crime generally and, consistent with the deterrence hypothesis, that homicide rates might be falling *relatively* more slowly than the rates of noncapital offenses. Even falling homicide rates after abolition might reflect deterrence if decreases were less precipitous than simultaneous decreases in noncapital offenses. The key test of offense deterrence, therefore, is whether homicide rate increases after abolition are greater (in absolute or relative terms) than any observed increases for noncapital crimes.

The offense deterrence hypothesis is examined in Table 30.3. This table compares changes before and after abolition for three time periods (one year, five years, and the maximum interval possible) for homicide and five noncapital offenses. Median offense rate changes for all cases are shown at the bottom of the table. Missing percentages indicate that the comparison could not be made for this offense during this particular interval using the data in the CCDF.

In general, the data run strongly counter to the hypothesis of offense deterrence. While this hypothesis predicts that capital crimes will increase more rapidly after abolition than noncapital offenses, precisely the opposite pattern obtains. No matter which time interval is examined, noncapital offense rates show increases greater than the changes observed for homicide rates. While noncapital crime rates increased following abolition – perhaps as a result of demographic or other changes – rates of homicide were stationary or declined.

This difference between capital and noncapital rate changes is striking, and it is difficult to imagine a result more in contradiction with deterrence theory. Under this hypothesis, one would have expected absolute homicide rate increases, or at least increases relative to any changes in noncapital offenses. Yet these cross-national findings fail to support the offense deterrence hypothesis and, in fact, provide strategic evidence that the death penalty has no discernible effect on homicide rates.

SUMMARY AND CONCLUSIONS

If capital punishment is a more effective deterrent than the alternative punishment of long imprisonment, its abolition ought to be followed by homicide rate increases. The evidence examined here fails to support and, indeed, repeatedly contradicts this proposition. In this cross-national sample, abolition was followed more often than not by

Table 30.3 Homicide levels before and after abolition using other offenses as control variables

Jurisdiction	One year						Five year						Maximum years possible*					
	Homicide	M†	R	A	Ro	T	Homicide	M†	R	A	Ro	T	Homicide	M†	R	A	Ro	T
Austria‡	-1%	+24	+12	-2	-9	+17	+32%	+57	+5	+8	+44	+55	+9%	+42	-3	+6	+72	+109
Canada	+38	+107	+32	+20	+42	—	+63	+11	+57	+76	+73	—	+67	+21	+68	+79	+78	—
Denmark	+5	—	0	+5	—	+8	—	—	—	—	—	—	+4	—	+25	—	+25	+34
England	3	+57	+28	+13	+44	+9	+18	+58	+56	+73	+102	+36	+27	+30	+86	+196	+248	—
Finland	-31	-27	+95	-10	-46	-43	-40	-44	+28	—	-80	-70	-59	-63	+102	—	-47	-9
Israel	-57	—	—	+40	-55	-6	-53	—	—	—	-75	+8	-65	—	—	—	-74	+60
Italy	-3	—	—	-10	+31	+4	-5	—	—	—	+32	—	-30	—	—	—	+35	+18
Neth Antilles	+54	—	-50	—	+51	+13	—	—	—	—	—	—	-4	—	-20	—	+87	+46
New Zealand	+100	—	+11	+27	-43	-4	+117	—	+16	+46	-46	+7	0	—	+100	—	-12	+10
Norway	+11	—	+36	-13	—	-10	—	—	—	—	—	—	-24	—	+100	-7	—	—
Sweden	-65	—	-58	-33	-36	—	—	—	—	—	—	—	-63	—	+123	-3	+19	-15
Switzerland	-21	—	+12	21	—	+7	-36	—	—	-36	—	-3	-46	—	—	-36	—	-3
Helsinki	-3	-35	+1	+3	-52	-42	-27	-42	+23	—	-86	+79	-57	-55	+73	—	-71	-43
Vienna	0	+30	+32	-2	-11	+22	+94	+100	+6	+20	+49	+53	+85	138	-3	+33	+100	+145
Median	-2%	+27	+12	-2	-11	+6	+7%	+34	+23	+33	+32	+22	-14%	+26	+71	+20	+35	+26

Notes

* For the number of years included in this comparison, see Table 30.2.

† Crime types: M (Manslaughter), R (Rape), A (Assault), Ro (Robbery). T (Theft).

‡ Homicide rates and year of abolition for each nation are given in Table 30.1.

absolute *decreases* in homicide rates, not by the increases predicted by deterrence theory. Further, the homicide rates of these nations also decreased relative to the rates of noncapital offenses after abolition. Both of these findings hold true whether comparisons are made for short, medium, or the longest feasible time periods. [. . .]

Clearly, the stakes in this debate are unusually high. Precisely for this reason, it seems fair to assume that the burden of proof is on the restorationists to show that a deterrent effect does exist – unless, of course, our society is prepared to shift from deterrence to retribution (or some other principle) as a justification for capital punishment. Given the extreme and irrevocable nature of capital punishment, the deterrent effect should be accepted as a sufficient basis for policy only if evidence shows this effect to be reliable, consistent, and large in magnitude. If the deterrent effect is anything less than this, executions cannot be expected to produce anything other than the deaths of the executed and the satisfaction of those who demand violent retribution. The exceptional nature of this burden of proof required of deterrence theory is cited in a study commissioned by the prestigious National Academy of Sciences:

> In undertaking research on the deterrent effect of capital punishment . . . it should be recognized that the strong value content associated with decisions regarding capital punishment and the high risk associated with errors of commission make it likely that any policy use of scientific evidence on capital punishment will require *extremely severe standards of proof*.
> (Blumstein, Cohen, and Nagin, 1978: 63; emphasis added)

Empirical support for the deterrence hypothesis, including the evidence presented here, obviously cannot meet this exacting standard. The evidence runs strongly contrary to deterrence theory and, while more research can of course be done, the mere existence of this consistently contrary evidence demonstrates that the deterrent effect – if one exists at all – cannot by definition be reliable, consistent, or large in magnitude. If the deterrent effect had these robust qualities, the effect surely would have surfaced vividly and repeatedly in these investigations.

The available evidence suggests that no deterrent effect exists at all, and surely no deterrent effect exists whose strength and size could possibly serve as a sufficient justification for capital punishment. [. . .]

As this chapter and other studies make abundantly clear, there is no extremely strong and overwhelming evidence for deterrence, and the contrary conclusions of existing research suggest that such evidence for deterrence will not be forthcoming. In the absence of thoroughly persuasive evidence, it seems inconceivable that our society would be willing to take the extreme step of executing people in pursuit of what is almost certainly a hopeless objective.

References

Archer, D. 1985. "Social deviance." Pp. 743–804 in G. Lindzey and E. Aronson (eds.) *The Handbook of Social Psychology* (3rd ed.). New York: Random House.

Bailey, W. C. 1975. "Murder and the death penalty." *Journal of Criminal Law and Criminology.* 65: 416–423.

Bailey, W.C. 1978a. "An analysis of the deterrent effect of the death penalty in North Carolina." *North Carolina Central Law Journal*. Fall: 29–49.

Bailey, W.C. 1978b. "Deterrence and the death penalty for murder in Utah: A time series analysis." *Journal of Contemporary Law*. 5: 1–20.

Bailey, W.C. 1979a. "Deterrence and the death penalty for murder in Oregon." *Willamette Law Review*. Winter: 67–85.

Bailey, W.C. 1979b. "The deterrent effect of the death penalty for murder in California." *Southern California Law Review*. March: 743–765.

Bailey, W.C. 1979c. "The deterrent effect of the death penalty for murder in Ohio: A time series analysis." *Cleveland State Law Review*. 28: 51–70.

Blumstein, A., J. Cohen and D. Nagin (eds.). 1978. *Deterrence and Incapacitation: Estimating the Effects of Criminal Sanctions on Crime Rates*. Washington DC: National Academy of Sciences.

Bowers, W.J. 1974. *Executions in America*. Lexington, MA: Lexington Books.

Bowers, W.J. and G.L. Pierce. 1975. "The illusion of deterrence in Isaac Ehrlich's research on capital punishment." *Yale Law Journal*. 85: 187–208.

Bowers, W.J. and G.L. Pierce. 1980. "Deterrence or brutalization: What is the effect of executions?" *Crime and Delinquency*. 26: 453–484.

Brier, S.S. and S.E. Fienberg. 1980. "Recent econometric modelling of crime and punishment: Support for the deterrence hypothesis?" Pp. 82–97 in S.E. Fienberg and A.J. Reiss (eds.), *Indicators of Crime and Criminal Justice: Quantitative Studies*. Washington, DC: U.S. Government Printing Office.

British Royal Commission on Capital Punishment. 1953. *Royal Commission Final Report on Capital Punishment*. London: Her Majesty's Stationery Office.

Bye, R. 1919. *Capital Punishment in the United States*. Philadelphia, PA: Committee on Philanthropic Labor of Philadelphia.

Calvert, E.R. 1931. *The Death Penalty Enquiry: A Review of the Evidence Before the Select Committee on Capital Punishment*. London: Camelot Press.

Dann, R.H. 1935. *The Deterrent Effect of Capital Punishment*. Philadelphia: The Committee of Philanthropic Labor of Philadelphia Yearly Meeting of Friends, Bulletin No. 29.

Ehrlich, I. 1975. "The deterrent effect of capital punishment: A question of life and death." *American Economic Review*. 65: 397–417.

Green, W.M. 1967. "An ancient debate on capital punishment." Pp. 46–54 in T. Sellin (ed.), *Capital Punishment*. New York: Harper and Row.

Hornum, R. 1967. "Two debates: France, 1791; England, 1956." Pp. 55–76 in T. Sellin (ed.), *Capital Punishment*. New York: Harper and Row.

Joyce, J.A. 1961. *Capital Punishment: A World View*. New York: Grove Press.

Klein, L.R., B. Forst, and V. Filatov. 1978. "The deterrent effect of capital punishment: An assessment of the estimates." Pp. 336–359 in A. Blumstein, J. Cohen, and D. Nagin (eds.) *Deterrence and Incapacitation: Estimating the Effects of Criminal Sanctions on Crime Rates*. Washington, DC: National Academy of Sciences.

Loftin, C. 1980. "Alternative estimates of the impact of certain and severity of punishment on levels of homicide in American states." Pp. 75–81 in S.E. Fienberg and A.J. Reiss (eds.), *Indicators of Crime and Criminal Justice: Quantitative Studies*. Washington, DC: U.S. Government Printing Office.

Passell, P. And J.B. Taylor. 1976. "The deterrence controversy: A reconsideration of the time series evidence." Pp. 359–371 in H.A. Bedau and C. Pierce (eds.), *Capital Punishment in the United States*. New York: AMS Press.

Reckless, W.C. 1969. "The impact of war on crime, delinquency, and prostitution." *American Journal of Sociology*. 48: 378–386.

Schuessler, K. 1952. "The deterrent influence of the death penalty." *Annals of the American Academy of Political and Social Sciences.* 217: 54–62.

Sellin, T. (ed.) 1959. *The Death Penalty.* Philadelphia: American Law Institute

Sellin, T. 1961. "Capital punishment." *Federal Probation.* 25: 3–11.

Sellin, T. (ed.) 1967. *Capital Punishment.* New York: Harper and Row.

Sutherland, E.H. 1925. "Murder and the death penalty." *Journal of Criminal Law and Criminology.* 15: 522–529.

Van den Haag, E. 1969. "On deterrence and the death penalty." *Ethics.* 78: 280–288.

Vold, G.B. 1932. "Can the death penalty prevent crime?" *The Prison Journal.* October: 3–8.

Vold, G.B. 1952. "Extent and trend of capital crimes in the United States." *Annals of the American Academy of Political and Social Sciences.* 217: 38–45.

Chapter 31

Charles J. Ogletree, Jr.

THE REHNQUIST REVOLUTION IN CRIMINAL PROCEDURE

From: Charles J. Ogletree, Jr. (2002), 'The Rehnquist revolution in criminal procedure', in Herman Schwartz (ed.), *The Rehnquist Court: Judicial Activism on the Right*, New York: Hill and Wang, pp. 55–69.

THE REHNQUIST COURT HAS had a tremendous impact on criminal justice issues, significantly rolling back the procedural rights of criminal defendants. This result owes much to the leadership of Chief Justice William H. Rehnquist, as can be seen in the way many of the Court's recent decisions on matters of criminal procedure were foreshadowed by his dissenting opinions prior to 1986, as Associate Justice. However, it would be an overgeneralization to assert that all the decisions of the Rehnquist Court have restricted the rights of criminal defendants. Rather, the current era can be seen as one of ideological tension between competing and fluid understandings of the scope of constitutional protections of a criminal defendant's procedural rights. While a criminal defendant today would certainly enjoy narrower procedural protections than sixteen years ago, there has been a certain amount of ideological back-and-forth in the Court's decisions over that period. One example of how this ideological tension has played out is in the issue of racial profiling, and the same tension will no doubt inform the Court's approach to the challenging and pressing questions of constitutional criminal procedure that arose in the aftermath of the September 11, 2001, terrorist attacks in Washington and New York.

What does it mean to talk about the jurisprudence of the Rehnquist Court? What responsibility can we attribute to the chief justice for the decisions of "his" Court? Normally, when we talk about the decisions of a particular Court, invoking the name of the presiding chief justice simply sets historical limits on the decisions we are considering. We may, in addition, attempt to discern the dominant legal philosophy characterizing the Court's decisions during his tenure. This practice has its uses: it provides neat comparisons for different periods of legal history and focuses analysis on the opinions, dissents, and concurrences in each case, rather than purely on the holding.

But the Court is, after all, composed of nine individual justices, each with his or her own legal philosophy. Furthermore, the Rehnquist Court is an extremely fractured one, reaching consistent and relatively predictable 5–4 votes along many issues, which makes it all the more difficult to talk in terms of a unitary, dominant judicial philosophy. It is with these caveats, then, that we can analyze the decisions of the Rehnquist Court as creating an identifiable corpus of criminal procedure law.

To better understand the criminal jurisprudence of the Rehnquist Court, we might consider that there are two models of criminal justice for the Court to draw upon: the *crime-control* model, which promotes deterrence and punishment of crime as the most important end of the criminal justice system, and the *due process* model, which is concerned with vindicating constitutional rights and maximizing individual freedom from government control. The crime-control model permits government agents considerable discretion in pursuing criminals, requires them to submit only to a relatively formal, uniform set of rules to control that discretion, and exhibits significant confidence in the government's identification of suspects as guilty of the crime with which they are charged. By contrast, the due process model requires stricter adherence to constitutional guarantees when the government is surveilling, detaining, and searching individuals; protects those constitutional guarantees through early judicial oversight of the police to ensure that the investigative process is free from bias or error; and emphasizes the presumption of innocence and the burden of proof in determining the guilt or innocence of a suspect.

While these models are neither exhaustive nor particularly sophisticated, they are useful as a framework for understanding different approaches to constitutional criminal procedure. To appreciate how these models apply in practice, it is worth considering the general features of a police investigation and arrest. The investigation typically begins with police observation of an individual's behavior. The Fourth Amendment's prohibition of unreasonable searches and seizures ensures that the police may not arrest people without good reason – what is commonly called "probable cause." A somewhat ambiguous and loosely defined concept, probable cause generally requires that the police have a "substantial basis" for believing that a search will provide evidence that the individual is guilty of an offense. A lesser standard is imposed when the search is likely to be less than ordinarily intrusive. For example, when an officer simply wishes to stop and perhaps frisk an individual at a roadblock or an airport security checkpoint the less onerous "reasonable suspicion" standard is used. Reasonable suspicion requires no more than some articulable reason to believe that a crime has been or will be committed.

Let us imagine that an officer has reasonable suspicion to stop and search you – she has information that someone driving the same make of car as you is planning to rob a department store, and you have driven slowly past that department store five times in the last half hour. With such evidence, the officer may detain you for a brief time, ask you questions, require you to exit your car, frisk you, and look around your car for weapons. You have a limited right to walk away, and at this stage of the investigation, anything you say to the police will be voluntary. If that investigation turns up sufficient information for the officer to establish that she has probable cause to believe that you plan to rob the store – for example, she sees a fake gun and a mask on the backseat – she may arrest you, impound your car, and take the mask and gun into police custody. To conduct a further search, including a search of your home, she must obtain a warrant from a magistrate, again based on probable cause.

Once she has decided to arrest you, the officer may continue to question you only after delivering a warning of your rights. This so called *Miranda* warning – familiar to all viewers of TV cop shows – informs you of your Fifth Amendment right to avoid self-incrimination and the right to obtain the assistance of an attorney during any questioning that takes place. These rights, however, can be waived. If you continue to talk after the warning and without your attorney – perhaps to tell the police that the mask and gun are your son's Halloween costume and that you were only looking at a particular pair of shoes in the store window – the police can use anything you say as evidence against you in a criminal trial.

The checks on the power of the police to search and seize are of relatively recent vintage. Although they are based upon, and arguably required by, the Fourth, Fifth, and Sixth Amendments, the three cases that created these protections – *Miranda v. Arizona, Massiah v. United States*, and *Mapp v. Ohio* – were decided by the Warren Court in the 1960s. They all reflected a marked shift in the Court's attitude toward the powers of the police vis-a-vis the rights of individual citizens and attempted to give some teeth to the elements of the due process model present in the Constitution. It is in contrast to the Warren Court, in particular, with its emphasis on vindicating the individual constitutional rights of criminal defendants, that the Rehnquist Court is usually presented.

There is little doubt that the Rehnquist Court is particularly conservative in the field of criminal law and has strongly endorsed the crime control model of criminal justice. In contrast to the Warren Court, with its due process leanings, the Rehnquist Court has, as Stanley H. Friedelbaum observes, "moved decisively to rework a wide array of judicially devised components of the criminal law by directly overturning or materially eroding their value as precedents."

No Court has been perfectly consistent in its application of jurisprudential models or in its ideological approach, mainly because of the fact-specific nature of many adjudications as well as shifts in majorities based on where along the ideological spectrum a particular case falls. For example, consider *Terry v. Ohio*, ironically a Warren Court decision and one of the most important contributors to the conservative erosion of the Warren Court's legacy. The facts presented in *Terry* are rather like the circumstances in the typical police investigation described above. An officer noticed Terry and another man on a street corner and observed an unusual pattern of behavior, in which they "pace[d] alternately along an identical route, pausing to stare in the same store window roughly twenty-four times; . . . followed immediately by a conference between the two men on the corner" and a discussion with a third man several blocks away. Based on these observations, the police officer stopped the three men and conducted a limited search for weapons. Guns were found, which formed the basis for Terry's conviction on charges of carrying a concealed weapon. The Court found that the police officer had acted reasonably in stopping the suspects, in part because the officer conducted not a full-blown search and seizure but only a "stop and frisk" for weapons. Although the Court limited the original rationale of *Terry* to a search for weapons and required some objective justification for the stop, subsequent decisions have substantially broadened its effect. The *Terry* decision has ultimately been used to authorize pretextual stops and has resulted in an increase in racial profiling.

In fact, this use of Warren-era precedent to erode Warren-era doctrine is a feature of the Rehnquist Court's conservative jurisprudence. Instead of disputing the content of the constitutional rights available to a citizen when stopped and questioned by the police, the Rehnquist Court has simply removed the adverse procedural consequences of police breaches of those rights.

For example, in *Caplin & Drysdale, Chartered v. United States*, a criminal defendant challenged a criminal forfeiture statute because, in taking his possessions, the state had left him without the means to retain the counsel of his choice. He claimed that this violated his Sixth Amendment right to counsel. The Court disagreed, noting, that he could retain an attorney – if one would work for free – and that the Sixth Amendment did not entitle him to the attorney of his choice, only to representation by counsel. The Court did not narrow the constitutional right to counsel – it simply adopted a rule that collaterally removed the defendant's meaningful enjoyment of the right.

The use of such judge-created procedural rules to limit the meaningfulness of constitutional rights is Chief Justice Rehnquist's own contribution to the jurisprudence of the Supreme Court. Three areas of law particularly demonstrate this impact: searches and seizures under the Fourth Amendment, the Fifth Amendment's right to avoid compelled self-incrimination, and the Eighth Amendment's prohibition on cruel and unusual punishment. In each area, Rehnquist's opinions during his tenure as an associate justice, often in dissent, foreshadowed the future direction of the Court.

The Warren Court determined that the only way to prevent police officers from violating the Fourth Amendment was to adopt a rule precluding the prosecution from using any evidence obtained in an unreasonable manner – in other words, without probable cause or without a validly issued warrant. That rule – called the exclusionary rule because such evidence was excluded from consideration at trial – is deeply unpopular with proponents of the crime-control model. Chief Justice Rehnquist has been extremely critical of the Fourth Amendment's exclusionary rule and has argued in dissent that *Mapp v. Ohio*, one of the principal Warren Court precedents developing this doctrine, be overruled.

Of particular importance for the Fourth Amendment is the rule that searches and seizures may ordinarily be conducted only after obtaining a warrant from an impartial magistrate based on probable cause. The strictest application of the warrant requirement was given by the Warren Court, which held that "searches conducted outside the judicial process, without prior approval by judge or magistrate, are *per se* unreasonable under the Fourth Amendment – subject only to a few specifically established and well-delineated exceptions." The contrary view, and one articulated strongly by Chief Justice Rehnquist, is that if the searches are "reasonable," the warrant requirement is redundant. Thus, if a suspect consents to a search, the officer may reasonably search anywhere he believes that consent would reach, including closed containers within the area to be searched.

The chief justice's adherence to the crime-control model of criminal justice and his disapproval of the due process model can be seen in his support for eliminating the exclusionary rule. His justification was based on a central element of the crime-control model: because admission of evidence from an unconstitutional search will injure only guilty defendants, not innocent ones, any evidence seized illegally should be permitted. In dissent, Rehnquist contended that "generally a warrant is not required to seize and search any movable property [such as "clothing, a briefcase or suitcase, packages, or a vehicle"] in the possession of a person properly arrested in a public place." In *Delaware v. Prouse*, again contrary to the majority's view, he would also have allowed random stops of motorists in order to check driver's licenses and registration, finding that the state had an interest in preventing unlicensed, unsafe motorists from driving. He has also argued that the police may execute an arrest warrant by searching the home of a third party even absent a search warrant, exigent circumstances, or consent and that police in carrying out a search warrant may frisk all patrons in a bar even without reasonable individualized suspicion that the patrons were armed. In *Dunaway v. New York*, he argued in dissent that a defendant was not "seized" where he had "voluntarily accompanied the police to the station to answer their questions" and where the police behavior "was entirely free of physical force or show of authority." Finally, he would have limited the circumstances in which courts may consider excluding evidence because of police misbehavior. In *Franks v. Delaware*, the central case entitling a defendant to a hearing to exclude or "suppress" illegally obtained police evidence, he would have held that probable cause could be based on a false statement and should not trigger an evidentiary hearing.

The approach to criminal justice manifested in these dissenting opinions bore fruit in the majority opinions of the Court once Rehnquist became chief justice. For example, one way of getting around the warrant requirement is for the criminal suspect to waive those rights – so police often have an incentive to induce waiver or to "encourage consent." Many people do not realize that they have a right to refuse to consent to a search, or to limit the scope of a search, pending a warrant from a magistrate. So, in the example that began this chapter, if you were the car's driver you could have refused to let the police officer search your car, particularly the trunk, without a warrant. However, if you mistakenly thought the officer was just being polite in asking and could search your car regardless of your consent, you might allow any search suggested by the officer. Chief Justice Rehnquist has not required that police inform suspects of their right to refuse consent: "The community has a real interest in encouraging consent, for the resulting search may yield necessary evidence for the solution and prosecution of crime, evidence that may ensure that a wholly innocent person is not wrongly charged with a criminal offense." So the chief justice's argument, which is now the law, is that "if [a suspect's] consent would reasonably be understood to extend to a particular [area or thing], the Fourth Amendment provides no grounds for requiring a more explicit authorization." The scope of a search is determined not by where you would have drawn the line but by where a reasonable police officer would have done so. What matters is the officer's interpretation – given police priorities in searching – of your consent.

The Rehnquist Court has extended this principle even further in the case of searches outside the home – it has crafted an "exception" to the Fourth Amendment's warrant requirement for packages in a car. In *California v. Acevedo*, the Court permitted the police to search a container located within an automobile if they have probable cause to believe it held contraband or evidence but don't have a warrant for the package or probable cause to search the vehicle as a whole. This is a direct application of the crime-control model that Chief Justice Rehnquist often articulated in dissent as an associate justice.

This same conception of criminal justice informs Chief Justice Rehnquist's approach to the Fifth Amendment. As an associate justice, Rehnquist often argued in dissent that the Fifth Amendment's protection against self-incrimination was being applied too broadly. One of the fundamental aspects of the right not to incriminate oneself (the "right to silence" or "taking the Fifth") is that a jury may not draw any adverse inferences from a defendant's refusal to testify. The burden is on the government to prove its case, not on the defendant to establish his or her innocence. In his dissenting opinion in *Carter v. Kentucky*, then-Justice Rehnquist would have eliminated this presumption and have held that there is no constitutional obligation on state trial judges to give "no adverse inference" instructions to the jury. And in *Doyle v. Ohio*, he would have affirmed the defendants' convictions even though the prosecutor attempted to use their post-*Miranda* silence against them at trial.

Under Chief Justice Rehnquist, the Court has evinced a deep skepticism about the validity of the *Miranda* decision itself. It has, for example, virtually eliminated the requirement that the *Miranda* waiver be given knowingly and intelligently. Such a requirement ensures that a suspect knows the consequences of starting to talk – that the evidence may be used to convict him – and so embodies a standard concern of the due process model of criminal justice. In *Colorado v. Connelly*, the Court refused to find that the waiver of a suspect's *Miranda* rights and his subsequent confession were involuntary, even though the suspect suffered from hallucinations rendering him unable "to make free and rational choices" at the time of his confession. Chief Justice Rehnquist's use of the crime-control model changed the scope of the inquiry; the previous standard, which inquired whether a waiver had been knowing, intelligent, and voluntary, was abandoned for an analysis of police coercion: so long as the confession was not a product of police coercion, there was neither a *Miranda* nor a voluntariness violation.

The constitutionality of *Miranda* finally came before the Court in 2000 in *Dickerson v. United States*. This case dealt with the question of whether *Miranda* was simply a set of prophylactic judge-made rules that could be overruled by an act of Congress or was instead a constitutional basis for the exclusion of evidence. For years, the Rehnquist Court had indicated that the *Miranda* warnings had no firm basis in the Constitution. Rather, the decision was often characterized as a judge-created procedural rule that could be repealed by appropriate legislation. Although Chief Justice Rehnquist had frequently characterized *Miranda* the same way, in *Dickerson*, writing for the Court, he ultimately conceded the constitutionality of the *Miranda* decision. *Dickerson* thus seems, at first glance, to be an entrenchment of the due process model and an anomaly in the general approach of the Rehnquist Court's jurisprudence.

Behind the chief justice's concession, however, stands a simple fact: the Court did not need to overrule *Miranda*, because it had already eviscerated most of its protections. The Rehnquist Court has burdened the assertion of *Miranda* rights with a variety of procedural impediments. One of the most important has been the "harmless error" rule – the legal equivalent of the phrase "no harm, no foul." Originally, where the courts found that evidence had been entered erroneously, they would reverse the verdict; the result was many technical acquittals. To evade this rule, subsequent courts developed the harmless-error doctrine: as long as a defendant's case is not substantially harmed by the introduction of tainted evidence, there is no reason for a court of appeals to reverse the conviction. The Supreme Court initially applied the federal harmless-error rule only to nonconstitutional errors. Under the Rehnquist Court, however, it was extended to include constitutional errors, even those that had previously been considered so fundamental as to require automatic reversal, such as the introduction into evidence of a coerced confession.

Confession evidence is often vital to a trial. Prosecutors will often not even go to trial without confession evidence because it establishes the government's case so compellingly. Coerced confessions, however, are unconstitutional – they have, by definition, been obtained in violation of the defendant's Fifth Amendment rights. And the confession has usually been coerced in a situation in which only the police and the defendant know the facts, and the defendant has just been discredited as a reliable witness because he has effectively convicted himself. If he retracts his testimony, he can be impeached because he must either be lying to the jury now or have lied to the police when he gave his initial testimony. How could such an error ever be harmless?

Chief Justice Rehnquist has argued that the answer to that question turns on the difference between "structural" and "trial" errors. Structural errors are those that make the trial as a whole a sham, such as a biased judge or the refusal to provide defense counsel. "Trial" errors do not render the trial qualitatively unjust, according to the chief justice, and can be cured – or rendered harmless – in a variety of ways, including permitting further cross-examination or by the judge's instructing the jury to ignore the error. There is thus no need for a per se rule of reversal for trial errors. So long as the evidence does not taint the jury's decision-making process, the error is in fact harmless and, because no legal "foul" has been committed, the verdict will be allowed to stand.

Given the inability of the defense to counter such evidence, the per se rule must apply to coerced confessions as well. Trials in which the verdict is premised upon unconstitutionally obtained evidence of the defendant that cannot effectively be challenged surely suffer from a structural defect every bit as damning as having a biased judge or being refused defense counsel. It is simply not true that "the admission of an involuntary confession is a 'trial error' similar both in degree and kind to the erroneous admission of other types of evidence," as Rehnquist claims. In most cases, the defense counsel must rely almost exclusively on procedural objections to the improper admission of the evidence. The trial becomes skewed, and appellate courts cannot meaningfully apply harmless-error analysis.

Chief Justice Rehnquist's approach here is another example of the crime-control model applied through a jurisprudence of "procedural narrowing." The chief justice does not change the right of a defendant to have his involuntary confession declared unconstitutional, but he does significantly narrow the number of occasions upon which that unconstitutionality will matter in practice.

Rehnquist's dissenting opinions as an associate justice also demonstrate a focus on restricting the constitutional protections established by the Eighth Amendment prohibition of cruel and unusual punishment and on limiting the scope of federal habeas corpus rules establishing a defendant's right to challenge the legal basis of his or her imprisonment.

The Eighth Amendment is particularly important because it has been used to attack the constitutionality of capital punishment. During the brief period between 1972 and 1976 during which the administration of the death penalty was often declared to violate the Eighth Amendment, Rehnquist joined the dissent in *Roberts v. Louisiana*, which argued that mandatory imposition of the death penalty does not amount to cruel and unusual punishment. He also would have upheld a state statute that eliminated a "guilty without capital punishment" verdict, the effect of which was a mandatory death sentence if the defendant was found guilty. Furthermore, he would have held that imposing the death penalty for rape, or for aiding and abetting a felony during the course of which a murder is committed, or on an insane prisoner, does not violate the Eighth Amendment.

Federal habeas law provides another example of the limitation of the constitutional rights of criminal defendants. Often defendants are represented by court-appointed counsel who – due to the lack of an effective public defender program, underfunding, or inexperience – are unprepared to mount an adequate defense of their client. As a consequence, they fail to raise important issues at time of trial. The consequences of this failure can be significant. Prior to *Wainwright v. Sykes*, the failure to raise a legal issue waived that issue only if there was an intentional relinquishment or abandonment of a known right or privilege. For example, if the failure to raise a claim was made for tactical reasons, the issue could not be presented on appeal or during habeas proceedings. If the issue was dropped inadvertently, however, it could still be raised on appeal. In *Wainwright*, Justice Rehnquist overturned this rule and instituted a new test for habeas claims, as a result of which a defendant can raise a new issue for the first time during a habeas proceeding only if he can establish some overriding reason why he did not do so before – which is extremely difficult to satisfy unless there has been a change in the law or the state has withheld facts – and that the failure to raise the claim actually prejudiced his case.

This restriction of access to collateral review has been extended even further during Rehnquist's tenure as chief justice. In *Teague v. Lane*, the justices decided an issue not briefed by the parties that drastically narrowed the scope of habeas relief. The issue was, again, a procedural one: whether a new constitutional rule could be applied in a petition for habeas corpus. *Teague* held that when a habeas petitioner argued for the application of a newly established rule of constitutional criminal procedure, a federal court could not decide the matter unless the new rule was one that would be applied retroactively. Moreover, in *Teague* and subsequent decisions, the Rehnquist Court has read the retroactive application exception very narrowly. The dramatic restriction effected by *Teague* can be seen in Justice Brennan's dissenting opinion, which lists many rights that were recognized for the first time on habeas corpus review. As James S. Liebman states, "If Warren Burger led 'The Counter-Revolution That Wasn't,' then *Teague* reveals William Rehnquist in the vanguard of the Thermidor that is."

Despite the general focus of its decisions on restricting the procedural rights of criminal defendants, it bears reemphasizing that the Rehnquist Court is not a monolithic entity. In fact, some commentators contend that the Rehnquist Court's more recent decisions have "reflect[ed] [its] efforts to refine its established conservative criminal justice doctrine." The Court has handed down a number of decisions that could be characterized as falling within the due process model of criminal procedure; in just the 1999–2000 term, for example, one observer notes, "the Rehnquist Court decided in favor of individuals in cases concerning such issues as Fourth Amendment searches and seizures, Sixth Amendment ineffective assistance of counsel, ex post facto laws, Miranda warnings, and the Fifth Amendment privilege against compelled self-incrimination." In these cases, in which the Court upheld a criminal defendant's constitutional rights, Chief Justice Rehnquist, however, found himself with the dissenters.

One effect of the Court's criminal policy has been to enlarge the potential for the use of racial profiling by the police. Its decisions increase the power of the police to arrest and search individuals and their automobiles for baseless, pretextual offenses. Unfortunately, the temptation for the use of racially motivated arrests and stops has proven far too great, and minorities have suffered accordingly.

Two decisions of the Rehnquist Court in 1996 and 2000 have made it particularly easy for the police to engage in racial profiling. In the first, *Whren v. United States*, the Court allowed police to stop a car and arrest the occupants for a minor traffic violation, such as turning without signaling, in order to follow up a suspicion that the occupants were engaged in something more serious. Since such minor violations are very common, the decision makes it very easy for the police to stop a car just because the occupants are black or Mexican. The lower courts, following the lead of the Supreme Court, have pushed the *Whren* case to its limits. In one case, they allowed police to arrest the driver of a truck with four black occupants for not signaling when changing lanes to avoid a police car deliberately driven close to the truck; in another case, a black driver was arrested for momentarily crossing a yellow line.

In the second case, *Illinois v. Wardlow*, a black man in "an area known for heavy narcotics trafficking" – a description of many African-American and Hispanic neighborhoods in the United States – looked in the direction of patrolling police officers and ran away. That was all, but it was enough for a 5–4 majority of the Court, in an opinion by Chief Justice Rehnquist, to allow the police to stop and frisk the man. Rehnquist called the man's action "unprovoked flight." As the dissenters pointed out, however, "among some citizens, particularly minorities and those residing in high crime areas, there is also the possibility that the fleeing person is entirely innocent, but, with or without justification, believes that contact with the police can itself be dangerous, apart from any criminal activity associated with the officers' sudden presence. For such a person, unprovoked flight is neither 'aberrant' nor 'abnormal.' "

Data demonstrate that racial profiling is not an illusory concern. Racial profiling and pretextual traffic stops, enabled by the *Terry* decision and facilitated by *Whren* and *Wardlow*, have become so endemic in many cities and on many highways that the offense has been termed "Driving While Black." The ACLU recently reported that almost 73 percent of motorists stopped and searched on 1–95 in Maryland in 1996 were black, even though black violators made up less than 17 percent of observed traffic violators. A review of police videotapes of stops by a Florida drug squad showed that black and Hispanic motorists made up 70 percent of the stops and 80 percent of vehicle searches on the Florida Turnpike; only nine of the more than one thousand recorded stops resulted in traffic citations, despite a Florida Supreme Court decision that allows traffic stops only for legitimate traffic violations.

Perhaps the most insidious application of racial profiling occurs when all members of a certain race are considered suspects for a crime committed by a person of color. In 1988, during a police hunt for a rapist known as the "Central City Stalker," described as an African-American man in his early twenties with a mustache, 5'6" to 5'8", weighing between 120 and 140 pounds, the police stopped and frisked several hundred men and arrested sixty more simply because they were African American.

In 1992, Oneonta College in upstate New York gave the names of 125 black students, its entire black male student body, to police officers investigating the attempted rape of an elderly white woman who alleged her assailant was a young black man. Thirty-seven of the students who were stopped and questioned by the police sued the city, and the lower courts denied their claims. Perhaps not surprisingly, the Supreme Court declined to review that decision.

After the September 11 terrorist attacks, many persons appearing to be of Arab descent or of the Muslim faith were treated as suspects by the government and by individual Americans. As of October 13, 2001, U.S. authorities had arrested or detained 698 people. As of October 2, 2001, the Council on American-Islamic Relations had received 785 reports of anti-Muslim incidents.

Laws have been proposed that would authorize the police and the federal government to restrict criminal procedure protections, beyond that which would normally be constitutional, in cases where a criminal investigation involves suspected terrorism. The Supreme Court's approach to the constitutionality of these proposed laws, as well as to the persistent and widespread practice of racial profiling of racial and ethnic minorities, will depend on whether it follows the dominant thread of the Rehnquist Court's decisions or some of the recent cases protecting constitutional rights.

Chapter 32

Robert J. Sampson and John H. Laub

STRUCTURAL VARIATIONS IN JUVENILE COURT PROCESSING
Inequality, the underclass, and social control

From: Robert J. Sampson and John H. Laub (1993), excerpts from "Structural variations in juvenile court processing," *Law & Society Review* 27(2): 285–311.

ALTHOUGH THERE IS A rich body of theory on crime causation, development of general sociological theory on criminal justice has been sparse (Hagan 1989). A major reason is that the criminal justice literature is dominated by a focus on individual-level case processing, in particular how "extralegal" factors such as race, social class, and gender influence court decisionmaking (for reviews see Hagan 1974; Hagan & Bumiller 1983; Gottfredson & Gottfredson 1988). The theoretical significance of these studies for criminal justice theory – especially at the macrolevel – has not been well developed. Hagan (1989) contends that the lack of theory is also related to the fact that criminal justice in the United States is organized as a "loosely coupled system," resulting in a seeming randomness in criminal justice decisionmaking (see also Hagan et al. 1979).

When one turns attention to the juvenile justice system, the theoretical landscape appears even more barren. Indeed, there is a surprising lack of research on the structural context of the juvenile court – the predominant mode of inquiry concerns individual-level variations *within* courts rather than macrolevel variations *between* courts (see Liska & Tausig 1979; Dannefer & Schutt 1982; Eisenstein et al. 1988:5; Feld 1991). Moreover, because of its long-standing commitment to individualized decisionmaking, the juvenile court can be characterized as more "loosely coupled" than the adult system. Studies of juvenile justice decisionmaking thus tend to leave more variation unexplained than comparable studies in the adult arena.

In addition to a theoretical bias in favor of individual-level explanations of juvenile case processing, there is a distinct lack of quantitative data on juvenile courts that are comparable across a large number of jurisdictions. Until recently, juvenile courts have been notoriously unsystematic about recordkeeping in a fashion that would facilitate cross-jurisdictional comparisons of case processing. . . . In fact, there is little research on the structural context of crime control in general. As Liska has argued (1987), most macrolevel research in this area has focused on deterrence (i.e., the effect of crime control on crime rates). [. . .]

This article addresses the lack of a macrolevel focus on juvenile justice by providing a theoretical framework and empirical assessment of the structural context of juvenile court processing in the United States. Specifically, we derive a macrolevel theory on inequality and official social control that poses the question: How does structural context – especially racial inequality and the concentration of "underclass" poverty – influence formal *petitioning*, predisposition *detention*, and *placement* (confinement) of juveniles? . . . Our goal is to lay the groundwork for a better understanding of the relationship between larger societal forces of increasing poverty and inequality (Wilson 1987, 1991) and formal systems of juvenile social control.

THEORETICAL FRAMEWORK

We argue that the juvenile court may be fruitfully analyzed by taking an explicitly macrostructural approach to official social control. As Empey (1982:320) has argued, juvenile justice is not a monolithic concept which operates uniformly throughout the United States. Instead, a fundamental fact is that the juvenile court is organized at the local (i.e., county) level, giving rise to potentially important *community-level variations* in juvenile justice (see also Eisenstein et al. 1988:22–27). . . . Consequently, Feld (1991:208) has argued that analyses and interpretations that ignore structural variations across court jurisdictions in justice administration may be systematically misleading. [. . .]

Although "randomness" may be typical in individual case processing, recognition of structural variations at the macrolevel opens a new window on the juvenile court. Generally speaking, a macrosociological perspective suggests that systematic differences in case processing will arise from the social attributes of the communities in which juvenile courts are located (Dannefer & Schutt 1982; Hasenfeld & Cheung 1985; Eisenstein et al. 1988; Myers & Talarico 1987; Feld 1991). This structural orientation has an analogy in research showing that styles of policing vary according to the demographic, organizational, and political structure of cities (Wilson 1968; Sampson & Cohen 1988). To organize our specific theoretical expectations with respect to juvenile court variations across structural contexts, we integrate three bodies of research.

Conflict theory: threatening populations and the social control response

Most criminal justice research has drawn on consensus and conflict theories of society (Hagan 1989). In the consensus view there is an assumption of shared values, where the state is organized to protect the common interests of society at large. Criminal law is seen as an instrument to protect the interests of all and punishment is based largely on legal variables (e.g., seriousness of the offense, prior record, etc.). In contrast, conflict theory views society as consisting of groups with conflicting and differing values, and posits that the state is organized to represent the interests of the powerful, ruling class. [. . .]

One proposition drawn from conflict theory is that groups which threaten the hegemony of middle- and upper-class rule are more likely to be subjected to intensified social control – more criminalization, more formal processing by the criminal justice system, and increased incarceration compared with groups that are perceived as less threatening to the status quo (see e.g., Brown & Warner 1992). Furthermore, conflict theorists have argued that minorities (especially blacks), the unemployed, and the poor represent such threatening groups (Liska & Chamlin 1984; Greenberg et al. 1985; Jackson & Carroll 1981). Irwin (1985:xiii) defines population groups that are deemed as threatening and offensive to the dominant majority as the "rabble class" – "detached and disreputable persons." Irwin argues that the primary purpose of jails is to manage society's rabble class and hence that this group will be subject to higher rates of confinement.

Although conflict theory has been applied to the realm of juvenile justice, it has been applied less often than to adult criminal justice. Extending the ideas of Platt (1977), Carter and Clelland (1979) argue that since its creation the juvenile court has sought to control lower class and minority youth in accordance with dominant class values. [. . .]

In one of the more comprehensive empirical studies relating macro-variables to micro-outcomes, Tittle and Curran (1988) examined juvenile justice dispositions in 31 Florida counties. They found differential sanctioning depending on the relative size of the nonwhite and young population, arguing that "non-whites and youth symbolize to white adults resentment-provoking or fear-provoking qualities like aggressiveness, sexuality, and absence of personal discipline" (p. 52). In a study of contextual characteristics of social environments and individual case decisionmaking, Dannefer and Schutt (1982) also found racial bias in police processing of juvenile cases in urban counties containing a large proportion of black residents.

In our view, what is important in these studies is the symbolic aspect of social threat. For instance, Tittle and Curran (1988:53) emphasize the perceptions of the threat that "provoke jealousy, envy, or personal fear among elites" rather than the actual threat these groups represent to the political positions of the elite. Similarly, Irwin (1985:17) notes the importance of the subjective perception of "offensiveness, which is determined by social status and context." Revising conflict theory, we argue that "the poor," "the underclass," and "the rabble" are perceived as threatening not only to political elites but to "mainstream America" – middle-class and working-class citizens who represent the dominant majority in American society. As such, we suggest that an assessment of the macrolevel response of the juvenile justice system to the evolving stereotype of threatening young black males dealing drugs in poor neighborhoods across the United States (see below) is especially timely and necessary.

Drugs and minorities: a symbolic threat

Peterson and Hagan's (1984) analysis of drug enforcement activity during the 1960s and 1970s documents the shifting concerns with drugs and crime in society and illustrates the need to consider historical context in understanding criminal justice operations related to race. More recently, Myers (1989) found increased punitiveness for nonwhite drug dealers, underscoring the need to examine race in conjunction with drug use and drug trafficking in a particular historical context.

Two trends emerged during the 1980s that reinforce these claims. The first was the increasing number of black males under correctional supervision (see Mauer 1990) and the second saw increasing punitiveness toward drug offenders, especially blacks and users of cocaine (Belenko et al. 1991; Blumstein 1993). . . . Moreover, the "war" on drugs in the 1980s embodied a different persona than earlier wars, leading to racially discriminatory practices by the criminal justice system (see also Jackson 1992; Feeley & Simon 1992:461–70). Particularly relevant to our thesis, Tittle and Curran (1988:52) found the largest discriminatory effects in juvenile justice dispositions for "drug/sexual offenses which represent overt behavioral manifestations of the very qualities [that] frighten white adults or generate resentment and envy."

Data from the 1980s support these concerns about the changing dynamics of race and drugs. For instance, while the number of arrests for drug abuse violations for white juveniles declined 28% in 1985 compared with 1980, the number of arrests for drug abuse violations for black juveniles increased 25% over the same time period (Federal Bureau of Investigation 1981, 1986). . . . Juvenile court data show that the number of white youth referred to court for drug law violations declined by 6% between 1985 and 1986; the number of referrals for black youth increased 42% (Snyder 1990). The disproportionate increase in the number of black youth detained also seemed linked to the increased number of black drug law violators referred to court (see also McGarrell 1993). More generally, Blumstein (1993) has shown that the dramatic growth in state prison populations during the 1980s was driven in large part by increasing admissions of blacks on drug convictions.

These trends suggest a recent and increasing punitiveness toward drug offenders – especially those perceived to be "gang" members from a growing "underclass" population (Jackson 1992:98–100; Feeley & Simon 1992:467–69). The existing studies are less clear, however, as to the nature of the juvenile justice system response to drug offenders, especially at the macrolevel. We fill this gap with an examination of the structural context of juvenile justice processing of drug cases.

Urban poverty and inequality: the changing urban landscape, 1970–1990

Wilson (1991:1) has documented "the rise of social dislocations in inner-city ghettos" over the last 25 years. As Wilson writes, "poverty in the United States has become more urban, more concentrated, and more firmly implanted in large metropolises, particularly in the older industrial cities with immense and highly segregated black and Hispanic residents" (ibid.). Reviewing a host of census data as well as focused studies on poverty, Wilson shows that "the 1970s witnessed a sharp growth in ghetto poverty areas, an increased concentration of the poor in these areas, a substantial rise in the severity of economic hardship among the ghetto poor, and sharply divergent patterns of poverty concentration between racial minorities and whites" (pp. 3–4). Sampson and Wilson (1993) also link an increase in poverty and joblessness to social dislocations in family life, community disorganization, and even lower feelings of self-efficacy. In short, research on urban poverty suggests that the social transformation of inner cities has resulted in a disproportionate concentration of the "truly disadvantaged" segments of the U.S. population – especially poor, female-headed black families with children. [. . .]

An extension of Wilson's (1987) concept of social isolation in inner-city areas of concentrated poverty to the larger macrolevel context of metropolitan areas and counties is supported by Land et al.'s recent (1990) findings on the relationships among structural covariates of homicide in the United States. Using principal components analysis, two clusters of variables were found to consistently covary over time and space (i.e., 1960, 1970, and 1980 for cities, SMSAs, and states). The first factor was termed a *population structure component* and consisted of population size and population density. The second factor was labeled *resource deprivation/ affluence*, and included three income variables – median income, percentage of families below the poverty line, and the Gini index of income inequality – in addition to percentage black and percentage of children not living with both parents. Although these variables seem to tap different concepts, Land et al. (1990) found they could not be separated empirically.

Land et al.'s results go beyond Wilson by suggesting that the clustering of economic and social indicators appears not only in 1980 and in neighborhoods of large cities but also for the two previous decennial periods and at the level of macrosocial units as a whole. Moreover, Land and his colleagues present evidence in support of Wilson's argument (1990:945) that concentration effects grew more severe from 1970 to 1980 – "the numerical values of the component loadings of percentage poverty, percentage black, and percentage of children under 18 not living with both parents are larger in 1980 than 1970." Recent data also point to the existence of a large underclass population in rural areas, especially the South. Therefore, indicators of disadvantaged "underclass" populations appear to be increasing in their ecological concentration and are present in macrosocial units such as counties and SMSAs – in highly urbanized as well as in rural areas.

The ideas of Wilson (1987, 1991) and the empirical research of Land and associates (1990) have not been integrated with the literature on criminal justice and juvenile justice processing. We believe this is a mistake, for the profound social changes taking place in the wider urban society have distinct ramifications for the major mechanisms of formal social control, namely, criminal and juvenile justice systems. The interesting question that emerges is: What effect do increasing concentrations of poverty and accompanying social dislocations have for juvenile justice processing? [. . .]

Hypotheses and strategy

Our theoretical integration of these heretofore separate research areas yields a core idea related to the macrostructural context of juvenile justice. That is, the rising concentration of the underclass corresponds precisely with that population perceived as threatening and the population at which the war on drugs has been aimed. Hence our major thesis is that, all else being equal, counties characterized by racial inequality and a large concentration of the "underclass" (i.e., minorities, poverty, female-headed families, welfare) are more likely than other counties to be perceived as containing offensive and threatening populations and, as a result, are subject to increased social control by the juvenile justice system. We further hypothesize that the concentration of racial poverty and inequality will exert macrolevel effects on punitive forms of social control that are larger for blacks than whites and for drug offenses than other delinquencies. [. . .]

To test these ideas we examine three post-intake decisions in the juvenile justice process that involve the increased penetration of official social control. Although the first step in

the juvenile justice system is referral to the juvenile court, the vast majority of these cases
($>$ 75%) stem from police referrals (Snyder et al. 1989:12). Drug offenses are most likely
to be referred by the police (91%). The remainder are referred by other social control
agencies (e.g., probation officers, schools) or by informal parties (e.g., parents). Hence
variations in rates of juvenile court referrals are shaped largely by differences in delinquent
offending and police decisionmaking, the latter a topic of considerable prior research.
By contrast, our purpose here is to study the more "hidden" and unexplored arena of
macrostructural variations in postreferral decisionmaking by the court, especially decisions
that involve coercive control and deprivation of liberty. To accomplish this goal our strategy
is to focus on formal *petitioning*, secure predisposition *detention*, and adjudicated *placement*
(confinement) of juveniles. We now turn to a description of the data and more explicit definitions and rationale for these three dimensions of social control.

DATA SOURCES

Our data stem from a larger project in collaboration with the National Juvenile Court
Data Archive (NJCDA), located at the National Center for Juvenile Justice in Pittsburgh.
A comparative, multijurisdictional approach to the study of the juvenile court was made
possible by transforming raw juvenile case records into a common format at the individual level. Specifically, each individual record in the national files created for the Juvenile
Court Statistics project (see Snyder et al. 1989) was recoded as a case disposed, eliminating interjurisdictional problems in case definitions. A case disposed represents a youth
processed by a juvenile court on a new referral regardless of the number of charges contained in that referral. "Disposed" means that some definite action had been taken, ranging from release to out-of-home placement. Since it is possible for a youth to be involved
in more than one case in a calendar year, the unit of count is not people but cases, thereby
taking into account repeat offending.

By aggregating these individual-level records within each juvenile court of jurisdiction,
a data base was created with counties as the unit of analysis. Counties with a minimum
population size of 6,000 youth aged 10–17 formed the sample. This cutoff corresponds
to a total population of about 40,000, and was selected to avoid unreliable demographic-
specific data in small counties with few juveniles. The states and original number of
counties are Alabama (23), Arizona (1), California (39), Connecticut (8), Hawaii (3),
Iowa (7), Maryland (15), Minnesota (15), Mississippi (15), Missouri (16), Nebraska (3),
New Jersey (19), New York (50), North Dakota (4), Ohio (1), Pennsylvania (45), South
Dakota (2), Tennessee (3), Utah (5), Virginia (24), and Wisconsin (24). All regions of the
country are represented, and there is a wide range in population size across the 21 states
(Sampson 1989).

Approximately 538,000 individual juvenile case records were aggregated to form
theoretically specified variables characterizing these 322 counties in 1985. The general
format resulted in the construction of variables relating to the key dimensions of *reason
for referral, detention*, and *disposition*. Then, to the extent the data allowed, variables were
classified by crime type and demographic characteristics of the juvenile (e.g., age, race,
sex). We rely here on the fourfold classification of crimes developed and validated in
Snyder et al. (1989: 120–23) – *crimes against property* (burglary, larceny, motor vehicle
theft, arson, vandalism, and stolen property offenses), *crimes against persons* (criminal

homicide, forcible rape, robbery, and assault), *drug offenses* (unlawful sale, distribution, manufacture, transport, possession, or use of a controlled substance), and *public order offenses* (drunkenness, disorderly conduct, contempt, weapons offenses, prostitution, statutory rape, probation and parole violations). Because of wide fluctuations across counties in reporting procedures for status offenses, the latter were excluded in the creation of court-processing variables and hence all rates refer to delinquency cases. The county-level juvenile court data consisting of both petitioned and nonpetitioned cases were merged with relevant sociodemographic and population data from two other data sets. The first was the Bureau of Census file on County Population Estimates by Age, Race, and Sex (1980, 1982, 1984). This data source provided detailed population estimates of age-race-sex breakdowns needed to create referral rates for counties. The second data file is the 1983 *County and City Data Book (CCDB)*, which contains social and economic variables describing each county in the United States.

Variable construction

Petitioning of cases

Cases may be placed on the official court calendar in response to the filing of a formal petition, a process that usually involves a hearing before a juvenile court judge. Alternatively, a case may be treated informally through a procedure whereby cases are screened out for adjustment prior to the filing of a formal petition. Depending on the court, this screening is conducted by judges, referees, probation officers, or other designated court personnel (Snyder et al. 1989:120).

Although less serious cases carry a higher likelihood of nonpetitioning (ibid., p. 54), there is still considerable variation across counties in the decision to petition a case formally even within the same crime type. When we control for crime type and "input" (i.e., referral rate), we argue that counties which channel a high proportion of cases to the juvenile court via a petition may be conceptualized as having a more formalized, bureaucratized system than counties which treat the same cases informally through a nonpetitioned procedure. In other words, the rate of formal petitioning or what Hasenfeld and Cheung (1985:806) call "judicial handling," may be seen as a quantitative indicator of the extent to which a county has formalized procedures for processing juveniles (see also Feld 1989). To capture these variations we created crime-specific variables representing the proportion of petitioned cases.

Secure predisposition detention

Before a case is disposed, a juvenile may be held in secure detention. Although this issue has been explored at the national level (see Schwartz 1989; Krisberg et al. 1989), it is central to the operation of juvenile courts at the local level. To address these county-level variations, we constructed proportions of secure detention by dividing the number of cases detained in a county by the total number of referrals in that county. As shown in Snyder et al. (1989:56), detained youth are twice as likely to be petitioned as youth not detained. In fact, many jurisdictions require a formal petition before a youth can be detained. As Snyder et al. thus argue, the decision to detain is closely intertwined with the decision to formally petition the case. As such, logits of secure detention were calculated separately for petitioned and nonpetitioned cases. . . . Because of our focus on the underclass and juvenile confinement, we also created race-specific logits of secure detention.

Analogous to adult imprisonment, the most serious form of social control exercised by the juvenile court is placement outside of the home. Virtually all such placements (99%) result from formal petitions. Therefore, to explore county-level variations in placement we constructed proportions that divided the number of petitioned cases placed out of the home by the sum of nonreleased, petitioned dispositions (i.e., placement, probation, referral, fine/restitution, and transfer to adult court). Placement rates were classified by type of crime and population subgroup in the same fashion as detention and then transformed into logits.

STRUCTURAL INEQUALITY AND CONTROL VARIABLES

Theoretical considerations coupled with principal components analysis of census data led us to construct three macrolevel variables relevant to assessing our explanatory framework on inequality and symbolic threat. The first is the concentration of resource deprivation, or what many have conceptualized as "underclass" poverty (Wilson 1987; Jencks 1992). To represent this dimension with respect to extant theory, we created a standardized scale from six interrelated indicators that, taken together, represent underclass concentration. The specific constituent variables in this scale are defined in Table 32.1. As was true of Land et al.'s (1990) findings, these variables were very highly correlated, clustered together on a single factor, and could not be separated empirically with statistical efficiency.

The second was a racial inequality dimension measured by two variables – the ratio of black to white poverty and the proportion of black families below the poverty level. We created a composite scale where a high value indicates black economic disadvantage relative to whites. Our third inequality-related measure taps the high end of the economic distribution – specifically, the wealth and economic resources of a county (see Table 32.1). The juxtaposition of wealth, racial inequality, and underclass poverty provides a unique opportunity to disaggregate the symbolic threat hypothesis. [. . .]

To account for competing theoretical perspectives we control for seven key variables. First, Feld (1989, 1991) has uncovered important urban-rural differences in juvenile justice administration. As Feld (1991:156) writes: "In urban counties, which are more heterogeneous and diverse, juvenile justice intervention is more formal, bureaucratized, and due process-oriented. By contrast, in more homogeneous and stable rural counties, juvenile courts are procedurally less formal and sentence youths more leniently." . . . We examine *urbanism* as a control variable (see also Myers & Talarico 1986, 1987).

Because of our focus on juvenile justice, it is possible that the proportion of youth in a county exerts a contextual influence on court processing. To control for this potential variation we thus created a second composite variable that measures the relative *density of youth* in a county.

Regional variation has always been an important aspect in the historical development of the juvenile justice system (see Sutton 1988), and there is contemporary evidence of the influence of region in both criminal and juvenile justice processing (Liska et al. 1981; Krisberg et al. 1984). Hence region (*West* and *South*) is controlled.

Table 32.1 Definitions and intercorrelations for structural characteristics of U.S. counties

A. Definitions

Underclass poverty	=	% AFDC + % black + % female-headed families with children + % persons in poverty + % families < $5,000 income + % non-married households + % female-headed families in poverty
Racial inequality	=	Ratio of black to white poverty + % black families in poverty
Wealth	=	% families > $50,000 income + median per capita income
Residential mobility	=	% moved households in past 5 years + % county population change 1980–84 + net county migration
Urbanism	=	% population in urbanized area + population size + population per square mile
Youth	=	% 15–18 + ratio of juveniles to adults
CJS $$$ resources	=	Per capita county revenues + per capita spending on police + per capita spending on state and local corrections
West	=	Dichotomous variable where 1 indexes Western region
South	=	Dichotomous variable where 1 indexes Southern region

B. Intercorrelations for structural characteristics of U.S. counties

	Inequality	Wealth	Mobility	Urbanism	Youth	CJS $$$	West	South
Underclass	.27**	−.20**	−.20**	.34**	−.00	.12**	.02	.34**
Inequality		−.10	−.16**	.08	−.06	−.04	−.11**	.14**
Wealth			.11**	.46**	−.19**	.33**	.14**	−.12**
Mobility				−.05	.04	.03	.55**	.12**
Urbanism					−.30**	.30**	.20*	−.14**
Youth						−.06	−.16*	.19**
CJS $$$							.37**	−.28**
West								−.23**

Notes

Multi-item scales were constructed based on Z-scores.

**Significant at the .05 level.

Extant theory further suggests that the referral rate will affect the response of the juvenile justice system. According to Hasenfeld and Cheung (1985:807), the higher the rate of referral, the more demand there is on court services. This creates the need for a "flexible processing technology" and results in more nonjudicial handling of cases. . . . On the other hand, Hasenfeld and Cheung argue that the more serious the caseload, the less informality in processing, resulting in the filing of more formal petitions. Whatever the exact relationship, it is crucial to account for *input* in assessing juvenile justice processing. . . . We thus control for the most relevant input to the system – crime and demographic-specific referrals. This strategy provides a test of the independent effects of social structure on juvenile processing.

In a similar vein, we take into account the *capacity and resources* of the crime control system in assessing the processing of cases. As Hasenfeld and Chueng found, factors relating to the external economy of the court – especially the level of resources – are significant in shaping case processing across decision points in juvenile courts. Although data are unavailable for resources allocated specifically to the juvenile court, we constructed a composite variable that taps per capita county revenues and resources allocated the police and corrections (see Table 32.1). In all likelihood criminal justice system (CJS $$$) resources are highly correlated with juvenile justice resources. In support of this notion, the wealth of a county is significantly correlated with our CJS resource variable ($r = .33$).

Finally, research from social disorganization theory has identified mobility as an important correlate of crime (Byrne & Sampson 1986). Preliminary analysis by Sampson (1989) on the structural sources of variation in juvenile justice processing has also shown that mobility is an important factor in juvenile justice decisionmaking at the macrolevel. We thus include *residential mobility* of the county as the seventh control variable.

RESULTS

Panel B of Table 32.1 displays descriptive data that provide an overview of the patterning among structural characteristics. Overall there are low levels of collinearity – the largest correlation is between mobility and Western region (.54). Importantly, correlations for our key structural variables show evidence of both construct and discriminant validity. [. . .]

The significant relationships between structural characteristics and region (both West and South) are noteworthy. Although Western region is not significantly related to underclass, the correlation between Southern region and underclass is .34. The underclass is often associated with large cities in the Northeast, Midwest, and West, yet these data remind us that underclass poverty is also rural and in the South (see Jencks 1992:252 n.4; O'Hare & Curry-White 1992). We would add that tests of conflict theory have also been limited largely to urban areas, truncating the full range of variation in the macrostructural contexts that are found in the United States.

Petitioning

Table 32.2 presents a multivariate regression of the logits of formal petitioning by type of offense. The variable most consistently related to formal petitioning is racial inequality, with all offenses but drugs showing significant positive coefficients. Racial inequality has the largest effect of all variables on personal and public order offenses. Somewhat surprising, neither underclass nor wealth is significantly related to formal petitioning for any of the four crime types. Also notable is the lack of explanatory power for key control variables such as criminal justice resources, youth density, urbanism, mobility, and Western region. Southern region exhibits large significant effects for property and drug offenses, while referral rates display significant negative effects for personal and property crimes. As anticipated by an organizational perspective, the proportion of variance explained across each of the four types of offenses is relatively low.

Confinement

Table 32.3 presents results for the structural sources of two types of predisposition confinement – petitioned and nonpetitioned secure detention. . . . In panel A of Table 32.3, we find that "underclass" poverty is significantly related to secure detention among petitioned cases only for drug offenses ($B = .26$). However, its effect is clearly larger than all other variables, supporting the theoretical framework on drugs and symbolic threat.

Table 33.2 Structural sources of variation in judicial handling of juveniles: formal petitioning by type of offense, U.S. counties, 1985[a]

| | Formal Petitioning | | | |
	Personal (N = 219)	Property (N = 220)	Drugs (N = 196)	Public Order (N = 217)
Underclass	−.00	−.10	−.09	−.16
Racial inequality	.22**	.19**	.10	.25**
Wealth	−.02	−.07	−.04	−.05
Referral rate[b]	−.22**	−.29**	−.14	−.06
Mobility	−.10	−.10	−.19*	−.13
Urbanism	.09	.08	.04	.06
Youth density	−.04	−.04	.04	−.03
CJS $$$ resources	.13	.14	−.11	.11
Western region	−.08	.04	.20*	.10
Southern region	.06	.25**	.29**	.14
R^2	.10	.17	.15	.08

Notes
[a] Entries are standardized regression coefficients (betas).
[b] Control for referral rate is offense specific.
* Significant at the .10 level.
** Significant at the .05 level.

Moreover, racial inequality is significantly related to both personal and public order offenses ($p < .10$). Once again the level of explained variance is relatively low, and most control variables show inconsistent or weak effects on detention. The exception is Western region, which appears strongly related to detention for all offenses except drugs.

The results for nonpetitioned detention in panel B are quite remarkable in their consistency. Controlling for referral rate and eight other characteristics of counties, underclass concentration is significantly and positively related to detention for all four offenses. For personal and property offenses, racial inequality and wealth significantly increase the detention rate as well. The consistent effects of underclass and also Western region are reflected in the noticeably larger proportions of explained variance for nonpetitioned compared to petitioned cases. Interestingly, then, the data suggest that for the more informal and hence largely hidden processing entailed by nonpetitioning, youth face a heightened risk of being detained prior to case resolution in counties characterized by racial inequality and underclass concentration.

Table 32.4 turns to the most serious sanction by the juvenile justice system – out-of-home placement. The results yield positive relationships between underclass poverty and two offense types – personal crimes ($B = .35$) and drug offenses ($B = .24$). Racial inequality and wealth of counties exhibit insignificant effects on rates of out-of-home placement. Of the control variables, mobility shows a strong positive effect for both personal and drug offenses while Southern region exhibits strong negative effects for all crime types except public order offenses. Similar to the results for detention, key control variables like urbanism, youth density, and criminal justice system resources reveal insignificant effects on rates of out-of-home placement.

Table 32.3 Structural sources of variation in secure predisposition detention by type of offense and petition status, U.S. counties, 1985[a]

A. Secure Detention, Petitioned Cases

	Personal (N = 188)	Property (N = 189)	Drugs (N = 167)	Public Order (N = 187)
Underclass	.12	.13	.26**	.09
Racial inequality	.15*	.12	.01	.17*
Wealth	−.01	−.06	.12	.02
Referral rate[b]	.06	−.08	.19**	.01
Mobility	.04	.06	.13	.02
Urbanism	−.01	−.00	.04	.02
Youth density	−.05	.04	−.02	−.06
CJS $$$ resources	−.02	.16	−.01	−.01
Western region	.25*	.25*	.11	.30**
Southern region	−.23**	−.08	−.13	−.01
R^2	.16	.17	.23	.14

B. Secure detention, nonpetitioned cases

	Personal (N = 183)	Property (N = 188)	Drugs (N = 173)	Public Order (N = 187)
Underclass	.19*	.29**	.22**	.25**
Racial inequality	.16**	.17**	.04	.09
Wealth	.19**	.24**	.13	.07
Referral rate[b]	.19**	.01	.21**	.17*
Mobility	.00	.16*	.00	.06
Urbanism	−.13*	−.13*	−.02	−.01
Youth density	−.09	−.01	.03	−.04
CJS $$$ resources	−.31**	−.10	−.25**	−.29**
Western region	.72**	.42**	.67**	.51**
Southern region	−.00	−.10	−.08	−.09
R^2	.36	.30	.46	.27

Notes
[a] Entries are standardized regression coefficients (betas).
[b] Control for referral rate is offense specific.
* Significant at the .10 level.
** Significant at the .05 level.

Race-specific processing

A major hypothesis stemming from our theoretical framework looks to interactions of structural context with the race of those processed by the juvenile justice system. To examine these interactions Table 32.5 displays the structural sources of variation in secure detention by race and type of offense. Based on the results in Table 32.3, we focus on nonpetitioned cases.

Table 32.4 Structural sources of variation in petitioned out-of-home placement by type of offense, U.S. counties, 1985[a]

| | Out-of-Home Placement | | | |
	Personal (N = 219)	Property (N = 220)	Drugs (N = 196)	Public Order (N = 217)
Underclass	.35**	.11	.24**	.09
Racial inequality	.02	.05	−.01	.10
Wealth	.07	−.09	.13	−.02
Referral rate[b]	−.05	−.05	.10	−.12
Mobility	.27**	.04	.37**	.10
Urbanism	.04	.00	.09	−.04
Youth density	.04	.08	.03	.05
CJS $$$ resources	.03	.14	−.03	.19
Western region	−.14	.07	−.21*	.09
Southern region	−.39**	−.19**	−.30**	−.14
R^2	.16	.09	.17	.08

Notes:

[a] Entries are standardized regression coefficients (betas).

[b] Control for referral rate is offense specific.

* Significant at the .10 level

** Significant at the .05 level

Although not substantially different, the R^2 statistics for all four offenses are larger for blacks than whites, suggesting that the detention of black juveniles is more tightly linked to county-level characteristics than it is for whites. One of these characteristics is clearly structural inequality – the concentration of underclass poverty is unrelated to white juvenile detention but has significant positive effects on the secure detention of black juveniles for personal, property, and public order offenses. Furthermore, racial inequality has a positive effect on black juvenile detention for drug and property offenses. Although the detention of whites for personal and property offenses is also influenced by variations in racial inequality, the raw coefficients reflecting inequality's effect on black property and drug detention are more than double the respective coefficients for whites. Even the upper tail of the economic distribution is salient in explaining differential variations in detention by race – wealthy counties detain more black juveniles for personal, property, and drug offenses, whereas county wealth has no relationship to white juvenile detention.

Some of the crime-specific models in Table 32.5 may suffer from collinearity among independent variables. For example, in the reduced sample of counties with valid data on black secure detention, underclass poverty is correlated .60 ($p < .01$) with racial inequality. We thus estimated reduced models of race-specific secure detention where the major explanatory variables were referral rate, region, urbanism, mobility, and underclass (table not shown). Consistent with Table 32.5, there was a significant ($p < .05$) effect of underclass concentration on the nonpetitioned detention of blacks for personal, property, drug, and public order offenses (Bs = .25, .25, .29, and .28, respectively). By contrast, among whites underclass was significantly related at the .05 level only to public order

Table 32.5 Structural Sources of Variation in Nonpetitioned Secure Detention by Race and Type of Offense, U.S. Counties, 1985[a]

A. Nonpetitioned Detention, Whites

	Personal (N = 156)		Property (N = 161)		Drugs (N = 145)		Public Order (N = 160)	
Underclass	−.04	−.07	.02	.05	−.00	−.00	.04	.07
Racial inequality	.43*	.16	.34*	.15	.15	.06	.35	.14
Wealth	.07	.04	.20	.12	.03	.01	.00	.00
Referral rate[b]	.15	.11	.01	.03	.38**	.28	.07*	.15
Mobility	−.04	−.03	.13	.11	.01	.01	−.06	−.05
Urbanism	.24	.13	.09	.06	.26*	.15	.31*	.17
Youth density	−.14	−.07	.12	.07	.10	.07	.02	.01
CJS $$$ resources	−.51*	−.29	−.26	−.17	−.37*	−.23	−.43*	−.25
Western region	6.84**	.76	4.87**	.62	5.82**	.71	5.67**	.65
Southern region	.85	.11	.12	.02	−.04	−.01	.13	.02
R^2		.35		.35		.58		.34

B. Nonpetitioned Detention, Blacks

	Personal (N = 119)		Property (N = 138)		Drugs (N = 71)		Public Order (N = 119)	
Underclass	.18**	.39	.10*	.19	.11	.21	.15**	.28
Racial inequality	.30	.10	.91**	.30	.84*	.24	.35	.10
Wealth	.36*	.21	.55**	.29	.42*	.25	.37	.18
Referral rate[b]	.06*	.16	−.00	−.03	.30**	.21	.05	.10
Mobility	.28*	.21	.07	.05	.21	.13	.09	.06
Urbanism	.50**	.27	.27	.13	.75**	.39	.16	.07
Youth density	−.03	−.02	.22	.12	.48**	.25	−.10	−.05
CJS $$$ resources	−.80**	−.46	−.26	−.14	−.47	−.25	−.47	−.24
Western region	5.38**	.61	4.72**	.53	5.68**	.69	6.93**	.72
Southern region	−.95	−.12	−.37	−.05	.61	.07	.83	.10
R^2		.44		.42		.60		.39

Notes

[a] Entries are metric coefficients and standardized regression coefficients (betas).

[b] Control for referral rate is offense and race specific.

* Significant at the .10 level.

** Significant at the .05 level.

detention, and the raw coefficient was approximately half that of blacks. Underclass had a weaker relationship to petitioned detention as expected from Table 32.3 but was significantly related to the confinement of blacks (but not whites) for property crimes.

In Table 32.6 our race-specific analysis of confinement turns to the social structural characteristics that predict rates of out-of-home placement, independent of the referral rate. Like Table 5, the results show important differences by race and crime type. For whites (panel A) we find that both underclass and wealth are significantly and *negatively* related to out-of-home placement for property offenses ($B = -.29$ and $B = -.20$, respectively). Racial inequality, on the other hand, is not significantly related to confinement among whites for any of the four crime types. Moreover, all control variables show weak or inconsistent effects for rates of white out-of-home placement.

The results in panel B again show that the explained variance is higher for blacks than whites in three out of four crime types. Substantively, the data suggest that despite controlling for "input" to the system (i.e., referral rate), criminal justice resources, and

Table 32.6 Structural sources of variation in juvenile confinement: out-of-home placement by race and type of offense, U.S. counties, 1985[a]

A. Out-of-Home Placement, Whites

	Personal (N = 179)		Property (N = 182)		Drugs (N = 157)		Public order (N = 180)	
Underclass	−.05	−.11	−.07**	−.29	−.04	−.06	−.02	−.04
Racial inequality	.16	.07	.10	.08	.39	.12	.28	.12
Wealth	−.13	−.08	−.17**	−.20	.21	.11	−.02	−.01
Referral rate[b]	.08	.08	.00	.00	.13	.09	−.02	−.04
Mobility	−.02	−.02	−.02	−.05	.16	.11	−.00	−.00
Urbanism	.11	.10	.03	.04	.12	.09	−.06	−.06
Youth, density	.17	.10	−.01	−.01	.31*	.14	−.05	−.03
CJS $$$ resources	.24	.15	.25**	.31	.55**	.28	.35*	.22
Western region	−.20	−.02	.21	.05	−.11	−.01	1.31	.16
Southern region	−2.42**	−.36	−.25		−.07	−1.04	−.12	−.26	−.04
R^2	.18		.13		.24		.10	

B. Out-of-Home Placement, Blacks

	Personal (N = 147)		Property (N = 162)		Drugs (N = 84)		Public Order (N = 144)	
Underclass	.22**	.43	.05	.10	.36**	.56	.10	.19
Racial inequality	.12	.04	.66**	.23	−.32	−.06	.19	.05
Wealth	.21	.11	.08	.04	.83**	.42	−.07	−.04
Referral rateb	−.01	−.03	.01	.10	.25	.17	.02	.03
Mobility	.42**	.28	−.08	−.06	.35	.19	−.16	−.10
Urbanism	.17	.13	.16	.14	.10	.08	.04	.03
Youth density	−.16	−.08	.09	−.05	.30	.13	−.33*	−.16
CJS $$$ resources	−.21	−.11	.21	.13	−.13	−.05	.24	.11
Western region	−1.26	−.13	.78	.09	1.99	.19	3.04*	.29
Southern region	−2.06**	−.25	.34	.05	−.32	−.03	.95	.10
R^2	.15		.18		.32		.18	

Notes

[a] Entries are metric coefficients and standardized regression coefficients (betas).

[b] Control for referral rate is offense and race specific.

* Significant at the .10 level.

** Significant at the .05 level.

other county characteristics, concentration of underclass poverty increases the placement rates of blacks for both personal offenses and drug violations. The positive effect of underclass poverty on drug placements of blacks is by far the largest ($B = .56$), and the unstandardized coefficient is seven times greater than for whites (difference significant at $p <. 01$). Note also that county wealth is strongly related to the placement of blacks for drug offenses ($B = .42$) and the only variable significantly related to black placement rates for property crimes is racial inequality ($B = .23$). Moreover, the effect of underclass poverty on placement for public order offenses is significant at the .05 level ($B = .22$) when the equation is reestimated dropping racial inequality (underclass and inequality are correlated .54 in this subset of counties). Consistent with the symbolic threat hypothesis, then, counties characterized by inequality and/or the presence of a large underclass produce the highest rates of confinement for blacks, particularly blacks adjudicated for drug offenses.

DISCUSSION

Our major finding is that structural contexts of "underclass" poverty and racial inequality are significantly related to increased juvenile justice processing. This pattern is especially pronounced for secure predisposition detention and adjudicated out-of-home placement. Moreover, our results reveal that the effect of macrolevel structure is generally larger for blacks than whites and appears for drug offenses as well as other delinquencies. Given this higher explained variance, it appears that juvenile justice outcomes are more tightly coupled when targeted against blacks. [. . .]

References

Belenko, Steven, Jeffrey Fagan, & Ko-lin Chin (1991) "Criminal Justice Responses to Crack," 28 *J. of Research in Crime & Delinquency* 55.

Blumstein, Alfred (1993) "Making Rationality Relevant," 31 *Criminology* 1.

Brown, M. Craig, & Barbara D. Warner (1992) "Immigrants, Urban Politics, and Policing in 1900," 57 *American Sociological Rev.* 293.

Byrne, James M., & Robert J. Sampson (1986) "Key Issues in the Social Ecology of Crime," in J. Byrne & R. Sampson, eds., *The Social Ecology of Crime*. New York: Springer-Verlag.

Carter, Timothy, & Donald Clelland (1979) "A Neo-Marxian Critique, Formulation and Test of Juvenile Dispositions as a Function of Social Class," 27 *Social Problems* 96.

Chambliss, William J., & Robert B. Seidman (1971) *Law, Order, and Power*. Reading, MA: Addison-Wesley.

Dannefer, Dale, & Russell K. Schutt (1982) "Race and Juvenile Justice Processing in Court and Police Agencies," 87 *American J. of Sociology* 1113.

Eisenstein, James, Roy B. Flemming, & Peter F. Nardulli (1988) *The Contours of Justice: Communities and Their Courts*. Boston: Little, Brown, & Co.

Empey, Lamar T. (1982) *American Delinquency: Its Meaning and Construction*. Homewood, IL: Dorsey.

Federal Bureau of investigation (1981) *Uniform Crime Reports for the United States*. Washington, DC: GPO.

——— (1986) *Uniform Crime Reports for the United States*. Washington, DC: GPO.

Feeley, M. and Simon, J. (1992) "The New Penology," *Law and Society Review*, 461–470.

Feld, Barry C. (1989) "The Right to Counsel in Juvenile Court: An Empirical Study of When Lawyers Appear and the Difference They Make," 79 *J. of Criminal Law & Criminology* 1185.

—— (1991) "Justice by Geography: Urban, Suburban, and Rural Variations in Juvenile Justice Administration," 82 *J. of Criminal Law & Criminology* 156.

Gottfredson, Michael R., & Don M. Gottfredson (1988) *Decision Making in Criminal Justice*. New York: Plenum Press.

Greenberg, David F., Ronald C. Kessler, & Colin Loftin (1985) "Social Inequality and Crime Control," 76 *J. of Criminal Law & Criminology* 684.

Hagan, John (1974) "Extra-legal Attributes and Criminal Sentencing: An Assessment of a Sociological Viewpoint," 8 *Law & Society Rev.* 357.

—— (1989) "Why Is There So Little Criminal Justice Theory? Neglected Macro- and Micro-Level Links between Organization and Power," 26 *J. of Research in Crime & Delinquency* 116.

Hagan, John, & Kristen Bumiller (1983) "Making Sense of Sentencing: A Review and Critique of Sentencing Research," in A. Blumstein, J. Cohen, S. Martin, & M. Tonry, eds., *Research on Sentencing: The Search for Reform*. Washington, DC: National Academy Press.

Hagan, John, John D. Hewitt, & Duane F. Alwin (1979) "Ceremonial Justice: Crime and Punishment in a Loosely Coupled System," 58 *Social Forces* 506.

Hasenfeld, Yeheskel, & Paul P. L. Cheung (1985) "The Juvenile Court as a People-processing Organization: A Political Economy Perspective," 90 *American J. of Sociology* 801.

Irwin, John (1985) *The Jail: Managing the Underclass in American Society*. Berkeley: Univ. of California Press.

Jackson, Pamela Irving (1992) "Minority Group Threat, Social Context, and Policing," in A. E. Liska, ed., *Social Threat and Social Control*. Albany: State Univ. of New York Press.

Jackson, Pamela Irving, & Leo Carroll (1981) "Race and the War on Crime: The Sociopolitical Determinants of Municipal Police Expenditures in 90 Non-Southern U.S. Cities," 46 *American Sociological Rev.* 290.

Jencks, Christopher (1992) *Rethinking Social Policy: Race, Poverty, and the Underclass*. Cambridge, MA: Harvard Univ. Press.

Krisberg, Barry, Paul Litsky, & Ira Schwartz (1984) "Youth in Confinement: Justice by Geography," 21 *J. of Research in Crime & Delinquency* 153.

Krisberg, Barry, Terence Thornberry, & James Austin (1989) *Juveniles in Custody: The State of Current Knowledge*. San Francisco: National Council on Crime & Delinquency.

Land, Kenneth C., Patricia L. McCall, & Lawrence E. Cohen (1990) "Structural Covariates of Homicide Rates: Are There Any Invariances across Time and Space?" 95 *American J. of Sociology* 922.

Liska, Allen E. (1987) "A Critical Examination of Macro Perspectives on Crime Control," 13 *Annual Rev. of Sociology* 67.

Liska, Allen E., & Mark Tausig (1979) "Theoretical Interpretations of Social Class and Racial Differentials in Legal Decision-Making for Juveniles," 20 *Sociological Q.* 191.

Liska, Allen E., & Mitchell B. Chamlin (1984) "Social Structure and Crime Control among Macrosocial Units," 90 *American J. of Sociology* 383.

Liska, Allen E., Joseph J. Lawrence, & Michael Benson (1981) "Perspectives on the Legal Order: The Capacity for Social Control," 87 *American J. of Sociology* 413.

McGarrell, Edmund (1993) "Trends in Racial Disproportionality in Juvenile Court Processing: 1985–1989," 39 *Crime & Delinquency* 29.

Mauer, Marc (1990) "Young Black Men and the Criminal Justice System: A Growing National Problem." Washington, DC: Sentencing Project.

Myers, Martha (1989) "Symbolic Policy and the Sentencing of Drug Offenders," 23 *Law & Society Rev*. 295.

Myers, Martha, & Susette Talarico (1986) "Urban Justice, Rural Injustice? Urbanization and Its Effect on Sentencing," 24 *Criminology* 367.

——(1987) *The Social Contexts of Criminal Sentencing*. New York: Springer-Verlag.

O'Hare, William P., & Brenda Curry-White (1992) "Is There a Rural Underclass?" 20 *Population Today* 6.

Peterson, Ruth D., & John Hagan (1984) "Changing Conceptions of Race: Towards An Account of Anomalous Findings of Sentencing Research," 49 *American Sociological Rev*. 56.

Platt, Anthony M. (1977) *The Child Savers*. 2d ed. Chicago: Univ. of Chicago Press.

Quinney, Richard (1970) *The Social Reality of Crime*. Boston: Little, Brown & Co.

——(1977) *Class, State, and Crime*. New York: D. McKay.

Sampson, Robert J. (1989) *Structural Sources of Variation in Juvenile Court Processing*. Final Report for the Visiting Scholars Program. Pittsburgh, PA: National Center for Juvenile Justice, National Juvenile Court Data Archive.

Sampson, Robert J., & Jacqueline Cohen (1988) "Deterrent Effects of the Police on Crime: A Replication and Theoretical Extension," 22 *Law & Society Rev*. 163.

Sampson, Robert J., & William Julius Wilson (1993) "Toward a Theory of Race, Crime, and Urban Inequality," in John Hagan & Ruth Peterson, eds., *Crime and Inequality*. Stanford, CA: Stanford Univ. Press.

Schwartz, Ira M. (1989) *(In)Justice for Juveniles*. Lexington, MA: Lexington Books.

Snyder, Howard N. (1990) "Growth in Minority Detentions Attributed to Drug Law Violators." Washington, DC: Office of Juvenile Justice & Delinquency Prevention, U.S. Department of Justice.

Snyder, Howard, Terrence Finnegan, Ellen Nimick, Melissa Sickmund, Dennis Sullivan, & Nancy Tierney (1989) *Juvenile Court Statistics, 1985*. Washington, DC: Office of Juvenile Justice & Delinquency Prevention, U.S. Department of Justice.

Sutton, John R. (1988) *Stubborn Children: Controlling Delinquency in the United States, 1640–1981*. Berkeley: Univ. of California Press.

Tittle, Charles R., & Debra A. Curran (1988) "Contingencies for Dispositional Disparities in Juvenile Justice," 67 *Social Forces* 23.

Turk, Austin T. (1969) *Criminality and Legal Order*. Chicago: Rand McNally.

Wilson, James Q. (1968) *Varieties of Police Behavior*. Cambridge, MA: Harvard Univ. Press.

Wilson, William Julius (1987) *The Truly Disadvantaged: The Inner City, the Underclass, and Public Policy*. Chicago: Univ. of Chicago Press.

——(1991) "Studying Inner-City Social Dislocations: The Challenge of Public Agenda Research," 56 *American Sociological Rev*. 1.

Chapter 33

Mary E. Vogel

PLEA BARGAINING AND ITS HISTORICAL ORIGINS

The courts, discretionary informality and the transition to democracy

From: Mary E. Vogel (1999), 'The social origins of plea bargaining: conflict and the law in the process of state formation, 1830–1860', *Law & Society Review* 33(1): 161–246, and Mary E. Vogel (2001), 'Lawyering in an age of popular politics', in Jerry Van Hoy (ed.), *Legal Professions*, London: Elsevier, pp. 207–252.

THOUGH HIGHLY CONTROVERSIAL, THE origins of plea bargaining are surprisingly obscure. While often thought to be either an innovation or a corruption of the courts after World War II, it has much deeper historical roots. My purpose here is to explain why plea bargaining arose and to show how those origins have shaped the way it has operated. The significance of plea bargaining lies in the fact that, by the late 19th century, most cases in the criminal courts were being resolved through this process. Although the popular image is one of jury trials with a presumption of innocence, a very different process has anchored the American courts.

To explain the rise of plea bargaining, I explore its beginnings in ante-bellum Boston – the first sustained instance of the practice known to exist. Boston was a national center of legal innovation from which many legal ideas and practices spread to other cities through diffusion (Novak 1996). Plea bargaining very probably was one such distributed legal innovation. An urban political elite, seeking to maintain its position of power, played a keyrole in its establishment. This privileged group responding to political challenge in a specific social and temporal context, shaped much of the imaginative construction of American legal ideas during this formative era. It was this elite's perception of crisis and threat, along with its effort to preserve social order, the legitimacy of self-rule and its own dominance, that produced in a single locale the practice of plea bargaining that would then become a national and, eventually, international phenomenon. Plea bargaining, thus, had its origin in a counter-revolutionary period of reaction to social change.

POST-INDEPENDENCE CONFLICT: CRISIS AND THE RE-MAKING OF POLITICAL AUTHORITY

In the years after the American Revolution, politicians worked to re-create political authority anew for a self-governing republican society. Yet their project faced the obstacle that this authority was to be anchored in popular self-rule but to be constructed during the 1830s which was a period when concentration of wealth and economic inequality increased more rapidly than any other time in the 19th century. Recently historians such as Gordon Wood (1992), have shown compellingly how intensely conflicted was the social and political landscape of the early American republic.

This "formative era" of American law was one of perceived crisis of unrest and political instability in the republic. Its timing was crucial because it occurred just as suffrage was "universally" extended. Together these events evoked new state responses to social conflict. As the voting public grew, uncertainty ran high as to whether self-governance would prove viable and what path politics might take. State response to the crisis was needed that would be defensible in a world of popular rule. Amidst a rescripting of legal practices that took place, one innovation, plea bargaining, achieved special prominence. Plasticity of institutions and practices at this creative time, when judges were forging legal institutions into a modern form much of which they retain today, facilitated creation of new legal mechanisms and, once formed, allowed them to achieve a permanence not otherwise possible.

During the 1830s and 1840s, rioting and unrest were widespread. The earliest factories were constructed which changed both forms of production and working conditions. City life brought diverse strangers of unequal rank into contact. These, coupled with new waves of immigrants, created a vibrant and tumultuous urban scene. Officials, already focused on the danger that conflict posed to property, social order and growth, grew anxious (Horwitz, 1977; Nedelsky, 1990). Religious beliefs, previously a source of cohesion, and social consensus, which had pervaded small scale community life, were also eroding (Nelson, 1981; Lockridge, 1981). Constant spatial movement and turnover among residents in city neighborhoods amplified the strains of inequality (Sellers, 1991). Irish immigrants began to coalesce as a major presence too. Amidst these pressures, conflict, unrest and violence, rather than harmony, was the order of the day.

Because self-rule was still new and local political capacity for responding to conflict was limited, there arose a sense of crisis and of threat to both the social order and to the elite power embedded in it. It was desire, in this context, to protect order and to reconsolidate the city elite's partisan control that elicited new state responses.

Spurred on by the election of Andrew Jackson to the Presidency, strikes by the Workingmen's movement swept the American northeast between 1833 and 1836 (Sellers, 1991, p. 338). Their crusade was for a ten-hour working day – a goal that, by 1836, had essentially been achieved (Sellers, 1991, p. 338). Yet, their discourse endured. Labor leaders charged that "capital divided society into two classes, the producing many and the exploiting few, by expropriating the fruits of labor" (Sellers, 1991, p. 338). Workingmen challenged growing inequality that let a privileged few flourish at the expense of many. Resentment simmered. By the 1830s, public concern was widespread about the future of republican self-rule. Workers began to use the language of republicanism in new ways that now viewed the holistic interests of the society through a new modestly socialist lens (Forbath, 1991). Social disorder, riots and strikes riveted elected officials. To defuse resentment and reassert control, they turned for help to the ideology of a "rule of law."

By this point, conflict had gripped the public imagination. Ethnic diversity and contention soared as did images of the Irish as one major source of the turmoil. Adding to these ethnic tensions was a palpable public fear of crime – especially violence. Addressing the Boston city council on September 18, 1837, Mayor Eliot decried the threat posed by "the incendiary, burglar and the lawlessly violent" which was "increasing at a ratio faster than that of the population" (cited in Lane, 1971, p. 34). Probably the clearest sign of public fear is that the Mayor requested and obtained funds to establish a paid police force for the city. Pointing to the "spirit of violence abroad," Eliot argued that the residents must be protected. Whether disorder and crime actually were rising or were simply perceived now as more threatening, it is clear that violence was pervasive.

During the 1830s, a remarkable series of riots and routs occurred. By then, city officials, who were very aware of similar events in England and on the Continent, were acutely sensitive to the political potential of such events (Lane, 1971, p. 30). In 1836 and 1837 an economic downturn, followed by financial panic, further fanned fears about the fragility of the new order. Unease created by daily contact among persons of diverse ranks in the city amplified fears as the lives of the poor impinged ever more on the consciousness of the affluent (Lane, 1971).

As labor unrest, ethnic conflict and crime mounted, shockwaves were buffered less than they had traditionally been by the erosion of shared religious values and cultural commonalities (Wiebe, 1966). Thus, during the 1830s, when social conflict grew, amidst weakened cultural consensus, it produced an acute sense of crisis in the new order. Response to this crisis was shaped by its timing which caused state actions to be devised in the context of two other key happenings (Poulantzas, 1975). Extension of the vote meant that any initiative must take a form that would sustain the popular consent crucial to self-rule. There was also emerging a new conscious campaign to promote social policy and the "people's welfare" through law (Horwitz, 1977). The fact that crisis emerged during this "formative era" of American law created a special window of opportunity for cultural change.

THE LEGAL ESTABLISHMENT AND THE LEGACY OF POST-REVOLUTIONARY FEDERALISM

Almost without exception, the Massachusetts bar, after the War of Independence, consisted of, first, Federalists and, then, Whigs (Warren, 1931, pp. 174, 178). During the "formative era," they achieved new influence after they recovered from an immediate post-Revolutionary period of disrepute. This political collegiality in the sympathies of the bar, combined with a long tradition of fraternity, practical exchange of ideas and fellow feeling, on the one hand, and, first, Federalist, and, later, Whig control of the Commonwealth's judicial appointments, on the other, to ensure that the courts were presided over by judges in step with the policies of these successive elite-dominated parties. [. . .]

Concern about lawyers' political allegiances was aggravated by the extensive part they were playing in state government. Nathaniel Ames argued that separation of powers was breached as lawyers wrought their influence simultaneously by their votes, their courtroom activities, and their candidacies for elected office (Warren, 1931, p. 179). This fear had some basis because "lawyers constituted the mainstay [and frequently also the candidates] of the Federalist party" (Warren, 1931, p. 179). Denouncing the lawyers' influence in colorful terms, Nathaniel Ames wrote: " . . . he that is not now a Lawyer, or tool of a Lawyer, is considered only fit to carry guts to a bear in New England" (Nathaniel Ames, *Columbian Minerva*, September 6, 1803; cited in Warren, 1931, p. 180).

Thus, the "law craft," as bastion of Federalism, possessed a distinctive ideological stance. As lawyers' status improved after the Revolution and they moved between careers in the bar, the judiciary and politics, they carried with them the unique political outlook of the Federalist/Whig elite and, with it, a clear commitment to their policies as ones that might best serve the "public good." As criminal courts innovated in their efforts to contain conflict, protect property and dampen the violence and rioting so destructive to prosperity, first, Federalist and, later, Whig ideas colored the thinking of judges about the need for order and what policies might achieve it.

POPULAR CHALLENGE TO THE COMMON LAW

Critique of lawyers, largely on grounds of their Federalist views, gradually came during the early 1800s to be associated in the public mind with opposition to the common law. Many states had, after the American Revolution, initially adopted much of British Common Law and public attitudes toward it had been positive. After 1800, however, things changed (Horwitz, 1977, p. 5). Previously the Common Law had been viewed as a fixed, customary standard. Judges envisioned their task as discovery and application of pre-existing rules (Horwitz, 1977, pp. 8–9). This produced a strict conception of precedent and a popular view of law as, if not always fair, at least known.

In the closing years of the 18th century, however, signs of change appeared in both criminal and civil spheres (Horwitz, 1977). Its roots were two. The first was states' rights constitutional theories which depicted lawfinding based on precedent as a form of "ex post facto" law. The second was new conceptions of the basis of legitimation of political authority which portrayed the customary approach of Common Law as outdated in light of popular sovereignty. Initially these sentiments generated calls for abandonment of the Common Law and a move to enacted statute. The codification movement sought to recognize primacy of "the people's" elected representatives and to move from case law to statutory enactments. . . .

Yet, judges, who were overwhelmingly Federalist-appointed, and political leaders resisted the move to statute precisely because of the power it would have given to legislative bodies dominated by the middling and lower classes (Horwitz, 1977, p. 21). Instead, they, together with what was then the Federalist elite, fought to maintain judicial discretion by preserving reliance on the common law (Horwitz, 1977, p. 21). Although the codification movement ultimately failed, it signaled public interest in reducing the discretion of judges and in simplifying and clarifying law, before the fact, and communicating knowable legal rules and procedures to the citizenry. In part the move-ment foundered due to a compromise proposal advanced by Joseph Story that "a digest [be prepared], under legislative authority of the settled portions of the common law" (Jones and Rogers, 1993, p. 35).

Complexity, a separate but related matter, also became a basis for challenge. In response to persistent criticism of lawyers, the courts and even the common law, Supreme Judicial Court Justice Theodore Sedgwick, a conservative from Stockbridge, urged reform arguing that only if the courts were "wise, simple and expedient" would people consider it "the most certain means of attaining justice" and use them rather than extra-judicial means for resolving conflicts (Jones et al., 1993, p. 30). [. . .]

EXTENSION OF THE FRANCHISE AND THE POLITICS OF CONSENT

By the end of Jackson's second Presidential term in the mid-1830s, "universal" suffrage was a fact of life and reconstituting politics. By easing restrictions, such as property ownership and the poll tax, states extended the vote to new segments of the laboring classes though a goodly share of Boston's citizens had already voted before. Artisans and workers now produced more representative assemblies though a lingering tradition of deference meant that the result was not immediate. Elected leaders, in turn, faced new constraints as their decisions increasingly required at least some broadbased popular consent. This abetted a move, already under way, to challenge the political control of Boston's Federalist elite (Lane, 1971). It also aroused worries about what other forms, particularly with respect to property, contestation would take. Joseph Story noted, at that point, that the lawyer's most "glorious and not infrequently perilous" responsibility was to protect the "sacred rights of property" from the "rapacity" of the "majority" (Story, 1829; cited in Mensch, 1982).

While proprietors complained that conflict marred quality of life, city leaders worried about even more far-reaching consequences (Lane, 1971). Familiar as they were with the rioting and revolt in Europe during the 1820s and 1830s, Boston's politicians worked feverishly to restore order, reconsolidate their partisan base, and cement popular commitment to the institutions of the republic. Because the franchise precluded solutions to disorder and unrest that jeopardized voter support, new responses had to be devised not only to violence, property crime and riot but to growing political tensions too.

The courts, which provided Americans' primary experience of the state before local political parties formed in the 1840s, now assumed a key role (Skowronek, 1982). Beginning in the 1820s, a first wave of court reform had established the Boston Police Court. It was a reform spearheaded by Boston's leading citizens and it aimed to re-establish the lower courts as a respected and well-used forum for resolving conflict (Hindus, 1980; Dimond, 1975). This responded both to the demands of the propertied for security and, even more, to the "claims [for a just forum on the part] of a [lower] class [whom they felt it] unsafe to deny" (Lane, 1971, p. 23). Additional changes followed.

By the 1830s, Boston's local officials were "no longer so firmly united by ties of class and [state] party [affiliation] as their predecessors (had been)" (Lane, 1971, p. 46). The city remained a one-party city where "candidates labeled Democrat . . . had [in most years virtually] no chance of . . . [electoral] success" (Lane, 1971, p. 47). However, the times were creating intractable dilemmas for these beleaguered [Federalist and, then, Whig] municipal authorities and "hopes for the material future were [increasingly] balanced by fear for the political" (Lane, 1971, pp. 47, 60). Under pressure, elite Bostonians experimented with new alternatives. To take one step "backward" to reconsolidate elite power, this city with its tradition of single-party Federalist/Whig control was forced to take several small steps forward in the service of consensus-building and reform.

Strategies to restore order were conceived, then, at a time that precluded politics as usual. The Whigs feared threats, not only to property per se, but even more to the stability in day to day affairs that investment and growth required. Fearing for the future, leaders worked to nurture order and predictability in public life and to cultivate the consent of citizens to both institutions of self-rule and the stewardship of their party. To this end, they approached social control, not through overtly coercive means, but in ways that underscored the party's claim to serve the will of the people.

City officials and elite civic leaders accomplished this by appealing to the pre-eminent social discourse of the day – that of a "rule of law." By common agreement, they argued, social life must proceed according to a body of rules specified in advance and oriented to fairness. Such rules, they contended, apply universally to every citizen and prescribe equal treatment for each accused person in court. Then, in a dramatic claim, it was argued that, even when such rules depart from popular opinion, they must, unceasingly, be observed. Only through adherence to legal principles and procedures, leaders argued, could the new project of self-rule be sustained. By appealing to the language of the widely revered "rule of law" as a basis for order, they hoped to bolster both social order and the legitimacy and authority of republican institutions. With order restored, they believed they could re-secure their hold on power.

The language in which the reforms were advanced reveals how officials viewed them. When, in 1822, the Police Court had been established, Mayor Josiah Quincy unveiled his plan by denouncing the potential for social conflict inherent in the previous system of Justices of the Peace. Quincy argued that "whenever confidence . . . [lapses] in the lower tribunals, there is no justice . . . [for] the poor, who cannot afford to carry their causes to the higher" ones (Quincy, 1822, pp. 7–8). Such injustice, he proclaimed, corrupts the morality and political commitment of citizens. Quincy referred, among other things, to the prior fee structure whereby magistrates had prospered the greater the number of cases heard. Anticipating a point later made by Max Weber, Quincy argued that where political authority anchors its legitimation in legal rules, the danger is especially great when that law is perceived as unjust. The risk is that laws, so viewed, may be treated as no law at all and that political authority itself will then be undercut. Following quickly upon court reform, other major new institutions including prisons and reformatories, a House of Industry and a professional police force were also set in place.

As new institutions moved into motion, judicial decision making and court procedure also changed – although more informally and incrementally. Judges' decisions took on a policy focus (Horwitz, 1977). In the criminal courts, pardons, the nolle prosse, the plea of nolo contendere and grants of immunity had already begun to be used in new, explicitly conditional ways to further specific policy goals. Plea bargaining now made its debut in the courts. Although the practice arose during a period of reform, it was not advanced as a unitary plan or formal initiative. Instead, it emerged as an informal and pragmatic accretion of small changes in the customary practice of the courts that was, only then, culturally codified.

LAW AS AN INSTRUMENT OF SOCIAL POLICY: JUDICIAL ACTIVISM

During the "formative era," judges began to reconceptualize American law as an instrument of social policy. This transformation in law, combined with state structure, made it likely that political response to crisis would come through the courts. As judges changed the way they envisioned their role, they increasingly crafted their decisions with an eye to policy implications beyond their case at hand (Horwitz, 1977). In private law, case decisions aimed to facilitate healthy markets and economic growth (Horwitz, 1977). In the criminal courts, judges sought to assure behavior that would uphold social order and, especially, foster the security and predictability needed for development (Vogel, 1999).

The early 1800s had been a "disruptive and potentially radical period" (Mensch, 1982, p. 19). As American leaders and jurists worked to re-establish post-independence political authority, they came to rely heavily on the courts where the role of judges was changing (Mensch, 1982, p. 19). It was the effort to reconcile the tension between judicial discretion and popular will, mentioned above in the context of the common law, that contributed mightily to what Horwitz (1977) has called the "transformation of American law." Judges increasingly bridged the gap between common law and "the people" by envisioning themselves as agents of "popular sovereignty." They came to view their role as that of activist and innovator functioning on behalf of the "common good" (Horwitz, 1977, p. 30). In the course of this change, judges began to view law as a policy instrument (Horwitz, 1977). Increasingly, judges articulated decisions and used law as a tool to shape the path of social change. In Mark DeWolfe Howe's words, "it was as clear to laymen as it was to lawyers that the nature of American institutions . . . was largely to be determined by the judges . . . (and that) questions of . . . law were . . . considered as questions of social policy" (Howe, 1947–1950; cited in Horwitz, 1977). Howe's words bespoke a conscious turn by the state to the courts, among other institutions, to promote its policies.

Judicial discretion, specifically in sentencing, was no exception. Mayor Josiah Quincy emphasized the existence of such discretion in his address to the Grand Jury of Suffolk County when he observed "There is, indeed, a discretion invested in judges" (Quincy, 1822, p. 12). That he believed such discretion should be informed by social policy in shaping sentencing Quincy left no doubt. He proclaimed that "The utility of a concentrated system of penal and criminal law in which punishment shall be graduated by the nature and aggravation of crimes, and *adapted to the actual state of society and public sentiment* [emphasis this author's], . . . [is] appreciated" (p. 14). That judges' discretion in the criminal sphere centered on sentencing policy, Quincy also emphasized. He noted that a judge's discretion included selecting "time and place [of imprisonment]" as well as other aspects of the severity of sanction (p. 12). Public knowledge of such policy uses of prosecutorial and judicial discretion in sentencing was widespread and the practice met with legislative approval (House Report, Massachusetts Legislature, No. 4, January 1845).

EMERGENCE OF PLEA BARGAINING: CHANGES IN THE PRACTICE OF LAW

[. . .]

Given the paucity of local political institutions and the many challenges of the day, during the early to mid-19th century, the courts emerged as central in shaping the relation of citizens to the state. At this point, they stepped forward as agents of the state to promote political stability, to enhance the legitimation of institutions of self-rule by nurturing political authority and to create conditions conducive to healthy economic development.

Reaching back into the traditions of the common law, the courts turned to mechanisms of discretionary, or episodic, leniency. Through these practices, leniency was frequently, but not always, accorded and so could not be counted on and taken for granted. What was unique about the tradition of leniency was that to qualify for it one relied on the intercession of what were essentially character witnesses to whom one was known. Thus the capacity to plea bargain was to some extent contingent on social capital – or embeddedness in webs of social relationships that empower one to realize her/his aspirations – as well as on economic capital and cultural capital. As Thompson (1975) and Hay et al. (1975) have shown, in England where litigation was also widespread, practices of leniency created incentives to appreciate, nurture and reciprocate social ties and bonds of patronage with those more privileged. In this way, one might benefit from the good will to cause a prosecution to be foregone or to have a powerful patron to plead for mercy if one ran afoul of the law. The result, in England, was a system of justice that reinforced the stability of the class structure, despite vast material inequality, through these social ties that it fostered at the same time that it bolstered political legitimacy by affirming a formal message of universality (i.e. law applies to all) and equality (i.e. formally equal treatment procedurally) before the law. In the United States, plea bargaining emerged as the most widespread form of episodic leniency – one which also promoted stability – but now in new ways in a context of popular electoral politics.

First signs of plea bargaining appear in the lower court of Boston in the 1830s (Vogel, 1988, 1999). Before that time, both bargained guilty pleas (either explicit or tacitly implicit) and, in fact, guilty pleas altogether were quite rare (Alschuler, 1979; Langbein, 1978). In fact, judges exhorted defendants to exercise the hard won rights of the republic against self-incrimination and warned of penalties if they failed to do so. Nor, according to prior research by John Langbein and others, did the practice exist in England or else-where before the 19th century. Although leniency in the form of pardons and grants of clemency has a long history, those did not involve direct exchange and never achieved the pervasive, routine use that plea bargaining did.

Yet, in Boston, during the 1830s and 1840s, this changed with the beginnings of plea bargaining. Guilty pleas, the first element of bargaining that appears together with concessions in disposition or sentencing, were first entered in significant numbers during the 1830s and, by 1840, were widely accepted – a pattern that continued into the 20th century (Vogel, 1999). Overall guilty pleas surged from less than 15% of all cases entered in the docket in 1830 to 28.6% in 1840 and then to a high of 88% in 1880 (Vogel, 1999). However, defendants' tendency to plead guilty varied among, different types of offenses with bargained pleas, initially, most common in the Boston court for property offenses and least for offenses against the moral order (Vogel, 1999). [. . .]

Turning to cultural traditions of the common law, Bostonians, during the late 1830s and 1840s, reworked elements of the tradition of discretion and episodic leniency into a creative legal practice which, while closing cases in a much and vociferously sought reform, retained for the courts considerable control over both sentencing and its implementation. Judges took standard vehicles of leniency, such as the pardon in which leniency was traditionally granted after conviction, and moved it up to a point before a decision was yet made – giving it a more contractual quality. In the case of pleas of nolo contendere which were used with some frequency, especially in regulatory cases, conditions might be specified explicitly for the grant of leniency. Much less complicated and almost always conditionless was the guilty plea bargain which emerged in criminal cases – especially those of larceny and assault. The simplicity of the plea bargain and absence of arcane legal formalities had broad popular appeal.

How, we might ask, could the bench and bar develop a shared sense of the policy concerns of the Whig party? Though informally constituted, the bar maintained its influence over the legal profession as an extremely powerful private club with strong personal ties and networks of connection between lawyers and judges. In addition to personal and family ties, along with lingering fondness for mentors of apprenticeship days, lawyers met at the Social Law Library and for meals, and, most importantly, "frequently corresponded with Supreme Judicial Court justices such as Lemuel Shaw, requesting copies of legal opinions and commenting on points of law" (Jones and Rogers, 1993, p. 38). For the circuit court, lawyers and judges rode together, stayed at the same inns and often dined together. Since many lawyers were also involved in politics, we have every reason to believe that judges' awareness of Federalist and, later, Whig policy objectives was high. Specific reforms, such as the 1841 request for a change in chancery rules, were sometimes proposed (Jones and Rogers, 1993, p. 32). Such exchange of ideas dated back to at least 1814 when the Court considered complaints from lawyers that the circuit delayed and, thus, denied justice in Suffolk County (Jones and Rogers, 1993, p. 33). A permanent court for the county was soon established.

Plea bargaining appears to have been espoused by old political and social elites whose electoral power was under siege because of the continued control it gave them, in a broad sense, through judicial discretion over sentencing policy. In Boston, during the early decades of the 19th century, virtually the entire Bar consisted of former Federalists – now Whigs. While committed to a "republican" vision, theirs, like that of many of Boston's elite Brahmin families, was a different, more forward looking variant of Jefferson's bucolic trust in the freeman farmer that accepted manufacturing, commerce and industrialization as the inevitable path of change. Thus, a fundamental commonality of political outlook, along with strong social and institutional ties, created both affinity and frequent mingling among the members of the bar, the judiciary and Boston's elite privileged inner circle.

Defendants, largely lower class persons in the lower court, accepted the practice because it held out a sense of leniency, the appearance of control over one's fate through negotiation, and the elimination of intrusive state oversight of the lives of defendants through what had been the increasingly frequent practice of leaving cases "open" on file. By offering leniency, closure of cases and some control over one's fate the Whigs hoped to draw conflicts into the courts before they could escalate in other realms – thus promoting the stability needed for growth. The opportunity to gain experience making decisions among structured options in public settings was also used as a process to educate the masses in both a conception of citizenship and a sense of the responsibilities it involved.

Plea bargaining emerged as a significant phenomenon during the 1830s and by 1840 the practice of granting concessions in cases where such a plea had been entered was set in place and continued into the 20th century (Vogel, 1999). Plea bargaining did not emerge as a full blown plan or scheme. Instead it was the product of gradual incremental improvisation by a Whig political elite seeking to bolster social order so vital to the healthy functioning of markets and to economic development and, with it, their own flagging political fortunes. Thus, the discretionary informality of plea bargaining emerged in a time of political reaction. Here Franz Neumann's observation in his essay "The Changing Function of Law in Modern Societies," which states that the rise of discretionary informality and expanded powers of judicial review in the German courts during the 1930s opened the way for their politicalization, provides an intriguing counterpoint.

Though informal, plea bargaining responded to various criticisms of criminal justice afoot in that day – namely claims that 18th century justice had been too expensive, hard to understand and slow. With its simplicity, rationality and regularity, plea bargaining offered a routinization that was appealing. In its exchange, albeit symbolic, the practice drew the attention of not only defendants but also the public to the precise costs of criminal acts in a way favored by consequentialists. Popular court vignettes appeared in city newspapers and communicated both case outcomes and often a moral lesson to readers on a daily basis. [. . .]

What then were the implications of acting through the courts to promote order? By working through the courts, political leaders appealed for legitimation to the ideology of the rule of law which was enormously powerful in that day (Tomlins, 1993). Court activity under the "rule of law" also repudiated overt coercion which might jeopardize the project of self-rule by undercutting claims to represent the popular will. Instead, use of the courts to promote order sought the consent of voluntary citizens to lawful action even when not immediately in their own interests. At the same time, however, it promoted on the part of those citizens a customary familiarity with the penalties for an offense that might deter.

THE MICROPOLITICS OF CONSENT

Besides providing advantages to city officials, to Boston's social elite, and to defendants, plea bargaining, once established, held out specific advantages for judges, prosecutors and defense attorneys. While not presented here as causes of the rise of plea bargaining, these advantages explain "bargaining's" acceptance by the court. For judges, the practice provided a rejoinder to criticisms of court discretion and reliance on precedent. While the codification movement, which had sought to restrict judicial discretion by moving to legislative statutes, had failed, the threat posed by its underlying sentiment remained. For judges, plea bargaining offered a new, more conciliatory, customary means of maintaining discretion – yet in a depersonalized, knowable and relatively predictable market-like form that was more palatable to the masses.

Justices in the lower courts, whose salaries were annually appropriated, also had reason to believe, rightly or not, that they faced subtle pressure for consonance with the policies of governor and legislature because of initiatives proposed in the legislature to examine the performance of judges individually during the appropriation process – an abortive attempt at political review of the judiciary. Politically motivated court reorganizations, that turned out all sitting judges and appointed new ones, had, as illustrated above, also historically been common. In this context, plea bargaining provided a low profile and implicit form of discretion that facilitated sentencing consistent with prevailing policies and purposes of punishment.

In addition to Whig influence through judicial appointments and social policy, there existed by 1840 a tradition of judges, justices of the peace and district attorneys who had careers that mixed judicial and political life. Eventually, after 1858, district attorneys were elected and prosecutors were linked to politics directly. This heightened the value of discretion plea bargaining accorded judges and prosecutors in cases that could color their political prospects. This is not to say that judges and prosecutors crafted positions with an eye to political gain. Reliance on plea bargaining, however, did accord them latitude in high profile situations of consequence. This connection between judges and prosecutors, on the one hand, and elected office, on the other, is not one that existed in England.

Plea bargaining also had other bureaucratic consequences that served prosecutors and defense attorneys as well. Cases in the lower courts were usually expeditiously handled by a judge alone with public prosecutors rarely involved before 1850. While district attorneys were salaried and so had no financial interest in case outcomes, the 1830s saw the legislature first require annual reports detailing court caseloads and dispositions. This appears to have been part of the court reform movement to establish impersonal and regularized justice. Such rationalized reporting meant that a process which inherently produced a high conviction rate grew desirable as the century wore on and public prosecutors handled more cases in the lower courts. While such required reports contributed to growing emphasis on efficiency and rational criteria of performance, their effect was limited in the lower courts where cases were typically handled without attorneys for either defense or prosecution. Perhaps most salient, bargaining provided a daily power resource for the prosecutor. For defense attorneys, criminal cases were not particularly lucrative, and so they stood to lose little in fees as a result of expeditious bargaining. Though attorneys often defended serious criminal cases, most lower court cases, before mid-century, were resolved without defense counsel so that attorneys lost virtually nothing at all. When defense attorneys did appear, plea bargaining enhanced their discretion as it did that of the prosecutor. Bargaining, thus, closely safeguarded the prerogatives of judges, and to the extent that they gradually came to serve in the lower courts, of prosecutors and defense attorneys too. Because plea bargaining served each actor well, it was variously embraced or tolerated, rather than opposed, within the courthouse.

Interestingly, while delay was a constant criticism in the higher courts, all signs are that cases moved quickly through the lower court – almost always reaching trial before a judge within one day in the early part of the century (Gil, 1837). This challenges the popular view that caseload pressure in the courts may have given rise to plea bargaining. The fact that caseload increased steadily over the last half of the 19th century, while concessions attendant to bargaining fluctuated, further challenges the power of caseload as a cause.

"TRIAGE": SOCIAL CLASSIFICATION

What was taking place was a form of "triage" or social sorting. This refers to the practice of distinguishing the victims according to the seriousness of their injuries and devising a differentiated rescue plan that tries to maximize the number of persons who can be saved. It is a practice, often witnessed at the scene of an accident, of identifying those who can be saved and treating them first. By relying on character witnesses, employment histories, family ties and criminal records, the court was clearly attempting to identify those who were hardworking family people who had simply made one misstep in an otherwise worthy life and who could be reclaimed as productive workers and responsible citizens. These the judges differentiated from marginals, transients and those with few ties who were more often sentenced to serve time at the House of Industry or, later, the House of Correction. In selecting judges for the Police Court, great care was paid to their educative capacities to convey this message of reconciliation across a broad range of social backgrounds.

In contrast to present day policy in the United States, where imprisonment is growing more and more widespread, the courts used the plea bargain initially almost like a form of symbolic surety – re-embedding the defendant, who is granted leniency, back into his or her world of work and family amidst that most powerful, for most persons, of all forms of social control – the web of watchful relationships of everyday life. Those who had testified symbolically staked their reputation on the defendant's future good behavior and, thus, had an interest in seeing the commitment kept. [. . .]

LEGITIMATING DEMOCRATIC INSTITUTIONS

As the American republic set off into the 19th century, self-rule was an extraordinary experiment and, though optimistic, no one knew whether it would survive. One dilemma was that, as in any democracy, it became particularly difficult for law to enforce order by coercion because the very need to use force challenged and undercut the claim of the regime to represent the "popular sovereignty" of the citizenry – the will of all. Thus, it became vital for the regime to win the consent of the people to its rule. In the new polity, governed no longer by monarchy but rather by self-rule, there was a realization that social order must rest, not on power or coercion, but instead on popular acceptance of sovereign commands and on a sense among the people of a duty to obey. That is to say that a vision of political authority was needed for a world of popular rule.

What emerged was, at first appearance, a conception of modern political authority rooted in the "rule of law." Yet, despite the basic modernity of the new republic, that authority, in practice, came to comprise a unique blend of what Weber would term rational-legal and traditional elements. The world's newest republic turned to some of mankind's oldest and "tried and true" approaches to bolster authority amidst the extraordinary adventure in self-rule. [. . .]

BLENDED FORM OF AUTHORITY: RATIONAL-LEGAL AND TRADITIONAL ELEMENTS

The result of this invocation of the rule of law and concomitant turn to episodic leniency was a move in the 19th century United States toward a vision of political authority that is, at first appearance, of a rational-legal sort – that is, authority whose legitimation is based in the enactment of rules in law and the specification of offices in law. Introduction of this guiding principle of a "rule of law" into a political world, first republican and then democratic, that was committed to popular sovereignty produced an inherently conflicted form of authority – producing an enduring tension between "law rule" and "self-rule." However, it was no more so than in most other modern democratic states and less so than in many.

Yet as judges focused on the problem of creating political authority anew, their reliance on tools of discretionary leniency, in addition to the powerful discourse of a "rule of law," was quite shrewd. Despite the basic post-Enlightenment modernity of the new "republic," they were crafting authority of a unique blend of modern rational-legal and traditional elements. There was a strong sense that ideology unsupported by the stabilizing influence of participation in an integrative network of social roles could prove a fragile basis on which to build social order. The Jacobin excesses in France had been vividly seared into the collective American political imagination and rioting in Britain prior to the Reform Act of 1832 was well noted too.

Local politicians sensed that, along with laws, the subjects of political authority that is solely rule-based require the normative guidance that comes from a secure place in the web and routines of social structure. During the excesses of the 1790s following the French Revolution, they believed those who had taken to the streets did so because they had become detached from their places in the habitual role structures and related rounds of activity of everyday life. Because religion, social consensus and the deference accorded status were all eroding apace, the established view was that hierarchy and a sense of social position had to be sustained lest the American masses be turned out as radically unconstrained individuals whose penchant for violence and excess might equal the French. If political stability could be had in America, the interconnected networks of social roles that honeycomb society (i.e. family, community and, especially, work) must, it was believed, play a vital part. New uses of leniency in the courts and the "symbolic suretyship" that I have been describing were well-suited to accomplish that embeddedness as defendants were turned back to the community under the watchful eye of their intercessors. In doing so, the plea bargain and other new forms of leniency linked the rule-based authority of the courts with the traditional authority that had historically served as a cornerstone of the socializing web of communal membership of everyday life.

Thus, the model of authority that emerged was a unique mix of modern rational-legal and traditional authority. The former based its legitimation, as noted a moment ago, in the enactment of its rules and specification of its offices in law which empowered a "rule of law." The latter, which relied on customary hierarchies and relationships (e.g. parents, spouses, employers, ministers, elders) legitimated its claims on the behavior of citizens through enduring regard for the sacredness of custom which endowed the relational web of membership of everyday life with a formidable capacity for social control. Amidst open turmoil of crime, riot and unrest, this was how the political leadership of the day faced the, if anything, deeper problem of translating the dreams of the framers of the Constitution, in practical terms, into an enduring social and political order capable of wise political action. American society, unlike France, had experienced political but not throughgoing social revolution (Wood, 1993). What we see here is the movement of old hierarchies to reconsolidate political power. Due to the prominence of the middling classes in the legislatures, old elite interests work instead through the courts where their presence is strong. Rather than seeking victory in individual cases, the quest is to supplant formal procedural rules with discretionary informality that can be used to craft enlightened sentencing policy and to nurture the restoration of social order.

References

Alschuler, A. (1979). Plea Bargaining and Its History. *Law and Society Review, 13*, 211–245.

Bendix, R. (1964). *Nation Building and Citizenship*. New York: Wiley.

Bentham, J. (1831[1827]). *Rationale of Judicial Evidence*, C. Ogden (ed.). Reprinted in 1995 by Fred B. Rothman and Co., Buffalo, NY.

Chitty, J. (1816). *Criminal Law*. Philadelphia, PA: Isaac Riley.

Council of Massachusetts Temperance Society (1834). Report.

DiFilippo, T. (1973). Jeremy Bentham's Codification Proposals and Some Remarks on Their Place in History. *Buffalo Law Review, 22*, 239–251.

Dimond, A. J. (1975). *A Short History of the Massachusetts Courts*. North Andover, Mass.: National Center for State Courts.

Ferdinand, T. N. (1992). *Boston's Lower Criminal Courts, 1814–1850*. Newark, DE: University of Delaware Press.

Forbath, W. E. (1991). *Law and the Shaping of the American Labor Movement*. Cambridge, Massachusetts: Harvard University Press.

Formisano, R. (1984). *Boston, 1700–1980: The Evolution of Urban Politics*. Westport, Connecticut: Greenwood.

Gil, T. (1837). *Court Vignettes from the Boston Morning Post*. Cambridge. Massachusetts: Widener Library Collection.

Gramsci, A. (1971). *Selections from the Prison Notebooks*. New York: International Publishers.

Gurr, T. (1981). Historical Trends in Violent Crime: A Critical Review of the Evidence. In: M. Tonry & N. Morris (Eds), *Crime and Justice: An Annual Review of Research* (Vol. 3, pp. 295–353). Chicago, Illinois: University of Chicago Press.

Handlin, O. (1979). *Boston's Immigrants*. Cambridge, Mass.: Harvard University Press.

Hay, D., Linebaugh, P., Rule, J.G., Thompson, E.P., and Werslaw, C. (1975). *Albion's Fatal Tree: Crime and Society in Eighteenth Century England*. New York: Pantheon.

Hindus, M. S. (1980). *Prison and Plantation: Crime, Justice and Authority in Massachusetts and South Carolina, 1767–1868*. Chapel Hill, North Carolina: University of North Carolina Press.

Horwitz, M. J. (1977). *The Transformation of American Law, 1780–1860*. Cambridge, Mass.: Harvard University Press.

House Report, Commonwealth of Massachusetts Legislature, number 4, January 1845.

Howe, M. D. W. (1947–1950). The Creative Period in the Law of Massachusetts. *Proceedings of the Massachusetts Historical Society, 69*, 237.

Jones, D. L. and Rogers, A. (1993). *Discovering the Public Interest*. Canoga Park, California: CCA Publications.

Lane, R. (1971). *Policing the City: Boston, 1822–1885*. New York: Atheneum.

Langbein, J. H. (1973). The Origins of Public Prosecution at Common Law. *The American Journal of Legal History, 17*, 313.

Langbein, J. H. (1978). The Criminal Trial Before the Lawyers. *The University of Chicago Law Review, 45*, 263–316.

Lockridge, K. A. (1981). *Settlement and Unsettlement in Early America: The Crisis of Political Legitimacy Before the Revolution*. Cambridge, England: Cambridge University Press.

Mensch, E. (1982). *The History of Mainstream Legal Thought in David Kairys. The Politics of Law*. New York: Pantheon.

Moley, R. (1929). *Politics and Criminal Prosecution*. New York: Minton, Balch.

Nedelsky, J. (1990). *Private Property and the Limits of American Constitutionalism: The Madisonian Framework and Its Legacy*. Chicago, Ill.: University of Chicago Press.

Nelson, W. E. (1981). *Dispute and Conflict Resolution in Plymouth County, Massachusetts, 1725–1825*. Chapel Hill, North Carolina: University of North Carolina Press.

Neumann, F. (1957). The Changing Function of Law in Modern Society. In *The Democratic and Authoritarian State*. New York: Free Press.

Poulantzas, N. (1975). *Political Power and Social Classes*. London, England: New Left Books and Sheed and Ward.

Quincy, J. (1822). Speech on July 4, 1822, Manuscript Copy, Statehouse Archives, Commonwealth of Massachusetts.

Sellers, C. (1991). *The Market Revolution*. New York, N.Y.: Oxford University Press.

Skowronek, S. (1982). *Building a New American State*. Cambridge, England: Cambridge University Press.

Smith, A. (1776). *The Wealth of Nations*. Lausanne: Societé Typographique.

Story, J. (1829). Discourse upon the Inauguration of the Author as Dane Professor of Law. Cornell Law School Collection.

Thompson, E. P. (1975). *Whigs and Hunters: The Origins of the Black Act*. New York: Pantheon.

Vogel, M. E. (1988). *Courts of Trade: Social Conflict and the Emergence of Plea Bargaining in Boston, Massachusetts, 1830–1890*. Doctural Dissertation, Harvard University.

Vogel, M. E. (1999). The Social Origins of Plea Bargaining: Conflict and the Law in the Process of State Formation. *Law and Society Review, 33*, 161.

Walker, S. E. (1980). *Popular Justice: A History of the American Criminal Justice*. New York: Oxford University Press.

Warren, C. (1931). *Jacobin and Junto*. Cambridge, Massachusetts: Harvard University Press.

Weber, M. (1978). In: G. Roth & C. Wittich (Eds), *Economy and Society*. Berkeley, California: University of California Press.

Wiebe, R. (1966). *The Search for Order*. New York: Hill and Wang.

Wood, G. S. (1992). *The Radicalism of the American Revolution*. New York: Vintage.

PART SEVEN

Reimagining criminal justice

ONCE LIPTON, MARTINSON AND Wilkes' book *The Effectiveness of Correctional Treatment* was misinterpreted as saying that in rehabilitative terms "nothing works," it took years to shift the focus of criminological debate back to considering the potential of rehabilitation. This was so despite a considerable body of evidence showing that numerous approaches showed positive treatment effects. Nonetheless the message that "nothing works" was taken up by the political right, under the banner of the Neo-Classical Revival, to claim the futility of rehabilitative initiatives. During the 1980s prisons expanded and by the 1990s one could say that criminal justice policy had experienced a "carceral turn." Gradually incapacitation and avoidance of risk emerged in what Simon and Feeley have called the "new penology."

This carceral turn has prompted much debate about its causes, especially in light of its being coupled, with what some see as a transfer of power to non-state institutions. In some quarters, there is talk of the "retreat" or "hollowing out" of the state. This book suggests that these changes have been so elusive to interpret because they are not about crime but rather about a political sea change, an Anglo-American vision of global leadership and the trans-Atlantic passage of the American "culture wars."

Why, then, did rehabilitation have such a long struggle back, since even in the Martinson, et al. study there was evidence that some programmes held promise? By the 1980s, stronger research methodologies were producing more robust findings to reinforce and elaborate those positive results. Increasingly, the message was that some things work for some people. Yet, the rhetoric of criminal justice policy continued to veer away from rehabilitation to urge a "tougher" stance on crime. By the 1990s, a third generation of quite sophisticated work was producing very interesting findings about both the positive effects of some preventive and rehabilitative initiatives and the damaging impacts of custodial sentences on prisoners and their families. At present, it is fair to say that a great deal is known about "what works." The issue now is clearly how that knowledge fits in politically.

In *Crime and Punishment*, Elliott Currie brings together much of the best of what is known about successes in preventing crime. Among the initiatives that he explores, special emphasis is placed on Operation Head Start which, perhaps more than any other program, has consistently been found to boost school achievement, school completion, relationship building, prospects for marriage and employment and to reduce the likelihood of juvenile delinquency.

In " 'What Works?' at the Millennium," Lynn Curtis agrees that we do very much know today "What Works" and the question is whether we want, as a socielty, to do that? Through his work with the Milton Eisenhower Foundation, Curtis draws on the strong research from the mid-1980s onward to highlight key findings about promising initiatives, such as family-based problem-solving for first time youthful offenders, to reduce reoffending. Lynn Curtis also highlights a growing assortment of findings about why prison programs, such as re-integration and post-release employment, are not working as well as they might and about the collateral damage that custodial sentences do to offenders and their families.

One problem policy-wise in attempting preventive initiatives in the United States has traditionally been that any programme that requires significant redistributive public spending is extremely unlikely to be accepted by American voters. In their seminal, historical work on social welfare policy in the United States, Weir, Skocpol and Orloff have shown that in America, historically, only programs that distribute benefits to middle class families as well as the disadvantaged (such as education initiatives) will receive political support. The logic bears some resemblance to a social democratic one. Their political insight into the dynamics of American social policy formation suggests the importance of dual-purpose initiatives, such as after school programmes for teens, that both educate and inhibit crime by changing routine activities during peak delinquency hours.

Taking a broader perspective, David Greenberg's research paints and tests a vision of an alternative criminal justice policy. He strikingly demonstrates that lower crime rates and lesser growth in crime have been found among the more welfarist social democratic countries than in Anglo-American societies experiencing the "carceral turn." Greenberg incorporates both social bond and strain approaches in his analysis of why this may be so. The implication of his study is a selective reconsideration of some of the more constructive welfarist initiatives of our relatively crime-free social democratic neighbors.

Beyond these programmatic steps, the dynamics of political participation, open dialogue and civic accountability are vital to a democracy. Arato and Cohen's work on civil society suggests some interesting prospects in that regard. Democracy, as they show, is not something that can be established once and for all and then left to its own devices. Democracy is a struggle. The effort required to sustain an open, authentic, participatory system in which civil liberties are honored never stops. A deliberative approach in a free and non-coercive public sphere is, as Jurgen Habermas has long argued, vital to such politics. When we stop saying what we think, it is all too likely that we stop thinking altogether. Perhaps nowhere has the Bush administration's impact been more evident than in its efforts, remarked on publicly by courageous statesmen such as Senator McDermott, of the state of Washington, to silence public debate through rapacious and often ad hominem attacks on those who speak out in dissent. Governments, like all bureaucracies, as Max Weber (1962) notes, tend toward control, secrecy and reliance on experts. This is, at least partly, because it leaves them freer to enact their preferred plans than does democratic public accountability. It safeguards bureaucrats' discretionary power.

Arato and Cohen show that the quest to sustain openness requires nothing less than a continuing and self-regulating ongoing social movement on the part of active members of a "civil society." Some query today whether the "green" or "environmental" movement could provide such a unifying force. The power of such movements is, perhaps, best illustrated by the "Velvet Revolution" that ushered in democracy to the Czech Republic without violence and brought the resistance leader, Vaclev Havel, to power. Movements from civil society and deliberative democracy could hardly present a starker contrast to the polarizing politics, neoliberal vision of global dominance, and mythic public life that are anchoring the "carceral turn" in the United States and, increasingly, Britain today.

Chapter 34

Elliott Currie

PREVENTION

From: Elliott Currie (1998), excerpts from 'Prevention', in Elliott Currie, *Crime and Punishment in America: Why the Solutions to America's Most Stubborn Social Crisis have not Worked — and What Will*, New York: Henry Holt, pp. 80–107.

[. . .]

GIVEN WHAT WE'VE LEARNED about crime prevention in recent years, four priorities seem especially critical: preventing child abuse and neglect, enhancing children's intellectual and social development, providing support and guidance to vulnerable adolescents, and working intensively with juvenile offenders. These aren't the only preventive strategies that can make a difference, but they are the ones that offer the strongest evidence of effectiveness. And they also fit our growing understanding of the roots of delinquency and violent crime.

I

The first priority is to invest serious resources in the prevention of child abuse and neglect. The evidence is compelling that this is where much of the violent crime that plagues us begins, especially the kinds of violence we fear the most. And it is increasingly clear that serious efforts to address the multiple problems of high-risk families can reduce rates of abuse and neglect, sometimes dramatically.

Child abuse is itself among the worst and most tragic of violent crimes. Nationwide, it results directly in up to 5,000 deaths per year, 18,000 permanent, severe disabilities, and 150,000 serious injuries. It is the fourth leading cause of death for American children aged one to four and second for black children that age. But its delayed effects are also devastating: children who suffer serious abuse or neglect are far more likely to turn to violence themselves as teenagers or adults. . . . Some striking evidence comes from a study by Carolyn Smith and Terence Thornberry of the State University of New York at Albany — part of a long-term project, the Rochester Youth Development Study, designed to uncover the roots of juvenile delinquency. Smith and Thornberry asked whether the youths in their sample who had been abused as children – measured by an official report to the county child-protective agency – were more likely than those who had not been abused to be delinquent once they reached junior high and high school age. It turned out that being abused or neglected had little effect, if any, on minor forms of delinquency. But for *serious* delinquency – and violent crime in particular – it mattered a great deal. The youths who had been abused were arrested almost twice as often, and reported almost twice as many violent offenses, as those without an official record of maltreatment.

The evidence from smaller, clinical samples of extremely violent youths is even more eloquent. The psychiatrist Dorothy Lewis and her colleagues studied fourteen death-row inmates sentenced for particulary heinous crimes they'd committed as juveniles and found that all but *one* had a history of severe and sometimes bizarre abuse. [. . .]

Preventing these tragedies can reduce violent crime. And there is encouraging evidence that comprehensive work with families at high risk – especially programs centered on "home visiting" by skilled and caring outsiders – can reduce abuse and neglect. . . . Recent resurgence of interest in home visiting in the United States can be traced mainly to one particularly influential experiment: the Prenatal-Early Infancy Program (PEIP) in Elmira, New York, launched in the late 1970s by a team led by the psychologist David Olds, then at the University of Rochester.

The Elmira program served vulnerable women – mostly white, poor, young, and unmarried – in a semirural community with some of the highest levels of child abuse and neglect in the state. The project had several related goals: to ensure more healthful pregnancies and births, improve the quality of parental care, and enhance the women's own development – in school, at work, and in family life. Registered nurses visited each woman during her pregnancy and for two years after the birth of her child. The visits took place weekly for the first six weeks after birth, decreasing to every six weeks by the last four months of the program. Five nurses, each working with twenty to twenty-five families, spent an average of about an hour and fifteen minutes with the mothers, providing parenting education, linking the families with other social services as needed, and generally building a long-term supportive relationship with women who had usually been allowed to fall through the cracks of the social-service system.

Unlike many programs aimed at low-income parents, this one was carefully evaluated from the start. Mothers who received home visits before and after giving birth were compared with a control group who did not. [. . .]

Among the mothers deemed at highest risk – those who were poor, unmarried, and teenaged – 19 percent of the control group, versus just 4 percent of the mothers in the program, had confirmed cases of abuse or neglect. . . . Once the program ended, however, the effects seemed to fade – a common pattern in many early intervention programs. . . . A more recent follow-up of the Elmira women, conducted when their children were fifteen years old, provides more encouraging evidence of the program's effectiveness. Over the whole fifteen-year period after the birth of their first child, the nurse-visited women were only about half as likely to be reported for child abuse as women in the comparison group. They were also considerably less likely to have serious problems with alcohol or drugs, and far less likely to be arrested. [. . .]

So far, the home-visiting approach has mostly been limited to one-time, short-term experiments, generally doomed to disappear once their funding runs out. The most important exception is Hawaii's statewide Healthy Start program. Healthy Start enrolls families considered at high risk of abuse and neglect – because of single parenthood, low income, unstable housing, poor education, inadequate prenatal care, depression, or a history of substance abuse or psychiatric care – immediately after the birth of a child. [. . .]

Like most other home-visiting programs, Healthy Start takes a comprehensive approach to the problems its clients face. The home visitors spend considerable time on parenting issues, but they also help the families deal with a broad range of troubles and crises – from difficulties in finding housing and jobs to the lack of transportation to medical and social-service appointments. There are also parent-support groups, respite child care for stressed parents, and counseling for drug abuse and domestic violence. Child-development specialists are available to help with more complicated parenting and developmental issues. [. . .]

After one year, the Healthy Start families accumulated only half as many reported abuse and neglect cases as the control group, and the few reports they did have were less serious. The Healthy Start parents, too, were doing a better job of parenting in general; they were more involved with and responsive to their children, for example, and less supportive of punishment. [. . .]

We do not yet know as much as we would like about just *how* these programs work – what exactly it is about home visiting that makes the difference. . . . We will need more research to answer these questions. But some conclusions are clear.

First, for home visiting to be effective, it must be carried out over a reasonably long period. [. . .]

Second, the home-visiting programs that work best are comprehensive: they go well beyond simply offering "parent education" to confront a wide range of problems that erupt in the lives of vulnerable families. [. . .]

II

The second priority in crime prevention is to expand and enhance early intervention for children at risk of impaired cognitive development, behavior problems, and early failure in school. Once again, the "why" is not mysterious. The link between these troubles and later delinquency is depressingly consistent. The success of some of the best early-childhood programs gives a very different, and far more hopeful, picture.

By far the best known of these efforts is the Perry Preschool program – a legacy of the Great Society, begun during the early 1960s in a low-income, mainly black neighborhood in Ypsilanti, Michigan. Poor children aged three and four were enrolled in preschool for two and a half hours a day. In addition, their teachers visited the children and their mothers at home once a week, for about an hour and a half. Most of the children stayed in the program for two school years, a few for just one. The preschool curriculum was distinguished by its commitment to an "active learning" approach, based heavily on the work of Jean Piaget. [. . .]

The Perry project was also distinctive in the care with which the experiment was designed and evaluated. The project randomly assigned 123 neighborhood children to the program group or to a control group that did not attend the program. Dogged efforts were made to keep track of these children as they grew up. . . . As of this writing, the evaluation has followed both groups until the youngest of the children were twenty-seven years old. The results are impressive; the Perry students were far more likely to be literate, off welfare, working and earning a decent living. They were only *one-fifth* as likely as the carefully matched control group to have become chronic criminal offenders (defined as having been arrested five or more times) and only about one-fourth as likely to have been arrested for drug-related crimes. [. . .]

As with the home-visiting programs, we do not know exactly what it was about the Perry approach that worked – whether the children's abilities improved as a result of the specific teaching strategy adopted in the preschool or whether teachers' visits to the *parents* counted for more. But the possibility that the Perry experiment worked at least in part by changing the behavior of the parents is supported by studies of other innovative family-oriented prevention programs that were inspired by progressive child development theories in the 1960s and 1970s.

One of the most successful of those programs, the Yale Child Welfare Research Program enrolled seventeen impoverished inner-city women expecting their first child. As in the Perry project, this was a highly vulnerable group: the majority of the women were unmarried, and more than half were entirely supported by welfare. The program offered them a variety of services over a period of thirty months, including regular well-baby exams and an average of twenty-eight home visits by a psychologist, nurse, or social worker. Like the successful child-abuse prevention programs, the Yale program placed a strong emphasis on immediate, tangible challenges – such as securing food and housing and helping mothers make decisions about school, marriage, and work. Most of the children also entered a center-based day-care program for an average of thirteen months. The curriculum focused on "social and emotional development," including learning to handle aggression. Each child was assigned a "primary caregiver," who worked closely with the parents. The ratio of children to caregivers at the center was never greater than three to one. The goal was to ensure "continuity of care by familiar and skilled professionals."

An early assessment, when the children were thirty months old, found few differences between program children and a control group, except that the former were doing better at language development. But a follow-up study ten years later showed far more varied and significant differences. Boys in the program, in particular, had adjusted to school far better than the controls. The control boys, in fact, typically displayed the kinds of problems that are widely acknowledged to be important "precursors" of delinquency. Their teachers rated them as likely to show "aggressive, acting-out, pre-delinquent behavior serious enough to require such actions as placement in classrooms for emotionally disturbed children or suspension from school." [. . .]

The program also had particularly encouraging effects on the *Parents*. But ten years after the program ended, the two groups had "diverged radically." Nearly all of the program families had become self-supporting, while the controls had essentially languished, many of them stuck on public assistance.

Once again, it is hard to untangle exactly what caused these differences. . . . We don't know. But a more recent analysis by the Yale researchers suggests that the program worked at least in part by improving the parents' capacity to raise their children. They tracked the later-born *siblings* of the initial study children over a three-year period, when the youngsters averaged a little under ten years old. By that age, the kinds of differences already noticed in the firstborns had become startlingly apparent. . . . The fact that positive effects occurred among children who did not actually participate in the initial program strongly suggests that there was a general improvement in the competence of the program parents, which translated into better prospects for all of their children.

What makes the Yale results encouraging from the standpoint of crime prevention is that the kinds of problems the program seems to have successfully prevented in pre-adolescents – poor school attendance and performance, aggressive behaviour toward family and peers – are precisely those that have been shown again and again to be forerunners of serious delinquency. And the few studies of early family-intervention programs that have followed the participating children into adolescence confirm that well-conceived intervention in early childhood can indeed prevent later delinquency. [. . .]

III

The third priority is to invest in programs for vulnerable adolescents that build their skills and keep them on track toward higher education or training. It has long been fashionable to argue that children are set in their path at a very early age and there's little we can do to change it. . . . For a long time, the pessimistic view was bolstered by the lack of con- vincing evidence that teenagers' lives could be changed for the better in ways that would reliably reduce crime and delinquency. Today, we know more.

One of the earliest programs for at-risk youth to show strong evidence of success was the federal Job Corps, an enduring legacy of the 1960s that, along with Head Start, is one of the only preventive programs that has survived, with significant funding, year after year. What set Job Corps apart from less successful programs was its strong emphasis on intensive skill training, coupled with a variety of supportive services for its participants. Evaluations showed that Job Corps found significantly reduced violent crime among its graduates, and the savings thus achieved more than repaid the costs of the program.

Some of the same principles also appear, in more sophisticated form, in the more recent Quantum Opportunity Program, which provided a comprehensive mix of services to high-school-age minority youths from welfare homes in several cities across the U.S. [. . .]

The students received substantial training in a variety of hightech skills in addition to regular schooling, and they engaged in community-service work. They were taken to the opera and theater and encouraged to read books and magazines. They were also given a small stipend as an incentive while they were in the program, which was matched dollar for dollar by money that was put into a fund they could draw on later to pay for college or advanced training. The program, in short, offered much more tangible supports to its young participants than past efforts had; it was also holistic, combining, as the organizers put it, "education, cultural, civic, and social development work and service."

The students were randomly selected to be in the program; this wasn't a case of self- selection by those who were probably going to do well anyway. Once in the program, they stayed in it for four years, working together in groups of twenty-five. One of the most innovative features of Quantum was that students were never dropped from the program. Even if they left it or failed to attend, they could always come back. The program sought to have a single adult coordinator for each group over the entire four years. [. . .]

Two years after the program ended, the average number of arrests for Quantum participants was half that of a control group. They were also only half as likely to be on welfare, and more than twice as likely to be enrolled in college. Nearly half of the control group members were neither at work, in school, or in training, versus just 14 percent of the Quantum participants. . . . The overall results are impressive, and they suggest that the potential of this kind of hands-on, holistic approach to poor teenagers is considerable. . . . We cannot expect the same results from programs that offer less. [. . .]

IV

The fourth priority in crime prevention is to invest time and attention in youths who have already begun a serious delinquent "career." [. . .]

It is a truism in criminology that a disproportionate amount of serious crime is committed by a relatively small proportion of offenders, who commit many offenses over the course of a "career" that often gets progressively more serious until they "mature out" of crime. Hence, keeping troubled youth from becoming "chronic" offenders by addressing, early on, whatever got them into trouble in the first place should be a crucial part of any serious preventive strategy against crime. [. . .]

The principle seems obvious. But in practice, this kind of work is astonishingly rare. That is partly because of the widespread belief that we "don't know how" to change the lives of young offenders – an argument that is also increasingly used to justify a "crackdown" on the troubled young, in the form of more money for youth prisons, more pressure to treat teenaged offenders as adults, and a "zero tolerance" approach to children who misbehave in school. James Q. Wilson, for example, has written, that "As for rehabilitating juvenile offenders, it has some merit, but there are rather few success stories. Individually, the best (and best-evaluated) programs have minimal, if any, effects." The element of truth in Wilson's exaggeration is that a great many programs marketed under the rubric of delinquency prevention really *don't* work. [. . .]

Here, then, it is critical to separate what is genuinely promising from what isn't, and to look for the underlying principles that help account for success.

Perhaps most importantly, many programs that purport to offer "rehabilitation" for offenders have tried to "treat" them in isolation from the broader social environment which surrounds them. That is a prescription for failure, but the exceptions show the way to a different approach.

The most impressive of these efforts goes under the rather formidable name of "multisystemic therapy" (MST). MST is rooted in the commonsense recognition that, as the psychologist Scott Henggeler and his colleagues put it, "individuals are nested within a complex of interconnected systems" – including family, peers, and school, and beyond them the broader community and its structure of opportunities and social supports. Accordingly, "treating" youth successfully requires dealing with whatever issues arise across these multiple systems, from individual learning problems to lack of supports in the community. [. . .]

Two systematic trials of this approach have been carefully evaluated; one in South Carolina, a later one in Missouri. Both are especially noteworthy because they achieved impressive success. . . . In South Carolina caseworkers addressed issues that arose in every institution that affected the youth's life – family, school, health care – with a special focus on family troubles. A little over a year after leaving the program, participating youths had roughly *half* the arrests of the control group and spent only a third as much time incarcerated. Two and a half years after the program ended, the same proportions held: the control youths were about twice as likely to be rearrested. What's more, the strategy seemed to work equally well for youths of all races and social classes, across genders, and for youths with widely different histories of past delinquency. The Missouri program produced even more striking results. [. . .]

If the delinquents fundamental problem is an abusive family or an unresponsive school environment, simply trying to help him "straighten out" is unlikely to change things much. [. . .]

Notes

p. 531   *child-abuse figures*   From U.S. Advisory Board on Child Abuse and Neglect, *A Nation's Shame: Fatal Child Abuse in the United States*, Washington, D.C., Government Printing Office, 1995, p. xxv; U.S. Public Health Service, *Report of Final Mortality Statistics, 1995*, Hyattsville, Md. Centers for Disease Control and Prevention, 1997.

p. 531   *Rochester study*   Carolyn Smith and Terence P. Thorn-berry, "The Relationship Between Childhood Maltreatment and Adolescent Involvement in Delinquency," *Criminology*, Vol. 33, No. 4, 1995, pp. 451–477. More evidence comes from a study by Cathy Spatz Widom of the State University of New York at Albany and her colleagues, who have found significantly higher rates of arrests – both for crime generally and for violent crime specifically – among youth who had been abused or neglected in childhood. In this study, both abuse and severe neglect seemed to have similar effects, and the impact was apparently even stronger for black youth. Cathy Spatz Widom, *The Cycle of Violence Revisited*, Washington, D.C., National Institute of Justice, 1996.

p. 532   *Lewis study*   Dorothy Otnow Lewis et al., "Characteristics of Juveniles Condemned to Death," *American Journal of Psychiatry*, Vol. 145, No. 5, May 1988, p. 588.

p. 532   *Elmira program*   See David L. Olds et al., "Preventing Child Abuse and Neglect: A Randomized Trial of Nurse Home Visitation," *Pediatrics*, Vol. 78, No. 1, 1986, pp. 65–78; David L. Olds et al., "Effect of Prenatal and Infancy Nurse Home Visitation on Government Spending," *Medical Care*, Vol. 31, No. 2, pp. 155–174; David L. Olds et al., "Effects of Prenatal and Infancy Nurse Home Visitation on Surveillance of Child Maltreatment," *Pediatrics*, Vol. 95, No. 3, March 1995, pp. 365–372; David L. Olds et al., "Long-term Effects of Home Visitation on Maternal Life Course and Child Abuse and Neglect: Fifteen-year Follow-up of a Randomized Trial," *Journal of the American Medical Association*, Vol. 278, No. 8, August 27, 1997, pp. 637–643.

p. 532   *Healthy Start*   Ralph B. Earle, *Helping to Prevent Child Abuse – and Future Consequences: Hawai'i Healthy Start*, Washington, D.C., National Institute of Justice, 1995; Center on Child Abuse Prevention Research, *Intensive Home Visitation: A Randomized Trial, Follow-up and Risk Assessment Study of Hawaii's*

Healthy Start Program, Chicago, National Committee to Prevent Child Abuse, 1996.

p. 533   *"some conclusions"*   cf. reviews of these programs in John M. Leventhal, "Twenty Years Later: We Do Know How to Prevent Child Abuse and Neglect," *Child Abuse and Neglect*, Vol. 20, No. 8, 1995, pp. 647–653; Harriett L. MacMillan et al., "Primary Prevention of Child Abuse and Neglect: A Critical Review, Part I," *Journal of Child Psychology and Psychiatry*, Vol. 35, No. 5, 1994, pp. 835–856; Weiss, "Home Visits."

p. 533   *Perry Project*   Lawrence Schweinhart, H. V. Barnes, and David Weikart, *Significant Benefits: The High/Scope Perry Preschool Study Through Age 27*, Ypsilanti, Mich., High/Scope Press, 1993; Deanna S. Gomby et al., "Long-Term Outcomes of Early Childhood Programs: Analysis and Recommendations," *The Future of Children*, Vol. 5, No. 3, Winter 1995.

p. 534   *Yale Program*   Victoria Seitz, "Intervention Programs for Impoverished Children: A Comparison of Educational and Family Support Models," *Annals of Child Development*, Vol. 7, 1990, pp. 84–87. See also the similarly encouraging results from the Houston Parent-Child Development Center, which also worked with both parents and children in a low-income community, in this case primarily Mexican-American. The program involved both home visiting and structured classes for both parents and children in a project center. At ages 5–8, the program children showed significantly less aggression than a control group. See Dale L. Johnson and Todd Walker, "Primary Prevention of Behavior Problems in Mexican-American Children," *American Journal of Community Psychology*, Vol. 15, No. 4, 1987, pp. 375–385.

p. 534   *sibling study*   Victoria Seitz and Nancy H. Apfel, "Parent-focused Intervention: Diffusion Effects on Siblings," *Child Development*, Vol. 65, 1994, pp. 677–683.

p. 535   *Quantum program*   Opportunities Industrial Centers of America, *Quantum Opportunity Program*, Philadelphia: OIC, 1995. For a journalistic account, see Celia W. Dugger, "Guiding Hand Through High School Helps Young People Out of the Ghetto," *New York Times*, March 9, 1995.

p. 536   *Wilson quote*   "What to Do About Crime," p. 289.

p. 536   *MST programs*   Charles M. Bourduin et al., "Multisystemic Treatment of Serious Juvenile Offenders: Long-term Prevention of Criminality and Violence," *Journal of Consulting and Clinical Psychology*, Vol. 63, No. 4, 1995, pp. 569–578; Scott W. Henggeler et al., "Multisystemic Therapy: An Effective Violence Prevention Approach for Serious Juvenile Offenders," *Journal of Adolescence*, Vol. 19, No. 1, 1996, pp. 47–61. [. . .]

Chapter 35

Lynn A. Curtis

THE OXBRIDGE LECTURE
What works at the millennium?

From: Lynn A. Curtis, excerpts from "What works at the millennium?" in the Eisenhower Foundation, *The Oxbridge Lecture*, Washington, DC: The Eisenhower Foundation.

> Whiles I am a beggar, I will rail
> And say there is no sin but to be rich;
> And being rich, my virtue then shall be
> To say there is no vice but beggary.
>
> King John II, i, 593

IN THE LATE 1960s after the big-city riots in America, the National Advisory Commission on Civil Disorders (the Kerner Riot Commission) and the National Commission on the Causes and Prevention of Violence (the National Violence Commission) submitted their final reports to President Johnson. In this paper, I would like to summarize trends in race, poverty, inequality, crime, prison building and justice in America since the Kerner Commission and Violence Commission, point out policy for the inner city and the truly disadvantaged that has and has not worked, and suggest ways in which we can overcome the disconnect in America between knowledge and action, by replicating what works to scale in politically feasible ways.

Trends

There are many indicators of progress since the 1960s. For example, among African-Americans and Hispanics, the middle class has expanded, entrepreneurship has increased and there has been a dramatic rise in the number of locally-elected officials. Yet there also have been many negatives. American leaders and media fail to sufficiently recognize them. Consider just a few:

During the 1980s, child poverty increased by 23%. Today, after almost a decade of economic expansion, the *only super power in the world still has about 1 out of every 4 children aged 5 and under living in poverty*, according to the National Center for Children and Poverty at Columbia University. That is incomprehensible. By comparison, the corresponding child poverty rate is about 15% in Canada, 12% in Japan, 7% in France,

4% in Belgium and 2% in Finland. At the new millennium, we have phenomenal prosperity in the United States. Yet the poor are barely better off than in the 1980s, in spite of the economic boom of the 1990s. And the extremely poor are worse off.

American leaders and media pundits in Washington boast of an unemployment rate of around 4%. Yet the Economic Policy Institute in Washington, DC estimates that the rate of underemployment is about 7.5% when one takes into account official unemployment rates, the number of people who have stopped trying to find jobs and who therefore are not counted, and persons working part-time who want to work full time. (Much of this underemployment is associated with temporary jobs that offer few, if any, benefits.) The United States Department of Labor has concluded, "The employment rate for out-of-school youth in high-poverty areas typically is less than 50 percent." The Center for Community Change in Washington, DC has estimated that the "jobs gap" is about 4.4 million jobs nationally. Of that, perhaps half of the jobs needed are in the inner city.

It is also true that, during the trickle-down, supply-side economics that dominated the 1980s in America, the rich got richer and the poor got poorer, according to conservative author Kevin Phillips and many others. The working class also got poorer. The middle class stayed about the same, so it lost ground to the rich.

In the 1990s, the large income gaps of the 1980s actually widened. The incomes of the best off Americans rose twice as fast as those of middle-income Americans, according to the Congressional Budget Office. The gap between rich and working income Americans rose even more. In Washington, DC during the overall economic boom from 1990 to 1999, income in rich (80th percentile) households increased by 8%, in middle class (median) households increased by 5% and in poor (20th percentile) decreased by 1%. Income differences between the haves and the have-nots are growing faster in America than in any industrialized democracy. In countries where reliable information exists, the United States is second only to Russia in having the smallest middle class and highest poverty rates.

The increase in wealth inequality during the Reagan years is virtually unprecedented. The only comparable period in America in the twentieth century was 1922–1929, before the Great Depression. During the 1980s, 99% of the wealth gained went to the top 20% of wealth holders in America – and the top 1% gained 62% of that. The median wealth of nonwhite American citizens actually fell during the 1980s. The average level of wealth of an African-American family in America today is about one-tenth of an average white family. Wealth inequality is much worse in the United States than in countries traditionally thought of as "class ridden," like the United Kingdom.

We know that, in 1980, the average corporate CEO earned 42 times as much as the average factory worker. We know that by 2000, and after the union busting of the 1980s, the average corporate CEO earned 419 times as much as the average worker.

We know that, according to Gary Orfield and his colleagues at the Harvard School of Education, America is resegregating in its neighborhoods and schools. Over two-thirds of all African-American and Hispanic students in urban areas attend predominantly segregated schools. Over two-thirds of those students cannot achieve minimally acceptable scores on standardized tests.

We know that today the states spend more on prison building than on higher education, whereas 20 years ago the opposite was true.

We know that, in the 1980s, prison building became our national housing policy for the poor. We more than quadrupled the number of prison cells, at the same time we reduced appropriations for housing the poor at the federal level by over 80%. The sound bite in America today is 2 million in the new millennium. That is the number of people incarcerated in America.

We know that, in the early 1990s, 1 out of every 4 young African-American men in America was in prison, on probation or on parole at any one time, according to the Sentencing Project in Washington, DC. That is a stunning statistic. Yet today and after a Presidential Commission on Race that did little in terms of practical policy impact, *1 out of every 3* young African-American men is in prison, on probation or on parole at any one time in America. In big cities, the number is *1 out of every 2*. Similarly, we know from Professor Milton Friedman, the conservative economist, that the rate of incarceration of African-American men in America today is 4 times greater than the rate of incarceration of black men in pre-Mandela, apartheid South Africa. Nonetheless, the fastest growing group of male prison inmates consists of Latinos.

One of the key reasons for this is the racial bias in our juvenile and criminal justice systems, including racial profiling by police and mandatory minimum sentences for drugs. For example, sentences for crack cocaine, used disproportionately by minorities, are much harsher than sentences for power cocaine used disproportionately by whites. As a result of these and related practices, America's prisons are disproportionately populated by minorities.

At the same time, prison building has become a job generating, economic development policy for rural white Americans who now send lobbyists with 6-figure incomes to Washington to fight for still more prisons, as part of the emerging prison-industrial complex. Yet we know, based on some of the most prestigious American studies of prison building to date, for example, by a panel of the National Academy of Science, that the criminal justice response to crime is, at most, running in place. To illustrate, in spite of recent declines, rates of violent crime and fear were roughly the same in 1999 as in 1969, when the National Violence Commission released its report.

Lack of knowledge?

Based on these trends in unemployment, child poverty, income, wealth, inequality, wages, resegregation, education, housing, prison building, racial bias, sentencing and white economic development through the prison-industrial complex, we can observe at least 2 breaches in the economic and social fabric of America as we enter the new millennium. The first breach, the one most talked about, is between those who have been left behind in the inner city, as well as those living in rural poverty, on one hand, and the rest of us, on the other. The second breach, not nearly discussed enough, because many politicians are afraid to touch it and much of the media has minimal interest, is the growing income and wealth gap between the poor, the working class and large portions of the middle class, on the one hand, and the rich and super rich, on the other hand.

What can we do to repair these breaches?

Part of the answer can be found in the public response in America after the 1992 riots in South Central Los Angeles associated with the verdict in the first Rodney King trial. A

The New York Times/CBS poll asked a national sample of Americans whether they would be willing to spend more on initiatives that worked in the inner city, especially on education and employment, even if it meant increased taxes. A majority of those polled answered yes. The next question in the poll was, "What is the major obstacle against doing more?" A majority of those polled around the nation said "lack of knowledge." Americans just don't believe we know what works.

But that is not true. To a considerable extent since the Kerner Riot Commission and National Violence Commission, we have learned a great deal about what doesn't work and what does work, based on scientific studies and careful evaluations. It therefore would make sense to stop doing what doesn't work and start doing what does work, but at a scale equal to the dimensions of the problem, to quote the Kerner Commission. Unfortunately, that seems too rational a policy right now for most American politicians and media. Let me redundant talk a bit more about what doesn't work and then about what works. My criteria for judging what works are 1) whether a policy or program has proven effective based on scientific evaluation and 2) whether a policy or program reduces inequality in America.

WHAT DOESN'T WORK?

I already have suggested that trickle-down, supply-side economics doesn't work – except, of course, for the rich. One part of supply-side economics in the 1980's was the Job Training Partnership Act (JTPA). We know from evaluations commissioned by the United States Department of Labor that JTPA failed for high school dropouts. Grossly underfunded, JTPA was more a "work first" than a "training first" program. Another form of supply-side economics is the Enterprise Zone, which we imported from England. Enterprise Zones are the notion that, for example, if you provide enough tax breaks, corporations will move to South Central Los Angeles and employ the young African-American men who rioted in 1992. It didn't happen. The failure of Enterprise Zones is carefully documented – for example, by the Urban Institute in Washington, DC and by the United States General Accounting Office. The failure also is well recorded in conservative journals like the *Economist* and *Business Week*. Among other reasons given by corporations for why they would not move back and employ inner-city youth was the opinion that youth were not adequately trained. (Hence, the need for "training first" programs for the hardest to employ at a time when the fashion is "work first.")

I also have suggested that prison building has not been particularly cost-effective. But has not crime gone down in America at the same time that prison building has surged? Since about 1993, F.B.I.-reported violent crime *has* gone down in many if not most big cities. What are the reasons, based on the best studies and evaluations available? Two leading (and interrelated) reasons have been the booming economy and the waning of the crack epidemic. Community-based groups appear to have been successful in some places, like Boston. The Brady bill, which controlled access to handguns by ex-offenders, appeared to have a national impact. So did community-based, problem-oriented policing (but not "Zero-tolerance" policing). Some of the decline in violent crime can in fact be explained by increased imprisonization (estimates are in the range of about

5% to about 30%). But the impact of prison building has been overstated by politicians and the media. And, as the Reverend Jesse Jackson likes to say, it costs more to go to jail than to Yale.

Nor has the recent fad of boot camps been successful. Its failure has been documented well in excellent studies by the University of Maryland that have been published by the United States Department of Justice, National Institute of Justice.

False rhetoric

So much for a few examples of what doesn't work. In the 1980s and 1990s, a false political rhetoric has been used to sugar coat policies that don't work. Here I refer to phrases such as voluntarism, partnership, self sufficiency, empowerment and "faith based." Often, these are helpful concepts at the street level – if applied with wisdom and discretion. But my concern is with their abuse by political ideologues.

For example, a highly-publicized 1997 national summit on voluntarism has been viewed with skepticism by many observers. The summit was held in Philadelphia. At the time of the summit, *The New York Times* interviewed residents in the impoverished Logan neighborhood of North Philadelphia. One resident thought that summit was a bit "naive" because "you need a certain expertise among the volunteers, and in communities like Logan, people don't have the expertise." The director of a non-profit community program in the neighborhood observed. "Volunteering is really good, but people need a program to volunteer for, and in order to do that, you have to have dollars." Pablo Eisenberg, former Executive Director of the Center for Community Change and now a Senior Fellow at the Georgetown University Public Policy Institute, concluded that "no matter whether you attract lots of volunteers, money is still the most important ingredient in reducing poverty and helping poor people. You need money even to organize volunteers." In an article on the new national organization created at the Philadelphia summit, *Youth Today* magazine asked whether the organization was "delivering for youth or fatally flawed." The executive director of one Midwest nonprofit community group concluded that, after 2 years, the new creation was "long on talk and hoopla and short on doing." A national nonprofit executive director called it "irrelevant window dressing." Along the same lines, after describing how volunteerism *increases* the gap between rich and poor (because most volunteers tend to stay in their immediate social and economic world). Sarah Mosle concludes a *Sunday New York Times* article by showing that public resources must drive private volunteerism: "Government spending causes volunteering. You can't have a volunteer in a school without a schoolhouse. Government institution-building increases volunteering."

Or take an international comparison. In the early 1990s. America won the war in the Persian Gulf because of large numbers of well-trained professional staff, large numbers of well-trained support staff and a huge amount of high-quality equipment. Yet, when it comes to the inner city and the truly disadvantaged, we are told that there is not enough money for adequate and adequately-paid professional staff, adequate and adequately-paid support staff, and good equipment, like computers and facilities in public schools and at the headquarters of the inner-city, grassroots community-based nonprofit organizations that are responsible for a great deal of what works. Instead, we are told that, for example, a grassroots community group ought to get grants from the public and private sectors for, say, 18 to 24 months. Then it ought to convert into "self-sufficient" operations by using a lot of (often poorly trained) volunteers from suburbia who "are here to help you." Volunteers should be combined with "partnerships" and "coalition building" among other financially competing and often penurious groups in the inner city. This, we are told, will somehow lead to the "empowerment" of our neighborhoods and our schools. Well, of course, it doesn't work that way – as anyone who labors in the trenches knows. This is the rhetoric of politicians who have a double standard. They are not prepared, financially or morally, to invest in our human capital, in our children and youth.

Similarly, it presently is fashionable in the private and public sectors to make grants to "faith-based" nonprofit groups. Yet no scientific evidence exists to prove that "faith-based" nonprofit organizations perform better than secular nonprofit organizations. Case studies by the Eisenhower Foundation underscore that "faith-based" groups have some potential, but not at the expense of secular groups. For example, one of the grassroots organizations presently receiving Foundation funding is secular, but its vision, energy and creativity come in part from the values of the local chief of police, who is an ordained minister. Yet success by this group also is greatly based on sound management and the hard work of secular civilians and police. Another organization that hosted an Eisenhower replication was secular, but the executive director was an ordained minister. The evaluation of this replication showed mixed results, particularly because management and relations with the community were not as sound as they might have been. A third group with which we replicated was faith-based. Importantly to us, the nun who ran it also was a very effective manager and received the cooperation of the police. A final illustration was a group led by another member of the clergy. This replication was an implementation failure, not because of any "faith-based" status, but because a new police chief would not necessarily agree to assign officers to the program as local match.

These case studies suggest that the keys to success are not necessarily based on secular versus "faith-based." More likely, one key is whether a grassroots nonprofit group has sound institutional capacity, for example, in terms of board leadership, staff management and good relationships with the community. Another key is whether the group can change the attitudes and behavior of youth into more positive directions. This requires "tough love," social support and perseverance. "Tough love" usually involves "doing the right thing," which has a moral imperative to it. But such a moral imperative is not by definition linked to a particular religion, as successes like the Argus Community, Delancey Street, the Dorchester Youth Collaborative and Job Corps have demonstrated. To create a more scientific grounding, we need to select a random group of "faith-based" grassroots nonprofits and a group of secular grassroots nonprofits. Then we need to undertake a long-term process and impact evaluation of the two groups.

Immorality

What exactly is "morality?" It usually is raised as a *private* sector issue. For example, grassroots nonprofit groups, we are told, should be driven by a moral imperative. And, if we as parents better teach right from wrong, we also are told, there will be much less need for youth development initiatives by grassroots community groups.

Of course parents and nonprofits should teach right from wrong. But what about *public* morality? When it comes to public policy that doesn't work:

- I suggest to you that it is immoral for almost a quarter of America's youngest children to live in poverty.
- I suggest to you that it is immoral to take from the poor and give it to the rich, as does supply-side economics, and for the federal government to do nothing about the growing inequality gap.
- I suggest to you that it is immoral for CEOs to earn 419 times as much as their workers.
- I suggest to you that it is immoral for the states to spend more on prison building than on higher education.
- I suggest to you that it is immoral for white corporations to profit from incarcerating minorities sentenced with racially-biased drug laws.
- I suggest to you that it is immoral for the rate of incarceration of African-American men in America today to be 4 times higher than the rate of incarceration of black men in pre-Mandela, apartheid South Africa.
- And I suggest to you that, through lack of campaign finance reform, it is immoral for America to create a one-dollar one-vote democracy, rather than a one-person, one-vote democracy.

We cannot give up the moral high ground.

WHAT WORKS?

So much for examples of what doesn't work, for the political sugar coating that often encases them, and for their not uncommon lack of morality. It is more hopeful to talk about what works. I want to give just a few interrelated examples. They cover preschool, safe havens after school, public school reform, training first jobs programs, community development, community banking and community policing.

Preschool

One of the best examples of what works is preschool. A recent state-by-state study by the Rand Corporation demonstrated that access to preschool increases student achievement, especially in impoverished communities. Earlier, the conservative CEOs on the Committee for Economic Development in New York asserted that, for every dollar invested in preschool. America gets almost $5.00 of benefits in return over the lifetime of a child who receives preschool. Those benefits include less involvement in crime, less involvement in drugs, less involvement in teen pregnancy, more likelihood to complete school, and more likelihood to become economically independent. Preschool makes economic sense. Yet less than half of all eligible poor children are enrolled in Head Start because, of course, we are told we don't have the money for our children, especially the almost 1 in 4 of the youngest who are living in poverty. At the same time, in many European countries, like France and Sweden, preschool is considered a basic human right.

Naysayers like to argue that, after a child leaves Head Start in America, benefits decline. Of course. If you only partially fund Head Start, decrease the amount of money available to Head Start programs for management and training (as has been the case in recent years) and throw a child back onto the mean streets at age 5 or 6 without any corresponding interventions, what do you expect? Most experts who work with children and youth have learned that we need a continuum of interventions from early childhood through adulthood. (See, for example, the views of Yale Professor Edward Zigler, considered the father of Head Start, in *National Policy Based on What Works*.)

Safe havens after school

That is one reason why, for children slightly older than preschoolers as well as for preteens, safe havens after school have worked, based, for example, on evaluations by Columbia University and the Eisenhower Foundation. Evolving from the formative Carnegie Corporation report. *A Matter of Time*, in 1992, safe havens have become known as places where kids can go after school for help with their homework, snacks, social support and discipline from adult role models. During the week, youth get into the most trouble from 3:30 p.m. to 10:00 p.m. in America. It does not take a rocket scientist to figure out why social support and discipline by paid adult staff during these hours will have a positive impact.

Public school reform

But this is after school. There are many good examples of public school reforms that work during school hours. One is the School Development Plan of Professor James Comer at Yale University. Parents, teachers and principals take over the management of inner-city schools, and additional investments in youth, like counseling and mental health services, are available. Evaluations have been positive, for example, in terms of less crime, less drugs, and higher grades in Comer Schools than in comparison schools. Professor Comer has widely replicated his plan, also with evaluated success. Similarly, "full service community schools," as articulated by Joy Dryfoos in her book *Safe Passage*, have begun to demonstrate their worth. A good model is Intermediate School 218 in the Washington Heights neighborhood of New York City. Such schools integrate the delivery of quality education with whatever health and social services are judged necessary by a specific community. For high schoolers, a good example of success is the Ford Foundation's Quantum Opportunities program. Well-trained adult mentors work one-on-one with inner-city high school youth, keeping them on track to good grades and high school completion, working out ways to earn money in the summer and providing venues for college education, if youth so choose. The original Brandeis University evaluation showed that Quantum Opportunity students did much better than controls, for example, in terms of less crime, less drugs, less drugs, less teen pregnancy, better grades, more likelihood to complete high school and more likelihood to go on to college.

These are all examples of public school reform. Advocates of private vouchers like to say that the issue is choice. That is not so. There are plenty of scientifically proven inner-city public school successes for a school system to choose from, like safe havens, the

Comer School Development Plan, full service community schools and Quantum Opportunities. The real issue is accountability. Private schools funded through vouchers are not accountable to the taxpayers whose public sector money finances them. For example, in Milwaukee, an African-American student who criticized her voucher school as racist was expelled. She sued on the grounds of free speech, but lost. The federal judge who wrote the opinion concluded that "restrictions on constitutional rights that would be protected at a public high school . . . need not be honored at a private school." As this illustration shows, voucher plans can reinforce inequality.

The inequality issue in education is, of course, also greatly linked to money, and expenditure per pupil. The rich, who tend to support vouchers, often say the issue is not money. But what do the rich do? They send their kids to Andover or Exeter – spending $20,000 a year on them. If it is good enough for the rich, why isn't it good enough for the poor, the working class and the middle class? What we need is public financing of education that allows the annual level of investment per child in American inner cities to be the same as the annual level of investment per child in the suburbs.

Training first job programs

When young people do drop out of high school, we know that there are alternatives to the old and failed Job Training and Partnership Act that can get them back on track. Often, these are "training first" initiatives.

One good example is the Argus Learning for Living Center in the South Bronx. Argus begins with "tough love" for inner-city dropouts, many of whom have drug problems. The priority is on changing attitudes, and then behavior. Considerable initial emphasis is on life skills trainings like how to manage money and how to resolve conflicts. Education and remedial education follow. When participants are ready, they move on to job training, focused on jobs for which there is a demand, like jobs in drug counseling. In the case of one replication of Argus by the Eisenhower Foundation, training is for good jobs repairing telecommunications equipment. After the training and job placement, there is follow-up to ensure retention. Retention is a crucial phase because there often are adjustments that need to be made once a person is in the workforce. Child care and transportation, for example, need to be in place. Sometimes help is needed with how to get along with fellow employees and with supervisors. Eisenhower Foundation evaluations of Argus and replications of Argus have demonstrated improved earnings, less crime and less drugs for enrollees versus comparison group members.

Another training first success is Job Corps, the intensive public sector training that takes seriously the need to provide a supportive, structured environment for the youth and welfare recipients it seeks to assist. Job Corps features classroom courses, which can lead to high school equivalency degrees, counseling, and hands-on job training. As in individual community-based, nonprofit programs like Argus. Job Corps carefully links education, training, placement and support services. Job Corps centers are located in rural and urban settings around the country. Some of the urban settings are campus-like. Others essentially are "street-based." In the original design, a residential setting provided sanctuary away from one's home. Today, nonresidential variations are being tried. Job Corps participants usually are about 16 to 22 years old, and often at risk of drug abuse, delinquency, and welfare dependency. The average family income of Job Corps participants is less than $6,000 per year, 2 of 5 come from families on public assistance and more than 4 of 5 are high school dropouts. The typical participant is an 18-year-old minority high school dropout who reads at a seventh-grade level.

In the 1990s, an evaluation by the Congressional Budget Office calculated that for each $10,000 invested in the average participant in the mid-1980s, society received approximately $15,000 in returns, including approximately $8,000 in "increased output of participants," and $6,000 in "reductions in the cost of crime-related activities." In 2000, an evaluation of almost 10,000 Job Corps participants and 6,000 controls by Mathematica Policy Research found that Job Corps participants were 20% less likely to be arrested, charged or convicted of a crime. If convicted, they served less jail time than control group counterparts, received more post participation non-Job Corps academic instruction and vocational training than control group members, received less in federal benefits than control group members, and were less likely to describe their health as "poor" or "fair."

Without a training first strategy based on the principles of successes like Argus and Job Corps, it is difficult to believe that America's present "work first" "welfare reform" will succeed for those who are the hardest to employ, including persons with drug problems. Nor has the new, disappointing Workforce Development Act understood the importance of training first.

Community development and community banking

Many of the jobs for such training first preparation can be generated by community development corporations in the private, nonprofit sector. Community development corporations were the brainchild of Robert Kennedy's Mobilization for Youth in the late 1960s. Initially, there were 10 such community development corporations – and now there are over 2,000. A favorite of mine is the New Community Corporation in the Central Ward of Newark, founded in the ashes of the 1960s riot there by Monsignor William Linder, who has received a MacArthur Foundation genius award. The New Community Corporation has generated thousands of economic development and associated services jobs in the Central Ward of Newark. One of its affiliates also owns the only Pathmark Supermarket in the Central Ward. Income streams from this for-profit operation help with the nonprofit operations.

The capital for community development corporations often can be secured via community-based banking. Here the model is the South Shore Bank in Chicago. Many banks do not bother with branches in the inner city. When they do, typically a bank will use the savings of inner-city residents to make investments outside of the neighborhood. South Shore does just the opposite. It uses the savings of the poor to reinvest in the inner-city neighborhoods where the poor live. And South Shore still makes a profit.

Community equity policing

My last example of what works is community-based, problem-oriented policing. This essentially means getting officers out of their cruisers and into foot patrols. They work shoulder-to-shoulder with citizen groups to focus on specific problems and solve them with sensitive efficiency.

I am not talking about "zero tolerance" policing, as practiced, for example, in New York City. Such policing, has, of course, created a tremendous amount of racial and community tension.

Opposite to "zero-tolerance" policing is the community-sensitive strategy of the Boston Police, as well as the community equity policing of the Eisenhower Foundation. Since 1988, the Foundation has replicated neighborhood police ministations that are housed in the same space as youth safe havens. (Neighborhood ministations were pioneered by the police in Japan, and after-school safe havens have been popularized in America by the Carnegie Corporation.) Grants are made to nonprofit grassroots youth development organizations, and police chiefs co-target 2 or 3 officers as local match. The officers are trained as mentors for youth. Officers on foot patrols are accompanied by citizens. The result has been drops in crime at least as great as with zero tolerance, along with improved racial and community relations.

Comprehensive interdependence

Look at how these few examples of what works interrelate, or can be made to interrelate through a wise national policy for the inner city and the truly disadvantaged. Problem-oriented, community equity policing can help secure a neighborhood. The security can help encourage community-based banking. Community-based banking can provide capital for community development corporations. Community development corporations can invest that capital in ways that generate good jobs for local residents. Inner-city youth can qualify for those jobs if they have been in job training, like that at Argus and Job Corps. Similarly, inner-city youth can stay in high school if they have been involved in human capital investments like the Ford Foundation's Quantum Opportunities mentoring program. They can get that far if they have been in Comer schools, full services community schools and after-school safe havens. And they can get that far if they have been in preschool. So what you see, when you ask what works based on scientific studies and careful evaluations, is what Lisbeth Schorr, at the Harvard University School of public Health, calls "multiple solutions to multiple problems."

The solutions then, are not single, narrow and categorical. The solutions are creative, comprehensive and interdependent.

NATIONAL POLICY

Such comprehensive interdependence is at the core of the national policy proposed in the Eisenhower Foundation's 30 year update of the Kerner Commission, composed of two publications – *The Millennium Breach* and *Locked in the Poorhouse* – and in the Foundation's 30-year update of the National Commission on the Causes and Prevention of Violence, *To Establish Justice, To Insure Domestic Tranquility*. Our policy concentrates on school and job reform, because that is what evaluations suggest is most important. Public opinion polls support school and job reform. (See the final section on common ground for political alliance.) So framed, our policy means expanding Head Start preschool to all qualified inner-city young people. It means replicating to scale proven public education reforms like safe havens, Comer schools, full service (public) community schools and Quantum

Opportunities. It means a new training first program for the hardest to employ, including out-of-school youth and persons on welfare.

To generate jobs, we need a commitment by the federal government to full employment for the inner city. As many of those jobs as possible should be generated by the private sector – especially through a new national community-based banking program modeled after the South Shore Bank. But many of those jobs need to be created by the public sector. A good many public jobs should be in the repair of decaying urban infra-structure – a result of the public disinvestment of the 1980s. America is far behind other industrialized democracies in investments in its public infrastructure. The new jobs also should be in constructing and repairing housing for the poor. Here, an excellent model is Youth Build USA, where founder Dorothy Stoneman, another MacArthur genius award winner, trains high school dropouts to rehabilitate housing. We also need public service jobs, many of which can be used to reform "welfare reform." There are hundreds of thousands of jobs needed for child care workers, assistance to teachers in inner-city schools, staff for nonprofit grassroots community-based organizations and drivers to get people to work.

Racial and criminal justice reform

To complement this school and job reform, we need racial and criminal justice reform. Here, one model is *The Shape of the River*, by the former presidents of Harvard and Princeton. The book provides some of the most comprehensive, cohort-based evidence on the cost-effectiveness of affirmative actions. Neither of the major candidates in the 2000 presidential election did particularly well in prep school. Yet both were admitted to elite Ivy League universities. Affirmative action is an accepted policy among the well-off. To eliminate the present double standard, affirmative action needs to be strengthened for the not-so-well-off.

We also need a new presidential commission to propose how to eliminate the racial biases in our juvenile and criminal justice systems, especially when it comes to drugs and mandatory minimum sentences. We need to acknowledge our defeat in the war on drugs in America. America spends 30% of its anti-drug resources on treatment and prevention and 70% on law enforcement. In many European countries, the percentages are just the opposite – 70% on prevention and treatment and 30% on law enforcement. We need a better balance. One model is the State of Arizona. Arizona held a referendum on the high cost of prison building. Voters decided to begin to divert non-violent offenders from the prison system into community treatment alternatives. An evaluation commissioned by the Supreme Court of the State of Arizona found recidivism rates for people so diverted to be lower and concluded that a considerable amount of money had been saved for the taxpayers of Arizona. If Arizona can begin to move in this direction, then less conservative states, like California, can do the same. Crucially, given that 400,000 to 500,000 persons are coming out of prison each year between 2001 and 2005 and given that there are few plans for educational and job preparation, we need to replication on a much broader scale the Delancey Street enterprise, began in San Francisco over 30 years age. Delancey Street is the premier American initiative for successfully reintegrating ex-offenders and dramatically reducing their recidivism.

Less affirmative action for the rich

That is the kind of comprehensive and interdependent policy – focused on education, employment, race and criminal justice – that we propose. The cost of replicating what works to scale. We estimate, is in the order of $50 to $60 billion dollars per year.

The Eisenhower Foundation believes that as much of this cost as possible should be borne by the private sector – especially when it comes to jobs and training. But we are not holding our breath. Given the failures of the private sector in supply-side economies, the Job Training Partnership Act and Enterprise Zones; given the huge salaries of corporate CEOs (over 400 times their workers): and given the enormous amount of corporate welfare high paid lobbyists have secured (see below). We believe that it is inevitable that the public sector must take the lead, at the local, state and national levels.

For its part, the federal government should *raise* funds, but then *re-target* them, not to the states, which have not been particularly successful when it comes to the inner city and the truly disadvantaged, but to the grassroots local level, and especially to private, nonprofit inner-city organizations, which are responsible for so much of what works, based on scientific evaluations.

How do we propose to finance such reform? Not through new taxes, through, as I have suggested, there is plenty of public opinion to suggest that Americans are willing to pay more taxes for school and job reform that works. Rather, at the federal level, we need to use a small fraction of the budget surplus such as the surplus that was created by President Clinton during the late 1990s. We also propose minor percentage changes in some budget line items. This can easily generate the $50 to $60 billion needed to begin replicating what works to scale.

Our first priority is one readucing affirmative action for the rich and corporate welfare. With an eye to the British East India Company, our founding fathers warned, in Thomas Jefferson's words, against the antidemocratic "aristocracy of our moneyed corporations." But today that aristocracy is alive and very well, indeed. The taxpayers of America spend somewhere between $100 and $200 billion per year on tax breaks and subsidies to the rich and to corporations. For example, in the 1980s, tens of billions of dollars of tax breaks were given out to the rich and to corporations, by way of liberalized depreciation and capital gains allowances. At the same time, we spend tens upon tens of billions of dollars per year on subsidies to corporations. These are federal grants. We subsidizes the nuclear power industry, the aviation industry, the media, big oil and gas, the mining industry and the timber industry. America subsidizes agribusiness to the tune of over $18 billion per year. We subsidize tobacco companies to give cancer to our children. I suggest to you that is neither cost-effective nor moral.

We also need to finance the replication of what works to scale through reductions in what doesn't work (like prison building and boot camps).

THE BOYS IN THE HOOD OR THE BOYS ON THE HILL?

At this point, just take a step back and ask yourself this question. If we really do know a great deal about what *doesn't* work, if we know a great deal about what *does* work, if we have learned a lot about how to replicate what works, if public opinion is in favor of much education and jobs reform, and if, at a time of unprecedented prosperity, we have the means to finance what works to scale, what is the problem?

In part, the problem has been not so much the boys in the Hood as the boys on the Hill. The problem has been one of political will and political inaction. For example, in recent years, many in Congress pressed for more funding of what *doesn't* work (like tax breaks for the rich and prison building for the poor) and less funding for what *does* work (like preschool and safe havens). In the 1990s, Congress often had it backwards. For its part, the Administration in the 1990s had a good understanding of what doesn't and does work, and should be praised for its economic policy. But, especially after the failure of healthcare reform, the Administration was not sufficiently willing to stand up on the bully pulpit and advocate for a policy that replicates what works on a scale equal to the dimensions of the problem.

Given this lack of political will and action in America, what can citizens and nonprofit organizations do to generate reform based on what works? In his book, *If the Gods Had Meant Us to Vote, They Would Have Given Us Candidates*, Hightower calls for grassroots citizen leadership. Consistent with this thinking, I would like to suggest 2 obvious grassroots venues: campaign finance reform and communicating what works.

The challenge in America, then, is to begin to build new political alliances around widespread support of education and training as well as not uncommon resentment of the idle rich. The challenge, above all, is to remember the dreams of our children – and never to forget how often the dreams of the children of the inner city have been deferred:

What happens   Does it stink like rotten meat?
To a dream deferred?   Or crust and sugar over
Does it dry up   Like a syrupy sweet?
Like a raisin in the sun?   May be it just sags
Or fester like a sore?   Like a heavy load.
and then run?   Or does it explode?

Langston Hughes
Harlem 2

Bibliographic sources

Alan Curtis, *Family, Employment and Reconstruction* (Milwaukee: Family Service America, 1995).

Alan Curtis and Fred R. Harris. *The Millennium Breach.* (Washington, DC: Milton S. Eisenhower Foundation, 1998).

Alan Okagaki, *Developing a Public Policy Agenda on Jobs* (Washington, D.C.: Center for Community Change, 1997).

Alan Wolfe, "The New Politics of Inequality," *The New York Times*, September 22, 1999, p. A27.

Alan Wolfe, "The New Politics of Inequality," *The New York Times,* September 27, 1999, p. A27.

Alfred Blumstein and Joel Wallman, editors, *The Crime Drop in America* (Cambridge: Cambridge University Press, 2000).

American Youth Policy Forum. *Some Things Do Make A Difference for Youth*. Washington, DC: American Youth Policy Forum, 1997.

Andrew Hahn, *Quantum Opportunities Program: A Brief on the QOP Pilot Program* (Waltham, Mass.: Center for Human Resources, Heller Graduate School, Brandeis University, 1995).

Barbara Miner, "Target: Public Education," *Nation*, November 30, 1998, p. 4.

Beatrix Hamburg, "President's Report," *Annual Report*, 1996 (New York: William T. Grant Foundation, 1997).

Bill Alexander, "On and Off the Wagon: America's Promise At Two," *Youth Today*, July/August, 1999.

Carnegie Corporation, *A Matter of Time* (New York: Carnegie Corporation, 1992).

Center for Community Change, *Newsletter* (Issue 19, Fall 1997); *Federal Register,* Volume 64, Number 105, Wednesday June 2, 1999, p. 29672.

Children's Defense Fund, *The State of America's Children* (Washington, DC Children's Defense Fund, 1994).

Christopher Wren, "Arizonal Finds Cost Savings In Treating Drug Offenders," *The New York Times*, April 21, 1999, p. A16.

Committee for Economic Development, *Children in Need: Investment Strategies for the Educationally Disadvantaged* (New York: Committee for Economic Development, 1987).

Doris L. Mackenzie and Clair Souryal, *Multiple Evaluation of Shock Incarceration* (Washington, DC: National Institute of Justice, 1994).

Dorothy Stoneman, "Replicating YouthBuild," Presentation at the National DS Senate Conference on *Locked in the Poorhouse,* Milton S. Eisenhower Foundation, Washington, DC (forthcoming, 2001).

Doug Henwood, "The Nation Indicators," *Nation*, March 29, 1999, p. 10.

Editorial "The Tide Is Not Lifting Everyone," *The New York Times,* September 30, 1997.

Editorial "Crack Sentences Revisited," *The Washington Post*, May 5, 1997.

Edward N. Wolff, *Top Heavy* (New York: The New Press, 1995).

Elliott Currie, *Crime and Punishment in America* (New York: Metropolitan Books, 1998).

Felicity Baringer, "Rich-Poor Gulf Widens among Blacks, *The New York Times*, Sept. 25, 1992.

Fox Butterfield, "Racial Disparities Seen As Pervasive in Juvenile Justice," *The New York Times*, April 26, 2000.

Fred R. Harris and Alan Curtis, co-editors, *Locked in the Poorhouse* (Lanham, New York and Oxford: Rowman and Littlefield, 1998).

Gary Orfield, "Segregated Housing and School Desegregation," in Gary Orfield, Susan E. Eaton and the Harvard Project on School Desegregation, *Dismantling Desegregation: The Quiet Reversal of Brown vs. Board of Education* (New York: New Press, 1996).

Glenn C. Loury, "Unequalized," *New Republic*, April 6, 1998.

Howell, James C., Editor. *Guide for Implementing the Comprehensive Strategy for Serious, Violent and Chronic Juvenile Offenders,* Washington, DC: US Government Printing Office, June, 1995.

James Bennett, "At Volunteerism Rally, Leaders Paint Walls and a Picture of Need," *New York Times*, April 27, 1997, p. Al.

James Brooke, "Prisons: Growth Industry for Some," *The New York Times*, November 2, 1997.

James P. Comer, *Waiting for a Miracle* (New York: Dutton, 1997).

Janofsky, Michael, "Police Chiefs Say Criticism Is Founded, and Vow to Regain the Public Trust," *The New York Times*, April 10, 1999.

Jared Bernstein and Ellen Houston, *Crime and Work: What Can we Learn From the Low Wage Labor Market* (Washington, DC: Economic Policy Institute, 2000).

Jason DeParle, "Richer Rich, Poorer Poor, and a Fatter Green Book," *The New York Times*, May 26, 1991.

Jeff Faux, "Lifting All Boats," chapter prepared for *To Establish Justice, To Insure Domestic Tranquility: A Thirty Year Update of the National Commission on the Causes and Prevention of Violence* (Washington, DC: The Milton S. Eisenhower Foundation, 1999).

Jeffrey A. Roth, "Understanding and Preventing Violence," in *Research in Brief* (Washington, DC: National Institute of Justice, 1994).

Jerry Jones, *Federal Revenue Policies That Work: A Blueprint for Job Creation to Support Welfare Reform* (Washington, DC: Center for Community Change, 1997).

Jim Hightower, *If the Gods Had Meant Us to Vote, They Would Have Given Us Candidates* (New York: Harper-Collins, 2000).

John Atlas and Peter Drier, *A National Housing Agenda for the 1990s* (Washington, DC: National Housing Institute, 1992).

Jonathan Kozol, "Saving Public Education," *Nation*, Feb. 17, 1997.

Josh Wilgoreh, "National Study Examines Why Pupils Excel," *The New York Times*, July 26. 2000, P. A14.

Joy G. Dryfoos, *Safe Passage: Making It Through Adolescence in a Risky Society* (New York: Oxford University Press, 1998).

Keith Bradsher, "Gap in Wealth in US Called Widest in West," *The New York Times,* April 17, 1995.

Kenneth Bredemeier, "Widening Gap Found Between Area's Rich, Poor" *The Washington Post*, November 29, 2000, p. E1.

Kevin Phillips, *The Politics and Rich and Poor* (New York: Random House, 1990).

Lawrence Mishel, Jared Bernstein and John Schmitt. *The State of Working America* (Ithica: Cornell University Press, 2000).

Lisbeth B. Schorr, "Helping Kids When It Counts," *The Washington Post*, April 30, 1997.

Lisbeth Schorr, *Within Our Reach: Breaking the Cycle of Disadvantaged* (New York: Doubleday, 1988).

Lynn A. Curtis, *Family, Employment and Reconstruction*; and *Sentencing Project, Crime Rates and Incarceration: Are We Any Safer?* (Washington, DC: Sentencing Project, 1992).

Mark Mauer, *Intended and Unintended Consequences: State Racial Disparities in Imprisonment* (Washington, DC: Sentencing Project, 1997).

Mark Mauer, *Young Black Men and the Criminal Justice System* (Washington, DC: Sentencing Project, 1990).

Mark Zepezauer and Arthur Naiman, *Take the Rich Off Welfare* (Tucson, Arizona: Odonian Press, 1996).

Michael Quint, "This Bank Can Turn a Profit and Follow a Social Agenda," *The New York Times*, May 24, 1992.

Milton Friedman, "There's No Justice in the War on Drugs," *The New York Times*, January 11, 1998.

Milton S. Eisenhower Foundation, *To Establish Justice, To Insure Domestic Tranquility* (Washington, DC: The Milton S. Eisenhower Foundation, 1999).

National Center for Children in Poverty. Columbia University. *Young Children in Poverty*, March, 1998.

National Research Council. *Losing Generations: Adolescents in High-Risk Settings.* Panel on the High Risk Youth, Committee on Behavioral and Social Sciences and Education. Washington, DC: National Academy Press, 1993.

Pam Belluck, "Urban Volunteers Strain to Reach Fragile Lives," *The New York Times,* April 27, 1997. p. A1.

Peter Applebone, "From Riots of the ?0s, A Report for a Nation with Will and Way for Healing," *The New York Times*, May 8, 1992.

Peter Edelman, "Who Is Worrying About the Children?" *The Washington Post*, August 11, 1999, p. A18.

Powell, Kenneth and Darnell F. Hawkins, Editors. "Youth Violence Prevention: Descriptions and Baseline Data from 13 Evaluation Projects." *American Journal of Preventive Medicine,* Supplement to Volume 12, Number 5, September/October 1996.

Price, Richard H., Emory L. Cowen, Raymond P. Lorion, and Julia Ramos-Mckay, eds. *14 Ounces of Prevention: A Case Book for Practitioners.* Washington, DC: American Psychological Association, 1988.

Richard A. Mendel, *Prevention or Pork? A Hard Look at Youth-Oriented Anti-Crime Programs* (Washington, DC: American Youth Policy Forum, 1995).

Robert D. Felner *et al.*, "The Impact of School Reform for the Middle Years," *Phi Delta Kappa*, March, 1997, 528–50.

Robert Suro, "More Is Spent on New Prisons Than Colleges," *The Washington Post,* February 24, 1997.

Robin Toner, "Los Angeles Riots Are a Warning, Americans Fear," *The New York Times*, June 14, 1992.

Sara Mosle, "The Vanity of Volunteerism," *New York Times Magazine*, July 2, 2000, p. 22.

Steven R. Donziger, *The Real War on Crime: Report of the National Criminal Justice Commission* (New York: Harper Collins, 1996).

The Milton S. Eisenhower Foundation, *Youth Investment and Police Mentoring* (Washington, DC: The Milton S. Eisenhower Foundation, 2000).

The Milton S. Eisenhower Foundation, *To Establish Justice, To Insure Domestic Tranquility* (Washington DC, The Milton S. Eisenhower Foundation, 1999).

The Milton S. Eisenhower Foundation, *Youth Investment and Police Mentoring* (Washington DC: The Milton S. Eisenhower Foundation, 2000).

The New York Times editorial, "Less Money Than Meets the Eye," July 9, 2000.

Timothy Egan, "Less Crime, More Criminals," *The New York Times*, March 7, 1999, p. 1.

Tom Furlong, "Enterprise Zone in L.A. Fraught with Problems," *Los Angeles Times,* May 19, 1992; "Reinventing America," *Business Week*, January 19, 1993; "Not so EZ," *Economist*, January 28, 1989. "Job Training and Partnership Act: Youth Pilot Projects," *Federal Register*, April 13, 1994.

U.S. Census, *Historical Poverty Tables* (Washington, DC: US Census, 1997).

United States Department of Labor, *National Job Corps Study: The Short Term Impact on Participants Employment and Related Outcomes* (Washington DC: U.S. Department of Labor, 2000).

Urban Institute, *Confronting the Nation's Urban Crisis: From Watts (1965) to South Central Los Angeles* (Washington, DC: Urban Institute, 1992).

Vince Stehle, "Vistas of Endless Possibility: Delancey Street Foundation Helps Felons and Addicts Rehabilitate Themselves into Responsible Citizens," *Chronicle of Philanthropy*, November 2, 1995, p. 59.

Vivien Stern, *The Future of A Sin* (Boston: Northeastern University Press, 1998).

William G. Bowen and Derek Curtis Bok, *The Shape of the River* (Princeton: Princeton University Press, 1998).

William J. Cunningham, "Enterprise Zones," Testimony before the Committee on Select Revenue Measures, Committee on Ways and Means, United States House of Representatives, July 11, 1991.

William Julius Wilson. *When Work Disappears: The World of the New Urban Poor* (New York: Knopf, 1996).

Chapter 36

David F. Greenberg

PUNISHMENT, DIVISION OF LABOR, AND SOCIAL SOLIDARITY

From: David F. Greenberg (1999), excerpts from 'Punishment, division of labor, and social solidarity', in William S. Laufer and Freda Adler (eds), *The Criminology of Criminal Law. Advances in Criminological Theory*, New Brunswick, NJ: Transaction Publishers, pp. 283–359.

INTRODUCTION

A LONG-STANDING SOCIOLOGICAL TRADITION considers the type of social control measures utilized in a society to be determined by its more fundamental features. For Durkheim (1933, 1992), it is the division of labor in a society and the degree of absolutism of its government that determine collective responses to violations of social rules. To social scientists inspired by Marx, the mode of production in a society, the demand for exploitable labor, and the kinds and intensity of class conflict are fundamental determinants (Rusche and Kirchheimer 1939; Fine 1980; Melossi and Pavarini 1980; Miller 1980; . . . Adamson 1984). In recent years Donald Black (1976) and his followers (Horwitz 1990) have been extending this research program by positing the influence of a number of social characteristics on levels and styles of social control.

At best, the insights furnished by this approach have been partial. One need not reject those insights to recognize that some recent developments in crime control policy cannot be fully understood in these reductionist terms. Without abandoning it altogether, I want to explore a different way of thinking about criminal sanctions by suggesting that some features of punishment policy and practices can be understood as components of political strategies for *changing* a society. It is an intended *future* social structure and culture, not its current condition, that shapes the strategies. These strategies are not directed to crime alone, but also to an array of other social issues, such as welfare, education, and immigration. [. . .]

TOUGH PUNISHMENT

Until the early 1970s, American prison populations rose and fell over the decades, yet remained within bounds, without any long-run trend (Blumstein and Cohen 1973;

Blumstein, Cohen and Nagin 1976). After declining appreciably for much of the 1960s, incarceration rates began to rise, and have been outpacing population growth steadily ever since. At the end of 1996, more than 1.6 million people were in prison or jail, and another 3.5 million were on probation or on parole. . . .

In 1972, there were 93 sentenced prisoners per 100,000 residents in state and federal institutions (Maguire and Pastore 1996:556); at the end of 1995, there were 409 (Gilliard and Beck 1996:3). This is the highest incarceration rate in the industrialized world. Many of those committed to prison have been convicted of relatively minor offenses (Austin and Irwin 1991). This enormous increase is all the more remarkable in that it has come at a time when governments have been facing strong pressures to cut budgets. . . .

Prison expansion is only one of many ways punishment policy has been toughening. Increasingly, states are adopting legislation allowing juveniles to be tried as adults, and are removing the confidentiality of juvenile court records (Butterfield 1996a). A number of states have started to hold parents responsible for offenses committed by their children (Kotlowitz 1994; Applebome 1996; Torbet et al. 1996). Educational programs for prison inmates are being eliminated in budget cuts (Kunen 1995). Federal legislation has excluded some addicts from Social Security benefits and from welfare payments. "Three strikes" legislation adopted by some states provides life sentences without parole for felons with two prior felony convictions, no matter how long ago, and sometimes without regard to the seriousness of the earlier offenses (Shichor and Sechrest 1996). In 1995, Alabama restored the chain gang (Bragg 1995), a form of penal servitude long regarded as an instrument of racial oppression. After a moratorium on executions between 1967 and 1977 while the U.S. Supreme Court was considering the constitutionality of the death penalty, executions have resumed; the number of prisoners currently awaiting execution now exceeds 3000. In another decision, the Supreme Court ruled that judges can legitimately extend someone's sentence on the basis of charges of which the defendant has been acquitted. [. . .]

EXPLAINING TOUGHENING

How to explain these developments? Homicide rates, considered the most accurate of all reported crime statistics, have changed little since 1980. Reported rates for other offenses did rise, but since victimization surveys show no parallel increase during the 1970s and 1980s, the increase in reported rates may reflect nothing more than an increased willingness of victims to notify the police (Orcutt and Faison 1981; O'Brien 1996).

That increases in reported crime rates do not necessarily lead to higher incarceration rates is demonstrated by the drop in prison populations during the late 1960s while reported crime rates were rising (at least partly for demographic reasons); and they are rising now, even though reported crime rates have been falling for five years in a row. [. . .]

A court can sentence to prison only those offenders who are actually brought into the criminal justice system. Could it be that more people are being imprisoned because the police are arresting more criminals? In 1972, the arrest rate for index offenses per 100,000 population was 883.4; in 1995 it was 1132.7 (FBI 1973:126, 1996:209). This increase of 28 percent can hardly explain a more than four-fold increase in the incarceration rate.

A very large increase in arrests on narcotics charges has certainly contributed. But imprisonment rates have increased for other offenses as well. Many states have adopted legislation mandating longer sentences for convicted criminals, and restricting or eliminating parole. Judges have been ladling out prison sentences more generously, and parole authorities have been revoking parole more readily (Shane-Dubow, Brown and Olsen 1985; Tonry 1988; Pillsbury 1989; Langan 1991; Wicharraya 1995; Marvell and Moody 1996). As a result, prison populations have grown at an historically unprecedented rate (Blumstein 1988; Langan 1991; Zimring and Hawkins 1995).

This trend is clearly inexplicable within the framework of Durkheim's (1933) model of legal evolution. That model sees the basis for social solidarity gradually shifting from "mechanical" to "organic" solidarity. In societies with mechanical solidarity, similarity in occupations and life circumstances is supposed to lead social members to identify strongly with one another, and to punish any infraction of social norms passionately, vigorously, and harshly. Societies with organic solidarity are supposed to be based on complementarity of function in a complex division of labor. Here demand for punishment is supposed to be milder, ameliorated by humanitarian sentiments; and social control places increased emphasis on restitution, less on retribution. Order is secured primarily through market exchanges rather than forcibly secured similarity, although punishment does not disappear.

It has long been known that long-term trends do not fit this model (Barnes 1965; Shelef 1975; Spitzer 1975), and it clearly furnishes no insights that would help us to understand increased punitiveness now. Though the division of labor in contemporary United States is complex, the demand for severe punishment is high. [. . .]

Increased punitiveness might, however, be explained by increasing inequality. Generalizing from diverse literatures, Donald Black (1976), has proposed that punishment will be more intense the higher the degree of economic inequality in a society, and that it will be harsher the lower the financial status of the person being punished. [. . .]

Although a number of crossnational studies of crime rates have found higher rates to be associated with economic inequality, this relationship is not found among the "high income" nations . . . . Though the United States is among the more stratified nations in this sample, its overall crime rate is not unusually high. [. . .]

Economic trends in the United States are consistent, however, with a positive relationship between income inequality and prison population. Over the past two decades, as the prison population has risen, the distributions of income and wealth have become appreciably more skewed (Winnick 1989; Burtless 1990; Phillips 1990:3–31; Karoly 1992, 1993; Krugman 1992, 1994; Danziger and Gottschalk 1993; Bradsher 1995; Westergaard 1995; Wolff 1995a,b; Head 1996). [. . .]

Trends for punishment and inequality are thus consistent with a cross-sectional relationship between inequality and punishment levels among the nations. Yet it is equally apparent from Figure 36.1 that the relatively high level of economic inequality alone cannot explain why the United States dishes out punishment so generously. Its prison population is far larger than can be explained by economic inequality alone. [. . .]

Others have offered explanations, but they can hardly be called satisfactory. Instrumental Marxists have argued that the ruling class in highly stratified societies must punish criminals harshly to prevent exploited and impoverished workers from rebelling against poverty and exploitation (Chambliss and Seidman 1980; Quinney 1977:131–34). The positive correlation found in time series and panel analyses between unemployment and the size of prison populations in a number of market economies (Greenberg 1977a; 1989; Jankovic 1977; Box and Hale 1982, 1985, 1986; Hale 1989; Inverarity and Tedrow 1987; Laffargue and Godefroy 1989; Sabol 1989; Yeager 1979; Wallace 1981;

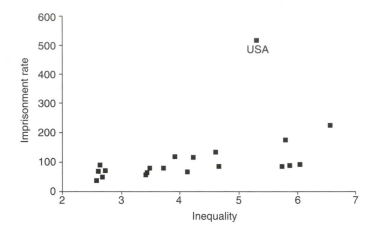

Figure 36.1 Imprisonment rates by inequality

Cappell and Sykes 1991) is consistent with this explanation. Yet the instrumental Marxist answer does not strike one as adequate in nations where the courts operate with a good deal of institutional independence from capitalist control, in which judges are not neces-sarily drawn from the capitalist class themselves, and in which the poor are not rebelling.

Moreover, the Marxist model, which attributes an expansive penal policy to a small ruling class, fails to account for the widespread belief among the American public that judges and parole boards are too lenient (Warr 1995). [. . .]

The extent of this support for severe punishments, however, does little to explain variability in the level of punishment across space and time. Why does the United States imprison so much more readily than other nations? Why so much more now than a quarter-century ago?

At first glance, it might seem that another of Black's generalizations could conceiv-ably be relevant: it is that punishment will be greater when there are large differences in status and culture between those who punish and those who are punishing. One would expect the dominant groups in society – those who make and enforce the laws – to punish those they regard as unlike them more harshly. Where groups are ranked hierarchically in prestige or moral repute, those in lower ranked groups should be more vulnerable to imprisonment.

In many countries, minority populations are disproportionately represented in arrest, conviction, and prison statistics (Home Office 1990; Carr-Hill 1987; Biles 1986; Albrecht 1987; Junger 1988; Hudson 1993; Tonry 1993, 1997; Chiricos and Crawford 1995; Jackson 1995). . . . Perhaps the United States has so much larger a prison population than the other high-income nations because the others do not have comparable racial-ethnic or class divisions.

Studies of sentencing in the criminal courts might be construed as failing to give con-sistent support to this idea. A number of statistical studies of criminal sentences have found that on average, the race of the defendant has little or no impact on the outcome (Hagan 1974; Kleck 1981; Blumstein, Cohen, Martin, and Tonry 1983; Wilbank 1987). On the other hand, other research has found evidence for invidious racial discrimination at various stages of criminal justice processing, unmitigated by the introduction of sentencing guidelines intended to eliminate prejudice (Chiricos and Crawford 1995; Jerome Miller 1996:78). [. . .]

If inequality is to be understood as a direct cause of the imprisonment rate, then it is immaterial why some nations are more unequal than others. Whatever the factors responsible for high inequality, it leads to more punishment. However, the relationship can be understood as something other than simply and directly causal. To consider this alternative possibility it becomes relevant to ask why inequality has grown in the United States. In considering this question, it is relevant to note that inequality has not grown in some of the other "high income" industrial nations such as England and France (Wolff 1995b:21–26). It is not an intrinsic feature of a technologically advanced economy. [. . .]

What is critical is that disposable incomes depend not just on extragovernmental social and economic factors, but also on the distribution of the tax burden and of governmental subsidies, including direct transfer payments and tax benefits. Constant exposure to condemnations of welfare for the poor makes it easy to forget that there are large (and largely unpublicized) subsidies to middle- and upper-income groups. Income tax deductions for interest paid on home mortgages are as much a subsidy as the provision of public housing. The federal government currently spends $66 billion a year on tax deductions for property taxes and interest paid on mortgages, quadruple the amount spent on low-income housing. According to DeParle (1996a), "more than two-thirds of it goes to families with incomes above $75,000." Bailouts for failing businesses are as much subsidies as unemployment compensation (Glasberg and Skidmore 1997). Federally guaranteed student loans, and payments to farmers for not planting their fields, are as much subsidies as unemployment compensation and AFDC (aid to families with dependent children) payments. Subsidies to business add up to $85 billion a year (Fischer et al. 1996:145). In addition to direct subsidies, such state interventions as minimum wage laws, tariffs, import quotas, and immigration policies affect economic outcomes indirectly through their effects on supply and demand for labor and commodities.

According to one estimate, in 1991, American households with incomes under $10,000 received a total of $5,690 in tax benefits and direct transfer payments, while households with incomes over $100,000 received $9,280 – almost twice as much. Were indirect subsidies and the provision of public goods and services that largely benefit middle-and upper-income households to be taken into account, the figures would change but the disparity would almost surely be even larger (Beeghley and Dwyer 1989).

This disproportionality has increased over time. Between 1980 and 1991 federal outlays to households with incomes under $10,000 dropped by 7 percent in constant dollars, while those to households with incomes over $200,000 doubled (Howe and Longman 1992). [. . .]

Income distributions, then, are as much an outcome of "politics" as of "economics." The direction and extent of state intervention to increase or reduce economic inequality may be taken as a measure of the degree to which a concern for the well-being of low-income strata has been made a goal of public policy. . . . Formally, that is, in law, the United States does not have a class state. Eligibility to vote and to hold public office are not restricted by class, and at least in principle, citizens of all classes are protected equally by law. Still, the benefits of citizenship are very unequally distributed. [. . .]

Opponents of redistributive economic policies point out that the more egalitarian European countries have higher levels of unemployment and lower levels of new job creation than the less egalitarian United States. In our sample, the correlation between inequality and GNP per capita is 0.31. Yet, a more systematic analysis of the evidence does not seem to support the antiredistribution argument. One reason the European countries have higher unemployment rates than the United States is that the United States more readily imprisons its unemployed, and prisoners are not counted in unemployment statistics (Western and Beckett 1999). Higher levels of inequality reduce nations' economic growth for reasons unrelated to redistribution (such as making education unaffordable to those in low-income brackets). In some circumstances, redistributive policies can enhance economic growth, or at least have no detrimental impact (Blank 1994; Chang 1994; Persson and Tabellini 1994; Fischer et al. 1996; Bénabou 1996).

Just as a society's concern for those with little money is manifested in its welfare policy, its willingness to execute and to imprison readily and for long periods indicates the extent to which the well-being of criminal offenders figures into governmental response to violations of the law. Many of those punished for law violation are drawn from low-income brackets, and so concern for the well-being of one group is not unrelated to concern for the other.

One may thus see the comparative leniency of the Dutch and Scandinavian criminal justice systems and their low degree of economic inequality (which is substantially a product of their generously funded welfare systems) as manifestations of a high degree of empathic identification and concern for the well-being of others. Where this identification and concern are high, citizens will tend to support social-democratic measures that partly detach economic well-being from fate in the marketplace. They will think that a member of the polity is entitled to an adequate standard of living simply by virtue of being a member of society, independently of any individually earned or inherited merit. Market outcomes themselves will be seen as the product of multiple contingencies, such as fluctuations in labor market conditions, that lie outside an individual's control and that should not play too large a role in determining someone's life chances. Principles of redistributive justice moderate commodification of labor in a market economy. [. . .]

The significance of both trends may be highlighted by recalling one of the critical insights of Durkheim's discussion of organic solidarity. Market exchanges, Durkheim observed, are not self-enforcing. Where they occur as part of an ongoing relationship, fairness may need no external guarantees because each partner will find it advantageous to retain the good will of the other. But in a complex market economy, many business dealings do not occur in the context of an ongoing relationship. And the informal pressures and constraints that might operate in a small-scale band or tribal society, or in a small town in a capitalist society into which the impersonality of the market has not fully penetrated, cannot be counted on to uphold transactions or ensure fairness. Thus parties may succumb to the temptation to back out of an earlier agreement, or to exploit or cheat others when it is advantageous. [. . .]

ABNORMAL FORMS OF THE DIVISION OF LABOR

Writing broadly of France at the end of the nineteenth century, Durkheim (1933:354–88) maintained that the division of labor brought about by the industrial revolution was neither mechanical nor organic. Instead, it was "abnormal." The growth of industry had been so rapid that new norms to govern industry had not had time to evolve; hence the division of labor was "anomic" – unregulated. In the absence of economic planning, investment decisions were vulnerable to miscalculation, triggering economic crises.

The scale of business enterprises had grown to the point where communication between workers and employers had broken down. Instead of cooperation, the classes fought.

In traditional society, people were, according to Durkheim, satisfied with the station in life into which they were born. Now no longer willing to stay in their customary place, they were nevertheless excluded from many career lines. Where there were no formal barriers, obstacles such as lack of educational qualifications and financial assets could still prevent them from taking up certain occupations. . . . (Durkheim 1933:378).

When individuals cannot choose their occupations on the basis of their interests and talents, roles are allocated inefficiently, and the division of labor is "forced." Inequalities of wealth also open the door to exploitation. Rewards are incommensurate with efforts: "If one social class is obliged, in order to live, to offer its services at any price, while the other can do without them, thanks to the resources at its disposal, which are not however necessarily due to any social superiority, the second unjustly dominates the first. In other words, there cannot be rich and poor at birth without there being unjust contracts" (Durkheim 1933:384). With an abnormal division of labor, "only an imperfect and troubled solidarity is possible."

Although several sociologists have stressed the theoretical importance of Durkheim's discussion of the abnormal forms of the division of labor (Taylor, Walton, and Young 1973; Pearce 1989), Durkheim's failure to incorporate the abnormal forms into his model of legal evolution has allowed sociologists to ignore them when explicating Durkheim's analysis of law.

Though deeply indebted to Marxian critiques of capitalism, Durkheim's decision to refer to the division of labor characteristic of his own day as "abnormal" suggested – contrary to Marxian analyses – that irrationality and exploitation were transient and ephemeral features of industrial capitalism, rather than essential to it (Schwendinger and Schwendinger 1974). They were, in other words, the result of an adaptive lag. Industrialization had taken place so rapidly that society had not had time to develop the institutions and norms needed to cope with the unprecedented problems it created. . . . Durkheim did not incorporate them into his model charting long-term trends in legal evolution. It is, however, not difficult to do so.

As Durkheim argued, early human societies had a relatively low division of labor, but that does not mean cooperation and mutual dependence was absent. Because every member of a small-scale society is important to the survival of the collective, and because members are linked to one another in long-lasting multiplex relationships that extend cooperation and dependence across different social functions (work, ritual, reproduction, socialization), dispute resolution tends to emphasize conciliation and restitution. Harsh punishment is rare because it would rupture these relationships and alienate those punished from the group, along with their families, friends and allies. Solidarity in such societies is based in part on interdependence (organic solidarity), but affiliation to kinship groups within a tribe (lineage or clan, for example) is also an important source of identity and loyalty, and strongly influences responses to norm violations. Culturally mandated redistributive processes may prevent stratification from destroying this solidarity. Such societies combine some of the features Durkheim links with organic solidarity with some of those he associates with mechanical solidarity.

As human societies become more productive, and as the size of the group increases, the division of labor becomes more complex. Inequalities of stratification and power appear, and with them the state forms as a specialized social agency (Engels 1942). States try, and often succeed, to establish their own authority and gain new sources of revenue by replacing retaliatory and conciliatory dispute-processing procedures with compulsory, punitive procedures under their own control. [. . .]

In societies where a forced division of labor is formally recognized in law, punishment will typically be harsher than in the more egalitarian small-scale primitive societies. The enlarged scale of the group means that individual norm violators may be considered expendable. The death penalty may be applied far more generously than in a band or tribal society. Punishment may also entail assignment to a degraded social status and to forced labor, e.g., penal slavery (Sellin 1976; French 1997).

In the usual case, offenses committed by individual members of the lower orders against their social superiors will be treated more harshly than vice versa, but this is not always the case. Elites may be expected to adhere to higher standards of conduct, and may be punished more heavily when they violate them. In the ancient Hindu Laws of Manu, for example, Brahmins are punished more harshly for certain infractions than members of other castes. [. . .]

Law has played a critical role in the transition toward a society in which occupational choice is unrestricted, and in which the conditions of work are not exploitative. It was through legal enactments that feudalism and slavery were abolished, and legal impediments to the employment of certain categories of people (such as women or members of religious and racial minorities) ended. Through legislation prohibiting discrimination in employment on the basis of race, sex, religion, and national origin, the state acted to remove long-standing public and private barriers to participation in the market economy.

In the United States, further legal steps were taken to remove the most glaring obstacles to full participation in social and political life. Voting rights were extended to blacks and women, and equality of citizens before the law was established as a constitutional principle. The Supreme Court struck down state legislation prohibiting racial intermarriage. The segregation of schools, public transportation, public facilities, and housing was ended. Public higher education expanded to give opportunities to classes of students who did not have them previously. [. . .]

All these steps can be seen as elements of a broad trend to move society from one with an abnormal, forced division of labor to one more closely approximating Durkheim's description of organic solidarity. In recent years this trend continued with the establishment of affirmative action programs in employment and education, and minority set-asides for government contracts, justified by the belief that in a society with a centuries-long history of legally enforced white supremacy, mere formal legal equality would not suffice to bring about equal outcomes or genuine organic solidarity in any reasonable time period.

Though these efforts have not brought about full parity of the races or sexes, though they have not removed all obstacles to freedom of occupational choice or advancement, or fully protected workers, they have had partial success. Welfare programs, denounced by conservatives for fostering dependency and sanctioning immorality, have made major inroads on poverty. Crossnational research shows that the higher the welfare benefits in a nation, the greater the ability of recipients to escape poverty (Duncan et al. 1993). A recent evaluation of such American welfare programs as food stamps, housing assistance, school lunch programs, the earned-income tax credit, Social Security, and Aid to Families with Dependent Children, based on Census Bureau data, concluded that: "federal and state antipoverty programs have lifted millions of children out of poverty. Many of those who remained poor were significantly less poor than they would have been without government assistance" (Primus et al. 1996:1; also see Ozawa 1995). [. . .]

Between 1971 and 1985, the black-white gap in high school completion narrowed dramatically – from 23 to 6 percentage points (with a slight widening – to 7 points – after that) (National Center for Education Statistics 1995:72–73). The black middle class is now substantially larger than it was a generation ago (Landry 1987) and larger than it would have been in the absence of such programs as subsidized loans for higher education, affirmative action, and federal civil rights legislation (Lavin and Hyllegard 1996; "A Small Ripple" 1996). [. . .]

Equally dramatic gains have been made in relation to gender equality. All the Western democracies have extended the right to vote to women. . . . The gap in wages between women and men has gradually narrowed (Kemp 1994:175). According to government figures, the number of women and racial minorities in corporate management has tripled over the last thirty years (Myerson 1997). [. . .]

The toughening of criminal justice policy reverses a number of these trends, just as reversals of incorporative trends are taking place on policies not directly related to crime, where the state has been promoting a transition from a forced division of labor toward organic solidarity. . . . Collectively, these measures represent a withdrawal from public commitment to transform society from an abnormal division of labor to one based on organic solidarity. Where regulatory enforcement is weakened, businesses operate anomically; the interests of consumers in purchasing safe and reliable products, of employees in working in a safe work environment, and of all residents in an environment that is not dangerously polluted, are sacrificed to profit maximization. [. . .]

Where prospects for lawful remunerative stable employment and upward mobility are restricted, the incentive to acquire income illegally through theft, prostitution, and the sale of narcotics is enhanced; and – leaving aside the effect of "repeat offenders" legislation – those with a criminal record have less to lose from a subsequent arrest or conviction. [. . .]

Individually and in the aggregate, levels of violence rise with poverty (e.g., Eberts and Schwirian 1968; Loftin and Hill 1974; Braithwaite 1979; Braithwaite and Braithwaite 1986; Messner 1980, 1982; Kick and LaFree 1985; Blau and Blau 1982; Bailey 1984; Simpson 1985; Avison and Loring 1986; Krahn, Hartnagel and Gartrell 1986; Rosenfeld 1986; Peterson and Bailey 1988; Maume 1989; Unnithan and Whitt 1992; Reiss and Roth 1993:130–31), and are reduced by government support for the poor (DeFronzo 1983; Rosenfeld 1986). Poverty increases the incidence of child abuse and domestic violence (Elmer 1967; Gil 1970; Gelles 1974; Maden and Wrench 1977; Straus and Gelles 1990; Straus, Gelles, and Steinmetz 1980). Thus, a decline in the economic well-being of the lower classes can be expected to increase levels of violence. To the extent that the prevention of victimization is a reason or a pretext for more punishment, the new anti-welfare policies will help to keep violence and victimization at appropriately high levels.

It could be objected that the deteriorating economic circumstances of the lower classes did not lead to large increases in theft and violence in the recent past. . . . Yet, crime rates might have grown a great deal for reasons having to do with the state of the economy, had the prison populations not risen.

WHY THE BACKLASH?

Social trends do not halt or reverse automatically. It is often easier to continue or expand an effort than to turn it around. Yet government crime policy did reverse course. [. . .]

Ask someone who supports the abandonment of egalitarian social policies and favors more punitive penal strategies why ameliorative policies lost favor, and you will be told that the old policies were obviously failing. Billions of dollars had been spent in the War on Poverty, yet welfare rolls rose, and so did crime. Instead of helping recipients to become self-supporting, welfare undermined the work ethic. Instead of bringing about integration, mandatory school bussing hastened "white flight," leaving schools segregated and cities deprived of tax revenues (Coleman, Kelly, and Moore 1975; Henig 1994:102). Liberal elitist judges were flouting the will of the people on such issues as school prayer, school desegregation, and abortion rights. Minimum wage laws and pollution control cost jobs. The breakdown of traditional morality, and Supreme Court decisions favoring criminals, were leading to promiscuity, illegitimacy, drug use and violence. Programs to rehabilitate criminals did not work. The public became aware of these difficulties, and demanded that politicians reverse course (Gilder 1981; Murray 1984; Van den Haag 1975; Wilson 1975; Mead 1992).

Many of these claims do not withstand close scrutiny. Efforts to reduce poverty and eliminate discrimination accomplished much, and would have accomplished more had more resources been devoted to implementation and enforcement. There is little evidence that overly generous welfare provisions increased welfare rolls, discouraged recipients from seeking jobs, or increased teenage pregnancies (Wilson 1987; Moffitt 1990; Hacker 1992; Jencks 1992; Tonry 1995:12–17; Luker 1996). Some research suggests that the minimum wage law, criticized by economists for increasing youth unemployment, does not in fact do so (Card and Krueger 1995; Blinder 1996). The bussing of school children probably had little impact on white flight (Rosell 1975–1976; Pettigrew and Green 1976). Many government initiatives and regulatory interventions have demonstrably improved public health and safety, and have benefitted the public in other ways (Kuttner 1996). [. . .]

Some of the support these measures receive from the public can be attributed to simple self-interest. It is quite rational for people who feel threatened by violence to suppose that they will be safer with more people in prison. If tax-payers are being squeezed by declining real incomes, cuts in welfare programs and taxes might sensibly be seen as offering relief. Part of the white opposition to affirmative action programs stems from the belief that they or their children are being denied access to good jobs and elite schools (Bobo and Kluegel 1993). It is advantageous to this constituency to argue that affirmative action programs discriminate against whites, and that college admissions and financial aid decisions should be made on the basis of "merit," not on the basis of allegedly irrelevant criteria such as race and ethnicity.

In the last two decades, middle-income voters have faced job insecurity and a gradual decline in real wages. As corporate "down-sizing" jeopardized white middle-class jobs (Newman 1988), whites became increasingly concerned with preserving their own class position, and less concerned with helping others. Thinking only of themselves and of the immediate short-run implications of admissions and hiring practices while forgetting the long-run social consequences, they have been less willing than before to foster upward mobility for the poor, and more vigorous in seeking tax cuts. Given this stance on social issues, it would be quite rational to want to put more criminals in prison. If re-distributive and preventive measures are to be excluded, what else can one do?

This reasoning, however, overlooks the high costs of the hard-line approach. Once these are figured in, it is not likely that the tough approach is rational when viewed in a purely material light. While self-interest may explain some opposition to welfare payments and affirmative action, it fails to account for the low-income citizens who oppose welfare, and those blacks who oppose affirmative action. Nor does it explain why some middle- and upper-class people have supported welfare, civil rights, and affirmative action. In the absence of support that extended beyond the beneficiaries, these measures would never have been adopted. [. . .]

If economic declines produce punitive feelings, one would have an explanation for the relationship between the business cycle and rates of admission to prison found in several capitalist countries, as well as the emotional appeal of punishments. The low sentences found in Scandinavia, the Netherlands, and Japan may reflect a lower popular demand for punishment in societies whose economic systems do not engender high levels of insecurity. In Scandinavia or the Netherlands the welfare system is relatively generous (dehaan 1990; Downes 1990), and in Japan unemployment is very low and jobs are often assured for life.

A direct test of this reasoning would require comparable data about levels of economic insecurity in different societies, and such data are not currently available. However, to focus too exclusively on fears about one's job or income may be to slight the process through which fears and anxieties are directed toward particular issues by politicians and the mass media. The emphasis they have given to crime, welfare, and affirmative action has focused anxiety on those issues, rather than – for example – on the military budget, or defects in the economic system.

In trying to explain why American prison populations soared, while those in West Germany declined modestly over the same years. Joachim Savelsberg (1994) has argued that politicians and the mass media play an important role in structuring popular beliefs about crime and crime control. Savelsberg notes that countries vary in the extent to which politicians and newspapers highlight crime as a social problem and call for harsher measures to deal with it. In the more corporatist societies, different political factions or bodies are formally recognized and represented politically. Attempts are made to accommodate their interests through explicit bargaining and concessions.

Politicians in such societies should be less likely to try to win support through inflammatory campaign rhetoric that exaggerates the magnitude of social problems. Because all the major parties share in the responsibility for dealing with these problems, they will not have strong incentives to misrepresent them. For the same reasons, they will refrain from attacking the existing policies as being outrageously misguided. Publics in these societies are not as fearful of crime, and are less likely to make demands on the state for more stringent penalties.

Differences in political arrangements make sense not only of the contrast between West Germany and the United States, but also of the low levels of incarceration in the Netherlands during the decades in which its "pillarized" political system was in place. In that system, major political decisions were made through behind-the-scenes agreements between the major political parties (Downes 1988; dehaan 1990). As this system has weakened in recent years, Dutch prison populations have risen, though not to the extent that they have in the United States.

A test of the importance of corporatism in structuring social responses to crime can be conducted using our sample of data for the affluent nations. When the per capita prison population is regressed on inequality, GNP, the crime rate, and a measure of corporatism measuring the extent to which different sectors of society engage in explicit bargaining and compromise agreements, (Pampel, Wiliamson, and Stryker 1990), corporatism is found to reduce the prison population significantly, while inequality no longer has a significant influence (see Table 36.1). The more corporatist societies are less punitive. The United States is the second least corporatist society in the entire sample, and the most punitive. [. . .]

The more corporatist societies are not only less punitive: they are also more egalitarian and have more far-reaching redistributive policies. . . . Welfare policies in the corporatist societies enjoy stronger public support. When asked whether the government should provide everyone with a "guaranteed basic income," support was far higher in Britain (59 percent), the Federal Republic of Germany (51 percent), and the Netherlands (48 percent) than in the United States (20 percent) (Smith 1990).

Obviously, these correlations pose a chicken-and-eggs problem. Corporatist political arrangements are not distributed among the nations at random, and they cannot necessarily be treated as exogenous to economic equality. It is in societies where it is considered important to accommodate diverse interests, including those of workers and people who cannot support themselves, that corporatist political arrangements tend to be found. The culture that gives rise to corporatism, and in turn to greater tolerance of deviance, shows a good deal of stability over time. [. . .]

However they come about, once corporatist political arrangements are in place, they tend to perpetuate themselves. [. . .]

On the other hand, sometimes political culture changes. For the first half of this century, the Netherlands had a higher incarceration rate than England and Wales, even though it had less crime (Downes 1988). Between 1968 and 1971, the value placed on social equality rose in national surveys of the American people; then in the 1970s it fell relative to such personal values as having a comfortable life, a sense of accomplishment, and excitement, possibly because awareness grew that equality came at a price. When real incomes began to fall, those costs came to be seen as unacceptable by a substantial fraction of the white population (Rokeach and Ball-Rokeach 1989). [. . .]

The emphasis on explaining differences in the standard social-science statistical procedures provides limited insights when it is a pattern of similarity one seeks to explain.

Table 36.1 Multiple regression of incarceration rates*

Variable	Standardized regression coefficients**	
Corporatism	−.80	−.78
	(2.15)	(2.20)
GNP	.63	.58
	(2.08)	(1.99)
Inequality	.00	.05
	(.00)	(.14)
Homicide Rate	−.08	
	(1.03)	
Total Crime Rate	−.193	
	(1.06)	
R^2	.68	.65
adjusted R^2	.56	.52

Notes

* Pairwise deletion. United States deleted from sample.

** Figures in parentheses underneath regression coefficients are student's *t* statistics.

In attitudes toward punishment and welfare, the most striking feature is not that there are some modest differences between the races, or between those holding different views of race relations, but the similarities. There is strong support for stiff punishment and cuts in welfare budgets among all groups. [. . .]

The notion that the courts are justified in punishing convicted criminals proportionately to the wrongfulness of their crimes has won a wide following among penological theorists in recent decades. Wrongdoers, they argue, should be punished because they deserve to be punished on the basis of what they have done. In so arguing, "just deserts" theorists do not contend that these principles are optimal for preventing crime, but rather that justice requires them. It is the wrongfulness of criminal acts, not social utility, that should govern the severity of punishment (Frankel 1972; Fogel 1975; Twentieth Century Fund 1976; von Hirsch 1976, 1985; Gross 1979). [. . .]

The same concern with justice figures prominently in reasons that supporters of the death penalty give to explain their support. "Murderers deserve punishment," they say: "an eye for eye; a life for a life" (Lotz and Regoli 1980; Finckenauer 1988; Steel and Steger 1988). [. . .]

These stands on punishment, . . . rest on assumptions about questions of fact that do not withstand close scrutiny, and on the applicability of particular normative framings. A desert-based punishment scheme based on criminal behavior alone assumes that it is equally easy for everyone to comply with the law. To the extent that this assumption is rendered false by the existence of discrimination and structured inequality not chosen by a defendant, equal proportional punishments no longer correspond to equal desert. [. . .]

Views of welfare also rest on assumptions about the recipients. Those who think welfare mothers are lazy, and believe that most people are poor because "they don't try hard enough to get ahead" are less sympathetic to welfare spending than those who think that people are poor "because they don't get the training and education they need" (Gilens 1996).

Contrary to claims made by critics of welfare policy and affirmative action, class origin has a large influence on tests that supposedly measure intellectual ability (Fischer et al. 1996:79–88), and expensive coaching can improve test scores substantially. Class and race also have large influences on someone's chances of being arrested, prosecuted, and convicted of crime. [. . .]

The assumption in many discussions of affirmative action that in the absence of special programs a "level playing field" exists runs counter to evidence about discrimination in hiring and promotion (Kilborn 1995). The importance role of friends and relatives in obtaining jobs is overlooked. [. . .]

We have then, not a push toward the reestablishment of a society based formally on racial or class distinctions. The opponents of affirmative action do not propose a return to Jim Crow law; whether honestly or hypocritically, they endorse legal equality, while opposing those measures that could make this equality more than formal. They see no inconsistency in this advocacy because they believe that remedial measures are no longer necessary.

If, as all indicators suggest, this view is mistaken, the result will be to leave in place a division of labor that is *de facto* forced, costumed as an organic division of labor based on complementarity. One of the very few tools left in such a society for managing the strains of actual inequality is punishment. . . .

With this conjunction of a culture of formal legal equality and social structure of high and stable inequality, the proportion of the population processed by the state punishment system expands, and the intensity of punishment increases. Inequality of social outcomes persists or increases, secured through legislation that appears to apply equally to all, but impacts differentially on different social strata; and through the discriminatory exercise of police, prosecutorial and judicial discretion. [. . .]

APPENDIX A: DATA SOURCES FOR THE HIGH-INCOME NATIONS SAMPLE

Homicide rates are for 1989–92, and are taken from United Nations (1995:484–503) except for Israel, Denmark and Switzerland, whose homicide rates are taken from Interpol (1992). Burglary and auto theft rates are taken from Interpol (1992). I have used 1990 rates except where unavailable. The Australian auto theft rate is from Clarke and Harris (1992). The Australian auto theft rate is for 1987/8; the burglary rate for New Zealand is for 1984, and for Belgium is for 1983. Income data represent income after taxes and transfer parents, and are from World Bank (1994:221). GNP per capita is for 1990, and taken from World Bank (1995). Imprisonment rates are taken from Mauer (1995b) except for Norway, whose rate is taken from Young and Brown (1993). The Israel prison population includes approximately a thousand Israeli "security prisoners," but excludes more than 3000 from the occupied territories.

References

Adamson, Christopher. 1984. "Toward a Marxian Penology: Captive Criminal Population or Economic Threats and Resources." *Social Problems* 31:435–53.

Albrecht, Hans-Jorg. 1987. "Foreign Minorities in the Criminal Justice System in the Federal Republic of Germany," *Howard Journal* 26:272–86.

Applebome, Peter. 1996. "Parents Face Consequences As Children's Misdeeds Rise." *New York Times* (April 10):A1, B8.

Austin, James and John Irwin. 1991. *Who Goes to Prison?* San Francisco: National Council on Crime and Delinquency.

Avison, William R. and Pamela L. Loring, 1986. "Population Diversity and Cross-National Homicide: The Effects of Inequality and Heterogeneity." *Criminology* 24:733–49.

Bailey, William C. 1984. "Poverty, Inequality and City Homicide Rates." *Criminology* 22:531–50.

Barnes, J. A. 1965. "Durkheim's Division of Labour in Society." *Man* N.S. 1:158–75.

Barrett, Wayne. 1997. "Not So Magic Stats: Did Rudy Cut the Murder Rate Himself?" *Village Voice* (January 14):15.

Beeghley, Leonard and Jeffrey W. Dwyer. 1989. "Income Transfers and Income Inequality." *Population Research and Policy Review* 8:119–42.

Bénabou, Ronald. 1996. "Inequality and Growth." *NBER Macro Annual* 11:11–74.

Berk, Richard A., Kenneth J. Lenihan and Peter H. Rossi. 1980. "Crime and Poverty: Some Experimental Evidence from Ex-Offenders." *American Sociological Review* 45:766–86.

Black, Donald. 1976. *The Behavior of Law*. New York: Academic Press.

Blau, Judith R. and Peter M. Blau. 1982. "The Cost of Inequality: Metropolitan Structure and Violent Crime." *American Sociological Review* 47:114–29.

Biles, David. 1986. "Prisons and Their Problems." In D. Chappell and P. Wilson (eds.) *The Australian Criminal Justice System, the mid-1980s*. Sydney: Butterworths.

Blank, Rebecca. 1994. "Does a Larger Social Safety Net Mean Less Economic Flexibility?" pp. 157–87 in R. Freeman (ed.) *Working under Different Rules*. New York: Russell Sage Foundation.

Blinder, Alan S. 1996. "The $5.15 Question." *New York Times* (May 23): A27.

Blumstein, Alfred. 1988. "Prison Populations: A System Out of Control?" pp. 231–66 in M. Tonry and N. Morris (eds.) *Crime and Justice: A Review of Research*, vol. 10. Chicago: University of Chicago Press.

Blumstein, Alfred and Jacqueline Cohen. 1973. "A Theory of the Stability of Punishment." *Journal of Criminal Law and Criminology* 64:198–207.

Blumstein, Alfred, Jacqueline Cohen, Susan E. Martin and Michael Tonry, eds. 1983. *Research on Sentencing: The Search for Reform*, vol. 1. Washington, DC: National Academy Press.

Blumstein, Alfred, Jacqueline Cohen and Daniel Nagin. 1976. "The Dynamics of a Homeostatic Punishment Process." *Journal of Criminal Law and Criminology* 68:317–34.

Bobo, Lawrence and James R. Kluegel. 1993. "Opposition to Race-Targeting: Self-Interest, Stratification Ideology, or Racial Attitudes." *American Sociological Review* 58:443–64.

Box, Stephen and Chris Hale. 1982. "Economic Crisis and the Rising Prison Population." *Crime and Social Justice* 18:20–35.

———. 1985. "Unemployment, Imprisonment, and Prison Overcrowding." *Contemporary Crises* 9:209–228.

———. 1986. "Unemployment, Crime and Imprisonment, and the Enduring Problem of Prison Overcrowding," pp. 72–96 in R. Matthews and J. Young (eds.) *Confronting Crime*. London: Sage.

Bradsher, Keith. 1995. "Widest Gap in Incomes? Research Points to U.S." *New York Times* (Oct. 27): D2.

Bragg, Rick. 1995. "Chain Gangs to Return to Roads of Alabama." *New York Times* (Mar. 26): I.16.

Braithwaite, John. 1979. *Inequality, Crime, and Public Policy*. Boston: Routledge and Kegan Paul.

———. 1981. "The Myth of Social Class and Criminality Reconsidered." *American Sociological Review* 46:36–57.

Braithwaite, John and Valerie Braithwaite. 1986. "The Effect of Income Inequality and Social Democracy on Homicide." *British Journal of Criminology* 20:45–53.

Burtless, Gary. 1990. "Earnings Inequality over the Business and Demographic Cycles," pp. 77–122 in G. Burtless (ed.) *A Future of Lousy Jobs?* Washington, DC: Brookings Institution.

Butterfield, Fox. 1996a. "States Revamping Laws on Juveniles as Feionies Soar." *New York Times*, Section 1 (May 12): 1, 24.

Cantor, David and Kenneth C. Land. 1985. "Unemployment and Crime Rates in the Post-World War II United States: A Theoretical and Empirical Analysis." *American Sociological Review* 50:317–23.

Cappell, Charles L. and Gresham Sykes. 1991. "Prison Commitments, Crime and Unemployment: A Theoretical and Empirical Specification for the United States, 1933–1985." *Journal of Quantitative Criminology* 7:155–99.

Card, David and Alan B. Krueger. 1995. *Myth and Measurement: The New Economics of the Minimum Wage*. Princeton, NJ: Princeton University Press.

Carneiro, Robert. 1970. "A Theory of the Origin of the State." *Science* 169:733–38.

Carr-Hill, Roy A. 1987. "'O Bring Me Your Poor': Immigrants in the French System of Criminal Justice," *The Howard Journal of Criminal Justice* 26.4:287–302.

Chambliss, WIlliam J. and Robert Seidman. 1980. *Law, Order, and Power*, 2nd ed. Reading, MA: Addison-Wesley.

Chang, Roberto. 1994. "Income Inequality and Economic Growth: Evidence and Recent Theories." *Economic Review* (Federal Reserve Bank of Atlanta) 79:1–10.

Chiricos, Theodore G. 1987. "Rates of Crime and Unemployment: An Analysis of Aggregate Research Evidence." *Social Problems* 34:187–212.

Chiricos, Theodore G. and Charles Crawford. 1995. "Race and Imprisonment: A contextual Assessment of the Evidence," pp. 281–309 in D.F. Hawkins (ed.) *Ethnicity Race, and Crime: Perspectives Across Time and Place*. Albany: State University of New York Press.

Chiricos and Miriam Delone. 1994. "Labor Surplus and Punishment: A Review and Assessment of Theory and Evidence." *Social Problems* 39:421–46.

Clarke, Ronald V. and Patricia M. Haries. 1992. "Auto Theft and Its Prevention," pp. 1–54 in M. Tony (ed.) Crime and Justice: A Review of Research, vol, 16. Chicago: University of Chicago Press.

Coleman, James S., S. Kelly, and J. Moore. 1975. *Trends in School Segregation, 1968–1973*. Washington, DC: The Urban Institute.

Danziger, Sheldon and Peter Gottschalk, eds. 1993. *Uneven Tides: Rising Inequality in America*. New York: Russell Sage Foundation.

DeFronzo, James. 1983. "Economic Assistance to Impoverished Americans: Relationship to Incidence of Crime." *Criminology* 21:119–36.

dehaan, Willem. 1990. *The Politics of Redress: Crime, Punishment and Penal Abolition*. Boston: Unwin Hyman.

DeParle, Jason. 1996a. "Class Is No Longer a Four-Letter Word." *New York Times Magazine* (March 17):40–43.

Downes, David. 1988. *Contrasts in Tolerance: Post-War Penal Policy in the Netherlands and England and Wales*. Oxford: Clarendon Press.

—— 1990. "The Case for Going Dutch: The Lessons of the Post-War Penal Policy." *Political Quarterly* 63:12–24.

Duncan, Greg J., B. Gustaffson, R. Hauser, G. Schmauss, M. Messenger, R. Muffels, B. Nolan and J. C. Ray. 1993. "Poverty Dynamics in Eight Countries." *Journal of Population Economics* 6:215–34.

Durkheim, Émile. 1933. *The Division of Labor in Society*. Trans. George Simpson. New York: Macmillan.

——. 1992. "Two Laws of Panel Evolution." Tr. T. Anthony Jones and Andrew T. Scull, pp. 21–49 in M. Gane (ed.) *The Radical Sociology of Durkheim and Mauss*. New York: Routledge.

Eberts, Paul and Kent P. Schwirian. 1968. "Metropolitan Crime Rates and Relative Deprivation." *Criminologica* 5:43–52.

Elmer, E. 1967. *Children in Jeopardy: A Study of Abused Minors and their Families*. Pittsburgh: University of Pittsburgh Press.

Engels, Frederick. 1942. *The Origins of the Family, Private Property and the State*. New York: International Publishers.

Federal Bureau of Investigation. 1996. *Crime in the United States – 1995*. Uniform Crime Reports, Department of Justice. Washington, DC: USGPO.

——. 1973. *Crime in the United States – 1972*. Uniform Crime Reports, Department of Justice. Washington, DC: USGPO.

Finckenauer, James O. 1988. "Public Support for the Death Penalty: Retribution as Just Deserts or Retribution as Revenge?" *Justice Quarterly* (March):81–100.

Fine, Bob. 1980. "The Birth of Bourgeois Punishment," *Crime and Social Justice* 13 (Summer):19–26.

Fischer, Claude S., Michael Hout, Martín Sánchez Jankowski, Samuel R. Lucas, Ann Swidler and Kim Voss. 1996. *Inequality by Design: Cracking the Bell Curve Myth*. Princeton, NJ: Princeton University Press.

Fogel, David. 1975. " . . . *We Are the Living Proof . . .* ": *The Justice Model for Corrections*. Cincinnati: W. H. Anderson.

Frankel, Marvin E. 1972. *Criminal Sentencing: Law Without Order*. New York: Hill and Wang.

French, Howard W. 1997. "The Ritual Slaves of Ghana: Young and Female." *New York Times* (Jan. 20):A1, A5.

Gallup, George. Jr. 1996. *The Gallup Poil: Public Opinion 1995*. Wilmington, DE: Scholarly Resources.

Galster, G. A. and L. A. Scaturo. 1995. "The U.S. Criminal Justice System: Unemployment and the Severity of Punishment." *Journal of Research in Crime and Delinquency* 22:163–89.

Gelles, Richard J. 1974. *The Violent Home*. Beverly Hills, CA: Sage.

Gil, David. 1970. *Violence against Children: Physical Child Abuse in the United States*. Cambridge, MA: Harvard University Press.

Gilder, George F. 1981. *Wealth and Poverty*. New York: Basic Books.

Gilens, Martin. 1996. " 'Race Coding' and White Opposition to Welfare." *Amercian Political Science Review* 90:593–604.

Gilliard, Darrel K. and Allen J. Beck. 1994. *Prisoners in 1993*. Bureau of Justice Statistics Bulletin. U.S. Department of Justice. Office of Justice Programs.

——. 1996. *Prison and Jail Inmates, 1995*. Washington, DC: U.S. Department of Justice. Office of Justice Programs.

Glasberg, Davita Silfen and Dan Skidmore. 1997. *Corporate Welfare Policy and the Welfare State: Bank Regulation and the Savings and Loan Bailout*. Hawthorne, NY: Aldine de Gruyter.

Goebel, Julius, Jr. 1976. *Felony and Misdemeanor: A Study in the History of Criminal Law*. Philadelphia: University of Pennsylvania Press.

Gordon, Diana R. 1990. *The Justice Juggernaut: Fighting Street Crime, Controlling Citizens*. New Brunswick, NJ: Rutgers University Press.

Gottfredson, Denise C. 1985. "Youth Employment, Crime, and Schooling: A Longitudinal Study of a National Sample." *Developmental Psychology* 21:419–32.

Greenberg, David F. 1977a. "The Dynamics of Oscillatory Punishment Processes." *Journal of Criminal Law and Criminology* 68:643–55.

——. 1980. "Penal Sanctions in Poland: A Test of Alternative Models." *Social Problems* 28:194–204.

——. 1989. "Unemployment and Imprisonment: A Comment." *Journal of Quantitative Criminology* 5:187–91.

Gross, Hyman. 1979. *A Theory of Criminal Justice*. New York: Oxford University Press.

Hacker, Andrew. 1992. *The Nations: Black and White, separate, Hostile, Unequal*. New York: Scribner.

Hagan, John, 1974. "Parameters of Criminal Prosecution – Application of Path Analysis to a Problem of Criminal Justice," *Journal of Criminal Law and Criminology*, 5:536–44.

Hale, Chris. 1989. "Unemployment, Imprisonment, and the Stability of Punishment Hypotheses: Some Results Using Cointegration and Error Correction Models." *Journal of Quantitative Criminology* 5:169–86.

——. 1991. "Unemployment and Crime: Differencing Is No Substitute for Modeling." *Journal of Research in Crime and Delinquency* 28: 426–29.

Hale, Chris and Dima Sabbagh. 1991. "Testing the Relationship between Unemployment and Crime: A Methodological Comment and Empirical Analysis Using Time Series Data from England and Wales." *Journal of Research in Crime and Delinquency* 28:400–17.

Head, Simon. 1996. "The New, Ruthless Economy." *The New York Review of Books* (Feb. 26):47–52.

Henig, Jeffrey R. 1994. *Rethinking School Choice*. Princeton, NJ: Princeton University Press.

Hershey, Robert D., Jr., 1997. "Clinton Aides Say That Income Gap Narrowed." *New York Times* Feb. 11, D3.

von Hirsch, Andrew. 1976. *Doing Justice: The Choice of Punishments*. New York: Hill and Wang.

———. 1985. *Past or Future Crimes: Deservedness and Dangerousness in the Sentencing of Criminals*. New Brunswick, NJ: Rutgers University Press.

Home Office. 1990. *Prison Statistics: England and Wales, 1989*. London: HMSO.

Horwitz, Allan V. 1990. *The Logic of Social Control*. New York: Plenum.

Howe, Neil and Phillip Longman. 1992. "The Next New Deal," *The Altantic* (April).

Hudson, Barbara A. 1993. *Penal Policy and Social Justice*. Toronto: University of Toronto Press.

Interpol. 1992. *International Crime Statistics, 1989–1990*. Saint Cloud. France: Interpol.

Inverarity, James, Pat Lauderdale and Barry C. Feld. 1983. *Law and Society: Sociological Perspectives on Criminal Law*. Boston: Little Brown.

Inverarity, James and L. M. Tedrow. 1987. "Unemployment, Crime and Imprisonment: A Pooled Cross Section and Time Series Analysis." Paper presented to the Society for the Study of Social Problems.

Jackson, Pamela Irving. 1995. "Minority Group Threat, Crime, and the Mobilization of Law in France." pp. 341–59 in D.F. Hawkins (ed.) *Ethnicity, Race, and Crime: Perspectives across Time and Place*. Albany: State University of New York.

Jacobs, David and Ronald E. Helms. 1996. "Toward a Political Model of Incarceration: A Time-Series Examination of Multiple Explanations for Prison Admission Rates." *American Journal of Sociology* 102:323–57.

Jankovic, Ivan. 1977. "Labor Market and Imprisonment." *Crime and Social Justice* 8:17–31.

Jencks, Christopher. 1992. *Race, Poverty and the Underclass*. Cambridge, MA: Harvard University Press.

Junger, Marianne. 1988. "Racial Discrimination in the Netherlands." *Sociology and Social Research* 72:211–16.

Jurik, Nancy C. 1983. "The Economics of Female Recidivism: A Study of TARP Female Offenders." *Criminology* 21:603–22.

Karmen, Andrew. 1996. "What's Driving New York's Crime Rates Down?" *Law Enforcement News* (Nov. 30):8–10.

Karoly, Lynn A. 1992. "Changes in the Distribution of Individual Earnings in the United States, 1967–1986." *Review of Economics and Statistics* 74:107–15.

———. 1993. "The Trend in Inequality among Families, Individuals, and Workers in the United States: A Twenty-five Year Perspective," pp. 1–97 in S. Danziger and P. Gottschalk (eds.) *Uneven Tides: Rising Inequality in America*. New York: Russell Sage Foundation.

Kemp, Alice Abel. 1994. *Women's Work: Degraded and Devalued*. Englewood Cliffs, NJ: Prentice-Hall.

Kick, Edward L. and Gary D. LaFree. 1985. "Development and the Social Context of Murder and Theft." *Comparative Social Research* 8:37–58.

Kilborn, Peter T. 1995. "White Males and Management: Report Finds Prejudices Block Women and Minorities." *New York Times* (Mar. 17): A14.

Kleck, Gary. 1981. "Racial Discrimination in Criminal Sentencing: A Critical Evaluation of the Evidence on the Death Penalty." *American Sociological Review* 46:783–805.

Knepper, Paul. 1991. "A Brief History of Profiting from the Punishment of Crime." Paper presented to the American Society of Criminology.

Kotlowitz, Alex. 1994. "Their Crimes Don't Make Them Adults." *New York Times* (Feb. 13): VI:40–41.

Krahn, Harvey, Timothy J. Hartnagel and John W. Gartrell. 1986. "Income Inequality and Homicide Rates: Cross-National Data and Criminological Theories." *Criminology* 24:269–95.

Krugman, Paul R. 1992. "The Rich, the Right, and the Facts." *The American Prospect* 11 (Fall): 19–31.

Krugman, Paul R. 1994. *The Age of Diminished Expectations*. Cambridge, MA: MIT Press.

Kunen, James S. 1995. "Teaching Prisoners a Lesson." *The New Yorker* (July 10):34–39.

Kuttner, Robert. 1996. *Everything for Sale: The Virtues and Limits of Markets*. New York: Alfred A. Knopf.

Laffargue, B. and T. Godefroy. 1989. "Economic Cycles and Punishment: Unemployment and Imprisonment." *Contemporary Crises* 13:371–404.

Land, Kenneth C., David Cantor and Stephen Russell. 1995. "Unemployment and Crime Rate Fluctuations in the post-World War II United States: Statistical Time Series and Alternative Models," pp. 55–79 in John Hagan and Ruth D. Peterson (eds.) *Crime and Inequality*. Stanford, CA: Stanford University Press.

Landry, Bart. 1987. *The New Black Middle Class*. Berkeley and Los Angeles: University of California Press.

Langan, Patrick A. 1991. "America's Soaring Prison Population." *Science* 251:1568–73.

Lavin, David E. and David Hyllegard. 1996. *Changing the Odds: Open Admissions and the Life Chances of the Disadvantaged*. New Haven, CT: Yale University Press.

Loftin, Colin and Robert H. Hill. 1974. "Regional Subculture and Homicide: An Examination of the Gastil-Hackney Thesis." *American Sociological Review* 39:714–24.

Lotz, R. and Robert M. Regoli. 1980. "Public Support for the Death Penalty." *Criminal Justice Review* 5:55–65.

Luker, Kristin. 1996. *Dubious Conceptions: The Politics of Teenage Pregnancy*. Berkeley and Los Angeles: University of California Press.

Lynch, Frederick R. 1989. *Invisible Victims: White Males and the Crisis of Affirmative Action*. New York: Greenwood Press.

Maden, M. F. and D. F. Wrench. 1977. "Significant Findings in Child Abuse Research." *Victimology* 2:196–224.

Maguire, Kathleen and Ann L. Pastore, eds. 1996. *Sourcebook of Criminal Justice Statistics 1995*. U.S. Dept. of Justice, Bureau of Justice Statistics. Washington, DC: U.S. Government Printing Office.

Marvell, Thomas B. and Carlisle E. Moody, Jr. 1996. "Determinate Sentencing and Abolishing Parole: The Long-term Impacts on Prisons and Crime." *Criminology* 34:107–28.

Mauer, Harc. 1995b. *Amercians Behind Baxs: The International Use of Incarceration, 1992–1993*. Washington, DC: Sentening Project.

Maume, David J., Jr. 1989. "Inequality and Metropolitan Rape Rates: A Routine Activity Approach." *Justice Quarterly* 6:513–27.

Mead, Lawrence A. 1992. *The New Politics of Poverty: The Nonworking Poor in America*. New York: Basic Books.

Melossi, Dario and Massimo Pavarini. 1980. *The Prison and the Factory*. London: Macmillan.

Messner, Steve F. 1980. "Income Inequality and Murder Rates: Some Cross-National Findings." *Comparative Social Research* 3:185–98.

———. 1982. "Societal Development, Social Equality and Homicide." *Social Forces* 61:225–240.

Michalowski, Raymond J. and Michael A. Pearson. 1990. "Punishment and Social Structure at the State Level: A Cross-Sectional Comparison of 1970 and 1980." *Journal of Research in Crime and Delinquency* 20:73–85.

Miller, Jerome. 1996. *Search and Destroy: African-American Males in the Criminal Justice System*. New York: Cambridge University Press.

Moffitt, Robert A. 1990. "The Distribution of Earnings and the Welfare State," pp. 201–30 in G. Burtless (ed.) *A Future of Lousy Jobs?* Washington, DC: Brookings Institution.

Murray, Charles. 1984. *Losing Ground: American Social Policy, 1950–1980*. New York: Basic Books.

Myerson, Allen R. 1997. "As Federal Bias Cases Drop, Workers Take Up the Fight." *New York Times* (Jan. 12): A1, A14.

National Center for Children in Poverty. 1997. *One in Four: America's Youngest Poor*. New York: Columbia University School of Public Health.

National Center for Education Statistics. 1995. *The Condition of Education, 1995*. Washington, DC: U.S. Department of Education.

Newman, Katherine. 1988. *Falling from Grace: The Experience of Downward Mobility in the American Middle Class*. New York: The Free Press.

O'Brien, Robert M. 1996. "Police Productivity and Crime Rates: 1973–1992." *Criminology* 34:183–208.

Orcutt, James D, and Rebecca Faison, 1981. "Sex-Role Attitude Change and Reporting or Rape Victimization, 1973–1985." *Sociological Quarterly* 29:589–604.

Ouimet, Marc and Pierre Tremblay. 1996. "A Normative Theory of the Relationship between Crime Rates and Imprisonment Rates: An Analysis of the Penal Behavior of U.S. States from 1972 to 1992." *Journal of Research in Crime and Delinquency* 33:109–125.

Ozawa, Martha N. 1995. "Antipoverty Effects of Public Income Transfers on Children." *Children and Youth Services Review* 17:43–59.

Pampel, Fred C., John B. Williamson and Robin Stryker. 1990. "Class Context and Pension Response to Demographic Structure in Advanced Industrial Democracies." *Social Problems* 37:535–47.

Parker, Robert Nash and Allan V. Horwitz. 1986. "Unemployment, Crime, and Imprisonment: A Panel Approach." *Criminology* 24:751–73.

Persson, Torsen and Guido Tabellini. 1994, "Is Inequality Harmful for Growth? Theory and Evidence." *American Economic Review* 48:600–21.

Peterson, Ruth D. and William C. Bailey. 1988. "Forcible Rape, Poverty, and Economic Inequality in U.S. Metropolitan Communities." *Journal of Quantitative Criminology* 4:99–119.

Pettigrew, Thomas F. and Robert C. Green. 1976. "School Desegregation in Large Cities: A Critique of the 'White Flight' Thesis." *Harvard Education Review* 46:1–53.

Pezzin, Liliana E. 1995. "Earnings Prospects, Matching Effects, and the Decision to Terminate a Criminal Career." *Criminology* 11:29–50.

Phillips, Kevin. 1990. *The Politics of Rich and Poor: Wealth and the American Electorate in the Reagan Aftermath*. New York: Harper Perennial.

Pillsbury, Samuel H. 1989. "Understanding Penal Reform: The Dynamic of Change." *Journal of Criminal Law and Criminology* 80:726–80.

Primus, Wendell, Kathryn Porter, Margery Ditto and Mitchell Kent. 1996. *The Safety Net Delivers*. Washington, DC: Center on Budget and Policy Priorities.

Quinney, Richard. 1977. *Class, State and Crime: On the Theory and Practice of Criminal Justice*. New York: David McKay.

Rainwater, Lee. 1995. "Poverty and the Income Package of Working Parents: The United States in Comparative Perspective." *Children and Youth Services Review* 17:11–41.

Reiss, Albert J., Jr. and Jeffrey A. Roth. 1993. *Understanding and Preventing Violence*. Washington, DC: National Academy Press.

Rokeach, Milton and Sancra J. Ball-Rokeach. 1989. "Stability and Change in American Value Priorities. 1968–81." *American Psychologist* 44:775–84.

Rosell, Christine. 1975–6. "School Desegregation and White Flight." *Political Science Quarterly* 90:675–95.

Rosenfeld, Richard. 1986. "Urban Crime Rates: Effects of Inequality: Welfare Dependency, Region, and Race." pp. 116–30 in J. M. Byrne and R. J. Sampson (eds.) *The Social Ecology of Crime*. New York: Springer-Verlag.

Rossi, Peter H., Richard A. Berk and Kenneth J. Lenihan. 1980. *Money, Work and Crime: Experimental Evidence*. New York: Academic Press.

Rusche, Georg and Otto Kirchheimer. 1939. *Punishment and Social Structure*. New York: Columbia University Press.

Sabol, William J. 1989. "The Dynamics of Unemployment and Imprisonment in England and Wales. 1946–1985." *Journal of Quantitative Criminology* 5:147–68.

Savelsberg, Joachim. 1994. "Knowledge, Domination, and Criminal Punishment." *American Journal of Sociology* 99:911–43.

Scull, Andrew T. 1977. *Decarceration: Community Treatment and the Radical View*. Englewood Cliffs, NJ: Prentice-Hall.

Schwendinger, Herman and Julia Schwendinger. 1974, *Sociologists of the chair: A Radical Analysis of the Formative years of North American Socoiology, 1883–1922*. Newyork: Basic Books.

Sellin, J. Thorsten. 1976. *Slavery and the Penal System*. New York: Elsevier.

Service, Elmer R. 1973. *Origins of the State and Civilization: The Process of Cultural Evolution*. New York: W. W. Norton.

Shane-Dubow, Sandra, Alice P. Brown, and Erik Olsen. 1985. *Sentencing Reform in the United States: History, Context, and Effect*. Washington, DC: U.S. Government Printing Office.

Shelef, Leon. 1975. "From Restitution to Repressive Law." *Archive Européenes de Sociology* 16:6–45.

Shichor, David and Dale K. Sechrest (eds.) 1996. *Three Strikes and You're Out: Vengeance as Public Policy*. Thousand Oaks, CA: Sage.

Simpson, Myles E. 1985. "Violent Crime, Income Inequality, and Regional Culture: Another Look." *Sociological Focus* 18:199–208.

Smith, T. W. 1990. "Social Inequality in Cross-national Perspective," pp. 21–31 in J. W. Becker, J. A. Dais, P. Estes and P. P. Mohler (eds.) *Attitudes to Inequality and the Role of Government*. Rijswijk, the Netherlands. Social en Cultural Planbureau.

Snell, Tracy L. 1995. *Correctional Populations in the United States, 1993*. NCJ-15621. Washington, DC: Bureau of Justice Statistics.

Spitzer, Steven. 1975. "Punishment and Social Organization: A Study of Durkheim's Theory of Penal Evolution." *Law and Society Review* 9:613–35.

Steel, Brent S. and Mary Ann E. Steger. 1988. "Crime: Due Process Liberalism Versus Law-and-Order Conservatism," pp. 74–110 in R. Tatalovich and B. W. Daynes (eds.) *Social Regulatory Policy: Moral Controversies in American Politics*. Boulder, CO: Westview Press.

Straus, Murray A. and Richard J. Gelles, 1990. *Physical Violence in American Families: Risk Factors and Adaptations to Violence in 8,145 Families*. New Brunswick, NJ: Transaction Publishers.

Straus, Murray A., Richard J. Gelles and Susan Steinmetz. 1980. *Behind Closed Doors: Violence in the American Family*. New York: Anchor.

Taylor, Ian, Paul Walton and Jock Young. 1973. *The New Criminology: For a Social Theory of Deviance*. New York: Harper and Row.

Thornberry, Terence P. and R.L. Christenson. 1984. "Unemployment and Criminal Involvement: An Investigation of Reciprocal Causal Structures." *American Sociological Review* 49:398–411.

Tonry, Michael. 1988. "Structured Sentencing," pp. 267–337 in M. Tonry and N. Morris (eds.) *Crime and Justice: A Review of Research*, vol. 10. Chicago: University of Chicago Press.

——. 1993. "Racial Disproportion in U.S. Prisons." *British Journal of Criminology*.

——. 1995. *Malign Neglect – Race, Crime, and Punishment in America*. New York: Oxford University Press.

——. 1997. "Ethnicity, Crime and Immigration," pp. 231–59 in M. Tonry (ed.) *Ethnicity, Crime, and Immigration: Comparative and Cross-National Perspectives*. Chicago: University of Chicago Press.

Torbet, Patricia, Richard Gable, Hunter Hurst IV, Imogene Montgomery, Linda Szymanowski and Douglas Thome. 1996. *State Responses to Serious and Violent Juvenile Crime*. Washington, DC: Office of Juvenile Justice and Delinquency Prevention.

Treviño, A. Javier 1996. *The Sociology of Law: Classical and Contemporary Perspectives*. New York: St. Martin's Press.

Twentieth Century Fund Task Force on Criminal Sentencing. 1976. *Fair and Certain Punishment*. New York: McGraw-Hill.

United Nations. 1995. *1993 Demographic Yearbook*. New York: Nations.

Unnithan, N. Prabha and Hugh P. Whitt. 1992. "Inequality, Economic Development and Lethal Violence: A Cross-Sectional Analysis of Suicide and Homicide." *International Journal of Comparative Sociology* 33:182–96.

Van den Haag, Ernest. 1975. *Punishing Criminals*. New York: Basic Books.

Votey, Harold, Jr. 1991. "Employment, Age, Race, and Crime: A Labor-Theoretic Investigation." *International Review of Law and Economics* 14:103–9.

Wallace, Don. 1981. "The Political Economy of Incarceration Trends in Late U.S. Capitalism: 1971–1977." *Insurgent Sociologist* 10:59–66.

Warr, Mark. 1995. "The Polls-Poll Trends: Public Opinion on Crime and Punishment." *Public Opinion Quarterly* 59:296–310.

Wessel, David. 1997. "America's Wealth is Being Distributed a Bit More Evenly, Fed Survey Shows." *Wall Street Journal* (January 24):A2.

Westergaard, John. 1995. *Who Gets What? The Hardening of Class Inequality in the Late Twentieth Century*. Cambridge, MA: Polity.

Western, Bruce and Katherine Beckett. 1999. "How Unregulated is the U.S. Labor Market? The Dynamics of Jobs and Jails, 1980–1995." *American Journal of Sociology* 104:1030–60.

Wicharraya, Tamasak. 1995. *Simple Theory, Hard Reality: The Impact of Sentencing Reforms on Courts, Prisons, and Crime*. Albany, NY: State University of New York Press.

Wilbank, William. 1987. *The Myth of a Racist Criminal Justice System*, Monterey, CA: Brooks/Cole.

Williams, David. 1980. "The Role of Prisons in Tanzania: An Historical Perspective." *Crime and Social Justice* 13 (Summer):27–38.

Wilson, James Q. 1975. *Thinking About Crime*. New York: Basic Books.

Wilson, William Julius. 1987. *The Truly Disadvantaged: The Inner City, the Underclass, and Public Policy*. Chicago, IL: University of Chicago Press.

Winnick, Andrew J. 1989. *Toward Two Societies: The Changing Distributions of Income and Wealth in the United States since 1960*. New York: Praeger.

Wolff, Edward N. 1995a. *How the Pie Is Sliced: America's Growing Concentration of Wealth in America*. New York: The Twentieth Century Fund.

——. 1995b. *Top Heavy: A Study of the Increasing Inequality of Wealth in America*. New York: The Twentieth Century Fund.

World Bank, 1994. *World Development Report 1994: Infrastructure for Development.* New York: Oxford University Press.

———. 1995. *World Tables, 1995.* Baltimore, MD Johns Hopkins University.

Yeager, Matthew G. 1979. "Unemployment and Imprisonment." *Journal of Criminology and Criminal Law* 70:586–8.

Young, Warren and Mark Brown. 1993. "Cross-National Comparisons of Imprisonment." pp. 1–49 in Michael Tonry (ed.) *Crime and Justice: A Review of Research 17.* Chicago: Universithy of Chicago Press.

Zimring, Franklin E. and Gordon Hawkins. 1995. *Incapacitation: Penal Confinement and the Restraint of Crime.* New York: Oxford University Press.

Chapter 37

Anthony Bottoms

ALTERNATIVES TO PRISON

From: Anthony Bottoms (2005), 'Alternatives to prison', *Criminology in Cambridge*, the Newsletter of the Institute of Criminology, University of Cambridge, Issue 6: 3, 14–15.

IN MARCH 2003, THE Esmée Fairbairn Foundation announced the establishment of an Independent Inquiry into Alternatives to Prison, chaired by Lord Coulsfield, a recently retired Scottish appeal judge. Later the same year, I was appointed as Research Director to the Inquiry.

The research task was a challenging one, but it was made easier by the Esmée Fairbairn Foundation generously providing significant funds to accomplish our goals. The main task was to provide a thorough and impartial review of relevant empirical research that could be drawn on by the Coulsfield Commissioners as they formulated their recommendations. Additionally, I was encouraged from the outset to consider undertaking a small piece of original empirical research that would inform the Commission's work.

Lord Coulsfield and the other commissioners were helpful and supportive through-out, and encouraged us to publish the research findings independently. So it was that, last November, a research volume entitled *Alternatives to Prison: Options for an Insecure Society* was released simultaneously with the Coulsfield Commission's report. Besides myself, the research volume had two other editors, one from each of the two universities in which I now work: Sue Rex from the Institute of Criminology, Cambridge (now of the Home Office) and Gwen Robinson from Sheffield University. We were also immensely fortunate to be able to assemble a group of leading scholars – representing ten U.K. universities in all – to provide well-researched chapters on a wide range of topics such as reparative and restorative approaches, rehabilitative and reintegrative approaches, electronic monitoring, dealing with substance-misusing offenders in the community, intensive projects for prolific and persistent offenders, factors guiding sentencing decisions, and sentence management.

What were the highlights of all this work? I would like to mention just four. The first concerns the use of prison. A thorough statistical review by Chris Lewis (Portsmouth University, formerly of the Home Office Research Section) on trends in crime, sentenc-ing, and prison populations, clearly showed that the large rise in the English prison population over the last decade was not the result of an increase in crime or its seriousness.

Rather, for any given offence, both the rate of imprisonment and the average length of sentence had increased. In 1993, for example, in the broad offence category of theft and handling (a category that includes many minor cases), 8 percent were imprisoned, 37 percent fined, and 25 percent received a community penalty. By 2002, the respective proportions were dramatically different – 22 percent, 19 percent, and 37 percent. These data also show another important trend, namely that, as well as an increased use of imprisonment, there has also been a strong recent tendency for courts in England and Wales to use community sentences instead of fines for more minor cases. This tendency, of course, has the unfortunate consequence of overloading probation service personnel with cases of lower strategic importance for the criminal justice system.

Simultaneously with the Coulsfield Inquiry's deliberations, the think-tank CIVITAS published a report arguing that the rise in the prison population in England and Wales was probably causally linked to the recent reduction in crime – that is, more severe punishments had created a reduction in crime through deterrent and incapacitative effects. My own review chapter in the Coulsfield volume examines this possibility in the light of, especially, the extensive US evidence on these topics. It concludes that the evidence for reductions in crime due to the deterrent effects of harsher sentencing is very weak. The evidence for incapacitation is stronger, but after a time of prison expansion (such as has recently been experienced in England) 'diminishing returns from incapacitation set in because the most serious and prolific offenders are already incarcerated'. Therefore, CIVITAS's argued policy case to the Coulsfield Commission – for a further increase in the prison population to achieve further reductions in crime – could not realistically be supported.

A second research highlight concerns the potential for various alternatives to prison to achieve reductions in re-offending. Unfortunately, some commentators have made some very rash statements on this topic in recent years – including the official Halliday Report of 2001, which dared to speak of a possible 16 percentage point reduction in the national re-offending rate if offender behaviour programmes were 'developed and applied as intended' (para 1.49).

More recent research results are substantially more modest. Nevertheless, the chapter by Peter Raynor (Swansea University) in the *Alternatives to Prison* volume emphasises that promising evidence for rehabilitative effectiveness does exist (both for programmes and for wider aspects of supervision). Raynor is, however, clear that there is no 'magic bullet', and that 'the [politically-inspired] rush to "go to scale" after hasty and incomplete evaluation must be slowed' (p. 217). Other modestly promising research results are also to be found scattered throughout the volume, for example, in relation to 'reintegrative' and constructive community service placements and restorative justice approaches (Gill McIvor, Stirling University); and a reduction in the rate of offending among prolific offenders while participating in (but not after leaving) intensive community-based projects (Anne Worrall and Rob Mawby, Keele University). The difficult task for policymakers is to recognise and build on modestly promising results of this kind, rather than succumbing to unrealistic demands for instant dramatic success stories.

A third matter well worth highlighting is sentence management, a vital but rather neglected topic considered in a chapter by Gwen Robinson and Jim Dignan (Sheffield University). Here a particularly important point concerns what the authors call the 'neglected asset' of the supervisor/supervisee relationship. In their own words: 'within a discourse which emphasises the "management" of offenders it has become unfashionable to talk about the "relational basis" of work with offenders . . . But in the face of a trend . . . toward specialist practice and the fragmentation of supervision, a growing body of research indicates that both the consistency and quality of offender/supervisor relationships are central to effective practice, in terms of promoting motivation and compliance (in the short term) and desistance (in the longer term' (p.322). In the light of the forthcoming changes to be brought about by the creation of the National Offender Management Service (see below), it is vital to acknowledge and build upon this set of research results.

Fourthly, our Coulsfield research volume is perhaps unusual among 'alternatives to prison' texts in placing strong emphasis on research into public opinion on sentencing. The editors' introductory chapter stresses that the contemporary 'alternatives to prison' debate cannot ignore the decisive shifts in the economic and social character of Western societies that have taken place in the last half-century; hence the subtitle of our volume ('options for an insecure society') was deliberately and carefully chosen. Within such a society, the issue of public opinion is pivotal, and it is examined in two chapters in the volume. Shadd Maruna and Anna King of the Institute of Criminology provide an overview of research findings, plus a glimpse of their research among various types of community in the south of England. They are able to show that certain core beliefs and values, such as 'offenders are redeemable,' or 'ultimately, crime is a choice', are strongly associated with attitudes in favour of, or against, community penalties. So too are expressive variables such as attitudes towards youth in contemporary societies, and perceptions of collective trust, or its absence, in a neighbourhood. Building on Maruna and King's work, and (with their permission) using some of the same questions, Andrew Wilson and I added a more explicitly 'community' dimension to the debate through empirical work in two high-crime areas in Sheffield. (This was the 'small piece of original empirical research' that the Esmée Fairbairn Foundation had encouraged us to conduct.) Although these two areas had very similar crime rates, the general public in one had markedly less punitive attitudes than was the case in the other. The two (linked) main explanations that we tentatively put forward to explain this very unexpected result were: first, that the more punitive area seemed to have more 'on-street disorders,' making the population more anxious (and therefore perhaps more punitive); and second, that the population in the less punitive area appeared to believe, to a significantly greater extent than in the other area, that the authorities listened to residents and were willing to put into place sensible social control policies. On this reading, then, the adequacy of general social control in an area is inextricably linked to the likelihood of being able to develop community penalties that command public confidence.

In the 'insecure society' in which we now live, the subject of alternatives to prison inevitably has a political dimension. This was emphasised, during the life of the Coulsfield Commission, by the publication of the Carter Report and the government's controversial decision to proceed with the creation of a new National Offender Management Service, in which the concept of 'contestability' is central.

How these plans will ultimately translate into local practice remains, at the time of writing, unclear. However, those of us who provided the research reviews for *Alternatives to Prison* believe and hope that our work will be of value not only to the Coulsfield Commissioners, but to those developing regional and local practice in this new context.

References

Bottoms, A.E., S. Rex, and G. Robinson, eds. 2004. *Alternatives to Prison: Options for an Insecure Society*. Cullompton: Willan.

Coulsfield Commision. 2004. *Crime, Courts and Confidence Reports of an Independent Inquiry into Alternatives of Prison*. London: Stationery Office.

Home Office. 2001. *Making Punishments Work: Report of a Review of the Sentencing Framework in England and Wales*. (The Halliday Report.) London: Home Office.

PART EIGHT

Governing through crime: coercion or consent?

PRISON EXPANSION AND ACCOMPANYING widespread fear of crime in America began at a time during the late 1980s when inequality had grown greater than at any time since the eve of the Great Depression. In Britain, it began about half a decade later. Jonathan Simon has described the United States as "governing through crime" so central had this phenomenon become by the 1990s. Disciplinary power operated in the shadows of juridico-political power, in Simon's view, to powerfully shape life chances through processes of classifying and social sorting. Such governance, through the carceral stance it embraced, designated the social problem of the day as criminal dangerousness in our midst and pointed to a particular population as a source of the problem to be targeted. Ultimately, the carceral turn became an end in itself as the purpose of rehabilitation was supplanted by an "actuarial justice" that targeted risk by means of a "managerialism" that simply "warehoused" offenders instead. This is a penetrating diagnosis that this volume embraces even as it seeks to complement it by building on and extending it and other explorations, such as those of David Garland, Bruce Western and Kathryn Beckett, Anthony Bottoms, and Barbara Hudson, of why this carceral turn has occurred.

The beginning of the carceral turn was also a time when conservative regimes, Reagan in America and Thatcher in Britain, built on financial strains in the welfare state to institute neo-liberal policies and to dismantle redistributive programmes. They were conditions that had previously led Jurgen Habermas, in his book *Legitimation Crisis,* to anticipate that social conflicts, long pacified by the meliorative policies of the welfare state, would resurface and precipitate a crisis of political authority where its legitimation is challenged.

During these years, technological change and de-industrialization combined to disadvantage the relatively unskilled residents of inner cities in new ways. As we have seen, these neighborhoods are disproportionately inhabited by ethnic minority groups both in America and also, I would add, in Britain. These are areas where residents experience the police as absent and where subcultural adaptations are relied on to enable youth to walk the streets safely. Devastated by disadvantage, these inner city residents also face laws, police and courts which they, particularly the young, believe to represent norms as well as interests at odds with their own.

It is said that regimes differ in terms of whether they govern primarily by power or authority. Under authority, commands are seen as legitimate and subjectively accepted. Thus, in democracies, authority assumes special importance because a resort to force by a regime weakens its claim to represent the will of the people. Authority can anchor its legitimation, which is the basis of its claim on the acceptance of a people, in one of three ways: tradition, the charisma of a leader, or legality. Unlike monarchies, which have drawn on the traditional awe in which kings and queens are held, democracies have relied on rational–legal authority – claiming that its officials are lawfully chosen and its rules legally drawn. Democracy therefore lacks the gravitational pull of acceptance through long habit and relies heavily on appeals to reasoned decisions of its people instead. This restricted capacity to resort to coercion, combined with reliance on the free choices of its citizens, makes democracy especially fragile.

Among the greatest dangers to the authority that binds together a democracy is that its laws may diverge from the norms held by its populace. Habermas has argued that laws, if they are to be viewed as legitimate, should embody norms whose acceptance all those bound could, through reasoned communication, under specific non-coercive conditions, ultimately come to hold. Habermas envisions law as evoking action of the sort that would unfold if all humans acted morally. The influence of law and acceptance of its legitimacy are fullest, he suggests, when laws are in harmony with beliefs and customs. When laws and norms diverge, we have the basis for a "legitimation crisis." This is because law – the legitimating basis of authority – is weakened.

As authority weakens in a context where conflicts resurface, Habermas argues, officials, lacking a welfarist alternative, tend to shift their reliance from participatory democratic dialogue, whose outcome they no longer dominate, to more coercive approaches of control, surveillance and policing. Specifically, democratic governance moves from a basis of consent toward coercion. While such power seeks to cloak itself in a mantle of authority, Habermas reminds us that the techniques remain inherently coercive. Sumner suggests that arguments to the contrary – that such techniques are needed to protect society – are hegemonic.

Colin Sumner points out that class tensions in western society have for many decades been eased by welfarist initiatives that ameliorated the worst hardships. In the 1970s, many advanced industrial societies entered a period of "fiscal crisis" due to the growing competitiveness of a globalizing world, economic inefficiencies, and the growing burden posed by the costs of supporting a welfare state. As redistributive social welfare has been cut back to ease this crisis, class tensions have reappeared and a sense of the hegemonic nature of political authority has strengthened in some quarters. The sense that "big money" is influential grew stronger. Political participation declined, as Robert Putnam has shown. As participation has waned, the struggle to hold political institutions accountable has also weakened. As a consequence, those institutions have been freed to shift toward their more familiar terrain of bureaucratic autonomy, secrecy and power. At times, the claim of democratic authority to represent the popular will has been openly challenged.

Increasingly, the state will has emphasized control and heightened policing, surveillance and the management of risk.

In the context of this historical trend, growing diversity is amplifying the challenge at hand. Economically, socially and ethnically diverse peoples hold dear quite different norms and values. Beliefs vary across cultures. Tyler has shown that this makes it inherently difficult for laws to reflect equally the norms of all groups. It is highly challenging, whatever the political will, to represent all sides of an array of conflicting and contradictory worldviews. It is therefore especially difficult to produce laws that satisfy all. Tyler has shown that where people believe laws to have been made in ways that are procedurally fair, they are more likely to accept them as legitimate whether they agree with the law or not. However, while procedural fairness can help, the underlying divergence of laws and norms remains a continuing problem. Where procedural guarantees are weakened or replaced by discretionary practices, the tensions build more intensely as they no longer have procedural fairness to ease them.

Declining civic participation also aggravates the crisis. Scholars have also begun to debate whether participation is declining, changing or both. Habermas claims that with the rise of a culture of consumption during the late nineteenth century, citizens became more politically passive. Since then, their capacity for genuine dialogue with the state that is so vital to democracy, has paled. Putnam counters that citizens have remained active but that work and lifestyle have changed so that, in contrast with earlier flowering of voluntary associations, more activity is undertaken alone.

Thus, the image that emerges of American society is of a people, large segments of whom feel increasingly estranged from a state whose authority is perceived, at least by some, as in crisis. In this context, what is happening to cause the United States to emerge as so draconian a power that it now imprisons the greatest share of its people of any nation in the world? My claim is that, amidst a crisis of which Habermas, Simon, Garland, Greenberg, Western and Beckett, and others have all described parts, a political transformation has been accomplished of significant proportions, whose roots lie equally in the Cold War, the Nixonian vision and Straussian political theory. Such politics, rife with creative subjectivity, seeks to redraw the contours of American and, indeed, democratic politics for the next century.

Now, the state is turning to a coercive repertoire of power and force in its quest for security. Drawing on concepts articulated by Carl Schmitt, as passed on through Leo Strauss, policymakers in America have moved in various ways to weaken the so-called "paralyzing neutrality of liberalism and its "rule of law" both internationally and domestically. Initially, this took the form of "culture wars" that contested the imagery of welfarism and transformed "dependency" into a trope of disadvantage. Later embracing "performativity" and a conception of our infinite capacity, like Madonna, to reinvent ourselves, the culture wars have gradually responsibilized the individual, no matter how disadvantaged, for what one is – depicting it as an accomplished, and thus chosen, "performance."

Drawing on a Schmittian "polarization" of the world into "friend" and "foe," the second Bush presidency has moved to divide American society, as it has the international community through its war-making, and to exacerbate and build on the repudiation of each segment by the other as the basis for a long term political vision. By drawing the line of division to isolate the most disadvantaged and problem-ridden segments of society and then responsibilizing such families culturally for their lifestyle, the effort is to depict those individuals as having chosen depravity. In the extreme version, this is portrayed as a moral flaw. By responsibiliz-ing individuals for such a lifestyle, this makes any defense of the "disadvantaged" or overture on their behalf by political opponents very risky. Like earlier Nixonian uses of "affirmative action" to consciously "polarize" the American electorate as far to the left as possible as a basis for moving to sweep the centre into his electoral camp, the "carceral turn" has simply inverted the strategy. These punitive policies have attempted to divide society as near to the bottom as possible, isolate that "dependent" group as having chosen depravity, and then associate that "unspeakable" lifestyle with Democratic politics. The goal is to mobilize the middle class in an "opposition of the decent" to the lifestyle of the disadvantaged.

Such policies find comfort in the erosion of rights and procedural quarantees and in the increasingly discretionary practices that guide the operation of criminal "justice." Suspension of rights, in the name of security, has grown more frequent. Whereas Schmitt initially spoke of "state of exception", wherein constitutional protections are suspended, as temporary, Agamben argues that the "state of exception" has now become a perma-nent paradigm for governing.

It is a domestic strategy that parallels a global one in which the "rule of law" is being replaced by what Pjeworsky terms the "rule by law" where law's power comes to be dominated by the powerful. Under the image of protecting society, incursions on peoples' right to self-determination are being made apace. Embracing cultural multiplicity, the culture wars dispute openly the possibility of truth in public life and query to what extent, if at all, it continues to make sense to speak of universal citizenship or whether the very notion of universalism always marginalizes some? This is not the colonization of the life world by rationalization described by Habermas. It is a conscious process wherein a regime works to occupy and then transform the culture and institutions of a society as a means of con-trol. In hundreds of small ways the infrastructure of our democratic institutions is being dismantled and the balance of power is shifting from public to private. One is reminded of Arendt's observation that the assault on rights almost always begins with the least popular groups.

Chapter 38

Jonathan Simon

GOVERNING THROUGH CRIME

From: Jonathan Simon (1997), excerpts from 'Governing through crime', in Lawrence M. Friedman and George Fisher (eds), *The Crime Conundrum: Essays on Criminal Justice*, Boulder, CO: Westview Press, pp. 171–189.

GOVERNMENT, PUNISHMENT, AND MODERNITY

THE CLAIM THAT OUR society is "postmodern" depends in the end on what one thinks has changed in the present that requires breaking the useful interpretive frames that have been associated with modernity. This paper proposes that one powerful candidate for such a change is the historic relationship between government, punishment, and modernity. [. . .]

Though Durkheim's evolutionary claims have been largely debunked, his essential insight that the division of labor makes it possible to coordinate individuals without as much reliance on the heavy hand of state coercion remains viable. Moreover, Durkheim's picture of a society whose very diversity, dynamism, and complexity made it capable of achieving a deeper level of coordination than simpler societies remains an important part of our self identity as moderns. In a number of different ways the long association of modernization with the diminution of crime and punishment as the central features of social order maintenance seems to be undergoing some kind of reversal.

As historians of crime and violence have largely come to agree, urban life in the past was more rather than less violent. While lacking statistical precision, scholars suggest that with scale of population taken into account, cities in Europe and its North American offshoots have experienced declines in violence from the sixteenth century on, and especially after the middle of the nineteenth century, a process that various scholars have credited to work discipline, moral education, and the deepening interiority of the self. This trend began to collapse in the 1940s and reverse itself, rising sharply in the 1950s and 1960s to levels that continue today.

Imprisonment rates in the United States fluctuated within a limited range from the beginning of reliable statistics in the 1920s through the late 1970s. Since then they have experienced an unprecedented upsurge that continues after tripling the portion of the population incarcerated to more than 409 per 100,000. Among African-American males the figure is ten times as great. When we look at total correctional supervision the figures are even more dramatic. More than two percent of the total adult population and more than thirty-three percent of young African-American male adults are in some form of custody or under some form of penal supervision on any given day.

One penal practice that acts with particular sensitivity as a marker of modernity is the death penalty, or rather its diminution. Limiting or abolishing the death penalty has been associated with the processes of modernization and democratization almost everywhere. Since World War II virtually all European nations have abandoned the practice altogether or reserved it for categories of atrocities that only rarely come to pass. In the United States, however, the practice of the death penalty is undergoing a resurgence. Political support for the death penalty has grown rapidly since the 1970s and now commands an overwhelming majority of virtually every relevant demographic group. [. . .]

Fear of crime has become a dominant theme of political culture. Because the incarcerated population, despite its unprecedented growth, is still small relative to other sites of governance like schools, businesses, and families, it is tempting to view it as a specialized sector. It is easy to show that incorporation into this sector is quite unequally spread and is among the most problematic differences in advanced industrial societies. But governing through crime seems to have a broader purchase in a number of ways that are harder to measure than the formal jurisdictional demography of the criminal justice system: A shift of attention to criminal justice system elements in the business of Congress and state legislatures; a dramatic over-representation of crime and punishment views as issues in election campaigns for all kinds of office, the more so the more central and powerful the position; the reinvigoration in all sorts of institutions, from colleges to businesses to families, of governance by rule and sanction; the obsessive media attention to crime and punishment that has both drawn on crime as the preferred metaphor for all forms of social anxiety and highlighted acts of punishment or retribution as the primary way of resolving disputes of almost any sort.

In summary, a historical diminution in the significance of crime and punishment to governance has ended. Indeed, something like a reversal is taking place. To a degree that would have surprised the sociological observers of modernity in the nineteenth and the first half of the twentieth century, we are governing ourselves through crime.

GOVERNANCE

The central argument of this essay is that advanced industrial societies (particularly the United States) are experiencing not a crisis of crime and punishment but a crisis of governance that has led them to prioritize crime and punishment as the preferred contexts for governance. I want to refer to this phenomenon as "governing through crime." By governance I mean not simply the actions of the state but all efforts to guide and direct the conduct of others. [. . .]

We govern through crime to the extent to which crime and punishment become the occasions and the institutional contexts in which we undertake to guide the conduct of others (or even of ourselves).

It has been obvious for some time that crime was casting a disproportionate shadow over what we primarily identify with governance, i.e., politicians and the electoral process of democracy. Every U.S. presidential campaign since Goldwater-Johnson in 1964 has been fought partly on the turf of crime. Since the reaction to the "Willie Horton" ad on behalf of George Bush in 1988, the salience of crime and its interconnection with race have been taken as given features of American politics. If crime kept a lower profile in the 1996 campaign, it was only because both candidates wholly gave themselves up to the public fixation on the "crisis" of crime. Although crime rates appear to have dropped significantly in recent years, a trend that has been exhaustively covered in the media and that may continue in the short term, a poll taken at the end of May 1996 showed crime as the top issue on the minds of the public. [. . .]

Less obvious are the ways in which crime has become a linchpin of governance within the less celebrated but more primary settings of governance. In schools, prevention of crime and drug use has arguably been the most significant agenda item for the last two decades (having replaced integration, among other concerns). Even school uniforms, now suddenly back in fashion, are justified in the name of identifying non-students attempting to infiltrate the school for gang or drug sales activities. In the workplace, non-crime themes still predominate, but drugs and crime are moving up on the margins of struggles about how work shall be governed. We see management testing employees for drugs and unions threatening to "drop a dime" on employers who violate environmental regulations. [. . .]

EXPLANATIONS

The priority of governing through crime might sensibly be thought to arise in response to a genuine increase in crime. As I suggested above, the long curve of declining violence in Western societies seems to have ended in the 1940s. But the steepest increases in crime, and violent crime in particular, came in the 1950s and 1960s. Since then, crime rates appear to have fluctuated within a relatively shallow range. The demand for punishment, however, escalated in the midst of this flat period. Even a political lag would not explain why the demand has actually grown stronger throughout the last decade and a half. This latecoming fixation on crime may be explained as a response to the selective crime reporting of the media. [. . .]

We might turn instead for an explanation to the resurgence of conservative political forces that began in the late 1970s in the United States and other mature industrial societies, and persisted through the early 1990s (at least). The rhetoric of conservatives suggests they favor the criminal law as a tool of state governance and regard highly punitive private norms to be the preferred strategy in other settings for governance. From this perspective we can see the crime and violence surge of the 1960s as mobilizing support for conservative policies and vindicating the conservative critique of liberal governments as overly "permissive."

There is doubtless some link between the conservative ascendancy and the trend toward governing through crime, but there are also reasons to doubt that the former explains the latter. For one thing contemporary liberals also find themselves drawn toward punishment as a locus for governance. Laws and institutional rules punishing racist speech, domestic violence, sexual harassment, and pornography, for example, have become major agenda items for some liberals. Likewise, twentieth century conservatives often embraced noncriminal approaches to governance as an alternative to social instability. It is interesting that in a period of conservative ascendancy during which the right has articulated aspirations to govern through patriotism, work, and family, as well as crime, it is largely with respect to crime and punishment that there has been significant legislative success.

Even if conservative ideology does not drive the trend toward governing through crime, conservatives in virtually all late- or postmodern societies have benefited politically from their ability to articulate the perception, shared by many of their fellow citizens, that traditional and traditionally modernist means of regulating youth — including families, schools, the labor force, churches, the military, etc. — have weakened. Voters in all these societies, but especially the United States, have affirmed the belief that social control is breaking down and that punishment of crime is the most promising strategy for checking that breakdown.

From this perspective it is helpful to recall that crime and punishment issues have long been associated with the difficulties of governing urban populations. Crime had literally mapped and written the cities during the nineteenth century. By the beginning of the twentieth century, however, the singular figures of the criminal and the homogeneous dangerous classes were no longer central targets of social policy because new practices and sciences made it possible to govern cities through new handles on industry, ethnicity and nationality, youthfulness, and ignorance. Even crime and punishment were reconfigured around these agendas. For much of the twentieth century, punishment of crime was displaced as the key to urban governance by a focus on housing, public health, social work, and education.

This family of strategies has been associated with a variety of terms and figures including Keynesianism, Fordism, collectivism, and the social. These new maps depicted social life as distributions of aggregate risks that could be governed by redistributing them. Elsewhere, I, along with others, have described some of the properties of these new governance strategies and of the new political technologies they deployed, including insurance, case work, and social statistics. One of the key elements in constructing this new approach to governing was the social response to industrial accidents and the quasi-industrial consumer accidents that have [involved] designing new ways to intervene in [a workplace embedded in] power relations. But the accident could play this role only after a long effort, never completed, to be free of the implication of crime.

When President Clinton repeated during his 1996 State of the Union Address that the era of big government was over, he was echoing the call made successfully by the Republican candidates for Congress in 1994 that the size of the federal government should be reduced. But he may also have been adverting to a less visible point. The era is over when it seemed plausible to govern society through "big-ness." That sense of scale is exactly what programs like unemployment insurance, worker's compensation, and the like were about: harnessing insurance and related technologies to balance the risks produced by industrial society with the very scale that seemed the source of much of this risk.

The era of "big government" went well beyond the state. It was a style of private sector organization as well, exemplified by the great unionized industries like automobiles and steel in which the control of large oligopolies over market conditions helped make possible a labor peace based on cooperative shifting of the cost onto the larger structures of consumption and investment. Insurance companies were once a symbol of this era and the sort of governance it promoted. The "good hands" of Allstate, for example, were giant hands that invited everybody in. Prudential invited Americans to link their precarious individual circumstances to the strength of its collective capital by owning "a piece of the rock." Their latest ad advises consumers to "be your own rock."

Lately we seem to be experiencing a crisis of these modes of governance. The United States and other advanced industrial societies have found themselves re-evaluating systems of collective risk distribution like welfare, public education, unemployment insurance, and worker's compensation. The failure of modest national health insurance in the United States in 1993 was a potent reminder of how muddled the basic narratives and rationalities supporting these governance modalities have become. Governing through crime, at its broadest, might be looked at as a response to this crisis, both a reaching back to real or imagined strategies for maintaining what appears to be a precarious social order, and a reaching forward toward new platforms to govern a social order that truly is undergoing remarkable demographic and economic change.

A number of scholars have begun to describe the emergence of a neo-liberal family of technologies of governing. In place of the great collectivist risk distribution systems, neo-liberal techniques re-emphasize the individual as a critical manager of risk, but do so through deliberate steering mechanisms rather than the threats and exhortations of traditional liberalism. Socializing risk inevitably undermined discipline (just as its critics said it would). The new strategies aim to hold individuals more accountable, or to "responsibilize" them, as some observers have aptly described it. Governing through crime is also a way of imposing this new model of governance on the population.

GOVERNING THROUGH SECURITY

An observer of political discourse in the United States might believe that people were increasingly governed by a logic that left virtually everything important in life to personal choice disciplined only by the fear of unremitting punishment for those who stepped across the lines drawn by the criminal law. What this picture would miss is how intensely we are regulated in the spaces where middle-class people spend most of their time. Spaces of work and consumption, and those hybrids like airports and shopping centers that are spaces of both, have become sites of extensive and detailed management. Private associations have increasingly filled in the regulatory gap left by official government. Some of this takes the shape of quasi-penal norms, like rules against smoking, playing radios, or skate boarding. Much of the new governance takes the shape of highly engineered environments that are designed to avoid recognized hazards and mitigate others without even seeking the compliance of the subject.

What the governments of many of these places share, besides the demands of a market economy, is a focus on the problem of security. They are focused on making people safe, for themselves and for others. Crime, of course, is a primary form of insecurity for these regimes, but one can govern crime without governing through crime. Governing through security focuses on the potential for harm rather than its source or explanations. While everything is open as a possible strategy for such a risk management approach, including punishments, there is no investment in punishment as a political ceremony. A security regime, in the end, is not there to enforce individual adherence to performance norms except where that is an effective way to minimize cost.

These techniques have been most widely adopted by private organizations responsible for maintaining the security of employees and customers. Perhaps the most famous such organization is the Disney Corporation, whose theme parks are world renowned for amusement. These sites also deserve to be seen as exemplars of risk management in which virtually every aspect has been designed to minimize harmful actions (accidental or otherwise) while at the same time minimizing any appearance of coercive social control, which would be highly incompatible with their primary business of selling family fun. Many of the same technologies are deployed in managing quasi-public spaces around and in large residential, commercial, and mixed-use spaces, which Shearing and Stenning call "mass private property." Another important site for the development of government through security has been international airports, which have had to create governance systems capable of dealing with multiple levels of hazard (every flight going in or out is a potential mass disaster) and a fluctuating human population with little in common besides the haste and anxiety attendant on air travel.

The implications of these risk management or security approaches to governance are a subject in their own right. They constitute an emerging alternative to the more collectivist risk distribution systems that are now in crisis. There are clear political dangers associated with this approach to governance. These techniques are easily turned toward exclusionary ends, something often demanded by the market. They are generally insensitive to the importance of spaces of deviation around which important forms of personal and political mobilization may take place. Here it is sufficient to note that they offer promising responses to those tendencies, discussed above, that seem to be driving the trend toward governing through crime.

Risk management techniques do not involve explicit pooling of risk and thus avoid the political problems that have beset efforts to extend the old collectivist risk distribution framework. Thus, theme parks and airports are utterly social in the sense that they have been designed with the collectivity of users in mind, but they require, among consumers at least, no formal association or common responsibilities.

Risk management techniques do not rely on intersubjectivity to produce order. These spaces are engineered to be navigable by those who share not even language. Airports and shopping centers have long had to cope with diverse users. Their technologies are spreading fast in societies where immigration and multiculturalism are undermining (or at least are perceived as undermining) traditional and modern sources of integration.

Risk management techniques do not invoke the form of sovereign power linked to the criminal law and its chain of discrediting and disabling experiences and associations. [. . .]

AMERICAN EXCEPTIONALISM

Some will argue that governing through crime is largely an American phenomenon. Virtually all of the evidence I have discussed here has been American. Still, for the reasons explored in the section on explanations, we should expect to find governing through crime to be a prominent feature of all societies that are undergoing the process of dismantling the governance strategies of industrial modernity, a process some have connected with the cultural experience of postmodernity.

But even if governing through crime does have corollaries in other societies, the American case is clearly unique in its degree. I can offer two provisional explanations. The first is race. The problem of race has been intertwined in the practices of crime and punishment almost since the beginning of the European settlement of the North American Atlantic coast. . . . Whether or not voters acknowledge such motives to pollsters, it is hard to ignore the continuities between the present situation and a traditional preference for governing predominantly African-American populations in distinct and distinctly less respectable ways.

The second provisional explanation arises from the commitment to democratization for which the United States has been long and justly famous. . . . There is a sense in which our commitment to governing through crime represents a continued commitment to democratic governance. In insisting that we invest in the apparatus that enables us to use punishment to achieve social order, we affirm the sovereignty of each individual. A society with less faith in the capacity of individuals to govern themselves would seek to constrain their behavior – not merely to punish their misbehavior. [. . .]

CONCLUSION: CRIME AND THE POLITICS OF GOVERNANCE

In the spring of 1997, the United States, at least, seems quite committed to governing through crime. The Republican party has declared itself irrevocably attached to this strategy. Republican policies call for massively enlarging the penal system while emphasizing such archaic punishments as the death penalty and highway chain gangs. So little concerned is the party of Lincoln with the impact of this strategy on the nation's racial politics that its congressional delegation has rejected the considered and conservative judgment of the United States Sentencing Commission that our current policy, which punishes dealers in crack cocaine far more harshly than those who traffic in its powdered form, is unjustified and discriminatory against African-Americans. The same party that a century and a quarter ago made unequal punishment, like slavery, an offense against our Constitution, now sneers at the sight of a large portion of the descendants of freedmen locked into a system that directly jeopardizes their ability to participate in a common national economic market and political society. [. . .]

Classical theorists recognized that criminal law was intimately related to the larger strategies of governing society. The leaders of our eighteenth century democratic revolutions gave priority to the abolition of monarchical procedures and the formation of new, lighter, more democratic modes of punishment. These leaders believed that free subjects would respond rationally not to the blunt command of the state, but to the incentive structure of its penal laws. The calculus of penalties urged by Beccaria and Bentham was a real alternative to the excessive punishments associated with monarchical codes – codes that, as far as shaping a free and productive society was concerned, were distinctly dysfunctional.

Are the harsher sentences of today meant to send a signal to free men? It would be hard to take this idea seriously. The implausibility of the classical ideal in the real conditions of urban poverty in America is apparent to those on all sides of the political spectrum. But instead of backing away from our commitment to governing through crime, we openly offer punishment for the purposes of warehousing the untrustworthy.

More ominously, crime and fear of crime continue to drive deeper levels of suburban isolationism. The emerging metropolitan form, with its combination of collapsed urban center and sprawling suburban edge city, with its overlays of race and demonization, constitutes a direct challenge to the ideal of democratic nationhood.

We cannot wish our real urban problems away, but we can make real choices among different orientations toward managing them. Crime will remain an important urban problem for a long time to come no matter what we do about it. But governing through crime reproduces the mentalities and strategies that have helped bring us to this impasse. With the right political choices, we could begin to change those mentalities and strategies tomorrow.

Bibliography

Foucault, M. (1977) *Discipline and Punish*. New York: Vintage.

Foucault, M. (1978) *Le Souci de soi*. Paris: Editions Gallimand.

Foucault, M. (1979) 'On Governmentality' *Ideology and Consciousness*, 6 (Autumn).

Foucaut, M. (1980) *Power/Knowledge*. New York: Pantheon.

Foucaut, M. (1981) 'Omnes et Singulatum' in S. McMurrin (ed.), *Tanner Lectures on Human Values II*. Salt Lake City, UT: University of Utah Press.

Foucaut, M. (1989) *Foucault Live: Interviews 1961–84*. Autonomedia.

Chapter 39

Alan Hunt and Gary Wickham

LAW, GOVERNMENT AND GOVERNMENTALITY

From: Alan Hunt and Gary Wickham (1994), excerpts from 'Law, government and governmentality', in Alan Hunt and Gary Wickham, *Foucault and Law: Toward a Sociology of Law as Governance*, London and Boulder, CO: Pluto Press, pp. 52–55.

ONE OF THE MOST important stages in the development of Foucault's work is the shift from a focus on discipline to government. He describes the general development of his project in terms that are worth quoting at length.

> It was a matter not of studying the theory of penal law in itself, or the evolution of such and such penal institution, but of analyzing the formation of a certain 'punitive rationality' . . . Instead of seeking the explanation in a general conception of the Law, or in the evolving modes of industrial production . . . it seemed to me far wiser to look at the workings of Power . . . I was concerned . . . with the refinement, the elaboration and installation since the seventeenth century, of techniques of 'governing' individuals – that is, for 'guiding their conduct' – in domains as different as the school, the army, and the workshop. Accordingly, the analysis does not revolve around the general principle of Law or the myth of Power, but concerns itself with the complex and multiple practices of a 'governmentality' which presupposes, on the one hand, rational forms, technical procedures, instrumentations through which to operate and, on the other hand, strategic games which subject the power relations they are supposed to guarantee to instability and reversal.
>
> (in Rabinow 1984: 337–338)

Modernity for Foucault is marked by the emergence of 'government' and 'governmentality'. As we have seen he uses the term 'government' in a way that is very different from the conventional sense of state executives and legislatures. One important implication of Foucault's conception of government is that it is consistent with his downgrading of the importance of the state and with it legal regulation. We return below to this relative neglect of the state since it has important implications for his treatment of law.

The reason that Foucault's discussion of 'government' and 'police' is important for our present concern with his treatment of law is that time and again he stresses the essentially non-legal character of his expanded conception of government. He insists that 'government' is

> not a matter of imposing laws on men, but rather of disposing things, that is to say to employ tactics rather than laws, and if need be to use the laws themselves as tactics.
>
> (G 1979: 13)

And again:

> the instruments of government, instead of being laws, now come to be a range of multiform tactics. Within the perspective of government, *law is not what is important*.
>
> (G 1979: 13; emphasis added)

The deployment of 'multiform tactics' is illustrated in the link that exists between 'government' and 'population' where a variety of experts (quantifying, calculating and codifying) scattered across a range of agencies generate social policies that operate both to constitute the 'social problems' at which governmental action is directed and actively to regulate, control and coordinate the targets thus created. Whether Foucault is correct in suggesting that in this context of modern government 'law is not important' . . . [is treated elsewhere].

Foucault abandons the historical distinction between the classical and modern period. In its place he adopts a set of historical stages that push the juridical state back into the feudal period, with the 'administrative state' grounded in 'regulation' emerging in the fifteenth century and the 'governmental state' in the seventeenth and eighteenth centuries (G 1979: 21). The governmental state is characterised by the importance of the themes he had previously announced, the central focus on the regulation of 'the population' (rather than territory) and the role of 'police'. He gives this stage a new designation when he speaks of society being controlled by apparatuses of 'security'. He tries to capture the new form of government by speaking of 'the governmentalisation of the state' by which he seeks to embrace the whole range of governmental activity, the 'multiform tactics'.

A significant implication of this treatment is that it amounts to a tacit renunciation of the view that absolutism marks a more or less sharp transition to the modern forms of power that he had previously encompassed within the 'disciplinary society'. Now there is no break or sharp transition, but rather an expansion in the range and scope of governmental institutions. But it is of the greatest significance that what gets missed in this protracted process, stretching from the eighteenth century to the present, is any attention to the democratisation of the representative institutions and, more generally, with forms of participation in governmental processes, whether it be the rise of political parties or participatory organisations such as trade unions. One further consequence is that there is no place in his treatment for the notion of citizenship and certainly nothing which corresponds to any idea of an expanded citizenship that moves from the formal civil rights of the eighteenth century to the securing of universal franchise . . . and the social citizenship, epitomised by the welfare state, by the mid twentieth century (Marshall 1963).

Foucault's focus is upon the emergence of a concern with 'security' within modern governmental rationality. The English word 'security' does not convey the sense of Foucault's discussion; the term 'welfare' is probably closer. It is embedded in the shift from a view of individuals as 'subjects' to one in which they are conceived as the bearers of 'interests', that is, they are economic subjects, subjects or, to be more precise, 'subjects of the state', considered only in so far as the state requires to regulate their conduct or to demand performance from them, military conscription and imposition of taxes being two central examples. The individual, when considered as a bearer of interests, requires the state to take cognisance of those interests, in their multiplicity and complexity. 'Security' functions not by negative prescription or refusal, but rather through the specification of a range of tolerable variation. Thus liberalism constructs a complex governance within which political, economic and juridical instances of subjectivity are dispersed.

The association of 'security' with 'liberty' marks not merely the rise to prominence of rights discourses but involves the idea that the systematic realisation of political and juridical rights are essential conditions of 'good government' which is itself a precondition for the persistence, stability and prosperity of both economic and political government. Gordon succinctly captures this governmental role of rights: 'disrespect of liberty is not simply an illegitimate violation of rights, but an ignorance or how to govern' (Gordon 1991: 20). It needs to be stressed that Gordon goes significantly beyond Foucault in giving weight to the juridical forms of liberty. This concern with rights and the conditions of prosperity can be seen as reaching a high point in Keynesian economic strategy in which the attempt to master cyclical economic crises and to secure the emblematic goal of full employment are conceived as preconditions of both economic prosperity and political stability. The 'security-liberty' characterisation of liberalism poses the question: *what part does law play in modern governmental rationality?*

Recall that Foucault asserts 'law is not important' (G 1979: 13). His account of the place of law is, in fact, more developed. The transition to modern governmental rationality involves a distinct and significant shift from some of the earlier positions associated with his expulsion of law discussed above. As has been demonstrated, in his major texts produced between 1975 and 1977, *Discipline and Punish, History of Sexuality* and *Power Knowledge*, he equates law with sovereignty and the juridical monarchy. He is at pains to stress not only the dispersion but the privatisation of disciplinary power.

However there are in this group of texts hints of a different conceptualisation, one we can locate as the retreat from a transition from 'law to disciplines' to a new focus on 'law and regulation'. One of his key formulations posits this historical shift from law to regulation. This transition occurs when he suggests that law does not simply 'fade into the background' (HoS 1978: 144). It is this insight that is developed in the 'late Foucault', the Collège de France lectures of 1978 and 1979, the essays 'Governmentality' (G 1979) and 'Omnes et Singulatim' (O&S 1981), the interest in 'liberalism' and more generally, in his concern with the 'government of the self. The root of this change of approach is the basic but important point that 'society' is an entity that had, during the course of the eighteenth and nineteenth centuries, to be discovered, whereas the nation conceived as a 'territory' was something that could be acted upon. But 'society' is a 'complex and independent reality that has its own laws' and thus cannot simply be acted upon (*Foucault Live* 1989: 261). Society necessitates 'good government', getting it right since undesired results and unintended consequences of any active intervention may actually make things worse. It is this caution about the desirability and even possibility of government that sparks his interest in liberalism. In this phase of his work the earlier expulsion of law from modernity is significantly modified. Now his conception of law focuses on the purposive rationality of the legislative output of representative legislatures. He emphasises the increasing particularism of regulatory instruments. The previous conception of law as a totalising and transcendent unity is superseded by the historically specific production of regulatory devices that mediate between state and civil society and between state and individual. Foucault never developed this line of thought, but its presence underpins our claim that the study of the part played by law in modern governance is consistent with and can draw stimulus from Foucault's work.

Bibliography

Burchill, G., C. Gordon and P. Rabinow (1991) *The Foucault Effect: Studies in Governmentality*. Chicago, IL: University of Chicago Press.

Foucault, M. (1979) 'On Governmentality' *Ideology and Consciousness*, 6 (Autumn).

Foucault, M. and P. Rabinow (1984) *The Foucault Reader*. New York: Pantheon.

Marshall, T. H. (1963) *Class, Citizenship and Social Development*. Garden City, NY: Doubleday.

Chapter 40

Jurgen Habermas

POSTSCRIPT (1994)

From: Jurgen Habermas (1996), excerpts from 'Postscript (1994)', in Jurgen Habermas, *Between Facts and Norms: Contributions to a Discourse Theory of Law and Democracy*, Cambridge, MA: MIT Press, pp. 447–453.

[. . .]

MODERN LAW IS FORMED by a system of norms that are coercive, positive, and, so it is claimed, freedom-guaranteeing. The formal properties of coercion and positivity are associated with the claim to legitimacy: the fact that norms backed by the threat of state sanction stem from the changeable decisions of a political lawgiver is linked with the expectation that these norms guarantee the autonomy of all legal persons equally. This expectation of legitimacy is intertwined with the facticity of making and enforcing law. This connection is in turn mirrored in the ambivalent mode of legal validity. Modern law presents itself as Janus-faced to its addressees: it leaves it up to them which of two possible approaches they want to take to law. Either they can consider legal norms merely as commands, in the sense of factual constraints on their personal scope for action, and take a *strategic* approach to the calculable consequences of possible rule violations; or they can take a *performative* attitude in which they view norms as valid precepts and comply "out of respect for the law." A legal norm has validity whenever the state guarantees two things at once: on the one hand, the state ensures average compliance, compelled by sanctions if necessary; on the other hand, it guarantees the institutional preconditions for the legitimate genesis of the norm itself, so that it is always at least possible to comply out of respect for the law.

What grounds the legitimacy of rules that can be changed at any time by the political lawgiver? This question becomes especially acute in pluralistic societies in which comprehensive worldviews and collectively binding ethics have disintegrated, societies in which the surviving posttraditional morality of conscience no longer supplies a substitute for the natural law that was once grounded in religion or metaphysics. The democratic procedure for the production of law evidently forms the only postmetaphysical source of legitimacy. But what provides this procedure with its legitimating force? Discourse theory answers this question with a simple, and at first glance unlikely, answer: democratic procedure makes it possible for issues and contributions, information and reasons to float freely; it secures a discursive character for political will-formation; and it thereby grounds the fallibilist assumption that results issuing from proper procedure are more or less reasonable. Two considerations provide prima facie grounds in favor of a discourse-theoretic approach.

From the standpoint of *social theory*, law fulfills socially integrative functions; together with the constitutionally organized political system, law provides a safety net for failures to achieve social integration. It functions as a kind of "transmission belt" that picks up structures of mutual recognition that are familiar from face-to-face interactions and transmits these, in an abstract but binding form, to the anonymous, systemically mediated interactions among strangers. Solidarity – the third source of societal integration besides money and administrative power – arises from law only indirectly, of course: by stabilizing behavioral expectations, law simultaneously secures symmetrical relationships of reciprocal recognition between abstract bearers of individual rights. These structural similarities between law and communicative action explain why discourses, and thus reflexive forms of communicative action, play a constitutive role for the production (and application) of legal norms.

From the standpoint of *legal theory*, the modern legal order can draw its legitimacy only from the idea of self-determination: citizens should always be able to understand themselves also as authors of the law to which they are subject as addressees. Social-contract theories have construed the autonomy of citizens in the categories of bourgeois contract law, that is, as the private free choice of parties who conclude a contract. But the Hobbesian problem of founding a social order could not be satisfactorily resolved in terms of the fortuitous confluence of rational choices made by independent actors. This led Kant to equip the parties in the state of nature with genuinely moral capacities, as Rawls would later do with parties in the original position. Today, following the linguistic turn, discourse theory provides an interpretation of this deontological understanding of morality. Consequently, a discursive or deliberative model replaces the contract model: the legal community constitutes itself not by way of a social contract but on the basis of a discursively achieved agreement.

The break with the tradition of rational natural law is incomplete, however, as long as *moral* argumentation remains the exemplar for constitution-making discourse. Then, as we find in Kant, the autonomy of citizens coincides with the free will of moral persons, and morality or natural law continues to make up the core of positive law. This model is still based on the natural-law image of a hierarchy of legal orders: positive law remains subordinate to, and is oriented by, the moral law. In fact, however, the relation between morality and law is much more complicated.

The argument developed in *Between Facts and Norms* essentially aims to demonstrate that there is a conceptual or internal relation, and not simply a historically contingent association, between the rule of law and democracy. As I have shown . . ., this relation is also evident in the dialectic between legal and factual equality, a dialectic that first called forth the social-welfare paradigm in response to the liberal understanding of law and that today recommends a proceduralist self-understanding of constitutional democracy. The *democratic process* bears the entire burden of legitimation. It must simultaneously secure the private and public autonomy of legal subjects. This is because individual private rights cannot even be adequately formulated, let alone politically implemented, if those affected have not first engaged in public discussions to clarify which features are relevant in treating typical cases as alike or different, and then mobilized communicative power for the consideration of their newly interpreted needs. The proceduralist understanding of law thus privileges the communicative presuppositions and procedural conditions of democratic opinion- and will-formation as the sole source of legitimation. The proceduralist view is just as incompatible with the Platonistic idea that positive law can draw its legitimacy from a higher law as it is with the empiricist denial of any legitimacy beyond the contingency of legislative decisions. To demonstrate an internal relation between the rule of law and democracy, then, we must explain why positive law cannot simply be subordinated to morality . . .; show how popular sovereignty and human rights presuppose each other . . .; and make it clear that the principle of democracy has its own roots independent of the moral principle . . . [. . .]

Moral and legal prescriptions each have different reference groups and regulate different matters. The *moral* universe, which is unlimited in social space and historical time, encompasses *all* natural persons in their life-historical complexity. To this extent, it refers to the moral protection of the integrity of fully individuated persons. By contrast, a spatiotemporally localized *legal community* protects the integrity of its members only insofar as they acquire the status of bearers of individual rights.

Morality and law also differ in their extensions. The matters that are in need of, and capable of, legal regulation are at once narrower and broader in scope than morally relevant concerns: they are narrower inasmuch as legal regulation has access only to external, that is, coercible, behavior; they are broader inasmuch as law, as a means for organizing political rule, provides collective goals or programs with a binding form and thus is not *exhausted* in the regulation of interpersonal conflicts. Policies and legal programs have a greater or lesser moral weight from case to case, for the matters in need of legal regulation certainly do not raise moral questions *only*, but also involve empirical, pragmatic, and ethical aspects, as well as issues concerned with the fair balance of interests open to compromise. Thus the opinion- and will-formation of the democratic legislature depends on a complicated network of discourses and bargaining – and not simply on moral discourses. Unlike the clearly focused normative validity claim of moral commands, the legitimacy claim of legal norms, like the legislative practice of justification itself, is supported by different types of reasons.

In summary, we can say that law has a more complex structure than morality because it (1) simultaneously unleashes and normatively limits individual freedom of action (with its orientation toward each individual's own values and interests) and (2) incorporates collective goal setting, so that its regulations are too concrete to be justifiable by moral considerations alone. As an alternative to the natural-law subordination of law to morality, it makes sense to view actionable positive law as a functional complement to morality: it *relieves* the judging and acting person of the considerable cognitive, motivational, and – given the moral division of labor often required to fulfill positive duties – organizational demands of a morality centered on the individual's conscience. Law, as it were, compensates for the functional weaknesses of a morality that, from the observer perspective, frequently delivers cognitively indeterminate and motivationally unstable results. This *complementary* relation, however, by no means implies that law enjoys moral neutrality. Indeed, moral reasons enter into law by way of the legislative process. Even if moral considerations are not selective enough for the legitimation of legal programs, politics and law are still supposed to be compatible with morality – on a common postmetaphysical basis of justification.

The doubling of law into natural and positive law suggests that historical legal orders are supposed to *copy* a pregiven suprasensible order. The discourse-theoretic concept of law steers between the twin pitfalls of legal positivism and natural law: if the legitimacy of positive law is conceived as procedural rationality and ultimately traced back to an appropriate communicative arrangement for the lawgiver's rational political will-formation (and for the application of law), then the inviolable moment of legal validity need not disappear in a blind *decisionism* nor be preserved from the vortex of temporality by a moral *containment*. The leading question of modern natural law can then be reformulated under new, discourse-theoretic premises: what rights must citizens mutually grant one another if they decide to constitute themselves as a voluntary association of legal consociates and legitimately to regulate their living together by means of positive law? The performative *meaning* of this constitution-making practice already contains *in nuce* the entire content of constitutional democracy. The system of rights and the principles of the constitutional state can be developed from what it means to carry out the practice that one has gotten into with the first act in the self-constitution of such a legal community.

If we have to undertake this reconstruction of law without the support of a higher or prior law enjoying moral dignity, then the foregoing considerations lead to two problems: . . . [first] how we should conceive the equal guarantee of private and public autonomy if we situate liberty rights, conceived as human rights, in the same dimension of positive law as political rights; . . . [and second] how we should understand the standard for the legitimacy of law, the discourse principle, if the *complementarity* of law and morality prohibits us from *identifying* it with the moral principle. [. . .]

Chapter 41

Colin Sumner

LAW, LEGITIMATION AND THE ADVANCED CAPITALIST STATE

The jurisprudence and social theory of
Jurgen Habermas

From: Colin Sumner (1983), excerpts from 'Law, legitimation and the advanced capitalist state', in David Sugarman (ed.), *Legality, Ideology and the State*, London: Academic Press, pp. 135–140.

[. . .]

THE LEGITIMATION CRISES OF ADVANCED CAPITALISM

HABERMAS'S THEORY OF CRISIS in advanced capitalist social formations posits crisis possibilities in all three main areas of social practice – the economic, the political and the cultural. . . . [He] believes that the economic crisis (industrial warfare, cyclical business crises, etc.) has been displaced, at least temporarily, into the political system (Habermas, 1976, p. 61). Two types of political crisis are possible – in rationality and in legitimation. "Rationality deficits" in public administration occur where the state cannot adequately perform its role of steering the economic system. In a nutshell, Habermas believes that state-accelerated accumulation creates tensions ("contradictory steering imperatives" in administrators' actions) due to the unavoidable parameters of capitalist production and the emergence of "foreign bodies" in the capitalist employment system such as workerist orientations in unproductive labour (e.g. welfare recipients, housewives) and radical professionalism in the public sector. Increasing public participation is no solution because it thematizes the parameters of decision-making. Failure to command obedience is not disastrous, but loss of control over "planning-related areas of behaviour" is. In short, state administration in advanced capitalism must always be plagued with "rationality deficits" but these only really produce social crisis inasmuch as they reduce the motivation and co-operation of the citizenry.

Because class domination no longer takes the politically anonymous form of the law of value, "it now depends on factual constellations of power whether, and how, production of surplus value can be guaranteed through the public sector, and how the terms of the class compromise look" (Habermas, 1976, p. 68). It also depends on the fact that motivation in normal social interaction patterns still remains tied to norms requiring justification; the legitimation of the political order has become the lynchpin of social integration. But, because social conflicts therefore undermine the legitimacy of the governors, it becomes necessary to distance the administration from the legitimating system. To this end, says Habermas enigmatically, instrumental functions become distanced from fundamental, expressive symbols. These generalizable symbols which release "an unspecified readiness to follow", are found in "strategies" such as "the personalisation of substantive issues, the symbolic use of hearings, expert judgments, juridical incantations, and also the advertising techniques (copied from oligopolistic competition)" (Habermas, 1976, p. 70). In Habermas's analysis the mass media are crucial in publicizing and withdrawing attention from legitimation themes, and therefore in guiding opinion formation. Like Kirchheimer (1961) and Hall *et al.* (1978), Habermas draws a strong link between the symbolic/ideological content of law (procedure and pronouncement) and its selective transmission in accentuated forms by the mass media. However, this separation of administrative and legitimation functions leaves the "cultural system" free from administrative control: "there is no administrative production of meaning". As Habermas says:

> Commercial production and administrative planning of symbols exhausts the normative force of counter-factual validity claims. The procurement of legitimation is self-defeating as soon as the mode of procurement is seen through.
>
> (1976, p. 70)

Moreover, once old traditions and standards are eroded by administrative action or advertising they are no longer available for legitimation purposes, and the state cannot guarantee the content of their replacement. Therefore, he argues, the expansion of state activity increases disproportionately the need for legitimation. Its encroachment into all areas of life inevitably thematizes for public discourse areas of practice which were previously totally self-legitimating and private (e.g. school curricula, family planning, marriage laws). Once the unquestionable, taken-for-granted, 'traditional' nature of certain beliefs, practices and institutions is destroyed, then their "validity claims" can only be stabilized "through discourse" (Habermas, 1976, p. 72). This means that civil privatism is threatened through the politicization of private/personal issues, yet as we have seen, civil privatism is a vital functional complement to the depoliticized public realm. Implicitly Habermas offers us clear reasons for the recent impact and general significance of political issues surrounding women and the family.

In sum, the interventionist welfare state demands much legitimation, but also creates substantial legitimation difficulties. These difficulties, however, would not lead to a legitimation crisis in themselves. People can be bought off in a social democracy through growth and redistribution. But, in the long run, this strategy cannot work because such growth can ultimately only be achieved within the priorities of profit maximization which clash with welfarism. "In the final analysis, *this class structure* is the source of the legitimation deficit" (Habermas, 1976, p. 73). Or, as he said more recently: ". . . class societies are structurally unable to satisfy the need for legitimation that they themselves generate" (1979, p. 163).

Legitimation difficulties would only become a legitimation crisis, in Habermas's view, if they combined with a motivation crisis, to the concept of which we now turn. Since 1945, expectations of affluence have increased and the state has been forced to the limits of its manoeuvrability and learning capacity within a capitalist mode of production.

> As long as the welfare-state program, in conjunction with a widespread, technocratic common consciousness (which, in case of doubt, makes inalterable system restraints responsible for bottlenecks), can maintain a sufficient degree of civil privatism, legitimation needs *do not have to* culminate in a crisis.
>
> (Habermas, 1976, p. 74)

From a technical systems-theory point of view, says Habermas, democratic modes of legitimation could equally be replaced with "a conservative authoritarian welfare state" or "a fascist authoritarian state". But, he says, both variants are "obviously" at odds with developed capitalist culture. The "sociocultural system" produces demands unmeetable by authoritarian systems and only negotiable within a multi-party, mass democracy. Only if the "socio-cultural system" became rigid and required rewards that the system could not deliver would a legitimation crisis occur for certain. In short, it needs a motivation crisis emerging from a discrepancy between attitudes demanded by the state and the motivations supplied by the socio-cultural system. Logically, however, as we have learnt in the UK over the last 10 years, it could also arise in a situation where the state's negotiation positions became tougher and less flexible despite the relative constancy of mass demands; Habermas did not consider this alternative.

'Tradition' is important for Habermas. The interventionist state erodes and supports it. Modern formal democracies require a political culture which 'screens out' expectations of participation. This is achieved via the continuation of pre-bourgeois authoritarian culture emphasizing particularism and subordination. However the socio-cultural system, says Habermas, cannot sustain the civil privatism necessary for effective social integration. One reason for this is that the erosion of tradition permits conditions to appear which contradict civil privatism. We have already mentioned the politicization of private troubles; another important aspect of it is the divorce of law and morality which comes with 'modernisation'. 'Positivised legal norms' have been separated from privatized moral norms. The umbrella of bourgeois law in the 'liberal' capitalist state was put up over a realm of autonomous private action, criminal prohibitions notwithstanding, thus releasing "norm-contents from the dogmatism of mere tradition". But as long as the present mode of socialization continues, founding action on justifiable norms not on conditioned responses, the only way that the authorities can ensure conformity between their laws and our morality is to subject all the norms to a system of "discursive will-formation". That, of course, is impossible because it would threaten the state structure and the whole social order. Whether it will ever occur is an interesting debating point.

Capitalism, in the meantime, has freed people from traditional, non-rational modes of justification and thus created its own legitimation problems. Morality has endured to a point today where it is dependent merely (but vitally) on discursive justice, that is, the abilty to redeem normative claims in a rational public discourse. Habermas hopes that the motivational crisis will be resolved this way, but seriously fears that social action could enter the evolutionary cul-de-sac of conditioned response behaviour, and that behaviour will become divorced from rationally justifiable motivations. The latter would be one precondition for a fascist mode of domination – one perfectly possible resolution of the pending legitimation crisis:

> . . . a legitimation crisis can be avoided in the long run only if the latent class structures of advanced capitalist societies are transformed or if the pressure for legitimation to which the administrative system is subject can be removed. The latter, in turn, could be achieved by transposing the integration of inner nature *in toto* to another mode of socialisation, that is, by uncoupling it from norms that need justification.
>
> (Habermas, 1976, pp. 93, 94)

From a jurisprudential angle, the danger is that rational-legal authority will become a mode of legitimation which is entirely procedural and divorced from "communicative ethics". Once procedural legitimacy is totally supreme, politics, and therefore legislation and adjudication, can begin to divorce themselves from public morality without fear of critique: another basis for fascism. Habermas criticizes Weber's conception of "rational authority" as a technical, sociological one resting entirely on the empirical presence of mass acceptance of the dominant justificatory system. He insists that every effective belief in legitimacy must have an immanent relation to truth, and therefore contains rational validity claims which are testable and criticizable in rational discourse. That is, the belief in legitimacy is (still) more than a belief in procedural legality: legality does not (and must never) equal legitimacy. Yet, says Habermas, modern philosophical attempts to resurrect Aristotelian natural law have failed and Marxist analysis of legitimacy has been subject to Weber's terms of reference. Somehow there must be a universally acceptable procedure for deciding between normative validity claims. Why that is so and what it is forms the basis of the next section, but let me just round off this discussion by explaining Habermas's most recent ideas on the legitimation problems of the modern state.

Developing the theme that legitimation problems of the modern state cannot be solved outside the inherited normative restrictions, Habermas argues that we need to look further into the origin of the modern state to understand the depth and range of its normative identity.

To begin with, he contends that only states need legitimating. Stateless societies organized power communally within reciprocal kinship relations and therefore its exercise needed no legitimation. Multinational corporations or the world market are also not justifiable (or legitimable); again because they are not founded upon rationally contestable validity claims (Habermas, 1979, pp. 178, 179). However, states *are* founded in this way, via the "successful stabilisation of a judicial position that permitted consensual regulation of action conflicts at the level of conventional morality" (Habermas, 1979, p. 161). Legitimate power crystallized around the administration of justice by judges who applied laws which were "intersubjectively recognised legal norms sanctified by tradition". When judges were no longer referees pragmatically deciding between competing constellations of power, and when they employed penal sanction rather than restitution, then the state had arrived. Once political domination through this elevated procedure of law had been established, says Habermas, the material production process could be uncoupled from kinship relations and reorganized via relations of domination (1979, p. 162). On the basis of political domination, class exploitation in production could begin. Thus, turning Marx on his head, the state becomes the basis of class society in Habermasian social theory.

Around the nucleus of this judicial power, the state emerges as the mechanism of social integration. Threats to its legitimacy are posed by class confrontations, but that is natural because the existence of the state is the fundamental precondition for "a class structure in the Marxian sense" (Habermas, 1979, p. 182). Class struggle only becomes the motor of social development, or the steering device of society, with the advent of capitalism and that system of exploitation can only develop when political domination through a state, or legitimate political inequality, has been established. This is why, says Habermas, class societies can never satisfy their own legitimation needs – their very origins in the state presuppose normative consensus – and this fact itself is "the key to the social dynamic of class struggle".

But the legitimation problems of the 'liberal' capitalist state were not limited to class inequalities, others were acquired owing to the historical logic of state development. Problems [arose] relating to secularization (requiring state power to be justified in political not religious terms), changing legal philosophy (requiring law to be legitimated procedurally not in terms of a religious or cosmological world-view), the conflict between the civil law based on universalistic principles and the particularistic needs of social classes, the nature of sovereignty (requiring legitimation in terms of the sovereignty of the people or 'the nation'), and nationalism (demanding political realisation and egalitarian expression).

The laws of the free market and the new ideology of national consciousness, or nation-building, could not stem the tide and conflicts were diverted into the political system of the welfare state, "as an institutionalised struggle over distribution". On this Habermas adds a topical comment to his earlier formulation. He says that the state's legitimation problem today is not how to conceal the relation between capitalism and state praxis through welfare ideology. This is now impossible: Marxism need not expose what is already exposed. What the state has to do is to present capitalism as the only alternative. This is difficult because of the increasingly high costs of welfare, rising Third World commodity prices, devolutionary movements, internal subversion and the increasingly obvious biases in the mass media. Legitimation must therefore become more and more difficult. [. . .]

Bibliography

Haberman, J. (1976) *Communication and the Evolution of Society.* Frankfurt: Suhrkamp Verlag.
Haberman, J. (1979 [1973]) *Legitimation Crisis.* London: Heinemann Educational Books.
Hall, S., C. Critcher, T. Jefferson and J. Clarke (1978) *Policing the Crisis.* London: Palgrave Macmillan.
Kirchheimer, O. (1961) *Political Justice.* Princeton, NJ: Princeton University Press.

Chapter 42

David Garland

THE CULTURE OF CONTROL
Social change and social order in late modernity

From: David Garland (2001), excerpts from *The Culture of Control*, London: Routledge, pp. 75–102.

THE CRIME CONTROL CHANGES of the last twenty years were driven not just by criminological considerations but also by historical forces that transformed social and economic life in the second half of the twentieth century. For our purposes it is useful to distinguish two sets of transformative forces:

First, the social, economic, and cultural changes characteristic of late modernity: changes that were experienced to a greater or lesser extent by all Western industrialized democracies after the Second World War and which became most pronounced from the 1960s onwards.

Secondly, the political realignments and policy initiatives that developed in response to these changes, and in reaction to the perceived crisis of the welfare state, in the USA and the UK from the late 1970s onwards. These changes in social and economic policy— a combination of free-market 'neo-liberalism' and social conservatism—had echoes in other states such as New Zealand, Canada, and Australia. But they were developed in their most thoroughgoing form in America under the Reagan and Bush administrations (1981–92) and in Britain under Prime Minister Thatcher (1979–92) and they have continued in more muted forms in the New Democrat administrations of Bill Clinton (1993–2000) and, in Britain, under the Conservative government of John Major (1992–7) and the New Labour government of Tony Blair from 1997 onwards.

Leaving aside for a moment the national differences that distinguished the American experience from that of Britain, one can summarize the impact of these developments as follows: The first set of forces—the coming of late modernity—transformed some of the social and political conditions upon which the modern crime control field relied. It also posed new problems of crime and insecurity, challenged the legitimacy and effectiveness of welfare institutions, and placed new limits on the powers of the nation-state. The second set of forces—the politics of post-welfarism—produced a new set of class and race relations and a dominant political block that defined itself in opposition to old style 'welfarism' and the social and cultural ideals upon which it was based.

Without this political realignment, the most likely response to the critique of correctionalism would have been incremental reform, improved safeguards, enhanced resources, the refinement of procedures. Instead, what occurred was a sharp reversal of policy and opinion and a remaking of the whole crime control field. This chapter will argue that the tunt against penal-welfarism took a 'reactionary', all-encompassing form because underlying the debate about crime and punishment was a fundamental shift of interests and sensibilities. This historical shift, which had both political and cultural dimensions, gave rise to new group relations and social attitudes—attitudes that were most sharply defined in relation to the problems of crime, welfare, and social order. These new group relations—often experienced and expressed as highly charged emotions of fear, resentment and hostility—formed the social terrain upon which crime control policies were built in the 1980s and 1990s.

The causes of this historical shift had little to do with criminal justice, but that did not prevent it from being massively consequential in its criminological effects. Broad social classes that had once supported welfare state policies (out of self-interest as well as cross-class solidarity) came to think and feel about the issues quite differently. Changes in demography, in stratification and in political allegiance led important sections of the working and middle classes to change their attitudes towards many of these policies—to see them as being at odds with their actuarial interests and as benefiting groups that were undeserving and increasingly dangerous. In this new political context, welfare policies for the poor were increasingly represented as expensive luxuries that hard working tax-payers could no longer afford. The corollary was that penal-welfare measures for offenders were depicted as absurdly indulgent and self-defeating.

If the searing experience of Depression and war had been the social surface on which the welfare state and penal-welfarism were built in the 1930s and 1940s, by the early 1980s that matrix of politics and culture was a dim historical memory. The politics of the later period addressed a different set of problems—many of which were perceived as being caused by welfarism rather than solved by it. I will argue that the gradual formation of new class interests and sensibilities came about in response to the crisis of the welfare state and the transforming dynamics of late modern social life, but I will also insist that this response was the result of political and cultural choices that were by no means inevitable. In the following pages I give an account of this social and political realignment. This account looks at the social and historical processes that have reconfigured the way that we live in the last third of the twentieth century and the ways in which we have come to think and act in relation to crime. It is the story of the development of late modernity, our political and cultural reactions to it, and the implications that these have had for crime, crime-control, and criminal justice.

My account is not intended as a history of the period, but rather as an exploration of social changes that influenced, or posed problems for, the crime control field. Much of what follows will be familiar to the reader—part of 'what everyone knows' about the late twentieth century. But it is important to recall it nevertheless. By calling to mind some of the great social facts of out recent history, I hope to unseat the 'presentist' mindset that so often dominates out discussions and diagnoses. All too often we tend to see contemporary events as having only contemporary causes, when in fact we are caught up in long-term processes of historical change and affected by the continuing effects of now-forgotten events. Our present-day choices are heavily path dependent, reflecting the patterns of earlier decisions and institutional arrangements, just as our habits of thought reflect the circumstances and problems of the periods in which they were first developed.

The theory of historical change I bring to bear in what follows is an action-centred, problem-solving one in which socially situated actors reproduce (or else transform) the structures that enable and constrain their actions. My substantive claim is that the political, economic and cultural supports that had previously underpinned modern crime control were increasingly eroded by late modern social trends and the intellectual and political shifts that accompanied them. These trends, in turn, posed novel problems, gave rise to new perceptions, and shaped a variety of practical adaptations, out of which gradually emerged the crime control and criminal justice practices of the present period. The theory assumes that the emergence of these practices is typically the outcome of practical problem-solving and of political and cultural selection. In consequence, it is a complex process in which competing accounts of problems and solutions are always in play, different interests and sensibilities are always at issue, and the capacity to select solutions on the basis of hard information is only ever partial at best.

THE DYNAMICS OF CHANGE IN LATE TWENTIETH-CENTURY MODERNITY

The large-scale social changes of the second half of the twentieth century have been the subject of much sociological reflection and debate. For some analysts these changes herald the coming of post-modernity and a form of social organization and consciousness that is quite distinct from modernity. Others, wishing to mark the distinctiveness of the world these changes have brought into being, but also to recognize its continuity with what went before, talk of 'late modernity', 'high modernity', or 'reflexive modernity'. Terms such 'New Times', 'post-Fordism', 'post-welfare', and 'neo-liberalism' also identify the peculiarities of the present, but the first of these is rather too vague and the others are rather too specific. My own preferred term is 'late twentieth-century modernity'—which indicates an historical phase of the modernization process without assuming that we are coming to the end, or even to the high point, of a centuries-old dynamic that shows no signs of letting up. Unfortunately such a phrase is even more cumbersome than the others and is of limited use for theoretical generalization. So I will use the term 'late modernity' for convenience, though readers should bear in mind the sense of my usage.

The major transformations that swept society in the second half of the twentieth century were at once economic, social, cultural, and political. To the extent that these can be disentangled, they can be summarized under the following headings: (i) the dynamic of capitalist production and market exchange and the corresponding advances in technology, transport and communications; (ii) the restructuring of the family and household; (iii) changes in the social ecology of cities and suburbs; (iv) the rise of the electronic mass media; and (v) the democratization of social and cultural life.

These great forces of historical change transformed the texture of the developed world in the second half of the twentieth century—all the way up to global economic markets and the nation-state system, all the way down to the daily lives and psychological dynamics of families and individuals. While the contours of capitalist, democracy modernity still frame our social existence, the second half of the twentieth century has ushered in profound changes in the way that life is lived—changes that have had important implications for issues of crime and its control. To begin a discussion of any one of these interwoven threads of social change inevitably leads on to all the others. Here I begin and end with what I take to be the most basic transformative forces of modern times: the economic force of capitalist competition and the political struggle for social and political equality.

The modernizing dynamic of capitalist production and market exchange

The must powerful and fateful of recent historical forces—as vigorous today as it was in the time of Karl Marx—was the unfolding dynamic of capitalist production and exchange. Directly or indirectly, all of the major transformations of the second half of the twentieth century can be traced back to the process of capital accumulation and the unceasing drive for new markets, enhanced profits, and competitive advantage. Military undertakings such as the arms race and the Cold War no doubt played a part, but it was the profit-motive above all else that drove the ultra-rapid transformation of technology, transportation and communications that has characterized the last forty years. Automobiles and aeroplanes, electronic valves and microchips, telephones and fax machines, personal computers and the Internet—each of these has had dramatic consequences for social relations and the texture of daily life. They gave rise to the 'information society' that we now inhabit; made possible the cities and suburbs in which we dwell; linked the four corners of the globe into a single accessible world; and created new social divisions between those who have access to the high-tech world and those who do not.

It was the mass production and mass marketing of goods that gave rise to the world of supermarkets and shopping malls, labour-saving devices and electronic gadgetry, hire purchase and extended credit, the fashion industry and built-in-obsoleseence—in short to a whole ethos of 'consumption' and 'consumerism' and the cultural attitudes that go with it. It was the iconoclasm of economic rationality that helped diminish age-old social divisions that had for centuries allocated men and women, blacks and whites, to different social roles. Contrariwise, it was these same 'bottom-line' considerations that allowed rampant inequalities and the social exclusion of groups who could not easily be turned to profitable use. It was the unending search for new markets, for higher returns, and for a more efficient division of labour that created international markets, non-stop flows of information and money around the planet, and a globalized economy in which nation-states are less and less able to control the economic and social destinies of their subjects.

The events of the late 1980s may have consigned Marx and Engels to the scapheap of failed ideologies, but their description of capitalist modernity in the *Communist Manifesto* remains as true today as it ever was:

> Constant revolutionizing of production, uninterrupted disturbance of all social conditions, everlasting uncertainty and agitation distinguish the bourgeois epoch from all earlier ones. All fixed, fast-frozen relations, with their train of ancient and venerable prejudices and opinions are swept away, all new-formed ones become antiquated before they can ossify. All that is solid melts into air, all that is holy is profaned, and man is at last compelled to face with sober senses, his real conditions of life, and his relations with his kind.

'The Golden Years': 1950 to 1973

For a quarter century after 1950 the economies of Britain and America—like most of the developed industrial world—experienced a remarkable and continuous process of growth and rising living standards. Thanks to the spread of mass production techniques, the expansion of consumer markets at home and abroad, the low cost of energy, and the success of Keynsian demand management, they succeeded in warding off the cyclical booms and slumps of previous eras and enjoyed almost three decades of uninterrupted expansion and prosperity. For the mass of working people 'full employment' and the new welfare safety net lent an unprecedented level of economic security to their lives, and the growth of trade unions, rising wage levels and progressive taxation had the effect of reducing the gap between the rich and the poor.

In the USA the spread of consumerism and middle-class affluence that had begun before Second World War resumed and accelerated in the years after, and the American suburban family quickly became a universal symbol of a comfortable and desirable 'lifestyle' equipped with all 'modern conveniences'. Once the period of post-war rationing and reconstruction was at an end, Britain embarked on the same trajectory, catching up with the new consumption patterns established across the Atlantic. By the 1950s the mass production of affordable consumer durables such as cars, washing machines, refrigerators, radios, and television sets, allowed large sections of the working population routine access to goods that had previously been available only to the very rich. By the 1960s, this *embourgoisement* had reached a level where many of the skilled working class took for granted luxuries—new cars, foreign holidays, homes of their own, fashionable clothes—that their pareuts had only dreamed of possessing. [. . .]

The Crisis Decades: 1970s and 1980s

What capitalist markets give, so also do they take away. With a sudden and unexpected jolt, the oil crisis of the early 1970s ushered in a period of economic recession and political instability throughout the Western industrialized nations. The re-appearance of 'negative growth', now complicated by a built-in inflation and the politically under-written expectations of unionized workers, exposed the underlying problems of the UK and US economies and opened them up to harsh competition from newly developing economies abroad. In this recessionary context, the tools of Keynesian demand management failed to bring supply and demand into line; wage and price inflation continued; production and trade fell precipitously; balance of payments crises appeared as public expenditures outran income; and bitter strife began to mar the relations between the erstwhile 'social partners' of government, employers and unions. Within a decade, mass unemployment re-appeared, industrial production collapsed, trade union membership massively declined, and the labour market restructured itself in ways that were to have dramatic social significance in the years to come.

This restructuring of the labour market—which had begun some time before but which now accelerated in response to the downturn—saw the collapse of industrial production, and with it the shedding of millions of jobs that were previously occupied by unskilled male workers. Where it continued, industrial manufacturing became more capital-intensive and technologically sophisticated, resulting in fewer jobs and demanding more skilled workforces. And as international investment markets grew, making capital more mobile and less closely linked to nations and regions, the pressure to increase productivity or decrease wages exposed the inefficiencies of the older industries and undermined the capacity of trade unions to protect their low-skilled members. When economic recovery came—as it did after recessions of 1973–5 and 1981–3—it was slower and more modest than before, and it was concentrated in service sectors and high technology. The result was a different kind of employment pattern: one that leaned towards low-paid, part-time, usually female workers, or else highly skilled, highly trained graduate employees.

From the late 1970s onwards, the labour markets of the USA and the UK became increasingly precarious and 'dualized'. The life-time job security that industries and the public sector had offered in the post-war years became a thing of the past as workers were forced to become more mobile, more willing to develop transferable skills, more used to retraining and relocating. The male wage-earner bringing home a family wage was increasingly displaced by female, part-time labour with little job-security and few benefits. And while the best-qualified strata of the work-force could command high salaries and lucrative benefits packages, at the bottom end of the market were masses of low-skilled, poorly educated, jobless people—a large percentage of them young, urban, and minority—for whom continuous unemployment was a long-term prospect. These new wage patterns, which in the 1980s were reinforced by increasingly regressive tax structures and declining welfare benefits, reversed the gains of the last half century, as income inequalities increased, and large sectors of the population (especially those with children) fell below the poverty line.

Nor were these changes temporary. Even in the 1990s, when a strong stock-market and low-wage costs led to a sustained period of growth and high levels of employment, whole sectors of the population—particularly inner-city youths in poor or minority communities—were systematically excluded from the labour market just as many of their parents had been before them. The consequence was a more sharply stratified labour market, with growing inequalities separating the top and bottom tiers; a diminished sense of shared interests as the power and membership of mass unions declined; greater contrasts in working conditions, lifestyle and residence; and ultimately, fewer ties of solidarity between these groups. [. . .]

Social forces operating outside as well as inside the family brought about these changes. Higher income levels, better healthcare, and increased welfare benefits allowed the elderly to live longer and more independently; enabled single parents to survive on benefits of with part-time jobs; provided teenagers with state funds to go to college; relieved families of some of their traditional caring tasks and gradually changed the norms and expectation that surrounded these. Changes in the labour market allowed more women to enters the workforce, and brought about the decline of the family wage. Movements in cultural and legal norms—particularly the rise of feminist ideals in the 1970s, the growing tolerance for 'alternative' family forms, and the diminishing stigma of divorce, illegitimacy and homosexuality—also contributed. And of course the relationship was reciprocal. As we will see, these changes in family structure brought about important practical consequences in every aspect of daily life.

As a result of these changes, households and families today look quite different, and operate quite differently from those that were typical of the 1950s or early 1960s. The question of what functional effects follow from these structural changes is, of course, one of the most contentious issues of our time. But what is not in doubt is that the question of the changing family and its social meaning has formed a central theme of political and cultural debate throughout the last quarter century. And these debates have repeatedly highlighted issues of crime and welfare.

Changes in social ecology and demography

The post-war decades saw two major developments in social ecology: the spread of the private automobile and the development of new dwelling patterns, the most important of which were suburban private housing tracts and public housing estates on the peripheries of large cities. [. . .]

These ecological shifts interacted with other demographic factors to bring about new forms of segregation and social division. In the USA one of the dynamics of suburbanization was 'white flight', as the mass migration of southern blacks to the Northern and Mid-Western cities from the 1940s onwards prompted many white city residents to move away. By the 1960s the combination of white suburbanization and extensive black in-migration had led to an unprecedented increase in the size of the ghetto in cities such as Chicago, Los Angeles, Newark, and Detroit. In the UK a similar, if less visible, segregation was effected as the housing policies of local authorities combined with the market choices of more affluent householders to produce a concentration of the worst-off residents in 'sink estates' and decaying inner city areas. In the 1980s the contrasts between the middle-class white suburbs and the poor, often black, urban neighbour-hoods, were exacerbated by the cut-back of government support associated with the 'New Federalism' of Reagan and Bush and the local government spending caps imposed by Mrs Thatcher's government.

The social impact of electronic mass media

If the automobile and the suburb transformed social space in physical terms, the coming of television and the broadcast media did so in a psychological sense that was equally profound and consequential. [. . .]

These changes in the media have helped create a greater level of transparency and accountability in our social and governmental institutions. Bad decisions and shoddy practices are now much more visible that ever before and there is a closer scrutiny of what is going on behind the scenes. Official secrecy and government privilege are increasingly challenged by an emboldened and popular press. As Meyrowitz observes:

> As the confines of the prison, the convent, the family house, the neighbourhood, the executive suite, the university campus and the oval office are all invaded through electronics, we must expect a fundamental shift in out perceptions of society, out authorities and ourselves.

The democratization of social life and culture

The 1950s, 1960s, and 1970s were decades in which democratic institutions in Britain and America were broadened and made more all-encompassing. The civil rights of groups such as blacks, women, gays, prisoners, and mental patients, were increasingly affirmed and extended in this period, and important shifts occurred in the balance of power between government and governed, employers and employees, organizations and consumers. These changes were the result of prolonged struggles by members of the disadvantaged groups and are testimony to the power of egalitarian ideals, the liberal mood of political elites, and the activism of reforming governments and, in the USA, of the Supreme Court. But they also had roots in the structural conditions of late modern society. Welfare state institutions, corporatist politics, the mass media, and the new culture of consumerism all contributed to this end. So did the functional democratization that grew out of the ever-lengthening chains of interdependency that characterized the division of labour, giving specialized workers, managers, and technicians a greater measure of power in the workplace, particularly where they were scarce or else well organized.

In this period the discourse of equality and the politics of equal rights came to play a major role in political culture, however often their claims were breached in practice. In principle, there was no reason why any individual should be treated unequally or denied the full benefits of citizenship. There was a cultural expectation of fair treatment for the individual in the face of authority or large organizations, and new mechanisms (employment tribunals, rent reviews, sex discrimination laws, TV consumer shows) were developed to enforce these claims. A similar expectation of equal rights and social inclusion transformed the expectations (if not always the life chances) of minority groups who had previously been assigned low rank and status. And while these new expectations did not always lead to the diminution of social distinctions and class barriers, they did produce a cultural effect that Ralph Miliband termed 'desubordination'—a decline in the levels of deference and respect for social superiors that previously reinforced the stratification system. In the 1960s and 1970s this push for democracy and egalitarianism extended beyond the political sphere into private domains of the family, the workplace, the universities, the schools—with major consequences for authority and control in these settings.

In many organizations, and especially in larger, well-run corporations and public institutions, this shift brought about a change in management styles and balances of power. 'Management by command', where a superior orders an inferior to behave in particular ways, was increasingly displaced by 'management by negotiation'. Workers, particularly skilled, organized workers, were no longer prepared to act like the servants of their employers. The clients of government bureaucracies began to act like customers. Women demanded more power in the home. Pupils and students and children and prisoners wanted some say in running the institutions that housed them. Experts and expert knowledge were subject to popular scepticism, even as the public became more and more reliant upon them. And although the result was often a change in form, rather than a real shift in status and power, these changing forms did make a difference—not least to people's expectations and their sense of entitlement. From the 1960s onwards, and in more and more social settings, absolute authority and top-down decision making became much more difficult to sustain.

In the post-war period, moral absolutes and unquestionable prohibitions lost their force and credibility, as the rigid and long-standing social hierarchies on which they relied began to be dismantled. This, in turn, weakened the moral powers of the church and the state, and encouraged the spread of a more relativistic, more 'situational' moral sensibility. In the course of a few years, quite radical changes occurred in the norms governing such matters as divorce, sexual conduct, illegitimacy, and drug taking. With the development of new social movements, and more and more groups asserting the legitimacy of their particular values and lifestyles, a much more pluralistic polities began to take shape. The result was an identity polities that disrupted the old political party system and a more diversified public opinion that questioned the possibility of moral consensus and the power of a singular dominant culture that it implied.

The 1960s assault on established social hierarchies and moral authorities also encouraged the development of a different intellectual culture and worldview—one that would become increasingly pervasive in the decades that followed. The characteristic thinking of this period tended to be more sceptical, more pragmatic, and more perspectival than before. The ending of absolutes and the development of a more pluralistic culture had consequences for intellectual life as well. 'Positivist' thinking became increasingly untenable—not just in criminology but in every sphere of social thought. The positivist notion that there were widely shared observations, a universally experienced reality, a given realm of real facts, the possibility of a theory-free science—none of this seemed very plausible once pluralism and relativism became part of the cultural atmosphere. Even 'rationality' was subject to challenge, as post-modern intellectuals and excluded groups rejected the idea of single shared standard. In cultural life, as in world of social institutions, the Enlightenment's legacy of scientific reason was increasingly pat in question and its social engineering ambitions were no longer viewed as an unquestioned human good.

One of the must profound consequences of these social and cultural changes was the emergence of a more pronounced and widespread moral individualism. In one setting after another, individuals were made less subject to the constraining influence of group demands and absolutist moral codes. More and more of the population were encouraged to pursue the goals of individual expression, self-fashioning, and gratification that the consumer society held out to everyone. The grip of tradition, community, church and family upon the individual grew more relaxed and less compelling in a culture that stressed individual rights and freedoms and which dismantled the legal, economic, and moral barriers that had previously kept men, women, and young people 'in their place'. The result was a shift in the balance of power between the individual and group, a relaxation of traditional social controls, and a new emphasis upon the freedom and importance of the individual. Some aspects of this new culture had an egoistic, hedonistic quality, linked to the non-stop consumption ethos of the new capitalism. But to the extent that it did entail a morality it was that of liberal individualism—a morality in which mutual toleration, prudent self-restraint, and respect for other individuals take the place of group commands and moral imperatives. In this moral universe, the worst sin was cruelty to individuals or the restriction of their freedom; obligations to the group or even to families were much more conditional.

It is true that as 'communities of fate' declined, and loosened their social grip upon individuals, new 'communities of choice' emerged—subcultures, consumer and lifestyle identities, professional associations, internet chat rooms—bringing people together in new ways, and subjecting them to new social norms. But these new forms of solidarity did not press so close in the controls that they exerted. They were not face-to-face, not local, not grounded in a shared sense of place or in the right bonds of kinship. They did not affect people in the same intimate ways as the old family and neighbourhood ties had done. Instead individuals checked in and out of multiple networks, relating to them in a segmental fashion, rather than as 'whole persons' who derive most of their identity from belonging to that particular group. Moreover, these new modes of association were not all encompassing. They excluded as well as included. Typically they operated to the exclusion of the poor, and minorities, many of whom were set apart from the community and controls of the workplace, the new social movements, and the legitimate sources of consumer identity. The declining hold of the family and the local community thus affected the poor more adversely than others.

THE IMPACT OF LATE MODERN SOCIAL CHANGE UPON CRIME AND WELFARE

The broad changes just described left their mark across the whole terrain of late modern social organization, and in every case, their impact was mediated by the ways in which policy makers and social actors understood and responded to the new developments. But before going on to outline the differing responses and adaptations that these changes provoked, I want to pause to consider some of the ways in which they impacted upon the two domains that are at the heart of this study: (i) crime and social control and (ii) the institutions of the welfare state.

Crime and social control

The transformative dynamics of late modernity had their most prouounced and dramatic effects in the two decades after 1960. That period coincided, more or less exactly, with a rapid and sustained increase in recorded crime rates—not just in the USA and the UK, but in every Western industrialized nation. The growth of crime in this period is a massive and incontestable social fact, no with standing the evidentiary problems inherent in criminal statistics and the possibility that these statistics were affected by changes in reporting and recording patterns. Between 1955 and 1964 the number of crimes recorded by the police in England and Wales doubled—from half a million a year to a million. It doubled again by 1975 and yet again by 1990. Recorded offences thus rose from about one per 100 people in 1950 to five per 100 in the 1970s to ten per hundred in 1994. In the USA, crime rates rose sharply from 1960 onwards, reaching a peak in the early 1980s when the rate was three times that of twenty years before, the years between 1965 and 1973 recording the biggest rise on record. Moreover, the increases occurred in all the main offence categories, including property crime, crimes of violence and drug offending.

This correlation between late modern social change and increased crime rates was no mere coincidence. The most likely explanation for a cross-national pattern of rapid and sustained increase is a social structural one that points to common patterns of social development. Despite considerable variation from place to place and in respect of the various offence categories, and despite the impact of different regimes of social and legal control, the evidence strongly suggests a causal link between the coming of late modernity and society's increased susceptibility to crime. Furthermore, one can give a plausible account of the mechanisms that link the specific social, economic and cultural changes of the late twentieth century with an increased susceptibility to crime. This increased susceptibility is by na means an inevitable, inexorable feature of late modern life. Some societies, most notably Japan and Switzerland, maintained a high and effective level of (largely informal) crime control, while most others eventually found methods of stemming the rising tide of crime. But the initial impact of late modernity was to make high rates of crime much more probable as a direct consequence of the new social and economic arrangements that it put in place.

Late modernity's impact upon crime rates was a multi-dimensional one that involved: (i) increased opportunities for crime, (ii) reduced situational controls, (iii) an increase in the population 'at risk', and (iv) a reduction in the efficacy of social and self controls as a consequence of shifts in social ecology and changing cultural norms. The consumer boom of the post-war decades put into circulation a mass of portable, high-value goods that presented attractive new targets for theft. This exponential increase in the number of circulating commodities created, as a matter of course, a corresponding increase in criminal opportunities. At the same, there was a reduction in situational controls as shops increasingly became 'self-service', densely populated neighbourhoods were replaced by sprawling suburban tracts or anonymous tower blocks, down-town areas became entertainment centres with no residents, and more and more well-stocked houses were left empty during the day while both wives and husbands went out to work. The coming of the motor car—which helped bring about this more spread-out, more mobile society—was itself a prime instance of its criminogenic properties. Within a few years, the spread of the automobile brought into existence a new and highly attractive target for crime, available on every city street at all times of the day and night, often completely unattended. Thefts of and from motor vehicles quickly became one of the largest categories of property crime.

Another ingredient for the 1960s rise in crime was the arrival of a large cohort of teenage males—the age group most prone to criminal behaviour. As a result of the changes described earlier, this generation of teenagers enjoyed greater affluence and mobility than earlier generations, as well as longer periods outside the disciplines of family life and full-time work. Teenagers were able to spend more time outside the home, had greater access to leisure activities, and were subject to less adult supervision, and more liable to spend time in subcultural settings such as clubs, cafes, discos, and street corners. This baby-boom generation, which grew up in a universalistic commercial culture and experienced a whole new level of desires, expectations, and demands for instant gratification, supplied most of the recruits for the crime-boom that followed in its wake.

Finally, one should add that this period also saw a relaxation of informal social controls—in families, in neighbourhoods, in schools, on the streets—partly as a result of the new social ecology, partly as a consequence of cultural change. Social space became more stretched out, more anonymous and less well supervised, at the very time that it was becoming more beavily laden with criminal temptations and opportunities. At more or less the same time, there was a questioning of traditional authorities, a relaxation of the norms governing conduct in the realm of sexuality and drug-use, and the spread of a more 'permissive', 'expressive' style of child-reating. For some sections of the population, especially the emerging voices of the new youth culture, 'deviance' came to be a badge of freedom, and 'conformity' a sign of dull, normalized repression. The old categories of 'crime' and 'delinquency' became less obvious in their behavioural reference and less absolute in their moral force.

Taken together these social trends had a definite and pronounced effect upon crime. The high crime rates of the 1960s and 1970s were a precipitate of these social changes—an unplanned but altogether predictable product of the interaction of these elements. Put more sociologically, the sharply increased crime rates were an emergent property of the converging social and psychological changes of the post-war period. The new social and cultural arrangements made late-modern society a more crime-prone society, at least until such time as new crime-control practices could be put in place to counter these structural tendencies.

The coming of late modernity also had immediate practical consequences for the institutions of crime control and criminal justice, quite aside from the impact that higher crime rates would eventually have. The automobile, the telephone and the stretching out of social space prompted the 1960s shift to what Americans call '911 policing'—a reactive policing style that took police officers off the streets and out of communities, placed them in patrol cars, and concentrated on providing a rapid response to emergency calls. The rise of the mass media, the universalizing of democratic claims, and what Edward Shils called the politics of 'mass society' put in place new laws and forms of accountability with regard to criminal justice authorities. The balance of power between the police and criminal suspects or between prison officials and prison inmates was altered slightly in favour of the latter and these institutions were subjected to greater levels of legal scrutiny and media exposure. Finally, the social deference and taken-for-granted moral authority that underpinned the idea of doing rehabilitative work with juveniles, in prisons and on probation ceased to be so readily available. As the ethies of work and duty lost their appeal and the idea of a moral consensus was progressively undermined, the idea that state employees could 'correct' deviants came to seem authoritarian and inappropriate rather than self-evidently humane. In the late modern context, the sullen, deep-seated resistance that working-class offenders and minority communities had often shown to the agents of the penal state, now took on an explicit, ideological aspect that made policing and punishing that much more difficult. The declining availability of work for ex-offenders after 1970 added further to the implausibility of the whole correctional project. [. . .]

POLITICAL DISCOURSE AND THE MEANING OF LATE MODERNITY

The changes brought about by the forces of late modernity in respect of crime, welfare, and every other aspect of social life appear in retrospect to have a material reality that is indisputable. But for those living through these changes their precise meaning and political implications were far from obvious. People in the post-war decades were very conscious that they were living through a period of rapid social change and there was an extensive, often anxious, literature reflecting on modernization and its discontents. There were, of course, many ways to 'read' and respond to these social developments, and different current of thought emerged in relation to them. As we will see, from the 1970s onwards, British and American political culture was characterized by a predominantly reactionary attitude towards late modernity and the social changes it ushered in: that is to say, by an attitude that generally regretted the changes and aspired to reverse them where possible. But it is worth pausing to recall that up until that point, the leading current of political thought was a social democratic one that largely embraced late modernity as an embodiment of economic progress and democratic social change.

The progressive reading

At least until the early 1970s the UK and US governments tended to view the direction in which social change was headed as an achievement rather than a problem. The governing parties of this period aimed not only to deliver continuing prosperity and full employment through a highly regulated economy but also to push ahead with a social agenda of extended welfare, expanded civil rights, and enhanced personal freedoms. There was, of course, deep-seated opposition to this agenda, particularly from tradition-ally conservative constituencies such as the Tory shires in England and the southern states in the USA, and from those sectors of capital and commerce that resisted regulation. But this opposition had less influence at the national level and was not formulated as an organized political ideology. The politics of expansion were in office. *Economic control and social liberation* were the watchwords of the day.

To the extent that the welfare state was problematized in these years, it was not in the name of a free market alternative, but in the cause of expanding its services and provision, allowing more community control and participation and taming the big government bureaucracies. The standard critique of the welfare state was that it was not doing enough, that its benefits were too meagre, its procedures too demeaning, its decision-making too inflexible, its experts insufficiently accountable. The preferred, progressive solutions involved transforming claims into social rights and entitlements, making benefits universal rather than means-tested, reforming the bureaucracy to make it more responsive, and rendering the whole process less patronizing and more empow-ering for clients and for poor communities. By the late 1960s this critical framework was a well established and increasingly influential position in social policy circles. A few years later, radical critics of criminal justice would, as we have seen, launch a critique of correctionalism in essentially the same terms.

Even the problem of rising crime rates failed to evoke much doubt or hesitation in the social democratic worldview. Although British and American crime rates increased every year from the mid-1950s onwards, and attracted much anxious commentary, the problem was often played down by government officials and treated with scepticism by criminological experts. Government reports attributed the rising rates to the dislocations of wartime, or the continuing problems of poverty and relative deprivation. Criminologists pointed to the pitfalls of official statistics, the effects of labelling and enforcement, or the media's over-reporting and moral panics. Many policy-makers and experts remained committed to the belief that the beneficial effects of welfare and prosperity would eventually reach into the inner cities and the poorest communities and remedy the crime problem. The penal-welfare paradigm and its criminological analysis thus continued to shape practical reasoning until the early 1970s, despite the emergence of facts that tended to contradict its claims.

The same penal-welfare paradigm shaped the predominant ways in which criminal justice institutions were regarded. Right up until the mid-1970s the most vocal reform proposals were for the improvement of rehabilitative services, the reduction of oppressive controls, and the recognition of the rights of suspects and prisoners. The demand was to criminalize less, to minimize the use of custody, to humanize the prison, and where possible to deal with offenders in the community. Radical proposals such as 'non-interventionism' and even 'abolitionism' emerged in these years—at the very height of the crime wave—and were influential in shaping the practice of juvenile justice, police cautioning, and prosecutorial diversion. This situation in which crime rates were rising and penal levels were being decreased would strike many subsequent commentators as absurd and self-defeating. But it made perfect sense within the prevailing penal-welfare framework which assumed that crime was primarily responsive to welfare interventions rather than to punitive ones. To the extent that the penal-welfare framework was seriously challenged during these years, it was a challenge from the left, pointing to the system's inadequate provision of treatment programmes and the limits of its individualistic, correctionalist approach.

The political discourse of social democracy thus embraced late modernity, down-played the problems of crime and the limits of the welfare state, and offered a vision of the future that stayed faithful to the fundamental values and assumptions of welfarism. It was precisely because of this constancy in the face of change that social democracy would come to appear so completely out of touch once political attitudes took a reactionary turn in the 1980s and 1990s.

The political watershed of the 1970s

Social democratic politicians may have refused to rethink their commitments in the light of late modern developments, but by the early 1970s, many voters were reconsidering their own allegiances. Even prior to the recession of 1973, sections of the working population in Britain and America had experienced a change in their economic position that had made them think differently about the welfare state and their relation to it. Voters who had previously been strong supporters of social democratic parties increasingly took the view that the welfare state no longer worked to their benefit. There was a sense of shifting actuarial interests as people became conscious that, in all probability, they would not have need of many of the state benefits that their ever-increasing tax contributions were paying for. For these recently arrived middle classes, there was also a growing anxiety that their hard-won success could be undermined by a dynamic of change that appeared to be running out of control. Social issues such as growing crime, worsening race relations, family breakdown, growing welfare rolls, and the decline of 'traditional values'—together with concerns about high taxes, inflation, and declining economic performance—created a growing anxiety about the effects of change that conservative politicians began to pick up on and articulate. One sees this from the mid-1960s onwards in the speeches of presidential candidates Goldwater and Nixon, even though the Republican party would remain Keynesian in its basic economic policies until Ronald Reagan took office in 1981. In the UK, the post-war social democratic consensus remained intact until the selection of Margaret Thatcher in 1979, but as early as the late 1960s Conservative politicians such as Enoch Powell began to articulate a reactionary (and sometimes racist) social vision that drew a great deal of popular attention.

These gradual shifts of interest and sentiment, which took place from the mid-1960s onwards, formed the background for the major political realignment that was eventually to follow. But it was not until the tumultuous events and economic collapse of the following decade, and the rapid shifts of public opinion that followed, that these under-lying conditions were given clear political expression. Televised images of urban race riots, violent civil rights struggles, anti-war demonstrations, political assassinations, and worsening street crime reshaped the attitudes of the middle-American public in the late 1960s, just as stories of 'mugging' and increased street crime, militant trade unionism, chronic industrial disputes, and long lines of unemployed workers eventually convinced many British voters that the politics of social democratic centrism had had its day. Together with the devastating economic impact of the mid-1970s recession, these factors triggered the collapse of the post-war political settlement. As social democratic governments around the world tried in vain to street a Keynesian course out of the recession, the parties of the right grasped their opportunity. At the end of the decade, Republican and Conservation governments swept into office on platforms that were explicitly hostile to welfarism and 'big government', to the 'permissive culture' of 1960s, and to the 'consensus politics' of social democracy that had governed for a quarter of a century.

What is striking about both the Reagan and the Thatcher election victories is that they owed less to the appeal of their economic policies—which at that state were con-spicuously underdeveloped—than to their ability to articulate popular discontent. Hostility towards 'tax and spend' government, undeserving welfare recipients, 'soft of crime' polices, unelected trade unions who were running the country, the break-up of the family, the breakdown of law and order—these were focal points for a populist that commanded widespread support. Appealing to the social conservatism of 'hard-work-ing', 'respectable' (and largely white) middle classes, 'New Right' politicians blamed the shiftless poor for victimizing 'decent' society—for crime on the streets, welfare expenditure, high taxes, industrial militancy—and blamed the liberal elites for licensing a permissive culture and the anti-social behaviour it encouraged.

Whereas post-war governments had taken it as their responsibility to deliver full employment and generalized prosperity, these New Right governments quickly abandoned both of these undertakings. Claiming that unemployment, like prosperity, was a market-generated phenomenon that reflected the underlying health of the economy—rather than a policy outcome in the grasp of the nation-state—these governments stood back and allowed market forces to operate largely unchecked, while simultaneously imposing severe public expenditure cuts. The predicable result was the rapid collapse of industrial production and the re-emergence of structural unemployment on a massive scale not seen since the 1930s. Both of these phenomena were turned to political effect as the Reagan and Thatcher governments took steps to weaken the trade unions shift power back towards managers and capital deregulate economic life, reverse the 'rights revolution', and 'roll back' the welfare state. Within a few short years, the progressive politics of the post-war decades had been displaced by political regimes that defined themselves in reaction to the welfare state and the social and cultural currents of late modernity.

The reactionary reading of late modernity

The political projects of the Thatcher and Reagan governments differed over time and from each other. However coherent they appear in retrospect, they were in fact more opportunistic, more contradictory, and less fully implemented than either their supporters or their critics supposed. Nevertheless, the policies and political ideologies of these governments had a thematic unity that allows us to characterize them, in a way that is abstract but not altogether inaccurate, as *reactionary* in a quite specific sense.

They were reactionary in that their policies were marked by a profound antipathy to the economic and social revolution that had transformed. Britain and America in the post-war decades: that is to say, to the politics of the welfare state and to the culture of late modernity. Both governments were absolutely committed to undoing many of the social arrangements that had been established in these years, and to attacking the economic and political orthodoxies that underpinned them. The often contradictory combination of what came to be known as 'neo-liberalism' (the re-assertion of market disciplines) and 'neo-conservatism' (the re-assertion of moral disciplines), the commitment to 'rolling back the state' while simultaneously building a state apparatus that is stronger and more authoritarian than before—these were the contradictory positions that lay at the heart of the Thatcher and Reagan regimes. They made ideological sense, and commanded extensive popular support—in spite of their incoherence—because together they represented a reversal of the progressive revolution of the post-war decades and a promise that the market would re-establish the economic prosperity that the interventionist state had failed to maintain. The framework of Keynesian social democracy ceased to be a catch-all solution and became, instead, the key problem to be attacked by government policy. Its faulty economic assumptions and permissive styles of thought lay at the root of all the new social and economic ills—low productivity, high taxes and inflation, the culture of dependency, declining respect for authority, the crisis of the family. The achievements of the welfare state were systematically discredited or forgotten, and instead its limitations and failures came to stand centre-stage.

Throughout the 1980s and much of the 1990s, these New Right politics dominated social and economic policy in the USA and the UK. Reversing the solidaristic solutions of the welfare state, with its concern for social equality; social security, and social justice, the new neo-liberal politics insisted on market fundamentalism and an unquestioning faith in the value of competition, enterprise, and incentives as well as in the salutary effects of inequality and exposure to risk. To this end, governments in both countries passed laws to tame the trade unions, reduce labour costs, deregulate finance, privatize the public sector, extend market competition and reduce welfare benefits. Tax rates for the rich were greatly reduced, and the resulting state deficits brought about further cuts in social spending. The result was a widening of inequalities and a skewed structure of incentives that encouraged the rich to work by making them richer and compelled the poor to work by making them poorer.

Neo-conservatism introduced into political culture a strikingly *anti-modern* concern for the themes of tradition, order, hierarchy, and authority. These themes were most clearly articulated by the American religious right, which developed as a political force from the mid-1970s onwards. But they were also argued with great force and influence by 'neo-con' intellectuals such as Irving Kristol, Gertrude Himmelfarb, Charles Murray, and James Q. Wilson, and by their British equivalents Roger Scruton, Digby Anderson, Norman Dennis, and Sir Keith Joseph. This brand of moral conservatism was implacably opposed to the liberal culture of the 1960s, and to the democratizing, liberating themes of the 'permissive era', which were blamed for all of the social and economic ills of the subsequent decades. By the 1980s, the demand to get 'back to basics', to restore 'family values' and to re-impose 'individual responsibility' had become familiar themes on both sides of the Atlantic. So too were calls for more discipline in schools and families, an end to 'libertarian license' in art and culture, condemnation of the new sexual morality, and a generalized return to a more orderly, more disciplined, more tightly controlled society.

These conservative calls for tighter order and control ought to have clashed head on with the policies of deregulation and market freedom that were, at precisely the same time, releasing individuals and companies from the grip of social regulation and moral restraint. That they did not is testimony to the success of their supporters in representing the problem of immoral behaviours as, in effect, a problem of poor people's conduct. Despite the all-encompassing rhetotic, the actual policy proposals that emerged made it clear that the need for more social control was not a generalized one, undoing the culture of late modernity, but instead a much more focused, much more specific demand, targeted on particular groups and particular behaviours. The well-to-do could continue to enjoy the personal freedoms and moral individualism delivered by post-war social change—indeed they could enjoy even more freedoms and choices as society became more marketized. But the poor must become more disciplined. Thus the new conservatism proclaimed a moral message exhorting everyone to return to the values of family, work, abstinence, and self-control, but in practice its real moral disciplines fastened onto the behaviour of unemployed workers, welfare mothers, offenders, and drug users.

If the watchwords of post-war social democracy had been *economic control and social liberation*, the new politics of the 1980s put in place a quite different framework of *economic freedom and social control*. And though this reactionary movement claimed to be undoing the political and the cultural regime that had been developing since the war, in reality its assault upon late modernity took a very particularized form and left the major social arrangements largely untouched.

The conservative call for a return to moral discipline and traditional values did result in a renewed discipline and a tightening of controls, but these were directed mainly at poor individuals and marginalized communities and did nothing to constrain the great majority of citizens. The neo-liberal call for an extension of market freedoms and the dismantling of the 'nanny state' certainly produced more freedom for those with the resources to benefit from a deregulated market, but it also resulted in chronic unemployment for the weakest sectors of the workforce and a growing sense of insecurity for the rest. The irony here was that even with meaner, more restrictive benefits, the fact of massive unemployment ensured that social spending was higher at the end of Reagan and Thatcher's terms than at the beginning. Moreover, the welfare programmes that most benefited the middle classes—cheap mortgages, social security, tax breaks, and education subsidies—remained firmly and expensively in place.

The politics of the 1980s and 1990s were heavily class-based in their impacts, even as they claimed to be generalized in their intent. And although the rich and the employed middle classes derived huge economic benefits from these new arrangements, the ending of solidaristic politics and the opening of class and race divisions had definite social costs that affected them too. Not the least of these was that the new politics produced a cultural mood that was defensive, atnbivalent, and insecure, in stark contrast to the confident, emancipatory culture of a few decades before. Introduced in the name of freedom, the politics of reaction gave rise to widespread insecurities, and would eventually produce a renewed obsession with control. One reason for this was that even those who were well placed to take economic risks and reap their rewards were less comfortable with other kinds of risks—such as the threat of crime and violence—that were inherent in the deregulated society. There was a dim but widespread awareness that the costs of the new market freedoms were largely being born by the poorest most vulnerable groups. And even if some could justify this by notions of desert and economic utility, it was hard to forget the implicit dangers involved in amassing a sizeable population of dispossessed youths and disaffected minorities.

In this situation, insecurity, group hostility, and some measure of bad conscience flourished and played a role in focusing discontent. Perhaps the pluralism of late modernity meant that living with 'difference' was everyone's irreversible fate and reactionary politics could do little to change this. As Émile Durkheim long ago pointed out, social arrangements of this kind pose acute problems of social order and call for the creation of governmental institutions and civic associations that can build social solidarity and ensure moral regulation. Complex societies need more organization, not less, and while markets can organize economic efficiencies, they do little to bring about moral restraint, social integration, or a sense of group belonging. In the absence of such initiatives, the new culture of diversity remained a source of frustration to many, and a constant source of grumbling cultural commentary. Among polite society at least, lipservice to multiculturalism and individual rights meant that objections to other people's lifestyles tended to be muted and displaced. But there were some behaviours and some people that did not have to be tolerated, and new and more coercive policies of social and penal control increasingly targeted these.

A central outcome of the politics of the 1980s was thus a hardening of social divisions. As neo-liberal policies reinforced rather than resisted the stratification produced by the global economy and a dualized labour market, stark new divisions emerged in the populations of the USA and the UK. The social and economic distance between the jobless and those in work, blacks and whites, affluent suburbs and strife-torn inner cities, consumers in a booming private sector and claimants left behind in collapsing public institutions grew ever greater in these years, until it became a commonplace of political and social commentary. In place of the solidaristic ideals of the Great Society or the Welfare State there emerged a deeply divided society—variously described as 'the dualized society', the 'thirty, thirty, forty society', the 'seduced and the repressed', or, in the USA where social divisions were overlayed by racial ones, 'American Apartheid'—with one sector being deregulated in the name of market enterprise, the other being disciplined in the name of traditional morality. These new divisions worked to further undermine the old solidarities of inter-class identification, of mutual sympathy across income divides, of a shared citizenship and mutual regard—these became increasingly unlikely as the lives and adaptive cultures of the poor began to look altogether alien in the eyes of the well-to-do.

In this new social context, it was hardly surprising to find that social problems such as violence, street crime, and drug abuse worsened, particularly in those areas where economic and social disadvantage were concentrated. So although property crimes in the USA began to decline after their peak in 1982, homicides and violent crime rose sharply in the second half of the 1980s, particularly among young people, and often in association with the growing market in hard drugs. In Britain under Mrs. Thatcher's law and order administration, the crime rate doubled in a decade.

But more important for our purposes is the way in which crime came to take on a new and strategic significance in the political culture of this period. Crime—together with associated 'underclass' behaviours such as drugs abuse, teenage pregnancy, single parenthood, and welfare dependency—came to function as a rhetorical legitimation for social and economic policies that effectively punished the poor and as a justification for the development of strong disciplinary state. In the political discourse of this period, social accounts of the crime problem come to be completely discredited. Such accounts, so it was said, denied individual responsibility, excused moral fault, watered down punishment, encouraged bad behaviour and in that respect were emblematic of all that was wrong with welfarism. Crime came to be seen instead as a problem of indiscipline, a lack of self-control or social control, a matter of wicked individuals who needed to be deterred and who deserved to be punished. Instead of indicating need or deprivation, crime was a matter of anti-social cultures or personalities, and of rational individual choice in the face of lax law enforcement and lenient punishment regimes.

In this watershed period, effective crime control came to be viewed as a matter of imposing more controls, increasing disincentives, and, if necessary, segregating the dangerous sector of the population. The recurrent image of the offender ceased to be that of the needy delinquent or the feckless misfit and became much more threatening—a matter of career criminals, crackheads, thugs, and predators—and at the same time much more racialized. And the compassionate sensibility that used to temper punishment now increasingly enhanced it, as the sympathy invoked by political rhetoric centred exclusively on the victim and the fearful public, rather than the offender. Instead of idealism and humanity, penal policy discussions increasingly evoked cynicism about rehabilitative treatment, a distrust of penological expects, and a new righteousness about the importance and efficacy of punishment. If 'radical non-interventionism' epitomized the progressive ideal of the 1960s, the term that best captures the new right's ideal is that of 'zero tolerance'. In the political reaction against the welfare state and late modernity, crime acted as a lens through which to view the poor—as undeserving, deviant, dangerous, different—and as a barrier to lingering sentiments of fellow feeling and compassion. In this reactionary vision, the underlying problem of order was viewed not as a Durkheimian problem of solidarity but as a Hobbesian problem of order, to which the solution was to be a focused, disciplinary version of the Leviathan State.

Chapter 43

Jean L. Cohen and Andrew Arato

CIVIL SOCIETY AND POLITICAL THEORY

From: Jean L. Cohen and Andrew Arato (1992), excerpts from *Civil Society and Political Theory*, Cambridge, MA: MIT Press, pp. 1–3, 15–17.

INTRODUCTION

WE ARE ON THE threshold of yet another great transformation of the self-understanding of modern societies. There have been many attempts from various points of view to label this process: the ambiguous terms "postindustrial" and "post-modern" society reflect the vantage points of economic and cultural concerns. Our interest is in politics. But from this standpoint, the changes occurring in political culture and social conflicts are poorly characterized by terms whose prefix implies "after" or "beyond." To be sure, for a variety of empirical and theoretical reasons the old hegemonic paradigms have disintegrated, as have the certainties and guarantees that went with them. Indeed we are in the midst of a remarkable revival of political and social thought that has been going on for the last two decades.

One response to the collapse of the two dominant paradigms of the previous period – pluralism and neo-Marxism – has been the attempt to revive political theory by "bringing the state back in." While this approach has led to interesting theoretical and empirical analyses, its state-centered perspective has obscured an important dimension of what is new in the political debates and in the stakes of social contestation. The focus on the state is a useful antidote to the reductionist functionalism of many neo-Marxian and pluralist paradigms that would make the political system an extension, reflex, or functional organ of economic (class) or social (group) structures of selectivity and domination. In this respect the theoretical move served the cause of a more differentiated analysis. But with respect to all that is nonstate, the new paradigm continues the reductionist tendency of Marxism and neo-Marxism by identifying class relations and interests as the key to contemporary forms of collective action. Moreover, the legal, associational, cultural, and public spheres of society have no theoretical place in this analysis. It thereby loses sight of a great deal of interesting and normatively instructive forms of social conflict today.

The current "discourse of civil society," on the other hand, focuses precisely on new, generally non-class-based forms of collective action oriented and linked to the legal, associational, and public institutions of society. These are differentiated not only from the state but also from the capitalist market economy. Although we cannot leave the state and the economy out of consideration if we are to understand the dramatic changes occurring in Latin America and Eastern Europe in particular, the concept of civil society is indispensable if we are to understand the stakes of these "transitions to democracy" as well as the self-understanding of the relevant actors. It is also indispensable to any analysis that seeks to grasp the import of such changes for the West, as well as indigenous contemporary forms and stakes of conflict. In order to discover, after the demise of Marxism, if not a common normative project between the "transitions" and radical social initiatives under established liberal democracies, then at least the conditions of possibility of fruitful dialogue between them, we must inquire into the meaning and possible shapes of the concept of civil society.

Admittedly, our inclination is to posit a common normative project, and in this sense we are post-Marxist. In other words, we locate the pluralist core of our project within the universalistic horizon of critical theory rather than within the relativistic one of deconstruction. At issue is not only an arbitrary theoretical choice. We are truly impressed by the importance in East Europe and Latin America, as well as in the advanced capitalist democracies, of the struggle for rights and their expansion, of the establishment of grass roots associations and initiatives and the ever renewed construction of institutions and forums of critical publics. No interpretation can do these aspirations justice without recognizing both common orientations that transcend geography and even social-political systems and a common normative fabric linking rights, associations, and publics together. We believe that civil society, in fact the major category of many of the relevant actors and their advocates from Russia to Chile, and from France to Poland, is the best hermeneutic key to these two complexes of commonality.

Thus we are convinced that the recent reemergence of the "discourse of civil society" is at the heart of a sea change in contemporary political culture. Despite the proliferation of this "discourse" and of the concept itself, however, no one has developed a systematic *theory* of civil society. This book is an effort to begin doing just that. Nevertheless, systematic theory cannot be built directly out of the self-understanding of actors, who may very much need the results of a more distanced and critical examination of the possibilities and constraints of action. Such theory must be internally related to the development of relevant theoretical debates. At first sight the building of a theory of civil society seems to be hampered by the fact that the stakes of contemporary debates in political theory seem to be located around different axes than the nineteenth-century couplet of society and state. It is our belief, however, that the problem of civil society and its democratization is latently present in these discussions and that it constitutes the theoretical terrain on which their internal antinomies might be resolved. [. . .]

REVIVAL OF THE CONCEPT OF CIVIL SOCIETY

The early modern concept of civil society was revived first and foremost in the struggles of the democratic oppositions in Eastern Europe against authoritarian socialist party-states. Despite different economic and geopolitical contexts, it does not seem terribly problematic to apply the concept also to the "transitions from authoritarian rule" in Southern Europe and Latin America, above all because of the common task shared with the oppositions of the East to constitute new and stable democracies. But why should such a concept be particularly relevant to the West? Is not the revival of the discourse of civil society in the East and the South simply part of a project to attain what the advanced capitalist democracies already have: civil society guaranteed by the rule of law, civil rights, parliamentary democracy, and a market economy? Could one not argue that struggles in the name of creating civil and political society especially in the East are a kind of repeat of the great democratic movements of the eighteenth and nineteenth centuries that created a type of duality between state and civil society which remains the basis for Western democratic and liberal institutions? And isn't this an admission that the elite theorists, the neoconservatives, or at best the liberals are right after all? Put this way, the revival of the discourse of civil society appears to be just that, a revival, with little political or theoretical import for Western liberal democracies. And if this is so, why would a civil-society-oriented perspective provide a way out of the antinomies plaguing *Western* political and social thought?

Several interrelated issues that have emerged in the current revival go beyond the model of the historical origins of civil society in the West and therefore have important lessons to offer established liberal democracies. These include the conception of self-limitation, the idea of civil society as comprised of social movements as well as a set of institutions, the orientation to civil society as a new terrain of democratization, the influence of civil on political and economic society, and finally an understanding that the liberation of civil society is not necessarily identical with the creation of bourgeois society but rather involves a choice between a plurality of types of civil society. All these notions point beyond a restriction of the theory of civil society merely to the constituent phase of new democracies.

The idea of self-limitation, all too often confused with the strategic constraints on emancipatory movements, is actually based on learning in the service of democratic principle. The postrevolutionary or self-limiting "revolutions" of the East are no longer motivated by fundamentalist projects of suppressing bureaucracy, economic rationality, or social division. Movements rooted in civil society have learned from the revolutionary tradition that these fundamentalist projects lead to the breakdown of societal steering and productivity and the suppression of social plurality, all of which are then reconstituted by the forces of order only by dramatically authoritarian means. Such an outcome leads to the collapse of the forms of self-organization that in many cases were the major carriers of the revolutionary process: revolutionary societies, councils, movements. Paradoxically, the self-limitation of just such actors allows the continuation of their social role and influence beyond the constituent and into the constituted phase.

This continuation of a role of civil society beyond the phase of transition can be coupled with domestication, demobilization, and relative atomization. That would mean convergence with society as the Western elite pluralists see it. But in the postauthoritarian settings actors who have rejected fundamentalism and raised civil society to a normative principle show that we do have a choice. While the total democratization of state and economy cannot be their goal, civil society itself, as Tocqueville was first to realize, is an important terrain of democratization, of democratic institution building. And if East European oppositionals were driven to this alternative at first only by blockages in the sphere of state organization, there is certainly a good chance that the idea of the further democratization of civil society will gain emphasis in the face of the inevitable disappointments, visible above all in Hungary, (East) Germany, and Czechoslovakia, with the emergence of the typical practices of Western democracies. Thus, the actors of the new political societies would do well, if they value their long-term legitimacy, to promote democratic institution building in civil society, even if this seems to increase the number of social demands on them.

The idea of the democratization of civil society, unlike that of its mere revival, is extremely pertinent to existing Western societies. Indeed, the tendency to see extra-institutional movements and initiatives in addition to settled institutions as integral parts of civil society is found earlier in Western than in Eastern experience, to which it is rapidly being extended primarily by new and old movements and initiatives. It is quite possible that some of the emerging Eastern constitutions will embody new sensitivity to an active civil society, a sensitivity that should in turn influence Western constitutional developments. These potential normative gains will confirm, in the East as well as the West, the idea that there can be very different types of civil society: more or less institutionalized, more or less democratic, more or less active. Discussions in the milieu of Solidarity in Poland raised these choices explicitly as early as 1980, along with the choice of political vs. antipolitical models of civil society. In the current wave of economic liberalism in Poland, Czechoslovakia, and Hungary, another question inevitably arises concerning the connection between economy and civil society and the choice between an economic, individualistic society and a civil society based on solidarity, protected not only against the bureaucratic state but also against the self-regulating market economy. This debate, too, will be directly relevant in Western contexts, as it already has been in Latin America, and conversely Western controversies around the welfare state and the "new social movements" should have much intellectual material to offer Eastern radical democrats hoping to protect the resource of solidarity without paternalism. [. . .]

Epilogue

ALTHOUGH CITIES SEE MORE violence, they are not alone. Suburbs are not as different from the cities as many people like to think. This work concludes by pointing to three portraits, in music and film, of the worlds we have been exploring. Tupac Shakur vividly portrays the world of the city as seen through the eyes of a young, poor, inner city black man with his lyrics for *Me Against the World* and *Dear Mama*. It is a world also painted evocatively in Boyz 'N the Hood. Eric Bogosian chillingly introduces us to another fraught world and its inhabitants in *Suburbia*.